AGENCY, PARTNERSHIPS, AND LLCs

Examples and Explanations

AGENCY, PARTNERSHIPS, AND LLCs

Examples and Explanations

Second Edition

Daniel S. Kleinberger

Professor of Law
William Mitchell College of Law

1185 Avenue of the Americas, New York, NY 10036
www.aspenpublishers.com

Permissions
Aspen Publishers
1185 Avenue of the Americas
New York, NY 10036

Printed in the United States of America

2   3   4   5   6   7   8   9   0

ISBN 0-7355-2468-8

Library of Congress Cataloging-in-Publication Data

Kleinberger, Daniel S.
    Agency, partnerships, and LLCs : examples and explanations /
Daniel S. Kleinberger.—2nd ed.
        p.   cm.
Rev. ed. of: Agency and partnership. c1995.
    Includes index.
ISBN 0-7355-2468-8
        1. Agency (Law)—United States.   2. Partnership—United States.
3. Private companies—United States.   I. Kleinberger, Daniel S.,
Agency and partnership.   II. Title.
KF1345.Z9 K6 2002
346.7302′9—dc21   2002026059

About Aspen Publishers

Aspen Publishers, headquartered in New York City, is a leading information provider for attorneys, business professionals, and law students. Written by preeminent authorities, our products consist of analytical and practical information covering both U.S. and international topics. We publish in the full range of formats, including updated manuals, books, periodicals, CDs, and online products.

Our proprietary content is complemented by 2,500 legal databases, containing over 11 million documents, available through our Loislaw division. Aspen Publishers also offers a wide range of topical legal and business databases linked to Loislaw's primary material. Our mission is to provide accurate, timely, and authoritative content in easily accessible formats, supported by unmatched customer care.

To order any Aspen Publishers title, go to *www.aspenpublishers.com* or call 1-800-638-8437.

To reinstate your manual update service, call 1-800-638-8437.

For more information on Loislaw products, go to *www.loislaw.com* or call 1-800-364-2512.

For Customer Care issues, e-mail *CustomerCare@aspenpublishers.com;* call 1-800-234-1660; or fax 1-800-901-9075.

Aspen Publishers
A Wolters Kluwer Company

to Carrie, the partner of my life,

and

*to Rachael and Sam, each in her or his own way
the finest Examples I have ever helped create.*

Summary of Contents

Contents

Contents

Contents

Contents

Contents

Contents

Contents

Contents

Contents

Contents

Contents

Contents

Preface to Second Edition

In the seven years since the publication of the first edition, the law of unincorporated business associations has undergone a revolution. The limited liability company ("LLC") has become the entity of choice for a myriad of enterprises, and the Revised Uniform Partnership Act ("RUPA") has revitalized the law of general partnerships. In some states, the annual number of newly-formed LLCs has exceeded the number of newly-formed corporations, and RUPA—with its tilt toward entity continuity and its provisions on limited liability partnerships ("LLPs")—has made the "shielded" general partnership as useable and interesting as an LLC.

In 2001, the National Conference of Commissioners on Uniform State Laws promulgated a new uniform limited partnership act—ULPA (2001). While the new act modernizes the law applicable to limited partnerships and also provides for limited liability limited partnerships ("LLLPs"), limited partnerships formed under predecessor statutes continue to serve thousands of ventures in which essentially passive investors rely on powerful, entrenched management.

Meanwhile, the common law of agency has been undergoing a recrudescence of its own. The American Law Institute is working through a Restatement (Third) of Agency, giving particular attention to agency issues *within* business entities and other modern organizations. By happenstance, agency law issues have also become relevant to the daily headlines. As this edition goes to press, those headlines contemplate accounting firms that have failed to detect massive corporate cheating and religious organizations allegedly rife with sexually abusive clergy. The auditors defend themselves, in part, by asserting that the corporations already "knew" of the cheating because, as a matter of agency law, a corporation knows what its top officers know.[1] The allegations of clergy abuse raise questions of a "master's" vicarious liability for the intentional torts of a "servant"[2] and a principal's direct liability for negligently hiring, training, supervising or retaining an agent.[3]

The matters covered by this book thus have great current importance, but such "relevance" accounts for only half the benefits of studying these

---

1. See section 2.4.
2. See section 3.2.6.
3. See section 4.4.1.

topics. Regardless of the use you plan to make of your legal training, studying agency law and the law of unincorporated business organizations will help you learn part of what is loosely called "thinking like a lawyer."

Such thinking includes a process I have labeled "categories and consequences"—analyzing situations by defining categories of behavior and then attaching consequences to those categories. This is not the only way in which lawyers understand the world, but it is certainly a fundamental one.

Agency law is an excellent way to learn about categories and consequences. Indeed, the analytic training that comes with understanding agency law's approach to issues rivals the analytic training available in confronting the Rule Against Perpetuities. Fortunately, mastering agency law is less traumatic.

The analytic benefits of studying partnership law come from several sources: applying the categories and consequences approach in more complex settings; seeing how themes from one area of law (i.e., agency) manifest themselves in a related but distinct area of law; developing familiarity with the concept and function of "default rules"; and learning to distinguish between issues within an organization (*inter se* issues) and issues between an organization and third parties.

To this mix of skills and concepts, studying the law of LLCs, LLPs, and LLLPs adds further experience in recognizing old themes in new settings (e.g., power to bind the organization; fiduciary duties within an organization) and further refinement of the distinction between *inter se* issues and third party issues (e.g., direct versus derivative claims, conflicts between an LLC's articles of organization and operating agreement).

I hope you will find this book useful, whether you are taking a course that considers its topics in depth or in passing.

August 2002   *Daniel S. Kleinberger*

Introduction

The structure of legal rules.   Law does much of its analysis by applying labels to facts.

Example: A multinational corporation lends millions of dollars to a local grain and seed company and tells that company how to run its business. The local company becomes insolvent, owing substantial debts to local farmers. The farmers try to recover from the multinational corporation. Whether they can do so depends on whether they can label the local company as the "agent" of the corporation.

Example: A national franchisor requires its local franchisees to follow a thick volume of operating regulations. A customer slips and falls while on the franchise's premises and attempts to recover from the national franchisor. Whether the customer can do so depends on whether the customer can label the franchisee as the "servant" of the franchisor.

The link between categories and consequences controls the structure of legal rules. Every legal rule can be stated as an IF/THEN proposition, with the IF component stating the elements and the THEN component stating the consequences.

IF: the facts of situation meet specified elements (i.e., if the situation fits a particular category)

THEN: specified consequences result

For example:

IF: • a party fraudulently makes an assertion of past or present fact concerning a proposed transaction,
        • another party justifiably relies on that assertion and is thereby induced to make a contract with the asserting party, and
        • the assertion is:
          —inaccurate and
          —material

THEN: the misled party may rescind the contract

Those who are more graphically inclined can think of each legal rule as a box. On top, the box has a name of a legal category, for example, "fraudulent inducement." The front panel of the box contains the "entrance criteria"— the elements that must be satisfied to qualify a situation to fit into the box. The right side panel contains the legal consequences created by the rule. If a situation fits "in the box," the consequences follow.[1] The figure below illustrates this approach.

In all events, you should keep in mind the link between labeling (categorization) and consequences. By doing so, you will synchronize your way of thinking with the way the law of agency approaches its subject matter.

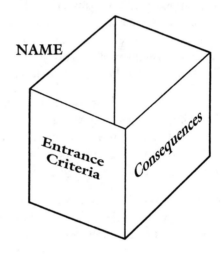

Name of the box (i.e., the legal category)
- fraud in the inducement

Entrance criteria (i.e., elements of the rule)
- a party fraudulently makes an assertion of past or present fact concerning a proposed transaction
- another party justifiably relies on that assertion and is thereby induced to make a contract with the asserting party
- the assertion is inaccurate and material

Consequences
- defrauded party may rescind contract

---

1. Perhaps this metaphor helps explain why lawyers are often accused of trying to pigeonhole everything and everybody.

Legal analysis for preventative lawyering.   Some of the questions in this book ask you to think proactively—that is, to consider a client's situation and goals, to identify potential legal problems, and to suggest a course of conduct that will prevent the problems from materializing. You may initially find these questions disconcerting, since law school analysis often operates from a post hoc, litigation perspective. That is, you consider a dispute that has already materialized, analyze each party's prospects, and predict the outcome of the dispute.

You may find the following protocol helpful in thinking preventatively:

1. Review the facts (e.g., the client's current situation and proposed conduct) and identify legal rules whose application might produce unpleasant consequences for the client.
2. For each such rule, identify the facts that are key to:
   a. making the rule applicable, and
   b. causing the rule to produce an unpleasant outcome for the client.
3. For each such fact, try to imagine a change that will make the problematic rule inapplicable or avoid the problematic outcome, but will not frustrate the client's goals.

Special Notice

Note on the Restatements of Agency and the Meaning of "Person"

Unless otherwise indicated, all references to the Restatement are to the Restatement (Second) of Agency (1958), promulgated by the American Law Institute ("ALI").[2] The ALI is currently working on a Restatement (Third) of Agency. References to that project contain the phrase "Restatement (Third)" and indicate a particular draft.

As of fall 2002, the ALI is approximately one-third (perhaps one-half) of its way through developing the Restatement (Third) of Agency. This edition makes numerous references to the Restatement (Third), but readers should keep in mind that the referenced provisions are merely tentative and remain subject to change until an ALI Annual Meeting gives final approval to the entire Restatement (Third).

Unless otherwise indicated, "person" means "legal person" and includes not only human beings but also organizations, such as partnerships, limited liability companies, and corporations.

---

2. The ALI is a private, nonprofit organization whose members are distinguished lawyers, judges, and law professors. The ALI has published a number of Restatements, each of which attempts to state and explain the law in a particular field. Each Restatement contains a large number of "black letter" propositions, accompanied by explanatory comments and illustrations. Adopted in 1958, the Restatement (Second) of Agency has been and continues to be very influential in courts throughout the United States.

AGENCY, PARTNERSHIPS, AND LLCs

Examples and Explanations

PART ONE

Agency

1

Introductory Concepts in the Law of Agency

§1.1 The Agency Relationship Defined and Exemplified; Its Players Identified

Agency is the label the law applies to a relationship in which:

- by mutual consent (formal or informal, express or implied)
- one person or entity (called the "agent")
- undertakes to act on behalf of another person or entity (called the "principal"),
- subject to the principal's control.

Agency relationships are everywhere in the commercial world and in noncommercial realms as well. Whenever a person or organization seeks to act through the efforts of others, the legal concept of agency likely applies. For example:

- A law student, rushing to prepare for graduation and the fabulous buffet party to follow, gives a friend a list of last-minute additions to the menu and asks her to "make sure the caterer includes these on the buffet." The friend agrees and becomes the student's agent.
- Miles Standish, seeking to court "the damsel Priscilla," entreats his friend, John Alden, to communicate to Priscilla the depth and direction of Standish's feelings toward her. Alden agrees and becomes Standish's agent.[1]

---

1. Henry Wadsworth Longfellow, "The Courtship of Miles Standish," in Hiawatha, the Courtship of Miles Standish, and Other Poems (Oxford U. Press 1925).

- A corporate shareholder, unable to attend the corporation's annual meeting, signs a "proxy" that authorizes another individual to cast the shareholder's votes at the meeting. By accepting the appointment, the proxy holder becomes the shareholder's agent.
- A landowner, preparing to leave for an around-the-world tour and wishing to sell Greenacre as soon as possible, gives a real estate broker a "power of attorney." This credential authorizes the broker to sell Greenacre on the owner's behalf and to sign all documents necessary to form a binding contract and to close the deal. The broker is the owner's agent.
- A supermarket chain that is about to purchase fancy new computerized cash registers retains a consultant to advise on what type of registers to buy and to arrange the purchase of the new machines on the chain's behalf. The consultant will act as the chain's agent.
- A bank, understanding that not all customers like dealing with ATM machines, hires tellers to handle customer deposits, withdrawals, and similar transactions. The tellers are agents of the bank.

In each of these situations someone (the *principal*) has asked someone else (the *agent*) to provide services or accomplish some task on behalf of the principal and subject to the principal's control. In each situation the agent has agreed to do so. To each situation, the label of "agency" applies.[2]

The agency relationship may at first appear to involve only the principal and the agent. But principals typically use agents to deal with others, so third parties figure prominently in the law of agency. Each of these players can be individual human beings or organizations, such as corporations, not-for-profit corporations, and partnerships.[3]

§1.2   Creation of the Agency Relationship

§1.2.1   *The Restatement's View of Creation*

The first section of the Restatement describes the creation of an agency relationship as follows:

> Agency is the fiduciary relation which results from the manifestation of consent by one person [the principal] to another [the agent] that the

---

2. The law of agency also applies when a party merely appears to be authorized to act for another. Sections 2.3 and 2.5 discuss the law of "apparent authority" and "agency by estoppel."

3. Agency law also subdivides the categories of principal and agent. In some circumstances, consequences vary depending on whether a principal is *disclosed, partially disclosed,* or *undisclosed.* See sections 2.2.2 (defining these terms), 2.2.4 (discussing contract claims and undisclosed principals), 2.3.8 (explaining why apparent authority is generally inapplicable to undisclosed and partially disclosed principals). Likewise, in some circumstances it matters whether an agent is a *general* or *special* agent. See section 2.6.2. In other circumstances it matters whether an agent is a *servant* agent or an *independent contractor* agent. See section 3.2.2.

other [the agent] shall act on his[4] [the principal's] behalf and subject to his [the principal's] control, and consent by the other [the agent] so to act.[5]

Several aspects of this description warrant special attention. Some relate to elements necessary to create an agency relationship. Others relate to the consequences that follow from the creation.

§1.2.2 *Manifestation of Consent*

The creation of an agency relationship necessarily involves two steps: manifestation by the principal and consent by the agent. The manifestation by or attributable to the principal[6] must somehow reach the agent; otherwise the agent has nothing to consent to. When the agent then manifests consent, an agency exists — even though the principal may initially be unaware of the manifestation.

> *Example:* Rushing to meet a publishing deadline, a law professor says to her student research assistant, "Please go to the corner and charge an extra large coffee to my account." The student says, "Sure," and an agency relationship comes into being. The principal has made a manifestation directly to the agent, and the agent has consented directly to the principal.

> *Example:* As the research assistant is leaving the law professor adds, "Do you know anyone who is good at authority checking?" The assistant answers, "Martha's great at that stuff." The professor says, "If you see her, ask her if she will authority check this chapter within the next couple of days." Later the assistant sees Martha and communicates the message. Martha then telephones the professor and says "Yes." An agency relationship exists. Even though the principal did not communicate the manifestation directly, the manifestation reached the agent. The agent directly communicated consent.

> *Example:* Another student, Carolyn, has long wanted to work for the professor. In class one day a question arises, and the professor says, "I'll have to look into that." After class Carolyn decides to research the question for the professor. Unbeknownst to Carolyn, the professor has decided to ask Carolyn's help and has left a message to that effect on Carolyn's answering machine. No agency relationship exists. The pro-

---

4. Like most legal writing of its era, the Restatement uses the masculine pronoun to include males and females, as well as genderless entities. This book strives for a gender-neutral or gender-balanced approach to pronouns but preserves the original usage in all quoted materials.

5. Restatement §1.

6. A manifestation can be "attributable to the principal" under the doctrines of agency law. See sections 2.2.2 and 2.4.8.

fessor has made a manifestation, but Carolyn is unaware of it. Carolyn's conduct, therefore, cannot be seen as consent.

§1.2.3 Objective Standard for Determining Consent

To determine whether a would-be principal and would-be agent have consented, the law looks not to their inner, subjective thoughts but rather to their outward manifestations.[7] Has the would-be principal done or said something that the would-be agent reasonably interpreted as consent that the would-be agent act for the would-be principal? Has the would-be agent done or said something that, reasonably interpreted, indicates agreement to act?

Typically it is the parties' words that evidence their reciprocal consents. However, given the law's objective standard, a party's conduct can also evidence consent. For example, an agent can manifest consent by beginning the requested task:

> *Example:* Rachael, the owner of Blackacre, writes to Sam: "Please act as my broker to sell Blackacre." Sam puts a "For Sale" sign on Blackacre. By beginning the requested task Sam has given the necessary manifestation of consent. An agency relationship exists.

The objective standard also means that, in the eyes of the law, two parties can be agent and principal even though one of them had no subjective desire to create the legal relationship. If, for instance, a person says something that someone else reasonably *mis*interprets as a request for services, an agency relationship may result.

> *Example:* Frustrated by the recalcitrance of Thomas Becket, the Archbishop of Canterbury, Henry II of England exclaims, "Will nobody rid me of this troublesome cleric?" Four of Henry's barons overhear the remark and proceed to kill Becket. Although Henry later protests that he never intended for anyone to kill the Archbishop, the barons nonetheless acted as his agents. In these circumstances Henry's outward manifestation, reasonably interpreted, indicated consent. Even assuming that Henry's protest is genuine, his subjective intent is irrelevant.

§1.2.4 Consent to the Business or Interpersonal Relationship, Not to the Legal Label

Agency is a legal concept—a label the law attaches to a category of business and interpersonal relationships. If two parties manifest consent to the type of business or interpersonal relationship the law labels "agency," then an agency relationship exists. The legal concept applies and the label attaches *regardless of whether the parties had the legal concept in mind and regardless of whether the parties contemplated the consequences of having the label apply.*

---

7. In this respect, agency law follows the modern approach to contract formation.

Sometimes when parties form a relationship they expressly claim or disclaim the agency label. For instance, franchise agreements[8] often include a statement to the effect that "This agreement does not create an agency relationship" or that "The franchisee is not for any purposes the agent of the franchisor." Courts do consider such statements when trying to determine just what relationship the parties actually established. However, the parties' self-selected label is never dispositive and is relevant only as a window on the underlying reality. For example, a disclaimer of agency status may help show that neither party consented to act on the other's behalf and subject to the other's control. However, if the actual relationship between two parties evidences the elements necessary to establish agency, then all the disclaimers in the world will not deflect the agency label. To paraphrase a former President of the United States, "You can hang a sign on a pig and call it a horse, but it's still a pig."[9]

§1.2.5 Agency Consensual, But Not Necessarily Contractual; Gratuitous Agents

Agency is not a subcategory of contract law; not all consensual relationships belong to the law of contracts. Although agents and principals often superimpose contracts on their agency relationship,[10] the agency relationship itself is not a contract.

Therefore, since the doctrine of consideration belongs exclusively to the law of contracts, an agency relationship can exist even though the principal provides no consideration to the agent. Agents who act without receiving any consideration are *gratuitous agents*. In most respects the rights and powers of gratuitous agents are identical to those of paid agents. The major exceptions concern the right of the parties to terminate the agency[11] and the standard of care applicable to the agent.[12]

§1.2.6 Formalities Not Ordinarily Necessary to Create an Agency

An agency relationship can exist even though the parties never express their reciprocal consents in any formal fashion. There is ordinarily no requirement

---

8. In a franchise agreement, one business ("the franchisor") authorizes another business ("the franchisee") to use the franchisor's name and trademark and to sell either a product produced by the franchisor or an array of services developed by the franchisor. In return, the franchisee typically pays an initial franchise fee plus an ongoing royalty, commission, or service fee. Franchise agreements typically obligate franchisees to operate their business in compliance with requirements set by the franchisor. These requirements can be quite detailed and comprehensive.

9. Bush Urges Racial Harmony, Attacks "Quota Bill," N.Y. Times, June 2, 1991, at A32 (George Bush objecting to certain aspects of the 1991 Civil Rights bill) ("You can't put a sign on a pig and say it's a horse.").

10. See sections 1.3, 4.1.6, and 4.3.3.

11. See section 5.2.3.

12. See section 4.1.4.

that the parties consent in writing. Indeed, as section 1.2.3 indicates, conduct alone can suffice; words themselves are not necessary.

In some jurisdictions, however, the "equal dignities" rule applies. The rule (1) is statutory, (2) pertains to transactions that must be in writing in order to be enforceable, and (3) provides that an agent can bind a principal to such transactions only if the agency relationship is documented in a writing signed by the principal. For example, Cal. Civ. Code §2309 states: "An oral authorization is sufficient for any purpose, except that an authority to enter into a contract required by law to be in writing can only be given by an instrument in writing."

§1.2.7 *Consent and Control*

To create an agency, the reciprocal consents of principal and agent must include an understanding that the principal is in control of the relationship. "Since the whole purpose of the relation of agency is that the agent shall carry out the will of the principal,"[13] agency cannot exist unless the "acting for" party (the agent) consents to be subject to the will of the "acted for" party (the principal). The control need not be total or continuous and need not extend to the way the agent physically performs, but there must be some sense that the principal is "in charge." At minimum, the principal must have the right to control the goal of the relationship.[14]

Often the manifestations creating a relationship do not expressly address the issue of control. If the issue is in question, courts will examine how the relationship actually operated in order to decide whether the "acting for" party consented to be controlled. The facts of the relationship may imply consent.

> *Example:* A hospital patient caught hepatitis from contaminated blood and sought to sue the blood supplier for breach of warranty. To succeed, the patient had to show that he was in privity with the blood supplier, but it appeared that the hospital, not the patient, had made the purchase from the supplier. The patient claimed he was nonetheless in privity, asserting that the hospital was acting as his agent when it obtained the blood. The court rejected the patient's claim, noting that there was no indication that the hospital was in any way subject to the patient's control.[15]

While this section treats "consent to control" as an element necessary to establish an agency relationship, issues of control also play major roles in at least three other parts of agency law. It is important to keep all four roles distinct from each other. The other three roles are:

---

13. Restatement, Chapter 5, topic 1, Introductory Note.

14. If the control characteristic is lacking, the relationship cannot be a true agency. See Chapter Six, and especially sections 6.1.2, 6.2, and 6.3.2.

15. *Krom v. Sharp and Dohme, Inc.,* 180 N.Y.S.2d 99 (1958).

1) *Control as a substitute method for establishing agency status.* When a creditor exercises extensive control over its debtor's business, that control can by itself establish an agency relationship. The law treats the debtor as the agent and the creditor as the principal. As a consequence, the creditor becomes liable for the debtor's debts to other creditors.[16]

2) *Control as an element of "servant" status.* Whether the principal has a right to control the physical performance of the agent's tasks determines whether the agent is a "servant" or "nonservant" agent. As discussed in Chapter Three, this distinction is crucial to determining the principal's liability for certain torts committed by the agent.

3) *Control as a consequence.* As a consequence of agency status (rather than as an element necessary to create that status), the principal has the power to control the agent. Even though the agent may have consented to give the principal only limited control, once the agency relationship comes into existence the principal has the power (though not necessarily the right) to control every detail of the agent's performance.[17]

§1.2.8 Consent to Serve the Principal's Interests

To create an agency relationship the agent must manifest consent to act *for* the principal; that is, the agent must manifest a recognition that serving the *principal's* interests is the primary purpose of the relationship. The facts of the relationship can and often do imply that recognition.

> **Example:** A law student, rushing to prepare for graduation and the fabulous buffet party to follow, gives a friend a list of last-minute additions to the menu and asks her or him to "do me a favor and make sure the caterer includes these on the buffet." The friend agrees. The friend has impliedly recognized that the endeavor's primary purpose is to meet the law student's needs, not to serve any separate agenda the friend may have.

§1.3 The Relationship of Agency and Contract

Although agency itself is not a contractual relationship, the parties to an agency can make contracts regarding their agency relationship. To take the most common example, the parties can agree that the principal will pay the agent for the agent's services. For further example, the parties can by agreement set a definite term to the relationship or limit the principal's right to control the agent with regard to matters connected with the agency.

---

16. See section 6.3 for an extensive discussion.

17. An understanding between the principal and the agent may limit the principal's *right* to exercise control. If a principal violates that understanding when exercising the *power* of control, the agent may sue for damages and may also terminate the agency relationship. See sections 4.1.3 and 4.1.6.

Example: A manufacturing company plans to build a large plant and retains a "construction management" firm to manage the project on behalf of the manufacturing company. The contract between the manufacturing company and the construction management firm states: "Using reasonable care, FIRM will select the various contractors to build the plant."

Contracts between agent and principal have limited impact. They can change the rights and duties that exist between agent and principal, but they cannot abrogate the powers that agency status confers on each party to the relationship. Thus, for example, despite any contract provisions to the contrary:

- the principal always has the power to control every detail of the agent's performance[18]
- the agent may have certain powers to bind the principal[19]
- both the principal and the agent have the power to end the agency at any time[20]

When an agent or principal exercises a power in breach of the other's contract right, the injured party can bring an action for damages. But the exercise of power cannot be undone or enjoined.

§1.4   Interaction Between Statutes and the Common Law of Agency

Although agency is a common law rubric, there is considerable interplay between statutory law and agency law. Statutes now govern key issues formerly left to the common law, and agency law labels and principles inform both the drafting and interpretation of statutes.

For example, one of the most important functions of agency law is to determine when information possessed by an agent is attributed to the principal.[21] However, if the principal is an organization, a business organization or commercial statute may provide the applicable rule.[22] Moreover, statutes have

---

18. See sections 4.1.3 and 4.1.6.

19. For example, if the principal allows the agent to run the principal's business and to appear as the owner, the agent has the power to bind the principal "through transactions usual in such businesses . . . although contrary to the directions of the principal." Restatement §195. For further discussion, see section 2.6.2. See also section 2.3 (apparent authority).

20. See section 5.1.1.

21. See section 2.4.

22. See, e.g., Revised Uniform Partnership Act (1997), §102(e) (stating rules as to when "a person other than an individual knows, has notice, or receives a notification of a fact"), Uniform Limited Partnership Act (2001), §103(g) (same) and UCC §1-201(27) (stating rules for "[n]otice, knowledge or a notice or notification received by an organization").

displaced much of the common law applicable to employment relations. The National Labor Relations Act (governing unionization) is perhaps the predominant example. In addition:

> Employment legislation has modified common-law doctrine concerning the fellow-servant rule,[23] under which an employer is not liable for injuries inflicted on one employee by the negligent acts of another, unless the act violates an employer's nondelegable duties. Employment legislation such as Title VII expands an employer's nondelegable duties substantially, subjecting the employer under some circumstances to liability for employee conduct, such as sexually harassing behavior, that usually falls outside the scope of the common-law doctrine of respondeat superior. Workers' compensation legislation likewise imposes liability on the employer in circumstances under which the common law did not.[24]

The interplay works in the opposite direction as well, as agency concepts make their way into statutory formulations. For example, the "servant" construct[25] helps set the scope for a wide range of statutes designed to regulate or tax the modern employment relationship. Thus, for example:

> *Nationwide Mutual Insurance Co. v. Darden* is the most important case for determining employee status under federal employment law. . . . [T]he case rejected legislative purpose as a reference for determining the scope and meaning of the term *employee*. [In the words of the U.S. Supreme Court,] "[w]here Congress uses terms that have accumulated settled meaning under . . . the common law, a court must infer, unless the statute otherwise dictates, that Congress means to incorporate the established meaning of these terms. . . . In the past, when Congress has used the term 'employee' without defining it, we have concluded that Congress intended to describe the conventional master-servant relationship as understood by common-law agency doctrine." The decision means in essence that the term "employee" is to be looked up in the dictionary of the common law.[26]

This interplay can produce confusing results, as when a statute uses a label taken from agency law but attaches consequences which are at odds with basic agency law principles. For example, under the common law of agency an agent always has the power, if not necessarily the right, to terminate the agency.[27] To exercise this power, an agent must communicate with the principal.[28] Yet several modern business law statutes refer to "an agent for service of

---

23. Discussed briefly in section 4.3.2.

24. Restatement (Third), Introduction (T.D. No. 2, 2001) (March 14, 2001).

25. Discussed in detail in section 3.2.2.

26. Daniel S. Kleinberger, "Magnificent Circularity and the Churkendoose: LLC Members and Federal Employment Law," 22 Okla. City U.L. Rev. 477, 494 (1997), discussing *Nationwide Mut. Ins. Co. v. Darden*, 503 U.S. 318 (1992).

27. See section 5.1.1.

28. See section 5.1.1.

process" while stating that the agent's resignation is effective only 31 days after the agent communicates with a specified public official.[29]

In sum, "[m]odern common law [agency] doctrines operate in the context of statutes," and statutes, both as drafted by legislatures and interpreted by courts, "incorporate definitions or doctrines that are drawn from the common law."[30]

§1.5   Major Issues in the Law of Agency

By way of an overview, the major issues in the law of agency can be organized according to the relationship among agency's three players: principals, agents, and third parties.

§1.5.1   *Between the Principal and the Agent*

Under what circumstances does an agency relationship exist?   As the Restatement explains, "agency is a legal concept which depends upon the existence of required factual elements."[31] Agency law is therefore fundamentally concerned with whether particular kinds of relationships qualify as agency relationships. For example, must both parties subjectively consent to the relationship? Must they intend to create the legal relationship? Must they even be aware that they are creating the legal relationship? Must the agent be promised contract-like consideration by the principal?[32]

What duties does the agent owe the principal?   The principal relies on the agent to get things done. How perfect must the agent's performance be? In dealing with the principal, may the agent follow the rules for "arm's-length" transactions, such as might apply to the parties to an ordinary contract? In carrying out the tasks of the agency, must the agent think only of the principal's interests, or may the agent also consider its own interests as well?[33]

What duties does the principal owe the agent?   Must the principal compensate the agent for the agent's efforts? If the agent somehow gets into trouble, must the principal help out the agent? Must the principal alert the agent to risks involved in the agent's task?[34]

---

29. Uniform Limited Liability Company Act §110 (1996); Uniform Limited Partnership Act §116 (2001).

30. Restatement (Third), Introduction (T.D. No. 2, 2001) (March 14, 2001) ("Common Law and Statutes").

31. Restatement §1, comment *b*.

32. See section 1.2.

33. See section 4.1.

34. See section 4.3.

§1.5.2 *Between the Principal and Third Parties*

If a third party has made a commitment to an agent, under what circumstances can the principal enforce that commitment?   People and organizations use agents to get things done, and often the agent's task involves making arrangements with third parties on the principal's behalf. For example, you might use a friend to make last-minute arrangements with the caterer you have hired for your graduation party. A bank might use its tellers to accept deposits from customers and give in return a paper evidencing the bank's resulting indebtedness (i.e., a deposit slip).

When an agency relationship involves this "arrangement making" function, it is essential that the principal be able to enforce commitments that third parties have made to the agent. Otherwise, the agent could not accomplish much for the principal. For example, it would do you little good to send a friend to deal with the caterer for your graduation party if the caterer could later ignore those dealings and say, "But that doesn't count. We weren't dealing with you directly." The ability to bind third parties to the principal is thus an essential aspect of the agent's role, and questions about that aspect are therefore very important in the law of agency.[35]

If an agent makes a commitment to a third party, under what circumstances may the third party enforce that commitment against the principal?   When an agency relationship involves the "arrangement making" function, it is essential that third parties be able to enforce against the principal commitments made by the agent. Otherwise agents could not accomplish much for principals; third parties would generally insist on "dealing direct."

Imagine, for example, that you go to Alice's Service Station to have your car repaired. You leave the car with Bob, a mechanic who works for Alice. Bob works on your car but the work turns out to be defective. When you complain to Alice, she says, "It's not my problem. You didn't deal directly with me." Would you ever again be willing to deal with one of Alice's agents? Or would you insist on dealing only with Alice? The ability to bind the principal to third parties is thus an essential aspect of the agent's role, and questions about that aspect are therefore very important in the law of agency.[36]

If the agent possesses certain information, under what circumstances will the law treat the principal as if the principal possessed that information?   In many situations the law cares whether and when a party has particular kinds of information. Since principals often act through agents, the law of agency must decide when to hold the principal responsible for information possessed by the agent.

---

35. Chapter Two deals with such questions.
36. Chapter Two also deals with such questions.

For example, Sam sells Blackacre to Rachael, innocently assuring her that Blackacre contains no toxic waste. Sam uses an agent to consummate the sale, and Sam's agent knows that a former owner of Blackacre buried loads of noxious chemicals on the land. The agent does not disclose this information either to Sam or to Rachael. In Rachael's subsequent fraud suit against Sam, will the law attribute to Sam the knowledge possessed by his agent?[37]

If the agent conveys certain information, under what circumstances will the law treat the principal as if the principal had conveyed that information?   In many situations the law cares whether and when a party communicates particular kinds of information. As with information *possessed* by an agent, the law of agency must decide when to hold the principal responsible for information *conveyed* by the agent.

For example, Sam uses an agent to sell Blackacre to Rachael. Without Sam's knowledge or consent the agent tells Rachael that Blackacre contains a lake "full of delicious trout." In fact, the lake contains nothing larger than minnows and the agent knows it. Will the law attribute the agent's statement to Sam?[38]

If an agent's acts or omissions cause tort injuries to a third party, under what circumstances can the third party proceed directly against the principal?   When an agent commits a tort, the injured party can of course proceed against the agent. The third party may, however, wish to pursue the principal. (For instance, the principal may have a deeper pocket or may make a less sympathetic defendant.) The law of agency must therefore determine under what circumstances a principal is liable for the tortious acts of its agent. For example, suppose the law student's friend, rushing to make last-minute arrangements with the caterer, drives negligently and runs over a dog. May the dog's owner recover damages from the law student? Or suppose the consultant who is being used by the supermarket chain to recommend new cash registers disparages a particular brand of register. May the company that sells the disparaged brand sue the supermarket chain?[39]

§1.5.3   Between the Agent and Third Parties

When an agent arranges a commitment between the principal and a third party, under what circumstances may the third party hold the agent responsible for the commitment?   This question is of great importance to both the agent and the third party. From the agent's perspective, the

---

37. See section 2.4.4.
38. See section 2.4.6. See also section 3.4.2 (misrepresentation by an agent).
39. For a discussion of these questions, see Chapter Three.

risks differ greatly as between merely arranging a contract for the principal and being personally liable for that contract's performance. From the perspective of the third party, it may well have been the reputation of the agent, not the principal, that induced the third party to make the commitment in the first place.[40]

---

40. See section 4.2.

2

Binding Principals to Third Parties in Contract and Through Information

§2.1   "Binding the Principal"

§2.1.1   *The Importance and Meaning of "Binding the Principal"*

Perhaps the most important consequence of the agency label is the agent's power to bind the principal to third parties and to bind third parties to the principal. The Restatement defines *power* as "the ability . . . to produce a change in a given legal relation (between the principal and third parties) by doing or not doing a given act,"[1] and, as explained previously, an agent's power to bind is central to an agent's ability to accomplish tasks on the principal's behalf.[2]

The concept of agency power is essentially a concept of attribution (sometimes called "imputation"). To the extent an agent has the power to bind, the agent's conduct is attributed to the principal. In the words of a venerable agency law maxim, *Qui facit per alium facit per se.*[3] Thus, when a third party as-

---

1. Restatement §6.

2. See section 1.5.2.

3. This maxim translates as "Who acts through another acts himself." Black's Law Dictionary 1249 (1990).

serts that an agent's act or omission has "bound the principal," the third party wants the principal treated legally as if the principal itself had acted or failed to act. Although the attribution rules differ depending on whether the underlying matter sounds in contract, sounds in tort, or concerns the possession or communication of information, the concept of attribution is ubiquitous.

Example: George, acting as agent for the Bronx Zoo, contracts with Martha, a "bring 'em back alive" hunter of wildlife, to procure a hippopotamus for exhibition at the Zoo. Later, Martha seeks to hold the Zoo to the contract, asserting that in making the contract George bound the Zoo. Martha wants the Zoo treated as if the Zoo itself had made the contract.

Example: A discount warehouse in Iowa contracts with a railroad to transport 150 tractors from Newark, New Jersey to the railroad's terminal in Iowa City. The contract between the warehouse and the railroad specifies that the warehouse must pick up the tractors "within three days after receiving notice of their arrival at the Iowa City terminal, and WAREHOUSE shall pay storage fees at a rate of $500 per day for any delay in pick up." The railroad gives notice of arrival by telephoning the loading dock at the warehouse after normal business hours and speaking to a janitor. The janitor fails to inform the warehouse, the warehouse fails to make a timely pick up, and the railroad claims storage fees. In assessing the storage fees, the railroad wants the warehouse treated as if the warehouse itself had received the notice.

Example: Sam sells Blackacre to Rachael, innocently assuring her that Blackacre contains no toxic waste. Sam uses an agent to consummate the sale, and Sam's agent knows that a former owner of Blackacre buried loads of noxious chemicals on the land. The agent does not disclose this information either to Sam or to Rachael. In Rachael's subsequent fraud suit against Sam, Rachael wants Sam treated as if he directly possessed and suppressed the information about the noxious chemicals.

Example: Walking into class, a law student slips, falls, and injures herself. The law school's maintenance crew had negligently overwaxed the floor. In her suit against the law school, the student seeks to legally attribute the crew's negligence to the school, that is, to have the school treated as if the school itself had been negligent.

Attribution can also work in favor of the principal, as when a principal seeks to hold a third party to a contract entered into by an agent or to information received or communicated by an agent.

Example: An art dealer's employee attends an auction on the dealer's behalf and makes the winning bid on a painting. Later the dealer tenders payment and seeks to compel the auction house to deliver the painting. The dealer seeks to be treated as if it itself had made the winning bid.

Example: A residential lease allows either party to terminate on 60 days' notice. The landlord's resident manager gives the proper 60-day notice to a tenant, but the tenant fails to vacate the apartment. In the subsequent eviction action, the landlord wishes to be treated as if it itself had given the requisite notice.

§2.1.2 *"Binding the Principal" and Questions of Agency Power*

Agency law uses its concept of power to analyze "binding the principal" questions. The question of "Under the law of agency did X's act or omission bind Y?" thus becomes "Under the law of agency, did X have the power to bind Y through that act or omission?" Agency law approaches questions of power through five attribution rules. An agent can have the power to bind a principal through:

(i)   actual authority (including express and implied actual authority),
(ii) apparent authority,
(iii) estoppel,
(iv) inherent power,[4] and
(v)   ratification.

More than one subcategory of agency power may apply in any particular situation. Indeed, in practice parties often argue attribution rules in the alternative. For example, "When X made this contract on behalf of Y, X had actual authority to do so. Y is therefore bound. And, even if X lacked actual authority, X had apparent authority and so Y is bound. And, even if X lacked both actual and apparent authority, X had the inherent power to bind Y, and so Y is bound. And if even X lacked both the authority and power to bind Y, estoppel applies and so Y is bound. And, even if X lacked both the authority and power to bind Y and estoppel does not apply, Y subsequently ratified X's act and so Y is bound."

This chapter discusses how each of the five attribution rules pertains to binding a principal in contract and also considers how, in contractual and similar matters, a principal can be bound by information that an agent or apparent agent receives, knows, ought to know, or communicates.

Chapter Three considers the attribution rules relevant to tort claims. In that context, the most important attribution rule is *respondeat superior*, an aspect of inherent power. Apparent authority is also relevant occasionally.

---

4. Inherent power is actually a collection of attribution rules, or a rule with several different facets. See section 2.6. Restatement (Third) proposes to eliminate the concept of inherent power, relying instead on concepts of apparent authority, estoppel, and restitution. Restatement (Third), Chapter 2, Introductory Note at 105.

§2.1.3 *Attribution Imputation: Transaction Specific and Time Sensitive*

Attribution (also called "imputation") is always transaction specific. For instance, the attribution question is not whether "*A* had apparent authority to bind *P*" but rather whether "*A* had apparent authority to bind *P* when *A* did *X*."

Because attribution is transaction specific, it is also time sensitive. With the exception of ratification,[5] all attribution rules are applied exclusively as of the time that relevant transaction occurred.

> *Example:* *T* claims that *P* is bound to a contract formed between *A* and *T* last Friday at 3 P.M. The attribution analysis focuses on whether *last Friday at 3 P.M. A* had the power to bind *P* to the contract.

> *Example:* *T* rents an apartment from *P* on a month-to-month lease. *T* claims to have given notice of termination to *A* on the last day of last month and further claims that the notice is effective against *P*. The attribution analysis focuses on whether *on the last day of last month A* had the power to bind *P* by receiving notices related to the lease.

§2.1.4 *Distinguishing the* Power *to Bind from the* Right *to Bind*

As will be discussed throughout this chapter and the next, various circumstances can *empower* an agent to bind the principal. An agent has the *right* to bind the principal only to the extent that the principal has authorized the agent to do so. A principal gives this authorization in the same way (and often at the same time) that the principal initiates the agency relationship—namely, by making a manifestation that reaches the agent.[6]

To the extent an agent has the right to bind a principal, the agent automatically has the power to do so. It is possible, however, for an agent to have the *power* to bind while lacking the *right*. In such circumstances, if the agent exercises the power and binds the principal, the agent wrongs the principal. Then, consistent with the right/power distinction:

- the agent is liable to the principal for the wrongful conduct, but
- the principal is nonetheless bound to the third party.

> *Example:* Rachael, the owner of Rachael's Service Station, promotes Sam to the position of general manager and puts him in charge of the Station's day-to-day operations. Although service station managers or-

---

5. Ratification occurs when a principal affirms a previously unauthorized act, and, consequently, ratification analysis has a dual temporal focus: the moment at which the unauthorized act occurs and the moment at which the principal affirms. Section 2.7 discusses ratification in detail.

6. The Restatement and the caselaw call this *authorized* power "actual authority." For a detailed discussion of actual authority, see section 2.2.

dinarily place orders for batteries, tires, and other accessories, Rachael instructs Sam to leave that ordering to her. Nonetheless, Sam orders batteries. Under the doctrines of apparent authority and inherent agency power,[7] Rachael is bound, even though Sam had no right (vis-à-vis Rachael, his principal) to place the order.

§2.2   Actual Authority

§2.2.1   *Actual Authority and the Agent's Authorized Power to Bind*

For an agency relationship to come into existence, the principal must manifest consent to have the agent act on the principal's behalf with respect to some task or goal. Therefore, at the core of any agency relationship is a zone of endeavor as to which the principal has authorized the agent to act. The principal's authorization creates "actual authority" in the agent; an agent has the power to bind the principal through any act or omission within the agent's actual authority. Authorized acts can include not only the making of agreements and the doing of tasks but also the receipt, possession, and communication of information.

§2.2.2   *Creation of Actual Authority*

Mechanics.   Paralleling the creation of the agency relationship itself, creation of actual authority involves:

- an objective manifestation by the principal
- followed by the agent's reasonable interpretation of that manifestation
- which leads the agent to believe that it is authorized to act for the principal.

In the words of §26 of the Restatement:

> authority to do an act can be created by written or spoken words or other conduct of the principal which, reasonably interpreted, causes the agent to believe that the principal desires him so to act on the principal's account.

Example: Two traveling salespeople, Bernice and Joe, are in the hotel bar. As Joe gets up to get another bowl of pretzels, Bernice says, "It's Happy Hour. While you're up, order another round of drinks for us and charge them to me." Joe orders the round and charges the price to Bernice's room. In doing so, Joe has acted within his actual authority. Bernice's statement constituted the necessary manifestation and Joe's action reflects his interpretation of that manifestation—that is, that Bernice

---

7. See sections 2.3 and 2.6.2. Restatement (Third) would treat this situation as involving only apparent authority.

(the principal) "desires him so to act on the principal's account." In the circumstances, Joe's interpretation is certainly reasonable.

Example: Same situation as above, except that when Joe gets to the bar he discovers that "Happy Hour" has ended and that prices have gone up. From the bar he conveys that information back to Bernice, who responds by waving her hand in a forward motion. When Joe charges the drinks to Bernice's room, he is again acting within his actual authority. By checking he has reinforced the reasonableness of his interpretation.

Source and nature of principal's manifestation.   A principal's manifestation can reach the agent directly or indirectly and, in some circumstances, can consist of inaction. Often the principal will communicate directly with the agent, but a manifestation that reaches the agent through intermediaries can still give rise to actual authority. Indeed, sometimes communication is typically indirect, as when the principal is an organization, such as a corporation or limited liability company. In those contexts, an agent normally receives communication "from" the principal via the conduct of co-agents.

The principal's inaction can constitute a manifestation when silence, reasonably interpreted, indicates consent. For example, when an agent takes particular action, the action comes to attention of the principal, and the principal makes no objection, the agent may well have actual authority to repeat the action in similar circumstances.

Example: For years the mechanics at Rachael's Service Station have, on an ad hoc basis, offered a 10 percent discount to regular customers on major service jobs. Rachael, the owner, never explicitly authorized the practice, but she has been aware of it and has not previously objected to it. As a result of Rachael's silent acquiescence, the mechanics have actual authority to offer the discount. The acquiescence satisfies the "manifestation" requirement.

Necessity, source, and nature of agent's belief.   For an agent to have authority to do a particular act, the agent must believe that authority exists, that belief must be based on some manifestation from the principal, and that belief must be reasonable. In the words of the Restatement §33:

> An agent is authorized to do, and to do only, what it is reasonable for him to infer that the principal desires him to do in the light of the principal's manifestations and the facts as he [i.e., the agent] knows or should know them at the time he acts.

Agency law determines the reasonableness of the agent's interpretation by considering the same sorts of information that figure into determinations of reasonableness in other areas of law. "All other matters throwing light upon what a reasonable person in the position of the agent at the time of acting would consider are to be given due weight."[8]

The Restatement's reference to "reasonable person" reflects an objective standard. In determining the scope of an agent's actual authority what matters is the principal's objective manifestation and the agent's reasonable interpretation of that manifestation. Any secret, subjective intent of the principal is irrelevant.[9]

Principal's control of agent's interpretation.   A principal can always cut back or countermand previously granted authority simply by making a manifestation to the agent and seeing that the manifestation reaches the agent. If it comes to the agent's attention that the principal desires to remove some or all of the agent's authority, the agent can no longer reasonably believe that it has the authority the principal desires to remove.

> *Example:* Rachael, the owner of Rachael's Service Station, decides that she can no longer afford the 10 percent discount. She calls the mechanics together and says, "Effective right now, no more 10 percent discounts." The next day, one of the mechanics, momentarily forgetting Rachael's instruction, offers the discount to a customer. In doing so, the mechanic has acted without actual authority. After Rachael's instruction, the mechanic cannot *reasonably* believe himself authorized to give 10 percent discounts.

In cutting back or countermanding previously granted authority the principal may be breaching a contract between the principal or agent.[10] The

---

8. Restatement §34, comment *a*. The text of §34 provides the following nonexhaustive list of factors that figure into determining the reasonableness of the agent's interpretation:

    (a) the situation of the parties, their relations to one another, and the business in which they are engaged;

    (b) the general usages of business, the usages of trades or employments of the kind to which the authorization [i.e., the principal's manifestation] relates, and the business methods of the principal;

    (c) facts of which the agent has notice respecting the objects which the principal desires to accomplish;

    (d) the nature of the subject matter, the circumstances under which the act is to be performed and the legality or illegality of the act; and

    (e) the formality or informality, and the care, or lack of it, with which an instrument evidencing the authority is drawn. Restatement (Third) §1.01, comment *e* at 30, suggests that the fiduciary character of agency influences the analysis of reasonableness. An agent's fiduciary duty means the agent "is not free to exploit gaps or arguable ambiguities in the principal's instructions to further the agent's self-interest, or the interests of another."

9. See section 1.2.3.

10. See sections 1.3, 4.1.3, and 4.1.6.

principal may also be leaving intact the agent's inherent power to bind the principal or an enforceable appearance of authority, or both.[11]

Irrelevance of third party knowledge.   The mechanics for creating actual authority involve the principal and the agent and have nothing to do with what third parties may or may not happen to know. As a result, in determining the existence and extent of an agent's actual authority, the law focuses on the relationship between the principal and the agent (the inter se relationship). An agent can have actual authority (and therefore power to bind the principal to third parties) even though at the time of the relevant occurrence the third party neither knows nor has reason to know the extent of the agent's authority. In contrast, the third party's view is pivotal to the existence of apparent authority.[12] Indeed, an agent can have actual authority even though at the time of the "binding" act or omission the principal is:

- only *partially disclosed* (i.e., the third party knows or has reason to know that the agent is acting for another, but not who that other is);[13] or even
- totally *undisclosed* (i.e., the third party does not know or have reason to know that the agent is acting as an agent).[14]

When a principal is undisclosed or partially disclosed, the third party will acquire evidence of the agent's actual authority only after the agent's exercise of that authority. Nonetheless, if the authority existed at the time of the transaction, the principal will be bound.

> *Example:* A power company authorizes a coal broker to buy coal for it. The broker contracts to buy the coal in its own name. When the coal seller later prepares to deliver the coal to the broker, the seller discovers that the broker has gone out of business. Then the seller discovers that the broker was making the purchase on the power company's behalf and had actual authority to do so. By asserting actual authority, the seller can

---

11. See sections 2.6.2 (inherent power) and 2.3 (apparent authority).

12. See section 2.3.5.

13. In such situations, the fact that there is a principal is disclosed (or at least reasonably knowable) but the identity of the principal is not. Disclosure is partial. Restatement (Third) §1.04(2)(c), at 91 substitutes the term "unidentified" for "partially disclosed" because the latter "misleadingly suggests that a portion of the principal's identity is known to the third party." Restatement (Third) §1.04, comment *b* at 94. Contrast a *fully disclosed* principal. For example, you bring your car into Rachael's Service Station and talk to Rachael's manager, Sam, to arrange for an engine tune-up. You know that Sam is acting for another, and you know who that other is. The principal, Rachael, is *fully disclosed*.

14. The third party cannot know or have reason to know who the principal is, since the third party does not even know or have reason to know that a principal exists. In limited circumstances a third party can escape claims made *by* an undisclosed principal. See section 2.2.4.

hold the *undisclosed principal* (the power company) to the contract. Because actual authority is at issue, it is irrelevant that at the time of contracting the seller was ignorant of the agency relationship.

Example: An attorney contacts an art dealer and contracts to buy a famous Picasso print. The attorney explains that she is acting for a client but declines to identify the client. (The client dislikes notoriety.) If the art dealer later learns the identity of the *partially disclosed* principal (the client) and can prove that the attorney acted with actual authority, then the art dealer can enforce the contract against the client.[15]

§2.2.3 *Actual Authority: Express and Implied*

In addition to the authority expressly indicated by the principal's words and other conduct, an agent may also have *implied* authority. Restatement §35 states: "Unless otherwise agreed, authority to conduct a transaction includes authority to do acts which are incidental to it, usually accompany it, or are reasonably necessary to accomplish it." Sometimes the implication is based on custom or past dealings. Other times, "the principal's objectives and other facts known to the agent" cause an agent to infer that a particular act is authorized.[16]

Comment *b* to §35 states the very simple rationale for the concept of implied authority. "In most cases the principal does not think of, far less specifically direct, the series of acts necessary to accomplish his objects." Implied actual authority fills in the gaps.[17]

Example: A company gave its plant manager express authority to purchase materials and supervise production of a product. Although the company expressed no instructions whatsoever concerning the handling of surplus raw materials, the manager had implied authority to act on the company's behalf and sell the surplus to a third party.

Example: An insurance broker acted as local agent for an insurance company, with express authority to conduct business for the company in the locality. Although the insurance company had given no express instructions to the broker on how to handle cancellation notices received from policy holders, the broker had implied authority to receive such notices. Accordingly, notice to the broker was notice to the insurance company.

The express manifestations of the principal can always negate implied authority.

---

15. Whether a principal is disclosed, partially disclosed, or undisclosed matters substantially as to the agent's liability on a contract. See section 4.2.1.

16. Restatement (Third) §2.01, comment *b,* at 107.

17. Restatement (Third) "treats implied authority as an aspect of the scope of the agent's actual authority and not as a separate type of authority." Restatement (Third), Chapter 2, Introductory Note at 105. This change does not affect the way the concept operates in practice.

§2.2.4 *Binding the Principal in Contract Through Actual Authority*

If an agent acting with actual authority makes a contract on behalf of a principal, then the principal is bound to the contract as if the principal had directly entered into the contract. In almost all circumstances, the third party is likewise bound on the contract to the principal.

> *Example:* Sam, a research scientist, instructs Irv, his lab manager, "Get me a maintenance contract on the electron microscope. Make sure that we have service 24/7/365. I don't care what it costs." Irv enters into a contract with Selma's Service Company, signing the contract, "Irv, as manager for Sam." Sam, the disclosed principal, is bound to the contract.

> *Example:* Same situation, except that Irv signs the contract in his own name, without having made any reference to Sam. Sam, the undisclosed principal, is bound to the contract.

> *Example:* Same situation, except that Irv enters into the contract through a phone conversation with Selma, explaining "I'm making this agreement for the lab's owner." Sam, the partially disclosed principal, is bound to the contract.

Special rules for contracts involving undisclosed principals.   When the principal is undisclosed, the third party is sometimes entitled to (i) insist on rendering performance to the agent, or (ii) escape the contract entirely.

Rendering performance to the agent.   The third party may insist upon rendering performance to the agent if the contract requires the third party to perform personal services or if in some other way rendering performance to the undisclosed principal would significantly increase or change the third party's burden. This rule makes sense, since when the third party entered into the contract it expected to render performance to the agent, not the principal. Deviating from that expectation is fair only if the deviation does not significantly alter the third party's burdens.

Escaping the contract entirely.   In a narrow range of circumstances a third party may escape entirely a contract made with an disclosed principal. Escape is possible if either:

- the contract between the third party and the agent provides that it is inoperative if the agent is representing someone, or
- the agent fraudulently represents that the agent is not acting for the principal, the third party would not have entered into the contract knowing the principal was a party, and the agent or undisclosed principal knows or should know that the third party would not have made the contract with the principal.

Active misrepresentation of the principal's role is insufficient. The third party must also show (i) that had the third party known of the principal's role, there would have been no contract and (ii) that the agent or principal had reason to know of the third party's aversion. Mere failure to disclose the principal's existence is always insufficient.

Example: A guitar maker has a guitar for sale. A musician wishes to buy, but knows that on account of a longstanding feud the guitar maker will refuse to sell the guitar to him. The would-be buyer therefore asks a friend to make the purchase. The guitar maker says to the friend, "I care about the guitars I make. I want to be sure that they're treated with respect." The friend responds, "Don't worry. I've wanted one of your guitars for a long time. I am looking forward to playing this one for years to come. I'll take good care of it." The guitar maker agrees to a deal, but learns the truth before turning over the guitar. The guitar maker is not obligated to go through with the sale. The agent affirmatively misrepresented the principal's role, that misrepresentation induced the seller to make the contract, and both the agent and the principal knew that the guitar maker would not have made a contract with the principal.

Example: A gay man, well-known as a gay rights advocate, seeks to buy a house for sale in a fashionable neighborhood, but fears that the owner, a well-known opponent of gay rights, will refuse to sell to him. The would-be buyer therefore secretly authorizes a friend to negotiate and consummate the purchase, ostensibly in the friend's name. It never occurs to the seller that the ostensible purchaser might be a front, and the seller asks no questions to that effect. The friend of course makes no comment on the subject. At closing the seller learns that the gay man is the undisclosed principal. The seller is nonetheless obligated to go through with the transaction. Although both the agent and the undisclosed principal had reason to know that the third party would have refused to deal with the principal, there was no affirmative misrepresentation.[18]

§2.3   Apparent Authority

§2.3.1   *The Misnomer of "Apparent Authority"*

"Apparent authority" is a misnomer. The term refers to the power to bind, not the right. The power derives from the *appearance* of legitimate authority; the doctrine exists to protect third parties who are misled by appearances.[19]

An apparent agent's intent is therefore immaterial. A person with apparent authority can bind the apparent principal to a contract even if the person does not intend to benefit the apparent principal and even if the person is lying about being authorized.

---

18. This Example assumes the transaction is not subject to a law prohibiting discrimination on account of sexual orientation.

19. For a more extensive explanation of the doctrine's rationale, see section 2.3.7.

§2.3.2   *Creation of Apparent Authority*

Mechanics.   Creation of apparent authority involves:

- an objective manifestation from one party ("apparent principal"),
- which somehow reaches a third party, and
- which causes the third party to reasonably believe that another party ("apparent agent") is indeed authorized to act for the first party (i.e., for the apparent principal).

In the words of the Restatement §27:

> apparent authority to do an act is created as to a third person by written or spoken words or any other conduct of the principal which, reasonably interpreted, causes the third person to believe that the principal consents to have the act done on his behalf by the person purporting to act for him.

Relationship to actual authority.   Apparent authority can coexist and be coextensive with actual authority.

Example: Two travelling salespeople, Bernice and Joe, are in the hotel bar. As Joe gets up to get another bowl of pretzels, Bernice says, "While you're up, order another round of drinks for us and charge them to me." Joe orders the round and charges the price to Bernice's room. If the bartender overheard Bernice's instructions, Joe had apparent as well as actual authority to charge the drinks.

Apparent authority can also extend an actual agent's power to bind the principal beyond the scope of the agent's actual authority.

Example: An Art Collector arranges for Broker to attend a forthcoming art auction and bid on certain items on Collector's behalf. Collector sends a letter to the Auction House, stating, "At your upcoming auction, Broker will represent me and is authorized to bid on my behalf." In the past Broker has often placed bids for Collector in excess of $50,000. This time Collector tells the Broker, "Don't bid more than $25,000 on any item." Collector does not, however, communicate this limit to the Auction House. Although the Broker's actual authority to bid is limited to $25,000 per item, the limit does not apply to the Broker's apparent authority.

Apparent authority can also exist where no actual agency exists.

Example: The Art Collector arranges for Broker to attend a forthcoming art auction and bid on certain items on the Collector's behalf. Collector sends a letter to the Auction House, stating, "At your upcoming auction, Broker will represent me and is authorized to bid on my behalf." Subsequently Collector changes his mind and instructs Broker not to bid for him. Collector neglects, however, to inform Auction House of this change. Although Broker has no actual authority to bind for Collector, Broker does have apparent authority.

The question of reliance.   When a third party seeks to bind an apparent principal by claiming apparent authority, must the claimant show that it relied to its detriment on the appearance of authority? The Restatement requires that the claimant's inference of authority be traceable to (and therefore, in some sense, rely on) the principal's manifestation, but does not require the claimant then rely to its detriment on the appearance of authority.[20] Many jurisdictions, however, do require the second, detrimental reliance. Indeed, some jurisdictions refer to apparent authority as *agency by estoppel*.[21] Figure 2-1 illustrates the two different occasions for reliance.

This doctrinal difference may have little practical significance. If a false appearance of authority does not cause a third party to act or omit to act to its detriment, then a claim will rarely be worth pursuing.

Figure 2-1. The Role of Reliance in Creating Apparent Authority

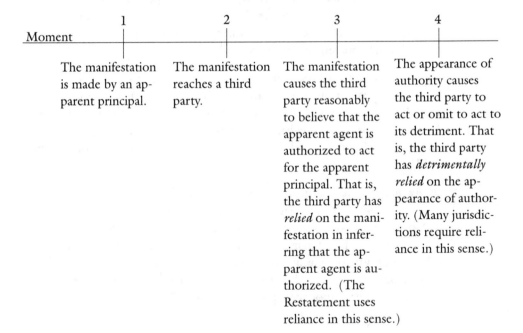

	1	2	3	4
Moment				
	The manifestation is made by an apparent principal.	The manifestation reaches a third party.	The manifestation causes the third party reasonably to believe that the apparent agent is authorized to act for the apparent principal. That is, the third party has *relied* on the manifestation in inferring that the apparent agent is authorized. (The Restatement uses reliance in this sense.)	The appearance of authority causes the third party to act or omit to act to its detriment. That is, the third party has *detrimentally relied* on the appearance of authority. (Many jurisdictions require reliance in this sense.)

20. Restatement §8, comment *d*. The word "traceable" does not appear in the Restatement but is part of the black letter of Restatement (Third) §2.03 at 151(defining apparent authority).

21. The Restatement also has a rubric of agency by estoppel, but the Restatement's concept of estoppel is subtly different from the doctrine of apparent authority. See section 2.5 (authority by estoppel).

§2.3.3   *The Necessary Peppercorn of Manifestation*

For apparent authority to exist, the third party must be able to point to at least some peppercorn of manifestation attributable to the apparent principal. This peppercorn must form the basis of the third party's reasonable belief that the apparent agent is actually authorized. Conduct by the apparent agent may bear on the reasonableness of that belief, but the belief must ultimately rest on some manifestation attributable to the apparent principal.

This requirement means that, with one rarely important exception (discussed below), the statements of the apparent agent cannot give rise to apparent authority.[22]

> *Example:* A silver-tongued salesman, nattily dressed and appearing for all the world to be precisely whom he claims to be, rings your doorbell and introduces himself as a representative of the Acme Burial Insurance Company. He shows you an impressive, glossy brochure and a printed contract form. You sign on the dotted line and give the man a $100 down payment. You later discover that the silver-tongued fellow had no connection whatsoever with Acme and that he had created the phoney brochures and contract forms as props. Unfortunately, you have no recourse against Acme. Although your belief that the salesman was acting for Acme may have been reasonable, you cannot point to any manifestation by or attributable to Acme, the apparent principal. Consequently, there is no apparent authority.

An apparent agent can supply the necessary peppercorn of manifestation only if the apparent agent (i) is actually authorized to act for the principal, and (ii) while actually authorized, accurately describes the extent of its authority. Every agent has the implied actual authority to accurately describe the agent's own actual authority,[23] and such accurate descriptions are therefore attributable to the principal.

> *Example:* You operate a horse ranch. One day a woman approaches you and informs you that she buys horses on behalf of Acme Rodeo Company and that she has the authority to pay up to $2,500 per horse. At that time, her statements are accurate. Two weeks later she returns and purports to commit Acme to purchase a quarter horse for $2,200. Unbeknownst to you, however, three days earlier Acme had expressly restricted her authority to purchases of $1,700 or less. You should be

---

22. A manifestation by one agent of a principal can, in contrast, give rise to apparent authority for another agent of the principal—if the first agent's manifestation is legally attributable to the principal. For a simple illustration of this phenomenon, see the first Example in section 2.3.4. See also section 2.8.

23. Restatement §27, comment *c*. The principal can remove this authority by directing the agent not to represent her authority.

able to hold Acme to the contract through an apparent authority claim. You can certainly show a manifestation attributable to the apparent principal. When the buying agent earlier described her buying authority, she acted within her implied actual authority. That description is therefore a manifestation attributable to Acme.

§2.3.4   *Noteworthy Modes of Manifestation*

Through intermediaries.   A manifestation that reaches the third party through intermediaries can still give rise to apparent authority.

> *Example:* Acting on instructions from the Art Collector, the Art Collector's personal secretary sends a letter to the Auction House stating: "On behalf of Art Collector, I am writing to inform you that, at your upcoming auction, Broker will be representing and bidding for Art Collector." Broker has apparent authority to bid for the Art Collector, even though the Art Collector herself (the apparent principal) never personally made the relevant manifestation. The secretary's letter constitutes a manifestation *attributable* to the Art Collector because the secretary's communication, made within the zone of actual authority, binds (i.e., is attributable to) the secretary's principal.[24]

It is not necessary that the intermediary be an agent of the apparent principal, although such is often the situation.

By position.   Sometimes the principal's sole manifestation to the third party may be to put an agent in a particular position. In light of local custom and standard business practices, that placement by itself may cause a third party to reasonably believe that the agent has certain authority. This type of apparent authority is sometimes called *authority by position*.

> *Example:* The owner of a dry cleaning store hires Ralph to work at the counter and expressly authorizes him to accept clothes for cleaning, give receipts, return cleaned clothes to customers, and accept payment from customers. Although the owner expressly forbids Ralph to promise to have any garment cleaned in less than two working days, Ralph promises a law student to have her "interview suit" cleaned "by tomorrow." The doctrine of apparent authority may hold the dry cleaning store to Ralph's promise. Ralph's position (as counter clerk) constitutes the necessary manifestation. The question is whether, based on that bare manifestation, the customer reasonably believed that Ralph had the authority to make the promise. Since it is customary for counter clerks to tell customers when clothes will be ready, and since 24-hour

---

24. For a more detailed discussion of this type of attribution, see section 2.8.

service is not unusual in the dry cleaning business, the answer is probably "yes."[25]

Example: After lengthy negotiations with a claims adjuster, an attorney purports to settle her client's insurance claim for $25,000. Unless the client has given the attorney actual authority to settle for that amount, the client is not bound. The mere position of an attorney does not create apparent authority to bind a client to a settlement.[26]

Apparent authority by position within organizations.   Large organizations dominate our economy, and those organizations inevitably distribute responsibilities across many positions. Moreover, even in a small organization employees can have substantially different functions which may be reflected in job titles.

It is necessary therefore to consider what apparent authority, if any, attaches to positions and titles within an organizational hierarchy. In general:

> [A]n agent is sometimes placed in a position in an industry or setting in which holders of the position customarily have authority of a specific scope. Absent notice to third parties to the contrary, placing the agent in such a position constitutes a manifestation that the principal assents to be bound by actions by the agent that fall within that scope.[27]

Example: Rachael is employed as a "purchasing agent" by Snerdly Manufacturing, LLC. Rachael has the apparent authority to make ordinary and usual purchases on Snerdly's behalf.

The particularities of an organization's structure may influence the apparent authority analysis.

> Observing a systematic hierarchy, a third party might reasonably infer that the organization is represented by a particular agent whose acts and statements are compatible with the agent's situation within the organization. Questions of apparent authority in this context often turn on the interplay between general definitions or authority associated [e.g., by custom] with specific positions and observed characteristics of how the organization actually functions.[28]

More particularly:

- *CEO or president* — apparent authority for transactions within the organization's ordinary course of business

---

25. As a "general agent," Ralph may also have bound the owner through inherent agency power. See section 2.6.2. Restatement (Third) would rely exclusively on apparent authority. Restatement (Third), Chapter 2, Introductory Note at 105, §2.01, comment *b* at 121 (explaining that Restatement (Third) does not use the concept of inherent agency power).

26. Some courts hold otherwise, but the Example reflects the majority view.

27. Restatement (Third) §1.03, comment *b,* at 73-74.

28. Restatement (Third) §1.03, comment *c,* at 80.

- *general manager*—apparent authority for transactions within the organization's ordinary course of business
- *vice president*—no apparent authority, because the title lacks any generalized meaning; however, a "vice president for/of [some specific function]" might have apparent authority to commit the organization to matters normally handled by the person in charge of that function
- *corporate secretary*—apparent authority to certify copies of corporate documents
- *branch manager*—in most jurisdictions, no per se apparent authority to bind the principal, but probably apparent authority to communicate decisions on significant matters made by the principal and in some jurisdictions apparent authority to make decisions ordinarily made at the branch level

Example: The CEO of Oz Balloon Tours, Inc. purports to commit the company to sell its sole balloon. The CEO has no apparent authority for this extraordinary transaction.

Example: Same facts, except that the company has 20 balloons, regularly buys new ones and sells used ones. The CEO has apparent authority to sell one or several used balloons.

Example: Rachael is the Vice President for Marketing for Sammada, LLC, a company that puts on rock tours and is known to spend tens of thousands of dollars in advertising. Rachael has apparent authority to enter into a $15,000 radio "buy" in a local media market to advertise a concert sponsored by Sammada.

An agent's apparent authority can be augmented if the organization provides the agent with standardized form contracts.

Example: Rosencrantz is a branch manager for the First Bank of Polonius, with actual authority to approve loans in amounts less than $50,000. The Bank provides Rosencrantz with copies of a form loan agreement, the first page of which carries the Bank's name and states in bold print: **NOT VALID FOR LOANS IN EXCESS OF $100,000.** Rosencrantz uses a copy of the form agreement to commit the Bank to lend Laertes $75,000. The Bank is probably bound. It is unclear whether Rosencrantz's position as branch manager suffices to create apparent authority for a $75,000 loan. However, Rosencrantz's possession of the form agreements, coupled with his position, probably does.

By acquiescence.   Sometimes the principal makes the necessary manifestation by acquiescing in an agent's conduct.

Example: On several occasions the caretaker of an apartment complex contracts with a roof repair service to fix a leaking roof. Each time the repair service sends an invoice to the owner of the complex, and each time

33

the owner pays. The repair service has no other contact with the owner. On the next service call, all goes as usual except that the owner refuses to pay. The owner claims "the caretaker has no authority to order repairs." Even if the owner is correct, the repair service can still collect. Regardless of whether the caretaker has actual authority to contract for repairs, the caretaker has apparent authority to order repairs from that particular repair company. By paying the previous invoices without comment, the owner of the complex has made the predicate manifestation.

Example: After the first two days of trial, attorneys for the two sides negotiate a settlement. With the parties present in open court, the two attorneys read the settlement into the record. Neither party objects. Both parties are bound to the settlement, regardless of whether either attorney had actual authority to settle. The clients' acquiescence imparted apparent authority to their respective counsel.

By inaction.   In limited circumstances, an apparent principal's inaction may constitute a manifestation. For an apparent principal's inaction to give rise to apparent authority, the following criteria must be met:

- Someone (including the apparent agent) must assert that the apparent agent has actual authority.
- The apparent principal must be aware of those assertions and fail to do anything to contradict them.
- The third party claimant must be aware of:
  —the assertions themselves,
  —the apparent principal's knowledge of the assertions, and
  —the apparent principal's failure to contradict the assertions.
- It must be the apparent principal's failure to contradict the assertions that causes the third party reasonably to believe that the apparent agent is authorized.[29]

In these circumstances, the apparent principal's silence amounts to acquiescence and is a manifestation that is known to the third party.

Example: Charlie goes to a trade show and approaches a booth displaying the products of Acme Widget Company. At the booth he meets Alice, the owner of Acme. Charlie asks, "Who shall I call to get a quote on prices on special orders?" Another customer, who has done business with Acme for years, interjects, "Oh, you want to call Brenda, their national sales manager. She's the one who gives those quotes." Brenda has been demoted and no longer has that authority, but Alice does not want to embarrass Brenda in front of customers. Alice therefore says nothing.

---

29. If this element is missing, the closely related doctrine of "estoppel" may help the third party. See section 2.5.

As to Charlie, Brenda has apparent authority to quote prices. The manifestation is not the customer's assertion but rather Alice's inaction in the face of that assertion.[30]

§2.3.5 The Third Party's Interpretation— The Reasonableness Requirement

Mere belief insufficient.   For apparent authority to exist, a manifestation attributable to the apparent principal must cause the third party to believe that the apparent agent has authority. Mere belief, however, is not enough. Apparent authority will exist only to the extent that the third party's belief is reasonable.

In determining whether a third party has reasonably interpreted the apparent principal's manifestations, the law of apparent authority considers the same kinds of information that are relevant to determining whether an agent has reasonably interpreted the manifestation of its principal.[31] Apparent authority analysis thus parallels actual authority analysis, except that apparent authority focuses on the interpretations of the third party, not the agent. We can therefore adapt Comment *a* to Restatement §34 to read: "All matters throwing light upon what a reasonable person in the position of the [third party] at the time of acting would consider are to be given due weight."

The third party's duty of inquiry.   In some circumstances, an apparent principal's manifestations may create an appearance of authority, yet it remains unreasonable for a third party to act upon that appearance without knowing more. The reasonable interpretation requirement thus imposes a duty of inquiry on the third party claimant. For instance, the manifestation itself may be ambiguous. Or, the apparent agent's conduct may be sufficiently unusual as to raise doubts. In such circumstances, the third party cannot reasonably interpret the manifestation as an indication of authority without first making some inquiry of the apparent principal.

> *Example:* A supplier of construction services and a general contractor dispute whether the general contractor is liable to the supplier for services furnished to a subcontractor. The president of the general contractor writes a letter denying liability. The supplier subsequently telephones the general contractor and talks with a vice president. Without consulting the president and without actual authority, the vice president acknowledges the liability and signs an agreement guaranteeing the subcontractor's payment. When the general contractor repudiates the vice president's action, the supplier claims that the vice president had

---

30. The same analysis applies to the other customer, who in addition can point to past experience as a manifestation attributable to the principal.

31. See section 2.2.2.

apparent authority to make the acknowledgement and sign the guarantee. A court holds otherwise, stating that "The fact that the [supplier] had been notified in writing by [the general contractor's] president that [the general contractor] denied liability for these services put the [supplier] on inquiry as to the authority of any other employee to countermand such a position."[32]

The role of the apparent agent's conduct.   With the one exception discussed in section 2.3.3 (the Example about the horse buyer), the apparent agent's conduct cannot satisfy the manifestation requirement. That conduct can, however, enter into the reasonableness determination. Plausible behavior by the apparent agent will buttress the third party's claim; implausible behavior will undercut it.

§2.3.6 *The Necessity of Situation-by-Situation Analysis*

Although an apparent agent may have apparent authority as to a wide range of acts and as to a wide range of third parties, each claim of apparent authority must be analyzed separately—even different claims from the same claimant. The reasons for this approach inhere in the elements necessary to create apparent authority. For any given claim of apparent authority, the third party must show that, at the relevant moment:

(1) a manifestation had occurred that was attributable to the apparent principal
(2) the manifestation had reached the third party
(3) the manifestation caused the third party to believe that the apparent agent was authorized
(4) the third party's belief was reasonable

If the apparent principal has made more than one manifestation, Element 1 may vary from claimant to claimant. Elements 2, 3, and 4 may vary depending on the identity of the third party claimant and on the specific act claimed to be authorized. For example, two different third parties may draw different conclusions from the same manifestations. Or, two different third parties may draw the same conclusion, but for one—possessing knowledge or expertise lacked by the other—the conclusion may not be reasonable. Similarly, even with regard to the same third party, one act may reasonably appear authorized while another act may not.

One implication of this situation-by-situation approach is that efforts to counteract an impression of apparent authority will be effective only to the extent that the counteracting manifestations reach the third party.

Example: Rachael, the owner of Rachael's Service Station, decides that she can no longer afford the 10 percent discount she has long offered to

---

32. *Truck Crane Service Co. v. Barr-Nelson*, 329 N.W.2d 824, 827 (Minn. 1983).

regular customers. She calls her mechanics together and says, "Effective right now, no more 10 percent discounts." The next day, one of the mechanics, momentarily forgetting Rachael's instruction, offers the discount to a customer. The customer accepts and leaves the car for servicing. When the customer returns to pick up the car, the mechanic says, "Hey, I'm sorry. I forgot. We don't give 10 percent discounts anymore." The customer is nonetheless entitled to the discount. Based on past dealings, the mechanic had apparent authority by acquiescence. Although the mechanic now lacks actual authority, the apparent authority remains intact because Rachael's counteracting manifestation has not reached the third party.

§2.3.7   Rationale of the Apparent Authority Doctrine

When a person purports to bind another in an interaction with a third party but lacks the actual authority to do so, the law must decide which of two relatively blameless parties (the apparent principal or the third party) will bear any resulting loss.[33] For two different (although compatible) reasons, if the purported agent had apparent authority, the law puts the loss on the apparent principal:

(1) So long as the third party has not been careless or silly, any loss resulting from the misapprehension of authority should be imposed on the party who could have prevented the misapprehension in the first place.

(2) Any loss should be imposed so as not to disrupt normal commercial operations.

The first rationale is reflected in the doctrine's requirement that the third party's belief be reasonable. The second rationale is served because the doctrine permits a commercial entity to rely on the appearance of authority so long as the appearance can be traced back to a manifestation of the apparent principal and the commercial entity acts reasonably in interpreting that manifestation.

§2.3.8   Apparent Authority and Principals That Are Not Fully Disclosed

An agent for an undisclosed principal can never have apparent authority, because by definition the third party is unaware that the agent is acting for

---

33. In a perfect world this question would perhaps be moot, because the apparent agent would "make good" any harm done. For the relevant legal theories, see sections 4.2.2 (warranty of authority) and 4.1.2 (duty to act within authority). In the real world, however, holding the apparent agent accountable costs time, effort, and money. Moreover, the apparent agent may be judgment-proof, beyond the jurisdiction of the court, or simply nowhere to be found.

any principal at all. It is therefore impossible for the third party to claim that, at the relevant moment, the agent appeared to be acting for the actual principal.

As to an agent for a partially disclosed principal, apparent authority is possible in theory but rare in practice. The third party must be able to point to some manifestation attributable to the principal which supports an inference that the agent has actual authority to act for *some* principal but which does not disclose the identity of the actual principal.[34]

> ***Example:*** P, an importer, has purchased a shipment of steel from Brazil and retains A, a customhouse broker, to clear the steel through customs. That task requires posting security for any custom duties which may be due, and customhouse brokers typically obtain security bonds on behalf of their clients. Without disclosing P's identity, A arranges for T, an insurance company, to post a surety bond for the duties on P's steel. A has apparent authority to bind P to pay T for the bond. P has provided A with the information about the shipment which A needs in order to arrange the bond, and T is aware that A has obtained that information for the owner of the steel. P has thus made a manifestation that A is authorized to act on P's behalf, even though neither the manifestation nor any other circumstances have disclosed P's identity.[35]

§2.3.9   *Binding the Principal in Contract Through Apparent Authority*

Apparent authority creates essentially the same results as to contracts as does actual authority.[36] If an apparent agent, acting with apparent authority, makes a contract on behalf of an apparent principal, then the principal is bound just as if the principal had itself entered into the contract. The third party is likewise bound to the contract.

§2.4   Attribution of Information

§2.4.1   *The Attribution Function and Its Connection with Non-Agency Law*

One of the most important functions of agency law is to treat the principal as if the principal knows, receives, or communicates information actually

---

34. If the manifestation discloses the principal's identity, the situation does not involve an undisclosed principal.

35. This Example is taken from Restatement (Third) §2.03, Illustration 15 at 171, which, according to the Reporter's Notes, is in turn based on *Old Republic Ins. Co. v. Hansa World Cargo Serv. Inc.,* 51 F. Supp. 2d 457, 495 (S.D.N.Y. 1999).

36. The exception for undisclosed principals, discussed at section 2.2.4, does not apply, because apparent authority cannot apply to an undisclosed principal.

known, received, or communicated by an agent. Other law determines the significance of the attributed information.

> *Example:* A contract between Hunter, Inc. and Rabbit, Inc. requires Hunter to provide Rabbit "48 hours advance notice of any deliveries." The shipping clerk of Hunter telephones Rabbit to give notice of a forthcoming delivery and speaks to a night janitor. Agency law determines whether that conversation constitutes notice to Rabbit. From there the contract and contract law take over and determine the significance of notice given or omitted.

> *Example:* A tort victim injured by a defective widget claims that the manufacturer should be liable for punitive damages, alleging that "said Defendant knew that the said widget design was defective and prone to inflict serious injuries and said Defendant had known of this defect and danger for at least five years before the sale of the widget which injured Plaintiff in that Defendant's chief engineer knew of said defect." Whether the manufacturer "knew" what the chief engineer knew is a question of agency law. Whether knowingly selling a dangerously defective product should result in punitive damages is a question of tort law.

§2.4.2 *Attribution as of When?*

Attribution of information is always time specific, with one party or another asserting that *at some relevant moment* some person knew, received or communicated some particular piece of information. Like the consequences of attribution,[37] the relevant moment is determined by other law. To borrow a famous comment from the Watergate crisis, agency law determines "what did he know and when did he know it."[38] Other law determines which "when" matters.

> *Example:* In the products liability Example involving the defective widget, tort law determines that the relevant moment is the moment at which the manufacturer sold the widget which injured the plaintiff. (If the jurisdiction recognizes a post-sale duty to warn, a later moment might be relevant as well.)

§2.4.3 *Attribution of Notice and Notification Received by an Agent*

Some legal rules and many contracts require or authorize one person to give "notice" of certain facts to another person or to send another person a "notifi-

---

37. See section 2.4.1.

38. According to Senator Howard H. Baker, Jr., the pivotal question in the Watergate crisis was "What did the President know, and when did he know it?" Fred Shapiro (ed.), Oxford Dictionary of American Legal Quotations (1993) at 13 (citing Sam J. Ervin, Jr., The Whole Truth: The Watergate Conspiracy at 174).

cation." Often a person will attempt to give notice or send notification to a principal by giving the notice or sending the notification to an agent. If the agent has actual or apparent authority to receive the notice or notification, then notice or notification to the agent has the same effect as notice made directly to the principal.[39] The attribution occurs regardless of whether the agent informs the principal of the notice or notification, unless when the agent received the notice or notification: (i) the agent was acting adversely to the principal, and (ii) the third party knew or had reason to know that the agent was so acting.

§2.4.4   *Attribution of Facts Known by an Agent*

Basic rule.   If an agent has actual knowledge of a fact concerning a matter within the agent's actual authority, the agent's knowledge is attributed to the principal. The attribution occurs regardless of whether the agent communicates the fact to the principal, unless at the relevant moment of attribution:[40] (i) the agent was acting adversely to the principal, and (ii) the third party claiming the benefit of the principal's attributed knowledge knew or had reason to know that the agent was so acting.

> *Example:* Caesar wishes to buy an apartment building for investment purposes and retains Brutus as his agent to find and negotiate the purchase of a good property. Brutus comes into contact with Anthony, who offers a seemingly attractive building for sale at an attractive price. However, when Brutus researches the neighborhood, he learns that the city has just approved a permit to open a half-way house across the street. Anthony offers Brutus $1,000 "so that what Caesar doesn't know won't hurt me." Brutus accepts, and Caesar buys the property. When Caesar subsequently claims fraud in the inducement, Anthony cannot successfully defend by claiming that Caesar knew about the half-way house. Beginning when he accepted the bribe and continuing through the closing of the deal, Brutus was acting adversely to Caesar and Anthony knew it.

Complexities as to source and permanence of agent's knowledge.   Suppose an agent learns a fact "off" the job—either (1) before becoming an agent, or (2) while an agent but while "off duty." Is the fact attributed the principal? Suppose that during the agency relationship an agent knows a fact related to his or her duties but by the time the fact is relevant to legal relations of the principal, the agent has forgotten the fact. Is the principal still "charged" with knowledge of the fact?

The answers to each of these questions is yes, and the rationale is straightforward. An agent's duties include communicating to the principal

---

39. Other law determines what the effect will be. See section 2.4.1.
40. See section 2.4.2.

any information which the agent has reason to know might be of interest or importance to the principal.[41] The rules for attributing information assume that the agent fulfills the duty and that the principal does not forget.

> *Example:* A bartender serves a patron a couple of drinks, after which the patron assaults another patron. The victim sues the bar for negligence, contending that (i) the bartender knew from her own "off the job" experience as the assailant's girlfriend that the assailant was prone to violence after a couple of drinks, and (ii) the bartender's knowledge was attributable to the bar, since the fact concerned a matter within the bartender's actual authority (making judgments about who could be served). The bartender's knowledge is attributed to the bar, despite the "off the job" source of the information.[42]

§2.4.5 *Information That an Agent Should Know But Does Not*

According to the Restatement and most courts, the unknown information is not attributed to the principal.[43]

> *Example:* P employs A, who is president of a bank, to purchase notes for him. A is a member of the discount committee of the bank and, if he attended to his duties properly, would know that B had obtained a specific negotiable note from T by fraud. Further, had he made the inquiries which his duty to P required, he would have learned this. Not having performed his duties properly, he does not know this fact and purchases the note from B for P. P does not hold the note subject to T's interest because of A's conduct, since there was no duty of care by P to ascertain the fraud in the original transaction.[44]

---

41. See section 4.1.5.

42. For a detailed discussion of this situation, see Daniel S. Kleinberger, Guilty Knowledge, 22 Wm. Mitchell L. Rev. 953 (1996).

43. Restatement §277 provides:

> The principal is not affected by the knowledge which an agent should have acquired in the performance of the agent's duties to the principal or to others, except where the principal or master has a duty to others that care shall be exercised in obtaining information.

Restatement (Third)—Council §5.03 takes a contrary position. "Notice is imputed to a principal of a fact that an agent . . . has reason to know if knowledge of the fact is material to the agent's duties to the principal. . . ." In support of this position, the Reporter's Notes at 99-100 cite *Southport Little League v. Vaugh,* 734 N.E.2d 261, 275 (Ind. Ct. App. 2000) as holding that "a principal is charged with the knowledge of that which his agent by ordinary care could have known where the agent has received sufficient information to awaken inquiry.

44. This Example comes verbatim from Restatement §277, Illustration 1.

However, even under the Restatement:

- *if*   —the principal has some independent duty to know, or use reasonable care to know, the information,
          —the principal delegates to an agent the task of acquiring the information, and
          —the agent fails to acquire the information,
- *then*   the principal may be liable on its independent duty.

§2.4.6 *Information Communicated by an Agent to Others*

If an agent acting with actual or apparent authority

- gives notice to a third party, or
- makes a statement or promise to a third party,[45]
- makes a misrepresentation to a third party,[46]

the information conveyed has the same legal effect under contract law as if the principal had conveyed the information directly.[47]

§2.4.7 *Direction of Attribution*

Agency law attribution works in only one direction—upward, from agent to principal. "Likewise, the legal consequences of knowing or having reason to know a fact, or having received or given notification, are not imputed downward."[48]

> *Example:* A patient brings a malpractice case against a hospital and several doctors who work as employees of the hospital. The hospital and doctors tender defense of the case to their professional liability insurer, under a policy naming as insureds both the hospital and its employee doctors. The insurance company desires to "reserve its rights"—i.e., take up the defense of the case while reserving the right to later assert that the case is not covered by the policy. Under the insurance contract, in order

---

45. Not all promises are enforceable, even if made directly by a principal. Agency law only attributes the agent's promise to the principal; contract law determines whether the promise is enforceable.

46. How can an agent have actual authority to make misrepresentations? Having actual authority to make accurate statements, that agent might make a misstatement innocently—reasonably believing the misstatement to be true. According to Restatement §162, comment *b*, that misstatement would come within the agent's actual authority. Other instances are also possible. A nefarious principal might indeed authorize fraud, and an innocent principal might authorize statements that turn out to be misrepresentations. In any event, where actual authority leaves off, inherent agency power takes over. An agent of a disclosed or partially disclosed principal has inherent power to make an inaccurate statement which, if accurate, would have been within the agent's actual authority. See section 2.6.3.

47. The impact under tort law is subtly different. See section 3.4.2.

48. Restatement (Third)—Council §5.01, comment *c* at 60.

to reserve its rights the insurance company must give notice to each insured. Assuming that the hospital will pass on the information to the doctors, the insurance company gives notice to the hospital but not individually to the doctors. The insurer has waived its reservation as to the doctors, because notice received by a principal (the hospital) is not attributed downward (to the employee doctors).[49]

Similarly, imputation does not work "sideways"—i.e., attribution is to the principal, and not to affiliates or owners of the principal.

Example: The sole shareholder of a corporation sold his stock in the corporation, warranting that, to his knowledge, the corporation was not in violation of any government regulations. In fact, the corporation was in violation, and its general manager knew of the violation. In the buyer's breach of warranty case, the court properly refused to attribute the general manager's knowledge to the shareholder.

§2.4.8   *Information Attribution Within Organizations*

Even most small businesses have multiple agents, and large organizations can have thousands. When a principal is an organization, information attribution can produce untoward effects—especially if "the left hand doesn't know what the right hand is doing." Attribution can occur even when the agent with the attributed knowledge is not the person acting for the principal in the transaction at issue.

Example: Sylvia, the Executive Vice President of Widget, Inc. ("Widget"), purchases a products liability insurance policy for Widget, and on Widget's behalf signs an application stating that Widget knows of no present facts which would give rise to a claim under the policy. Sylvia has canvassed all top level Widget employees via email and knows of no such facts. Unfortunately, Widget's risk assessment coordinator does know of one potential claim but has neglected to tell Sylvia. The facts as to the claim are relevant to the risk manager's authorized tasks and are therefore attributed to Widget. Widget's application therefore contains a material, false statement, and the insurance company is entitled to an appropriate remedy.[50]

§2.5   Estoppel

To establish apparent authority, a third party must show some manifestation of authority attributable to the principal. But what if an asserted principal has

---

49. This Example is based on *Knox-Tenn Rental Co. v. Home Ins. Co.,* 2 F.3d 678, 682 (6th Cir. 1993), cited in Restatement (Third)—Council §5.02, Reporter's Notes at 72.

50. This Example is based on Restatement (Third)—Council §5.03, Illustration 12 at 88.

made no such manifestation but has merely sat by while someone else has claimed an agency relationship? What if these claims of authority have lead third parties to extend credit, incur costs, or otherwise change their position? What if the asserted principal knew of the claims and of the danger to third parties and yet did nothing?

In such situations, apparent authority is rarely applicable, because only in very narrow circumstances can the asserted principal's inaction serve as a manifestation.[51] To prevent injustice beyond those narrow circumstances, the Restatement and some courts use the concept of *estoppel*. In the words of the Restatement, estoppel imposes liability on a person for:

> a transaction purported to be done on his account . . . to persons who have changed their positions because of their belief that the transaction was entered into by or for him, if
>
> (a) he intentionally or carelessly caused such belief,
>
> or
>
> (b) knowing of such belief and that others might change their positions because of it, he did not take reasonable steps to notify them of the facts.[52]

In concept, the distinction between apparent authority and estoppel is clear enough. Unlike apparent authority, estoppel can apply even though the claimant can show no manifestation attributable to the asserted principal.[53] Estoppel liability can arise from the asserted principal's mere negligent failure to protect against a misapprehension.

Unfortunately, the case law often blurs this distinction. Many jurisdictions make detrimental reliance an element of apparent authority and even refer to apparent authority as "agency by estoppel." Moreover, most situations that give rise to apparent authority also give rise to estoppel. If an asserted principal makes a manifestation sufficient to support a reasonable inference of authority (i.e., to create apparent authority), the asserted principal can probably be said to have "intentionally or carelessly caused such belief" (i.e., estoppel).[54]

The distinction between apparent authority and estoppel is probably best illustrated by an example.

> *Example:* Emma Posster arrives with great fanfare in the mid-sized city of Regionville. She purports to be the personal representative of

---

51. See section 2.3.4 (manifestation by inaction).

52. Restatement §8B(1).

53. For jurisdictions that follow the pure Restatement view of apparent authority there is another distinction: apparent authority can exist without a showing of detrimental reliance. See section 2.3.2 for a discussion of the Restatement's view of apparent authority. As noted in that section, many jurisdictions differ with the Restatement on this point.

54. The quoted language is from Restatement §8B(1)(a).

Mo Gull, a millionaire tycoon who lives in Metropolis, a large city some 250 miles away from Regionville. Posster claims that Gull is interested in developing Regionville's riverfront property and is looking to her to make the preliminary "go/no go" recommendation. Posster is wined and dined by Regionville's political leaders. On the strength of her purported relationship to Gull, she takes the most expensive suite at Regionville's most expensive hotel and opens and uses charge accounts at several of the city's most exclusive restaurants and shops. In fact, Posster has no relationship whatsoever with Gull, and Gull has no interest in Regionville's riverfront.

Posster's style is flamboyant, and a wire service runs a story about her, her work for Gull, and the contemplated riverfront project. The story runs in the Metropolis paper, and Gull reads it. Rather than doing anything to alert people in Regionville, Gull merely chuckles, sits back, and says to himself, "What a bunch of chumps." Shortly after the story runs, Posster (still on credit) throws an extravagant party for Regionville notables, buys a new mink coat from a Regionville furrier, and disappears without paying any of the bills. The irate merchants seek payment from Gull. They will not succeed with a claim of apparent authority, because they cannot point to any manifestation legally attributable to Gull. However, for amounts charged *after* Gull read the story in the Metropolis paper, the merchants can succeed with a claim of estoppel. After reading that story, Gull knew that Regionville merchants believed Posster to be acting on his behalf. Yet "knowing of such belief and that others might change their positions because of it, he did not take reasonable steps to notify them of the facts."[55] Since the merchants did in fact change their positions "because of their belief,"[56] Gull is estopped from denying Posster's authority to bind him.

What of the third party's own carelessness or unreasonable credulity? The Restatement does not expressly contemplate the issue, but in other legal contexts estoppel requires reasonable or justifiable reliance.[57]

§2.6   Inherent Agency Power

§2.6.1 A "Catch-All" Doctrine Based on Fairness

In some situations, an agent has neither actual nor apparent authority, estoppel does not apply, and yet the agent has the power to bind the principal.

---

55. Restatement §8B(1)(b).

56. Restatement §8B(1).

57. See, e.g., Restatement (Second) of Contracts §90 (promissory estoppel available to enforce promise to the extent justice requires if "promisor should reasonably expect" that promisee will rely).

Example: Paul purchases Eli's Dry Cleaning, does not change the business' name and hires Eli to manage the dry cleaning store. Although dry cleaning stores customarily order cleaning solvent in large quantities, Paul instructs Eli never to buy more than $50 worth of solvent at a time. Disregarding these instructions, Eli places a phone order for solvent costing $450. The seller of the solvent believes that Eli is still the owner. Eli has acted without actual authority; his principal's manifestations expressly prohibit the order Eli made. Eli has also acted without apparent authority; there can be no apparent authority by position when the principal is undisclosed.[58] Nonetheless, agency law will bind Paul on the order.

Example: An agent, acting within her authority, negotiates a contract with a third party under which the agent's principal will sell widgets to the third party. During the negotiations the agent falsely describes the widgets. The principal has not authorized the agent to make misstatements, and, arguably at least, nothing in the principal's manifestations to the third party created an appearance of such authority. Nonetheless, agency law will attribute the misstatements to the principal.

In neither of these situations is the principal responsible on account of its own culpable conduct. To the contrary, in each situation the agent has caused mischief while acting counter to the principal's wishes. Yet the third party is also without blame, and so a legal and policy issue arises: As between the principal and the third party, who should bear the risk of the agent's misconduct? Who should have the burden of pressing claims against the agent or absorbing the harm the agent has caused?[59]

To deal with this issue, the Restatement and some courts use a catch-all agency doctrine labelled *inherent agency power.*[60] In a wide range of situations, the doctrine imposes *enterprise liability,* that is, it places the loss on the enterprise that stands to benefit from the agency relationship. As explained by the Restatement:

> It is inevitable that in doing their work, either through negligence or excess of zeal, agents will harm third persons or will deal with them in

---

58. For an explanation of this point, see section 2.3.8.

59. In a perfect world, free of transaction costs, both parties could look to the agent. The world, however, is not perfect. See supra note 33. If the principal is not relatively blameless (e.g., it has negligently hired an agent with a background of misbehavior), other doctrines will place the loss on the principal. For a discussion of a principal's liability for direct negligence, see sections 4.4.1 and 4.4.2.

60. Some courts call the doctrine "inherent agency authority." Restatement (Third) proposes to eliminate the concept of inherent power, relying instead on concepts of apparent authority, estoppel, and restitution. Restatement (Third), Chapter 2, Introductory Note at 105, §2.01. For instance, as to the widget Example above, Restatement (Third) would probably apply apparent authority, reasoning that the agent had apparent authority to describe the widgets and therefore the descriptions—whether true or false—are attributable to the principal.

unauthorized ways. It would be unfair for an enterprise to have the benefit of the work of its agents without making it responsible to some extent for their excesses and failures to act carefully. The answer of the common law has been the creation of special agency powers or, to phrase it otherwise, the imposition of liability upon the principal because of the unauthorized or negligent acts of its servants and other agents.[61]

Inherent agency power plays a major role in attributing tort liability to principals, and those attribution rules are discussed in Chapter Three. With regard to topics covered in this chapter, inherent power performs two important functions: It holds a principal responsible for (1) certain unauthorized acts of an agent whom the principal has entrusted with ongoing responsibilities, and for (2) certain false representations of an agent or apparent agent.

§2.6.2 A Rule of Inherent Power: Unauthorized Acts by a General Agent

When a principal entrusts an agent with ongoing responsibilities, the notion of an enterprise fairly applies. As a result, the agent has the inherent power to take certain actions even though the principal may have forbidden those actions. Agency law uses the category of "general agent" as the entrance criterion to this type of inherent power.

General and special agents defined.   If a principal authorizes an agent "to conduct a series of transactions involving a continuity of service,"[62] the law calls the agent a *general agent*. If, in contrast, a principal authorizes the agent only to conduct a single transaction, or to conduct a series of transactions that do not involve "continuity of service," then the law calls the agent a *special agent*. Perhaps the simplest example of a general agent is an employee in charge of a store, a factory, or other place of business. It is not necessary, however, to have wide-ranging or important responsibilities in order to be a general agent. A fulltime photocopy clerk is a general agent with regard to photocopying duties.

In theory, the "special vs. general" distinction is an "either/or" matter. That is, with regard to any particular responsibility, an agent must be either a general agent or a special agent. In practice, however, this either/or categorization encounters many grey situations.

It is possible for an agent to be a general agent with regard to some matters and a special agent with regard to others. The key factor separating general agency status from special agent status is whether the agent has an ongoing responsibility.

---

61. Restatement §8A, comment *a*.
62. Restatement §3(1).

Example: A bank employs Larry as a teller. One day the bank asks Larry to deal with a caterer and arrange refreshments for a retirement party. With regard to his teller duties, Larry is a general agent. With regard to the party arrangement, Larry is a special agent.

Inherent agency power of general agents.   Under the doctrine of inherent agency power:

- if the agent is a general agent with actual authority to conduct certain transactions,
  - — the agent is acting in the interests of the principal, and
  - — the agent does an act usual or necessary with regard to the authorized transactions,
- then the act binds the principal regardless of whether the agent had actual authority and even if the principal has expressly forbidden the act.

Although this rule applies in slightly different forms to all principals, it makes the most difference for undisclosed and partially disclosed principals. With a disclosed principal, apparent authority by position will typically produce the same result as inherent power. With an undisclosed or partially disclosed principal, however, apparent authority is of no help.

Example: Sylvia decides to enter the silk importing business. The trade is notoriously biased against women, and she fears that her company will suffer if her interest in it is known. She therefore hires Phil as her general manager, but sets up the company so that Phil appears to the outside world as the owner. It is common in this trade for silk importers to sell to large customers on credit, but Sylvia instructs Phil never to extend more than $50,000 of credit to any customer without Sylvia's approval. One day, in order to close an important deal, Phil agrees without consulting Sylvia to extend $150,000 of credit to one customer. Although Phil acted without actual or apparent authority, Sylvia, the company's true owner and Phil's undisclosed principal, is bound. "An undisclosed principal who entrusts an agent with the management of his business is subject to liability to third persons with whom the agent enters into transactions usual in such businesses and on the principal's account, although contrary to the directions of the principal."[63]

Policy based limitations to the rule.   This rule of inherent agency power has two policy-based limitations. It does not apply if either (i) the third party knows that the agent is acting without authority or (ii) the agent is not acting

---

63. Restatement §195 (acts of manager appearing to be owner). See also Restatement §161 (unauthorized acts of general agents) and §194 (acts of general agents). Restatement (Third) would undoubtedly reach the same result, probably by applying notions of estoppel.

in the principal's interest. If the third party knows of the lack of authority, then the third party is not innocent and the rule's rationale does not apply.[64] If the agent acts on its own behalf, the conduct is not part of the enterprise from which the principal stands to benefit and again the rule's rationale does not apply.

§2.6.3 A Rule of Inherent Power: False Statement by an Agent

Under this aspect of inherent power, an agent's false statements are attributable to the principal if:

- the principal is disclosed or partially disclosed, and
- a true statement concerning the same subject would have been within the agent's actual or apparent authority.

Once the doctrine of inherent power attributes the agent's misstatements to the principal, the principal faces the same contract law consequences that would result from the principal making the misstatement directly—namely, breach of contract claims and, in appropriate circumstances, rescission.[65]

This rule does not apply to false statements about the scope of the agent's authority. That is, although an agent ordinarily has actual authority to *truthfully* describe its authority, an agent has no inherent power to *falsely* describe that authority. Without this exception, inherent power would give every agent unlimited ability to create apparent authority.[66]

§2.7 Ratification

§2.7.1 The Role, Meaning, and Effect of Ratification

Ratification occurs when a principal affirms a previously unauthorized act. Ratification validates the original unauthorized act and produces the same legal consequences as if the original act had been authorized. If, for instance, a party ratifies a contract, the ratification binds both that party and the other party to the contract.

Example: Ralph is a janitor in a large residential apartment complex. He has neither actual nor apparent authority to act for the owner of the complex in renting apartments. He also lacks inherent agency power. Nonetheless, he shows apartment 101B to Alice and agrees to rent the

---

64. Recall from section 2.6.1 that inherent agency power functions to allocate the risk between two relatively blameless parties.

65. For the subtly different implications under tort law, see section 3.4.2.

66. See section 2.3.3 (explaining how an agent's actual authority to truthfully describe the agent's authority can create apparent authority).

apartment to her on a six month lease. Later, when Alice telephones the rental office to check on her move-in date, she speaks to the actual owner. The owner says, "Well, you know Ralph had no business renting that apartment to you. He's just the janitor. But your application looks okay, so go ahead." The owner has ratified Ralph's previously unauthorized actions, and Alice and the owner are both bound to the lease.

With one exception, ratification also releases the purported agent from any liability for having made an unauthorized contract.[67] If the principal ratifies only to "cut his losses," the purported agent is not released from liability to the principal.

Example: Acting without authority, Edmund sells and delivers to Lucy goods belonging to Peter. Lucy then resells the goods to an innocent third party and fails to pay Peter. Peter files suit against Lucy for the contract price, in essence ratifying the sale. Edmund remains liable to Peter for any damages resulting from the unauthorized sale.

Ratification typically concerns "the making or breaking of a contract"[68] and in theory is relevant only when no other attribution rule applies. If an actor has actual or apparent authority, or inherent agency power, or if estoppel applies, there is no need to retroactively validate the act. In practice, however, parties often argue ratification in the alternative.

§2.7.2 *Mechanics of Ratification*

For ratification to occur, two requirements must be met. Certain preconditions must exist, and the purported principal must purposely embrace the previously unauthorized act ("affirmance").[69]

---

67. See section 4.1.2 (agent's duty to act within authority) and 4.2.2 (agent's warranty of authority).

68. Restatement §84, comment *a*. The Restatement also contemplates the ratification of tortious acts, and there are indeed a *few* cases that cite ratification as the reason for holding one party liable for another's tort. Most of those cases seem to involve the ratification of a course of conduct that happened to include a tort, rather than a purposeful embracing of the tort and its attendant liability.

For example, suppose the friend of the owner of a coal delivery service takes the friend's delivery van and makes a coal delivery. While delivering the coal, the friend carelessly breaks a window. The owner does not ordinarily employ the friend, and in fact when delivering the coal (and breaking the window) the friend acts without the consent or knowledge of the owner. The owner does, however, bill the customer for the delivered coal and in due course receives payment. The owner has ratified into existence a master-servant relationship and is consequently liable for the broken window.

For the rules of master-servant liability, see section 3.2. For the case that served as the model for this example, see *Dempsey v. Chambers,* 28 N.E. 279 (Mass. 1891) (Holmes, J.).

69. Restatement (Third) §4.01(2)(a) eschews the term "affirmance" and refers instead to a person "manifesting assent that the [previously unauthorized] act shall affect the person's legal relations." The change is apparently intended to emphasize the objective nature of the analysis.

Preconditions.   Ratification can occur only in the context of certain preconditions:

- Someone ("the purported agent") must have purported—either expressly or impliedly—to act on behalf of another (the "purported principal") in some transaction with a third party;
- the purported agent must have acted without either agency authority or agency power and estoppel must not apply;
- at the time of the act the purported principal must have existed and must have had capacity to originally authorize the act;[70] and
- at the time of the attempted ratification, the third party must not have indicated—either to the purported agent or to the purported principal—an intention to withdraw from the transaction (i.e., the transaction must still be available to ratify).

Affirmance—the act (or inaction) of ratification.   If the necessary preconditions exist, a purported principal affirms by either:

- making a manifestation that, viewed objectively, indicates a choice to treat the unauthorized act as if it had been authorized, or
- engaging in conduct that is justifiable only if the purported principal had made such a choice.

In the simplest of situations, a purported principal affirms just by stating a choice.

> **Example:** Having read that car dealers generally make better deals for male customers than for female customers, Sally hires Ralph to purchase a used car on her behalf. She specifically instructs him, however, not to buy any foreign-made car. Purporting to act on Sally's behalf, Ralph makes a great deal on a used BMW. When Sally hears of the deal, she says, "Okay, for a deal like that I don't have to 'Buy American.' I'll take the car." Sally has ratified the deal.

Affirmance occurs when the manifestation occurs. The manifestation need not reach the third party to be effective.[71]

A purported principal can also affirm through inaction, that is, by failing to repudiate the act "under such circumstances that, according to the ordinary experience and habits of men, one would naturally be expected to speak if he

---

70. This precondition explains why a corporation cannot ratify a contract made on the corporation's behalf before the corporation came into existence. See section 2.7.5, which contrasts ratification with novation and assumption.

71. This rule parallels the rule governing an agent's consent to act on behalf of a principal. See sections 1.2.2-1.2.3. In that case also, the manifestation is viewed objectively and need not reach the other relevant party to be effective.

did not consent."[72] Such failure to repudiate creates a situation resembling agency by estoppel.

> *Example:* Acting without either authority or power to bind the owner of an apartment complex, Ralph, the janitor, offers a resident manager job to Felix. The landlord learns of the offer and also hears that Felix is planning to quit his current job so he can become resident manager. The landlord says nothing to Felix, and Felix quits his current job. By this inaction, the landlord has ratified Ralph's offer.

A purported principal can also ratify by accepting or retaining benefits while knowing that the benefits result from an unauthorized act. If the purported principal accepts benefits *without* the requisite knowledge, the third party may have an action in restitution or quantum meruit. Ratification is usually preferable for the third party, however, because ratification entitles the third party to the full benefit of the bargain. Restitution or quantum meruit, in contrast, entitles the third party only to the value of the benefit actually conferred.

> *Example:* Ralph, the self-aggrandizing janitor, offers to rent an apartment to Mike for a year at $50 per month off the regular monthly rent if Mike agrees to keep the grass well mowed. During his first month as a tenant, Mike mows the grass four times. If the landlord knew of the unauthorized offer, the landlord has ratified the agreement by accepting the services. Mike may therefore hold the landlord to the full bargain (i.e., to a lease and a rent reduction for a year). If, however, the landlord did not know of the offer, Mike has a right only to restitution or quantum meruit (i.e., only to be paid for the fair value of the mowing work he has already done).[73]

The "All or Nothing" Rule.   Ratification occurs on an "all or nothing" basis. If a purported principal attempts to ratify only part of a single transaction, then either the entire transaction is ratified or there is no ratification at all.

> *Example:* Acting without authority, Rebecca purports to sell Vladi's car to Michael for $500. Rebecca also purports to extend a 90-day warranty on the car. Vladi cannot ratify the sale without also ratifying the warranty.

Whether ratification has occurred is a question of fact, depending essentially on whether the purported principal:

---

72. Restatement §94, comment *a*.

73. If a third party has fully performed an unauthorized contract, the difference may well be immaterial. In theory, the measure of recovery will be different—benefit of the bargain versus value of services conferred—but in practice courts often use the contract price to measure the benefit.

- has manifested an intent to ratify and sought to impose some exclusions or qualifications (in which case the entire transaction has been ratified and the sought-after exclusions and qualifications are ineffective), or
- has manifested an intent to be bound only if the exclusions or qualifications are part of the transaction (in which case there is no ratification and neither the purported principal nor the third party is bound, unless the third party manifests consent to the conditions).

This fact determination resembles the determination made under §2-207(1) of the Uniform Commercial Code. That "battle of the forms" provision distinguishes between "a definite . . . expression of acceptance . . . which . . . states terms additional to or different from those offered" and an expression in which "acceptance is . . . made conditional on assent to the additional or different terms."

The role of consideration.   An affirmance almost never needs consideration to be effective, because the contract being ratified provides consideration to the purported principal. In the BMW Example on page 51, for instance, Sally's consideration is the car dealer's promise to deliver her a BMW.[74]

When, however, an allegedly ratified transaction provides no benefit to the principal, the third party must indeed establish some independent consideration. "Independent consideration" cases are interesting in the abstract, and several authorities refer to the concept. However, actual reported cases are extremely rare.

§2.7.3 *Principal's Ignorance of Material Facts*

According to the Restatement, "If, at the time of affirmance, the purported principal is ignorant of material facts involved in the original transaction, and is unaware of his ignorance, he can thereafter avoid the effect of the affirmance."[75] Many courts, however, treat the purported principal's knowledge of material information as a precondition to ratification. That is, the purported principal cannot effectively ratify if ignorant of material facts. The difference is more than semantic; it determines the burden of proof.[76]

---

74. Even when a purported principal affirms by accepting benefits, the ratified contract still provides the essential consideration. Conceptually, the role of the benefits is to estop the purported principal from denying that it has made an affirmance.

75. Restatement §91(1).

76. If the principal must assert ignorance to avoid the ratification, the principal has the burden of proof. Otherwise, the party seeking to enforce the ratification must prove the principal's knowledge. Restatement (Third) §4.06 at 404 takes the latter view, describing it as present in "[m]any contemporary cases." Restatement (Third) §4.06, comment *b* at 405.

Materiality defined.   The Restatement defines *material facts* as those that "so affect the existence and extent of the obligations involved in the transaction that knowledge of them is essential to an intelligent election to become a party to the transaction."[77] The Restatement then confines this normally broad concept by specifically excluding knowledge:

- of the legal effect of ratification
- about the value of the transaction or the transaction's desirability, other than knowledge of important representations made by the agent or third party as they entered into the transaction.

Restatement (Third) takes a much simpler and broader approach: "The point of materiality is the relevance of the fact to the principal's consent to have legal relations affected by the agent's act."[78]

Ignorance defined.   At first glance, the ignorance requirement seems straightforward. Ignorance is a state of mind. What should matter, therefore, is whether the purported principal lacks subjective knowledge of material facts, not whether the purported principal has reason to know those facts.

However, both the Restatement and case law eschew this conceptually pure approach:

- If the principal knows information that would cause a reasonable person to infer the missing information, then the trier of fact can conclude that the principal did indeed "know" the missing information.
- If the principal faces a situation in which a reasonable person would first inquire and the principal affirms without inquiry, then the principal has assumed the risk of ignorance.[79]

The first proposition seems quite close to a "reason to know" standard, and the second is a "duty to inquire" standard. Restatement (Third) explicitly embraces the second proposition.[80]

Principal's ignorance vs. third party's reliance.   The principal's ignorance ceases to be a factor if the third party has learned of and detrimentally relied on the principal's affirmance.[81]

---

77. Restatement §91, comment *d*.

78. Restatement (Third) §4.06, comment *c* at 406 (stating "[f]or definitions of materiality, see Restatement (Second), Torts, §538(2)(a); Principles of Corporate Governance: Analysis and Recommendations §1.25").

79. See, e.g., Restatement §91, comments *c* and *e*.

80. Restatement (Third) §4.06, comment *d* at 407 (stating that ignorance does not preclude ratification if the principal "had knowledge of facts that would have led a reasonable person to investigate further, but . . . ratified without further investigation").

81. Restatement §91, comment *b*.

§2.7.4 *The Third Party's Right of Avoidance*

Ordinarily, a purported principal's affirmance binds not only the purported principal but also the third party. As explained previously, a third party can *preclude* ratification by giving notice of withdrawal from the transaction *before* the purported principal affirms.[82] In two situations, the third party can also *avoid* an otherwise binding affirmance.

Changed circumstances. The third party may avoid a ratification if, before the purported principal ratifies, circumstances change so materially that holding the third party to the contract would be unfair. Obviously, at some point the third party will have to inform the purported principal of the changed circumstances. However, it is not necessary that the third party give notice before the affirmance.

The Restatement gives the classic example:

> Purporting to act for *P* but without power to bind him, *A* contracts to sell Blackacre with a house thereon to *T*. The next day the house burns. A later affirmance by *P* does not bind *T*.[83]

Conflicting arrangements. A third party can also avoid ratification if the third party:

- learns that the purported agent acted without authority,
- relies on the apparent lack of authority, and
- makes substitute, conflicting arrangements or takes some other action which will cause prejudice to the third party if the original transaction is enforced.[84]

For the necessary reliance to exist, the third party must act before learning of the purported principal's affirmance.

§2.7.5 *Ratification Contrasted with Adoption and Novation*

Cases often confuse and interchange the terms *ratification, adoption,* and *novation.* Many of those cases involve contracts made by corporate promoters on behalf of corporations not in existence when the contract is made. To the extent the three terms have separate meanings, those meanings are as follows:

---

82. See section 2.7.2.

83. Restatement §89, Illustration 1. This is a curious example and perhaps a redundant concept. Since ratification relates back to the moment of contract formation, any relevant changed circumstances must occur after contract formation. In that case, however, contract law doctrines are available to allow the principal to avoid the contract. See Restatement (Second) of Contracts §§261 (impracticability) and 265 (frustration of purpose).

84. Restatement §95, comment *b.*

Ratification.   As described in this section, *ratification* is the retroactive approval of a previously unauthorized act. Subject to the conditions and exceptions discussed in this section, ratification binds both the purported principal and the third party to the original undertaking and discharges the purported agent from any liability on that undertaking.

Adoption.   *Adoption* occurs when:

- a purported agent has purported to bind a purported principal to an agreement while lacking the power to do so;
- the purported principal cannot ratify the purported agent's unauthorized act, typically because at the time of the act the purported principal either did not exist or lacked capacity to authorize the act;
- the original agreement made by the purported agent and the third party expressly or impliedly empowers the purported principal to choose to receive the benefits and assume the obligations of the agreement; and
- the purported principal manifests—either expressly or through a course of conduct—its desire to receive the benefits and assume the obligations of the agreement.

Like ratification, adoption binds both the principal and the third party to the original agreement. *Unlike* ratification, adoption does not relate back in time to the unauthorized act. So, if for any reason the starting date of the relationship between the adopting principal and the third party is important, that date is the date of the adoption, not the date of the unauthorized act. Moreover, adoption does not release the purported agent from any liability it may have to the third party on account of the original agreement, unless the original agreement contemplates that the principal's adoption will indeed release the agent.

Novation.   A *novation* is a new, independent agreement between the principal and the third party. Novations arise from the same circumstances that give rise to adoptions, and it is often the original, unauthorized contract that causes the purported principal and the third party to consider doing business with each other. The terms of the novation may be and often are identical to the terms of the prior, unauthorized agreement.

Nonetheless, a novation reflects an entirely separate process of contract formation. Once formed, the novation contract completely displaces the original, unauthorized contract and relieves the purported agent from any liability it may have had to the third party on account of that prior contract.

Whether the new arrangement is an adoption (which does not release the purported agent) or a novation (which does) is a question of the parties' intent.

Example: Rachael decides to go into business with a 1950s-style hamburger joint. She plans to incorporate the business under the name of

"Sam's Place, Inc." She signs a lease for the restaurant, however, before actually forming the corporation. In signing the lease she purports to act as "President of Sam's Place, Inc." and neglects to inform the lessor that Sam's Place, Inc. has not yet come into existence.

Since a nonexistent corporation cannot authorize anyone to do anything, Rachael's act in signing the lease is unauthorized and does not bind the corporation. As of that moment, Rachael, not the corporation, is liable to the lessor on the lease.[85]

When Rachael does form the corporation, the corporation may decide to take responsibility for the lease. However, the corporation cannot by itself take Rachael off the hook. Ratification would release Rachael, but ratification is not possible: At the time of the lease signing the corporation did not exist, so one of the necessary preconditions to ratification is absent. The corporation can adopt the lease, but that adoption will not release Rachael. If the corporation later defaults, she will still be liable.

If the lessor agrees, the corporation and the lessor can make a novation. A new contractual relationship between the lessor and the corporation will replace the original lease, the corporation will be bound, and Rachael will no longer be liable.

§2.8   Chains of Authority

§2.8.1   *Multilevel Relationships*

For the most part, the examples used in this chapter so far have been "flat." The principals act through a single agent, and agents draw their authority directly from manifestations made by the principal. Third parties claim apparent authority from manifestations made directly by a principal.

Real life relationships tend to be more intricate.

Example: Marcia is the manager of an airport office of a rental car company. As part of her job, she hires, supervises, and when necessary, fires the people who staff that office. Those people are agents of the rental car company, not of Marcia, even though (1) it was Marcia who told each of them, "You're hired," and (2) the company itself has never made any direct manifestation to any of them.

Example: Seeking to increase business, Marcia retains the services of Abitatruth, Inc., an advertising agency. Acting on behalf of the rental car company, Marcia authorizes the agency to spend $10,000 to rent advertising space around the airport on the company's behalf. The agency assigns the work of renting the advertising space to Alan, one of its

---

85. See section 4.2.2.

employees. Alan has the power to bind the rental car company, even though (1) Marcia has never made any manifestation to Alan, and (2) Marcia does not even know that Alan exists.

Each of these examples involves a "concatenation" of responsibility. That is, in each situation a *chain* of relationships or events makes the rental car company the principal and gives the person at the bottom of the chain the power to bind. Thus, a person can be an agent without ever having met or communicated directly with the principal.

For instance, in the first example (Marcia hires the staff), the employees are agents of the rental car company because another agent of the company (Marcia), acting within her actual authority, has made manifestations (attributable to the company) that the company (as principal) desires the employees to act on the company's behalf and subject to the company's control. See Figures 2-2 and 2-3.

Figure 2-2. Concatenating Authority — The Practical Structure

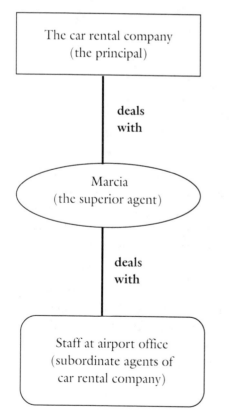

The car rental company
(the principal)

deals with

Marcia
(the superior agent)

deals with

Staff at airport office
(subordinate agents of car rental company)

(Principal wishes to maintain an office at airport and to hire employees to staff that office.)

(Marcia is appointed office manager. Her job description includes hiring and firing office staff. Marcia acts for car rental company in dealing with employees. She and each member of the office staff are co-agents of the car rental company.)

Figure 2-3. Concatenating Authority—The Agency Structure

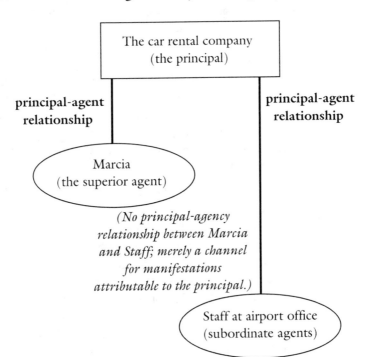

Agency law handles such complexity in characteristic fashion. It establishes categories, labels the categories, and attaches consequences to the categories. In matters of contract and communication, the key labels are *superior agents, subordinate agents,*[86] and *subagents.*

§2.8.2 Superior and Subordinate Agents

The categories. As section 2.8.1 illustrates, a principal can use one of its agents to appoint, direct, and discharge other agents of the principal. Using

---

86. Neither the Restatement nor the case law provide any names for these important links in the chain of agency authority. For the first edition of this book, the author coined the terms "intermediary" and "subordinate." Restatement (Third) uses the terms "superior and subordinate co-agents," §1.04(10) at 93, and this edition follows that usage.

"superior agents" to deal with "subordinate agents" is merely a specific instance of a principal acting through its agents. The principal uses one (or more) of its agents to manifest its desires to the principal's other agents.

This concatenated, hierarchical structure is commonplace. Only the smallest of organizations can operate without the "top dog" delegating some responsibility to superior and subordinate agents. Moreover, the delegation often works through several levels (in military terms, the "chain of command"), with agents being simultaneously superior agents vis-à-vis those "below" them, and subordinate agents vis-à-vis those "above" them. Superior agents and subordinate agents are "co-agents" of the principal. A subordinate agent is never the agent of a superior agent.

> *Example:* Marcia's actual authority to run the airport office might derive as follows: The car company's regional manager appointed her to the position and generally described to her the duties and authority of the position. The regional manager obtained the actual authority to make such manifestations on behalf of the company when the Vice President for Leasing Operations appointed him to the regional manager position. The Vice President, in turn, obtained her actual authority to manifest the company's choice of regional managers (and to manifest the company's wishes as to the duties and authority of those managers) when the Chief Executive Officer appointed her as Vice President and outlined the duties and authority of that position. The company made the necessary manifestations to appoint and authorize the CEO when the company's Board of Directors elected the CEO.[87] See Figure 2-4.

A principal can also authorize a superior agent to formulate the principal's desires for it, and then to manifest those desires as necessary to the principal's other agents and to would-be agents.

> *Example:* The board of directors of Rollerskating, Inc. adopts a resolution instructing its CEO to "develop and implement a plan for aggressively marketing the company's new generation of in-line skates." Acting within the resulting actual authority, the CEO decides on a marketing approach, interviews various advertising agencies that wish to provide services to implement the concept, selects an agency for the project, and delegates numerous tasks to various Rollerskating employees.

No matter how much authority and discretion a superior agent has, however, the superior agent acts on behalf of the principal and not on the agent's

---

87. As to the conduct of a corporation's day-to-day affairs, the board of directors has the ultimate authority and power. See, e.g., Revised Model Business Corporation Act §8.01(b) ("All corporate powers shall be exercised by or under the authority of, and the business and affairs of the corporation managed under the direction of, its board of directors. . . .")

Figure 2-4. The Rental Car Company's Chain of Command

Board of Directors

*manifests the Company's consent and
establishes actual authority in*

the Chief Executive Officer [a superior agent]

*who, acting within his actual authority as an agent of the Company,
did an act attributable to the Company, namely — appointing*

the Vice-President for Leasing [a subordinate
agent and simultaneously a superior agent]

*who, acting within her actual authority as an agent of the Company,
did an act attributable to the Company, namely — appointing*

the Regional Manager [a subordinate agent
and simultaneously a superior agent]

*who, acting within his actual authority as an agent of the Company,
did an act attributable to the Company, namely — appointing*

Marcia, the manager of the airport office [a subordinate
agent and simultaneously a superior agent]

own account. So long as a superior agent acts with actual authority, apparent authority, or inherent agency power, the superior agent's manifestations—whether to the subordinate agents or to third parties—are attributable to the principal.

A subordinate agent's power to bind the principal.   A subordinate agent binds its principal under the same rules applicable to "plain" agents. The key questions are therefore the same, namely, did the subordinate agent act with actual authority? apparent authority? inherent agency power? under circumstances giving rise to estoppel? Answering these questions involves looking at the conduct attributable to the principal, including any manifestations made by superior agents within the scope of their actual authority, apparent authority, or inherent agency power.

Example: Marcia, the manager of the rental car company's airport office, has engaged Abitatruth, an ad agency, to develop advertising for the rental car company. Marcia brings along Sara, one of her assistants, to a series of conferences with Abitatruth. During these conferences Marcia repeatedly seeks Sara's opinion as to choices posed by the ad agency and occasionally defers to Sara's judgment. Later, when the ad agency cannot get in touch with Marcia, it asks Sara to approve the content of several advertising posters. Although Marcia has stated privately to Sara that Marcia plans to approve all posters, Sara tells the ad agency, "Go ahead."

This approval binds the rental car company. Although Marcia's private statements to Sara preclude a claim based on actual authority, Sara did have apparent authority. Apparent authority presupposes a manifestation *of the rental car company,* which Marcia's conduct supplies. Consulting with and relying on subordinates—even in the presence of others—was certainly within Marcia's actual authority. That conduct is therefore, by attribution, the conduct of the rental car company. Coupled with the ad agency's resulting, reasonable belief in Sara's authority, this attributed manifestation gave Sara apparent authority to approve the posters on the rental car company's behalf.

Superior agent's limited responsibility for the misconduct of subordinate agents.   All agents owe a duty of care to their principal,[88] and superior agents must exercise care in selecting, directing, and discharging subordinate agents. If a superior agent fails to do so and that breach of duty proximately causes injury to the principal, the superior agent is liable to the principal for resulting damages.

Example: Marcia hires Henry to drive the courtesy van that takes passengers between the airport and the car rental office. Marcia carelessly fails to check Henry's references and driving record. The references are false, and the record includes several drunk driving convictions. One day Henry drives the van while drunk and causes an accident. Under the doctrine of respondeat superior, the car rental company is liable for any damage Henry caused to others.[89] Marcia is liable to the car rental company for its obligations to others, plus any damage to the company's courtesy van. She breached her duty of care in selecting and supervising a subordinate agent.

A superior agent is not, however, the guarantor of the subordinate agent's performance.

Example: Same situation, except Henry's references are okay, his driving record is clean and Marcia uses reasonable care in hiring and supervising Henry. The car rental company remains liable to others for harm

---

88. See section 4.1.4.
89. See section 3.2.

caused by Henry's drunken driving, but Marcia is not liable to the car rental company.

§2.8.3 Subagents

The category.   When a principal engages an agent to perform a task, the principal has in effect delegated the task to the agent. If the agent, acting with authority, in turn redelegates part or all of that task to an agent of its own, then the second agent becomes a subagent of the original principal.

> *Example:* P retains A, a real-estate broker, to sell Blackacre. P knows that A employs sales people to show property to prospective purchasers and to state the terms on which the property is for sale. The sales people are A's employees, not P's employees. The sales people are also P's subagents.[90]

The agent's authority to redelegate.   As a general rule an agent has no authority to delegate its tasks to another. However, a principal can authorize its agent to delegate, and the general rules for creating actual authority apply to determine whether the principal has done so.

Consistent with those rules, implied actual authority to delegate exists when: (i) the delegation relates merely to the mechanical aspects of the agent's tasks; (ii) the agent is a corporation, partnership, limited liability company, or other organization; or (iii) it is customary for agents in similar situations to delegate. As with all instances of implied actual authority, a manifestation of the principal can restrict or even completely negate the implied authority. However, when the agent is a corporation or other legal entity, some authority to delegate must remain. Legal "persons" can act only through the endeavors of natural persons.

> *Example:* Sylvia, a rock singer, retains David, a well-known agent, to arrange on her behalf the facilities and amenities to be made available to Sylvia on an upcoming tour. David has several assistants, and they normally handle such "logistical details." Sylvia, however, says, "I want your personal touch on this. Don't let anyone else work on it." David has no authority to delegate the work.

> *Example:* Sylvia, a rock singer, retains Pauline's Representation, Inc. ("Pauline's") to arrange bookings. Pauline's is a corporation, with the necessary right to delegate the task. Sylvia, however, imposes a condition, saying, "Make sure whoever works on my account has been with you for at least five years."

A subagent's power to bind the principal.   Assuming that an agent has the authority to delegate tasks to a subagent, determining the scope of a subagent's power to bind the principal in contract involves a two-stage analysis:

---

90. This Example is taken verbatim from Restatement (Third) §1.04, Illustration 3 at 98.

1. What is the scope of the agent's power to bind the principal?
2. Of that scope, what has the agent authorized the subagent to perform?[91]

Example: The car rental company (acting via Marcia) gives Abitatruth actual authority to spend up to $10,000 in renting advertising space [stage 1]. Moe is a junior vice president of Abitatruth, with actual authority (from Abitatruth) to make leasing commitments of $1,000 or less [stage 2]. Moe has neither apparent authority nor inherent agency power to exceed the $1,000 limit while acting for Abitatruth [stage 2]. Moe purports to commit the car rental company to space Alpha for $800 and to space Beta for $1,250.

In each instance Moe has acted as an agent for Abitatruth and subagent for the car rental company. The commitment on space Alpha binds the car rental company, because the commitment was within Abitatruth's authority vis-à-vis the company [stage 1] and within Moe's authority vis-à-vis Abitatruth [stage 2]. The commitment on space Beta does not bind the car rental company, because that commitment exceeded Moe's authority vis-à-vis Abitatruth [stage 2].

To bind the principal, a subagent's act must be both within the subagent's power to bind the agent and within the agent's power to bind the principal.

Agent the guarantor of the subagent's performance.   When an agent delegates all or part of its responsibilities to a subagent, the agent remains "on the hook" to the principal. Delegation does not relieve the agent of its responsibilities. If the subagent's performance satisfies the obligations the agent owes to the principal, then the agent, acting through the subagent, has performed its responsibilities as agent. If, however, the subagent's performance fails to satisfy the agent's obligations, then the agent is directly responsible to the principal.[92]

§2.8.4   *Distinguishing Subordinate Agents from Subagents*

The concepts of subordinate agent and subagent both presuppose a hierarchy with:

- the principal at the top,
- the subordinate agent or subagent at the bottom, and
- an intermediary (either a superior agent or an agent) in between.

---

91. Restatement §5, comment *d*.

92. The rule stated here closely parallels a rule of contract law: When an obligor delegates its performance obligations to another, that delegation does not by itself discharge the obligor's duties to the obligee.

Nonetheless, the two concepts reflect very different relationships with very different legal consequences. It is therefore important to distinguish one relationship from the other.

The crucial point of distinction is the manifestation that the principal makes to the intermediary. Ideally at least, that manifestation, reasonably interpreted, will lead the intermediary to believe either that:

- the principal wishes the intermediary to retain or supervise another agent *of the principal*—in which case the intermediary is to be a superior agent, the other agent is to be a subordinate agent, and both the superior and subordinate agents are to be co-agents of the principal;

or

- the principal wishes to retain the intermediary as the principal's agent and recognizes that the agent may delegate some or all of its responsibility to another person—in which case that other person is an agent of the agent and simultaneously a subagent of the principal.

Example: A landlord retains a management company to manage 150 separate apartment buildings owned by the landlord. The landlord wants a resident caretaker in each building and expects these caretakers to be employees of the management company. The caretakers will be agents of the management company and subagents of the landlord.

Superior and subordinate agents are usually part of the same company, as in the Examples in sections 2.8.1 and 2.8.2 involving Marcia and the car rental company. However, that circumstance is *not* an element of the superior/subordinate agent analysis.

Example: The management company's contract with the landlord has significantly increased the company's obligations, and the company needs interim help recruiting and supervising resident caretakers. On an interim basis, the management company retains Carolyn, an experienced real estate attorney, to interview applicants for caretaker positions and gives her authority to hire applicants she considers appropriate. The management company also retains Carolyn to supervise the applicants she hires. Like her, the caretakers she hires will be agents of the management company.[93] When she supervises, she will be acting as a superior agent viz à viz subordinate agents.

PROBLEM 1

Captain Miles Standish loved the fair damsel Priscilla, but Standish's intense shyness prevented him from speaking to her. One day Standish lamented the

---

93. Unlike her, the caretakers will probably also be servants of the management company. See section 3.2.2. However, that distinction is immaterial here.

situation to his friend John Alden, and Alden offered to speak to Priscilla and on Standish's behalf invite her to an upcoming community dance. Standish responded, stroking his beard reflectively, "I dunno. That might be a good idea." Alden took that comment as assent and rode off to see Priscilla. Actually, however, Standish did not intend to consent. Right after Alden rode off, Standish wrote in his diary, "Told Alden that I would think about his offer. Have done so and will reject it as soon as I next see him."

Before Standish saw Alden again, however, Alden saw Priscilla. Alden explained Standish's great love, and—purporting to act on Standish's behalf—invited Priscilla to accompany Standish to the dance. Priscilla accepted. Later, Standish saw Alden and told him not to talk to Priscilla. Alden told Standish, "Too late, fellow; you're going to the dance."

Assume that, as a matter of contract law, contracts to attend dances are valid and enforceable. Is Standish bound?

EXPLANATION

Standish is bound only if Alden had actual authority to extend the invitation.[94] The creation of actual authority requires (i) a manifestation by the principal, (ii) the agent's reasonable interpretation of that manifestation as a request that the agent acts for the principal, and (iii) the agent's manifestation of consent to act. The first and last certainly occurred. Standish's comment ("That might be a good idea") suffices as a manifestation. Alden's action reflects his consent. The question of the agent's interpretation, however, is more difficult. Although Standish's subjective intent is irrelevant, Standish's response was objectively ambiguous. Especially given what Alden knew of Standish's shyness, it was probably unreasonable for Alden to consider himself authorized without having first sought clarification. Therefore, no actual authority existed and Standish is not bound on the contract.

PROBLEM 2

A tenant rents her apartment on a month-to-month tenancy, with each term beginning on the first of the month. Under local law, the tenant can terminate the tenancy by giving a full calendar month's notice. For example, for the tenancy to end on March 31, the tenant must give notice before March 1. The building is managed by a resident manager, whom the landlord has authorized to receive notices from tenants. On December 28, the tenant gives proper notice to the resident manager, stating that the tenant will vacate by January 31. Unfortunately, the resident manager fails to pass the notice on to the landlord until January 3. Will the tenancy end on January 31?

---

94. Since there is no indication of Priscilla's being aware of any manifestation by Standish, there can be no apparent authority. Since Alden is not a general agent, there can be no inherent power. Since Priscilla has not changed position to her detriment, there can be no estoppel. (The facts do not indicate that she has bought a new dress or rejected other invitations.)

EXPLANATION

Yes. When an agent has actual authority to receive a notice, receipt of that notice is attributable to the principal. The agent's failure to communicate the information to the principal may be a breach of the agent's duty to the principal[95] but has no effect on the attribution rule.

PROBLEM 3

A railroad company wishes to acquire three parcels of land for a new line. The company fears that the landowners will ask too much money if they learn that the railroad needs the land. It also fears the same result if the landowners are contacted by someone representing an unnamed principal. The company therefore uses three different "straw men." Each of these agents individually approaches one of the landowners. Each of the agents affirmatively states that he or she is acting on his or her own account. Each negotiates for and signs a land purchase contract in his or her own name. Later, before the purchases are closed, the landowners learn that the railroad is the actual purchaser. Are landowners obliged to go through with the deals?

EXPLANATION

Yes. A contract made by an agent acting for an undisclosed principal is binding both on the undisclosed principal and the third party. A third party can escape a contract with an undisclosed principal only if (i) there has been an affirmative misrepresentation as to the undisclosed principal's status, and (ii) either the undisclosed principal or the agent had reason to know that the third party would refuse to deal with the principal. In this situation the first factor is present, but the second is not. The agents did actively misrepresent the role of the undisclosed principal, but neither the agents nor their undisclosed principal had reason to know that the third parties would refuse to contract with the principal. To the contrary, both the agents and principal thought the third parties would be delighted to contract with the railroad—but at a substantially higher price.

PROBLEM 4

Mr. and Ms. Yup, high-powered corporate lawyers, mesh their schedules and arrange a week's vacation hiking in the Andes Mountains. To babysit their offspring ("Little Yup") and to housesit their house, the Yups hire a babysitter ("Babysitter"). The Yups provide the babysitter, among other information, the name, office phone number, and office address of Little Yup's pediatrician. They also leave a health insurance card that indicates a health insurance account number for Little Yup. Unfortunately, while the Yups are away, Little Yup becomes seriously ill. The babysitter takes Little Yup to the hospital,

---

95. See section 4.1.5.

where expensive medical procedures enable Little Yup to recover. In order to have the hospital provide the services, Babysitter shows the health insurance card and signs a contract with the hospital. Queried about the child's parents, Babysitter responds, "They're backpacking in the Andes. I am babysitting for their child for this week." Babysitter signs the hospitalization contract: "I.M. Babysitter, for Mr. and Ms. Yup." Are Mr. and Ms. Yup bound on that contract?

EXPLANATION

The Yups are bound, certainly on actual authority and perhaps on apparent authority as well. Merely by entrusting the child to Babysitter for a week and leaving the country, the Yups manifested consent to have Babysitter arrange for necessary medical care. Providing the name of the pediatrician and the health insurance card reinforced that basic manifestation. The Yups did not specifically mention hospitalization and did not specifically authorize Babysitter to sign hospital contracts on their behalf, but Babysitter certainly had implied actual authority to arrange hospitalization in an emergency and to sign all reasonably necessary documents for that purpose.

The argument for apparent authority is also strong. The hospital must be able to point to some manifestation of the Yups which, reasonably interpreted, led the hospital to believe that Babysitter was authorized to bind the Yups. The hospital can identify three manifestations: the Yups' entrusting of their child to Babysitter; the Babysitter's possession of the insurance card; the Babysitter's statement about her responsibilities. The first manifestation arguably establishes apparent authority by position, although babysitters do not customarily commit parents to large hospital bills. The possession of the insurance card made it more reasonable for the hospital to believe that the parents had given Babysitter authority to arrange for medical services. It is the third manifestation—Babysitter's statement—which is perhaps the strongest point. Had that statement been made directly by the Yups, there would have been no question of Babysitter's apparent authority. When Babysitter accurately described her authority, she was acting within her actual authority. As a consequence, her statement had the same effect as if the Yups had made it themselves.

PROBLEM 5

Pickwick owns an antique store which occupies the first three floors of a four-story brownstone. Pickwick lives on the fourth floor, has security cameras throughout the first three floors and has a rather lackadaisical attitude toward maintaining personal surveillance over the store premises. He customarily leaves the store door unlocked even when he is upstairs having lunch or taking a nap. A large sign just inside the store entrance advises: "For assistance, pull on cord to ring bell."

One day two newlyweds enter the store and are promptly approached by a respectable looking lady who identifies herself as "Mrs. Pickwick." With Mrs. Pickwick's assistance, the newlyweds examine several large antiques and decide to purchase two of them. The newlyweds give Mrs. Pickwick $200 in cash as a down payment and arrange for a delivery day. Mrs. Pickwick takes from a roll-top desk a sheet of letterhead of "Pickwick & Company" and writes out a receipt.

"Mrs. Pickwick" is in fact an imposter. Is Mr. Pickwick bound to the purported contract? If not, is Mr. Pickwick obliged to make good the $200?

EXPLANATION

Although the imposter lacked actual and apparent authority,[96] Mr. Pickwick is probably liable via estoppel at least for the $200. The newlyweds "changed their position because of their belief that the transaction was entered into . . . for" Mr. Pickwick and Mr. Pickwick "carelessly caused such belief" through his lackadaisical attitude toward security.[97] At minimum, the newlyweds are entitled to their reliance damages and perhaps to their expectation interest as well.

PROBLEM 6

Henry comes to town one day looking for some land to purchase. He learns that Eleanor has a parcel of lakefront property that she wishes to sell. Henry meets Eleanor, explains that he is "in town acting for a group of investors who are looking for lakefront in this area" and goes with Eleanor to inspect the property. Henry appears impressed, but says to Eleanor, "I'm just the gofer. I'll have to check with the folks in charge." The next day Henry comes back and tells Eleanor that he is authorized to pay her $30,000 for the property. Eleanor thinks the price is a fair one, and together they go to a local stationery store and buy a legal form entitled "Contract for the Sale of Land." They fill in all the blanks, Eleanor signs as seller and Henry signs as "agent for the Aquitaine Corporation, Buyer." As completed and signed, the contract indicates that on behalf of Aquitaine Corporation Henry has put $100 down and that the corporation will deliver the rest of the purchase price within 30 days.

Two weeks after the contract is signed, Eleanor sees Henry walking down a street in town. Walking with Henry is a man whom Henry introduces as Richard, President of the Aquitaine Corporation. (This man is indeed Richard, and Richard is indeed President of Aquitaine.) After casual remarks about the weather, Eleanor asks, "Does Henry do a lot of work for your corporation, Richard?" Richard responds, "We've used him on a number of occasions. He's quite a go-getter."

---

96. No manifestation attributable to Mr. Pickwick, the principal.
97. Restatement §8B(1)(a), discussed in section 2.5.

Thirty days pass after the signing of the contract, and Eleanor receives no payment. When she contacts the Aquitaine Corporation, it denies that Henry was authorized to act on its behalf. It truthfully states that: (i) it never made any manifestation to Henry regarding Eleanor's parcel; and (ii) Henry never had any ongoing responsibilities with Aquitaine but instead occasionally received specific assignments. Aquitaine denies any responsibility for the Eleanor-Henry transaction and flatly refuses to pay.

Henry being nowhere to be found, Eleanor brings suit on the contract against Aquitaine Corporation. Assume that the ("equal dignities") rule does *not* apply in the jurisdiction. Assume also that Richard's comments to Eleanor are attributable to Aquitaine. What result in Eleanor's suit?

EXPLANATION

Eleanor will lose. She will be unable to attribute Henry's actions to Aquitaine.

Since Aquitaine never made any manifestation to Henry regarding Eleanor's parcel, actual authority did not exist. Since Henry's role with Aquitaine never involved any "continuity of service," he was never a general agent. Consequently, he had no inherent agency power to enter into contracts on Aquitaine's behalf. The doctrines of apparent authority and estoppel are Eleanor's only hope, and that hope is forlorn.

The problem with apparent authority is one of timing: The apparent principal's manifestation came too late. To establish apparent authority, Eleanor must show some conduct attributable to Aquitaine that—*as of the moment of contract formation*—caused her to reasonably believe that Henry had authority. Until just prior to the execution of the form contract, Eleanor did not even know who the supposed principal was. Even when Henry disclosed Aquitaine's identity, Eleanor's inference that Henry had authority was based solely on Henry's remarks, not on any conduct of Aquitaine.

In some circumstances, an apparent principal's silence in the face of an apparent agent's known conduct will suffice as a manifestation. However, in this case there is no indication whatsoever that at the time of contract formation Aquitaine Corporation was aware of Henry's claim of agency status.

The conversation between Eleanor and Richard cannot salvage the situation for Eleanor. Even if Eleanor reasonably interpreted Richard's comments to mean that Henry had authority, there remains the problem of timing. Even under the Restatement view, the claimant must link the manifestation to a reasonable belief that existed *as of the moment of the relevant act*. A post hoc manifestation cannot justify an ante hoc belief. By the time Eleanor spoke with Richard, Eleanor had already executed the contract.

The Eleanor-Richard conversation will be likewise unavailing for a claim of estoppel. Even assuming that Richard's casual remark "intentionally or carelessly" caused Eleanor to believe that Henry had acted with authority,[98]

---

98. Restatement §8B(1)(a), discussed at section 2.5.

that belief did not cause any relevant harm. Eleanor had already signed the contract. Unless she can show that she suffered some additional prejudice subsequent to her conversation with Richard (e.g., turning down another potential buyer), she cannot establish estoppel.[99]

PROBLEM 7

A small real estate company is planning to rent office space to an entrepreneur who needs "a place to hang my hat, pick up my mail, and get telephone calls." The real estate company's premises are small and its phone system very basic. The entrepreneur's calls will come through the main switchboard without a dedicated line, and her desk will be located in the same open space used by employees of the company. How can the real estate company minimize the chances that it will be held responsible for its tenant's dealings with third parties?

EXPLANATION

Perhaps the most important safeguard is to expend the time and effort necessary to check into the *bona fides* of the would-be tenant. Problems will arise only if the entrepreneur cheats her customers or suppliers.

As for the agency law analysis, apparent authority is the key concept. Under that concept the main risks would come from (i) ambiguous manifestations by the real estate company, and (ii) reasonable misinterpretations by third parties. Due to the limitations of the phone system and the office setup, certain manifestations are inherent in the proposed arrangement. The key, therefore, is to preclude reasonable confusion. The safest approach is to make sure that an appropriate clarification accompanies each potentially confusing manifestation. For example, when the receptionist receives a call for the entrepreneur, the receptionist should use a greeting that indicates that the entrepreneur is not employed by the real estate company. As for the office setup, a sign on the office entrance should indicate the entrepreneur's independent, unassociated status.

PROBLEM 8

The resident building manager in an apartment building serves regularly as the information "go-between" between the tenants and the landlord. On January 25 the landlord fires the manager, effective immediately, and gives the manager until the end of the next month to vacate his apartment. The next day a month-to-month tenant gives notice to the resident manager, stating that the tenant will vacate her apartment by the end of February. Angry and

---

99. To assert that Richard's comments caused a ratification is too much of a stretch. Ratification requires a manifestation of affirmance, and the purported principal's manifestation must relate specifically to the unauthorized act being ratified.

embarrassed about the firing, the fired manager accepts the notice, says nothing to the tenant about being fired and purposely does not pass the notice on to the landlord. Is the notice effective against the landlord? If so, what could the landlord have done to avoid being bound by a notice the landlord never actually received?

EXPLANATION

The notice is effective. Although the firing terminated the manager's actual authority to receive notices, the apparent authority continued. The landlord's past use of the resident manager as a channel of communication satisfies the manifestation requirement. So long as the former manager remained in the same apartment and no one told any of the tenants of the firing, it remained reasonable for the tenant to believe the former manager was authorized to receive notices for the landlord.

The landlord had available a simple preventive measure—promptly notifying the tenants of the change and directing them not to give notices to the former manager. No tenant who received this message could have reasonably believed that the former manager remained authorized.

PROBLEM 9

Jeffrey is a buyer's broker in the recycled newspaper business. On behalf of various newsprint manufacturers, he locates and purchases recycled newspapers. Each time Jeffrey makes a purchase, he is acting on behalf of a particular customer. He nonetheless makes each purchase in his own name.

For the past five years, one of Jeffrey's customers has been Amalgamated Newsprint. During that time Jeffrey has made about four purchases per year for Amalgamated. On each occasion Jeffrey and Amalgamated have followed the same procedure: Amalgamated places an order with Jeffrey, stating a quantity and a maximum price. When Jeffrey finds the necessary newspapers, he purchases them in his own name and informs Amalgamated of the delivery date and price. Amalgamated then wires funds to Jeffrey, and Jeffrey pays the vendor. A commission structure rewards Jeffrey for bringing in an order below the maximum allowed price. Jeffrey understands that he is not authorized to make any purchases for Amalgamated without first having an order in hand.

Nonetheless, after five years Jeffrey has begun to anticipate Amalgamated's needs. Last week he saw a great purchase opportunity and, expecting an order from Amalgamated, he agreed to make the purchase. Although as always Jeffrey made the purchase in his own name, he noted the purchase on his books as "for Amalgamated." If Jeffrey is unable to pay for the purchase, can the vendor enforce the contract against Amalgamated?

EXPLANATION

Probably not. Since Jeffrey lacked the right to purchase for Amalgamated without first having an order and since Amalgamated was an undisclosed principal, neither actual nor apparent authority apply. Also, since the vendor and Amalgamated were unaware of each other, there can be no estoppel.

The vendor's only hope is inherent agency power. The vendor must (i) label Jeffrey as Amalgamated's general agent, (ii) delineate Jeffrey's agency function as acquiring newspaper for Amalgamated on an ongoing basis, and (iii) characterize the purchase contract as "usual or necessary" to Jeffrey's authorized activities.[100]

The vendor will likely fail in all three respects, because it will fail in the first. Jeffrey is not a general agent. He is not "authorized to conduct a series of transactions involving a continuity of service."[101] To the contrary, he receives and needs separate authorization for each individual transaction. As a result, Jeffrey has no "ongoing" authorized responsibilities and the unauthorized purchase was not "usual or necessary" to any authorized activity.

PROBLEM 10

Jeffrey makes the unauthorized purchase described in Problem 11, but in doing so tells the vendor that the purchase is being made on behalf of Amalgamated. Jeffrey then calls Amalgamated and reports his "great find." Amalgamated shocks Jeffrey by saying, "Nothing doing. No order with us, no deal from us."

Jeffrey immediately contacts the vendor, seeking a brief delay on delivery. "I bought this for a customer," he explains, "and I didn't exactly have their OK in advance. They're balking a bit. I've got to make nice with them." Jeffrey then calls Amalgamated again, apologizes profusely and extols the benefits of this bargain. After a 45-minute conversation, Amalgamated relents and says, "Alright. We'll take it."

Jeffrey immediately calls the vendor back and says, "No problem. We're fine." The vendor responds, "I'm fine anyhow. As soon as I learned that you were a go-between and had no authority, I went looking for another buyer. Just two minutes ago I sold the goods to somebody else."

Can Amalgamated enforce the original agreement against the vendor?

EXPLANATION

No. Amalgamated did eventually affirm Jeffrey's unauthorized act, and ordinarily that affirmance would bind both the vendor and Amalgamated to the contract. In this instance, however, the vendor can avoid the ratification. In reliance on Jeffrey's lack of authority, the vendor changed its position and bound itself to another buyer. The fact that Amalgamated ratified before that change in position took place is irrelevant. What matters is that the vendor changed position before learning of the ratification.

---

100. Restatement §194 (inherent agency power of general agent of undisclosed principal), discussed at section 2.6.2.

101. Restatement §3(1) (general agent defined), discussed at section 2.6.2.

PROBLEM 11

January 1, 1999	Elvira enters into an oral contract with three entrepreneurs who are founding a community theater. The contract calls for Elvira to begin work managing the theater on March 1, 1999 and to work in that capacity for one year. All parties understand that the entrepreneurs plan to form a corporation to own the business and that the corporation will take over Elvira's contract.
March 1, 1999	Elvira begins work as manager.
May 1, 1999	The entrepreneurs form Community Theatre, Inc. ("CTI") and elect themselves as the board of directors. Acting as the board, they appoint Roberta as chief executive officer and formally (albeit orally) agree to have CTI "take over the management contract with Elvira."
May 2, 1999	Roberta informs Elvira of CTI's formation, Roberta's appointment as CEO, and the board's action to take over Elvira's contract. Roberta says, "As of now, your management contract is with CTI."
May 31, 1999	Elvira receives her monthly salary check, this time drawn on a CTI checking account.
June 30, 1999	Elvira receives her monthly salary check, drawn on a CTI checking account.
July 10, 1999	Roberta terminates Elvira as manager.

Elvira subsequently sues CTI for breach of contract, asserting that under the contract CTI was obligated to continue her employment through February 29, 2000. CTI defends in part invoking the statute of frauds, noting that the original agreement contemplated performance that would extend more than one year beyond the making of the contract.

Elvira responds that: (a) the original agreement with the three entrepreneurs may have been within the statute, but she is not suing them; (b) when CTI "took over" the contract, the contract called for less than a year of performance, and therefore (c) the statute of frauds does not apply to CTI's obligations.

CTI rejoins that: (i) by "taking over" the contract, CTI ratified the original agreement; (ii) ratification relates back to the time of the action being ratified, and therefore (iii) CTI's ratification results in a contract that is within the statute of frauds.

Who is right?

EXPLANATION

Elvira. A party can ratify a prior act only if the party existed at the time of the act. A corporation can therefore never ratify an act taken on its behalf before the corporation came into existence.

PROBLEM 12

The board of directors of Rollerskating, Inc. adopts a resolution authorizing the CEO "to appoint such officers, managers, and employees of the corporation as the CEO deems appropriate and to prescribe their respective duties, subject only to the numerical limits established by the board of directors from time to time." Aware of the resolution, Rollerskating's CEO appoints Rachael to be its purchasing agent. The CEO provides Rachael with a four-page memo, outlining the internal approvals necessary before Rachael may place an order. For instance, orders costing less than $50,000 can be approved by the CEO; orders costing less than $25,000 may be approved by any vice president; orders costing less than $5,000 may be approved by any department manager. Rachael receives a request from a vice president to order a Model 5400 Wodget from Samuel Equipment Corporation ("Samuel Equipment") at a price of $15,000, and she places the order. Does the order bind Rollerskating?

EXPLANATION

Yes. In placing the order, she is acting with the reasonable belief that she is authorized to do so. Her belief is based on manifestations from a superior agent (her appointment to the position of purchasing; the memo of internal procedures). Those manifestations are within the superior agent's actual authority and are therefore attributable to the principal. In short, Rachael has actual authority.

PROBLEM 13

Over the next three months, Rachael places several more orders with Samuel Equipment Company, each properly requested by a Rollerskating vice president and each costing between $10,000 and $24,000. In due course Samuel Equipment delivers the equipment and bills Rollerskating. The bills come to the Rollerskating comptroller, whom the CEO has made responsible for reviewing and approving for payment all invoices over $1,000. The comptroller reviews the invoices, notes that each order was properly authorized and has been fulfilled, okays the payment, and signs and sends to Samuel Equipment a payment for the invoiced amount.

Subsequently, Rachael is promoted out of the purchasing department and is replaced by Herman. Rachael's last responsibility as purchasing agent is to brief Herman on his new responsibilities. Rachael does so, directing Herman's attention to the CEO's memo on internal approvals. Herman reads the memo but promptly forgets its provisions.

The next day Herman receives a rush request to order another Model 5400 Wodget from Samuel Equipment Company at a price of $15,000. The request comes from a department manager, not a vice president, but Herman places the order anyway. Does Herman's order bind Rollerskating?

EXPLANATION

After having read the CEO's memo, Herman lacked actual authority to place the order. He could not *reasonably* have believed himself authorized. He did, however, have apparent authority. Rollerskating is therefore bound.

The apparent authority arises from manifestations attributable to Rollerskating, Herman's principal. Those manifestations were (i) Herman's position as Rollerskating's purchasing agent, and (ii) Rollerskating's conduct on past orders placed with Samuel Equipment by a Rollerskating purchasing agent. On each prior occasion, Rollerskating's comptroller approved and sent payments. The comptroller was acting within her actual authority, so her actions are attributable to Rollerskating. The sequence of events—order from a purchasing agent followed by payment without protest—presumably led Samuel Equipment to believe that Rollerskating purchasing agents have authority to place such orders. In light of the past events, that belief was certainly reasonable.

Herman may also have had inherent agency power. He was a general agent, acting in his principal's interest. Ordering the Model 5400 could be seen as an act usual or necessary to serving Herman's authorized purpose.[102]

PROBLEM 14

A large corporation is facing a large number of products liability suits venued around the country but involving the same product. For efficiency's sake, the corporation hires a large firm of experienced and expensive lawyers ("Big Firm") to serve as national coordinating counsel to the corporation. In that capacity Big Firm acts on the corporation's behalf to (i) retain local counsel to represent the corporation in the various lawsuits, (ii) facilitate and coordinate the exchange of information and work product among the various local counsel, and (iii) to supervise the work of the local counsel.

Big Firm uses due care in carrying out its duties. Unfortunately, however, one of the local counsel commits discovery abuses which result in a $50,000 sanction being assessed against the corporation. Is Big Firm liable to the corporation for some or all of this amount?

EXPLANATION

No, because local counsel is a subordinate agent of the corporation, and not a subagent of Big Firm. Distinguishing between a subordinate agent and a subagent involves focusing on the manifestations of the principal. In this in-

---

102. In one respect, this Explanation is unrealistically "flat." The third party, Samuel Equipment, has no mind in which to form or harbor beliefs and therefore cannot *directly* believe anything about Herman's authority. The relevant beliefs are those of Samuel Equipment's agents, which are attributable to their principal according to agency law. Whether those attributed beliefs are reasonable depends in part on what Samuel Equipment knows or has reason to know. Since Samuel Equipment cannot *directly* know anything, what it knows or has reason to know likewise depends on the attribution rules of agency law.

stance, the principal (the corporation) told the intermediary (Big Firm) "retain local counsel to represent the corporation"—i.e., to retain counsel to act as agents of the corporation. Therefore, Big Firm and local counsel are co-agents of the corporation, and Big Firm is a supervisory agent viz à viz local counsel. In that capacity, Big Firm is not the guarantor of local counsel's conduct and would be liable for local counsel's mistakes only if Big Firm had breached its duty of care in supervising local counsel.

PROBLEM 15

The _____ Law School Exam Conflict and Make-Up Policy, printed in the Student Handbook, states in part:

> Students will take exams at the time and place announced in the exam schedule unless:
> (1) A student is prevented from taking the exams because of his or her illness or illness or death in the student's immediate family;
> (2) A student has two exams scheduled on the same day;
> (3) A student has three exams scheduled within a period of three calendar days;
> (4) A student has two exams scheduled to begin within 23 hours of each other;
> (5) A student has exceptional circumstances that, in the discretion of the Dean of Students, justify a rescheduling. Exceptional circumstances must relate to personal situations, not to a burdensome examination schedule.
>
> No make-up exam will be given more than one week after the end of the regular exam period, except when such a delay is necessitated by illness or other exceptional circumstances.
>
> No student shall take any exam before the regularly scheduled time for the exam.

On account of a serious illness in the immediate family, a student requests permission to reschedule an exam. Due to long-standing and significant employment responsibilities, the only practical time for the make-up exam is three days before the regularly scheduled time. The Dean of Students grants the request, and the student buys two nonrefundable airline tickets. The Dean is aware that the student will be purchasing airline tickets but not that the tickets will be nonrefundable.

Subsequently, the professor whose exam is involved learns that an unidentified student will take a make-up in advance of the rest of the class. The professor objects and asserts that an advance make-up violates the Policy quoted above. Has the action of the Dean of Students bound the College to allow the advance make-up?

EXPLANATION

The Dean can bind the College through some form of agency power (actual authority, apparent authority, inherent agency power) or through estoppel. In this matter, none of these attribution rules apply and the College is not bound.

For actual authority to exist, some manifestation of the principal must cause the agent to reasonably believe the agent has the right to bind the principal. The most salient manifestation given by the facts is the Student Handbook. That Handbook expressly precludes the scheduling of advance make-ups. The Dean's discretion, mentioned in item 5, relates to adequate cause for a make-up and does not override the subsequent, express prohibition on advance make-ups. The Dean could not reasonably believe that he or she has the right to schedule advance make-ups.

For similar reasons, apparent authority will not help the student. For apparent authority to exist, some manifestation of the principal must cause the third party (here, the student) to reasonably believe the agent has the right to bind the principal. Arguably, at least, the Dean's position constitutes a manifestation, as does the Handbook's reference to the Dean as the person who authorizes make-ups. However, those who rely on the appearance of authority have a duty of reasonable diligence. For a law student, that duty encompasses knowing the contents of the Student Handbook. Therefore, the student could not *reasonably* believe that the Dean has the authority to violate the Policy.

Inherent authority also will not help the student, even though the Dean is a general agent (i.e., authorized "to conduct a series of transactions involving a continuity of service"). In some circumstances a general agent has the inherent power to bind its principal even through an unauthorized act. However, the power does not exist when the third party has reason to know that the act is unauthorized.[103]

Estoppel is likewise unavailing. The student may have believed the Dean authorized to permit an advance make-up, but—given the clear statement in the Student Handbook—the College cannot be said to have "intentionally or carelessly caused such belief."[104] Moreover, through the Student Handbook, the College had taken "reasonable steps to notify [the student] of the facts."[105]

---

103. It would be a mistake to argue that the Dean's approval of an advance makeup constituted a misrepresentation about the scope of the Dean's actual authority and thereby bound the College through inherent agency power. Inherent agency power extends to misstatements concerning the subject matter of the transaction (e.g., quality of goods being sold) and not to the scope of the agent's authority. To argue otherwise means that an agent would always have the power to expand the scope of its power to bind. See section 2.6.3.

104. Restatement §8B(1)(a), discussed in section 2.5.

105. Restatement §8B(1)(b), discussed in section 2.5.

3

Binding the Principal in Tort

§3.1 Overview

In a modern economy, most principals work through agents and most tortious conduct is committed by agents.

> *Example:* A delivery company uses appropriate care in selecting, training, and scheduling its drivers. On the way to make a delivery, one of the company's drivers drives negligently and injures a third party. The driver's conduct is directly tortious, but the company's is not.

> *Example:* The owner of an office building hires a real estate broker to sell the building. The broker finds a prospect and, in extolling the building's virtues, purposely misrepresents several material matters. The owner is unaware of the misrepresentations and certainly has not authorized them. The broker's conduct is fraudulent, but the building owner's is not.

In the two circumstances just described, and in many others, the principal will be responsible for the agent's tort. Agency law contains rules for attributing an agent's tort to its principal, even though the principal has not itself engaged in any wrongful conduct.[1]

These attribution rules divide roughly into two categories, according to the nature of the agent's conduct and the nature of the third party's injury. If an agent's physical conduct causes physical harm to a third party's person or property, then the concepts discussed in Chapter Two are largely irrelevant

---

1. If a principal does engage in wrongful conduct, *direct* liability results. For a discussion of the direct duties of principals to third parties, see section 4.4.

and the applicable doctrine is *respondeat superior*. This rule of inherent agency power applies only to a subcategory of agents known as "servants." A principal is generally not responsible for the physical torts of its nonservant agents.[2]

In contrast, if the agent's misconduct consists solely of words and the third party suffers harm only to its emotions, reputation, or pocketbook, the servant/nonservant distinction is rarely relevant. Respondeat superior is largely inapposite,[3] and attribution occurs according to the same rules of actual authority, apparent authority, and inherent agency power that apply to contractual matters.

§3.2   Respondeat Superior

§3.2.1   *The Rule Defined*

Respondeat superior is a venerable doctrine which imposes strict, vicarious liability on a principal when:

- an agent's tort has caused physical injury to a person or property,
- the tortfeasor agent meets the criteria to be considered a "servant" of the principal, and
- the tortious conduct occurred within the servant's "scope of employment."[4]

When triggered, respondeat superior automatically renders the principal (referred to as "the master") liable for the servant agent's misconduct regardless of whether the master (i) authorized the misconduct, (ii) forbade the misconduct, or (iii) even used all reasonable means to prevent the misconduct. Most respondeat superior cases involve claims that a servant has been negligent, but the doctrine also applies to intentional torts involving physical harm.

The scope of respondeat superior thus depends on the definition and application of two key concepts: *servant status* and *scope of employment*. The more expansively each is defined, the broader the scope of the rule. As a result, disputes between an injured third party and an alleged master typically involve battles over characterization. Was the tortfeasor a servant? Was the tortious conduct within the scope of employment?

---

2. Liability may exist when the work involved is inherently dangerous.

3. Respondeat superior is relevant in certain borderline areas, such as malicious prosecution and intentional interference with business relations. See section 3.4.4.

4. The injured party may also assert claims of direct responsibility against the principal. See section 4.4. In any event, the tortfeasor agent will be directly liable. See section 4.2.3.

§3.2.2 *Servant Status*

Servant defined.   Under Restatement §220(1), an agent is a servant if the principal controls or has the right to control the agent's "physical conduct in the performance of the [agency] services."

> *Example:* Dennis works as a baker's assistant in Suzanne's bakery. Suzanne provides all the necessary equipment, sets Dennis's hours, assigns his particular tasks, and supervises his performance. Dennis is Suzanne's servant agent, and Suzanne is the master.

> *Example:* Dennis decides to quit work and hires Eli, an attorney, to work out a "severance package" with Suzanne. Dennis tells Eli what kind of package he wants, but the details of the negotiations are up to Eli. Eli is Dennis's nonservant agent.

In the agency law sense, the term *servant* has nothing to do with servile status or menial tasks. Servants are everywhere in modern society: A maid may be a servant, but so too are the top executives in any large corporation. Neither the exercise of responsibility nor the possession of professional skills negates servant status.[5] A carpenter employed by a general contractor is likely a servant, as is the skilled staff physician employed by a hospital. The typical modern employee is, in agency parlance, a servant.

Servant contrasted with independent contractor.   Agency law applies the label "independent contractor" to a nonservant who provides services or undertakes tasks for others. As a result, respondeat superior disputes often begin with a struggle over labels—servant versus independent contractor.[6] As stated previously, the ultimate determining factor is whether the principal controls or has the right to control the agent's "physical conduct in the performance of the [agency] services."[7] The Restatement provides ten factors to aid in making that determination:

> (a) the extent of control which, by the agreement, the master may exercise over the details of the work;

---

5. However, in some circumstances an alleged servant's skills can argue against servant status, especially when the alleged master lacks the necessary expertise to effectively exercise control. See section 3.2.2.

6. In theory, there should be a preliminary question. At least according to the Restatement, a servant is a type of agent. Yet cases determining servant status rarely, if ever, consider the threshold question of whether the party in question actually qualifies as an *agent*. Instead, the decisions typically skip directly to the issue of servant versus independent contractor. History may explain the omission. The notions of servant status and respondeat superior predate the modern law of agency, and perhaps, given that history, the doctrine of respondeat superior should be seen as an autonomous area of law. Within that autonomous area, a servant is a servant—pure and simple. The notion that servant status is a subcategory of agent status may be disregarded as a modern and distracting gloss.

7. Restatement §220(1).

(b) whether or not the one employed is engaged in a distinct occupation or business;

(c) the kind of occupation, with reference to whether, in the locality, the work is usually done under the direction of the employer or by a specialist without supervision;

(d) the skill required in the particular occupation;

(e) whether the employer or the workman supplies the instrumentalities, tools, and the place of work for the person doing the work;

(f) the length of time for which the person is employed;

(g) the method of payment, whether by the time or by the job;

(h) whether or not the work is a part of the regular business of the employer;

(i) whether or not the parties believe they are creating the relation of master and servant; and

(j) whether the principal is or is not in business.[8]

No single factor is determinative, and the language of an agreement will not prevail over the reality of the relationship. Formal independence will be discounted if the master's right to fire results in practical control.

> *Example:* A pizza shop contracts with a driver to provide home delivery. A written agreement between the shop and the driver has the following terms: it labels the driver an "independent contractor"; it permits the pizza shop to terminate the contract at any time without cause; it requires the driver to provide his own car, car insurance, and uniform; it requires the driver to know the streets of the delivery area and to choose his own route on each delivery; it provides for payment by delivery, not by the hour. The contract also permits the driver to have other jobs, even for other pizza shops, so long as the driver is available at times scheduled by the pizza shop. The driver, however, has no other employment. While making a delivery the driver has an auto accident. The other driver sues the pizza shop, successfully invoking respondeat superior. Despite the driver's formal freedom of action and the contract's label of "independent contractor," the pizza shop's right to terminate at any time gave the shop effective control of the driver's performance. Given the driver's dependence on the job, the driver was likely to obey any "suggestions" the shop happened to make. Given the unskilled nature of the work, the shop had whatever expertise was necessary to actually make suggestions or give orders. Moreover, the driver has no distinct occupation and the work is an integral part of the pizza shop's business.

The right to terminate is not by itself dispositive, however. It carries weight only to the extent that it creates the practical ability to control the agent's performance.

---

8. Restatement §220(2).

Example: Suzanne, the baker, hires Paul, a carpenter, to remodel the front of the bakery. Suzanne provides a detailed plan for the remodelling and agrees that Paul will work on a "time and materials" basis. That is, Paul will charge her for the materials he uses, plus an hourly fee for the time he spends working. Paul agrees that Suzanne can end the job at any time for any reason. Despite Suzanne's right to terminate, Paul is an independent contractor, not Suzanne's servant. Carpentry is a skilled occupation, and Suzanne lacks the expertise to control the details of the work. Moreover, Paul supplies his own tools, the work is not part of Suzanne's regular business, and Paul is engaged in a distinct occupation.

Example: Paul wants to speed up the remodelling, so he hires Dorothy to work on the project. Like Paul, Dorothy is a skilled carpenter. Paul agrees to pay Dorothy an hourly wage, and Dorothy understands that Paul can fire her at any time. Despite Dorothy's skill, she is Paul's servant. His right to fire her gives him effective control over her performance. His expertise will allow him to exercise that control. (The hourly wage also argues in favor of servant status.)

The impact of servant status on other areas of law. The servant concept helps set the scope for a wide range of statutes designed to regulate or tax the modern employment relationship. In areas ranging from civil rights to payroll taxes, these statutes typically cover "employees" but neglect to define the term. Courts must therefore develop a definition, and many have turned to the agency notion of servant. Some decisions make explicit reference to the law of agency; others use its concepts without attribution.

Servant concepts have influenced the reach of statutes in the following areas, among others:

- discrimination in employment
- unemployment compensation
- workers' compensation
- social security
- payroll taxes

§3.2.3 *Scope of Employment*

The rationale and reach of the concept. *Scope of employment* is the other main respondeat superior battleground. Even if the tortfeasor is a servant, vicarious liability results only if the tort occurred within the scope of employment.[9] This restriction arises from the rationale of the rule. Respondeat

---

9. A master may nonetheless face direct liability. For example, if a resident manager rapes an apartment tenant, that conduct is probably outside the scope of employment. See section 3.2.6 (discussing respondeat superior and intentional torts). However, if the manager had an extensive criminal record involving violence toward women and the landlord overlooked that record, the landlord may be directly liable on a claim of negligent hiring or for failure to provide safe premises. See sections 4.4.1-4.4.2.

superior is a doctrine of inherent authority, and the "scope of employment" element seeks to confine the master's liability to risks that inhere in the servant's assigned tasks.

According to the Restatement, a servant's conduct is within the scope of employment only if:

  (a) it is of the kind he is employed[10] to perform;
  (b) it occurs substantially within the authorized time and space limits;
  (c) it is actuated, at least in part, by a purpose to serve the master, and
  (d) if force is intentionally used by the servant against another, the use of force is not unexpectable by the master.[11]

Example: Early one morning, Dennis, the baker's assistant, is at his job kneading dough in the bakery. He notices that a stray cat has wandered in and is about to jump on a counter that is covered with freshly baked cookies. Dennis scoops the cat up and gently tosses it out the door into the alley. Unfortunately, the cat lands atop a crate packed with cut glass that belongs to the china shop next door. The crate falls over and the glass breaks. Dennis has acted within the scope of his employment. He was doing the kind of work he was employed to perform, in his usual (and therefore authorized) place and during the usual (and therefore authorized) time. He acted to serve his master's interests. Using force against a cat is not, in Restatement terms, using force "against another."[12]

Example: After work one day Dennis stops by a bookstore, looking for a book on baking techniques. He wishes to improve his own skills so that he can do a better job at the bakery. While browsing through the aisles he trips over a step-stool and bumps another customer. This accident was not within the scope of his employment. Although he was "actuated, at least in part, by a purpose to serve the master," he was not doing the type of work for which he was hired. Moreover, he was outside the authorized time and far from his authorized place of work.

Factor analysis.   The Restatement lists ten factors to be considered in determining whether a servant's conduct is within the scope of employment:

  (a) whether or not the act is one commonly done by such servants;
  (b) the time, place, and purpose of the act;

---

10. In ordinary parlance, the word "employment" describes a business relationship that agency law classifies as master-servant. In contrast, the Restatement uses "employment" as a term of art, to mean a principal's engagement of an agent to accomplish some task or provide some service. Thus, in Restatement terms, a principal can "employ" a nonservant agent.

11. Restatement §228(1). Some jurisdictions omit the "actuated in part" element when considering intentional torts. See section 3.2.6.

12. Although respondeat superior applies, the china shop will prevail against Suzanne only if it can demonstrate that Dennis's act was tortious.

(c) the previous relations between the master and the servant;

(d) the extent to which the business of the master is apportioned between different servants;

(e) whether or not the act is outside the enterprise of the master or, if within the enterprise, has not been entrusted to any servant;

(f) whether or not the master has reason to expect that such an act will be done;

(g) the similarity in quality of the act done to the act authorized;

(h) whether or not the instrumentality by which the harm is done has been furnished by the master to the servant;

(i) the extent of departure from the normal method of accomplishing an authorized result; and

(j) whether or not the act is seriously criminal.[13]

As these factors indicate, scope of employment is not limited to the servant's proper or authorized conduct. To be within the scope of employment, "conduct must be of the same general nature as that [actually] authorized, or incidental to the conduct authorized."[14] However, the notion of "incidental" goes a long way. It is foreseeable that servants will on occasion transgress and that some of the misconduct will occur on the periphery of the servant's authorized work. An act can therefore be within the scope of employment even though (i) the master has expressly forbidden the act, (ii) the act is tortious,[15] or (iii) the act constitutes a minor crime.

Example: A bar owner instructs a bouncer never to use a certain chokehold in restraining obstreperous customers. One night the bouncer overreacts to an especially troublesome patron and uses the hold. The patron subsequently files a civil suit against the bar owner and seeks to press criminal charges against the bouncer. Nonetheless, the bouncer acted within the scope of employment; the relevant conduct fits within the general guidelines of Restatement §228(1).[16] The alleged tort does not change the outcome. Respondeat superior exists to attribute the torts of servants. The use of a forbidden tactic also is immaterial here. Unauthorized conduct can be within the scope of employment. Likewise, the alleged simple assault does not matter. "The master can reasonably anticipate that servants may commit minor crimes in the prosecution of the business."[17]

---

13. Restatement §229(2).

14. Restatement §229(1).

15. If tortious acts were necessarily outside the scope of employment, respondeat superior would never impose vicarious liability. The doctrine operates to attribute the servant's tort to the master.

16. Quoted above at note 11. Restraining patrons is the kind of work a bouncer is "employed to perform." The bouncer's purpose was to serve the bar owner (by quieting a disruption), and the actions occurred when and where they were supposed to. A bouncer's use of force should come as no surprise to a bar owner.

17. Restatement §231, comment *a*.

The relationship of the master's control to the scope of employment.
The principal's right to control determines whether a party is a servant but as
a general matter does not influence the servant's scope of employment. A principal must have a certain amount of control over the agent's physical performance in order for servant status to exist, but that control will not necessarily
extend to every aspect of the servant's tasks. It is therefore possible for a servant's scope of employment to include areas in which the master does not exercise control.

> *Example:* Suzanne, the baker, employs Sarah, an expert wedding cake
> designer. Suzanne pays Sarah a weekly salary and provides the location
> and all necessary equipment and materials for Sarah's efforts. Suzanne
> determines Sarah's working hours and working conditions and assigns
> Sarah particular cake orders to fill. In short, Sarah is Suzanne's servant.
> Nonetheless, Suzanne and Sarah both expect Sarah to use her own judg-
> ment, discretion, and expertise in designing, baking, and constructing
> wedding cakes. On one occasion, Sarah leaves a small metal wire inside
> an apparently edible portion of a cake, and a customer is injured. Sarah's
> negligence is within the scope of her employment. Even though the
> negligence occurred outside the master's zone of control, the conduct
> was nonetheless "of the same general nature as that [actually] author-
> ized, or incidental to the conduct authorized."[18]

§3.2.4   The Rule's Rationale

The doctrine of respondeat superior rests on three rationales: enterprise liability, risk avoidance, and risk spreading. It sometimes seems, however, that the
doctrine's real purpose is to "find the deep pocket."

Enterprise liability.   As explained in more detail in Chapter Two, this rationale attempts to link risks to benefits and hold accountable for risk-creating
activities the enterprise which stands to benefit from those activities.[19] A servant—subject to detailed control both as to means and ends—is integrally
connected to the master's enterprise. A servant's scope of employment com-
prises those activities that are fairly considered part of the master's enterprise.

Risk spreading.   According to this rationale, the master should strictly and
vicariously bear the risk of its servants' misconduct because the master can
(i) anticipate the risks inherent in its enterprise, (ii) spread the risk through insurance, (iii) take into account the cost of insurance in setting the price for its
goods or services, and (iv) thereby spread the risk among those who benefit
from the goods or services.

---

18. Restatement §229(1).

19. See section 2.6.1 (discussing enterprise liability as a rationale for inherent agency
power).

Risk avoidance.   According to this rationale, respondeat superior serves to protect society from dangerous occurrences. Since the existence of servant status means that the master has the right to control the servant's physical performance, the master is well positioned to prevent the servant from engaging in careless or otherwise improper conduct. Imposing strict liability creates a strong incentive for the master to use its position of control to achieve "risk avoidance."

Viewed from this perspective, the rule may seem overbroad. If we are looking to encourage "safety-producing" conduct by masters, why impose liability even if the master has taken reasonable care in selecting, training, and supervising its servants? Why, that is, have strict liability? Why not impose liability only when the master has failed to properly select, train, or supervise?[20]

In part the answer is that both the *enterprise liability* and *risk spreading* rationales support a broad approach. Expediency is also involved. A narrowly tailored rule would present significant problems of proof, and those problems of proof would make a narrowly tailored rule ineffective. The difficulty of proving direct negligence on the part of the master warrants a rule of vicarious, strict liability.[21]

The deep pocket theory.   In modern society, the typical master-servant relationship is that of employer and employee. The overwhelming majority of servants therefore have fewer resources than do their masters. It may be tempting to look to this economic reality and characterize the doctrine of respondeat superior as a mere guise for reaching non-negligent defendants with convenient deep pockets.

Indeed, a few cases have expressly sought to justify respondeat superior as a mechanism for assuring victim compensation, and the rule does owe its practical importance to the deep pockets of masters. However, as discussed above, the doctrine has independent theoretical justification.

§3.2.5 *Scope of Employment and a Servant's Travels*

Commuting, the "special errand" exception, and necessary travel.   In general, a servant's trips to and from work are not within the scope of employment. Commuting may be a precondition to the servant performing his or her tasks, but the commute is not normally part of those tasks.

However, if, at the master's request, the servant undertakes an errand while going to or from work, the entire trip may become part of the scope of employment.

---

20. A master (or other principal) can be directly liable on this basis. See section 4.4.1.

21. In this regard this rationale for respondeat superior parallels one of the rationales for strict product liability. See, e.g., *Phipps v. General Motors Corp.,* 363 A.2d 955, 958 (Md. 1976) (strict liability warranted in part due to the difficulty of proving producer negligence).

Example: As the company's receptionist is leaving work at the end of the day, the office manager asks him to "Drop off this bottle of scotch" at the house of one of the company's major customers. The receptionist agrees, delivers the scotch without incident and is driving straight home from the customer's house when an accident occurs. The drive home (and the accident) are within the receptionist's scope of employment.[22]

In addition, where the servant's work necessarily involves travel from place to place, and the master establishes a schedule that effectively, even indirectly, controls the time and place of the travel, the travel itself can be within the scope of employment.

Example: A professional wrestler entered into a contract under which (1) the promoter controlled when, where and against whom the wrestler would wrestle and who would win; (2) winning had no effect on the amounts due the wrestler; (3) the schedule required the wrestler to travel by car from venue to venue, with the wrestler wrestling in thirty different towns in four or five states in one thirty-one day period; and (4) the wrestler could not wrestle for anyone else without the promoter's permission and could be terminated at any time. While driving from one venue to another, the wrestler negligently caused an auto accident. Even though the next day was a day off for the wrestler, he was within the scope of employment at the time of the accident.[23]

Other factors which can establish "in transit" scope of employment include: providing the servant a vehicle for traveling, reimbursing the servant for travel expenses, paying the servant for travel time.

Tangential acts — frolic and detour.   An act can come within the scope of employment even though it is merely tangential to the authorized work, so long as there is some connection. The servant must be "actuated, at least in part, by a purpose to serve the master."[24] When a servant does something purely for its own reasons, that conduct is outside the scope of employment.[25]

Example: Nick and Nora drive a delivery van for Acme Delivery Company. During their lunch break, they take the company truck and drive to the Opera House to buy tickets to "La Boheme" for their own use. During this trip they are not acting within the scope of their employ-

---

22. This Example is based on *Trejo v. Maciel,* 48 Cal. Rptr. 765 (Cal. Ct. App. 1966).
23. This Example is based on *White v. Frenkel,* 615 So. 2d 535 (La. Ct. App. 1993).
24. Restatement §228(1)(c).
25. In the context of intentional torts, recent cases have somewhat attenuated this rule. See section 3.2.6 (respondeat superior and intentional torts).

ment. To use a term first introduced in an 1834 English case, they are on a *frolic* of their own.[26]

Scope of employment can, however, cover situations in which the servant has temporarily detoured for some personal reason while still essentially serving the master's purposes.

> **Example:** On their way to make a delivery for Acme, Nick and Nora realize that they are hungry and that the city's best deli is just two blocks off their direct route. They are entitled to a full lunch break but know that the customer is anxiously awaiting delivery. They decide just to get something "to go" at the deli. On their brief trip to the deli, they remain within the scope of their employment. Although they are temporarily on business of their own, they remain "actuated, at least in part, by a purpose to serve the master." In traditional terms, they are merely on a "detour."

Frolic and *detour* are powerful labels. They determine whether respondeat superior applies. Unfortunately, neither the cases nor the commentators provide coherent, specific guidance for determining when which label applies. One famous case requires the conduct to be at least "incidental" to the servant's duties.[27] But how to determine whether a detour is incidental enough to avoid being a frolic? One prominent commentator has suggested, "A temporary deviation from one's work can be incidental to one's task; a temporary abandonment cannot be."[28] But how to distinguish between a deviation and a temporary abandonment?

There are no simple answers to these questions. The cases sometimes refer to the distinction being "a matter of degree" or to the determination necessarily being made on a "case-by-case basis." Such expressions are really a code for "we know the difference when we see it (maybe), but we cannot articulate any rule to allow lawyers (or law students) to easily predict outcomes."

In the face of this uncertainty, those seeking to predict outcomes should read a range of "frolic or detour" cases, try to develop a sense of their "flavor," and keep in mind the following themes:

- Servants predictably engage in small-scale deviations from single-minded concentration on the master's interests. Ordinary, expectable deviations are likely to be considered mere detours.

---

26. *Joel v. Morrison, England, Nisi Prius (Exchequer)*, 6 Car. & P. 501, 172 Eng. Rep. 1338 (1834).

27. *Fiocco v. Carver*, 137 N.E. 309, 311 (N.Y. 1922).

28. J. Hynes, Teacher's Manual to Agency and Partnership: Cases, Materials, Problems 41 (3d ed. 1989).

- Deviations that pose risks of harm of a type significantly different than the types inherent in the servant's task are more likely to be considered frolics.[29]
- If the servant's deviating conduct occurs far outside the "time and space" authorized by the master, the deviation is more likely to be a frolic.
- If the master instructs or controls a servant as to matters that would otherwise be the servant's purely personal concern (e.g., personal hygiene, off-duty recreational activities), the servant's conduct in those matters is neither a detour nor a frolic. The master's instructions bring the matters directly within the scope of employment.

Ending the frolic. Frolics rarely last forever. At some point, the servant will be, in Restatement terms, "re-entering employment"[30] and respondeat superior will again apply. Re-entry has certainly occurred once the servant is fully back in the master's service, that is, once the servant is

- again actuated at least in part (or in some jurisdictions, predominantly) by a desire to serve the master's interest,
- again within the authorized space and time limits, and
- actually is taking (or has taken) some action in the master's interests not necessitated by the frolic itself.

Example: After purchasing their opera tickets, Nick and Nora get back into the Acme delivery van, drive to their next delivery stop, and begin unloading packages. One of the packages falls and lands on the toe of a passerby. Assuming that Nick and Nora have been negligent, respondeat superior will apply. Nick and Nora's frolic has ended, and they have re-entered employment.

The analysis is murkier, however, if a servant negligently causes harm while merely "on the way back" to employment. Indeed, the law here is as difficult to pin down as the law distinguishing frolic from detour. The following themes provide some guidance:

- A servant has not re-entered the scope of employment merely by deciding to return to serving the master's interest.
- In most jurisdictions the servant must be at least "reasonably near the authorized space and time limits" for re-entry to occur.[31] In some jurisdictions, merely starting back toward a place where servant duties are to be performed suffices to re-enter the scope of employment. In

---

29. Respondeat superior is a doctrine of inherent agency power, and this theme is consistent with that doctrine's rationale, i.e., imposing liability on the principal only for risks inherent in the enterprise. See section 3.2.4.

30. Restatement §237, comment *a*.

31. Restatement §237.

other jurisdictions, the servant must have actually returned to the authorized "time and space."

- A servant does not necessarily have to return to the point the frolic began in order to re-enter the scope of employment.

Example: Nick and Nora's trip to the opera house has taken them a half-hour off their regular delivery route. After purchasing their tickets, they get back into the Acme delivery van and head for their next stop. As they are pulling away from the curb, they negligently hit another car. In some jurisdictions, respondeat superior will apply, since the servants have started back to their authorized work location (i.e., the next delivery stop). In other jurisdictions, the distance between that location and the accident site will preclude a finding of re-entry into employment.

§3.2.6 *Intentional Torts*

Although most respondeat superior cases involve torts of negligence, the doctrine's rationale and reach also extend to intentional torts. When a servant, acting within the scope of employment, commits an intentional tort causing physical harm, the master is vicariously liable. Overly aggressive barroom employees provide prime examples.

Example: Seeking to remove an unruly patron, a bar's bouncer applies an overly aggressive wrist lock. The bar's owner is vicariously liable for the intentional tort of battery.

Example: A customer in a bar refuses to pay for a drink. Outraged, and seeking to collect on the debt owed the bar's owner, the bartender strikes the customer. The bar's owner is vicariously liable for the intentional tort of battery.

As with any respondeat superior claim, the third party in an intentional tort case must show that the servant acted within the scope of employment. For many years the key question in this respect was whether the servant was motivated at least in part by a desire to serve the master.[32]

Example: During a horse race, two horses are struggling for the lead. One of the jockeys strikes the other and thereby gains a competitive advantage. The striking jockey's employer is vicariously liable for the intentional tort. The servant was seeking, albeit wrongfully, to advance the master's interests.

Example: Throughout a lengthy bus ride a passenger is noisy and disruptive. After the bus arrives at the terminal and the passenger has disembarked, the bus driver grabs the passenger and punches him. The bus

---

32. Restatement §228(1)(c), discussed in section 3.2.3, makes this an entrance criterion to scope of employment.

company is not vicariously liable.[33] Since the trip is over and the passenger's misbehavior no longer affects the master's interest, the servant could not be actuated by a desire to serve the master.

The "purpose rule" has always been pliable. "Judge Learned Hand concluded that a drunken boatswain who routed the plaintiff out of his bunk with a blow, saying 'Get up, you big son of a bitch, and turn to,' and then continued to fight, might have thought he was acting in the interest of the ship."[34] One court has even found the necessary "purpose to serve the master" when a police trainee, practicing his quick draw inside the police station, accidentally shot a fellow officer. The court held that the trainee was trying to improve his firearms techniques, to the benefit of his employer.[35]

Some more recent cases go beyond manipulating the purpose test and look instead to foreseeability, that is, "whether such conduct should fairly have been foreseen from the nature of the employment and the duties relating to it,"[36] or "whether the risk was one that may fairly be regarded as typical of or broadly incidental to the enterprise undertaken by the employer."[37] In the most well reasoned of these cases, the courts identify some special characteristic of the servant's assigned task as facilitating or at least occasioning the abusive conduct.

> *Example:* A psychologist employed by a clinic engages in sexual relations with a patient. The patient later asserts that the psychologist's emotional control over her vitiated any apparent consent and that the psychologist's conduct constituted an intentional tort. She sues both the psychologist and the clinic. The clinic may well be liable vicariously, because the psychologist's conduct was both foreseeable and incidental to his job. "[S]exual relations between a psychologist and a patient is a well-known hazard and thus, to a degree, foreseeable and a risk of employment. In addition, the . . . situation would not have occurred but for [the psychologist's] employment; it was only through his relation to [the patient] as a therapist that [the psychologist] was able to commit the acts in question."[38]

---

33. If the bus company owns the terminal, it may be directly liable for failing to provide safe premises to business invitees.

34. *Ira S. Bushey & Sons v. United States,* 398 F.2d 167, 170 (2d Cir. 1968), *citing Nelson v. American-West African Line,* 86 F.2d 730 (2d Cir. 1936), *cert. denied,* 300 U.S. 665 (1937).

35. *Thompson v. United States,* 504 F. Supp. 1087 (D.S.D. 1980).

36. *Marston v. Minneapolis Clinic of Psychiatry and Neurology, Ltd.,* 329 N.W.2d 306, 311 (Minn. 1983).

37. *Whitson v. Oakland Unified School District,* 123 Cal. App. 3d 133, 142 (1981) (citations and internal quotations omitted).

38. Marston, supra note 36, at 311.

§3.3 Liability for Physical Harm Beyond Respondeat Superior

In general, a principal is not vicariously liable for physical harm caused by the torts of a nonservant agent. Respondeat superior controls most such cases, and it applies only to servants. In a few situations, however, other rules apply, and these rules impose liability for the torts of nonservants.

§3.3.1 *Principal's Direct Duty to a Third Party*

If a principal owes a direct duty of care to a third party and relies on an agent for the necessary performance, the agent's conduct may result in liability for the principal. Section 4.4 discusses such situations.

§3.3.2 *Intentional Torts of Nonservant Agents*

When a nonservant agent commits an intentional tort and causes physical injury, the relevant law is muddy. According to some authorities, the principal is not liable unless (i) the principal intended or authorized the result or the manner of performance,[39] or (ii) the principal owed a duty to the injured party to have the agent's task performed with due care. Notable exceptions exist to this rule. For example, store owners often face liability when their hired guard service falsely arrests or imprisons a customer of the store. The liability comes despite the store owner's protestation that the guard service acted as an independent contractor. Some of the cases that impose liability rest on a finding of control. Others assert that the principal ratified the guard service's wrongful act (e.g., by not terminating services of the independent tortfeasor). Other cases hold the store liable for breaching its duty to protect its customers from unwarranted attack.[40] Still other cases simply hold that independent contractor status does not bar vicarious liability for an agent's *intentional* (as distinguished from negligent) torts.

§3.3.3 *Misrepresentation by an Agent or Apparent Agent*

If (i) a person has actual or apparent authority to make statements concerning a particular subject, (ii) the person makes a misstatement of fact concerning that subject, (iii) a third party relies on that misstatement, and (iv) the third

---

39. In such circumstances, a master would also be liable for the intentional tort of its servant. The master's intent would bring the servant's act within the scope of employment.

40. Under this theory, the store is not vicariously liable for the guard service's intentional tort. Rather, the store is directly liable for having breached its duty to provide safe premises for its business invitee. See section 4.4.2.

party suffers physical harm as a result, then the actual or apparent principal is liable to the third party.[41]

> *Example:* Office Realty Inc. ("Realty") is substantially remodelling an office building that it owns and wishes to allow prospective tenants to see the work in progress. Realty has hired a construction manager to supervise the remodelling work and instructs that manager to tell prospective tenants which sites within the building are safe to view. One day the construction manager makes a mistake and sends Bill, a prospective tenant, into an unsafe stairwell. Bill is injured. Realty is vicariously liable, regardless of whether the construction manager is a servant or independent contractor. Realty's agent had actual authority to identify the safe locations, and the agent's misstatement on that subject caused Bill physical harm.[42]

> *Example:* Realty tells Alice, another prospective tenant, "If you want to see how the place will look, go over to the building. It's under construction, but one of our people will tell you where it's okay to go." Alice goes over to the building and meets a security guard, who is employed by a guard service hired by Realty. Neither the guard service nor its employees have actual authority to direct prospective tenants. However, when Alice asks, "How do I get to look at some redone offices?" the guard responds by directing Alice into the unsafe stairwell. If Alice is injured as a result, she can hold Realty vicariously liable. The guard's statement was made with apparent authority.[43]

§3.3.4   *Negligence of Apparent Servants*

In one area, the doctrine of respondeat superior meshes with the law of apparent authority and produces vicarious liability for those who merely appear to be masters. In the words of the Restatement:

> One who represents that another is his servant or other agent and thereby causes a third person justifiably to rely upon the care or skill of such apparent agent is subject to liability to the third person for harm caused by the lack of care or skill of the one appearing to be a servant or other agent as if he were such.[44]

---

41. Restatement §251(b) contains the rule for statements made with actual authority. Restatement §266 contains the rule for statements made with apparent authority and also refers to statements made within the apparent scope of employment. The latter notion seems to add little, if anything, beyond apparent authority. That is, any statement within a person's apparent scope of employment will likely be within the scope of that person's apparent authority as well.

42. Bill may also have another theory of recovery: Realty's direct liability for failure to use reasonable care to protect business invitees. See section 4.4.2.

43. For the rules for establishing apparent authority, see section 2.3.

44. Restatement §267.

Example: An oil company conducts a national advertising campaign, encouraging customers to have their cars serviced at service stations carrying the company's logo. In the words of the ad campaign: "You can trust your car to the man who wears the star." Some of the service stations are, in fact, independently owned and operated. In agency parlance, they are independent contractors, not servants. One such independent contractor negligently repairs a car, and the customer suffers injury as a result. The injured customer may well have a claim against the oil company. The ad campaign may have created an appearance of servant status and the customer may indeed have "trusted" to that relationship in choosing the service station. If so, the oil company will be vicariously liable.[45]

This rule is increasingly important; in the modern economy more and more businesses present themselves to the marketplace as economically integrated enterprises while substituting independent contractors for traditional employees.

§3.4   Torts Not Involving Physical Harm

§3.4.1   *The Basic Paradigm: Closer to Contracts Than to Physical Torts*

If an agent's misconduct consists solely of words and the third party suffers harm only to its emotions, reputation, or pocketbook, the agency analysis resembles the approach used for contractual matters. The key rules are those of actual authority, apparent authority, and inherent agency power.[46] Except for the borderline areas of malicious prosecution and intentional interference with business relations, respondeat superior is largely irrelevant.

§3.4.2   *Misrepresentation*

The attribution rule.   A principal is vicariously liable for an agent's tort of misrepresentation if:

- the agent makes a misstatement that is tortious under the law of the relevant jurisdiction,
- the misstatement comes within the agent's actual authority, apparent authority, or inherent agency power, and
- a third party relies on the misstatement and suffers harm as a result.[47]

---

45. *Gizzi v. Texaco, Inc.,* 437 F.2d 308 (3d Cir. 1971) (directed verdict for defendant reversed; jury question as to whether ad campaign induced reasonable reliance).

46. For a detailed discussion of these rules, see Chapter Two.

47. Restatement §257.

Example: Rebecca retains Michael to sell a plot of land she owns near the river. She gives him the authority to truthfully describe the land and its vicinity. Michael shows the land to Samantha, who seems quite interested. She asks, "Has there ever been any trouble with flooding from the river?" Michael knows that, in fact, almost every spring the river floods at least a little and that often the water temporarily covers a quarter of Rebecca's plot. However, fearful of losing the sale, he responds, "Oh no. Not at all." Samantha agrees to buy the land and signs a purchase agreement. Planning to build a house near the river, she hires and pays an architect to do preliminary plans. She then learns the truth about the flooding and, pursuant to contract law, rescinds the purchase agreement.[48] The architect's plans are now worthless to Samantha, and she may recover their cost from Rebecca. Michael, Rebecca's agent, made a material misstatement with intent to deceive and thereby committed the tort of intentional misrepresentation.[49] Since Michael had the actual authority to truthfully describe the flooding situation, he had the inherent agency power to give a false description.[50] Samantha relied on the false statement and as a consequence suffered injury. Rebecca is therefore vicariously liable in tort.

When a misrepresentation is made with apparent authority, the principal is liable even if the person making the misrepresentation "acts entirely for his [sic] own purposes, unless the [third party] has notice of this."[51] In general, "A principal who puts a servant or other agent in a position which enables the agent, while apparently acting within his authority, to commit a fraud upon third persons is subject to liability to such third persons for the fraud."[52]

Tort attribution contrasted with contract attribution.   Besides saddling a principal with tort liability, an agent's misstatements can also give rise to contractual claims against the principal, particularly claims for breach of warranty and rescission.[53] The tort attribution rules differ from the contract rules, however, with regard to what is being attributed and, consequently, with regard to the role of innocent misstatements.

For tort law purposes, the principal's liability is vicarious, and the attribution involves a complete tort: a material misstatement made by an agent

---

48. Michael's misstatement as to the flooding is attributed to Rebecca, so Samantha can rescind for fraud in the inducement. See section 2.6.3.

49. Michael is also liable. See section 4.2.3.

50. See section 2.6.3.

51. Restatement §262.

52. Restatement §261.

53. See section 2.6.3 (for contract law purposes, misstatement attributable to principal if made within agent's actual authority, apparent authority, or inherent agency power; if agent has actual authority to make true statement on a subject, agent has inherent power to make false statements on that subject).

with the requisite state of mind (e.g., intent, negligence), followed by a third party's injurious reliance. Establishing the principal's liability involves two steps: tort law recognizes a tort as committed by the agent; agency law attributes that completed tort to the principal. Therefore, since innocent misstatements do not constitute torts, an agent's innocent misstatements do not trigger the tort attribution rules.

The process works differently with contractual claims. Unless the principal is undisclosed, no contractual claim is complete at the agent's level and no complete claim exists to be attributed.[54] Instead, agency law attributes the agent's statement, and contract law then imposes liability as if the principal had itself made the statement. The principal's liability is direct ("on the contract"), even though one of the elements creating liability (the misstatement) is satisfied only by attribution. For contract law purposes, therefore, an agent's misstatement is attributed regardless of whether the misstatement was innocent, negligent, reckless, or intentional. Indeed, the attribution occurs essentially as if the statement were accurate.[55] For a graphic explanation, see Figure 3-1 on next page.

Often, the same situation supports both contract and tort claims. Whether the third party prefers one claim over another often depends on issues outside of agency law, such as which remedy is the most desirable or whether the statute of limitations has run on one claim but not on the other.

§3.4.3 Defamation

A principal is liable for an agent's defamation if the agent acted with actual or apparent authority in making the defamatory statement. It is not necessary that the agent be actually or apparently authorized to commit defamation, but rather that the agent be actually or apparently authorized to make the statement. For apparent authority to be relevant, the agent must have appeared authorized to "those hearing or reading the statement."[56]

> *Example:* A credit bureau authorizes its employees to report to subscribers information contained in the bureau's data base. A bureau em-

---

54. If the principal is undisclosed, the agent is a party to the contract and the third party's claim will be valid against the agent as well as the undisclosed principal. See section 4.2.1.

55. Assume, for example, that a principal authorizes an agent to sell the principal's car and to describe the car's characteristics to prospective purchasers. The agent says to a third party, "This car will get at least 25 miles per gallon on the highway," and in reliance the third party agrees to buy the car. Agency law attributes the mph statement to the principal, and under contract law the statement creates a warranty that binds the principal. If the statement happens to be true, contract law gives the buyer no claim against the principal. If the statement happens to be false, contract law will provide the buyer several remedies (e.g., rejection, revocation of acceptance, action for damages for breach of warranty). The distinction drawn in the text parallels a distinction between contract law and tort law. Under contract law, innocent misstatements by a party can be actionable. Under tort law, they are not.

56. Restatement §247.

Figure 3-1. Comparison of Tort and Contract Attribution Paradigms

	Agent's Level	*What Is Being Attributed*	*Principal's Level*
Tort	Agent commits a tort of mis-representation (which necessarily involves a non-innocent mis-statement).	Agent's tort	Vicarious Liability for the attributed tort of Agent
Contract	Agent makes a statement which may be a misstatement, which in turn may be innocent.	Agent's (mis)statement	Direct Liability, in part due to the attributed (mis)statement of Agent

ployee receives a call from a subscriber who is seeking information about James Hobbs. The employee consults the data base and reports, "Two convictions for larceny, and 12 bounced checks." In fact, the data base is completely wrong, and, up to this moment, Mr. Hobbs's reputation has been unblemished. The credit bureau is liable for defamation. The employee had actual authority to make the report which turned out to be defamatory.

Example: A newspaper columnist has written a series of columns harshly criticizing the city parking commissioner. The newspaper's publisher becomes concerned that the columns are getting perilously close to the "actual malice" necessary to allow a public figure to recover for defamation. The publisher therefore orders the columnist to cease writing about the commissioner. Assuming that the columnist will obey, the publisher neglects to mention the order to the paper's managing editor. The columnist disobeys the publisher's order, and another column appears that contains scurrilous statements that are clearly defamatory. The newspaper is liable to the commissioner for defamation. Although the columnist lacked actual authority to write on the subject, to the newspaper's readers the columnist appeared to be authorized.[57]

The example of the columnist highlights the policy behind using apparent authority as an attribution rule for defamation. In the words of the Restatement:

---

57. The newspaper's manifestation was, of course, the running of the column.

[D]efamation is effective, in part at least, because of the personality of the one publishing it. Thus, one who appears to have authority to make statements for the employer gives to his statements the weight of the employer's reputation.[58]

§3.4.4 *Malicious Prosecution and Interference with Business Relations*

These torts often involve both words and actions, and in this borderline area respondeat superior is the chief rule.

> *Example:* Todd is a salaried sales rep for the Nickel Surgical Products Company ("Nickel"). Nickel trains its sales reps to pursue business aggressively. Todd persuades Ace Hospital to stop buying its surgical drapes from Amalgamated Hospital Supply ("Amalgamated") and buy instead from Nickel. Ace's decision and subsequent purchases from Nickel breach a contract with Amalgamated. Todd has tortiously induced that breach of contract, and Nickel is vicariously liable.[59]

§3.5 Attributing Torts in Complex or Multilevel Relationships

Respondeat superior attributes a servant's tort to the master, that is, the principal with a right to control the servant's performance. In some situations, however, it may be difficult to identify the responsible master. For example, one master's servant may come under the temporary control of another party, as when an equipment leasing company lends an equipment operator to a construction company or when a surgeon conducts an operation with the assistance of nurses employed by a hospital. Agency law analyzes such situations using the *borrowed servant* doctrine. Another type of problem arises when the servant of one master commits a tort, that master itself is subject to substantial control by another party, and the tort victim seeks to recover from that other party. These *chain of masters* situations arise most often in franchise relationships, although they also occur frequently in the construction industry. Agency case law and the Restatement offer several different views on that subject.

Borrowed servant.   This concept is best introduced by example.

> *Example:* Hoister Crane Company ("Hoister") owns and leases out large cranes used in major construction projects. Operating such a crane

---

58. Restatement §247, comment *c*.

59. For a discussion of the factors used to determine scope of employment, see section 3.2.3.

requires considerable skill, so Hoister employs a staff of trained, full-time operators and assigns an operator to run each leased crane. Hoister charges its customer a single fee that includes both the use of the crane and the services of the operator.

Hoister rents a crane to General Contractor, Inc. ("General Contractor"), a construction company building a large office building. At the worksite, Hoister's operator runs the crane, but General Contractor's site supervisor tells the operator what tasks to do and when to do them. When the crane is in operation, the site supervisor uses hand signals to direct the operator. While lifting a load of steel bars, the operator negligently allows three bars to fall. They injure a passerby. Whether respondeat superior implicates Hoister or General Contractor depends on whether, at the time of the accident, the crane operator was General Contractor's borrowed servant.

Example: Jeff Couteau, a surgeon, has operating privileges at Morgan Hospital ("the hospital") but is not a hospital employee. When he performs surgery at the hospital, he is assisted by operating room nurses who are hospital employees. During the course of an operation these nurses take orders from whatever physician is in charge.

At the end of one of Couteau's operations, a nurse neglects to make a proper sponge count and the patient is closed with one sponge still inside. In the subsequent malpractice action, the patient asserts that respondeat superior makes Couteau liable for the nurse's negligence. Whether this claim succeeds depends on whether, during the operation (and more particularly, at the time of the negligent sponge count), the nurse was Couteau's borrowed servant.

The precise contours of the borrowed servant doctrine vary from jurisdiction to jurisdiction, and application of the rule is always very fact-intense. In most jurisdictions a party invoking the rule must show that:

- the regular master (sometimes called "the general employer") assigned or allowed its servant to work for and under the supervision of another party (sometimes called "the special employer");
- at the time of the servant's tortious conduct
  - the special employer had the right to control in detail the performance of the servant's work, and
  - the general employer retained no significant right of control over the servant, including the right to reassign the servant to other tasks.[60]

---

60. Sometimes it is the injured party who asserts the theory, seeking to impose vicarious liability on the more solvent defendant. Sometimes the general and special employers contest the issue, each seeking to place vicarious liability on the other. Sometimes an allegedly borrowed servant will him- or herself invoke the doctrine,

The doctrine is relevant only when a servant is alleged to have committed a tort, so "the important question is not whether or not [the servant] remains the servant of the general employer as to matters generally, but whether or not, as to the act in question, [the servant] is acting in the business of and under the direction of [the general employer] or [the special employer.]"[61]

Although the borrowed servant doctrine can be described as an exception to respondeat superior, the doctrine is better understood as an application of respondeat superior principles. Respondeat superior attributes a servant's negligence to the servant's master, and the borrowed servant doctrine redirects that attribution away from the regular master ("the general employer") to a temporary master ("the special employer"). The redirection is appropriate because the special employer has a transitory but complete right to control the servant. Since respondeat superior rests on the master's right to control, vicarious liability should follow the control. When the general employer allows the special employer to control the servant's performance, the "borrowed" servant's torts should be attributed to the special employer.

As for the case of the crane operator, courts have gone both ways.[62] Some have looked to the general contractor's detailed control over the operator (e.g., the hand signals) and have found the operator to be the general contractor's borrowed servant. Other courts have held to the contrary, following a Restatement comment that "a continuation of general employment is indicated by the fact that the general employer can properly substitute another servant at any time, that the time of the new employment is short, and that the lent servant has the skill of a specialist."[63]

As for the medical malpractice case, if the hospital lacked the right to re-assign the nurse during the operation, the borrowed servant doctrine probably applies.

---

seeking to escape the constraints of the workers' compensation statute so as to assert tort claims against the servant's regular employer. (Ordinarily an employee cannot sue its employer in tort and must instead pursue the less remunerative remedies of the workers' compensation system. However, if at the time of the accident the employee is the borrowed servant of the special employer, the workers' compensation statute applies not to the general employer but rather to the special employer. The employee therefore receives workers' compensation benefits from the special employer and is free to pursue tort remedies against the general employer.)

61. Restatement §227, comment *a*.

62. Compare *DePratt v. Sergio,* 306 N.W.2d 62 (Wis. 1981) (holding crane operator who obeyed hand signals to be a borrowed servant) and *Gulf, Colorado & Santa Fe Co. v. Harry Newton, Inc.,* 430 S.W.2d 223 (Tex. Civ. App. 1968) (holding crane operator not to be a borrowed servant even though operator was following instructions of the special employer).

63. Restatement §227, comment *c*. Presumably the operator's skill makes it less practical for the special employer to assert effective control. See section 3.2.2 (when agent possesses special skills that principal lacks, principal is less able to exert control and less likely to be a master).

Chain of masters.[64]   In this area too the issues are best introduced with examples.

> *Example:* A franchisor licenses a local company to run a hotel using the franchisor's name, logo, business practices, and national reservation system. The franchise agreement requires the franchisee to abide by a thick book of regulations on topics ranging from style of linen to lawncare. One winter a custodial employee of the *franchisee* carelessly shovels a sidewalk and leaves behind a thin sheet of ice. A customer of the franchisee slips and falls. The customer sues not only the franchisee but also the franchisor.

> *Example:* A construction company ("the general contractor") wins a bid to build a new apartment building. It subcontracts the electrical work to an electrical subcontractor and the plumbing work to a plumbing subcontractor.[65] Concerned about workplace safety, the general contractor has its own site supervisor regularly check on the work of all the subcontractors. An electrician, employed by the electrical subcontractor, negligently leaves some equipment lying around, and an employee of the plumbing subcontractor trips and suffers injury. The injured employee sues not only the electrical subcontractor but also the general contractor.

The outcome of each of these situations depends on whether the plaintiff can find a chain of attribution that links the tortfeasor (i.e., the custodian and the electrician) to the distant party (i.e., the franchisor and the general contractor). Unfortunately, many of the cases in this area fail to articulate a complete analysis. For example, courts in franchise cases often (i) note that the tortfeasor is the servant of the franchisee, (ii) determine that the franchisee is the servant of the franchisor, and (iii) on that basis alone hold the franchisor liable for the tortfeasor's misconduct. These courts neglect to explain why the franchisor is responsible for the torts of its servant's servant.

At least three different theories could apply. First, the tortfeasor could be deemed the subservant of the distant party. According to the Restatement, if a master's servant engages servants of its own to conduct the master's business, then the servant's servants are subservants of the master.[66] In that event, re-

---

64. Unlike "borrowed servant," this phrase does not appear in the Restatement or in case law. It is instead the author's shorthand.

65. Sometimes a business that is providing services or producing a product will delegate or "subcontract" part of the work to another business. The reasons for this practice vary. The delegating party may lack the necessary in-house expertise; it may have the expertise, but its own employees may be busy on other projects; it may be able to save money by delegating work to a company that is more efficient or that pays its employees lower wages. Subcontracting is characteristic of the construction industry and increasingly prevalent in the manufacturing sector.

66. Restatement §5(2).

spondeat superior attributes the subservant's torts (if within the scope of employment) directly to the master.[67] Under this approach, the franchisor and the general contractor would be masters, the franchisee and the electrical contractor would be servants, and the custodian and the electrician would be subservants. See Figure 3-2.

The problem with this analysis is that, for a subservant to exist, the master must have expressly or impliedly authorized the servant to engage servants of its own to do the master's business. Moreover, the master will have the "prerogative of overriding his servant in giving directions [to] the subservant."[68] In the situations under discussion, neither of these elements is present. The distant party (i.e., the franchisor and the general contractor) does not consider the intermediate party (i.e., the franchisee and the electrical contractor) to be its servant. To the contrary, the typical franchise agreement and the typical construction subcontract expressly disclaim any agency status whatsoever. It is therefore unlikely that the distant party has consented to having the intermediate party engage *sub*servants. Likewise, the intermediate parties see themselves as independent contractors, especially when it comes to control of

Figure 3-2. Subservant Analysis

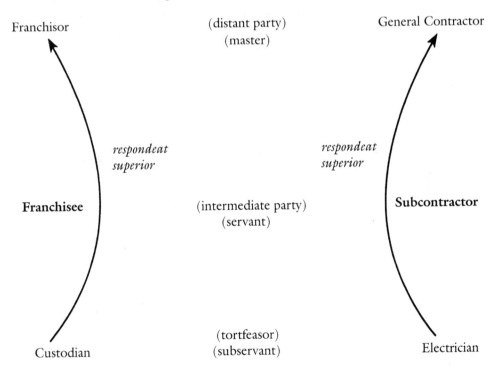

67. Restatement §5(2), comment *e*.
68. Id.

their employees. They would hardly view the distant party as having the "prerogative" to directly control their employees.

The second approach follows more closely the actual business relationships and involves two steps of attribution. Under this approach the tortfeasor (i.e., the custodian and the electrician) is seen simply as the servant of the intermediate party (i.e., the franchisee and the electrical contractor), and the intermediate party is seen as the servant of the distant party (i.e., the franchisor and the general contractor). Respondeat superior then operates twice: The tortfeasor's negligence is attributed to the intermediate party, and the intermediate party's (attributed) negligence is attributed to the distant party. See Figure 3-3.

The third approach is the most direct, holding that the distant party has retained or exercised a direct right to control the intermediate party's employees and is accordingly the tortfeasor's master. Respondeat superior therefore applies directly. See Figure 3-4. In most circumstances, there will be no express evidence of the distant party's right of control. Indeed, the typical franchise agreement and the typical construction subcontract will state to the contrary. However, the parties' conduct may belie their formal manifestations. If, for example, the general contractor's site supervisor regularly issues orders to the employees of the electrical subcontractor and those employees obey, then the right to control is present and respondeat superior may well apply. Similarly, if the franchisor regularly sends out inspectors, these inspectors give orders directly to the franchisee's employees, and the employees obey, then

Figure 3-3. Master of Master Analysis

Franchisor	(distant party) (master)	General Contractor
↑ *respondeat superior*		↑ *respondeat superior*
Franchisee	(intermediate party) (servant of distant party; master of tortfeasor)	**Subcontractor**
↑ *respondeat superior*		↑ *respondeat superior*
Custodian	(tortfeasor) (servant of intermediate party)	Electrician

Figure 3-4. Direct Control Analysis

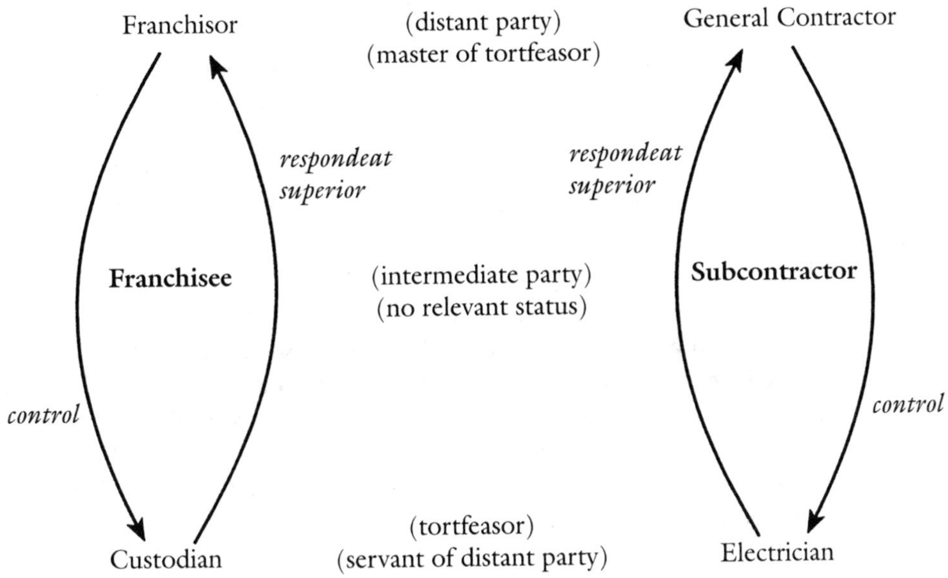

Franchisor   (distant party)   General Contractor
                          (master of tortfeasor)

                    respondeat   *respondeat*
                    superior   *superior*

Franchisee   (intermediate party)   **Subcontractor**
                          (no relevant status)

control   *control*

Custodian   (tortfeasor)   Electrician
                      (servant of distant party)

the franchisor may well find itself at the receiving end of respondeat superior liability.

PROBLEM 16

Rachael hires Alex, an experienced attorney, to represent her in a commercial dispute. Driving to a settlement conference, Alex negligently hits a pedestrian. The pedestrian sues Rachael, asserting respondeat superior. What result?

EXPLANATION

The pedestrian's claim will fail. For respondeat superior to apply, the tortfeasor must be a servant. For servant status to exist, the principal must have the right to exercise detailed control of the agent's manner of performance. A lawyer's client does not have that right. The client sets the goal and may make major strategy decisions. Tactics, however, are the lawyer's domain.

PROBLEM 17

Samuel buys new vinyl tile for his kitchen floor from Athos Floor Coverings Unlimited ("Athos"), a discount retailer of carpet, linoleum, tile, and other floor coverings. Athos does not have any installers on staff, but tells Samuel that it will arrange to have the tile installed by one of the "licensed, bonded contractors who do this sort of work for us." Athos arranges for Michael Planchet to install Samuel's tile. Planchet runs his own small contractor business and does jobs for various retailers and directly for homeowners. Athos does not guarantee him any regular work and pays him a flat fee per square yard on each installation. (The fee does vary depending on the floor covering being installed.)

In due course, Planchet arrives at Samuel's kitchen with the tile and the installment materials. Those materials include an effective but highly volatile adhesive for securing the tiles to the subfloor. Unfortunately, Planchet fails to read or follow the instructions on the adhesive can, and a fire breaks out. Samuel sues Athos, asserting respondeat superior. What result?

EXPLANATION

Samuel will lose. Planchet is an independent contractor, not Athos's servant.

Virtually all the factors listed in Restatement §220(2) indicate Planchet's independence. Athos, the alleged master, has no control "over the details of the work." Planchet, the alleged servant, is skilled, "is engaged in a distinct occupation or business," and supplies his own tools. The employment is episodic, not sustained, and payment is by the job. Moreover, Athos and Planchet do not consider themselves master and servant.[69]

PROBLEM 18

A newspaper provides its customers home delivery through a network of "independent delivery agents." A written contract between the newspaper and each agent (i) assigns each agent a particular route, (ii) provides the agent a percentage commission based on the subscription price of papers delivered, (iii) allows the newspaper to terminate the relationship at any time without cause, and (iv) expressly disclaims any master-servant relationship. The newspaper conducts training programs on how to make deliveries and increase sales. Although the contract does not mention these programs, the newspaper considers regular attendance to be mandatory. Each delivery agent supplies his or her own car or van to make the deliveries. Many of the routes are quite large, and many of the agents have no other gainful employment. The newspaper does not withhold social security taxes from the commission checks and does not pay the employer's portion of social security on the commission amounts.

While delivering papers one morning, one of the agents loses control of the car and crashes into a building. The building owner sues the newspaper, asserting respondeat superior. What result?

EXPLANATION

The building owner may well prevail, although several Restatement factors point the other way.

---

69. Restatement §§220(2)(a), (b), (d), (e), (f), (g), & (i), respectively. Samuel may have a successful contract claim, however, if he can establish that his contract with Athos included installation. See section 4.4.3.

The parties apparently did not consider themselves master and servant. The contract expressly disclaimed that relationship, and the principal did not withhold or pay social security taxes on account of the commissions.[70] The newspaper did not pay a set wage or salary,[71] and the delivery agent supplied the key instrumentality (i.e., the car).[72]

The key question, however, is the right to exercise control. The newspaper's right to terminate without cause and without advance notice suggests that, practically speaking, the newspaper had considerable control over the agents' performance. The fact that few of the agents were "engaged in a distinct occupation or business"[73] made each especially susceptible to the threat of termination. That the threat carried weight is evidenced by the required attendance policy.

Although the Restatement factors may thus point in opposite directions, the policies underlying respondeat superior clearly favor a finding of servant status. Home delivery is an integral part of the newspaper's enterprise, and that enterprise should bear the costs of accidents foreseeable in that phase of the business. As for risk avoidance, the training sessions demonstrate that the newspaper can and already does influence the agents' manner of performance. Moreover, as for risk spreading, the newspaper is far better able to anticipate, calculate, and spread the cost than are the individual agents.

PROBLEM 19

A manufacturing company employs a staff of full-time research scientists. Each scientist receives a salary, a well-equipped laboratory, and necessary materials. Each scientist reports to the company's Director of Research, who assigns research projects and keeps tabs on research progress. According to company policy, however, all scientists are to spend at least 20 percent of their time on projects they have conceived. The company believes that this "bootleg research" will spur creativity and innovation. The Director of Research does not review the bootleg projects in any detail, but instead merely inquires on occasion as to their subject matter.

One afternoon, a company research scientist leaves the lab and goes to a city park. As part of a bootleg project, the scientist wishes to test a new waterproofing substance in the brook that runs through the park. (It's also a nice day for a walk.)

Although the scientist is certain that the substance is stable and nontoxic, the substance disintegrates in and pollutes the brook. Clean-up costs total $35,000. The city sues the manufacturing company, alleging respondeat superior. What result?

---

70. Restatement §220(2)(i).
71. Id. §220(2)(g).
72. Id. §220(2)(e).
73. Id. §220(2)(b).

EXPLANATION

The city will prevail. The scientist is the company's servant and was acting within the scope of employment.

Servant status is evident. The only possible contrary factor is Restatement §220(2)(c)—the great degree of "skill required in the particular occupation." That skill does not, however, undercut either the master's right or ability to control. The Director of Research, who acts for the master,[74] has ample expertise to supervise the scientist.

The scope of employment issue is almost as clear. Although the scientist was away from the authorized workplace,[75] the work was (i) within the authorized time,[76] "of the kind [the scientist was] employed to perform,"[77] and "actuated at least in part by a purpose to serve the master."[78] The bootleg nature of the project is immaterial. Although the master did not exert active control over the project, the master certainly retained the right to do so. Nothing prevented the company from changing or eliminating the bootleg policy. Moreover, in determining the scope of employment, what matters is the zone of the servant's endeavors, not the zone of active control.

PROBLEM 20

Sandpit Gravel Company ("Sandpit") is excavating a deposit of gravel from a large open pit. Among the Sandpit servants working in the pit are a group of dump truck drivers. There are two ways to drive out of the pit: one safe but very time-consuming, the other quick and quite dangerous. Sandpit has repeatedly instructed the drivers to take the safe route and has repeatedly forbidden them to use the dangerous one. The drivers are generally happy to comply, since the company pays them by the hour. At closing time, however, the drivers have a different attitude. When the closing whistle blows, the drivers are "off the clock" and want to get themselves home as soon as possible. Nonetheless, they obey the rules and take the slow way out, until one day, when a driver in a big rush tries the fast route. The truck slides off and rolls over, crushing the leg of an OSHA inspector. The OSHA inspector sues Sandpit, alleging respondeat superior. What result?

EXPLANATION

Sandpit is liable. A servant's act can come within the scope of employment even though forbidden by the master. In this case, the driver was conducting the mas-

---

74. Under the terminology developed in Chapter Two, the Director of Research is the master's superior agent. See section 2.8.2.

75. Restatement §228(1)(b).

76. Id.

77. Id. §228(1)(a).

78. Id. §228(1)(c). The scientist was also actuated in part by a personal desire to take a walk in the park.

ter's business, with an "instrumentality . . . furnished by the master;"[79] the act
was quite similar "in quality . . . to the act authorized;"[80] "the departure from
the normal method of accomplishing an authorized result"[81] was moderate; and
"the master [had] reason to expect that such an act [would] be done."[82]

PROBLEM 21

A shopping mall employs its own staff of private security guards. These guards
receive regular wages, wear uniforms supplied by the mall, report to the mall's
Director of Security, and work shifts assigned by the Director. The mall,
through the Director, has forbidden the security guards to carry guns.

One day a guard disobeys that policy and brings an unlicensed gun to
work. While at work the guard has a scuffle with an unruly patron, and the
gun inadvertently discharges and wounds a patron in the leg. The patron sues
the mall, alleging respondeat superior.[83] What result?

EXPLANATION

Assuming that the patron can establish the guard's underlying tort, vicarious
liability will probably exist. Dealing with unruly patrons is central to the
guard's responsibilities, and as shown in Problem 20, a forbidden act can be
within the scope of employment. The servant's illegal act—carrying an unlicensed weapon—will undercut the patron's claim only if that act is considered
"seriously criminal" and even then only if the act is considered unforeseeable.

PROBLEM 22

Domestic Safari, Inc. ("Safari") takes teenagers on summer camping treks
throughout the country. For each trek Safari employs a trek leader and a group
of counselors. During one trek, the leader sends a counselor into town to buy
food for the next week's camping. The counselor takes a Safari jeep and drives
to a shopping mall. While at the mall the counselor also buys a few items for
her personal needs. Returning to the campsite, the jeep runs into another car.
That car's driver sues Safari, asserting respondeat superior. What result?

EXPLANATION

If the driver can prove the counselor negligent, then the driver will win. Even
assuming that the counselor's purchase of personal items constituted a frolic,

---

79. Restatement §229(2)(h).

80. Id. §229(2)(g).

81. Id. §229(2)(j).

82. Id. §229(2)(f). The master saw a need to repeat the prohibition, suggesting that
the master considered the prohibited conduct to be at least somewhat attractive to the
drivers.

83. The patron would probably also assert direct claims, such as failure to provide reasonably safe premises to customers and negligent hiring. See section 4.4.2.

she had reentered the scope of employment by the time of the accident. Since Safari had authorized the trip to and from the mall, the return trip was well within "the authorized space and time limits."[84] Moreover, since the counselor was transporting the sought-after food, she was again "acting with the intention of serving [her] master's business."[85]

PROBLEM 23

A major league pitcher is having a bad day on the mound. Not only are the opposing batters doing well, but a heckler in the stands is increasingly obnoxious. Finally, distracted beyond endurance, the pitcher whirls and fires the ball straight at the heckler. This pitch is right on target, hitting the heckler on the head. The heckler sues the pitcher's employer, the ballclub. What result?

EXPLANATION

This intentional tort may be one instance in which the incidental/foreseeable test is worse for the plaintiff than the more traditional purpose test. Beaning a spectator is hardly incidental to pitching a ball game, and there is nothing in the nature of a pitcher's task that makes the assault foreseeable. It might be established, however, that the pitcher's purpose was in part to serve the master. The heckling was distracting the pitcher and interfering with his ability to perform well for his employer. To silence the heckler therefore was to advance the master's interests. The result will thus depend on whether the court uses the purpose test and, if so, how malleable the court considers that test to be.[86]

PROBLEM 24

A large school district, serving tens of thousands of students and with thousands of employees, assigns a custodian to work at a high school. Subsequently, the custodian sexually assaults a student at the high school. The student sues the school district, asserting respondeat superior.[87] What result?

EXPLANATION

If the jurisdiction uses the purpose test, the student will inevitably lose. By no stretch of the imagination can a sexual assault be said to serve the school district's interests.

---

84. Restatement §237.

85. Id.

86. In any event, the heckler may have a direct claim against the owner of the ballpark for failing to provide reasonably safe premises to a customer, see section 4.4.2, and can certainly sue the pitcher for battery. See section 4.2.3.

87. The student would probably assert direct claims as well, such as failure to provide safe premises and negligent hiring and supervision. See sections 4.4.1-4.4.2.

Even if the jurisdiction uses some form of the incidental/foreseeable test, the student's chances are slim. Abstractly, it may be foreseeable that an organization that has a large enough number of employees will inevitably employ some "bad apples." However, for an intentional tort to be foreseeable in the sense of respondeat superior, there must be something about the nature of the servant's job or the master's enterprise that facilitates or occasions the harm. Unlike the psychologist-patient relationship discussed previously,[88] a custodian's role does not make the victim especially vulnerable to sexual assault. Sexual assault is not incidental to custodial work.

PROBLEM 25

Your adult son, though employed, is mentally handicapped. Ordinarily, you drive him to and from work, but over the next several weeks you will be out of town for a number of days. You decide to have a particular taxicab company fill in for you, and you make the necessary arrangements through a telephone call to the company's dispatcher.

You believe the cab company employs cab drivers as well as dispatchers, and your belief comes from the company's trade name, trade dress, advertisements, signage, and published telephone numbers. This appearance plays a role in your decision to have this particular company dispatch drivers to transport your son.

In due course, you leave town and the cab company dispatches cabs to transport your son. Unfortunately, one of these cabs is involved in an accident, the driver is at fault, and your son is injured. Only when you seek compensation for your son from the taxicab company do you discover that the company does not in fact employ the drivers. Contrary to appearances, the drivers in those distinctively marked cabs are all independent contractors. The taxicab company denies any legal responsibility for the driver's negligence and for your son's injuries. Is the taxicab company correct?

EXPLANATION

No. Under the stated facts, the drivers are the apparent servants of the taxicab company. Through its "trade name, trade dress, advertisements, signage, and published telephone numbers," the taxicab company "represent[ed] that another [was] his servant," and that representation justifiably caused you to "rely upon the care or skill of such apparent agent."[89] According to Restatement §267, therefore, the taxicab company "is subject to liability . . . for harm caused by the lack of care or skill of the one appearing to be a servant . . . as if he were such."[90]

---

88. Supra section 3.2.6.

89. Restatement §267.

90. Id. This Problem is based on Daniel S. Kleinberger and Peter Knapp, *Apparent Servants and Making Appearances Matter: A Critique of Bagot v. Airport & Airline Taxi Cab Corp.*, 28 Wm. Mitchell L. Rev. 1527 (2002).

PROBLEM 26

A hotel franchisor is concerned about apparent servant liability, but still wants its franchisees to make abundant use of the franchise name, logo, and trademarks. Consistent with that business purpose, how can the franchisor reduce its exposure to apparent servant liability?

EXPLANATION

The core of apparent servant liability is the appearance of servant status. Therefore, the simplest solution, at least in concept, would be to eliminate the appearance at its source. The legal problem would disappear if the franchisees were to remove all insignia that make their hotels appear to belong to the franchisor and that make their employees appear to be the franchisor's servants. This would be legally perfect treatment—after which the patient (i.e., the business) would unfortunately die. A less pure but more practical solution would be to leave the insignia in place but act affirmatively to avoid the misapprehension. For example, the franchisor could require all its franchisees to prominently indicate that their hotel, although part of the national chain, is "independently owned and operated." The proclamation might appear on all significant signage, the hotel's stationery, and on all check-in and check-out documents.

PROBLEM 27

An air conditioning manufacturer is about to ship a valuable load of equipment to a developer that is constructing a new office building. The manufacturer is, however, concerned about the developer's ability to pay for the equipment. The developer assures the manufacturer, "No problem. We've got a loan commitment from First National Bank that will cover the entire cost of construction. Why don't you call the Bank's Vice President for Commercial Loans and get that confirmed?"

The manufacturer takes the suggestion and calls the Vice President. The Vice President confirms that the Bank has committed to a loan up to $10 million and that current cost projections total only $8.5 million. Satisfied, the manufacturer ships the equipment.

Unfortunately for the manufacturer, the Bank had made no loan commitment. The Vice President lied in return for a $5,000 bribe from the developer. The office building project eventually folds, the manufacturer's equipment is nowhere to be found, and the developer is bankrupt. Can the manufacturer recover from the Bank?

EXPLANATION

Yes. The Bank's agent, its Vice President for Commercial Loans, committed the tort of intentional misrepresentation. That tort will be attributed to the Bank if the agent had actual authority, apparent authority, or inherent agency power to make the statement in question. The Vice President had apparent authority by position. It is customary for Bank officers to provide the type of information the Vice President provided, so it was reasonable for the manufacturer to believe the Vice President was speaking for the Bank. The Vice President's ulterior motive is immaterial. Apparent authority can exist even though the apparent agent does not intend to serve the interests of the apparent principal.[91]

PROBLEM 28

You are planning on selling your house through a real estate agent. You know that your agent will put the house on the local multiple-listing service, which means that literally hundreds of other agents may be showing your house and making representations about it. You fear that, carelessly or otherwise, one of these agents may make a misrepresentation about the house which may come back to haunt you. Keeping the house off the multiple-listing service is impractical. What else might you do?

EXPLANATION

As explained in Chapter Two, your listing agreement will expressly or impliedly authorize your broker to enlist the services of other brokers. Those other brokers will be your subagents, and their torts of misrepresentation, if made within their authority or power, will be attributed to you.[92]

It is not practical to check the *bona fides* of hundreds of brokers whom you have never met. Your preventative actions must therefore go toward (i) reducing their authority and power to make inaccurate statements and (ii) making sure that inaccurate statements do not become tortious. You can accomplish both by having the purchase agreement conspicuously state that: (a) the purchase agreement contains the parties' entire understanding; (b) no broker has any authority to make any representations different from or additional to the purchase agreement; and (c) the buyer is not relying on any statements, descriptions, or other representations outside of the purchase agreement. Against the background made by point "a," point "b" undercuts any claim of agency authority or power, and point "c" may prevent a misrepresentation from becoming tortious. (A representation is tortious only if it induces justifiable reliance.)

PROBLEM 29

Morgan Hospital has an in-patient psychiatric ward that is run under the direction of Dr. Stanley, a board-certified psychiatrist who is a full-time em-

---

91. See section 2.3.1 (apparent agent can bind apparent principal even though apparent agent intends to take for itself the benefits of the transaction).

92. See section 2.8.3 for a discussion of subagents and their authority and power to bind the principal.

ployee of the hospital. Dr. Stanley has become increasingly frustrated with Medical Indemnity Company, an insurance company that provides health insurance coverage to many people in Morgan's vicinity. Medical Indemnity has been disallowing a large number of claims made by patients treated in Morgan's in-patient psychiatric ward. Dr. Stanley believes that most of these disallowances are unjustified, and he faults two psychologists who review patient claims for Medical Indemnity. Dr. Stanley's job has never involved public relations, but he decides that "enough is enough." In a fit of frustration and without discussing the matter with any of Morgan's higher-ups, he fires off a letter to the local medical association, the local association of clinical psychologists, and the President of Medical Indemnity. The letter, written on Morgan Hospital letterhead and signed by Stanley as "Director, In-Patient Psychiatry Unit, Morgan Hospital," scathingly criticizes the two psychologists. Embarrassed and humiliated, the two psychologists sue both Dr. Stanley and Morgan Hospital for defamation. Should Morgan Hospital be worried about the psychologists' claim?

EXPLANATION

Yes. If the letter was indeed defamatory, the hospital is probably liable. An agent's defamatory statement is attributable to the principal if the agent had actual or apparent authority to make the statement. Dr. Stanley probably lacked actual authority. Nothing in his job implied the authority to speak for Morgan Hospital on matters of public concern, and Dr. Stanley did not receive any specific authorization before sending the letter. To those who received the letter, however, Dr. Stanley may have appeared to be speaking on Morgan Hospital's behalf. Morgan arguably manifested as much when it clothed Dr. Stanley with an impressive title. Certainly, Dr. Stanley's use of the title added weight to the comments and power to the defamation.

PROBLEM 30

Ziegler Limo Leasing and Sales, Inc. ("Ziegler") sells and leases limousines and also provides limousine service on an hourly, daily, and weekly basis. Newly wealthy, Irv is considering buying a limousine from Ziegler. Selma, Ziegler's owner, says, "Tell you what, I'll let you use a limo and a driver for a week for free. It's kinda slow for us right now, and you'll get a feel for what it's like to have a limo at your beck and call. Then you can decide. Just one thing, though—if business heats up I'll have to take the limo back."

Irv happily agrees to the arrangement, and Selma assigns Jeffrey, one of her best drivers, to drive a stretch limo for Irv. Selma tells Jeffrey, "Listen. Show him our best red carpet service. That way, if he decides not to buy, he'll know we're the only place to rent from. But also—you know how new millionaires sometimes get aggressive. Remember our safe driving policy."

Two days later Jeffrey is driving Irv to a party, when a sports car cuts them off. Enraged, Irv yells to Jeffrey, "That [expletive deleted] can't do that to us. Catch him and pass him." Ziegler's operating rules require all Ziegler drivers to obey speed limits and strictly prohibit "aggressive driving." Irv is insistent, however, and Jeffrey gives in. In the rush to catch the sports car, the limo sideswipes another car. Assuming that Jeffrey has been negligent, can the driver of the other car successfully invoke respondeat superior against Irv?

EXPLANATION

Probably not. At the time of the accident, Jeffrey probably was not Irv's borrowed servant. Although Jeffrey's general employer (Ziegler) had assigned Jeffrey to work for Irv, Ziegler retained considerable control over Jeffrey's conduct. Selma had reminded Jeffrey that Ziegler's safe driving rules still applied. Moreover, Ziegler had retained the right to reassign Jeffrey at any time. When Irv successfully urged Jeffrey to speed up, Irv was merely persuading Jeffrey to violate the general employer's rules. Irv was not establishing the type of total, temporary control that establishes a special employer.

PROBLEM 31

A city hires an electrical contractor to remove above-ground electrical lines that had once served a trolley system. The contract gives the contractor total control and responsibility for the work, provided only that the contractor minimizes interference with traffic. However, the city's manager of public works worries incessantly about safety on the job. The manager repeatedly makes surprise visits to the worksites and often speaks directly to the contractor's employees. The employees report these contacts to the contractor. The contractor is fearful of losing the contract by offending the public works manager and instructs its employees to take the manager's suggestions "unless they're dangerous, expensive, or off the wall."

Midway through the project, a live line falls on a passing car. Fortunately, no one is injured, but the car is severely damaged. Assuming the conduct of the public works manager binds the city[93] and that the accident resulted from the negligence of an employee of the contractor, does the car owner have a claim against the city?

EXPLANATION

Yes. The city's interference in the performance of the work demonstrates a right to control the employees of the contractor. Those employees are therefore servants of the city, and respondeat superior accordingly applies.

PROBLEM 32

When a business contracts out work, for quality control and safety reasons the business may wish to closely supervise the contracted work. If an accident oc-

---

93. For a discussion of this type of question, see Chapter Two.

curs, however, the injured party will point to the close supervision and seek to invoke respondeat superior. By acting on its concern for quality and safety, the delegating party will have risked vicarious liability. Propose a solution to this conundrum.

EXPLANATION

The problem cannot be totally resolved, because a tension will always exist between the amount of control and the amount of risk. The key is to find ways to influence performance that stop short of actionable control. The first step, whenever possible, is to reduce the risk by avoiding mishaps. The delegating party should therefore find contractors that have good safety records and justified reputations for quality work. Second, the delegating party should limit its review of the work to inspection and suggestion. This step will, perhaps, prevent the delegating party from being deemed the master of the contractor. Third, the delegating party should avoid any direct instructions to the contractor's employees. This step will, perhaps, prevent those employees from being deemed servants of the delegating party.

4

Duties and Obligations of Agents and Principals to Each Other and to Third Parties

§4.1 Duties and Obligations of the Agent to the Principal

§4.1.1 Duty of Loyalty: Hallmark of Agent Status

Agency is emphatically not an arm's length relationship. The Restatement, in its very first blackletter line, labels agency a "fiduciary relation,"[1] and the duty of loyalty is a hallmark characteristic of agent status. The agent's role is a self-less one, and the principal's objectives and wishes are dominant. The agent is important merely as a means to accomplish the principal's ends.[2] Except when the principal has knowingly agreed to the contrary or when extraordinary

---

1. Restatement §1(1). Likewise, Restatement (Third) §1.01, at 19 begins "Agency is the fiduciary relationship. . . ." and Restatement (Third) §1.01, comment *e*, at 27 explains: "The word 'fiduciary' appears in the black-letter definition to . . . emphasize that an agency relationship creates the agent's fiduciary obligation as a matter of law." Nonetheless, Restatement (Third), Introduction at 3-4 accurately recognizes that: "The fiduciary character of the relationship does not explain all of the doctrine included within agency law. For example, the bases for the respondeat superior doctrine are not necessarily linked to the bases for treating agents as fiduciaries." For a further discussion of this point, see section 3.3.2, n.6.

2. This legal characteristic does not always comport with the practical reality. In the lay sense, the agent may be the "star" and the principal merely the supporting context. Consider, for example, Itzhak Perlman serving for a season as first violinist of a metropolitan orchestra or Barry Bonds playing baseball for the San Francisco Giants.

circumstances exist,[3] the agent is obliged to prefer the principal's interests over its own and to act "solely for the benefit of the principal in all matters connected with [the] agency."[4]

The duty of loyalty is so deeply ingrained into agency law that few cases address the rationale underlying the duty. Some modern commentators speak in terms of economic efficiency. It would certainly be woefully inefficient if agent and principal had to negotiate their expectations in detail prior to the formation of each agency relationship. Having a standard set of loyalty rules thus reduces transaction costs. In addition, a strict regime of selflessness probably reduces the principal's monitoring costs.[5]

This perspective finds little voice in the case law, however. When judges explain the duty of loyalty, they do so with a decidedly moralistic tone. When a principal engages an agent, the principal reposes trust and confidence in that agent and the agent accepts a position of trust and confidence. To allow an agent to violate that confidence, betray that trust, and then profit from the abuse is simply unacceptable.[6]

The duty of loyalty applies regardless of how grand or menial an agent's role may be and unquestionably encompasses all modern day employees:

> As agents, all employees owe duties of loyalty to their employers. The specific implications vary with the position the employee occupies, the nature of the employer's assets to which the employee has access, and the degree of discretion that the employee's work requires. However ministerial or routinized the work assignment may be, no agent, whether or not an employee, is simply a pair of hands, legs, or eyes. All are sentient, and, capable of disloyal action, all have the duty to act loyally.[7]

An agent's duty of loyalty includes a number of specific duties of selflessness, all serving to protect the principal's economic interests.

---

3. See infra this section for discussion of "Reshaping the duty of loyalty by consent" and "The agent's legitimate disloyalty."

4. Restatement §387.

5. "Monitoring costs" are the principal's costs of keeping guard against misconduct by the agent. The stricter the rules of loyalty, the easier it will be to establish misconduct and obtain a right of recovery. The most important monitoring costs, however, relate not to recovering for misconduct but rather to preventing it. It is not clear how strict loyalty rules reduce those costs.

6. Justice Cardozo's comment in *Meinhard v. Salmon,* 164 N.E. 545, 546 (N.Y. 1928), exemplifies this tone: "Many forms of conduct permissible in a workaday world for those acting at arm's length are forbidden to those bound by fiduciary ties. A trustee is held to something stricter than the morals of the market place. Not honesty alone, but the punctilio of an honor the most sensitive, is then the standard of behavior." *Meinhard* concerned a joint venture but the case is often cited and Cardozo often quoted in cases concerning an agent's duty of loyalty.

7. Restatement (Third) §1.01, comment *g* at 43.

Unapproved benefits. Unless otherwise agreed, an agent may not benefit from its efforts on behalf of the principal. This rule applies regardless of whether the benefit is received from the principal or from a third party.

Of course, in most agency relationships the principal agrees to compensate the agent for the agent's efforts, so the agent has the right to receive and retain those benefits. An agreement to allow the agent to profit may be express or implied.

Confidential information. An agent has a duty to safeguard the principal's confidential information and not to use that information for the agent's own benefit or the benefit of others. Confidential information includes any information that is not generally known and that either carries an economic benefit for the principal, or could, if disclosed, otherwise damage or embarrass the principal. Trade secrets, customer lists, unique business methods, and business plans are examples of confidential information.

The duty of nondisclosure and nonuse applies to any confidential information the agent acquires or develops during the course of the agency relationship. The duty applies even if the confidential information does not relate to the subject matter of the agency. The duty does *not* encompass any special skills that the agent develops while performing agency tasks.

> *Example:* Ralph works as a waiter in an upscale restaurant. None of Ralph's duties involve preparing food. One day, while standing in the kitchen waiting for an order, Ralph sees and reads the restaurant's secret recipe for stuffed mushrooms. Ralph may not use the recipe or disclose it to others. Even though his role as an agent does not involve preparing food, Ralph must keep the recipe confidential.

> *Example:* Bernice works as an assistant cook in the same restaurant. She learns all of the restaurant's special recipes and also learns how to make pate brisée (a type of pastry that is standard in upscale cooking but very difficult to make well). Bernice may not use the recipes outside her job, because they are confidential information. Bernice's knowledge of how to make pate brisée, however, is an expertise, not confidential information. Subject to her duty not to compete (discussed below), Bernice may make pate brisée wherever she likes.

The duty to respect confidential information continues even after the agency ends. Confidential information belongs to the principal, and the end of the agency relationship does nothing to alter the principal's property rights in the information.[8]

No competition. Unless otherwise agreed, the agent has a duty not to compete with the principal in any matter within the scope of the agency rela-

---

8. For further discussion of this point, see section 5.3.4 (use of confidential information following termination of agency).

tionship. This noncompetition duty follows from the theme of selflessness and applies regardless of whether:

- the agent uses the principal's facilities, property or confidential information to find or pursue the opportunity
- the agent finds or pursues the opportunity "on its own time."

This aspect of the duty of loyalty runs counter to a strong public policy in favor of open competition. Once the agency relationship ends, that public policy reasserts itself. As a matter of agency law, the noncompetition duty ends. The duty to respect the principal's confidential information remains, but otherwise agency law allows a former agent to compete with its former principal.[9]

No acting for others with conflicting interests.   Unless otherwise agreed, an agent may not act for anyone whose interests might conflict with the interests of the principal. The mere existence of a dual agency violates the duty of undivided loyalty. Moreover, the dual agent risks specific conflicts of duty as to a myriad of individual issues. The fact that these individual conflicts may be irreconcilable does not justify the agent ignoring one duty or the other. Rather, if any such specific conflict materializes, the agent is destined to be liable to one principal; the other, or both.

> *Example:* A real estate broker agrees to help Sam locate and purchase a new house. The broker knows that Rachael is interested in selling her house. The broker contacts Rachael and agrees to help sell her house to Sam. Since Rachael's and Sam's interests are in some ways conflicting, the broker has breached a duty of loyalty to both Sam and Rachael merely by acting for both simultaneously.

> *Example:* Same situation as above, plus Rachael wishes not to disclose to Sam certain information which in an arm's length transaction she is privileged to withhold. Rachael mentions the information to the broker but instructs the broker not to tell Sam. The broker's duty of obedience to Rachael compels compliance,[10] while the broker's duty to provide to Sam requires disclosure.[11]

If an agent arranges a transaction in violation of the dual agency rule:

- if neither principal knows about the dual agency, either principal may rescind;
- if one principal knows, the other principal may either (i) affirm the transaction and seek damages from the agent and the knowing principal, or (ii) rescind.

---

9. For further discussion of this point, see section 5.3.4 (post-termination competition).
10. See section 4.1.3.
11. See section 4.1.5.

Dealing with the principal. When a principal uses an agent to arrange a transaction, the agent may not become the other party to the transaction unless the principal consents. In Restatement terminology, without the principal's consent the agent may not be "the adverse party" and may not "act on his own account."[12]

> *Example:* Horace wishes to go into the restaurant business and retains Elizabeth to locate a restaurant that Horace can purchase. Elizabeth happens to own a restaurant and wishes to sell it to Horace. She may do so only if she discloses her ownership to Horace, and he consents. She may not hide her ownership and make the sale through a "straw man."

Even if the principal does consent, the duty of loyalty continues to affect the transaction. In an arm's-length transaction, each party is obliged merely to avoid misstatements. When an agent acts as the adverse party, the agent has an affirmative duty to disclose all facts that the agent knows or should know could affect the principal's decision.

Good conduct. The agent's conduct can reflect on the principal, so the agent must not act in a way that brings disrepute on the principal. This aspect of the duty of loyalty extends not only to the agent's performance of the tasks of agency, but also to other behavior.

> *Example:* Charlie works as a manager at a clinic that specializes in teaching people to quit smoking. On the job, Charlie is completely smoke-free. Outside of work, however, he is often seen smoking. Patrons and potential patrons of the clinic begin making remarks like "Some clinic. Its business manager smokes." Since public smoking can reflect adversely on his principal, Charlie's duty of good conduct requires that he refrain at least from smoking where the public can observe him.[13]

The agent's legitimate disloyalty. An agent may legitimately act against the principal's interests "in the protection of [the agent's] own interests or the interests of others."[14] The notion of self-protection seems straightforward. The agent may assert its contract rights against the principal and may defend itself if the principal makes accusations of misconduct. The notion of protecting others is far vaguer. For instance, must the other party's interest be espe-

---

12. Restatement §389, comment *d*.
13. If Charlie fails or refuses to refrain and the clinic fires him, it is a separate question whether he is entitled to unemployment compensation. Although unemployment compensation statutes typically model their concept of "employee" on the agency law concept of "servant," see section 3.2.2, they have their own, somewhat narrow notion of what constitutes disqualifying misconduct.
14. Restatement §387, comment *b*.

cially substantial in order to warrant the agent being disloyal? If the disloyalty will undermine one of the principal's significant interests, must the other party's interest be even more substantial?

In extreme circumstances, the answers seem clear enough.

Example: Arnold works for a real estate development company in the land acquisition department. He knows that his friend, Alice, is about to give Ralph an option to buy some land she owns. Through his work Arnold knows that (i) the real estate company plans to develop the area in which Alice's land is located, (ii) the value of Alice's land is therefore destined to rise sharply, and (iii) the option Alice plans to grant will allow Ralph, rather than Alice, to profit from the increase in value. Arnold may not disclose his principal's confidential information to Alice.

Example: Through his work in the land acquisition department, Arnold discovers that the real estate company is engaged in a pattern of criminal fraud that, if unchecked, will cost innocent land owners thousands of dollars. Arnold may disclose the information not only to the land owners but also to the police.

Between the extremes, however, the rule is obscure. A court might consider the following factors to determine whether "the protection of . . . the interests of others"[15] justifies an agent's act of disloyalty:

- the legitimacy of the other party's interest and the importance of that interest to that other party;
- the extent to which the other party reasonably expects that the interest will be respected by the world in general and by the principal in particular;
- the legitimacy of the principal's interest and the importance of that interest to the principal; and
- the extent to which the agent might have protected the other party's interests while using means that were either less injurious or less disloyal to the principal.

Reshaping the duty of loyalty by consent.   Agency law allows a principal and agent wide latitude to reshape the duty of loyalty. Agreements can limit or even eliminate each of the specific duties discussed in this section. For instance, a principal can always consent to the agent's disclosure of confidential information or allow the agent to profit from agency efforts.

Two qualifications do exist, however. First, the duty of loyalty applies to the manner in which an agent obtains agreement from the principal. The overall relationship remains a fiduciary one, so arm's length bargaining is in-

---

15. Id.

appropriate. When an agent seeks agreement from the principal, the agent must refrain from overreaching and must disclose to the principal all material information.

Example: A real estate broker agrees to help Sam locate and purchase a new house. The broker already has in mind a house owned by Rachael. Without disclosing that information, the broker asks Sam, "If I find a house, would you mind if I also worked with the seller to work out a deal you both can live with?" Sam agrees, but the broker's conflict of interest problem remains. Since the broker breached its duty of disclosure in obtaining Sam's consent, the consent is ineffective.

The second qualification is both more theoretical and more fundamental. The fiduciary duty of loyalty is at the essence of an agency relationship. If a contract negates all duties of loyalty, that contract may indicate that no agency relationship exists.

§4.1.2 *Duty to Act Within Authority*

Although, as discussed in Chapter Two, an agent may have the power to act beyond the scope of actual authority,[16] an agent does not have the *right* to do so. To the contrary, the agent has a duty to act only as authorized.[17] An agent who violates this duty is liable to the principal for any resulting damage. A parallel rule applies to nonagents who purport to be agents and thereby bind the apparent principal.

If an agent has reason to doubt the scope of authority, except in emergency situations the agent has a duty to inquire of the principal.

Example: Sally arranges for Ralph to buy a car on her behalf. She specifies, "Buy American." Ralph finds a good deal on a car assembled in the United States from components made almost exclusively overseas. Before buying the car for Sally, Ralph should check with her.

§4.1.3 *Duty to Obey Instructions*

The principal always has the *power* to instruct the agent concerning the subject matter of the agency. Accordingly, an agent has a duty to obey instructions from the principal unless the instructions call for the agent to do something improper.

Example: Sam works for a car dealership in the used car department. He reports to the owner that he cannot sell a particular used car at the desired price because the car has too many miles on it. The owner re-

---

16. See sections 2.3 (apparent authority) and 2.6 (inherent agency power).

17. The scope of that authority is determined objectively, based on the agent's reasonable interpretations of the principal's manifestations. See section 2.2.2.

sponds, "Well, just roll back the odometer a bit." Despite being the owner's agent, Sam has no duty to comply. Rolling back an odometer is illegal, and Sam has no duty to obey instructions that call for wrongful conduct.

The agent's duty to obey instructions is consistent with the agent's duty to act within authority. Instructions from the principal are manifestations from the principal, and the agent's authority comes from the agent's reasonable interpretation of the principal's manifestations. Therefore, if an agent disregards the principal's instructions, the agent is in effect acting without authority.

The duty to obey instructions exists even if the principal has contracted away the *right* to instruct. The agent may have a claim for breach of contract but nonetheless is obliged either to obey the principal's instructions or resign.[18]

§4.1.4   *Duty of Care*

An agent has a duty to act with "due care." How much care is due depends on (i) whether the agent is paid or unpaid (gratuitous), and (ii) any relevant agreement between the principal and agent.

For paid agents, due care is usually ordinary care; a standard of ordinary negligence applies. The determination of what constitutes ordinary negligence is quite similar to the determination made under the "negligence" rubric in the law of torts. What would a reasonably careful person in similar circumstances do? As with tort law, a person with special skills or knowledge has a duty to make reasonably careful use of those skills and knowledge. For example, in judging the response of a paid babysitter to a medical emergency, a reasonable care standard will demand more of a trained nurse than of a high school student. Also as with tort law, a person's lack of ordinary skills or knowledge does not relax the due care standard.

For gratuitous agents, the standard of care is the same standard that applies to other gratuitous actors (e.g., gratuitous bailees). That standard is often one of gross negligence.

> ***Example:*** Mark is driving home from college for the holidays. Melinda, who comes from the same home town, is not. She asks Mark, as a favor, to bring home for her the CD player and the laptop that she had borrowed from her parents. Mark agrees. On the way home, he stops at a restaurant, leaving the CD player and the laptop in the back seat, with the car unlocked. When he returns to the car, he discovers that the CD player is missing. Again leaving the car doors unlocked, he goes back into the restaurant and calls the police. By the time he again returns to the car, the laptop is also gone.

---

18. See section 4.1.6.

Mark is probably liable to Melinda for the loss of the laptop but not for the CD player. As a gratuitous agent ("as a favor"), Mark is responsible only for damage caused by his gross negligence. The loss of the CD player probably reflects only ordinary carelessness. But the loss of the laptop—coming after the first theft gave Mark clear warning—resulted from gross negligence.

An agreement between the principal and agent can change the amount of care owed by the agent. For instance, a principal might agree (i) that a paid agent is obliged only to avoid gross negligence, or (ii) not to hold the agent responsible for harm caused by ordinary negligence (an "exculpatory agreement").

Public policy limits the validity of some "care reducing" agreements. For example, ethical rules prohibit lawyers from making "an agreement prospectively limiting the lawyer's liability to a client for malpractice."[19] In some states, exculpatory provisions relating to negligence are void or subject to strict construction.

It is theoretically possible for an agent to agree to raise the general standard of care, but such agreements are rare. More common are agreements under which an agent promises to produce certain results. In that case, the agent is contractually obliged to produce the promised results and cannot excuse failure by claiming the exercise of due care.[20]

§4.1.5 Duty to Provide Information

If an agent possesses information and has reason to know that the principal may need or desire the information, the agent has a duty to provide the information to the principal. This duty underlies the attribution rule that binds a principal on account of information possessed by its agent.[21] An agent's duty of care may require the agent to acquire information for the principal.

§4.1.6 Contractual Overlay

As the previous sections have discussed, an agent has obligations to its principal as a matter of agency law. Those obligations are only part of the story, however. A contractual relationship usually overlays the agency relationship, and so an agent typically owes duties in contract as well as under agency law.[22]

Not every agency relationship has a contractual overlay. As explained in Chapter One, an agency relationship is consensual, but not necessarily contrac-

---

19. Model Rules of Professional Conduct Rule 1.8(h) (1983).

20. For precisely this reason, agents (as well as independent contractors) prefer to promise "reasonable efforts" to produce specified results.

21. See section 2.4.

22. Likewise the principal may have contractual obligations to the agent. See section 4.3.3.

tual.[23] Typically, however, the reciprocal consents that create an agency relationship also reflect an exchange of consideration. The agent undertakes to perform some task or achieve some objective for the principal, and the principal undertakes to compensate the agent for the agent's efforts. Thus, a process of contract formation typically accompanies the process of "agency formation."[24]

Rights and duties created by contract often supplement the rights and duties existing under agency law. For example, a contract may set performance standards for the agent, and the agent will then have to satisfy those standards as well as agency law's duty of care.[25] A contract may also define or circumscribe duties arising under agency law. For example, a contract can delineate the scope of an agent's duty of care by specifying the scope of the agent's endeavors. A contract can also waive an agent's agency law duties. For instance, as discussed previously an agent has a duty not to compete with its principal, unless the principal consents.[26] A contract can embody that consent.

There are, however, certain agency law duties that a contract cannot waive. For example, under agency law the principal always has the power to control the goals of the agency relationship and the means by which the agent pursues those goals.[27] A contract may limit a principal's rights in these matters but cannot abrogate the power. Accordingly, when a principal exercises the power of control, the agent has an agency law duty either to comply or to resign. If the principal's exercise of agency law power violates the agent's contractual rights, then the agent may pursue contract law remedies.

> *Example:* Ralph hires Sally, a real estate broker, to sell his house. The brokerage agreement gives Sally the right to decide when to show the house. Ralph subsequently decides that he does not want the house shown on weeknights. Sally has a duty to abide by Ralph's decision or to resign. In either case, however, she can sue Ralph for breach of contract. (To recover, of course, she must prove damages).

In like fashion, the principal always retains the power, if not the right, to terminate the agency relationship.[28]

§4.1.7   Principal's Remedies for Agent's Breach of Duty

Damages.   If an agent's breach of duty to the principal causes damage to the principal, the principal can recover those damages from the agent. If an

---

23. See section 1.2.5.
24. As with most contracts, terms may be implied by custom and usage.
25. Section 4.1.4 discusses the agent's duty of care.
26. See section 4.1.1.
27. If the principal also has the *right* to control the means, then the agent is likely a servant. See section 3.2.2.
28. See section 5.2.

agent's breach of duty renders the principal liable to a third party, the agent must indemnify and hold harmless the principal from that liability.

Additional remedies for breach of the duty of loyalty. If the agent breaches a duty of loyalty, the principal's remedies include not only *damages* (if provable) but also *disgorgement* of any profits derived by the agent from the disloyal transaction and *rescission* of any transaction between the principal and agent, if the breach infected that transaction.

> *Example:* Mikki is selling her hobby farm to a shopping mall developer and must therefore dispose of five horses. Four of the horses are quite old, but the fifth is quite valuable. Helen approaches Mikki and proposes to sell the four older horses for a five percent commission and then buy the fifth horse for herself at a below-market price. Mikki agrees, on condition that Helen sells to "people who will care about my horses." Helen accepts the condition.
>
> Within a few days Helen reports that she has sold the horses to "some real nice folks." After those horses are shipped, Helen collects her commission and pays for and takes the fifth horse.
>
> Mikki later discovers that Helen sold the four horses to a glue factory. Because Helen gained the commission through dishonesty to her principal, the commission is subject to a constructive trust. Because Helen's disloyalty infected her purchase of the fifth horse, Mikki may rescind that transaction.

Both disgorgement and rescission are considered equitable remedies, and both are available without proof of damage. Courts ordering disgorgement often do so by imposing a "constructive trust" on the agent's ill-gotten gains. A court will order disgorgement even though the remedy leaves the principal better off than the principal would have been had the agent complied with its duty of loyalty.

> *Example:* A blockbuster adventure movie creates intense demand for a line of toys based on the movie. Williams Manufacturing, Inc. ("Williams") has the exclusive right to manufacture the toys. Although it raises its prices to take advantage of the demand and increases production, for several months Williams has more orders than it can fill. During this time, Max, Williams's national sales manager, gives order preference to those customers willing to "make it worth my while." The gratuities range from cash to cases of wine to airline tickets. No one else at Williams is aware of what Max is doing. If Williams can prove that Max's conduct damaged Williams's good will, Williams can recover from Max the amount of the damage. Even without proof of damage, Williams can recover from Max the value of the gratuities. By profiting without his principal's consent, Max breached his duty of loyalty. He

must disgorge all benefits resulting from that breach. Williams may also be able to recover from Max whatever salary he received during his period of dishonesty.

In many jurisdictions, breach of the duty of loyalty can support a claim for punitive damages. Also, in many jurisdictions the statute of limitations incorporates some form of the "discovery" rule—that is, the time period does not begin until the principal knows or has reason to know of the breach.

§4.2   Duties and Obligations of the Agent to Third Parties

§4.2.1   Obligations "On the Contract"

Rules for determining agent's liability.   Agents often make contracts on behalf of principals, and agency law provides rules for determining whether the agent is liable on such contracts.[29] The analysis turns on whether the agent's principal is disclosed.[30]

If the principal is disclosed, then the agent is not liable on the contract. The rationale for this rule is straightforward. With a disclosed principal, the third party enters into the contract knowing that the agent is merely a representative and that the principal will be the obligor. The agent is not promising any performance of its own,[31] and the third party may look only to the principal for performance.

This rule applies even if the third party bases a warranty claim on a statement made by the agent.

> *Example:* A patron at a gambling casino approaches the roulette wheel and asks the employee operating the wheel, "Is this game honest?" The employee responds, "As honest as the day is long." The patron places several bets, losing each one. Subsequently the patron discovers that the wheel is rigged and claims breach of warranty against both the employee and the casino. The claim against the employee will fail.[32] The patron's bets were transactions between the patron and the casino, and the employee's principal was disclosed. The employee is therefore not liable on

---

29. Agency law also determines whether the principal is liable. See Chapter Two.

30. Section 2.2.2 (in creation of actual authority, third party knowledge of principal-agent relationship is irrelevant).

31. The agent is, however, implicitly promising that the principal will be obligated. If the principal is not obligated, the agent will be liable. See section 4.2.2 (agent's warranty of authority).

32. The claim against the casino will prevail, however, since the employee's statement is attributed to the casino. See section 2.4.6 (agent's statements attributable to the principal for contract law purposes).

the contract—even though the employee's statement gave rise to the breach of warranty claim.[33]

If the principal is only partially disclosed, then the agent is almost always liable on the contract. The rationale is again one of expectations. Without knowing the identity of the principal, the third party is presumably relying on the trustworthiness, creditworthiness, and *bona fides* of the agent.

Example: An attorney contacts an art dealer and contracts to buy a famous Picasso print. The attorney explains that she is acting for a client but declines to identify the client. (The client dislikes notoriety.) The attorney is liable on the contract.[34]

Expectations also explain the "auctioneer" exception to this rule. When an auctioneer sells an item for an unidentified owner, no one expects the auctioneer to "stand behind" the goods.[35]

When the principal is undisclosed, the agent is liable *a fortiori.* As far as the third party knows, the contract is with the agent and none other.

Example: A power company authorizes a coal broker to buy coal for it. The broker contracts to buy the coal in its own name, without disclosing its status as agent for the power company. The broker is liable on the contract.[36]

These rules on contract liability are default rules. They can be overridden by express or implied agreement between the agent and third party.

Example: Return to the roulette wheel scenario (above), adding the following dialogue to the conversation between the patron and the employee:

Patron: Are you sure this wheel is as honest as the day is long?
Employee: I personally guarantee it. I wouldn't work at a crooked wheel.

The conversation reflects an agreement by the employee to guarantee one aspect of the principal's performance—namely, that the wheel will operate honestly. That agreement overrides the default rule, and the employee is liable, together with the principal.

---

33. If the employee made the misstatement negligently or intentionally, the employee may be liable in tort. See section 4.2.3.

34. The client is liable, too. See sections 2.2.2 and 2.2.4.

35. Restatement (Third) §1.04, Reporter's Notes, section *b* at 99-100. The situation might be different if the auctioneer has a reputation for probity and is known to check items for authenticity before offering them at auction.

36. The power company is liable too. See sections 2.2.2 and 2.2.4 (in creation of actual authority, third party knowledge of principal-agent relationship is irrelevant). As for the relationship of the broker's liability to the power company's liability, see infra this section.

Example: An attorney hires a doctor to serve as an expert witness in a personal injury lawsuit. Although the expert witness will serve the interests of the attorney's client and the client's identity is fully disclosed, the attorney may nonetheless be responsible to the doctor for the expert witness fees. Custom in the locality may imply a promise by the agent (the attorney) to guarantee payment by the principal (the client).[37]

The agent's liability and available defenses.   Unless otherwise agreed, an agent's contractual liability is as a *guarantor.* The agent partakes of any of the principal's defenses that arise from the transaction, plus any personal defenses or setoffs the agent may have vis-à-vis the third party. The agent may not assert defenses or setoffs that are personal to the principal (i.e., defenses arising from other transactions between the principal and the third party).

§4.2.2 *Warranty of Authority*

When a person purports to bind another person to a contract, the law implies a warranty of authority, that is, a promise that the purported agent actually has authority to act for the purported principal. If the purported principal is not bound, then the purported agent has breached the warranty of authority and is liable to the third party for expectation damages as well as reliance damages.

The warranty applies:

- both to true agents who act outside their authority and to mere purported agents who have no actual authority at all;
- regardless of whether the purported principal is disclosed or partially disclosed;[38] and
- even though the third party could have discovered the lack of authority by exercising reasonable care.

The warranty does *not* apply if:

- the purported agent disclaims having authority to bind or indicates that it doubts its own authority, or
- the third party knows for some other reason that the purported agent lacks authority.

---

37. This analysis runs counter to some old cases but reflects a modern trend. To avoid uncertainty and unwanted liability, an attorney should have a written understanding with the expert that specifies who is responsible for the expert's fees.

38. With a partially disclosed principal, the purported agent will be bound whether or not a contract is formed. If the principal is bound, a contract results and the agent is liable as a guarantor. See section 4.2.1. If the principal is not bound and no contract is formed, then the agent is liable under the warranty of authority. With an undisclosed principal, the warranty does not apply because the agent is not purporting to act on behalf of another. See section 2.2.2 (defining undisclosed principal). However, the agent is bound on the contract. See section 4.2.1.

Example: An employee of Harris, Inc. ("Harris") purports to retain Pauline, a real estate broker, to sell two acres of land that Harris owns. The employee signs an engagement letter, purportedly on Harris's behalf, agreeing that Harris will reimburse Pauline's reasonable expenses and will pay a commission in the event Pauline finds a buyer willing and able to pay the asking price. Pauline finds such a buyer, who signs and delivers an offer letter to her. She takes the letter, making clear that she has no authority to accept the offer on Harris's behalf. When Pauline brings the offer to Harris, she discovers that (i) the Harris employee acted without authority in dealing with Pauline and (ii) Harris does not wish to sell the land. If the deal does not go through, the Harris employee will be liable to Pauline for breach of the warranty of authority. The liability will include not only Pauline's reasonable expenses but also the commission she would have earned on the sale. Pauline, in contrast, will not be liable to the disappointed buyer, since she never represented that she had authority to bind Harris.

If a purported agent acts without actual authority but manages to bind its purported principal through apparent authority, inherent agency power, or estoppel,[39] the warranty of authority is not breached. The third party has received just what the purported agent promised — a binding contract with the purported principal.[40] Likewise, no breach occurs if the purported principal ratifies the contract.[41]

Example: The counter clerk in a dry cleaner promises to have your interview "power suit" ready by the next day. The clerk has made comparable promises to you before, and the dry cleaner has always fulfilled them. Last week, however, the owner instituted a new policy, depriving employees of the authority to promise next-day service. Although the clerk lacks actual authority to bind the dry cleaner to a contract for next-day service, the clerk's apparent authority binds the principal. Therefore, there is no breach of the warranty of authority.

§4.2.3 Obligations in Tort

A tort is a tort is a tort. Being an agent does not immunize a person from tort liability. A tortfeasor is personally liable, regardless of whether the tort was committed on the instructions from or to the benefit of a principal. A tortfeasor cannot defend itself by saying, "Well, I did what I did to serve my principal."[42]

---

39. For a discussion of these attribution rules, see sections 2.3 (apparent authority), 2.6 (inherent agency power), and 2.5 (estoppel).

40. The purported agent may be liable to the purported principal. See section 4.1.2.

41. For a discussion of ratification, see section 2.7.

42. The principal may well be liable too. The liability may be vicarious, see Chapter Three, or direct, see section 4.4 (principal's direct duties), or both.

For example, if a supermarket employee negligently drops a carton of cans on a customer's foot, the customer has a negligence claim against the employee.[43] Similarly, an agent who intentionally misstates a material fact while selling its principal's goods is personally liable for misrepresentation,[44] and, in some jurisdictions, can also be liable for aiding and abetting the principal's fraud. For aiding and abetting to apply, the agent must know of the fraudulent plan and give substantial assistance. The assistance need not involve directly fraudulent conduct.[45]

> *Example:* Al's Used Cars advertises for sale an automobile with interiors of "fine Corinthian leather." In response to that ad, a customer comes in and talks with Emily, a salesperson for Al's. Emily knows that the interiors are not leather and that the ad was a purposeful "come on." However, she closes the deal without mentioning the interiors. She is liable to the buyer for knowingly assisting in her principal's fraud.

Agency-related rights and duties that negate or give rise to torts. Although agency status does not create tort immunity, rights created by agency status can negate the very existence of a tort. For example, an agent acting within the scope of authority may exercise and benefit from its principal's privileges. Those privileges can transform otherwise tortious conduct into lawful behavior.

> *Example:* The owner of Sherwood Forest allows none but his guests to enter the Forest. Robin purchases the right to enter the Forest to collect certain examples of local fauna. Acting as Robin's agent, Tuck enters Sherwood Forest to collect specimens. Tuck's conduct is proper. He benefits from Robin's right to enter the land. Were Tuck entering for his own purposes, he would be committing the tort of trespass.

Agency status can also give rise to duties, the breach of which will constitute torts.

> *Example:* The owner of Sherwood Forest is leaving the country on an extended sabbatical. She hires John Little to conduct hunting expedi-

---

43. For tactical reasons the customer may decide not to assert this claim, instead relying exclusively on claims against the principal (e.g., respondeat superior, failure to provide reasonably safe premises to business invitees). Tactical considerations could include: the small chance of collecting any substantial judgment from the employee; removing the employee as a party to allow the jury to see the matter as a David versus Goliath conflict (i.e., injured "ordinary folk" versus rich, impersonal mercantile establishment); eliminating the employee's financial incentive to justify its own conduct.

44. If the agent innocently passes on the principal's misrepresentations, the agent is not liable. For the tort of intentional misrepresentation, most jurisdictions require intent to deceive or at least reckless disregard of truthfulness. Some jurisdictions also recognize a claim for negligent misrepresentation.

45. If the agent assists in the fraud by purposely making misstatements, then the agent will be liable for misrepresentation as well as for aiding and abetting.

tions into the Forest and gives him complete authority to manage the Forest premises. As a matter of tort law, Little has a duty to use care in maintaining the Forest.[46] Little's duty arises from his control of the premises, and that control comes from his authority as an agent.

§4.2.4 Breach of Duty to Principal Not by Itself a Breach to Third Party

When an agent breaches a duty of care or proper performance to its principal and the principal suffers harm, the agent is liable to the principal for damages.[47] The same misconduct may also harm a third party, but an agent's breach of duty to its principal does not automatically create a damage claim for the third party.[48] Rather than simply "borrowing" the principal's breach of duty claim, the third party must transform that duty and breach into a duty and breach running directly to the third party. To do so, the third party must show that:

1. The agent has undertaken to perform tasks for the principal that involve protection of a third party's physical safety or the safety of a third party's tangible property.
2. Either the principal or the third party (or both) have relied on the agent to provide the protection.
3. Without excuse the agent failed to provide the protection, causing injury to the third party or the party's physical property.
4. Either:
   - the agent acted with the intent to harm the third party or the third party's property, or
   - the agent's failure to perform created an unreasonable risk of harm and the agent should have recognized that risk.

The third party may recover only for injury to the person or tangible property (i.e., not merely for lost profits).

> *Example:* The city hires Sandy to serve as a lifeguard at a small municipal pool. One afternoon, while the sole lifeguard on duty, Sandy takes an unauthorized break, leaving the pool unsupervised. During that break, a child drowns, and Sandy may well be liable to the child's estate. She undertook a duty for her principal (the city) that involved protecting swimmers from physical danger (Element #1). Her principal cer-

---

46. How much care is due depends on the jurisdiction and, in some jurisdictions, on the status of the injured party (e.g., business invitee, trespasser).

47. The duty of care arises from the agency relationship. See section 4.1.4. A duty of proper performance may arise from a contract between the principal and agent. See section 4.1.6. Section 4.1.7 discusses the damage remedy.

48. The principal may well be liable to the third party, either vicariously, see section 3.2 (respondeat superior), or directly, see section 4.4.

tainly relied on her. For the time at issue it hired no one else to perform the protective function. The parents of the child may have relied on Sandy as well (Element #2). Through her unauthorized break Sandy failed to provide the expected protection and that failure arguably caused the child to drown (Element #3). Sandy's unauthorized break created an unreasonable risk of harm, and Sandy should have recognized that risk (Element #4).

§4.3   Duties and Obligations of the Principal to the Agent

§4.3.1 Principal's Duty to Indemnify

When an agent acts on behalf of its principal, the agent may incur expenses, make payments, suffer injury, and even offend the rights of third parties. As a matter of agency law,[49] a principal has a duty to indemnify its agent for:

- payments made or expenses incurred within the agent's actual authority,
- payments made to the principal's benefit, but without authority, if:
  - the agent acted in good faith, mistakenly believing itself to be authorized, and
  - under the principles of restitution it would be unjust not to require indemnity[50]
- claims made by third parties on contracts entered into by the agent, with authority, and on the principal's behalf
- claims made by third parties for torts allegedly committed by the agent, if:
  - the agent's conduct was within the agent's actual authority, and
  - the agent was unaware that the conduct was tortious.

No duty to indemnify exists for:

- payments made or expenses incurred that are neither within the agent's actual authority nor of benefit to the principal;
- losses resulting from the agent's negligence or from acts outside the agent's actual authority;
- losses resulting from the agent's knowing commission of a tort or illegal act.

---

49. Although the Restatement calls the duty to indemnify "primarily contractual in nature," Restatement §438, comment *a*, that description is confusing. No particular words or circumstances are necessary to obligate the principal. To the contrary, the duty exists because the agency relationship exists. A contract between the principal and agent can, however, modify the duty.

50. Note that a mistaken belief of authority does not by itself qualify the resulting loss or expense for indemnity.

A duty to indemnify is a duty to hold harmless: to reimburse the agent for payments made, to compensate the agent for losses suffered, to protect the agent from third party claims. Protecting against claims means (i) providing or paying for a defense, including reasonable attorney's fees and other costs of litigation ("the duty to defend"), and (ii) paying for any liability, including reasonable settlements.

To invoke the principal's duty to defend, the agent must give the principal reasonable notice of the claim, allow the principal to manage the defense, and cooperate with the principal in the defense. If the agent fails to notify the principal, the principal is not responsible for the costs of defense and will be responsible for the agent's liability only if the agent made a reasonable defense.

Example: Alvin, an up-and-coming rock singer, hires Dave as road manager for Alvin's new tour. On Alvin's instructions, Dave uses his credit card to book Alvin into the fanciest suite in the fanciest hotel in each of the tour stops. Alvin has a duty to indemnify Dave for the room charges. Alvin's instructions gave Dave actual authority to incur the expenses.

Example: Following a concert, Alvin directs Dave to bring back to the hotel a new amplifier that Alvin used during the concert. The amplifier actually belongs to the owner of the concert hall, and the owner subsequently sues Dave for conversion. Dave promptly notifies Alvin. Although Dave may well be liable for conversion,[51] Dave is entitled to indemnity from Alvin. Dave did not know he was committing a tort, and, as between Dave and Alvin, taking the amplifier was an authorized act. Alvin must therefore (i) defend Dave or pay Dave's reasonable costs of defense, and (ii) cover any liability.

Example: Although Dave's responsibilities only relate to the road tour, Dave has visions of getting Alvin a recording contract. Without checking with Alvin, Dave starts wining and dining various record company executives. Dave's efforts are fruitless, but he does manage to run up $2,000 in "entertainment" expenses. Alvin has no duty to indemnify Dave. Dave had no actual authority to incur the expenses, and the expenses were of no benefit to Alvin.

§4.3.2 *Principal's Duties in Tort (Physical Harm to the Agent)*

Nonservant agents.[52] A principal owes its nonservant agent whatever tort law duties the principal owes to the rest of the world. In addition, a principal

---

51. Conversion is a strict liability tort. Therefore, Dave's innocent state of mind is irrelevant to the owner's suit.

52. For the rules that determine whether an agent is a servant, see section 3.2.2.

has a duty to warn its nonservant agent of any risk involved in the agent's tasks if the principal knows or should know that (i) the risk exists and (ii) the agent is unlikely to be aware of the risk.

> *Example:* Rachael owns and runs her own hauling service, and Samuel hires her on commission to sell and deliver firewood. To pick up the firewood Rachael must come on Samuel's property, and, in most jurisdictions, Samuel will owe her a duty of reasonable care. That duty arises from Rachael's status as nontrespassing entrant on land and not from her status as Samuel's agent.

> *Example:* On Samuel's land, the shortest route to the stacks of firewood crosses an old wooden bridge. After one of Rachael's trips to pick up firewood, Samuel notices a hairline crack in the bridge's supporting structure. The crack is not visible from the road. Samuel has reason to know that the bridge is dangerous and that Rachael is unlikely to be aware of the danger. He therefore has a duty to inform Rachael of the risk before she makes her next trip to the stacks of firewood.

Servant agents.   Before the advent of workers' compensation statutes, the common law delineated a master's liability for work-related, physical injuries suffered by its servants. The common law was complex and confusing. In theory, the master had a duty to provide reasonably safe working conditions for its servants. In reality, three doctrines combined to eviscerate that duty and tilt the law strongly toward the master:

The "fellow servant" rule—This rule prevented servants from holding their masters vicariously liable for the tortious conduct of a "fellow servant." The Restatement defined fellow servants as "servants employed . . . in the same enterprise or household and so related in their labor that, because of proximity or otherwise, there is a special risk of harm to one of them if the other is negligent."[53] The definition (and therefore the rule) swept broadly. For instance, if a master operated several tugboats within a harbor and the negligence of a servant on one boat happened to cause injury to a servant on another, the fellow servant rule barred recovery. Since many workplace injuries resulted, at least in part, from the negligence of fellow employees, this rule left many injured servants without a remedy.

Assumption of risk—At one time this doctrine applied generally within tort law. In the master-servant context, it barred servants from recovering for injuries arising from the ordinary dangers of their work, because servants were said to have assumed the risk of such injuries. The more dangerous the work, therefore, the less likely a servant was to recover.

---

53. Restatement §475.

Contributory negligence—At one time this doctrine also applied generally within tort law. In the master-servant context, it barred recovery whenever an injured servant's own negligence had helped cause the injury.

Today, workers' compensation statutes provide a no-fault compensation regime, and preempt the common law.

§4.3.3 *Contract-Based Duties*

As explained previously, a contract between agent and principal can overlay the agency relationship and impose contractual duties on each party.[54] For principals, the most common contract-based duty is compensation. Indeed, agency law subdivides agents into two categories depending on whether the principal has agreed to pay the agent for the agent's efforts.[55]

Although the rules for construing a principal's contract-based duties are for the most part identical to the rules for construing the duties of any party to any contract, the concept of implied terms does require some special attention. As with contracts generally, the law can supply a term ("implied in law") and terms can be implied "in fact" from the (i) express terms of the agreement; (ii) the parties' conduct (before or after contract formation); and (iii) other circumstances (including usages of trade). However, no implication arises from the fact that an agency relationship exists or from the fact that the principal has promised to pay the agent.

> *Example:* Dave hires Alvin for a job in a music studio. Dave knows that Alvin lacks the technical knowledge necessary to perform adequately. These circumstances imply a contract-based duty for David to train Alvin.

> *Example:* Dave hires Theodore to do the "mixing" work on a new record. Based on this express understanding, Dave has an implied duty not to unreasonably interfere with Theodore's efforts.[56]

> *Example:* Dave hires Simon for a low-level job at the music studio, promising to pay Simon the statutory minimum wage. A month later, Dave terminates the agency relationship. Simon complains, contending that Dave: (i) never gave him any on-the-job training, (ii) did not give him enough hours per week to work, and (iii) had no right to fire him without "cause." As a matter of agency law, Simon's complaints are un-

---

54. See section 4.1.6.

55. See section 1.2.5 (defining gratuitous agents).

56. Dave nonetheless has the power to interfere. See section 4.1.3 (agent's duty to obey instructions even when principal breaches contract by giving the instructions).

founded. The mere promise to compensate an agent does not by itself imply a promise to train, a promise to provide any particular amount of work, or a promise to retain the agent for any particular length of time.[57]

§4.4   Duties and Obligations of the Principal to Third Parties

§4.4.1   *Agency Law Duties*

Duty to properly select and use agents.   As discussed in Chapters Two and Three, the acts and omissions of agents often cause principals to be obligated to third parties. In these instances agency law works in tandem with some other area of law, typically contracts or torts. Agency law provides the attribution rules, and the other area of law supplies the rules of obligation. For example, when an agent signs a contract on behalf of its principal, agency law determines whether the signature binds the principal and contract law determines whether that signature has formed a contract. Similarly, when a servant injures a third party, agency law determines whether the servant's conduct is attributable to the master while tort law determines whether the servant's conduct is actionable.

Agency law also imposes some obligations of its own on principals with regard to third parties. A principal has a duty to use reasonable care in choosing, informing, training, and supervising its agents. If a principal breaches this duty of care and a third party suffers harm, the principal is liable. This liability results from the principal's direct duty to the third party and exists even though the most proximate cause of the harm was the act or omission of an agent, and regardless of whether the agent's conduct was negligent.

> *Example:* The "Speedy Delivery" Company uses college students to deliver messages on bicycles. Speedy does not supply the bicycles, pays per delivery (not by the hour), does not control routes, and requires only that students give at least 48-hour notice of when they plan to work. One day Speedy gives a delivery assignment to a student who is obviously intoxicated. The student rides carelessly and runs into the dean of the law school. The dean drops her portable computer, which breaks. The dean will not succeed with a respondeat superior claim against Speedy, because the student is not a servant. The dean will succeed, however, with a direct claim based on the principal's duty of care. Speedy breached that duty by selecting an obviously intoxicated person to make a delivery and will therefore be

---

57. As a separate matter of statutory law, Simon may have the right to receive unemployment compensation. As for a principal's right to terminate without cause the services of an agent who is an employee, see section 5.2.

directly liable to the dean. The liability will exist even though it was the student's negligence that most proximately caused the dean's loss.

Example: The servant agent of a private snow-plowing company drives one of the company's trucks to a customer's residence in order to plow snow from the driveway. Unbeknownst to the agent, the company has installed a new module to control the snowplow attached to the front of the truck. When the agent arrives at the customer's residence and attempts to lower the plow to street level, the plow lowers so quickly that it gouges a hole in the city street. The company is liable to the city for the cost of the street repair, even though the agent has not been negligent. The relevant negligence is that of the company, which failed to properly instruct and inform its agent.

The fact that an agent has acted negligently does not by itself establish that the principal breached its direct duty of care.

Example: Harris Carpeting sells floor coverings and provides installation services through various nonservant agents. It is customary for Harris to deliver the floor covering to the customer's location and for the installer to arrive separately. Harris uses only skilled installers and follows up with customers to determine their satisfaction both with the carpet and the installation. Harris therefore sees no need to incur the expense of supervising the installers.

One of Harris's regular installers is Albert, who has done installation work for 15 years and has an exemplary record. One day Albert uses a new type of adhesive to install vinyl tile and carelessly fails to read the instructions. He therefore fails to ventilate the room properly, and a fire results. Despite Albert's negligence, Harris has not breached its duty of care. In light of Albert's experience and reputation, it was reasonable to select Albert and to allow him to work without supervision.[58]

Relationship of principal's direct duty to principal's vicarious liability. The principal's liability under the direct duty of care is different from the principal's vicarious liability under the doctrine of respondeat superior. The two liabilities can, however, overlap. If a principal negligently selects, informs, trains, or supervises a servant agent and that servant agent negligently injures a third party, the principal will be liable to the third party on two counts: directly, for a breach of the duty of care, and vicariously, through the doctrine of respondeat superior.

Besides overlapping, the two liabilities can create a double-bind for principals who hire agents to do potentially dangerous work. If the principal

---

58. The customer may have a contract claim against Harris, however. See section 4.4.3.

adopts a hands-off attitude and something goes wrong, the principal may be liable for failure to adequately supervise, train, inform, or instruct. If, in contrast, the principal seeks to avoid such a result with a hands-on approach, the law will take the principal's right of control to mean that the agent is a servant. If so, any negligence of the servant will make the principal vicariously liable.

The following table shows how the principal's direct and vicarious liability relate to each other and also how the principal's liability in tort is affected by the negligence of the principal, the negligence of the agent, and the status of the agent as servant or nonservant. The table assumes that conduct of the agent has caused physical injury to the person or property of a third party.

	Principal **Breached** *Duty of Care*	*Principal* **Did Not Breach** *Duty of Care*
Agent's Conduct **Negligent**	Principal liable on direct claim. Also liable vicariously *if* agent was a servant and was acting within scope of employment.	Principal not liable on direct claim. Liable vicariously *if* agent was a servant and was acting within scope of employment.
Agent's Conduct **Not Negligent**	Principal liable on direct claim only, regardless of whether agent is a servant.	Principal not liable.

§4.4.2 "Nondelegable" Duties Imposed by Other Law

Nonagency law sometimes imposes duties on account of a person's status or relationship to others. For example, in most jurisdictions the owner of a business has a duty to use reasonable care to make the premises safe for customers. Although the law sometimes calls such obligations "nondelegable duties," the term is usually a misnomer. With most such duties a person may indeed delegate the responsibility to others. For example, a store owner may appoint a store manager and leave her in charge of the premises. The mere fact of delegation breaches no duty.

A better, albeit more cumbersome, name for these duties would be "duties that may be delegated but that are not discharged merely by delegation." When a person delegates to an agent, the delegating person's relationship with the person accepting the delegation is a matter of agency law. However, neither the delegation nor the law of agency affect the original duty. Regardless of the care the principal uses in selecting, informing, training, and supervising the agent, the principal remains on the hook until and unless the agent properly performs the delegated tasks. If the agent does so, then the principal has satisfied its obligations under nonagency law. If, however, the agent does not perform properly, the principal is liable. The principal may have a claim against the agent, but that claim does not excuse the principal.

> *Example:* Under a statute governing the leasing of residential premises, a landlord owes a tenant a duty to maintain the premises in "habitable" condition. The landlord hires a resident manager and instructs the manager "to do whatever is necessary to keep this place in good condition." The resident manager neglects the job, and a tenant sues the landlord for breach of the statutory "warranty of habitability." The landlord cannot successfully defend by blaming the resident manager, because delegating the responsibility did not discharge it.[59]

§4.4.3   *Duties Assumed Under Contract*

In any contract the parties undertake duties to each other, and in most situations a contract obligor may delegate performance of a duty to someone else.[60] When a contract obligor does delegate performance to an agent,[61] agency law relates to that delegation in the same way it relates to the delegation of duties imposed by law. The delegation does not discharge the duty. The obligor remains strictly responsible to the obligee, even if the obligor uses the greatest care in selecting, supervising, and instructing the agent.

> *Example:* Mikki is under contract with Samantha to mow Samantha's lawn by Saturday at noon, in time for a big outdoor party Samantha is hosting. Mikki directs Horace, one of her employees, to do the lawn mowing on Saturday morning. Horace has always been one of Mikki's most responsible employees, and Friday evening Mikki reminds Horace of the job. Unfortunately, at breakfast on Saturday Horace gets food poisoning and is hospitalized before he can warn Mikki to send a replacement worker. The lawn is not mowed, and Mikki has breached her contract with Samantha. Delegating the duty did not discharge it, no matter how reasonable the delegation. Horace's sudden illness is irrelevant.

PROBLEM 33

In his first meeting with Friar Tuck, Robin Hood compels Tuck to carry him across a stream. Hood uses his sword as the instrument of coercion. Tuck un-

---

59. The results are the same when a person delegates a duty to a non-agent. See, e.g., Restatement (Second) of Contracts §318(3) (unless otherwise agreed by the obligee, delegation does not discharge the obligor's duty to the obligee).

60. Sometimes the nature of the obligation (e.g., personal service) precludes delegation. Sometimes the contract validly prohibits delegation. In such circumstances, contract duties are genuinely "nondelegable," and the obligee need not accept the delegated performance.

61. It is possible and quite common to delegate duties to non-agent independent contractor. See section 6.1.2 (distinguishing agents from independent contractors).

dertakes the task, but midway across purposely drops Hood into the stream. Has Tuck breached his duty of loyalty? Would it matter if Tuck's conduct were grossly negligent rather than intentional?

EXPLANATION

Tuck has not breached his duty of loyalty, because none exists. For an agency relationship to exist, *inter alia* the agent must manifest consent to act on the principal's behalf. Tuck made no such manifestation, but merely yielded temporarily to coercion.

PROBLEM 34

Travelling across country by car after the death of her husband, Alice stops at a roadside diner for lunch. The diner is in chaos. The one waitress has just quit, and Mel, the owner and cook, has a room full of increasingly irate customers. Sensing a job opportunity, Alice says to Mel, "Hey, I can wait tables. Want some help?" Mel responds, "Minimum wage. You're hired. Your shift ends at 7 P.M."

Alice works hard and extremely well. By the end of the day, she has collected $150 in tips. She is shocked when Mel says, "The tips belong to me. I didn't saying nothing about you keeping the tips." Is Alice obliged to surrender the tips?

EXPLANATION

No. Although an agent must have the principal's consent to profit from the agency, custom may imply the necessary consent. It is certainly customary for waitresses and waiters to retain their tips.

PROBLEM 35

Victoria commissions Albert to get a contracts casebook for her at the used bookstore. She specifically instructs him that she wants him to buy a book that was previously used, underlined, and annotated by someone who received at least a B-plus in the contracts course. She promises to pay Albert a $5 fee if he succeeds in purchasing for her a book that meets her specifications.

Albert goes to the bookstore and initially attempts to perform his task. However, the bookstore clerk tells Albert that the bookstore has no way of knowing how well the former owner of any particular book did on any particular exam. Not wanting to lose a sale and always on the lookout for a little personal gain, the clerk suggests a little scam. The clerk will telephone Victoria and tell her that the bookstore does indeed have a book which was owned by someone who received an A in contracts. The clerk will also tell Victoria that, since the book has such a good pedigree, the book costs $15 instead of the regular used price of $12. If Albert will back up the story, the clerk will split the extra $3 with him, fifty-fifty. Albert agrees.

The scam works. Victoria gives Albert $20 ($15 for the supposed price of the book and $5 for Albert's commission.) Twelve dollars of Victoria's money goes into the bookstore's cash drawer. The clerk splits the other $3 with Albert. Albert also pockets the $5 commission.

But not for long. The scam unravels when Victoria learns that the former owner of the book flunked out of law school without ever having achieved a grade above C-minus. Threatened with dire consequences, the clerk spills his guts and tells Victoria the whole sordid story. Victoria rescinds her purchase. The clerk returns to Victoria the full $15 purchase price, taking $12 from the bookstore's cash drawer and the other $3 from his own pocket. Victoria then goes after Albert. She sues him not only for the return of the $5 commission, but also to disgorge the $1.50 kickback. Albert concedes the $5 and pays it back to Victoria. Albert contests the $1.50, however. He points out that he has paid the $5 and the clerk has paid the $15, so Victoria is now "whole." According to Albert, Victoria has recovered whatever damages she suffered and is now looking for a windfall. What result?

EXPLANATION

Albert must disgorge the $1.50. When an agent profits by breaching the duty of loyalty, the law imposes a constructive trust in favor of the principal. It is irrelevant that Victoria can prove no damages, and it is immaterial that disgorgement will make Victoria "more than whole" financially. It is better that the principal receive a windfall than the agent profit from a breach of fiduciary duty.

PROBLEM 36

After graduating from law school, Beth goes to work for a law firm. Several months later, an uncle contacts Beth and asks her to handle a closing on the sale of some land. Beth says, "I'd be delighted. When would you like to come down to the office?" The uncle responds, "Oh, I don't want to get your office involved. I don't really want to pay downtown lawyer fees. Why don't I just come by your house tonight?"

Beth explains that she is really obligated to work through her firm, but her uncle is insistent. Finally, Beth hits upon a solution. "Listen, uncle," she says, "You're family. Let me do this closing as family, no charge. We'll call it an introductory offer." Her uncle agrees.

Beth spends about six hours preparing for and attending the closing, and all goes well. Two weeks later, she receives at home a beautiful silver necklace, with a note from her uncle: "Dear Beth, With thanks to my favorite niece. Love, Your uncle." The necklace is worth approximately $900. What should Beth do?

EXPLANATION

Beth faces a difficult situation. Presumably, she does not want to hurt her uncle's feelings, and for sentimental, aesthetic, and financial reasons she may well want to keep the necklace for herself. However, as Beth explained to her uncle, she is obliged to do her legal work through her firm. Her duty of loyalty precludes her acting in competition with her principal. No matter how earnest her efforts to avoid a problem and how pure her motives, she cannot retain benefits made through competitive activity unless she has her principal's informed consent.

That analysis dictates Beth's next steps. She must either return the necklace to her uncle or disclose the situation to the firm and seek the firm's permission to retain the necklace.

PROBLEM 37

Sam obtains from a video game distributor the right to place its video games in bars, restaurants, and video parlors throughout a tri-state area. The right is quite valuable, because this manufacturer has several very popular video games and rations the number of games allowed in any one geographic area. Sam retains Eli to represent him in locating the best possible locations for the games and to negotiate with the owners and managers of those locations. Eli makes a number of recommendations, which Sam follows. Per their agreement, Sam pays Eli a fee of $500 per location selected.

The games do not produce the revenue Sam expected, and after about six months he looks more carefully into the locations Eli recommended. Sam discovers that (i) half of the locations are owned by Interactive Display Outlets, LLC ("IDO"); (ii) during the time that Eli was advising Sam, Eli was also on retainer to IDO as a management consultant; (iii) many of the IDO locations are not in high traffic areas; and (iv) Eli could easily have arranged superior, non-IDO placements that would have produced better revenues for Sam. What recourse does Sam have against Eli?

EXPLANATION

By acting for IDO, a potentially adverse party, without having Sam's consent, Eli breached his agent's duty of loyalty. He is liable to Sam for damages, that is, the present value of the additional revenues that would have been produced by the easily-arranged, superior, non-IDO placements. Eli may also have to disgorge the compensation he received from Sam, as well as any compensation he received from IDO for having gotten Sam's video games into IDO locations.

PROBLEM 38

Sandy agrees to go to an auction for Ralph and bid for a particular picture. Ralph authorizes Sandy to bid up to $20,000. Both Sandy and Ralph expect the auction to end by 6 P.M. The auction runs late and Sandy must leave to pick up a child from day care. The day care center closes at 6:30 P.M. After Sandy leaves, the picture Ralph wanted is sold for $18,000. Ralph later buys the picture from the purchaser for $20,000. He learns that the purchaser would have stopped bidding at the auction when the price hit $19,000. Ralph then sues Sandy for $1,000—the difference between what would have been a winning bid at the auction and the price Ralph had to pay to get the painting after the auction. What is Ralph's theory of recovery? What will Sandy argue? What will Ralph respond?

EXPLANATION

Ralph will argue that (i) Sandy was his agent; (ii) Sandy owed Ralph an agent's duty of loyalty, which Sandy breached by leaving the auction before the bidding finished (or at least before the $20,000 limit was reached on the picture); and (iii) Sandy is liable for the $1,000 of damages proximately caused by Sandy's breach of fiduciary duty.

Sandy will make two arguments. First, Sandy will argue that, by at least tacit agreement of the parties, the agency (and Sandy's fiduciary duty of loyalty) terminated at 6 P.M., when both the principal and agent expected the auction to be over. Second, Sandy will argue that even assuming the agency continued past 6 P.M., the agent's duty of loyalty yields when necessary to protect important interests of others. Preventing a child from being abandoned at a day care center should qualify as such an interest. Protecting children is certainly a legitimate social value and should outweigh some relatively minor financial harm to the principal.

Ralph will respond that Sandy had available at least two alternatives for protecting the child's interest without sacrificing the principal's. First, by anticipating the problem and disclosing it in advance to Ralph, Sandy would have allowed Ralph to make other arrangements for covering the auction. Second, when the auction appeared to be running long, Sandy could have asked for a brief recess, called the day care center, and tried to arrange for a late pick-up.

PROBLEM 39

Sylvia decides to enter the silk importing business. The trade is notoriously biased against women, and she fears that her company will suffer if her interest in it is known. She therefore hires Phil as her general manager, but sets up the company so that Phil appears to the outside world as the owner. It is common in this trade for silk importers to sell to large customers on credit, but Sylvia instructs Phil never to extend more than $50,000 of credit to any customer without Sylvia's approval. One day, in order to close an important deal, Phil extends $150,000 of credit to one customer without consulting Sylvia. The customer makes only $20,000 of payments and then defaults. Assuming that Phil's judgment about the customer's creditworthiness was reasonable, does Sylvia have any claim against Phil?

EXPLANATION

Yes. Phil owes Sylvia $130,000. He breached his duty to act within his authority, and he is liable to his principal for the resulting harm. The reasonableness of Phil's judgement about the customer's creditworthiness is irrelevant. Sylvia is not claiming breach of the agent's duty of care.

PROBLEM 40

The owner of a car dealership appoints Rachael to manage the used car department. The owner promises that Rachael can have a "free hand" running the department. Rachael decides to open the department on Sundays. Although Sunday openings are not against the law, the owner considers them "inappropriate." The owner instructs Rachael to stay closed on Sunday. Must Rachael comply?

EXPLANATION

Although this instruction breaches the agreement between the owner and Rachael, Rachael has a duty either to obey or to resign. If Rachael can prove damages, she may recover for breach of contract.

PROBLEM 41

Sidney hires Sam, a private detective, to locate and deliver to Sidney a valuable statue of a bird. Sidney agrees to a fee of $200 per day, plus reasonable expenses, with a $15,000 bonus if Sam succeeds in finding and delivering the statue. Sam is on the verge of locating the statue when Sidney learns that Sam is carrying a gun. Sam is properly licensed to do so, but Sidney tells Sam, "I abhor violence. You may not carry that thing when you are working for me." Must Sam obey? Does he have any recourse against Sidney?

EXPLANATION

A principal always has the power to control the agent, so Sam must either obey or resign. Sam may nonetheless have a claim against Sidney for breach of contract. If, for example, the local custom is for detectives to use whatever lawful tactics they choose, that custom may have implied an agreement requiring Sidney to respect Sam's discretion. If so, and if Sam could for instance prove that his lack of a gun cost him the opportunity to retrieve the statue, Sam could recover the $15,000 bonus from Sidney.

PROBLEM 42

Esther seeks to sell her business and enlists Harry to locate and help evaluate prospective buyers. With Harry's advice, Esther decides on a price of $1.5 million. She is willing to finance the sale (i.e., to receive payments in installments) but only with a down payment of at least 10 percent. Both Esther and Harry believe that buyers are more likely to succeed if they have some of their own money at risk.

Initially Harry has difficulty locating qualified buyers, but after three months he presents an offer from JoDot Enterprises ("JoDot"). JoDot offers to pay $1.5 million, with $150,000 down. Esther accepts the offer, and the sale goes through.

Unfortunately, JoDot cannot operate the business at a profit and defaults on its obligations to Esther. Esther then learns that (i) JoDot did not actually have the $150,000 needed for the down payment and had to borrow $75,000 from a third party, and (ii) Harry was aware of that fact when he presented JoDot's offer to Esther. Does Esther have any recourse against Harry?

EXPLANATION

Yes. Harry breached his duty to provide information to Esther, his principal. Harry understood both the importance of the down payment and Esther's view of the subject. He therefore knew or should have known that Esther would want to know that the prospective buyers lacked a true down payment.[62]

Esther can compel Harry to disgorge any commission he earned on the deal. If she can prove causation, she can also collect damages.

PROBLEM 43

An attorney contacts an art collector, seeking to buy a famous Picasso print on behalf of a client. The attorney explains to the collector that she is acting for a client but declines to identify the client. (The client dislikes notoriety.) The attorney has actual authority to offer up to $450,000 for the print, and she persuades the collector to sell for $415,000. It is late Friday afternoon, and the attorney can have a cashier's check for the contract price by 10 A.M. Monday morning. The attorney wishes, however, to sign a binding sale agreement with the art collector, so that the collector cannot change his mind over the weekend. The attorney has $5,000 of her own money immediately available that she is willing to use as an earnest deposit. The attorney does not, however, wish to be liable on the contract itself. What should she do?

EXPLANATION

The attorney's potential problem comes from a rule of agency law. When an agent makes a contract for a partially disclosed principal, the agent is liable to the third party as a guarantor of the principal's performance—unless the agent and the third party have agreed otherwise. This rule dictates the attorney's strategy. The sale agreement must let her off the hook.

From the attorney's perspective, the ideal solution would be to include in the sale agreement an express statement that the attorney is not liable. It seems possible, however, that the collector would balk at such a term. After all, he

---

62. It is also possible to view Harry's conduct as a breach of his duty to obey instructions. This view assumes that Esther instructed him to bring her only offers from "qualified" buyers, that is, buyers capable of meeting the 10 percent down payment requirement.

would be committing to take the print off the market in return only for a promise to pay from a party whose creditworthiness he is unable to assess. The attorney could respond to this concern by limiting the duration of the collector's risk. The agreement could require payment by cashier's check by Monday at noon and provide that any delay in payment would entitle the collector to rescind the agreement. If the collector required further inducement, the agreement could provide for a nonrefundable "earnest money" payment of $5,000.

PROBLEM 44

Rose's Marina rents berths to various boat owners and also does boat and engine repair. The Marina does not ordinarily sell boats. Phil rents a berth at the Marina for his cabin cruiser. He happens to mention to Rose that he is thinking about selling his boat. Phil then leaves town on a two-week vacation. Three days later Rose meets Irv, who is interested in buying a cabin cruiser just like Phil's. Rose shows Phil's cruiser to Irv, and Irv immediately offers to pay $25,000 for the boat. Overcome by her enthusiastic desire to help Phil, Rose says, "OK. He'll take it. Give me $500 earnest money." Irv does so, receiving in return a receipt from Rose: "Received from Irv, nonrefundable down payment on Phil's boat. By Rose, acting for Phil."

When Phil returns to town, he refuses to go through with the sale. Assuming that Phil is not bound,[63] does Irv have any recourse against Rose?

EXPLANATION

Yes. When Rose purported to act on Phil's behalf in selling the boat, she impliedly warranted her authority to bind Phil. In fact, she was not Phil's agent and lacked any power to bind him. She has breached her warranty of authority and is liable to Irv for both reliance and expectation damages.

PROBLEM 45

Jerry, the owner of Jerry's Gas, Service, and Repair Station, instructs Leah, one of his employees, to "pick up the blue Chevy station wagon parked in the driveway of 1346 Lincoln Avenue. Customer called and says it won't start and we should get it and fix it." Leah takes the Station's tow truck and does as in-

---

63. According to the rules discussed in Chapter Two, Rose had no power to bind Phil. He made no manifestation that could have *reasonably* caused her to believe that he wanted her to sell his boat. Therefore, she had no actual authority. He made only one manifestation that reached Irv—leaving the boat at the Marina. That manifestation was insufficient to cause Irv to *reasonably* believe that Rose was Phil's authorized agent. Therefore, Rose had no apparent authority. Cf. U.C.C. §2-403(2) (power of merchant who deals in goods of the kind to transfer entrusters title to a buyer in ordinary course). Inherent power is inapplicable, because Rose was not Phil's agent, much less his general agent. Estoppel will not work because Phil neither knew of nor carelessly caused Irv's misapprehension.

structed. On the way back from the driveway, a semitrailer crosses a median strip and smashes into the station wagon. Fortunately, no one is injured, but the station wagon is totalled. Moreover, it later develops that Jerry made a mistake on the address: The customer who authorized the repair work lives at 1436 Lincoln. Is Leah liable to the owner of the station wagon?

EXPLANATION

Yes. Leah is liable for conversion, a strict liability tort. That she acted on her principal's instructions and without negligence is irrelevant to the question of her liability. Leah certainly has a right to be indemnified by her principal, and her principal is doubtlessly liable to the wagon's owner.[64] Nonetheless, she remains responsible for the tort she committed.

PROBLEM 46

Tim and May hire Bob, a general contractor, to build them a two-story beach cottage. The contract calls for the cottage to be "fully plumbed, with all plumbing fixtures properly installed and operational." A separate Exhibit to the contract specifies the quality, quantity, and location for various fixtures.

Bob subcontracts the plumbing work to Forrest, an expert plumber. Bob has worked with Forrest before and knows that Forrest takes great pride in his work. Bob does not supervise Forrest's work.

When Tim and May take possession they discover that Forrest plumbed the laundry room incorrectly and that they cannot hook up a washing machine. Correcting the problem will cost $500, and Bob is nowhere to be found. Can Tim and May recover from Forrest?

EXPLANATION

No. Forrrest's mistake with the plumbing presumably breached a duty to Bob, but that breach creates no direct liability to Tim and May. Even assuming that Forrest is Bob's agent, an agent's breach of duty to its principal cannot create a claim for a third party when the third party suffers only monetary loss.[65]

PROBLEM 47

Seller owned five acres of land on which he had built stables, corrals, fencing, and other improvements useful for raising horses. He retained Broker to sell the land on his behalf. Seller walked the property with Broker, showing Broker the various improvements and the property lines. Together they found most of the boundary markers but could not find some. On the east side of

---

64. This liability rests on respondeat superior. See section 3.2.

65. Tim and May could try to recover as third party beneficiaries. They would assert that, when Bob subcontracted his duty of performance to Forrest, they became intended beneficiaries of that subcontract. See Restatement (Second) of Contracts §302(1)(b). This argument would likely fail, however.

the property, they found the northeast marker but could not find the southeast one. A line of trees seemed to confirm Seller's description of the east boundary. Moreover, Seller assured Broker, "I know where my land is and where I built. All my improvements are on my property." Broker did not independently verify the boundary lines.

When Broker showed the land to the eventual Buyers, Broker represented that all the improvements were within the property. After closing, the Buyers discovered that a corral on the east side of the property encroached several feet into the neighboring parcel. The cost for moving the improvements was $6,000. Was Broker liable for that amount?

EXPLANATION

No. An agent is not liable for an innocent misrepresentation. The third party must show either intentional or negligent misrepresentation. There is no case here for intentional misrepresentation. Broker actually believed its own statements about the boundaries. Nor do the facts support a finding of negligent misrepresentation. Broker had no reason to doubt Seller's assurances, especially when the land's natural features (i.e., the trees) and what markers could be found seemed to support those assurances.

PROBLEM 48

In an attempt to get better booking for his client, Dave (Alvin's road manager) threatens a booking agent with imminent bodily harm. The booking agent sues Dave for assault and for intentional infliction of emotional distress. Is Alvin obliged to indemnify Dave?

EXPLANATION

No. The suit arises from a tort knowingly committed by an agent. The principal therefore has no duty to indemnify.[66]

PROBLEM 49

Tim and May hire Bob, a general contractor, to build them a two-story beach cottage. The contract calls for the cottage to be "fully plumbed, with all plumbing fixtures properly installed and operational." A separate Exhibit to the contract specifies the quality, quantity, and location for various fixtures.

Bob subcontracts the plumbing work to Forrest, an expert plumber. Bob has worked with Forrest before and knows that Forrest takes great pride in his work. Bob does not supervise Forrest's work.

On the very first night after taking possession of the beach cottage, Tim takes a bath in the second-floor bathroom. Everything goes well until Tim

---

66. Alvin may yet get involved, however, since the booking agent may have a respondeat superior claim. Dave's intentional tort may have been within his scope of employment. See section 3.2.6.

starts to drain the tub. Then, gallons of water pour through the first floor ceiling into the living room. Later inspection reveals that Forrest had neglected to connect the tub drain to the drain pipe.

Tim and May demand that Bob pay them $2,500: $300 for fixing the plumbing and $2,200 for repairing the damage caused by the cascade of dirty bath water. Bob responds, "I'm real sorry about the trouble, but your complaint is really with Forrest. I trusted him, and I had no reason not to. He's always done excellent work. This time he messed up. You have to go after him, not me." Must they?

EXPLANATION

No. Bob's analysis is coherent, but irrelevant. He is essentially making an independent contractor argument and asserting that he is neither vicariously nor directly liable for Forrest's negligence.[67] But Tim and May are not trying to hold Bob accountable for Forrest's negligence. They are asserting Bob's failure to perform his direct obligations under contract. Bob did not escape those obligations merely by delegating them to Forrest.

---

67. Rephrased into agency terminology, Bob's argument runs as follows: Bob had no right to control the details of Forrest's performance, so Forrest was not Bob's servant and Forrest's negligence is not attributable to Bob. Moreover, given Forrest's excellent track record, Bob was not negligent in selecting or supervising Forrest and therefore is not directly liable either. For present purposes, it is immaterial whether Bob seeks to characterize Forrest as a complete independent contractor or merely as an independent contractor (i.e., nonservant) agent.

5

Termination of the Agency Relationship

§5.1   Ending the Agency Relationship

An agency relationship may end in numerous ways.

§5.1.1   *Through the Express Will of Either the Principal or the Agent*

In a true agency situation, both the principal and the agent have the *power* to end the relationship at any time.[1] Either party can exercise this power simply by communicating to the other that the relationship is at an end. The principal's exercise of this power is sometimes called *revocation* (as in revocation of the agent's authority), while the agent's exercise is sometimes called *renunciation*. Like other agency manifestations, communications of revocation and renunciation are judged by an objective standard.

> *Example:* The City Opera Company signs Maestro Donna Prima to an agreement under which Ms. Prima agrees to conduct exclusively on behalf of the Company throughout the upcoming season. Like the opera star stereotype, Ms. Prima is a mercurial personality and is given to emotional outbursts. At one rehearsal, during which the violin section makes several mistakes, she loudly proclaims, "I am sorry, but I cannot

---

1. As discussed previously, power is not the same as right. See sections 1.3, 4.1.3, and 4.1.6. Whether a particular revocation or renunciation is "rightful" depends on the contract overlaying the agency relationship. See section 5.2. If the principal lacks the power to terminate, no true agency exists. See section 6.2 (power coupled with an interest; authority [or power] given as security).

tolerate mediocrity. I resign." On two prior occasions she has made similar announcements during rehearsals only to return a few hours later. Viewed objectively, in light of what the Opera Company knows of Prima's personality and her past conduct, this latest pronouncement does not constitute a renunciation and does not terminate the agency relationship.

Example: The sheriff of a Western town is well known as a man slow to make decisions but resolute once a decision is made. Despite receiving no support from the townspeople, the sheriff has just survived a gunfight with several outlaws. As the townspeople come out of hiding and try to congratulate the sheriff, he looks at them with disgust, takes off his badge, and throws it into the dirt. The sheriff has renounced his agency.

§5.1.2 *Through the Expiration of a Specified Term*

Principal and agent can and often do specify that the relationship will last for a particular period of time. If they do, the relationship automatically terminates at the end of the specified period unless the parties agree to an extension or renewal. That agreement can be inferred from the parties' conduct.

Example: Mark retains Tonya to find a buyer for Mark's condominium. They agree that Tonya will have the exclusive agency for 90 days. They also agree that during those 90 days Tonya will have the authority to accept any cash offer of at least $90,000. On the 101st day, Tonya purports to accept a cash offer for $92,000. Tonya lacks the actual authority to accept the offer on Mark's behalf. That authority, and Tonya's role as agent, terminated at the end of 90 days.

Example: Same facts, except that following the 90th day, Mark and Tonya continue to discuss the condo, and Tonya, with Mark's knowledge, continues to show the condo to prospects. The conduct of Mark and Tonya implies an agreement to extend the agency.

§5.1.3 *Through the Accomplishment of the Agency's Purpose*

If the manifestations that create an agency indicate a specific objective, achieving that objective ends the agency. Without further manifestations from the principal, the agent has no basis for believing that either its authority or its agency continues.

Example: Capitalist, Inc. hires Veronica to lobby for the passage of a bill in Congress. As part of her lobbying efforts Veronica "wines and dines" Congressional staff members. She sends the bills to Capitalist. On October 12th, the bill passes and is sent to the President. The next day, Veronica takes three staffers out to a "thank you for all your hard work" lunch. Without some additional manifestation from Capitalist,

Veronica may not bill this lunch to Capitalist. Her agency relationship with Capitalist ended when the goal of the agency was accomplished.

Sometimes an agent will continue to exert effort for the principal even after accomplishing the agency task. The principal's acceptance or even acknowledgement of those efforts may manifest consent for the agency to continue or resume.

Example: Irv hires Jeff to help arrange a loan to finance Irv's acquisition of a business. Jeff arranges a loan and receives a fee from Irv. Jeff keeps in touch with the lender and some months later learns that Irv is having difficulty meeting his payments. Without first talking to Irv, Jeff contacts the lender to talk about refinancing the loan. At this point, Jeff is not acting as Irv's agent.[2] Subsequently, Jeff talks to Irv and says, "I understand from your lender that the payments are too large. I think I can work something out. Do you want me to try?" Irv replies, "Sure. Why not?" From that point, Jeff is again acting as Irv's agent.

§5.1.4 *By the Occurrence of an Event or Condition*

Sometimes the manifestations that create an agency indicate that a particular event or condition will end the agency. If so, once the event or condition occurs the agent can no longer reasonably believe itself authorized to act on the principal's behalf. The agency therefore terminates.

Example: Larry hires Howie to sell hot dogs at the beach, "but only until my daughter gets here from summer school." When Larry's daughter arrives, Howie's agency ends.

The same rationale applies if the original manifestations call for the agency to end if a particular event or condition does not occur.

§5.1.5 *By the Destruction of or the End of the Principal's Legal Interest in the Property*

If the agent's role is predicated on some particular property and the property is no longer practically or legally available to the agent, the agency ends.

Example: Larry hires Howie to skipper Larry's yacht during the summer. In June the yacht sinks. Howie's agency ends.

Example: Larry hires Howie to skipper Larry's yacht during the summer. In June Larry sells the yacht. The yacht still exits, but Larry no longer has a legal interest in it. Howie's agency ends.[3]

---

2. Jeff may nonetheless have the apparent authority to bind Irv. See section 5.3.1.

3. If the end of the agency means that Larry has breached an agreement with Howie, Howie may pursue contract remedies. See section 5.2. Nonetheless, the agency ends.

§5.1.6 *By the Death, Bankruptcy, or Mental Incapacity of the Agent or Principal*

Under traditional common law rules, any of these events terminates the agency relationship. However, modern statutes allow for substantial exceptions, and the Restatement (Third) of Agency proposes to reformulate the common law to "follow[] the lead set by statutes of broad applicability."[4] Section 5.3.1 discusses the Restatement (Third)'s proposed reformulation.

§5.1.7 *By the Expiration of a Reasonable Time*

Where the original manifestations set no specific term, the agency relationship expires automatically after a reasonable time has passed. What constitutes a reasonable time depends on a number of factors, including:

- the manifestation of the parties when the agency is created
- the extent and nature of the communications between the parties after the agency is created (including indications by a party that it wishes to end the agency or that it believes the agency has ended)
- the particular objective of the agency
- past dealings, if any, between the principal and agent
- the custom, if any, in the locality with regard to agency relationships of the same or similar type

§5.2 Power versus Right in Termination

As previously indicated,[5] both principal and agent always have the *power* to end a true agency relationship. Whether either has the *right* to do so depends on the content of any contract overlaying the agency relationship as well as on concepts of detrimental reliance and good faith.

§5.2.1 *The Role of Contract*

Contractual terms can, *inter alia:*

- set a specific duration for the agency, during which neither party may rightfully end the relationship without having cause
- provide for the agency to continue indefinitely, until ended by either party giving notice
- define "cause" sufficient to allow one party, or the other, or both to end the agency

---

4. Restatement (Third) §3.06 (T.D. No. 2, 2001) (March 14, 2001) (Termination of Actual Authority—In General), comment *d.*

5. See section 5.1.1.

- provide for the agency to continue so long as the agent meets certain performance requirements

Regardless of its terms, a contract leaves intact the parties' *power* to end the agency relationship. If a principal revokes or an agent renounces in breach of contract, the other party may seek contract damages but cannot avoid the destruction of the agency. In any damage action, ordinary contract rules (e.g., assertions of prior breach, the duty to mitigate) will apply.

Example: Marge enters into a contract calling for her to serve as Mountain Fleece, Inc.'s East Coast Regional Sales Representative for 18 months. Despite the contract, Mountain Fleece terminates the agency a mere six months later. As a matter of agency law, Marge cannot compel Mountain Fleece to continue the relationship.[6] She can, however, sue for damages.

Example: Same situation, except that Marge prematurely renounces. As a matter of agency (and contract) law, Mountain Fleece cannot compel Marge to serve. It can sue her for damages.

§5.2.2 *Implied Terms*

For the most part, the rules on implying terms in an agency contract are identical to the rules for implying terms in any contract. A difference exists, however, with regard to terms restricting the right of the parties to terminate the relationship.

An express term can certainly restrict either party's right to terminate the agency. For example, most collective bargaining agreements expressly preclude the principal (i.e., the employer) from terminating a servant agent (i.e., an employee) without "just cause." Courts will not, however, easily imply such a restriction. To the contrary, most agents have the right to renounce at will and most serve at the will of the principal.[7]

Courts are most likely to find an implied, contractual limit on termination when:

- the agency relationship is outside the employment context,
- the limitation is asserted against the principal, and

---

6. Nonagency law may provide for such compulsion. For example, a state statute may protect sales representatives against unfair termination and may allow a court to order Marge's reinstatement.

7. In the employment context, this situation is known as *employment at will,* and the employment at will doctrine dates back more than a century. Many modern commentators have attacked the doctrine, and some courts have created exceptions relating, for example, to retaliatory firing of whistleblowers and to promissory estoppel. Statutory developments have also made inroads. Statutes prohibiting employment discrimination, for instance, do not directly require an employer to have "good cause" to terminate an employee but do prohibit an employer from terminating an employee for bad cause—i.e., in violation of the statutory rules prohibiting discrimination. For the most part, however, the employment at will doctrine remains intact.

- either
  - —the principal's manifestations are the source of the implication, or
  - —the agent has reasonably incurred costs in undertaking the agency and needs time to earn back those costs.

Example: A manufacturer retains a salesperson as the manufacturer's selling agent and states, "We will supply all the widgets you can sell during the next year." A court may imply a term under which, during that next year, the manufacturer has the right to terminate the agency only for cause.

Example: A manufacturer retains a salesperson as the manufacturer's selling agent. Nothing is said about duration, but the salesperson does buy from the manufacturer demonstration equipment costing $4,200. The manufacturer may be contractually obliged either to buy back the demonstration equipment or to let the agency exist long enough to allow the agent to recoup the $4,200 through commissions.

§5.2.3   *Non-Contract Limitations on the Right to Terminate*

The gratuitous agent.   If the agency is gratuitous, then by definition the agent's right to terminate is not limited by contract.[8] However, principles akin to promissory estoppel impose some restrictions. If a gratuitous agent (i) makes a promise or engages in other conduct that causes the principal to refrain from making different arrangements, and (ii) the gratuitous agent had reason to know that the principal would so rely, then:

- if alternative arrangements are still possible, the agent has a duty to end the agency only after giving notice so the principal can make alternative arrangements, and
- if alternative arrangements are not possible, the agent has a duty to continue to perform the agency as promised.

Like any other agent, a gratuitous agent always has the power to renounce. However, if a gratuitous agent improperly leaves the principal in the lurch, the agent will be liable for damages.

The principal.   Even if a principal has the right to terminate the agency at will, the principal may not exercise that right in bad faith. Most bad faith cases arise when a principal seeks to snatch some benefit away from the agent.

Example: Marcia tells Teri, "Find me a bona fide buyer for my restaurant and help put the paperwork together, and I'll pay you a finder's fee

---

8. Although an agency can exist without consideration, a contract generally requires consideration to be enforceable.

of $10,000." Teri finds a prospect. As soon as Marcia learns of the prospect, she tells Teri, "Changed my mind. Think I'll wait awhile." Marcia then contacts the prospect directly and arranges the sale. Even though the agency relationship contained no express limitations on Marcia's right to terminate the relationship, Marcia will be liable to Teri for the finder's fee. Marcia terminated the relationship in bad faith.

§5.3   Effects of Termination

§5.3.1   *Effects on Agent's Authority and Power to Bind Principal*

According to traditional common law principles, the agent's actual authority to bind the principal terminates when the agency terminates. Any inherent agency power also ends, because that power presupposes the status of general agent.

The fate of the agent's apparent authority depends on the reason the agency terminated. If the principal has died or lacks capacity, the agent's apparent authority terminates immediately. In other circumstances, the agent's apparent authority terminates as to any particular third party only when (i) the third party learns that the agency has ended, or (ii) in light of other information, the third party can no longer reasonably believe that the agent is authorized to act.

> *Example:* Melinda is a rancher. Sam is a horse breeder. On Monday, Melinda introduces Rebecca to Sam as "my agent for buying horses." On Tuesday, as Rebecca is negotiating with Sam, Melinda dies. Unaware of the death, Rebecca and Sam reach agreement on a horse purchase and Rebecca purports to bind Melinda. Melinda's estate is not bound, however, because Melinda's death terminated Rebecca's apparent as well as actual authority.[9]

> *Example:* Same situation, but Melinda does not die. Instead, Melinda fires Rebecca for insubordination but fails to tell Sam. The next day, Rebecca purports to buy a horse from Sam for Melinda. Rebecca's action binds Melinda, although the firing ended Rebecca's actual authority. Because neither death nor incapacity caused the agency relationship to end, Rebecca's apparent authority remained intact.

> *Example:* Jeff is a long-time customer of Hunter Brokerage Company ("Hunter") and has always done his investing through Dottie, one of Hunter's agents. One afternoon, unbeknownst to Jeff, Hunter fires Dottie. That night Dottie calls Jeff with a "hot tip" and urges Jeff to make a

---

9. Rebecca is therefore liable for breach of the warranty of authority. See section 4.2.2.

quick investment of $5,000. Dottie explains that the opportunity may disappear "overnight" and persuades Jeff to bring the $5,000 to Dottie's home. Dottie has never before tried to rush Jeff's decision, and Jeff has sent all past investment funds to the offices of Hunter. Jeff probably cannot hold Hunter accountable for Dottie's actions. The termination of the agency relationship has ended Dottie's actual authority to bind Hunter, and Dottie probably lacks apparent authority as well. Given Dottie's two deviations from standard practice, Jeff could no longer reasonably believe that Dottie was authorized to act for Hunter.

In some jurisdictions, statutes have changed the common law, providing that upon a principal's death or incapacity the agent's actual authority continues until the agent knows of the death or incapacity and the apparent authority continues until the third party knows.[10] Other statutes allow principals to execute documents creating agency powers that survive the principal's disability or incapacity, even after the disability or incapacity becomes known.[11]

The Restatement (Third) of Agency proposes to reformulate the common law rules in this area:

> The impact of the principal's death on an agent's actual authority has the potential to create harsh consequences because the agent, unaware of the principal's death, may continue to act in good faith following it. The agent risks claims from third parties that the agent breached express or implied warranties of authority. . . . Third parties risk the loss of transactions to which the agent committed the principal. Legislation has long mitigated the common-law result. Widespread adoption of consistent legislation of general applicability is a reliable measure of contemporary policy. The residual common-law rule should reflect the policy judgments reflected in legislation such as the Uniform Commercial Code, the Uniform Durable Power of Attorney Act, and contemporary partnership statutes.[12]

Accordingly, Restatement (Third) §§3.07(2) and 3.08(1) state that:

> The death of an individual principal terminates the agent's actual authority. The termination is effective only when the agent has notice of the principal's death. The termination is also effective as against a third party with whom the agent deals when the third party has notice of the principal's death.[13]
>
> An individual principal's loss of capacity to do an act terminates the agent's actual authority to do the act. The termination is effective only

10. Uniform Durable Power of Attorney Act §4 (1979) (applicable to written powers of attorney).

11. Uniform Durable Power of Attorney Act §2 (1987).

12. Restatement (Third) §3.07 (T.D. No. 2, 2001) (March 14, 2001) (Death, Cessation of Existence, and Suspension of Powers), comment *d*.

13. Restatement (Third) §3.07(2) (T.D. No. 2, 2001) (March 14, 2001) (Death, Cessation of Existence, and Suspension of Powers).

when the agent has notice that the principal's loss of capacity is permanent or that the principal has been adjudicated to lack capacity. The termination is also effective as against a third party with whom the agent deals when the third party has notice that the principal's loss of capacity is permanent or that the principal has been adjudicated to lack capacity.[14]

As to apparent authority, Restatement (Third) §3.11, comment *b*, states: "A principal's death or loss of capacity does not by itself or automatically end the agent's apparent authority."[15]

> *Example:* Same facts as in the Example on page 159 involving Melinda's death. Subject to any contrary provisions of applicable estate law, Melinda's estate is bound. Neither the agent (Rebecca) nor the third party (Sam) had notice of her death, so at the time of the transaction the agent had both actual and apparent authority.

§5.3.2 *Agent's Obligation to Cease Acting for Principal*

Once the agency relationship ends, the former agent has a duty not to act for the principal. If the former agent violates this duty and binds the former principal, the former agent will be liable for damages.[16]

§5.3.3 *Principal's Duty to Indemnify Agent*

The termination of the agency relationship does not eliminate any right of indemnity that the agent may have on account of events that occurred before the termination.

> *Example:* As an authorized part of her lobbying for Capitalist, Inc., Veronica "wines and dines" important people. She periodically submits her bills to Capitalist for reimbursement. Capitalist one day decides that having lobbyists is not good for its image and therefore terminates its relationship with Veronica. At that time, Veronica has $500 of reimbursement claims submitted but as yet unpaid and $400 of expenses incurred but not yet submitted for reimbursement. Veronica is entitled to both the $500 and the $400. Both amounts relate to events that occurred before the termination of the agency relationship.

---

14. Restatement (Third) §3.08(1) (T.D. No. 2, 2001) (March 14, 2001) (Loss of Capacity).

15. Restatement (Third) §3.11 (T.D. No. 2, 2001) (March 14, 2001) (Termination of Apparent Authority), comment *d*.

16. This duty is similar to an agent's duty not to act without or beyond its authority. See section 4.1.2. When it reaches this issue, the Restatement (Third) will presumably provide that the former agent's duty begins only when the agent has notice that the relationship has ended. In particular, when the principal dies or becomes incapacitated, the agent's duty to cease acting for the principal will begin only when the agent has notice of the death or incapacity. See section 5.3.1.

§5.3.4 *Agent's Right to Compete with Principal*

While an agency relationship exists, the agent's duty of loyalty precludes competition with the principal. Unless the principal consents, the agent must refrain from engaging in any competitive activity that relates to the scope of the agency relationship.[17]

Once the agency relationship ends, however, so does the absolute barrier to competition. Public policy strongly favors free competition, and the former agent has a right to compete with its former principal. A former agent may even recruit customers from the former principal's clientele.[18]

The right to compete does, however, have three limitations: a prohibition against using the former principal's confidential information; the duty to "get out clean"; and the obligation to abide by any valid "noncompete" agreements.

Prohibition against using the former principal's confidential information. The agent's duty not to disclose or exploit the principal's confidential information[19] clearly continues after the agency relationship ends. Disputes about the duty center around the question of just what kinds of information are protected from use.

Although in theory the same question exists during the agency relationship, at that juncture the question has far less practical import. Most alleged misuses involve some form of competition, and during the agency relationship competition is itself barred. As a result, during the relationship a claim of misuse of confidential information is often just a "tag along" to a claim of improper competition. The question of whether allegedly misused information is truly confidential (and therefore protected) is unlikely to be crucial.

Post-termination competition, however, is not by itself improper,[20] and a claim of information misuse can therefore be crucially important in a conflict between former principal and former agent. In that context the question of what constitutes confidential information can be dispositive.

Analyzing that question can involve two different but complementary perspectives:

1. Does the information warrant protection as a trade secret? That is:
   - Has the principal expended effort and incurred expense to obtain or create the information?
   - Does the principal derive economic advantage from the information not being generally known?

---

17. See section 4.1.1.

18. However, customer lists can be confidential information. If so, a former agent will breach a duty by making use of the lists to compete with the former principal.

19. See section 4.1.1.

20. A valid "noncompete" agreement can make post-termination competition improper. See below.

- Has the principal used reasonable efforts to protect the confidentiality of the information?
2. Does the information consist of facts or specialized techniques as distinguished from general expertise that an agent might develop while performing agency tasks?

Duty to "get out clean."   During the agency relationship an agent may properly contemplate post-termination competition with the principal. An agent may not, however, disregard its current loyalty obligations to further its post-termination plans. Put colloquially, the agent must "get out clean."

This duty has two major aspects. First, the agent has a duty not to begin actual competition while still an agent. During the agency relationship, discussions with customers or potential customers of the principal violate the duty of loyalty. Also, attempts to enlist other key agents of the principal may violate the duty of loyalty. The agent may, however, have discussions and even make agreements with parties *other than customers, potential customers, and key fellow agents* of the principal. For instance, the agent may properly have stationery printed, rent an office, and apply for a license.

Second, the agent may not actively deceive the principal as to the agent's reasons for terminating the agency relationship. The agent probably has no affirmative duty to provide reasons or even to respond if the principal asks "Why are you quitting?" The agent may not, however, lie to conceal its plan to compete. Moreover, subject to its right not to reveal its plans for the future, the agent must continue to provide agency-related information to the principal[21] right up to the moment that the agency ends.

An agent who fails to "get out clean" may be liable to the former principal both for damages and for disgorgement.[22]

> *Example:* May works as the headmaster of a private school. Frustrated by policies set by the board of trustees, she decides to start her own school. Before resigning, she discusses her plans with several of the private school's major donors and obtains commitments from them for start-up funding. She also copies the private school's mailing list of the families of current students. Her actions breach her duty of loyalty. She has the right to compete with the private school for donations, but only after she terminates her agency relationship. She never has the right to purloin her principal's mailing list.

Noncompetition obligations imposed by contract.   A contract between the principal and agent can restrain the agent from competing after the relationship ends, although the law's strong pro-competition stance causes courts

---

21. See section 4.1.5.

22. See section 4.1.7 for a discussion of the principal's remedies for an agent's breach of the duty of loyalty.

to scrutinize such agreements carefully. The restraints must be reasonable with respect to the scope of activities foreclosed, the geographic area foreclosed, and the duration of the foreclosure. In some states, overbroad restraints are simply unenforceable. In most states, however, courts will "blue-pencil" over-broad "noncompetes"—carving the restraints back until they are reasonable.

Despite the judicial skepticism, contractual noncompetes are common and quite important whenever an agent is likely to develop strong relationships with the principal's customers.

> *Example:* A wholesale tire company assigns a three-state territory to a sales representative and instructs that representative "to get to know every potential buyer in the territory. Get them to know us and like us." As the sales rep fulfills those instructions, there will almost necessarily develop a personal relationship between the sales rep and the tire whole-saler's customers. It makes little sense for the tire wholesaler to pay the sales rep to develop all this "good will," if the sales rep can simply resign and take the business to a competing wholesaler.

PROBLEM 50

For the past several years Ventura Company ("Ventura") has been acting as a buying agent for Ilan Enterprises ("Ilan") in the U.S. soybean market. Ventura has had authority to make purchases up to $250,000 without prior approval from Ilan.

Recently, Ilan discovered improprieties in Ventura's conduct. Ilan wishes to terminate the relationship immediately and wants to know how to do so. Ilan is also concerned about its responsibility if Ventura continues to trade on Ilan's account even after Ilan terminates the relationship. Advise Ilan how best to proceed.

EXPLANATION

Ilan can terminate the agency simply by giving notice to Ventura. A principal always has the power to terminate an agency. In this instance Ilan also has the right to do so, since the facts reveal no express or implied agreement as to term. Ilan should make the notice in writing and use some means of transmission that allows proof of delivery. (Agency law does not require written notice. The writing and delivery precautions are to simplify proof.)

As for the possibility that Ventura will bind Ilan through post-termination trading, the termination notice will end Ventura's actual authority and inherent agency power.[23] Ilan should be concerned, however, with Ventura's lingering apparent authority. If Ilan has a list of traders and other parties with whom Ventura has dealt, Ilan should send each a brief notice, stating in effect that "Effective [date of termination] Ventura Company is no longer authorized to sell, buy, make trades, or conduct any other business for Ilan Enter-

---

23. See section 5.3.1.

prises."[24] This notice will prevent the recipients from reasonably believing that Ventura remains authorized and will thereby stop them from claiming apparent authority as to any future transactions.

Ilan must also consider the rest of the marketplace. It is possible that Ventura possesses apparent authority in the soybean market generally—even with parties who have never dealt with Ventura. Ventura may have previously and accurately described itself as having authority, and that description is attributable to Ventura's principal.[25] Moreover, the Ventura-Ilan relationship may be generally known, with that knowledge traceable to the fact that Ilan has followed through on deals made by Ventura.

Because this aspect of the problem relates to a possible public perception, public preventative measures are necessary. Ilan should identify some trade publication or other medium of communication that reaches those who participate in the soybean market and insert in that medium the same "no longer authorized" notice just described.

Besides addressing the apparent authority concerns, Ilan's private and public notices will also block attempts to claim agency by estoppel. Knowing that market participants might believe Ventura is still authorized to act for Ilan and that they "might change their position because of it," Ilan will have taken "reasonable steps to notify them of the facts."[26]

PROBLEM 51

Roseanne gets a job at a posh new restaurant in an upscale mall where the waitstaff all wear uniforms. Each uniform costs $55 dollars, and the restaurant requires Roseanne to buy four before starting work. Three days after Roseanne starts work the restaurant manager decides that the staff is too large for the current volume of business. He fires the newest employee—Roseanne. Does Roseanne have any recourse?

EXPLANATION

The answer will probably depend on how strongly the relevant jurisdiction adheres to the employment-at-will doctrine. Roseanne will argue that, by requiring her to buy so many uniforms, the restaurant impliedly agreed not to terminate her without cause at least until she had worked long enough to

---

24. As a matter of agency law, the notice need not explain why this change has occurred; as a matter of *defamation* law, the notice *should* not explain. (Even if the explanation were accurate and even though truth is a defense to a defamation claim, why invite trouble?)

25. See section 2.3.3 (agent has implied actual authority to accurately describe its authority to act for the principal).

26. Restatement §8B(1)(b). See section 2.5. Note that this Explanation does not mention that Ventura would be breaching a duty if it purported to act for Ilan after receiving a termination notice. Although that assertion is correct, see section 5.3.2, the breach of duty is not relevant to the issue presented.

make the uniform purchase an economically rational act. As a fall-back, she will argue that the restaurant must buy the uniforms back from her.

PROBLEM 52

Eli is a regional sales agent for Maurice Ball Bearing, Inc. ("Maurice"). Eli and Maurice have a written agreement that (i) grants Eli an exclusive territory in which to promote and solicit orders for Maurice products, (ii) provides that Eli has no authority to accept any order on behalf of Maurice and that all sales will be made by Maurice directly to customers, (iii) establishes a commission schedule, (iv) requires Eli to follow lawful and ethical business practices but otherwise allows him complete discretion in how he conducts his operations, and (v) allows either party to terminate the relationship without cause on seven days' notice. Under the commission schedule, Eli qualifies for a $25,000 bonus in any calendar year in which he books orders aggregating more than $3 million.

It is October. So far Eli has booked $2.8 million, and he will certainly reach the bonus level by year's end. However, Maurice has decided for its own reasons to "go direct" in Eli's region. That is, Maurice wishes to use its own employees, rather than Eli, to solicit orders. The CEO of Maurice wishes to terminate Eli immediately and asks you for legal advice. Provide it.

EXPLANATION

Maurice has the power to terminate its agent at any time and appears to have the right to do so simply on seven days' notice. However, with Eli so close to qualifying for the bonus, a precipitous termination could raise suspicions of bad faith. A principal has no right to terminate an agency merely to deprive the agent of benefits that the agent is on the verge of earning.

Even if Maurice succeeds in demonstrating a good faith reason for terminating Eli, Eli might still make trouble by claiming breach of an implied agreement. He could argue that the agreement, which offers a large bonus based on a calendar year's effort, impliedly prohibits Maurice from terminating at year's end any agent who is about to earn the bonus, unless the agent has engaged in misconduct.

If Maurice believes it essential to terminate the agency before year's end, in the long run Maurice may find it less expensive and less stressful to send with the termination notice an offer to pay the $25,000 bonus.

PROBLEM 53

May works as an agent for Broker, Inc., a company that, for a commission, helps U.S. firms sell goods to foreign governments. May's responsibilities include traveling around the United States to try to persuade U.S. companies to use Broker's services. During one trip May decides to go into business for herself. Aware (because Broker has told her) that the government of Argentina is seeking bids for major construction projects, May contacts a number of U.S. companies. She gets "in the door" as a representative of Broker, but once in she tells the companies that she will soon be providing the same services as Broker—and for a lower commission. She does not, however, close any deals for herself. At the end of the trip, May returns to Broker's home office and resigns. She explains her resignation by saying that her brother-in-law has offered her a job in the family upholstery business. May then promptly sets up her own firm, pursues the contacts she made on the last trip, and lands a number of lucrative contracts related to the Argentine project. Does Broker have any recourse against May?

EXPLANATION

Broker has a claim for disgorgement of May's profits. In two and perhaps three ways, May has breached her duty of loyalty. First, by promoting her own services in contrast to Broker's, she began to compete while still an agent. Second, she lied to her principal about her reasons for leaving. Third, her pursuit of contracts related to the Argentine project *may* have been a misuse of Broker's confidential information. Broker's information about the project certainly was of economic importance to Broker, but Broker would have to show in addition that (a) the existence of the project was not generally known, (b) Broker had expended effort or expense to obtain the information, and (c) Broker used reasonable means to protect the information.

PROBLEM 54

Captain Miles Standish found himself deeply in love with "the damsel Priscilla." Unfortunately, Captain Standish was a shy fellow (except in matters of war) and could not find within himself the strength to approach Priscilla on his own behalf. He turned, instead, to his good friend John Alden. He asked Alden to visit Priscilla and express to her Standish's feelings.

Alden also loved Priscilla, but did not mention that fact to Standish. Instead, "[f]riendship prevailed over love," and Alden agreed to act on Standish's behalf. Alden went to Priscilla's house and explained his mission. Priscilla responded with the immortal words, "Why don't you speak for yourself, John?" Consistent with the principles of agency law, could he? If not, what could he have done to free himself to speak?

EXPLANATION

Alden may not speak for himself right away. He has consented to act on Standish's behalf. He is therefore Standish's agent and has a duty of loyalty that bars selfish conduct. That he is acting gratuitously affects neither his status as agent nor his duty of selflessness. While he remains Standish's agent, Alden simply cannot advance his own cause adverse to his principal's interests.

If Alden wishes to respond to Priscilla's invitation, he must first "get out clean" from his agency. To do so, he must notify Standish that he (Alden) can no longer represent Standish's interests to Priscilla. Although Alden probably has no duty to disclose that he intends to compete for Priscilla's attention, he probably does have a duty to report to Standish what Priscilla has said. That information came to Alden during his agency, and he has reason to know that his principal would consider the information important. He therefore must communicate that information to his principal.

Once has he done so, he may terminate the agency. Then he may indeed speak for himself.[27]

---

27. It might seem at first glance that Alden may not use his knowledge of Priscilla's interest, because he gained that information during the agency. However, the information is not Standish's property; it is not confidential to Standish. Priscilla can rightfully disclose the information as she sees fit.

6

Distinguishing Agency from Other Relationships

§6.1   Agency and Other Beneficial Relationships

§6.1.1   The Existence and Meaning of the Issue

There are a myriad of relationships in which one party benefits another, but not all "beneficial" relationships qualify as agency relationships. Consider, for example, the relationship between you and:

- the dry cleaner that cleans your wool sweater,
- the firefighter who carries you out of a burning building,
- the stationery store that provides you legal pads,
- the law school that provides you a legal education,
- the bank that provides you a student loan,
- the trustee who administers the trust fund established for you by your late, lamented, rich aunt.

In each of these relationships, the other party provides you benefits (goods, services, money), without becoming your agent. Likewise, an executor of an estate benefits the heirs and the conservator of a person benefits the conservatee, but neither the executor nor the conservator are agents.

Agency *vel non*[1] is often a high stakes issue because the agency label carries significant legal consequences. Indeed, disputes about the label are essentially

---

1. This Latin phrase means "or not" and is a very useful term of art because so many points of legal analysis involve "yes/no" characterizations.

disputes about those consequences. The consequences can follow from agency law itself or from the interaction of agency status and some other body of law.

Example: A grain elevator goes bankrupt owing money to local farmers and to the multinational company that provided the elevator a line of credit. The farmers try to establish that the elevator acted as the agent of the multinational company and not merely as a debtor. The farmers care about the "agent" label only as a means of establishing that the multinational company is liable for the debts incurred by the elevator.

Example: A cattle rancher sells cattle to a cattle company, which resells the cattle to a meat packer. The meat packer pays the cattle company, but the cattle company fails to pay the rancher. The rancher seeks to characterize the cattle company as the meat packer's agent and not an independent buyer/reseller, so that agency law attribution rules will make the meat packer liable for the unpaid contract.

Example: A manufacturer markets its products by delivering them to intermediaries who then sell them to the ultimate users at a price dictated by the manufacturer. Accused of an antitrust violation known as "resale price maintenance," the manufacturer asserts that the intermediaries are its agents and not distributors and so the resale price maintenance rule does not apply.

Example: A service station operator obtains gas from an oil company and sells it to customers. The operator fails to pay for the gas and is charged with embezzlement. The prosecution asserts that the operator was the oil company's agent and therefore: (i) the proceeds from the sale belonged to the oil company, minus only the operator's agreed-upon commission, and (ii) the operator had a fiduciary duty to turn the proceeds over to the oil company. The operator defends by denying an agency relationship and asserting that a *buyer's* failure to pay for goods is not criminal.

§6.1.2 *Distinguishing Agency from Other Similar Relationships*

Disputes over the existence of an agency relationship usually relate to one of the two fundamental characteristics of an agency: the principal's right of control and the fiduciary nature of the relationship. For an agency to exist, the party receiving the benefits must have the right to control at least the goals of the relationship and the person providing the benefits must be acting "on behalf of" the person receiving the benefits.[2] A beneficial relationship that lacks either or both of these characteristics is not an agency.

---

2. These characteristics are introduced in sections 1.2.7 and 1.2.8.

Figure 6-1. The Universe of Those Who Provide Benefits to Others

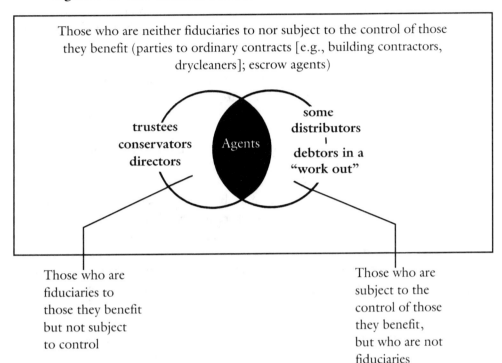

Those who are neither fiduciaries to nor subject to the control of those they benefit (parties to ordinary contracts [e.g., building contractors, drycleaners]; escrow agents)

trustees
conservators
directors

Agents

some
distributors
|
debtors in a
"work out"

Those who are
fiduciaries to
those they benefit
but not subject
to control

Those who are
subject to the
control of those
they benefit,
but who are not
fiduciaries

Agency *vel non* disputes typically have an either/or structure. One party asserts an agency, while the other seeks to place the relationship into some non-agency category. For example, in the case of the bankrupt grain elevator, the plaintiff farmers contended "agent," while the multinational company asserted "debtor." In the gas station embezzlement case, the prosecution asserted "agent," while the defense contended "independent distributor."

Following are examples of beneficial relationships that resemble agencies closely enough to supply the "or" in the typical either/or analysis. (For graphic representation of the following material, see Figure 6-1 above.)

- **Party Providing the Benefit Is a Fiduciary But Is Not Subject to Control.**
  — *Trustee of a trust and the trust beneficiary.* The trustee is obliged to act solely for the benefit of the beneficiary, but the beneficiary does not have the right to control the trustee.[3]

---

3. The Restatement (Second) of Trusts §8 (Trust and Agency) states in its black letter that "An agency is not a trust" and in its comment provides a more elaborate explanation of why:

   a. Title. A trustee has title to the trust property; an agent as such does not have title to the property of his principal, although he may have powers with respect to it.

—*Conservator and conservatee.* Appointed by a court to take care of the financial affairs or personal decisions (or both) of an incompetent person, the conservator is obliged to act in the best interests of the conservatee. The conservatee has neither the right nor power to control the conservator.

—*Directors of a corporation and the corporation.* Although the directors do owe duties of loyalty to the corporation, the corporation does not control the directors. To the contrary, the directors control the corporation.[4]

- **Party Providing the Benefits Is Subject to Control But Is Not a Fiduciary.**

  —*Distributor of goods and its supplier.* Some distribution agreements give the supplier considerable control over the distributor, regarding, for example: (a) where the distributor can resell the goods, (b) how the distributor may advertise the goods, (c) what kinds of after-sale service the distributor must provide. The distributor is not the supplier's agent, however, because the relationship's primary purpose is not to benefit the supplier. In this arm's-length transaction, each party's own interest is primary to that party.[5]

  —*Supplier of specially designed goods and its customer.* Sometimes a customer may exercise considerable control over its supplier. For example, if the customer is buying components from the supplier to incorporate into the customer's own products, the customer may: (i) design the component, (b) specify the raw materials the supplier is

---

b. Control. An agent undertakes to act on behalf of his principal and subject to his control; a trustee as such is not subject to the control of the beneficiary, except that he is under a duty to deal with the trust property for his benefit in accordance with the terms of the trust and can be compelled by the beneficiary to perform this duty.

c. Liability. An agent may subject his principal to personal liabilities to third persons; a trustee cannot subject the beneficiary to such liabilities.

d. Consent. An agency is created by the consent of the principal and the agent; a trust may be created without the knowledge or consent of the beneficiary or of the trustee.

e. Termination. An agency can be terminated at the will of either the principal or the agent and is terminated by the death or incapacity of either. A trust is not ordinarily terminable at the will of either the beneficiary or the trustee or by the death or incapacity of either. The mere fact that by the terms of the trust a power of revocation is reserved to the settlor does not make the trustee an agent.

(Citations and cross references omitted.)

4. Some commentators describe directors as the agents of the shareholders (i.e., of the people and organizations who own stock in the corporation). Although used in this way the agency concept helps analyze certain corporate law issues, the usage does not fit with the legal definition of agency. Shareholders have the right to exercise only limited and intermittent control over the directors.

5. Moreover, some arguably crucial aspects of control are lacking, such as the power to set the distributor's resale price.

to use, and (c) even insist on the right to approve the supplier's methods for producing the component. The supplier is not the customer's agent, however, because the relationship's primary purpose is not to benefit the customer. In this arm's-length transaction, each party to the relationship seeks its own benefit, and neither party's benefit is primary.[6]

- **Party Providing Benefits Is Not a Fiduciary and Is Not Subject to Control.**

  —*Parties to an ordinary contract ("independent contractors" or "non-agent service providers").* An ordinary contract is a so-called "arm's length" relationship. Neither party has consented to serve primarily the interests of the other; to the contrary, each party has entered into the contract to further its own interests. Neither party has agreed to act "on behalf" of the other, and the contract does not contemplate one party having any "power to subject the [other party] to personal liability" to third parties.[7] Both parties are subject to the obligations of the contract, but that control device is a product of the agreement between the parties.

  In the terminology of the Restatement (Second) of Agency, a person who provides benefits to another under a *non-agency,* contractual relationship is an "independent contractor."[8] That usage is confusing because the Restatement (Second) also uses the same term to describe *agents* who are not servants—i.e., independent contractor agents.[9] The Restatement (Third) of Agency proposes to use "non-agent service provider" instead of non-agent "independent contractor."[10]

  A building contractor is often described as the classic example of an independent contractor (in Restatement (Third) terms: a non-agent service provider). However, *most* commercial and consumer relationships involve non-agent service providers:

Example: Exhausted but exalted after completing your final exams, you decide to go to a local shopping mall for some "R & R." Contemplating the eventual consumption of alcoholic beverages, you decide to take the bus rather than drive. The bus company is a non-agent service provider.

---

6. Some courts, seeking the liability consequences that attach to the agency label, will ignore the fiduciary element of the agency relationship and find agency based on control alone. See sections 3.2.4, n.6 and 4.1.1, n.1 (for respondeat superior purposes, servant status need not be considered a subcategory of agent status) and section 6.3 (Restatement §14 O and *Cargill*).

7. Restatement (Second) §12 (Agent as Holder of a Power).

8. Restatement (Second) §14 N, comment *b*.

9. Restatement (Second) §14 N, comment *a*.

10. Restatement (Third) of Agency Reps. Mem. (T.D. No. 1, 2000) (March 20, 2000). The Restatement (Third) also proposes to eliminate the servant/independent contractor terminology.

When you are at the mall, you enter "Sharon's Custom T-Shirts" and purchase a custom-made T-shirt that says, "I Survived the Rule Against Perpetuities." Sharon's relationship to you as she prepares and sells the T-shirt is that of an independent contractor. Slipping on your new T-shirt, you proceed to "Don't Doubt This Thomas—Homemade Desserts," where you purchase a dish of peach cobbler, which is handed to you by Malika, the general manager of the store. Malika is an agent of the store, but the store is acting as an independent contractor when it provides you the peach cobbler.

> —*Escrow holder and parties to the escrow agreement.* When two parties agree that a third will hold an item of value (e.g., money, stock, a deed) until specified conditions are met and then deliver the item per the agreement, the item is considered in escrow and the third party is the escrow holder. Neither of the escrow parties has a right to control the escrow holder, who is obligated only to perform as the escrow agreement requires. The escrow holder does not act primarily for the benefit of either party to the escrow agreement, but rather acts to fulfill its own obligations. The escrow holder is therefore not an agent.

§6.2   Ersatz[11] Agency

In two related circumstances, what may appear to be an agency is in fact a different, irrevocable, non-agency relationship. In each situation:

- one person grants another the right to bind the grantor and lacks the power (not merely the right) to revoke that grant;
- the authority to bind is granted *not* to benefit the grantor (i.e., the party who seems like a principal), but rather to benefit the grantee (i.e., the party who seems like the agent), and
- the grantee (not the grantor) is in charge.[12]

The two circumstances go under the names of "agency (or power) coupled with an interest" and "authority (or power) given as security."[13]

---

11. From the German, meaning "seeming proper but actually not genuine."

12. This description states the default rules. The parties may agree to provide the grantor a right of revocation.

13. The Restatement (Third) of Agency proposes to treat the former concept as encompassed within the latter. Tentative Draft No. 2 (March 14, 2001), §§1.04(7) and 3.12(1) each define "Power given as security" as "A power given as security is a power to affect the legal relations of its creator that is created in the form of a manifestation of actual authority and held for the benefit of the holder or a third person. It is given to protect a legal or equitable title or to secure the performance of a duty apart from any duties owed the holder of the power by its creator that are incident to a relationship of agency. . . ." Section 1.04, comment *g* states "A power coupled with an interest is an instance of a power given as security." See also §3.12, comment *c.*

§6.2.1 Power Coupled with an Interest

For a power to be coupled with an interest:

- the grantee's power (i.e., the authority to bind, which appears like agency authority) must relate to some particular right or other property, and
- the same transaction that establishes the grantee's power must also provide the grantee some "interest" in that particular right or other property.

Example: Ophelia owns 200 acres of land. To cause Hamlet to sell the land for her, she gives him an undivided one-tenth interest in the land, coupled with an irrevocable power of attorney to sell her interest at any price above $500 per acre. Hamlet's power relates to the land, and he has received that power at the same time he has received an interest in the land. The power is coupled with an interest and is irrevocable. Hamlet is not Ophelia's agent.

For the power to be "coupled with an interest," the power and the interest must relate to the same aspect of the particular property. If the grantee receives an interest not in the underlying property itself but rather in the proceeds that result from the grantee's exercise of the granted power, then a true agency results and the grantee's authority is revocable.

Example: As above, Ophelia owns 200 acres of land and wishes to have Hamlet sell them for her. Instead of giving him an interest in the land, however, she sends him a letter (i) giving him a right to 30 percent of the sale price over $300 per acre and (ii) purporting to grant him irrevocable authority to sell the land for $300 or more per acre. Hamlet's power is not coupled with an interest. His power relates to the land and his interest relates only to the proceeds of the sale of the land. Hamlet is Ophelia's agent, and despite the letter his authority is revocable.[14]

§6.2.2 Authority (or Power) Given as Security

If (i) an obligor owes a debt or other obligation to an obligee, and (ii) in order to provide the obligee with security the obligor grants the obligee a power to bind the obligor, then:

- no agency is created,
- the power is "given as security," and
- the power is irrevocable during the life of the obligor.

---

14. "The agent's interest in being paid a commission is an ordinary incident of agency and its presence does not convert the agent's authority into a power held for the agent's benefit." Restatement (Third), Tentative Draft No. 2 (March 14, 2001), §3.12 (Power Given as Security; Irrevocable Proxy), comment *b*. The letter probably does obligate Ophelia to refrain from revoking. She nonetheless retains the power to revoke. See section 5.2 (power versus right to terminate).

Example: Ophelia, in Dunsinane, appoints Hamlet as her agent to sell 700 crates of oranges being stored in a warehouse in Elsinore. Hamlet informs Ophelia that $500 of storage fees must be paid or the oranges will be sold by the warehouse. Ophelia has no funds available, and Hamlet agrees to advance the $500. To secure her obligation to repay Hamlet, Ophelia grants him the irrevocable right to collect all payments on the oranges and to repay himself from those proceeds before sending any money to Ophelia. The relationship between Ophelia and Hamlet is no longer an agency. Instead, Hamlet possesses a power given as security, which is irrevocable except through the death of Ophelia.

In this Example, the power given as security is *not* a power coupled with an interest. Hamlet has no interest in the underlying property (i.e., the oranges). Often, however, circumstances will satisfy both concepts, and a power given as security will also be a power coupled with an interest.

Example: Hamlet borrows money from Ophelia, and as collateral grants Ophelia a security interest[15] in 100 shares of stock in Birnam Forest, Inc. Hamlet also grants Ophelia his proxy to vote the stock. The proxy is "given as security" for the debt and is therefore irrevocable except by Hamlet's death. Moreover, since the same transaction that granted Ophelia the proxy also gave her a security interest in the underlying property, the proxy is "coupled with an interest." The proxy is therefore irrevocable even if Hamlet dies.[16]

§6.3   Constructive Agency

§6.3.1   *The* Cargill *Case and Restatement §14 O*

Sometimes a court construes a seemingly arm's-length arrangement into an agency relationship. The case of *A. Gay Jenson Farms v. Cargill, Inc.*[17] provides one of the best known examples of such *constructive agency.*

Cargill arose from the financial collapse of the Warren Grain & Seed Co. ("Warren"), a grain elevator located in rural Minnesota. Warren was in the business of buying grain from farmers and then reselling that grain on the market or directly to grain companies. Cargill, Inc. financed the operations of Warren (i.e., Cargill loaned the elevator money with which to operate) and also bought substantial amounts of grain from Warren. As Warren's debt to Cargill increased, Cargill exercised more and more control over Warren's operations.

---

15. A security interest is like a mortgage on personal rather than real property.

16. By its terms the proxy will likely be automatically revoked when the underlying debt is paid.

17. 309 N.W.2d 285 (Minn. 1981).

Warren's owners diverted large amounts of the company's money to their personal ends, and Warren's business eventually collapsed. At the time of the collapse Warren owed $2 million to farmers who had sold grain to Warren but had not been paid. Warren also owed $3.6 million to Cargill.

The farmers sought to recover their $2 million from Cargill, contending that (i) Warren was Cargill's agent, and (ii) Cargill, as principal, was liable on any grain contracts made by its agent. The jury, the trial judge, and the Minnesota Supreme Court all agreed.

Although *Cargill* also quoted and purported to apply §1 of the Restatement, the decision turns on §14 O. The comment to the latter section states in part:

> A security holder who . . . takes over the management of the debtor's business . . . and directs what contracts may or may not be made . . . becomes a principal, liable as any principal for the obligations incurred thereafter in the normal course of business by the debtor who has now become his general agent. The point at which the creditor becomes a principal is that at which he assumes de facto control over the conduct of his debtor, whatever the terms of the formal contract with his debtor may be.

The *Cargill* decision held that Cargill had indeed taken over the management of the debtor's business and had consequently become liable as a principal for Warren's debts to the farmer plaintiffs.

§6.3.2 *Conceptual Confusions and Practical Concerns*

The *Cargill* case is troubling both conceptually and practically. The court tries to justify its decision under §1 of the Restatement as well as under §14 O and thereby confuses constructive agency with true agency. Practically, the decision is dangerous for any creditor that eschews immediate foreclosure of a problem loan and tries instead to guide its debtor through a workout.[18]

Constructive versus genuine agency.   *Cargill* is confusing because it misunderstands the relationship between Restatement §§1 and 14 O. Although both sections concern agency creation, they apply to quite different situations and state different and even inconsistent rules.

For an agency to exist under §1, the principal must manifest consent for the agent to act on the principal's behalf, and the agent must manifest consent to do so. Section 15 states that "an agency relation can exist *only*" under such circumstances.[19] Yet §14 O, which also establishes agency status, nowhere mentions consent. Instead, it focuses exclusively on control.

---

18. When a debtor has difficulty paying its major lender, the lender can typically demand immediate payment of the full amount due, foreclose on any collateral, and put the debtor out of business. However, with that approach lenders rarely recover the full amount owed. Lenders therefore often try to help the debtor work its way out of its financial difficulties. Hence the term *workout*.

19. Emphasis added.

The inconsistency exists because the Restatement is using the same label ("agency") to describe two different kinds of situations:

(1)   "garden variety" situations, in which the parties act in a manner that reasonably suggests they intend to establish the consensual and fiduciary relationship of true agency, and

(2)   extraordinary situations, in which for policy reasons the law wishes to treat creditors and debtors *as if* they had manifested consent to the garden variety of agency.

The situations share a key consequence[20]—the principal's liability on contracts made by the agent—but the criteria that trigger the consequence are fundamentally different: For the garden variety situation, mutual consent; for the extraordinary situation, overbearing control.[21]

The rationales underlying the rules are likewise different. With a true agent, acting within its actual authority, liability arises at least in part from consent. In the extraordinary, §14 O situation, liability arises for reasons akin to the rationale for inherent agency power. That is, liability follows control, because: (1) those who exercise control have the ability to avoid harm and should therefore be liable when avoidable harm occurs; and (2) when an undertaking causes harm to others, the cost of that harm should be borne by those who stand to benefit from the undertaking and typically it is those in control who stand to benefit.

The *Cargill* case concerns an extraordinary situation, and the decision becomes confusing when it seeks to apply the garden variety rule (manifestation of consent; fiduciary relationship) as well as the extraordinary rule (exercise of control). Referring, for instance, to the *principal's* manifestation of consent, *Cargill* states, "By directing Warren to implement its recommendations, Cargill manifested consent that Warren would be its agent." This assertion seems to equate control with consent. If party *A* controls party *B,* then through that control *A* manifests consent that *B* act for *A in dealing with third parties*. Although such an inference may often be reasonable, it is not necessarily so. For example, a department store may control in detail the work assignments of a custodian without consenting to the custodian placing orders with dress manufacturers.

Equally troubling is the decision's treatment of the *agent's* manifestation of consent. In this respect the question is whether Warren manifested consent to place Cargill's interests above its own, that is, consented that the primary purpose of the relationship was to serve Cargill, not Warren. The *Cargill* court never mentions any direct evidence on this point. Instead the

---

20. In the extraordinary situation, the agency label does not produce all of the consequences that attend that label in the garden variety situation. No one suggests that under §14 O the debtor, as agent, owes a fiduciary duty to its principal, the creditor.

21. The control is "overbearing" in the sense that the creditor "takes over the management of the debtor's business." Restatement §14 O, comment *a*.

decision states: "Cargill believed that Warren was not free to become Cargill's competitor, but rather conceded that Warren owed a duty of loyalty to Cargill." The logic here is flawed. An agent's duty of loyalty includes the duty not to compete, but an agreement not to compete does not by itself establish either a full-fledged duty of loyalty or a fiduciary relationship. A party's agreement to defer to another party's interest in one specific area neither constitutes nor implies an agreement to defer to that other party's interest throughout the relationship. To the contrary, noncompete agreements occur in many arm's-length relationships.

The *Cargill* court would have made matters considerably clearer had it simply stated, "This situation warrants constructive agency analysis. Restatement §14 O applies, and therefore §1's garden variety criteria for establishing true agency are irrelevant."

Dangers for workouts. In applying Restatement §14 O, the *Cargill* court noted a number of factors that evidenced Cargill's control over Warren. The court acknowledged that many of these same factors appear in ordinary debtor-creditor transactions, but assured the banking community that ordinary delinquent loans were not destined to turn into principal-agent relationships.

To support its assurances, the Court noted the following differences between the Warren-Cargill relationship and an ordinary lending situation: (i) Cargill aggressively financed Warren; (ii) Cargill "was an active participant in Warren's operations rather than simply a financier"; (iii) Cargill's relationship with Warren was "paternalistic"; and (iv) Cargill's purpose in lending money to Warren "was not to make money as a lender but rather to establish a source of market grain for its business."

Of the four distinctions noted by the court, the first three (aggressive financing, involvement in the debtor's operations, a "paternalistic" attitude) occur in most workouts. The fourth purported distinction—that Cargill was really "in it" not for the interest but rather to obtain a supply of grain—is irrelevant under §14 O. That provision makes no reference at all to the creditor's purpose in becoming a creditor. Moreover, there are many lending relationships in which the lender seeks more than interest payments. A company like GMAC, for example, lends money to General Motors car dealers in part to allow them to buy cars from GM and lends money to the dealers' customers in order to allow them to buy GM cars from the GM dealers. Is GMAC in it just for the interest, or does GMAC have the ulterior motive of increasing the marketability of GM cars?

In sum, the *Cargill* court's attempt to distinguish the Cargill-Warren situation from normal debtor-creditor relationships is unpersuasive. For lenders considering workouts, the case is a cautionary tale.[22]

---

22. Although any informed lender's attorney will worry about *Cargill*, few other reported cases have taken the *Cargill* approach. Fewer than ten reported decisions have

PROBLEM 55

A housebuyer ("Would-Be") contacts a real estate broker ("Broker") and solicits her assistance in locating a suitable property. Would-Be seeks a modern, upscale house with enough land to allow the installation of a swimming pool. Over the next two months, Broker calls Would-Be frequently to discuss possible purchases, and occasionally goes with Would-Be to view properties. Eventually she locates a house that Would-Be decides to purchase. As Would-Be contemplates making the purchase, Broker explains that "my fee comes from the seller. It's no big deal. That's the way we do it. So you can figure out the price you're willing to pay without worrying about a commission."

Would-Be makes the purchase and subsequently discovers that his neighbors will raise zoning law objections to any pool. He also learns that the lower portion of his land is subject to flooding during the early spring. He sues Broker for not having informed him of these problems.

Assume that:

- Broker never thought of herself as Would-Be's agent, and never intended to act on Would-Be's behalf. She saw herself as acting at "arm's length" from him.
- Would-Be, in contrast, believed all along that Broker was "on my side, looking out for my interests."
- When Would-Be expressed serious interest in the house he eventually purchased, Broker contacted the seller and arranged to act as the seller's agent in the transaction.
- Other than her comment about the seller paying her fees, Broker never explained to Would-Be her view of her relationship to Would-Be. She never disclosed that she was acting as the seller's agent.
- Broker's view of the relationship is consistent with the way real estate brokers in the locality ordinarily approach similar matters.
- Broker knew that the neighbors would probably object to the building of a pool but never mentioned anything about that problem to Would-Be.
- Broker did not know about the flooding but could have discovered the problem through the exercise of ordinary care.

---

discussed Restatement §14 O. Only one affirmed recovery for the plaintiff, and another reversed summary judgment for the defendant. One case, Buck v. Nash-Finch Co., 102 N.W.2d 84 (S.D. 1960), acknowledged that a major creditor had controlled substantial portions of the debtor's operations but denied recovery because the major creditor had not controlled the particular area of operations that gave rise to the plaintiff's claim. Compare section 3.2.3 (respondeat superior liability attaches to servant's scope of employment not to master's zone of control). Another case held that Section 14 O imposed liability only when the controlling creditor had engaged in wrongdoing. Mere control was insufficient. Lubrizol Corp. v. Cardinal Construction Co., 868 F.2d 767 (5th Cir. 1989).

- Broker never made any representations to Would-Be concerning the pool or the flooding.
- There are no statutes or government regulations relevant to this situation.

Can Would-Be recover from Broker?[23]

EXPLANATION

Since Broker made no representations about the pool or the flooding, Would-Be can recover from Broker only if he can establish that Broker had an affirmative duty to disclose. Moreover, as to the flooding problem, Would-Be will also have to establish that Broker had a duty to inquire.

Both duties existed if Broker was acting as Would-Be's agent.[24] To establish that agency relationship, Would-Be must show (i) some manifestation from him that, reasonably interpreted, indicated his desire to have Broker act on his behalf, and (ii) some manifestation from Broker that, reasonably interpreted, indicated Broker's "consent . . . to so act."[25] The first showing is easy: Would-Be expressly and specifically solicited Broker's assistance. As for Broker's manifestation, her two months of effort provide at least a "peppercorn."

Broker's subjective view of the situation is irrelevant. What matters is the reasonableness of Would-Be's interpretation, and on that point the evidence is mixed. The local custom *as known to brokers* may weigh against reasonableness, but reasonableness is determined from the perspective of an ordinarily prudent person *in the position of the principal*. The facts do not indicate whether the brokers' custom is generally known and understood by ordinary homebuyers.

The payment arrangement may also weigh against reasonableness. If Broker was looking out for Would-Be's interests, why would someone else — especially the adverse party — be paying the fee? Although with the principal's consent an agent may receive compensation from a third party, arguably the circumstances were unusual enough to prompt a reasonable person to inquire.

Despite this negative evidence, Would-Be may still prevail by pointing to Broker's conduct as a whole. Would-Be sought out Broker and asked for her assistance. For two months Broker provided that assistance without once indicating her arm's length attitude. Moreover, when — at the crucial moment — Broker pledged allegiance to the adverse party, she failed to warn or even advise Would-Be. To the contrary, she induced his continuing trust by treating the fee question as "no big deal." Taking all these circumstances together, perhaps it was reasonable for Would-Be to believe that Broker had agreed to act on his behalf.

---

23. Many jurisdictions now have statutes or regulations governing this type of situation.

24. See sections 4.1.5 (agent's duty to disclose information which agent knows or should know is of interest to the principal) and 4.1.4 (agent's duty of care).

25. Restatement §1.

If so, Broker was acting as Would-Be's agent and was subject to duties of disclosure and due care. Broker would therefore be liable for damages suffered by Would-Be due to Broker's failure to disclose the zoning difficulty and for her failure to discover and disclose the flooding problem.[26]

PROBLEM 56

Tim buys a new truck from a local car dealer. The dealer purchases its truck inventory from the manufacturer under a dealership agreement. That agreement (i) states that the dealer is an independent contractor and not the agent of the manufacturer, (ii) acknowledges that the dealer, not the manufacturer, controls the management of the dealer's business, (iii) describes the three-year warranty that the manufacturer extends to customers who purchase the manufacturer's trucks through the manufacturer's network of dealers, (iv) obligates the dealer to provide service under the manufacturer's warranties at no charge to the customers, and (v) provides that the dealer will bill the manufacturer for this warranty service at specified rates. Each new truck comes with an owner's manual that describes the manufacturer's warranty and directs customers to have warranty service performed at any of the manufacturer's authorized dealers.

Tim is quite happy with his purchase for the first week. Then a problem develops in the truck's steering. Tim immediately notifies the dealer and brings the truck in for repair. Over the next two years, the truck has a series of problems with its steering mechanism. Each time a problem occurs, Tim brings the truck back to the dealer, and the dealer attempts to fix the problem. Each time the dealer assures Tim that "this is under warranty" and there is no charge. After two years, however, Tim has had enough. He decides to sue the dealer for breach of warranty and wishes also to sue the manufacturer.

Under the jurisdiction's version of the Uniform Commercial Code, a remote buyer (such as Tim) can bring a breach of warranty claim against the remote seller (such as the manufacturer) if the remote buyer has given timely notice of the defect to the remote seller or the remote seller has knowledge of the defect.[27] Tim has told the dealer of the problems as they have occurred, so the dealer has known of the defect since one week after the sale. Tim has never informed the manufacturer, however. Under the jurisdiction's case law, it is now too late to first notify the manufacturer. May Tim nonetheless bring a warranty claim against the manufacturer?

---

26. Note that if Broker was acting as Would-Be's agent, she has a "dual agency" problem. See section 4.1.1 (no acting for others with conflicting interests).

27. See Uniform Commercial Code §2-318 (third party beneficiaries of warranties) and §2-607(3)(a) (buyer must give timely notice of breach or be barred from remedy) and comment 5 (requirement of timely notice applies to remote buyer making third party beneficiary claim).

EXPLANATION

To safeguard his claim against the manufacturer, Tim must show that his notice to the dealer suffices as notice to the manufacturer. To do that he must use the attribution rules of agency law.

The agreement between the manufacturer and dealership expressly disclaims agency status, but the parties' actual relationship belies their words at least with regard to the manufacturer's warranty program. Through its customer warranty, the manufacturer undertook to provide services to Tim. Through its dealership agreement, the manufacturer manifested consent for the dealer to provide those services on the manufacturer's behalf and the dealer manifested consent to do so. For the purposes of providing warranty service, the dealer is indeed the manufacturer's agent.

Under this agency relationship, the dealer may have implied actual authority to receive notices of defects on the manufacturer's behalf. Implied actual authority exists as acts "which are incidental to . . . , usually accompany, . . . or are reasonably necessary to accomplish" expressly authorized acts,[28] and a customer typically invokes the manufacturer's warranty (and triggers the dealer's expressly authorized act) by communicating with the dealer. Notice received within an agent's actual authority (express or implied) binds the principal.

Even if the dealer is not authorized to receive notice on the manufacturer's behalf, the dealer's knowledge of the defect binds the manufacturer. The defect information certainly concerns a matter within the dealer's actual authority and is therefore attributed to the principal.[29]

PROBLEM 57

Fred Hornet ("Hornet") is a mid-level manager at Commerce Bank whose responsibilities include evaluating applicants for business loans. For the past several years, Hornet has been trying to persuade the Loan Committee (i.e., a committee of five senior managers that must approve any business loan) to take a more accommodating attitude toward loan applications from female- and minority-owned start-up businesses. The discussion has proceeded through several stages, with the key points being roughly as follows:

Hornet: Our regular evaluation criteria make it highly unlikely that we will approve loan applications from minority-owned or female-owned busi-

---

28. Restatement §35. See section 2.2.3.

29. See section 2.4.4. Tim might also assert that the dealer has apparent authority to receive notices for the manufacturer. This argument seems weaker than the actual authority arguments, because Tim can point to only two relevant manifestations of the principal: the appointment of the dealer as an authorized seller of the manufacturer's trucks and the direction in the owner's manual that customers have warranty work done at the manufacturer's authorized dealers. From these manifestations it is reasonable to believe that the dealer is authorized to act for the manufacturer in providing warranty service, but not necessarily that the dealer is authorized to accept pre-suit notices on the manufacturer's behalf.

nesses. We put a lot of weight on whether the key people in the new business have any significant prior entrepreneurial experience. It's a matter of history that, for women and minorities, access to that type of experience has been far more difficult to obtain. It's important morally, and for the social stability of our country, that we increase the access. As a practical matter, that access depends fundamentally on being able to borrow money. The way we're going now, though, it's a vicious circle. Can't borrow the money because not enough experience. Can't get experience running a small business because can't borrow any money to get one started. This bank quite rightfully prides itself on being "a good corporate citizen." To live up to our own ideals we need to relax our emphasis on prior entrepreneurial experience.

Loan Committee: We're with you in spirit, but we also have a responsibility to our stockholders and our depositors not to be careless in lending money. We have found that a lack of "prior entrepreneurial experience" tends to increase the likelihood of a loan going bad. What can you suggest to offset the increased risk?

Hornet: First, more rigorous attention to the application process—the applicant's proposed business plan, for instance. But, more importantly, I suggest an increased commitment at the bank to keeping an eye on these businesses. If we think that trouble is developing, we'll get in and work with the people—provide them advice, make sure they're using sensible business practices. In other words, if we find out that a lack of entrepreneurial experience is beginning to cost them (and threatening their ability to pay us back) we'll temporarily roll up our sleeves and help provide them the expertise that comes with experience. I realize that this approach involves an extra commitment of resources, but I think it's worth it.

Loan Committee: What if the borrowers don't want our help?

Hornet: I think for this program to work we have to be up front with the people, and tell them when they apply what might happen if things go sour later on. Also, we have to choose to lend to people whom we think will be willing to take help. Finally, under our standard loan agreements, if push comes to shove, we have the right to take control.

The Loan Committee is just about convinced to give Hornet's approach a try. Assume that they turn to you, as the Bank's lawyer, and ask, "Are there any legal wrinkles?" Advise them by (i) identifying and explaining any legal risks involved in Hornet's proposal, and (ii) suggesting changes in the proposal that will decrease those risks without sacrificing the business objectives.

EXPLANATION

Cargill and Restatement §14 O appear to create a Hobson's choice for the bank. Measures designed to meet the bank's business needs seem destined to increase the bank's legal risk. Moreover, the legal risks will be most substantial just when the business needs are the most intense. The bank is most likely to exert control when a borrower has fallen behind in its loan payments. At that juncture, the borrower is likely also to be falling behind in its obligations to other creditors. Exerting control will create a *Cargill* claim, and the other obligations will constitute the damages.

The solution to this conundrum lies in analyzing Hornet's proposal and separating, as follows, the tactical objective, the tactics proposed to achieve that objective, and the rationale that links those tactics to that objective:

- *Tactical objective:* Increase the quality of the borrower's management, especially at times of financial distress.[30]
- *Rationale:* All other things being equal, inexperienced management is likely to be less effective than experienced management. A firm, experienced hand is especially necessary when a business is trying to "workout" from under financial difficulties.
- *Tactics:* Empower the bank to be that firm, experienced hand.

This analysis indicates the source of the legal risks within Hornet's proposal and thereby suggests a way to reduce those risks. Section 14 O problems arise from control, and within Hornet's proposal the only flavor of control comes from the proposed tactics. Taking the tactical objective and the rationale as given,[31] the lawyer's challenge is to find substitute tactics that lack that flavor. In other words—to find another firm, experienced hand.

For example, the loan agreement might require the borrower to designate an experienced business consultant, acceptable to the Bank, to advise the borrower on an on-going basis, and temporarily turn over management of the business to that consultant (or some other independent business expert chosen by the Bank), if (i) the borrower falls behind in its loan payments or gives the Bank other reasonable grounds for insecurity and (ii) the Bank elects to require the management change. These arrangements would of course require the agreement of the specified consultant and experts, but that agreement could be obtained in advance. The loan agreement could also provide mechanisms for choosing replacements in case the designated individuals become unable or unwilling to serve.

In all events, it would be essential for the consultant and the expert to remain independent of the Bank. If the Bank controls them, they could be deemed the Bank's agents and *Cargill* could apply by attribution. The loan agreement should therefore provide that the consultant and the expert will each (i) work for and be paid by the borrower, not the Bank and (ii) have a duty to serve the best interests of the borrower, not the Bank. It should also provide that the Bank will have no right to control the advice given or the de-

---

30. The tactical objective is intended to make possible the pursuit of another objective—increasing the bank's lending to minority- and female-owned businesses.

31. It might be possible to propose additional options for the Bank by challenging the rationale. That approach is not pursued here, however, because that kind of analysis presupposes considerable familiarity with the way businesses function.

cisions made by either the consultant or the expert. The rationale and importance of these provisions should be explained to those Bank employees who deal with the borrower, so that the Bank's conduct (through those employees) conforms to these restrictions.

This structure is admittedly more cumbersome than Hornet's proposal and certainly provides less direct control for the Bank. The structure's virtue is that it significantly reduces the Bank's legal exposure while still serving the basic tactical objective of Hornet's plan.[32]

---

32. This approach will not work, however, if the Bank's objectives include causing the borrower to prefer the Bank's claims over the claims of other creditors. If that is an objective, *Cargill* exposure is probably inevitable and appropriate.

PART TWO

Partnerships and LLCs

7

Introductory Concepts in the Law of General Partnerships

§7.1   The Role, Structure, and Relationship of the Uniform Partnership[1] Act and Revised Uniform Partnership Act

§7.1.1 General Partnership: Creature of Contract and of Statute

A general partnership is a creature both of contract and of statute. Unlike most other business organizations, a general partnership is *not* created by filing a public document pursuant to an "organic" statute.[2] Instead, a general partnership arises when two or more persons manifest an intention to associate as co-owners in a business for profit. Their manifestations—whether by word or conduct or both—create what is essentially a contract between or among them.

---

1. U.S. law encompasses two forms of partnership: general partnerships and limited partnerships. Each of these forms has a version with a corporate-like liability shield for the owners: in the case of a general partnership, a limited liability partnership (LLP); in the case of a limited partnership, a limited liability limited partnership (LLLP). Whenever this book uses the term "partnership" by itself, the term refers to a general partnership without a liability shield. For a discussion of limited partnerships, see Chapter Twelve. For a discussion of LLPs and LLLPs, see Chapter Fourteen.

2. In the modern parlance of business entity law, an "organic" statute is a statute under which a business entity is created and whose provisions govern the internal relationships ("internal affairs") of those who own and operate the business entity.

Many general partnerships have detailed written partnership agreements, some running hundreds of pages long, while many other general partnerships have no written agreement at all. Regardless, one fundamental aspect of a general partnership is the contract-based relations among the partners.

Another equally fundamental aspect is the statutory context in which such contracts arise and exist. In every state, a partnership statute provides that context:

- determining whether a partnership exists,
- governing the relationship of the partnership and its partners with outsiders,
- governing—largely subject to the partnership agreement—the relationship among the partners and between the partners and the partnership, and
- determining when a partnership ceases to exist and what then happens to the partners' interests, the partnership's assets and the partnership's liabilities.

§7.1.2   *History and Prevalence of the UPA, Advent of RUPA*

For almost all of the twentieth century, the Uniform Partnership Act ("UPA") was the backbone of partnership law. Promulgated in 1914 by the National Conference of Commissioners on Uniform State Laws ("NCCUSL"), the Uniform Partnership Act was adopted in 49 states.[3]

In 1992 the National Conference of Commissioners on Uniform State Laws adopted a new uniform partnership act. NCCUSL made changes to the new Act in 1993, approved the revised version in 1994, made further revisions in 1996 and again in 1997. NCCUSL refers to each of these versions as Uniform Partnership Act ([year NCCUSL approved the version]), but almost all practitioners and commentators refer to the new act as the Revised Uniform Partnership Act—i.e., "RUPA."

RUPA is in many ways a major improvement over the UPA, although some of RUPA's provisions—especially those relating to fiduciary duty—have been controversial. What is uncontraverted is that RUPA is far more detailed and longer than the UPA.[4] As of August 2002, more than 30 states have adopted RUPA, repealing the UPA.

Although this book describes many UPA and RUPA provisions in detail and analyzes several in depth, *no secondary source can ever replace your own careful reading of each statute.* Each time you consider a section of this book which

---

3. Louisiana was the lone hold out. The District of Columbia, Guam, and the Virgin Islands also adopted the UPA. Some states adopted nonuniform provisions.

4. The text of RUPA is approximately 25 percent longer than the text of the UPA, but that comparison is only half of the story. Both the UPA and RUPA contain official Comments, but the Comments to the UPA are scant while the Comments to RUPA are copious.

deals with a section of either statute, you should compare this book's analysis with the statute's actual language.

§7.1.3 The Role of Case Law

Case law is also extremely important in the law of partnerships, perhaps more than one might expect in a field covered by an apparently comprehensive statute. This phenomenon has at least three causes. First, both the UPA and RUPA incorporate certain areas of judge-made law. The UPA provides generally that "In any case not provided for in this act the rules of law and equity, including the law merchant, shall govern"[5] and specifically that the law of estoppel and of agency "shall apply under this act."[6] In particular, "the rights and liabilities of partners with respect to each other and to third persons are largely determined by agency principles"[7] or by UPA provisions consistent with those principles. RUPA takes a comparable approach, stating even more generally that "Unless displaced by particular provisions of this [Act], the principles of law and equity supplement this [Act]."[8]

Second, many of the UPA and RUPA rules are "default" rules that can be displaced by agreement.[9] Numerous cases consider the existence and effect of such agreements. Third, flaws in the UPA's language have invited and even necessitated judicial clarification. A few UPA provisions are so vague or recondite as to be virtually unintelligible.

§7.1.4 UPA and RUPA Flexibility: Default Rules and Agreements Among Partners

The rules of both the UPA and RUPA can be divided into two categories:

- those that govern the relationship among the partners (inter se rules), and
- those that govern the relationship between the partnership (and its partners) with outsiders (third party rules).

These categories carry an important practical distinction. Inter se rules are "default" rules, applicable only in the absence of a contrary agreement among the partners. Such an agreement may be express or implied, written or oral.[10]

---

5. UPA §4.

6. UPA §5.

7. Restatement §14A, comment *a*.

8. RUPA §104(a).

9. For a more detailed discussion of this point, see section 7.1.4.

10. According to the weight of authority, the statute of frauds does not apply to most inter se agreements. It may apply to agreements to enter into a partnership, or to admit someone into a partnership, if (1) the partnership is alleged to have a term of more than one year, or (2) the admission is allegedly conditioned on some performance by the would-be partner and that performance cannot be accomplished within a year.

Table 7-1. Default and Mandatory Rules

Rules Governing Inter Se Relationships	Rules Governing Relationships with Third Parties
"default rules"	"mandatory rules"
can be changed by agreements among partners	cannot be changed by agreements among partners
<u>Examples:</u>	<u>Examples:</u>
UPA §18(a); RUPA §401(b) (partners share profits equally)	UPA §9(1); RUPA §301 (partner has power to bind partnership through acts apparently for carrying on the business of the partnership in the usual ordinary way)
UPA §18(e); RUPA §401(f) (all partners have equal right to manage partnership and its business)	UPA §13; RUPA §305 (partner's wrongful act binds the partnership)

To the extent the default rules are to be changed by the initial partnership agreement, unanimous consent is required. As a matter both of partnership and contract law, *adopting* a partnership agreement always requires unanimity. However, a partnership agreement can provide for its own amendment on a less-than-unanimous basis (e.g., majority vote of the partners). With such a provision in place, subsequent changes to the default rules can be accomplished with less-than-unanimous consent.

In contrast, third party rules are mandatory rules. An agreement among the partners cannot change them.[11] See Table 7-1.

The default structure of both the UPA and RUPA provides a basic set of operating rules for partners who do not want to spend the time and money to develop their own "rules of the game." At the same time, the default approach provides great flexibility. To the extent partners wish to accept the default rules, they may do so.[12] But partners who wish to deviate from the default structure may tailor their relationship virtually as they see fit.

The special tailoring does have some limits. Deviating too far from the default rules may negate the existence of a partnership. For example, if an agreement labels a person a partner but denies that person any share in the profits, that person would not be a partner.[13] In addition, rules dealing with

---

11. As a matter of contract law, a third party may agree with a partnership or a partner to waive rights created under one of the mandatory, third party rules.

12. Indeed, those who become partners by inadvertence are stuck with those rules wholesale, at least initially. (Formation of a partnership requires no special formalities and may occur even though the participants in a business relationship are unaware that the law labels their arrangement a partnership. See section 7.2.2.)

13. See section 7.2.3. However, if a third party knew of the label, the person might be liable to that third party *as if* a partner. See section 7.5 (partnership by estoppel).

partner-to-partner fiduciary duty can be shaped by agreement but not abrogated.[14]

Under the UPA, limitations on the power of the partnership agreement are mostly a matter of case law.[15] RUPA, in contrast, devotes a major statutory provision to the question. RUPA §103 states as a general rule that "relations among the partners and between the partners and the partnership are governed by the partnership agreement."[16] This general rule is subject to a list of specific exceptions—mostly constraints on the partnership agreement's power to: (1) reshape the fiduciary duties which partners owe each other and the partnership; and (2) limit the ability of partners to "dissociate" themselves from the partnership.[17] The section also states that, as to relations among the partners and the partnership, "[t]o the extent the partnership agreement does not otherwise provide, this [Act] governs."[18]

In any event, under both the UPA and RUPA, partnership agreements have broad latitude. Flexibility in structuring inter se relationships is a prime attraction of the partnership form.

§7.2   Partnership Described

§7.2.1   *Key Characteristics*

Partnership is the label that the law applies to a particular kind of business relationship. In the words of the UPA, "A partnership is an association of two or more persons to carry on as co-owners a business for profit."[19] RUPA provides, "the association of two or more persons to carry on as co-owners a business for profit forms a partnership, whether or not the persons intend to form a partnership."[20]

The paradigmatic partnership is:

- an unincorporated[21] business, intended to make a profit,
- which has two or more participants, who may be either individuals or entities,

---

14. See section 9.9.1.

15. UPA does contain a few statutory limitations. For example, under UPA §31(2) the partnership simply cannot prevent a partner from wrongfully causing the dissolution of the partnership by "express will." See sections 11.2.1 and 11.6.

16. RUPA §103(a).

17. RUPA §103(b). For a more specific discussion of these constraints, see sections 9.9.1 (fiduciary duty) and 11.9.2 (dissociation).

18. RUPA §103(a).

19. UPA §6(1).

20. RUPA §202(a).

21. A business that complies with the formalities necessary to become a corporation cannot be a partnership, even if in every other respect the business matches the key characteristics of a partnership.

- each of whom "brings something to the party," such as efforts, ideas, money, property, or some combination,
- each of whom co-owns the business,
- each of whom has a right to comanage the business, and
- each of whom shares in the profits of the business.

Partnerships appear in a wide variety of forms and engage in a wide variety of businesses. Some partnerships have only two partners; others have hundreds.[22] Some partnerships are based on complicated partnership agreements. Others arise from a handshake or a course of conduct. Many small retail establishments are partnerships, as are many businesses that own real estate. At one time, lawyers wishing to combine their efforts and share profits had no choice but to form partnerships, and even today most law firms, as well as other professional practices, are organized as partnerships.[23]

Creating a partnership involves no special formalities. There are no magic words that must be said or documents that need be signed or filed. If a business structure has the essential characteristics of a partnership, then the business *is* a partnership.

§7.2.2 *The Consent Characteristic*

Both the UPA and RUPA refer to a partnership as "an association."[24] That term connotes voluntariness, and the law has always considered a partnership to be a consensual relationship. For a partnership to exist, there must be a business relationship whose participants intend the kind of arrangement that the law calls a partnership. The participants must agree to that arrangement, either expressly or by their conduct.

It is not necessary, however, that the participants intend or agree to the *legal label* of partnership. A partnership can exist even though the participants have no idea that the legal label applies to them. Indeed, a partnership can exist among participants who have expressly disclaimed the partnership label.[25]

> *Example:* Sid has fallen on hard times. He receives the following letter from his brother, Jules:

---

22. Partnerships with large numbers of partners are uncommon. Unless the partnership is a limited liability partnership ("LLP"), see Chapter Fourteen, partners are personally liable for the debts of the partnership. See section 7.3. Regardless of LLP status, the partnership is liable for the misconduct of its partners. See Chapter Ten. The larger the number of partners, the greater is this risk of vicarious liability. Also, UPA partnerships are susceptible to dissolution, and increasing the number of partners increases the problems inherent in that susceptibility. See Chapter Eleven.

23. See section 7.3.2 (restrictions on business forms available to professionals).

24. UPA §6(1); RUPA §202(a).

25. RUPA makes this point explicitly. See §202(a), quoted in section 7.2.1.

Dear Sid,

I am sorry to hear that you've lost your job. Things are very tight here, otherwise I'd be happy to send you some money to tide you over.

I do have another idea, though. You know that land I own up by the lake? I think it would make a good resort, if I could just get some cabins built on it. If you'd be willing to move up there with your family and build the cabins, I would pay for all the materials, and for food and necessities for you and your family. I couldn't afford to pay you any wages, but once we got the resort up and running I'd give you half of the profits for the first 5 years.

Let me know how you feel about this.

/s/Jules

Sid's letter may be the blueprint of a partnership.

Example: Caesar lends money to Julio, who personally owns a company that produces and markets cheese. The loan agreement provides that, until the money is repaid Caesar (i) will receive a share of the company's profits in lieu of interest, (ii) may have the marketing rights for 50 percent of the company's output, and (iii) may have his own accountant check the company's finances weekly and approve any payments to be made by the company in excess of $100. The loan agreement also expressly states that Caesar and Julio are not partners in the cheese company but rather are creditor and debtor. Nonetheless, a court may find that a partnership exists.[26]

Partnerships that arise inadvertently are likely to be problematic. The parties will have created a legal relationship without having thought about, much less worked through, key business issues. At least initially, statutory default rules will govern their relationship,[27] but those rules may fail to match the deal the parties would have made for themselves. In any event the applicability of those rules will come as quite a surprise.

When a partnership arises despite an express disclaimer, there is another unpleasant consequence. Disputing the disclaimer is worthwhile only when money is at stake, so in these situations the label "partner" is invariably costly. In the cheese company Example above, for instance, if Caesar is deemed a partner of Julio, then Caesar will be personally liable for the cheese company's debts.[28]

---

26. The parties' self-description is not necessarily useless. The parties' label can be influential in "close call" situations. See section 7.4.3.

27. As explained in section 7.1.4, the partners can displace the default rules, but they can do so only by agreement.

28. See section 7.4 (contesting and establishing the existence of partnerships). Since the participants do consider themselves partners, they will not obtain the liability protection of an LLP. See section 14.2.

§7.2.3   *The Profit Sharing Prerequisite*

For participants in a business to be partners they must have the right to share in the business's profits. It is not necessary that the business actually have profits, and profit sharing is not irrefutable evidence of partner status,[29] but the right to share whatever profits exist is a necessary precondition to being a partner.

> *Example:* Carolyn opens an art supply store in a building she rents from Sylvia. As part of her rent, Carolyn pays Sylvia 30 percent of Carolyn's monthly revenues. Carolyn and Sylvia are not partners because they do not share profits.

Since sharing in revenues does not satisfy the profit-sharing prerequisite, it is important to understand the difference between profit sharing and revenue sharing. A business's revenue (or proceeds, or receipts, or gross income) consists of all the money the business takes in. A business's profit equals the amount of its revenue, less the amount of expenses the business has incurred in generating that revenue.

> *Example:* The Acme Widget Company manufactures and sells widgets. In 2000, it sold 50,000 widgets, for which it received $500,000. In order to make and sell the widgets, in 2000, the Company spent $100,000 on materials, $150,000 on salaries, wages and sales commissions, $20,000 in energy costs and $30,000 in legal fees for total expenses of $300,000. In 2000, the Company had $500,000 of revenue (or gross receipts), but only $200,000 of profits ($500,000 minus $300,000 of expenses equals $200,000).[30]

Having a share of profits tends to produce a different attitude than having a share of revenues. Someone with a share merely of revenues tends to focus on making sales, worrying little about the rest of the enterprise. For someone who shares profits, in contrast, sales (and revenues) are only part of the equation; a profit will exist only if the whole business is functioning well.

> *Example:* Sylvia is a partner in the Acme Widget Company with a right to ten percent of the profits. Phil is a salesperson for the Company, with a five percent commission on all revenue collected from the sales he makes. Phil has a customer who is willing to buy 5,000 widgets if Acme can ship within two weeks. Acme can make that deadline only by paying its workers substantial amounts of overtime pay. For Phil the main con-

---

29. See sections 7.4.3 and 7.4.4, which discuss other business relationships that may involve profit sharing.

30. For simplicity's sake, the example lists only a few of the costs an actual company would incur. The concepts being illustrated would apply as well in a realistically complicated situation.

cern is booking the order and seeing that Acme meets the shipping deadline. Sylvia, in contrast, wants to know how much the extra overtime costs will add to the cost of manufacturing.

The profit-share prerequisite thus fits well with two other key partnership characteristics: comanagement and co-ownership. Those who share profits tend to view their economic fate as linked with the fate of the enterprise as a whole. As a consequence, they will wish to involve themselves in controlling the enterprise and will tend to see the enterprise as belonging in part to them.

§7.2.4 The Role of Loss Sharing

Express agreements to share losses certainly intensify the comanagement and co-ownership inclinations just discussed,[31] and in all jurisdictions such agreements are very strong evidence of a partnership. In some jurisdictions, an express agreement to share losses is actually a prerequisite to a finding of partnership.

The majority rule, however, is to the contrary. Neither the UPA nor RUPA mentions loss sharing as a prerequisite. Instead, both statutes treat loss sharing as a consequence of partnership status.[32]

> *Example:* Carolyn opens an art supply store in a building she rents from Sylvia. As part of her rent, Carolyn agrees to pay Sylvia 20 percent of Carolyn's yearly profits. The agreement says nothing about Sylvia's obligation to pay Carolyn if Carolyn loses money. Regardless of whether the UPA or RUPA applies, the absence of an express agreement to share losses does not preclude a finding that Carolyn and Sylvia are partners.

> *Example:* Julie and Evelyn operate a dance school as partners. They specifically agree to share profits 50/50, but do not consider what will happen if they lose money. The applicable partnership statute implies an agreement to share losses 50/50.[33]

§7.2.5 A Meaning for "Co-Ownership"

Co-ownership is a key characteristic of a partnership, but the concept can be quite confusing. The confusion exists because neither the UPA nor RUPA defines the term and because the concept has a different meaning depending on whether it is used to (i) help determine whether a partnership exists (i.e., as an entrance criterion to partner status), or (ii) describe certain legal rights that follow from partner status.

---

31. Section 7.2.3.
32. UPA §18(a); RUPA §401(b) (unless otherwise agreed, losses to be shared in the same proportion as profits are shared). See section 8.3.1.
33. UPA §18(a); RUPA §401 (b).

To understand co-ownership as an entrance criterion to partnership status,[34] consider two entrepreneurs who go into business together. They agree (as partners do) that they will jointly control whatever property the business uses ("the assets") and will decide together which assets to select, what use to make of those assets, and whether, when, and for what price to dispose of the use and control of those assets. They also agree that they will share the economic benefit (or detriment) that eventuates from their control, use, and disposition of those assets (i.e. they will share profits).

In a functional sense the two entrepreneurs co-own the assets of the business. By their agreement they have arranged to share the two predominant characteristics of property ownership: the right to control use and disposition, and the right to benefit (or suffer) economically from the exercise of that right of control. Such functional co-ownership is characteristic of a partnership.[35]

§7.2.6   *Partnership Types and Joint Ventures*

Partnership types.   There are three basic types of partnership, categorized according to when the partnership rightfully comes to an end.[36]

- *Partnership at will*—each partner has the right to cause the partnership to come to an end, at any time and without having to state or have "cause."[37]
- *Partnership for a term*—the partnership comes to an end at the end of the time period specified in the partners' agreement.
- *Partnership for a particular undertaking*—the partnership comes to an end when the particular task or goal specified in the partners' agreement has been accomplished.

Example: Paul, Suzanne, and Sarah form a partnership to practice law. They make no agreement about the duration of the partnership. Each partner has the right to leave the partnership at any time, causing the partnership to come to an end. The partnership is at will.

Example: Paul, Suzanne, and Sarah form a partnership to invest in a strategically located parcel of real estate. They agree that the partnership will hold the property for five years, after which the partnership will sell the property and come to an end. The partnership is for a term.

---

34. For a discussion of the co-ownership "consequences" of partnership, see Chapter Eight.

35. Legal ownership of a partnership's assets is quite another matter. See section 8.8.8.

36. Recall from sections 4.1.3 and 4.1.6 the difference between *power* and *right*. Under the UPA, each partner always has the *power* to call an end to the partnership. See section 11.2.1. The situation is different under RUPA. See sections 11.10 and 11.11.

37. A partner's fiduciary duty may limit this right. See section 11.7.1.

Example: Paul, Suzanne, and Sarah form a partnership to develop a subdivision of single-family houses. They agree to remain partners until all construction is complete and all the houses have been sold. The partnership is for a particular undertaking.

Joint ventures. The term *joint venture* provides more confusion than enlightenment. Under the law of most states, a joint venture is distinguished from a partnership by having a more narrow scope than a partnership formed to conduct an on-going business. But that distinction makes little sense, since both the UPA and RUPA recognize limited-scope partnerships as partnerships for a particular undertaking. Moreover, under the law of most states, joint ventures are analogized to partnerships and therefore governed by partnership law.

§7.2.7 Entity or Aggregate? (And Why Care?)

The question of "entity vs. aggregate" has long vexed the law of partnerships. Is a partnership a separate legal person, with a legal identity distinct from its individual partners? Or is a partnership merely an aggregation of its individual partners, with no separate legal identity of its own?

UPA's schizoid approach. The problem inheres in the UPA. When the Act was being drafted reasonable minds differed on the issue. As the drafting project began, the principal drafter favored the entity approach. He died, however, in the middle of the project, and his replacement favored the aggregate view.

The UPA as promulgated includes both approaches. Some provisions reflect an entity concept. UPA §9(1), for example, begins: "Every partner is an agent of the partnership. . . ." Other provisions reflect the aggregate notion. For instance, UPA §29 characterizes partnership dissolution as "the change in the relation of the partners caused by any partner ceasing to be associated in the carrying on . . . of the business." Still other provisions combine the two approaches.[38]

Understanding that the UPA embodies two discordant themes helps make sense of some of the Act's provisions. The themes can also have an impact in determining how nonpartnership law treats partners and partnerships.

Example: A state statute prohibited banks from making loans to their own directors. A bank made a loan to a partnership in which one of the bank's directors was a partner. A court held that the bank had not violated the statute, since the partnership was an entity separate from its partners. A court in another state reached the opposite conclusion in an essentially identical situation. The state had a similar statute, but this court considered

---

38. E.g., UPA §25 (partners have no individual rights in property owned by the partnership but do have collective rights to use and possess the partnership's property for partnership purposes).

the partnership to be a mere aggregation of individuals. As a result, the court saw the bank's loan to the partnership as a loan to each individual partner, of whom one was a director of the lending bank.

RUPA's simple answer.   Matters are far simpler under RUPA. Its drafters cut the Gordian knot: "A partnership is an entity distinct from its partners."[39]

§7.3   The Hallmark Consequence of an Ordinary General Partnership: Partners' Personal Liability for the Partnership's Debts

Until the very end of the twentieth century, the most important consequence of general partner status had been simply this: *All partners are personally liable for all debts and other obligations of the partnership.* In an ordinary general partnership it does not matter whether a particular partner participates or approves the conduct that creates the obligation. The liability results merely from the status of "partner" and is automatic, strict, and vicarious.

In the modern commercial world, this situation is remarkable and—for partners and potential partners—harrowing. Being a partner is tantamount to giving a personal guarantee to everyone with a claim or potential claim against the business.

Today, partners can avoid this risk by causing their general partnership to be a limited liability partnership. LLP status severs the automatic connection between partner status and liability for the partnership's debts, and partners in a "full shield" LLP are no more liable for the partnership's debt than shareholders in a corporation are liable for the corporation's debts.[40]

However, it is still necessary to understand the liability rules for ordinary general partnerships. For one thing, even under RUPA many of the statutory default rules reflect the assumption that the partners are liable for the partnership's debts. For another, many, many general partnerships are not LLPs. (Regulatory barriers may exist, or the partners may simply not know that LLP status is available or understand the dangers of eschewing that status.[41])

§7.3.1   *Exhaustion, Joint and Several Liability, Inter Se Loss Sharing*

The rule of personal liability has three separate areas of complexity: an exhaustion rule, the question of joint and several liability, and the issue of how part-

---

39. RUPA §201(a). This approach also allows RUPA to simplify partnership law's approach to partnership property. See section 8.8.3.
40. Chapter Fourteen explains limited liability partnerships.
41. See section 7.3.2.

ners' liability to third parties relates to partners' obligations to share losses among themselves.

Exhaustion rule.   In some UPA jurisdictions, as a matter of case law a creditor of the partnership may not pursue individual partners without first exhausting the assets of the partnership. In RUPA jurisdictions, the exhaustion rule applies per the statute.[42]

Joint liability and joint and several liability.   In most UPA jurisdictions, partners are jointly and severally liable for certain kinds of debts and jointly liable for others. Under UPA §15, partners are jointly and severally liable for partnership debts arising from partner misconduct and merely jointly liable for all other partnership debts.[43]

The distinctions between the two types of liability relate not to the extent of each partner's personal responsibility but rather to the steps a creditor must take to pursue the partners. Under both forms of liability, each partner may be held individually responsible for the full amount of the partnership's debt.[44] When the liability is joint *and* several, the creditor may pursue any one of the partners individually. That is, the creditor does not need to include all the partners as defendants in the same lawsuit. Moreover, the creditor may release its claim against one of the partners without undermining its claim against the others. In contrast, when the liability is joint *but not* several, the creditor must sue all of the partners in order to sue any of them. Likewise, if the liability is merely joint, the creditor's release of any partner releases all of them.

Under RUPA the rule is simpler. In an ordinary general partnership, "all partners are liable jointly and severally for all obligations of the partnership."[45]

Relationship of partners' liability to third parties and partners' inter se loss sharing.   As discussed in Chapter Eight, partners typically share losses among themselves. Their inter se loss sharing has, however, absolutely no effect on a third party's claim against any particular partner.

> *Example:* Under their partnership agreement, Larry, Moe, and Curley agree to share losses 60/20/20. Shemp has a $100,000 claim against the partnership on which each partner is jointly and severally liable. Shemp

---

42. RUPA §307(d).

43. For a discussion of how a partner's misconduct could give rise to a partnership debt, see sections 10.4 and 10.5. For a discussion of other ways in which partners can bind their partnership to third parties, see sections 10.2 and 10.3. In addition, a partnership can be bound through the conduct of its agents.

44. Of course the creditor cannot collect more than the amount owed. That amount will be reduced to judgment. Once the creditor has collected the full judgment amount, the judgment is satisfied.

45. RUPA §306(a). Under both the UPA and RUPA a new partner's personal liability does not extend to a partnership obligation incurred before the person became a partner. UPA §17; RUPA §306(b). The question of when a partnership obligation is actually incurred is complex and a matter of case law. See section 14.2.5.

sues only Larry, seeking to recover the entire amount. Larry cannot defend by saying, "At most, my liability is $60,000 [i.e., 60 percent]."[46]

§7.3.2 *Why Risk It?*

Why would anyone form a general partnership instead of a corporation? Forming a corporation is a simple matter, and the corporate entity shields its owners from the debts of the business. Of course even with the corporate form, owners of start-up businesses often have to give personal guarantees to particular, important creditors (e.g., banks, major suppliers). However, such particularized guarantees cause far less exposure than does the simple fact of partner status. Why would anyone take the risk of partnership?

That question has a five-part answer: (i) tax advantages; (ii) greater flexibility in structuring the "deal" among the participants; (iii) legal restrictions on the business forms available to professionals; (iv) inadvertence; (v) poor or no legal advice. The first answer is of great, although now waning importance. The second and third are for the most part mere vestiges of past practices. The fourth and fifth have perhaps the greatest lasting significance.

Tax advantages.   For decades, tax advantages have been a substantial reason for organizing a business as a partnership rather than a corporation. Most corporations are taxable entities and therefore face double taxation when distributing profits. The standard corporation can pay dividends to its shareholders (i.e., distribute profits to its owners) only in after-tax dollars. In essence, the corporation must first pay corporate income tax on its corporate profits before distributing any of those profits as dividends. The shareholders must in turn pay income tax on the dividends.

A partnership, in contrast, is a "pass through" entity. Tax law treats the partnership's profits as allocated among (i.e., passed through to) the partners. The partnership pays no tax; only the partners do. Partners thus face only a single level of taxation. Losses also pass through. When a partnership loses money, the partners obtain tax deductions for use on their own income taxes.

For some businesses, the tax advantages of a partnership have been substantial enough to warrant the risks of personal liability. This has been especially so when the risks are either small or insurable.[47]

---

46. Larry will, however, be entitled to indemnity from the partnership and, if the partnership lacks the necessary funds, will have a claim against Moe and Curley for their respective shares of the loss. See sections 8.4 (partner's right to indemnity) and 8.3.1 (loss sharing applied when third party has collected from one partner and the partnership has failed to indemnify).

47. For a detailed discussion of the advantages of partnership tax status, see section 13.2.

Greater flexibility in structuring the deal. As discussed previously,[48] partners have almost unlimited flexibility in structuring their relationship with each other. With this flexibility, they may predetermine the various aspects of their deal. For example, they may agree in advance which partners will work in the business and how much, if any, extra remuneration those partners will receive for doing so. They may, in contrast, establish a flexible mechanism for allocating profits. They may subject particular business decisions to the veto of each partner, or they may give complete management authority to one or more managing partners.

At one time, the corporate form did not allow comparable flexibility. Some courts invalidated predetermined deals as attempts to "sterilize" the corporation's directors, who under traditional corporate norms are supposed to exercise independent judgment in managing corporate affairs. Modern court decisions and modern corporate statutes have changed matters, however. In most jurisdictions, shareholders in a closely-held corporation (i.e., a corporation with few owners) can do just as much predetermination as the partners in a partnership. In these jurisdictions, business people who want to set their deal in advance no longer have to expose themselves to the personal liability that comes automatically with partner status.

Restrictions on business forms available to professionals. At one time, states prohibited professionals from practicing in corporate form. Professional status was seen as carrying a special responsibility, so the corporate liability shield was inappropriate for a professional practice. According to this view, professionals were properly saddled with the all-encompassing, vicarious liability of a partner. Professionals who wished to practice together and co-own their practice had only one organizational choice—a partnership.

Today, in contrast, almost every state permits professionals to practice in entities which shield their owners from partner-like vicarious liability. These entities include professional corporations, professional associations, professional limited liability companies, and professional limited liability partnerships.[49] Consequently, professionals who today choose the partnership form do so for reasons other than necessity.

Inadvertence. Since creating a partnership requires no special formalities, partnerships can arise inadvertently.[50] Indeed, partnership is the "default" organizational status. If:

- a court determines that two or more persons in fact co-own a business, and

---

48. Section 7.1.4.
49. For a discussion of limited liability companies, see Chapter Thirteen. For a discussion of limited liability partnerships, see Chapter Fourteen.
50. See sections 7.2.2 and 7.4, and also Chapter 8.

- that business has not formally chosen to be some other form of entity, then

the law classifies the business as a partnership and treats the owners of the business as partners. Thus many partners assume the harrowing risk of personal liability without understanding that they are doing so.

Poor or no legal advice.   Some persons knowingly become partners without appreciating the liability risk that accompanies partner status. These persons have either not sought legal advice or have received bad advice.

§7.4   Contesting and Establishing the Existence of a Partnership

§7.4.1   *Why a Contest?*

Some of the most important partnership cases involve disputes over whether a particular business relationship constitutes a partnership. These disputes usually relate to one of two major attributes of partnership status: the fact that partners are personally liable for the debts of the partnership or the fact that partners share profits with each other.

The liability attribute interests creditors seeking a "deep pocket." If the party who owes a debt cannot pay, the creditor may seek a more solvent business associate of the debtor and try to characterize that business association as a partnership.

> *Example:* A manufacturing plant defaults on its obligation to buy power from a power company. Another creditor of the plant has exerted some control over the plant's business and has received a share of the plant's profits. The power company claims that the other creditor is in fact a partner in the plant's operations and as such personally liable for the plant's debt. Note that, since the participants do not consider themselves partners, they will not think to obtain the liability protection of an LLP. LLP status is not available retroactively.[51]

The profit-sharing attribute interests those seeking a bigger piece of a business's pie. If a person who participates in a business can establish partner status, that person stakes a potentially valuable claim. As a partner, the person is entitled to a share not only of profits made in the future but also of any profits distributed in the past (i.e., while the individual was in fact a partner although not recognized as such).

---

51. See sections 14.2.2 and 14.2.5.

Example: Bob owns and operates a tree farm. He induces Ted to work on the farm as manager, and Ted holds that position for six years. Ted then claims that Bob had promised him a 50/50 partnership after three years. During years 4 through 6 Bob took $200,000 in profit out of the business. A court sides with Ted and orders Bob to pay Ted $100,000 in back profits. (After that payment, Bob's profit from years 4 through 6 will be reduced to $100,000, so the two partners will have profited equally.)

§7.4.2 The Pivotal Question: The Character of the Profit Sharing

The right to share profits is a prerequisite to partner status, and both the UPA and RUPA give profit sharing a pivotal role in most disputes concerning the existence *vel non* of a partnership. RUPA §202(c)(3) provides:

> A person who receives a share of the profits of a business is presumed to be a partner in the business, unless the profits were received in payment:
>
> (i) of a debt by installments or otherwise;
>
> (ii) for services as an independent contractor or of wages or other compensation to an employee;
>
> (iii) of rent;
>
> (iv) of an annuity or other retirement or health benefit to a beneficiary, representative, or designee of a deceased or retired partner;
>
> (v) of interest or other charge on a loan, even if the amount of payment varies with the profits of the business, including a direct or indirect present or future ownership of the collateral, or rights to income, proceeds, or increase in value derived from the collateral; or
>
> (vi) for the sale of the goodwill of a business or other property by installments or otherwise.

UPA §7(4) contains a very similar list, although using the concept of prima facie evidence rather than a presumption.

These statutory provisions conduce toward one basic structure of analysis:

1. The party asserting the existence of a partnership must establish that each participant in the alleged partnership had a right to share in profits.
2. The parties will joust over how to characterize the profit sharing. E.g., did the profit share reflect the remuneration of a co-owner (a partner) or the payment on a debt, or rent, etc.?
3. If the profit share does not fit into one of the "protected categories,"[52] under RUPA the arrangement is presumed to be a partnership.[53]

---

52. RUPA §202, Comment 3.
53. RUPA §202(c)(3).

Under the UPA, the profit sharing is prima facie evidence of a partnership.[54] In either event, the partnership *vel non* determination is a question of fact.[55]

Since no one can be a partner without a right to share in profits, disputes about the existence of partnership inevitably focus on the characterization issue.

§7.4.3   *Factors in the Contest of Characterization*

There is, unfortunately, no bright line test for resolving disputes over the characterization of profit sharing. It is, however, possible to identify the following five factors which tend to influence courts.

Control.   Comanagement is a key characteristic of a partnership. The more an alleged partner participates in management decisions or exercises control over the business, the more likely is a finding of partnership. The control factor can be especially problematic for creditors who receive profits "[a]s interest on a loan."[56] Many loan agreements permit the creditor a voice in or even control over management decisions if the debtor has trouble making payments. A creditor who takes a profit share and then exercises such rights faces substantial risks if the debtor's business fails. *Other* creditors will use that exercise of control to characterize the profit sharing as a partner's remuneration. Since in an ordinary general partnership all partners are liable for the partnership's debts, this characterization will make the profit-sharing creditor liable *on the other creditor's claims* against the debtor.

Control is a less useful factor when the alleged partner provides the business full-time services, rather than money or credit. Many key employees exercise substantial discretion in the conduct of their employer's business. Some key employees even have contract rights which oblige the employer to respect that discretion. Control can therefore be equivocal when trying to distinguish between profits received as a partner and payments received "for services as an independent contractor or of wages or other compensation to an employee."[57]

---

54. UPA §7(4).

55. The official Comment to RUPA §202 characterizes the difference between prima facie evidence and a presumption as merely "a more contemporary construction." However, unlike a presumption, prima facie evidence does not shift the burden of proof. Prima facie evidence means that a party has submitted enough evidence to satisfy the burden of proof, but, as the fact finder considers all the evidence, the burden of persuasion remains on the party seeking to establish partnership status. A presumption means that the party *contesting* partnership status has the burden of persuasion.

56. UPA §7(4)(d). In RUPA, the comparable language is "in payment . . . of a debt by installments or otherwise." RUPA §202(c)(3)(i).

57. RUPA §202(c)(3)(ii). UPA §7(4)(b) refers to profits received "[a]s wages of an employee."

Agreements to share losses. As previously explained,[58] an express agreement to share losses is strong evidence of a partnership. Such agreements rarely, if ever, exist in the arrangements between creditor and debtor, employer and employee, or in any of the other relationships that, according to UPA §7(4) and RUPA §202(c), involve profit sharing but not partnership.

Business participants can and sometimes do share losses without having an express agreement to do so. That course of conduct probably implies a loss-sharing agreement and in any event is itself strong evidence of a partnership.

Contributions of property to the business. If a party has contributed property to the business, that contribution favors the partnership characterization. As discussed more fully in Chapter Eight, partners often "buy into" a partnership by transferring ownership of something such as land, patents, or money to the business.[59] They give up ownership rights in the property in return for a share of the profits and a right to receive back the value of the property (but not the property itself) if and when the partnership comes to an end.

A contribution of property is not a prerequisite to a finding of partnership, and many partners bring only their talents, skills, and labor.[60] However, a property contribution does tend to rule out any of the non-partnership "protected categories" under UPA §7(4) and RUPA §202(c). Property transfers do occur in some of those relationships, but the transfers are of a different nature. For example, a landlord transfers to a tenant the property right to occupy and use the leased premises, but: (i) the transfer is only temporary, (ii) the landlord has a right to regain the same property and not just its value, and (iii) the return of the property ordinarily occurs at a time certain or upon specified notice, not merely when the partnership happens to come to an end. Similarly, a lender transfers to a borrower the right to use and dispose of the loaned funds, but the timing of the repayment ordinarily does not depend solely on the ending of the partnership.

The extent to which the profit share constitutes the recipient's only remuneration from the business. If a profit recipient receives no other remuneration from the business, that fact favors the partnership characterization. If, in contrast, the profit share is just a bit of "icing" on top of some other payments, courts are more inclined toward one of the protected categories.

Example: Sylvia manages the widget factory of the Acme Widget Company. She receives no salary. Her only compensation is a 20-percent share of profits. (She can "draw" a certain amount each month against her profit share, but if at the end of the year her draws have exceeded her

---

58. Section 7.2.4.
59. See sections 8.1 and 8.6.
60. See section 8.7.

share she must repay the excess.) Phil, the national sales manager of the company, receives a salary of $50,000 per year, plus one percent of the Company's profit as an incentive. A court is far more likely to find Sylvia to be a partner than Phil. All of her remuneration comes in the form of profits. For Phil, the profit share is small and is a mere add-on to his salary.

The parties' own characterization of their relationship. Although the parties' own labels are never dispositive, in close situations some courts look to how the participants in a business relationship have characterized that relationship. This factor is probably more influential when the characterization dispute involves only the participants. When someone outside the relationship (e.g., a creditor seeking to find a deep pocket) challenges the participants' self-labelling, courts are more likely to see the label as self-serving.

§7.4.4   *Handling the Factors (A Mode of Analysis)*

Legal analysis involving factors is always difficult. Which factor is the most important? What if one factor points strongly in one direction, while two other factors point weakly in the other? Unfortunately, no simple, mechanical paradigm exists for ordering the characterization factors. However, you may find the following perspective helpful.

All disputes about the character of profit sharing are either/or disputes. The parties do not contest the general paradigm of a partnership but instead struggle over whether a particular person is a partner or merely a participant in one of the protected categories of UPA §7(4) and RUPA §202(c)(3). In one case, for example, the alleged partner will be either a partner or a wage earner receiving profits as wages. In another case, the alleged partner will be either a partner or a lender receiving profits as interest.

To decide these either/or questions, courts can look to the factors discussed in section 7.4.3. If all the factors point in the same direction, the analysis is simple and the answer is clear. The analysis gets complicated only when the factors point in opposite directions.

You can handle that complexity by thinking of each either/or choice as involving a multi-layered continuum. Each layer reflects one of the five characterization factors. At one end of the continuum sits the "ideal type"[61] of a partner. At that end, at each layer of the continuum, the facts indicate "partner." At the other end of the continuum sits the "ideal type" of the arguably applicable protected category. At that end, at each layer of the continuum, the facts indicate "wage earner," or "lender," or whatever the category may be. For example, when the characterization choice is either "partner" or "wage earner," the continuum might look like Table 7-2.

---

61. An "ideal type" possesses all the key attributes described by a concept; it epitomizes the concept.

Table 7-2. Partner versus Wage Earner

"Partner" ◄————————————► "Wage Earner"		
participates in all important decisions	*Control*	obeys instructions; has no important discretion
has expressly agreed to share losses	*Express Loss Sharing Agreement*	has never agreed to share losses; when losses occur, payout does not change
contributed property to the business	*Contribution*	merely works in the business
all payout via profit share	*Importance of Profit Share*	profit share is only icing on the cake
called a partner	*Self-Labelling*	called an employee

Although in any particular case one factor (or layer) or another may predominate, courts rarely decide on the basis of one factor alone. Instead, they look at the overall picture: The more each layer of the disputed situation leans toward one end of the applicable continuum, the more likely the court is to come down on that side of the either/or fence.

The analysis is inevitably imprecise. Since the law declines to make one factor (or combination of factors) dispositive, courts are left essentially to decide whether the disputed situation "looks" more like one end of the continuum or the other.

§7.5 Partnership by Estoppel; Liability of a Purported Partner

§7.5.1 The Basic Approach

It is possible for a person to have partner-like liability for an enterprise's obligations without truly being a partner. UPA labels the applicable rule *partnership by estoppel;* RUPA uses the caption "Liability of Purported Partner."

Unfortunately, the UPA rule is byzantine, and RUPA made only a few changes.

Under both statutes, however, the basic concept is fairly simple and consistent with ordinary estoppel principles:

If • a person represents itself as being a partner in an enterprise (or allows others to make the representation)

and • a third party reasonably relies on the representation and as a result does business with the enterprise,

Then • the person who was represented as a partner is personally liable on the transaction, even though that person is not in fact a partner, and

- others who have either made or consented to the representation are bound by the person's acts.

The rule rests on common beliefs about a partner's responsibilities and powers. Before the advent of limited liability partnerships, partner personal liability was a well-known fact of business life. To represent oneself as a partner (or to allow someone else to make the representation) was therefore to impliedly promise to be "good for" any debts of the enterprise just like any other partner.[62]

When a false representation of partner status induces a third party to deal with the enterprise, the third party cannot invoke genuine partner liability against the person whose status was misrepresented. (That person is not, in fact, a partner.) The third party can, however, invoke UPA §16 or RUPA §308, which will function to make good that person's implied promise of responsibility.

The "power to bind" aspect of the rule rests on a similar rationale. It is well known that partners have certain powers to bind the partnership.[63] When a person is represented to be a partner with others, third parties will naturally believe that the person can bind the partnership and, on account of each partner's personal liability, can bind those others as well. To the extent that those others consent to the representation, a partner-like power to bind should apply.

§7.5.2 *The Details*

Liability of person whose status is misrepresented (UPA §16(1); RUPA §308(a)). This part of the rule is straightforward in concept:

If: • a person represents itself, or consents to others representing it, as a partner in an enterprise, and
          • a third party relies on that representation and enters into a transaction with the supposed partnership,[64]

Then: • the person is liable to the third party on the transaction.

---

62. If the partnership is an LLP, no partner is personally liable for the partnership's debts, so no *partnership-based* liability will attach to the person making the misrepresentation. However, other common law claims might be available; e.g., misrepresentation, fraud in the inducement.

63. For a discussion of the rules that underlie this perception, see Chapter Ten.

64. UPA §16(1) refers specifically to liability to a third party "who has, on the faith of such representation, given credit." Case law has expanded the liability to favor those who have detrimentally relied in other ways. RUPA codifies that case law, creating a claim for any "person, relying on the representation, [who] enters into a transaction with the actual or purported partnership." RUPA §308(a).

The reliance element has two components. The third party must believe the misrepresentation, and the misrepresentation must cause the third party to act.

Example: Rachael and Samuel are partners in The Egg Company, a chicken farming operation. Together with Carolyn, the partnership's farm manager, Samuel goes to the local feedstore to buy chicken feed. At the store Samuel explains that he is a partner in the Egg Company and that the Egg Company wishes to buy chicken feed on credit. The store owner is initially reluctant to make a credit sale but then sees Carolyn and says, "Oh, is she one of you?" Samuel nods his head, and Carolyn says nothing. The store owner then agrees to sell on credit. Carolyn is personally liable on the sale. By her inaction she consented to being misrepresented as a partner; in reliance on that representation a third party entered into a transaction.

If a person's status as partner has been misrepresented publicly, either by the person or with the person's consent, then a third party may rely on the reverberations of that public misrepresentation. That is, a third party may invoke UPA §16(1) or RUPA §308(a) without having relied on a misrepresentation *directly* made or *directly* consented to by the person whose status is being misrepresented.

Example: Rachael and Samuel send Carolyn to a chicken auction to buy baby chickens for The Egg Company. So that Carolyn will have no trouble getting her bids accepted, Rachael and Samuel indicate on the bidder's registration form that Carolyn is a partner. Carolyn acquiesces in this tactic. The chicken auction provides all auctioneers and registered sellers a list of registered bidders and their status. Although Carolyn may be unaware of this list, the listing of her as a partner will satisfy the misrepresentation element of UPA §16(1) and RUPA §308(a).

UPA §16(1) and RUPA §308(a) each concern only the person whose status was misrepresented. If others have made or consented to the misrepresentation, their liability depends on UPA § 16(2) or RUPA § 308(b).

Liability of others who make or consent to the misrepresentation (UPA §16(2); RUPA §308(b)). UPA §16(2) and RUPA §308(b) impose liability on those who misrepresent another person's status as partner or who consent to that misrepresentation. The nature of the liability depends on whether a genuine partnership exists and, if so, whether all the genuine partners have made or consented to the misrepresentation. The following three-part rule restates the recondite formulation found in both provisions.

1. *If:* • a partnership exists, and
   • all the partners make or consent to the misrepresentation of a person's status as partner,

Then:
- the partnership is liable on the transaction, and
- the partners are each liable under the ordinary rules of partner liability—i.e., UPA §15 and RUPA §306.

2. *If:* • a partnership exists, but
      • not all the partners make or consent to the misrepresentation,

Then:
- the partnership is not liable, and
- those partners who made or consented to the misrepresentation are jointly (UPA) or jointly and severally (RUPA) liable on the transaction.

3. *If:*   no partnership exists,
    Then: those who made or consented to the misrepresentation are jointly (UPA) or jointly and severally (RUPA) liable on the transaction.

Example: Recall the chicken feed Example above. Samuel is jointly liable with Carolyn under UPA §16(2) and RUPA §308(b), since he made the misrepresentation that Carolyn was a partner. Rachael is not liable, because she neither made nor consented to the misrepresentation.[65]

Example: Recall the chicken auction Example above. Under both the UPA and RUPA, all of Carolyn's bids will be binding on the partnership. A genuine partnership does exist, and all the partners have consented to the misrepresentation.

PROBLEM 58

Ralph wants to open a riding stable but does not have enough money. He approaches Sally, who has both experience managing start-up businesses and some money to invest. They agree that: each will own a half-interest in the business; Ralph will run the day-to-day operations while Sally will "handle the books"; all major decisions will be made jointly; Sally will invest $50,000; Ralph will get 40 percent of the profits and Sally 60 percent. Sally is concerned with the liability that comes with being a partner, so the agreement between Ralph and Sally states clearly: "This relationship shall not be deemed to be a partnership." What legal effect will that disclaimer have on claims by creditors?

EXPLANATION

The disclaimer will be useless. Sally and Ralph have created precisely the type of business relationship that the law considers to be a partnership. They co-

---

65. However, if Samuel's act in buying the feed bound the partnership, then Rachael will be liable on this transaction as for any other partnership obligation. UPA §15(b); RUPA § 306(a). For the power of partners to bind the partnership, see Chapter Ten.

own, they comanage, and they share profits. In the face of a claim by a creditor, the disclaimer will be disregarded as inaccurate and self-serving.

PROBLEM 59

Mark is the treasurer of the Zenith Vending Machine Company. In that capacity he prepares all the Company's tax returns. The Company is a partnership, and each year its partnership tax returns list the partners as Allen, Betty, Charlotte, and Ralph.[66] As part of his remuneration, Mark receives a share of Zenith's profits. If he later claims that he is a partner in the company, what role will the partnership tax returns play in the dispute?

EXPLANATION

The returns will argue strongly against him, because they list the partners and do not include Mark. As the preparer of the returns, Mark evidently assented to the exclusion. This situation therefore differs from efforts to use disclaimers against third parties.

PROBLEM 60

For ten years Paul has operated "PAUL's," an automobile salvage business. The business buys wrecked automobiles from insurance companies or at auction and then either rebuilds them or cannibalizes them for parts. PAUL's sells rebuilt and used parts to car dealers, service stations, and the public.

For the past three years Eli has been working in the business with Paul. Eli has only a third grade education but is an excellent, street smart auto mechanic. He is active in almost all aspects of the business: bidding at auctions, buying cars from insurance companies, and fixing cars and parts. Only Paul, however, sets the prices on cars and parts that the business sells. Paul also maintains all the business's records and takes care of the business's various tax returns.

Paul first approached Eli to come to work with him when Paul learned that Eli had won $9,000 at the racetrack. Eli gave the money to Paul, who used it to buy cars at an auction. Those cars were then used in the salvage business. Paul promised Eli 50 percent of the business's profit for as long as Eli would "work as hard, sweat as much, and do as much as I do."

Ever since Eli began work at PAUL's, the company's records have shown him as an employee. His salary has been calculated based on 50 percent of the profits, and social security has been withheld from his checks. The company has paid social security and unemployment compensation taxes on account of Eli and has maintained worker's compensation coverage for him. Both the

---

66. Even though partnerships do not pay taxes, see section 7.3.2, they must nonetheless file tax returns.

company's various tax returns and its insurance policies list Eli as an employee.

Is Eli an employee of or a partner in PAUL's?[67]

EXPLANATION

Eli is a partner. He shares in the profits and has made a capital contribution. Although Paul has exclusive responsibility in two areas, Eli shares management authority over other areas that are crucial to the business.

The company's books and tax returns do describe Eli as an employee, but that fact does not undermine Eli's partner status. Parties' self-descriptions can give insight into their intents, but only when the parties genuinely assent to the description. There is no evidence that Eli was aware of the way he was described in the company's records, other than the withholding of social security from his checks. With his lack of formal education, Eli was probably unaware of what that withholding implied about his status.

PROBLEM 61

As a sole proprietor, Dave runs a dry-cleaning store called "Dave's Drycleaning." He is in deep financial trouble. His bank will no longer give him any credit and is threatening to call his loans (i.e., demand immediate payment of all money owed). Dave also owes money to various trade creditors (i.e., businesses which have supplied him goods and services). Dave approaches Susan, a well-known venture capitalist, and asks her to refinance his business. Susan reviews his books and his operations and says, "Listen, you're a great dry cleaner but a lousy businessman. I'll bail you out, but we have to divide up the responsibilities a bit. If we're going to make this business work, we have to be more hardnosed about it. First, no more credit to law professors. They're lousy risks. Second, I want to determine who gets paid when. One of the arts of staying in business is stretching out your accounts payable. So, before you pay anyone, you check with me. Also, I want some upside potential. So long as you owe me money, I want 12 percent interest on what you owe or 10 percent of the profits, whichever is higher. You pay me the 12 percent monthly, and quarterly I'll decide whether to keep the past three months' interest or take my share of the past three months' profits."

Dave accepts Susan's terms, with one condition: "We have to pay our people [i.e. the employees] on time. If we have the money, we pay them." Susan accepts Dave's condition, pays off the bank, and provides additional working capital to the business.

---

67. This question will have great practical importance if, for example, Paul attempts to "fire" Eli. See sections 11.4.2 (partner's right to compel liquidation of UPA partnership business), 11.7.1 (partner's right to damages for UPA dissolution done in bad faith), and 11.5.3–11.5.4 (UPA partner's right to distribution upon dissolution) and 11.11 (RUPA).

The business continues to operate under the same name, and no one except Dave knows of Susan's role in the business. Dave stops extending credit to law professors. Each month Susan reviews Dave's accounts payable and sets the priorities for payment as follows: (i) pay Susan the interest owed her, (2) pay overdue bills from people Dave intends to buy from again, (3) pay overdue bills from other people who are threatening suit, (4) pay others. Susan never does take a percentage of the profit, because the 12 percent interest figure is always higher.

Dave makes all decisions about which tradespeople to buy from. He also makes all personnel decisions (e.g., hiring, firing, salaries). After a year the business fails. Dave owes Susan $350,000; he owes creditors a total of $175,000 (trade creditors—$150,000; three employees—$25,000 in back wages). Dave has no money.

Can these other creditors collect from Susan? Consider Chapter Six as well as Chapter Seven in analyzing this Problem.

EXPLANATION

Two different theories hold promise for the creditors—partnership law and constructive agency under Restatement §14 O. If the creditors can establish that Susan is Dave's partner, UPA §15(b) or RUPA §306(a) will make Susan liable with Dave for the partnership's debts. If the creditors successfully invoke §14 O, Susan will be liable to the creditors as Dave's principal.

Although it is unlikely that Dave and Susan thought of their relationship as a partnership, they may nonetheless have formed one. Their thoughts about the legal label are largely immaterial. What matters is the nature of the business relationship they have intentionally created.

The other creditors will contend that the business relationship fits most of the paradigmatic characteristics of a partnership. Most importantly, Susan has a right to share profits. That right—rather than the actual receipt of profits—is the fundamental prerequisite to partner status. Susan has also "brought something to the party"—not only essential working capital, but also key management services. Moreover, like a paradigmatic partner, Susan has helped run the business, exercising management control over key financial issues. She has not contributed any property, because she has a contractual right to be repaid her loan. But not all partners contribute property. There is no express agreement to share losses, but most jurisdictions do not require one. Dave and Susan have shared control over the business and its assets. They have linked their economic fate to each other and to the business by agreeing to share profits. They have thus arranged to "carry on as co-owners a business for profit."[68]

Susan's response will be to characterize her right to share profits as mere "interest on a loan" and therefore not probative of partner status.[69] Both the

---

68. UPA §6(1); RUPA §202(a) (definition of partnership).

69. UPA §7(4)(d); RUPA §202(d)(3)(i).

profit-sharing agreement and the circumstances leading up to that agreement support this characterization. Susan's agreement with Dave gave her the right to take either interest at a fixed rate or a profit share. This arrangement demonstrates that profits, if chosen, were to take the place of conventional interest. The origins of the profit right indicate likewise. Susan did not seek an interest in Dave's business, but rather demanded an option on profits as a condition to making a loan.

The biggest problem with Susan's argument is the type of control she exercised. While many loan agreements give the lender extraordinary power over the debtor's affairs in the event of a default, Susan asked for, obtained, and began exercising *mundane* control *as a condition of granting the loan.* This deviation from standard lending practice may well tip the balance against Susan.

In any event, Susan has troubles under agency law. If a creditor asserts enough control over a debtor to take over the management of the debtor's business, Restatement §14 O makes the creditor liable for the debts of the business. Mere veto power is not enough; extensive involvement is necessary.

Susan may well have asserted the necessary control and undertaken the necessary involvement. She was certainly involved in the business; she spoke specifically of "divid[ing] up the responsibilities." Moreover, she controlled some very important aspects of the business—namely, when and what accounts would be paid and what customers would be allowed to buy services on credit. Susan can, however, point to large areas of the business that she did not control, namely, all personnel matters and the selection of vendors.

With the fact question of control a close one, a court may be influenced by the striking similarity between Susan's situation and the situation in *Cargill.* The creditor in *Cargill* kept the Warren grain elevator in business, obtaining grain while the elevator's debts to farmers mounted. Susan kept the dry cleaning enterprise in business and then used her control to make sure that she was paid before all creditors other than employees. In both situations, the creditor used its control to obtain a benefit at the expense of other creditors. Such an abuse of power simultaneously (a) demonstrates that the creditor did substantially interfere with the management of the debtor's business and (b) provides a policy reason for making the controlling creditor liable to the other creditors.

If Susan is liable under Restatement §14 O, the extent of that liability depends on whether the court follows *Cargill* or *Nash-Finch*.[70] *Cargill* follows §14 O faithfully and makes the creditor-principal liable for all debts incurred in the business after the creditor took control. Under *Cargill*, therefore, Susan would be liable to all creditors for all amounts arising after she refinanced and took control of the business.

Under *Nash-Finch,* in contrast, the principal's liability extends only to debts arising within areas of the business controlled by the creditor. Under

---

70. See section 6.3.2 n.22.

that approach, Susan would not be liable to the three employees. She did not control their selection, training, supervision, or payment. She did control payment to trade creditors and would be liable to them.

PROBLEM 62

From 1979 to 1993 attorneys Smith and Jones practiced law as a partnership. They had their offices on the tenth floor of a downtown office building. Outside their office they hung a beautiful mahogany sign that read:

SMITH & JONES
Attorneys at Law

In 1993 Smith and Jones terminated their partnership. They continued to share offices and office staffs, however. They also left in place their mahogany sign. They considered taking the sign down but "we never got around to it."

In 1994 a bookseller, J. A. Proofrock, came to Smith's office and sold her a new, expensive treatise on limited liability companies. Smith failed to pay and later became insolvent. Can Proofrock hold Jones liable for the debt? What additional facts would Proofrock have to prove?

EXPLANATION

Proofrock may be able to hold Jones liable on a theory of partnership by estoppel (UPA) or liability of purported partner (RUPA). By allowing the sign to remain up, Jones represented that he and Smith were partners. Under the UPA, Proofrock would also have to prove that "on the faith of such representation" she extended credit to Smith.[71] Under RUPA, she would have to show that "relying on the representation, [she] enter[ed] into a transaction with the . . . purported partnership."[72] The required showing is identical under both statutes and has two components: (i) that Proofrock believed Smith and Jones to be partners, and (ii) that the belief caused Proofrock to enter into the transaction. Both components concern Proofrock's state of mind. The facts provide a little outward evidence on the first component. The shared office space and staff show that Proofrock had no reason to disbelieve the sign. The facts provide no outward evidence on the causation issue.

---

71. UPA §16(1).
72. RUPA §308(a).

8

Financial Aspects of a Partnership (Creation and Operation)

§8.1 The Practical Background

Like any other business, a partnership needs two types of inputs in order to function: the working efforts of human beings ("labor") and the use of at least some property, be it as elaborate as a $30 million factory or as simple as paper on which to write out bills ("capital"). Partnerships can and often do obtain inputs from outsiders (i.e., from nonpartners). A partnership can, for example, rent office space from a landlord, borrow money from a bank, and engage servant agents (colloquially called *employees*), nonservant agents, and even nonagent independent contractors.

Partnerships also depend on inputs from the partners. A partnership typically obtains both labor and capital from its partners, although not every partner necessarily provides both.[1] Of course, a partner who provides something of value to the partnership will want something in return. Both the UPA and RUPA provide a comprehensive set of default rules that determine how and when partners receive a return,[2] and this chapter

---

1. In some partnerships, for example, one partner provides all the capital, while the other partner provides only labor. See section 8.7.

2. As explained in section 7.1.4, default rules apply except to the extent the partners have agreed otherwise.

discusses how those rules apply to the creation and operation of a partnership.[3]

§8.2   The Partner's Basic Return

Absent a contrary agreement, a partner's financial return has two components: (1) a right to share in the profits of the partnership, if any, and (2) a right, when the partnership ends, to receive the value of any property that the partner *contributed* to the partnership.[4] A partner also has the right to be indemnified against expenses and liabilities incurred in the service of the partnership.[5]

A partner may also have other financial arrangements with the partnership. For example, a partner may rent property to the partnership or loan it money. But such arrangements result from particular agreements between the partner and the partnership. They do not inhere in partner status.

§8.3   Rules for Sharing Profits and Losses

§8.3.1   *The Size of the Share (Percentages)*

Profits.   Both the UPA and RUPA have a simple default rule on the size of each partner's profit share. Absent a contrary agreement, each partner receives an equal share.[6] The rule applies regardless of how much individual partners have contributed to the partnership and regardless of how much individual partners work for the partnership.

> *Example:* Larry, Moe, and Curley form a partnership to manufacture and sell whoopee cushions. To get the business started, Larry and Curley each contribute $10,000. They each work in the factory 60 hours per week. Moe, in contrast, contributes $0 and works 20 hours per week "closing big deals." Despite these differing contributions and efforts, the partners share profits equally (i.e., a third each). Absent a contrary agreement, the default rule applies.

---

3. For UPA, §18 contains most of the default rules relevant to this chapter. In RUPA, §401 is the main section. When a partnership comes to an end, other financial aspects surface and other UPA and RUPA provisions become relevant. Chapter Eleven discusses those aspects and provisions in detail.

4. As discussed in detail in section 8.6, a partner contributes property to the partnership by transferring ownership of the property to the partnership.

5. See section 8.4.

6. UPA §18(a); RUPA §401(b).

Losses. Absent a contrary agreement, partners share losses in the same percentage as they share profits. UPA §18(a) states: "Each partner . . . must contribute towards the losses . . . sustained by the partnership according to his share in the profits." RUPA §401(b) says the same thing in gender neutral language: "Each partner . . . is chargeable with a share of the partnership losses in proportion to the partner's share of the profits."

If there is no inter se agreement addressing profits or losses, then—because the default rule on profits provides for equal profit sharing—the partners will share losses equally. If a partnership agreement establishes profit-sharing percentages but neglects to address loss sharing, the loss sharing percentages will mirror the profit-sharing percentages.

> *Example:* Larry, Moe, and Curley form a whoopee cushion partnership. The partnership agreement gives Moe a 60 percent share of profits and Larry and Curley each a 20 percent share. The agreement does not mention losses. If the partnership suffers losses, the partners will share the losses 60/20/20. Because the default rule applies, the loss shares match the profit shares.

No impact on third party claims. In an ordinary general partnership, loss sharing arrangements *among* partners do not affect the personal liability of each partner to creditors. If the partnership is not an LLP, each partner is either jointly liable or jointly and severally liable for each partnership debt regardless of the inter se situation.[7]

Inter se arrangements can, however, affect what happens if a creditor does succeed in collecting a partnership debt from an individual partner. If the partnership lacks the funds to indemnify that partner,[8] then the inter se arrangements will determine how much each of the other partners must compensate the partner who took the hit.

> *Example:* The Larry-Moe-Curley partnership goes out of business. The partnership is not an LLP, and a creditor of the partnership subsequently collects $21,000 from Curley on a debt owed by the partnership. The partnership has no funds to reimburse Curley. The partners had agreed to share losses equally. Curley has a right to collect $7,000 each from Larry and Moe.

---

7. UPA and RUPA rules governing relationships with outsiders cannot be changed by agreements among partners. See section 7.3.1 (relationship between partners' liability to third parties and partners' inter se loss sharing). Under RUPA, liability is always joint and several. Under the UPA, some liabilities are joint and others are joint and several. See section 7.3.1. In an LLP, the rules on loss sharing are changed somewhat to protect the liability shield. See section 14.2.6.

8. See section 8.4.

§8.3.2 *Timing*

Determining when profits are paid.   Neither the UPA's nor RUPA's default provisions on profit sharing specify how often profits are to be calculated and distributed, although the UPA provision can be read to suggest that a partnership must repay the value of all contributions and discharge all liabilities before it pays out any profit: "Each partner shall be repaid his contributions . . . and share equally in the profits and surplus remaining *after* all liabilities . . . are satisfied. . . ."[9]

In practice, however, such an approach would be extremely unusual. Partnerships typically repay contributions only when a partner withdraws from the partnership or when the partnership business comes to an end.[10] Profits, in contrast, are typically recognized and allocated on an annual basis. This approach is consonant with tax law requirements.[11]

As for when profits are actually *distributed,* the UPA provides no definitive answer and RUPA has only a Comment. That Comment states: "Absent an agreement to the contrary, . . . a partner does not have a right to receive a current distribution of the profits credited to his account, the interim distribution of profits being a matter arising in the ordinary course of business to be decided by majority vote of the partners."[12]

In any event, in most partnerships the timing of interim distributions is a matter of agreement—either express or through a course of conduct—and most such agreements contemplate some sort of annual distribution. Likewise by express agreement or by custom, partners in many partnerships make "draws" throughout the year against their anticipated annual profit share. Under most such arrangements, matters are evened up at year's end. If a partner has overdrawn, the partner must repay the excess. If a partner has drawn too little, the partner may then withdraw the remainder.[13]

Annual reconciliation is not mandatory. For example, a partnership agreement can appoint a later time for the "evening up" process or provide that overdraws simply be subtracted from the value of any contributions the partner has made to the partnership. Likewise, a partnership agreement could allow partners to leave in some or all of their profit share and have that amount treated as if the partners had contributed it back to the partnership.[14]

---

9. UPA §18(a) (emphasis added).

10. See Chapter Eleven.

11. Although a partnership pays no tax, it must annually provide each partner a "K-1" form. This form indicates each partner's share of profits or losses from the past tax year.

12. RUPA §401, Comment 3. An "interim distribution" is one that occurs before the winding up and termination of the partnership. For a discussion of partner management rights, See Chapter Ten. For a discussion of winding up and termination, see Chapter Eleven.

13. Profit draws are thus quite different than salary and wages. Salary and wages reflect a definite commitment by the partnership to pay a fixed amount, regardless of

14. See section 8.6.3 (contributions) and section 11.5.3 (capital accounts).

Determining when losses are "shared." Neither the UPA nor RUPA specifies the timing of loss sharing. Typically the partnership's books keep track of loss allocations on an annual basis, as required by tax law, and the recorded losses affect what each partner receives when the partnership comes to an end.[15]

§8.4 A Partner's Right to Indemnity

UPA §18(b) states, as a default rule, that:

> The partnership must indemnify every partner in respect of payments made and personal liabilities reasonably incurred by him in the ordinary and proper conduct of its business, or for the preservation of its business or property.

This rule closely resembles an agent's right of indemnity from its principal.[16] RUPA contains essentially the same provision, except with gender neutral wording and the words "reasonable" and "proper" omitted.[17] RUPA's official comments do not explain the omissions, explaining only that "Subsection (c) is derived from UPA Section 18(b)."[18]

> *Example:* In the Larry, Moe, and Curley whoopee cushion partnership, all partners share in the marketing work. A potential customer comes to town to discuss the possibility of placing a large order. Moe spends $300 wining and dining the customer, but the customer decides against placing the order. The partnership must reimburse Moe. His efforts were reasonable in light of the shared marketing responsibilities, and the amount of expense was reasonable in light of the potentially large order.

> *Example:* Same situation, except the partners have agreed that Larry alone will handle marketing efforts and sales promotion.[19] Under the UPA, that agreement means that Moe's payments for wining and dining

---

how much profit (if any) the partnership makes. Absent a contrary agreement, no partner has a right to wages or salary for work done for the partnership. See section 8.5.

15. Section 11.5.3 explains both the recordkeeping process and the eventual effect of the allocated losses.

16. See section 4.3.1.

17. RUPA §401(c) states that "(c) A partnership shall reimburse a partner for payments made and indemnify a partner for liabilities incurred by the partner in the ordinary course of the business of the partnership or for the preservation of its business or property."

18. RUPA §401, Comment 4.

19. For the enforceability of such agreements inter se the partners, see section 9.6. For the effect of such agreements on the *power* of partners to bind the partnership to third parties, see sections 10.1–10.3.

expenses have not been "made . . . in the ordinary and *proper* conduct of [the partnership's] business." UPA §18 (emphasis added). Under the UPA, therefore, he is not entitled to reimbursement. Under RUPA, the result is probably the same, since the agreement puts Moe's entertaining outside the "the ordinary course of the business of the partnership." RUPA §401(c).

§8.5   Remuneration for Labor Provided by Partners to the Partnership

If partners spend time and effort furthering the partnership's business, what compensation do they receive? Under both UPA §18(f) and RUPA §401(h), the default rule is simple. Absent a contrary agreement—be it express or implied—they receive nothing beyond their share in the profits: no wages, no salary, no extra compensation of any kind.[20]

> *Example:* Larry, Moe, and Curley form a partnership to manufacture and sell whoopee cushions. They agree to share profits equally. To get the business started they each contribute $5,000 to the partnership. Larry and Curley each work in the factory 60 hours per week. Moe works 20 hours per week "closing big deals." Larry and Curley contend that they should get "something extra" for working more. They are incorrect, unless they can show either an express or implied agreement.

Although in concept the mechanism for determining whether a partner has a right to additional compensation is clear-cut, in practice fact disputes about alleged implied or oral agreements can be quite intense.

§8.6   Remuneration for Capital Provided by Partners to the Partnership

§8.6.1   *Overview*

Providing capital may be some or all of what a partner brings to the table when forming or entering a partnership.[21] Under both the UPA and RUPA, default rules on remunerating partners for capital are far more complicated than the rules for remunerating partners for labor because partners can provide capital to the partnership in three different ways:

---

20. This rule has one exception. Under RUPA, each partner is entitled to "reasonable compensation for services rendered in winding up the business of the partnership." RUPA §401(h). Under UPA §18(f), the exception is narrower; reasonable compensation for winding up is available only to a sole surviving partner.

21. Absent a contrary agreement, a partnership cannot compel those already partners to provide *additional* capital.

- They may *contribute* property, transferring their ownership interest in the property to the partnership.
- They may *furnish* property, providing the partnership only the use of the property for either the duration of the partnership or some other period of time, retaining title to the property and receiving no remuneration beyond a share in the profits.
- They may *lease* or *loan* the property, providing the partnership the use of the property for either the duration of the partnership or some other period of time, retaining title to the property and receiving rent, interest, or royalties as compensation.

The property involved can be any property—real or personal, tangible or intangible—in which the partner holds an interest.

> *Example:* Larry, Moe, and Curley form a partnership. Larry *contributes* $10,000 in cash. Moe has a right under a lease to occupy certain business premises, and he *furnishes* those premises to the partnership. Curley *leases* his truck to the partnership.

The remuneration rules are essentially the same under the UPA and RUPA and, under both statutes, vary depending on the mode a partner has used to provide capital.

§8.6.2 *Distinguishing the Modes of Providing Capital*

UPA approach.[22]   The UPA contains no rules for distinguishing the modes of providing capital.[23] The rules come from the case law, which is plentiful. Whether a partner has leased, loaned, furnished, or contributed property to a partnership depends on the intent of the parties, that is, of the partner providing the property and the partnership. Intent is a question of fact, to be determined objectively from the parties' manifestations. Express agreements provide the clearest manifestation.

In the absence of an express agreement, a court is unlikely to find a lease or a loan unless the partnership has in fact made payments that can be fairly construed as rent, interest, or royalties. As for distinguishing *contributed* property (ownership transfers to the partnership) from merely *furnished* property (partner retains ownership), the following factors indicate *contribution*:

---

22. This section is drawn from Kleinberger & Wrigley, Who Owns the Christmas Trees? The Disposition of Property Used by a Partnership, 39 Kansas L. Rev. 245, 256–57 (1991).

23. UPA §8(2) does provide a rule for characterizing property purchased with partnership funds. "Unless the contrary intention appears, property acquired with partnership funds is partnership property."

- the use of the property in the partnership business, especially if the property is crucial or central to that business;
- the use of partnership funds in improving, maintaining, insuring, or paying taxes on the property;
- indications in the partnership's books that the property belongs to the partnership; and
- nonreceipt of rent or other compensation by the partner who provided the property.

The factors just listed do not include the partnership holding formal legal title to the property. There are at least two reasons. First, only real property and a few forms of personal property (e.g., motor vehicles, stocks) even *have* record title. Second, in many states, prior to the enactment of the UPA a partnership could not hold title to real property in the partnership's name.[24] It was therefore common for individual partners, or for partners jointly, to hold title to real estate that in a functional and equitable sense belonged to the partnership. As a result of custom and inertia, such arrangements have continued even under the UPA.

RUPA approach.   RUPA changes the law on this subject and places considerable emphasis on title. The change is consistent with RUPA's entity approach as well as with RUPA's concern to clarify record title for real estate.[25] The RUPA rules have two facets: one relating to the formalities of property acquisition (i.e., in whose name); the other relating to the assets used to accomplish the acquisition (i.e., who paid for it). The first facet is controlling. That is, the rules relating to who paid for the property apply only if the rules relating to formalities of acquisition do not determine the question.

Formalities of acquisition.   Property is partnership property if acquired:

- in the name of . . . the partnership"[26]

or

- in the name of "one or more partners" if "the instrument transferring title to the property" indicates "the person's capacity as a partner or . . . the existence of a partnership."[27]

Example: Rachel executes a deed to a parcel of land, with the transferee shown as "Eli, a partner." Eli is a partner in the Eli-Ilan Scissor Company, a RUPA general partnership. The land belongs to the partnership.

---

24. This disability reflected the aggregate approach to partnerships. See section 7.2.7.
25. See section 10.3.5 (discussing statements of authority, limitation, and denial).
26. RUPA §204(a)(1).
27. RUPA §204(a)(2).

Assets used to accomplish the acquisition.   If the just stated rule does not determine ownership, then the source of funds or credit used to acquire the property raises an ownership presumption.

- "Property is presumed to be partnership property if purchased with partnership assets."[28]
- "Property acquired . . . without use of partnership assets, is presumed to be separate property, even if used for partnership purposes."[29]

Although RUPA rules work best with property with record title, they apply with equal force to all forms of property—e.g., real, personal, tangible, and intangible.

§8.6.3 *Determining a Partner's Remuneration for Property Provided to the Partnership*

This remuneration analysis is the same under the UPA and RUPA and has two aspects: (i) what compensation, if any, the partner receives for providing property to the partnership, and (ii) whether the partner ever receives back the property provided. Inherent in the second question are two more questions: (i) if the property depreciates while being used by the partnership, who bears the loss? (ii) if the property appreciates, who takes the gain?

For property leased or loaned.   A partner who leases or loans property to the partnership receives compensation according to the terms of whatever agreement establishes the lease or loan. When the lease or loan period ends, the property returns to the partner. Absent a contrary agreement, if the value of the property has decreased (for reasons other than abuse) or increased during the loan/lease period, that detriment or benefit belongs to the partner who owns the property.

> *Example:* A partner leases to the partnership several new pieces of construction equipment, and the partnership agrees to pay rent of $5,000 per month. After five years, the partnership comes to an end and the lease terminates. The partner regains the right to possess, use, and dispose of the equipment. Although the equipment is now far less valuable than it was originally, the partnership is not obliged to compensate the lessor/partner for the decrease.[30] Absent a contrary agreement, the risk of diminishing value stays on the party who owns the leased property.

---

28. RUPA §204(c).

29. RUPA §204(d).

30. Of course, if the lessor/partner has figured the lease payments rationally, those payments will have taken the depreciation into account. Nonetheless, as a formal matter the risk of depreciation stays with the owner.

For property merely furnished.   A partner who merely furnishes property to the partnership receives no compensation beyond a share in the profits; allowing the partnership to use the property is part of what the partner brings to the party in return for that profit share. When the partnership ends, the property returns to the partner who furnished it. Absent a contrary agreement, if the value of the property has decreased (for reasons other than abuse) or increased, that detriment or benefit belongs to the partner who owns the property.

> *Example:* A partner furnishes to the partnership the royalty-free use of a patent. After five years the partnership dissolves, and the partner regains full rights in the patent. In that five years, the patent has become more valuable because a major competitive product has been discontinued as unsafe. The partnership has no right to share in that increased value. Absent a contrary agreement, the benefits of increasing value stay with the party who owns the property.

For property contributed.   A partner who contributes property to the partnership receives no on-going compensation beyond a share in the profits—no lease payments, no royalties, no interest.[31] However, when the partnership comes to an end, the partnership owes the contributor the *value* of the contribution, measured as of the time contribution occurred.[32] In a well-run partnership the partners specify that value by agreement. Otherwise, if a dispute occurs, valuation becomes a question of fact.

Absent a contrary agreement, the contributor has no right to the return of the property itself. If after contribution the property has decreased or increased in value, that detriment or benefit belongs to the partnership.[33]

> *Example:* To help the Larry-Moe-Curley partnership get started making whoopee cushions, Moe contributes equipment worth at the time $500,000. A year later the equipment breaks down and becomes worthless. When the partnership later comes to an end, the partnership owes Moe $500,000.

> *Example:* Larry contributes to the partnership land worth $400,000. The land appreciates during the partnership's existence and is worth $1,000,000 when the partnership comes to an end. Larry has no right to the return of the land; it belongs to the partnership. Larry does have

---

31. UPA §18(d); RUPA §401(d).

32. There may be other facts which create debits or offsets against this amount. See section 11.5.3.

33. To keep track of their financial rights and obligations, partners use a device called "capital accounts." Although the term may seem frightening to those unfamiliar (or phobic about) accounting, it merely labels a set of conventional rules for tracking what is due each partner from the partnership and vice versa. Section 11.5.3 explains capital accounts in more details and illustrates their function.

a right to the return of the original value of his contribution, that is, $400,000. The $600,000 in appreciation belongs to the partnership.[34]

§8.7   Special Problems with K-and-L Partnerships

§8.7.1   *K-and-L Partnerships Described*

A partner may "buy into" a partnership by providing or promising to provide capital, labor, or both. There is no requirement, however, that each partner provide both capital and labor. In some partnerships one partner provides all the capital (the *K* partner) and another partner provides all the labor (the *L* partner).[35] In the context of such K-and-L partnerships, courts occasionally have difficulties applying the statutory default rules on remuneration and loss sharing.

§8.7.2   *Problems with Loss Sharing*

The UPA and RUPA default provisions apply regardless of the inputs the partners provide to "buy into" the partnership. Therefore, if a K-and-L partnership loses money, the *L* partner (i.e., the one who provided only labor) will receive nothing from the partnership (since there will be no profits to share and since UPA §18(f) and RUPA §401(h) preclude any other compensation for *L*'s labor). In addition, the *L* partner will have to pay the *K* partner so as to share losses with that partner (since UPA §18(a) and RUPA §401(b) provide for loss sharing).[36]

> *Example:* Cliff and Lilith form a partnership to run a dating service. They do not make any agreements displacing the remuneration and loss default rules. Lilith provides $250,000 in start-up money and does not work in the business. Cliff works full-time in the business, but contributes no capital. The partnership comes to an end after a year, having lost $250,000. (That is, the partnership manages to pay off all creditors, but then has nothing left over. Since the partnership began with $250,000, the partnership has suffered a $250,000 loss.) For his year of work, Cliff has received nothing. There are no profits, and the statute (be it UPA §18(f) or RUPA §401(h)) bars any other form of compensation. Lilith appears to have lost $250,000, but the UPA's default rule on loss sharing is in effect. That rule provides that Cliff and Lilith share losses as they would have shared profits; that is, equally. For Cliff's *out-of-pocket* losses to equal Lilith's, $125,000 must make its way from Cliff

---

34. Larry may receive some of the $600,000 as shared profits. See section 11.5.3.

35. In the shorthand used by economists, *K* represents capital and *L* represents labor.

36. Technically, the *L* partner would pay the partnership, which would then distribute the money to the *K* partner. See section 11.5.3.

to Lilith. Cliff will pay $125,000 to the partnership, which will then distribute that amount to Lilith. Both Cliff and Lilith will then have lost $125,000.

This result may appear harsh. After all, without loss sharing Cliff and Lilith appear each to have lost roughly comparable value. They have lost, that is, the value they provided the partnership in return for becoming partners. (The statutory default rules seem to assume that those values are roughly comparable, because under those rules Cliff and Lilith qualified for equal shares of the profits.) Accordingly, if Cliff has to transfer $125,000 to Lilith, his loss of value will exceed hers.

Seeking to avoid such apparently harsh results, some courts have held that the *L* partner shares losses only if he or she has expressly agreed to do so. Appearances can mislead, however, and those courts have misunderstood the balance of losses between K-and-L partners. In the example above, Cliff lost whatever value he could have derived from using his labor elsewhere during the partnership's year of operation. Lilith had a parallel loss—whatever income she could have derived from investing the $250,000 elsewhere for a year. In addition, without loss sharing, Lilith also lost the $250,000 itself.

Whether the statutory default rule is unfair to Cliff (or perhaps unfair to Lilith) will depend on how the value of Cliff's forgone labor opportunity compares with the value of Lilith's forgone capital opportunity. If Lilith could have earned 10 percent interest by investing her money elsewhere for a year, and if Cliff's lack of skills and odd personality mean that he could have earned no more than $20,000 in salary in some other position, then even after Cliff pays Lilith $125,000 Lilith will have suffered greater detriment than Cliff. Cliff will have lost $125,000 out-of-pocket, plus the forgone opportunity to earn $20,000 by working elsewhere for the year. Total detriment: $145,000. Lilith will have lost $125,000 out-of-pocket ($250,000 contributed, offset partially by Cliff's $125,000), plus the forgone opportunity to earn $25,000 interest on her capital. Total detriment: $150,000.

In any event, the language of UPA §18(a) and RUPA §401(b) expressly mandates loss sharing.

§8.7.3 *Problems with Appreciation*

Under the statutory default rules, when a partner contributes property to the partnership and that property subsequently increases in value, the partnership—not the partner—benefits.[37] Eventually, when the partnership realizes the appreciation, that value either offsets business losses or adds to profits. To the extent the appreciation adds to profits, all partners share in the benefit according to their respective profit shares. The partner who originally contributed the property has no special claim on the appreciation.

---

37. See section 8.6.3.

Occasionally, courts dealing with K-and-L partnerships ignore or misunderstand the default rules and allocate all the appreciation to the *K* partner (i.e., the partner who contributed the property). They do so either by miscalculating the amount they award each partner or by returning the appreciated asset itself to the *K* partner.

> *Example:* Cliff and Lilith form a partnership to raise chickens, agreeing to share profits equally. Cliff contributes a small farm worth $50,000. Four years later the partnership comes to an end. By selling all of its assets other than the farm the partnership has enough cash to exactly pay off its debts. During the life of the partnership, land values have increased sharply, so the partnership manages to sell the farm for $200,000. How the proceeds are divided will depend on whether the court follows the applicable partnership statute:
>
> - *Applying the Default Rules of the UPA and RUPA*—The partnership pays $50,000 to Cliff, returning to him the value of his contribution.[38] The remaining $150,000 represents postcontribution appreciation and is therefore profits. Cliff and Lilith each receive half.
> - *Overcompensating the K Partner*—The partnership either allocates all $200,000 to Cliff or simply transfers ownership of the farm back to him. In either event, Cliff gets the benefit of all the appreciation.

§8.8 Partner's Interests in Partnership Property

§8.8.1 Partnership Property

Reflecting the entity approach,[39] both the UPA and RUPA allow partnerships to own property, and partnerships typically do so. Partnerships acquire ownership of property either by accepting contributions or by purchase. Funds for purchase can come from contributions, from business operations (including the sale of other partnership property), or from loans.

As for a partner's interest in partnership property, the UPA and RUPA each reach the same result—although the two statutes differ substantially in how they state their respective rules.

§8.8.2 UPA's Approach: Partner's Property Rights in the Partnership

According to UPA §24, each partner has three *property* rights in the partnership: "(1) his rights in specific partnership property, (2) his interest in the partnership, and (3) his right to participate in the management."

---

38. See section 8.6.3.
39. See section 7.2.7.

As to the first and third rights, the "property" label borders on the bizarre; the rights relate to management prerogatives, not property interests. The key to understanding the UPA approach is therefore to disregard the label and attend instead to the specific content of the rights being described.

Management prerogatives disguised as property rights.   A UPA partner's "property" rights include two management prerogatives: (i) the right to use the assets of the partnership in furtherance of the partnership's business (UPA §25); and (ii) the right to participate in the management of the partnership (UPA §24).[41]

The upshot is a fairly straightforward and common sense notion. Absent a contrary agreement each partner has the right to possess and use partnership property for the purposes of the business, but no partner has the right to use partnership property for other purposes. Unfortunately, UPA §25 states this notion in an unnecessarily intricate way. Taking an aggregate approach, the provision describes the right to use business assets for business purposes as "co-tenancy in partnership."

The partner's interest — the partner's economic rights.   A UPA partner's "interest in the partnership" consists of a right to share in the profits of the partnership and the right to receive, when the partnership ends, the value of any property contributed to the partnership.[40] Although labelling these rights "property" is not misleading, it is redundant. UPA §18(a) independently establishes that being a partner involves having a right to share in the profits of the business. Likewise, UPA §18(a) provides that "[e]ach partner shall be repaid his contributions."[42]

§8.8.3   RUPA Approach

RUPA replaces the UPA's oblique approach with two straightforward pronouncements:

- "A partner is not a co-owner of partnership property and has no interest in partnership property which can be transferred, either voluntarily or involuntarily."[43]

---

40.   UPA §26 (share of profits and surplus).

41.   A partner's "right to participate in the management" under UPA §24(3) is redundant of UPA §18(e). Sections 9.2.1, 9.3, 9.4.2, and 9.5.1 discuss UPA §18(e) in detail.

42.   As for a partner's right to receive back the value of its contribution, see section 8.6.3 and section 11.5.3 (describing how UPA §40 implements UPA §18).

43.   RUPA §501.

- "A partner may use or possess partnership property only on behalf of the partnership."[44]

As for a RUPA partner's property rights, there is only the partner's "transferable interest," which is "the partner's share of the profits and losses of the partnership and the partner's right to receive distributions."[45]

§8.8.4 Assignability and Creditors' Rights

Assignability.   Despite all the so-called property rights of a UPA partner, the UPA and RUPA take essentially the same approach to the assignability of a partner's interest. Under the statutory default rules of UPA §§25–28 and RUPA §§501–504, only a partner's economic rights are freely assignable ("transferable" in the terminology of RUPA). A partner may not assign or transfer to someone else the right to participate in management or the right to use partnership property for partnership purposes, unless an agreement among the partners allows the assignment. Such an agreement may be made in advance and apply generally or may consist merely of consent to a particular assignment or transfer.

> *Example:* Larry wants to assign his right to receive profits in the Larry-Moe-Curley partnership to the First National Bank. The Bank wants the assignment as security for a loan it is about to make to Larry. The Bank also wants the right to exercise Larry's management rights. The partnership agreement is silent on the subject. To assign the management rights to the Bank, Larry needs the consent of Moe and Curley.

> *Example:* The partnership agreement of the Larry-Moe-Curley partnership states that all partners must agree on any purchase whose price exceeds $10,000. The agreement also provides: "If a partner assigns all of his interest in profits, the partner may also assign to that same assignee the right to vote on proposed purchases whose price exceeds $10,000." Under that provision, when Larry assigns his profit interest to the First Bank, he may—without further consent from Moe and Curley—also assign the right to vote on purchases in excess of $10,000.

The statutory default approach to assignment/transfer is consistent with the statutes' default approach to adding new partners. To assign or transfer management and asset-use rights is tantamount to bringing the assignee or

---

44. RUPA §401(g).
45. RUPA §502.

transferee into the partnership. Under UPA §27(1) a partner cannot assign a complete partnership interest (and thereby make the assignee effectively a member of the partnership) "in the absence of agreement" with the copartners. Likewise, under UPA §18(g), absent a contrary agreement: "No person can become a member of a partnership without the consent of all the partners."[46] Similarly, under RUPA §401(i), "A person may become a partner only with the consent of all of the partners." As for transferability, "The only transferable interest of a partner in the partnership is the partner's share of the profits and losses of the partnership and the partner's right to receive distributions."[47] Moreover:

> A transfer . . . of a partner's transferable interest in the partnership . . . is permissible [but] does not, as against the other partners or the partnership, entitle the transferee, during the continuance of the partnership, to participate in the management or conduct of the partnership business, to require access to information concerning partnership transactions, or to inspect or copy the partnership books or records.[48]

Agreements among partners can also work to restrict transferability, limiting or eliminating partners' rights to assign their economic interests.

Creditors' rights — the charging order.   Creditors seeking to collect on a claim against an individual partner may reach only the partner's economic rights.[49] The creditors may not attach or levy on the partnership's property, for: (i) under the UPA, an individual partner's rights to that property are inalienable without the agreement of the other partners;[50] and (ii) under RUPA, an individual partner has no rights in partnership property.[51]

To reach a partner's economic rights, the creditor must use a *charging order*, a special device first created by UPA §28 and essentially replicated in RUPA §504. The charging order first functions as a type of garnishment. The creditor applies to a court for an order that, if granted, obligates the partnership to pay to the creditor any amounts that would otherwise be paid to the debtor partner.[52]

A charging order also functions as a judgment lien. The other partners can use their own, separate funds to redeem the charged rights, and partner-

---

46. An assignment of a complete partnership interest would not effectively admit a new partner if the assignee were already a partner. However, UPA §27(1) applies regardless of whether the assignee is already a partner.
47. RUPA §502.
48. RUPA §503(a)(1) and (3).
49. UPA §§28(1), 26; RUPA §504.
50. UPA §25(2)(c). Creditors seeking to collect a debt of the partnership can, in contrast, levy on the partnership's property. Id.
51. RUPA §501.
52. UPA §28(1); RUPA §504(b).

ship funds may be used with "the consent of all the partners whose interests are not so charged or sold."[53] If "the circumstances of the case . . . require,"[54] the court may order the charged interest foreclosed and sold. In that event, the economic rights of the debtor partner are sold just like any other property subject to a judgment lien.

> *Example:* The Larry-Moe-Curley partnership owns considerable property, including a modern factory and a large inventory of whoopee cushions. Moe personally owes Shemp $500,000, and that amount has been reduced to judgment. Shemp cannot levy against the factory or the inventory, since that property belongs to the partnership. Shemp can, however, obtain a charging order against Moe's economic rights in the partnership. With that order in place, Shemp will receive any distributions the partnership would otherwise make to Moe.

A charging order and any foreclosure and sales relate only to the debtor partner's economic rights. Neither the creditor nor any foreclosure purchaser obtains any rights to participate in the management of the partnership or to possess or use partnership property.

> *Example:* Although the Larry-Moe-Curley partnership enjoys good long-term prospects, the business is not currently making any profits. Shemp wishes to collect on his judgment now and persuades a court to foreclose the charging order. The charged interest is sold at auction to Lucille, who in essence now owns whatever economic interests Moe had as a partner. However, neither the foreclosure nor the sale make Lucille a partner or entitle her to participate in the operation and management of the business.

PROBLEM 63

The partnership agreement of a law firm provides a complicated formula for determining each partner's annual profit share. The formula takes into account billable hours, payments actually received on account of work billed, and work brought into the firm ("rainmaking"). At the end of one year, one partner seeks "a more egalitarian approach" and contends that the partnership statute requires partners to share profits equally. Is that partner correct?

EXPLANATION

No. UPA §18(a) and RUPA §401(b) each provide for equal profit shares but only as a default rule. When partners displace the default rule by agreement, the agreement governs.

---

53. UPA §28(2)(b). See also RUPA §504(c)(2) and (3).
54. UPA §28(1). See also RUPA §504(b).

PROBLEM 64

Paul and Dennis operate a basketball camp as an ordinary general partnership. Theirs is a handshake deal; they have no written agreement.

A camper who is hurt at the camp successfully sues the partnership for negligence and recovers a judgment of $250,000. The partnership has no money, and the camper collects the entire amount from Paul. Assuming that the partnership has sustained no other losses but has no money with which to reimburse Paul, how much, if anything, can Paul collect from Dennis? Can Dennis successfully argue that "the losses should lay where they fall"?

EXPLANATION

Dennis owes Paul $125,000. Absent a contrary agreement, partners share losses as they do profits—equally. Collection by a third party does not change how losses are allocated.

PROBLEM 65

In 1983, Larry, Moe, and Curley became partners in an entertainment business. Their partnership agreement set a term of ten years and stated:

> Profits shall be calculated and paid on an annual basis, with the fiscal year being the calendar year. For any profit made in any fiscal year, Larry will receive 60%, Moe 25%, and Curley 15%. Losses will be shared as provided in the Uniform Partnership Act.

Each year in the period 1983 through 1987, the partnership broke even. In 1988, the partnership lost $100,000. How should that loss be apportioned? Would the result be different under RUPA?

EXPLANATION

The loss should be apportioned 60/25/15. Under UPA §18(a), absent a contrary agreement losses are apportioned the same way as profits. RUPA would produce the same result. RUPA §401(b) is essentially identical to UPA §18(a).

PROBLEM 66

Suzanne and Bernard run a dance school as a partnership. The school serves children between the ages of 4 and 14. The highlight of each year is a splendiferous dance recital held at a public auditorium rented by the partnership. Suzanne takes care of the business side of operations, and Bernard has agreed that Suzanne alone has the right to sign checks and make payments for the partnership. Bernard handles the artistic side of the business.

This year disaster threatened the school. On the night of the big recital Bernard arrived at the auditorium and found it locked. After some frantic telephoning he located the auditorium manager who said that she had never received the dance school's rental check. (It had apparently been lost in the mail.) The manager refused to open the auditorium without a check in hand. Suzanne was out of town, so Bernard wrote a personal check for the rental fee. Under RUPA, is Bernard entitled to reimbursement from the partnership, or does his foray into the business side of the partnership disqualify the expense? Under the UPA?

EXPLANATION

Cancelling or rescheduling the recital at the last minute could have been disastrous for the dance school's business. While Bernard's payment (his "foray") was probably not "in the *ordinary* course of the business of the partnership," RUPA §401(c) (emphasis added), the payment *was* "for the preservation of [the partnership's] business." Id. Therefore, Bernard is entitled to reimbursement.

The result is the same under the UPA. Like RUPA §401(c), UPA §18(b) provides for reimbursement for "payments made . . . for the preservation of [the partnership's] business or property."

PROBLEM 67

Rachael and Alyssa go into partnership together to own a natural foods store. They each put up $5,000 and jointly select a storefront to rent. During the first year Alyssa is the "silent" partner. She does no work for the business. Rachael, in contrast, works about 50 hours per week in the store, with no vacation. At the end of the year, the partnership has made a profit of $30,000. Rachael proposes a profit split of $20,000 for herself and $10,000 for Alyssa. She explains, "I put in at least 2,500 hours this year, and our lowest paid clerk got $4 per hour. I figure I'm worth at least that. Four times 2,500 is $10,000, leaving another $20,000 which we split equally." Is Alyssa obliged to agree to Rachael's proposal?

EXPLANATION

No. Absent a contrary agreement, Rachael's work in the partnership business brings her no right to extra remuneration.[55] Absent a contrary agreement, the partners split profits equally.[56]

PROBLEM 68

Joseph owns 500 acres of land on which he grows pine trees for harvest and for sale each year at Christmas time. The land is worth $500,000, and land values in the region are increasing steadily. Joseph asks Charles to operate the Christmas tree business for him. In return for Charles's promise to stay for five years, Joseph promises Charles an annual salary of $10,000 plus half the profits.

Assume that (i) Charles makes a number of changes to the land, including harvesting some trees, planting others, and building a few dirt roads;

---

55. UPA §18(f); RUPA §401(h).
56. UPA §18(a); RUPA §401(b).

(ii) at all times relevant title to the land is in Joseph's name; and (iii) a court finds that the arrangement between Joseph and Charles constitutes a partnership with a five-year term. If the UPA governs, at the end of the five years, will Joseph still own the land? Does the result differ under RUPA?

EXPLANATION

Under both statutes, the answer depends on whether Joseph has contributed the land to the partnership or merely furnished its use. The land was of central importance to the partnership, and the partnership did (through Charles) make some improvements to the property.

However, it seems unlikely that Joseph intended to give up ownership of the land. In most states, a partnership can own land in its own name, and Joseph never transferred title to the partnership. More importantly, to view the land as contributed is to construe into existence an extraordinary sweetheart deal for Charles. Charles brought to the partnership only his labor, for which he received not only a salary but also a share of profits. At minimum, Joseph furnished the use of land worth $500,000 and contributed any trees that Charles harvested from the land. For that, Joseph received in return less than Charles—merely a profit share.

If Joseph *contributed* the land, then the deal is even sweeter for Charles. The land itself belongs to the partnership; any appreciation will belong to the partnership; and Charles will have a right to half of that appreciation. That deal seems too good to be either true or intended.

Under RUPA the result would be the same, with the analysis buttressed by the presumption established by RUPA §204(d):

> Property acquired in the name of one or more of the partners, without an indication in the instrument transferring title to the property of the person's capacity as a partner or of the existence of a partnership and without use of partnership assets, is presumed to be separate property, even if used for partnership purposes.

PROBLEM 69

This Problem is based on a children's poem by Eugene Field:

> Wynken, Blynken, and Nod one night
>   Sailed off in a wooden shoe—
> Sailed on a river of crystal light,
>   Into a sea of dew.
> "Where are you going, and what do you wish?"
>   The old moon asked the three.
> "We've come to fish for the herring fish
>   That live in this beautiful sea;
>   Nets of silver and gold have we!"
>   Said Wynken,
>   Blynken,
>   And Nod.

Assume that Wynken, Blynken, and Nod are partners. Last year, before the partners divided profits, the "nets of silver and gold" were purchased using some of the revenues generated by the sale of herring fish. Wynken is taking her family fishing and wants to take one third of the nets with her on the outing. Under the UPA, does she have the legal right to do so?

EXPLANATION

No—not without the consent of her fellow partners. The nets belong to the partnership, not to the partners. "Unless the contrary intention appears, property acquired with partnership funds is partnership property."[57] Under UPA §25(2)(a), Wynken has an equal right to possess partnership property but only for partnership purposes. To use partnership property for personal purposes requires the consent of the other partners.

PROBLEM 70

Although the Rachael/Alyssa health food store partnership is doing well enough, Alyssa has fallen on hard times. One of her personal creditors is about to sue her. To avoid that embarrassment, Alyssa persuades the creditor to release the claim in return for "an assignment of all of my rights in the partnership I co-own with Rachael." The creditor then approaches Rachael and insists upon a voice in running the health food store. If RUPA governs, is Rachael obliged to accede?

EXPLANATION

No. Absent a contrary agreement, Alyssa may transfer her economic rights in the partnership—her "transferable interest"—but cannot transfer her rights to participate in management.[58]

PROBLEM 71

Samuel, Philip, and Sylvia operate a dental supply business as partners. Samuel and Philip are the "outside salesmen," and Sylvia runs the office. Samuel and Philip both do a lot of driving, and every two years, partnership money is used to buy them each a new car. Title to the cars is in the partnership's name, and the partnership pays for the car insurance. However, the price of the each car is reported as profit on Samuel's and Phil's respective K-1 forms. A judgment creditor of Samuel's tries to levy on the car he currently drives. What result under the UPA? Under RUPA?

---

57. UPA §8(2).
58. RUPA §§502, 503(a)(1) and (3).

EXPLANATION

Under either statute, the levy will be successful only if the car is not partnership property. A personal creditor of a partner cannot levy on partnership property.[59]

Under the UPA, several factors suggest that Samuel's car is partnership property. Partnership funds were used to purchase and to insure it. Title is in the partnership's name. Moreover, the car is of central use in the partnership's business.

The question is, however, ultimately one of the partners' intent, and the K-1 forms argue strongly that the car is Samuel's personal property. By treating the price of the car as profit allocated to Samuel, the K-1 form effectively characterized the car as his personal property. It is hard to dismiss that characterization as self-serving or artificial, because (i) it was integrally connected with the way the partners structured their relationship and (ii) it created tax liability for Samuel.[60]

Under RUPA, the result is different, because RUPA §204(a)(1) controls. That provision states: "Property is partnership property if acquired in the name of . . . the partnership." Because the car is titled in the partnership's name, it is evident that the car was acquired "in the name of the partnership."

---

59. UPA §25(2)(c); RUPA §504(e).
60. See section 7.3.2 (profits allocated to a partner are taxable income for that partner).

9

Management Issues and Fiduciary Duties

§9.1   The Panoply of Management Rights

Comanagement is a key attribute of a partnership, and—under the default rules of both the UPA and RUPA—each partner has a full panoply of management rights:

- the right to know what is going on in the partnership,
- the right to be involved in conducting the business,
- the right to commit the partnership to third parties,[1]
- the right to participate in decision making, and
- the right to veto certain decisions.

§9.2   The Right to Know

Under both the UPA and RUPA each partner has a right to obtain from the partnership and from fellow partners full and complete information concerning the partnership and its business.

---

1. Just as an agent can have the *power* to bind its principal without having the right to do so, see section 2.1.4, a partner can have the *power* to bind its partnership without having the *authority* to do so. Section 9.4 considers a partner's authority to bind. Chapter Ten considers the power.

§9.2.1   Under the UPA

Under the UPA the right to information rests on four sources. UPA §§19 and 20 provide the most direct authority. UPA §19 states that "every partner shall at all times have access to and may inspect and copy any of [the partnership books]." UPA §20 states: "Partners shall render on demand true and full information of all things affecting the partnership to any partner. . . ."[2]

UPA §18(e) provides authority by implication. That provision gives each partner an equal right "in the management and conduct of the partnership business," and a partner who lacks information cannot meaningfully manage or conduct business. For the UPA §18(e) right to be meaningful, therefore, it must by implication encompass access to all relevant business information.

The concept of fiduciary duty also provides authority by implication. As discussed below,[3] partners are mutual fiduciaries. Each partner owes fellow partners a duty of loyalty, which includes a duty of candor. If Partner *A* owes Partner *B* a duty of candor, by implication Partner *B* has a right to whatever information Partner *A* is duty bound to provide.

§9.2.2   Under RUPA

In general.   RUPA §403 contains a comprehensive set of information access rules which recognize three categories of information: information in the partnership's books and records, information which one partner is obliged to volunteer to another, and information which one partner is entitled to demand and receive from another. The rules can be as succinctly quoted as paraphrased:

> (b) A partnership shall provide partners and their agents and attorneys access to its books and records. . . . The right of access provides the opportunity to inspect and copy books and records during ordinary business hours. A partnership may impose a reasonable charge, covering the costs of labor and material, for copies of documents furnished.
>
> (c) Each partner and the partnership shall furnish to a partner, and to the legal representative of a deceased partner or partner under legal disability:
>
> (1) without demand, any information concerning the partnership's business and affairs reasonably required for the proper exercise of the partner's rights and duties under the partnership agreement or this [Act]; and
>
> (2) on demand, any other information concerning the partnership's business and affairs, except to the extent the demand or the information demanded is unreasonable or otherwise improper under the circumstances.

---

2. In some situations, a partner has an affirmative duty to disclose information to a fellow partner, even without a demand. Section 9.8 discusses those situations.

3. Section 9.8.

RUPA does not require a partnership to maintain any formal records,[4] recognizing that "general partnerships are often informal or even inadvertent."[5] However, the official Comment to Section 403 counsels:

> In general, a partnership should, at a minimum, keep those books and records necessary to enable the partners to determine their share of the profits and losses, as well as their rights on withdrawal. . . . The partnership must also maintain any books and records required by state or federal taxing or other governmental authorities.[6]

If books and records do exist, a partner is entitled to access under RUPA §403(b) without having to demonstrate, state, or even possess a proper purpose. The Comment explains that "A partner's unlimited personal liability justifies an unqualified right of access to the partnership books and records."[7] However, nothing in the statutory text or Comments qualifies this right when a partnership is an LLP.[8]

As to the duty under subsection (c)(1) to volunteer information, that duty *is* confined to information related to a particular purpose — namely, information "reasonably required for the proper exercise of the [recipient] partner's rights and duties." This phrase reaches not only to the conduct of the partnership business but also to some partner-to-partner interactions.

Example: Rachael and Sam are each partners in a general partnership, and Rachael is considering selling her transferable interest to Sam. While the two partners are negotiating over price, Sam learns some business information that suggests that the partnership is about to enter a "boom" period. Because Rachael's transfer of her transferable interest is her right under RUPA §503(a)(1), Sam's disclosure of that information is "reasonably required for the proper exercise of [Rachael's] rights . . . under . . . this [Act]."

If a particular item of material information is apparent in the partnership's records, whether a partner is obliged to disseminate that information to fellow partners depends on the circumstances.[9]

---

4. RUPA §403(a) (referring to a partnership's "books and records, *if any*") (emphasis added).

5. RUPA §403, Comment 1.

6. RUPA §403, Comment 1.

7. RUPA §403, Comment 2.

8. The same Comment states that "An abuse of the right to inspect and copy might constitute a violation of the obligation of good faith and fair dealing for which the other partners would have a remedy." For a discussion of this obligation, see section 9.8.4. If the information is misused in connection with a violation of a partner's duty of care or loyalty, the partnership and other partners might have a remedy for a breach of those duties. See section 9.10.

9. This passage, including the two following Examples, is taken from the official Comments to the Uniform Limited Partnership Act (2001), §407(b)(1).

Example: A partnership has two partners: each of whom is regularly engaged in conducting the limited partnership's activities; both of whom are aware of and have regular access to all significant partnership records; and neither of whom has special responsibility for or knowledge about any particular aspect of those activities or the partnership records pertaining to any particular aspect of those activities. Most likely, neither partner is obliged to draw the other partner's attention to information apparent in the partnership's records.

Example: Although a partnership has three partners, one is the managing partner with day-to-day responsibility for running the partnership's business. The other two meet periodically with the managing partner, and together with that partner make "all decisions relating to any substantial change in policy." Most likely, the managing partner has a duty to draw the attention of the other partners to important information, even if that information would be apparent from a review of the partnership's records.

In any event, under RUPA §403(c)(1) the pivotal question is whether the disclosure by one partner is "reasonably required for the proper exercise of [another's] partner's rights and duties."

There may, however, be some circumstances in which another RUPA section comes into play and some other question is pivotal. RUPA §404(d) codifies the common law obligation of good faith and fair dealing,[10] and Comment 4 to §404 states, somewhat cryptically, "In some situations the obligation of good faith includes a disclosure component. Depending on the circumstances, a partner may have an affirmative disclosure obligation that supplements the Section 403 duty to render information."

A departure from prior law — duty to inform not a fiduciary duty.   At least some pre-RUPA authority characterized as a fiduciary duty a partner's obligation to provide information to fellow partners. In contrast, RUPA makes clear that its information access duties are not fiduciary.[11] RUPA §404(a) states: "The only fiduciary duties a partner owes to the partnership and the other partners are the duty of loyalty and the duty of care set forth in subsections (b) and (c)." The duty to provide information is "set forth" in §403, not subsection (b) or (c) of §404.

The difference between RUPA and prior law is more than a matter of labels.[12] Courts typically take an expansive approach to construing and applying fiduciary duties. They are rarely as liberal when imposing liability under a

---

10. See section 9.8.4.

11. Fiduciary duty is discussed in detail in section 9.8.

12. But see White v. Panic, 783 A.2d 543, 556 (Del. 2001) (conflating good faith and fiduciary duty; stating that "a board [of directors] may breach its fiduciary duty of good faith by issuing false public statements").

statute. Moreover, a breach of fiduciary duty can support a claim for disgorgement and, in egregious circumstances, for punitive damages.[13] In contrast, one who breaches a statutory duty typically risks only a claim for ordinary damages.

§9.3   The Right to Be Involved in the Business

Each partner has the right to be involved in the business: to get his, her, or its[14] hands dirty, to actually take part in the work of the partnership. This right brings no extra compensation, because under the default rules of UPA §18(f) and RUPA §401(h) working in the business does not increase a partner's remuneration. The right to participate can, however, be psychologically important. Moreover, working in the business can be a very effective way to keep "in the know."

A partner's right to be involved in a UPA partnership rests on two provisions of the statute. UPA §18(e) states the right expressly: "All partners have equal rights in the management and *conduct* of the business."[15] UPA §25(2)(a) buttresses the point with its concept of cotenancy in partnership: Each partner has, as a property right, "an equal right with his partners to possess specific property for partnership purposes."

Under RUPA, as previously discussed,[16] management rights do not masquerade as property rights. RUPA §401(f) states unequivocally: "Each partner has equal rights in the management and conduct of the partnership business."

§9.4   The Right to Bind the Partnership

§9.4.1   *The Issue's Significance*

A partner's right to bind the partnership is significant in two contexts. First, the right affects the power to bind. When a partner acts with actual authority (i.e., with the right to act), the partner's act binds the partnership. (Unauthorized acts may bind the partnership as well. In logical terms, authority is sufficient but not necessary to bind the partnership. See Figure 9-1.)

Second, the question of actual authority is significant inter se the partners. A partner who enters into a transaction without actual authority risks several negative consequences. If the unauthorized act binds the partnership

---

13. See section 9.10.

14. A partner that is an organization (e.g., a corporation) would take part through its agents.

15. Emphasis added.

16. See section 8.8.3.

Figure 9-1. Authority to Bind the Partnership Is Sufficient But Not Necessary for the Power to Bind the Partnership

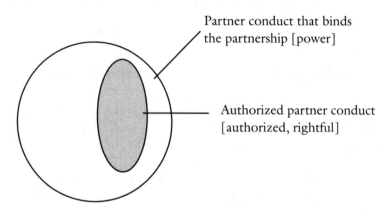

Partner conduct that binds the partnership [power]

Authorized partner conduct [authorized, rightful]

to the partnership's detriment, the partner will be liable to the partnership for damages. If, to the contrary, the unauthorized act does not bind the partnership, the partner will be liable to the third party for damages.[17] Moreover, in egregious situations, the partner may be subject to expulsion.[18]

In addition, a partner who acts without authority ordinarily acts without a right to indemnity. UPA §18(b) provides for indemnification "in respect of payments made and personal liabilities *reasonably* incurred by [a partner] in the ordinary and *proper* conduct of [the partnership's] business."[19] It will rarely be reasonable or proper for a partner to act without authority. The result should be the same under RUPA, even though its indemnification provision omits the words "reasonably" and "properly."[20] Except in unusual circumstances *inter se* the partners, unauthorized acts are beyond "the ordinary course of the business of the partnership."[21]

---

17. If the partner made the commitment while purporting to bind the partnership, the partner would be liable for a breach of the warranty of authority. See section 4.2.2. If the partner made the commitment in its own name, without reference to the partnership, the partner would be liable directly on the contract. See section 4.2.1 (agent liable on the contract when principal is undisclosed).

18. See sections 11.2.1, 11.7.2, and 11.9.2 (expulsion). If the unauthorized conduct is sustained and seriously affects the partnership business, dissolution can result. See sections 11.8 and 11.12.

19. Emphasis added. Section 8.4 discusses a partner's right to indemnity.

20. See section 8.4.

21. RUPA §401(c). Under the UPA, indemnification will be available if a partner acts without authority but "reasonably . . . for the preservation of [the partnership's] business or property." UPA §18(b). RUPA §401(c) includes comparable language, although lacking any express requirement of reasonableness.

§9.4.2 *Deducing the Extent of Actual Authority*

The basic scope. Partners may by agreement define the authority of each partner to bind the partnership, and partnership agreements often do so. Such definition is wise, for the statutory default rules are deficient in this area; they do not directly address the subject. It is, however, possible to infer the default scope of a partner's actual authority from the language of various statutory provisions. The scope is the same under both statutes, although the analysis differs slightly because the relevant language differs.

Under the UPA. UPA §§9(1), 18(e), 18(b), and 18(h) combine to imply the default scope of each UPA partner's authority.

Although §9(1) deals primarily with a partner's power to bind a partnership, it does contain a clause relating to authority: "Every partner is an agent of the partnership for the purpose of its business. . . ."[22] An agent has implied actual authority to commit its principal to third parties to the extent that the commitments are "incidental to, usually accompany . . . , or are reasonably necessary to accomplish" the objectives of the agency.[23] In the default mode, therefore, a UPA partner has the authority to make commitments "incidental to, [which] usually accompany . . . , or are reasonably necessary to accomplish" the partnership's business.

UPA §§18(e) and 18(b) support this position from a different angle. As a practical matter, at least one partner must have *some* authority to bind the partnership. As a legal matter, UPA §18(e) provides that *all* partners have "equal rights in the management and conduct of the partnership business." Therefore, absent a contrary agreement, *all* partners have *some* authority to bind the partnership.

The extent of that authority is suggested by §18(b). That provision delimits the acts that qualify for indemnification. Presumably the acts that qualify for indemnification are the acts that are authorized, and vice versa. If so, absent a contrary agreement, a UPA partner is authorized to make those commitments "reasonably [made] in the ordinary and proper conduct of [the] partnership's business."

Under RUPA. The RUPA analysis is similar to the UPA analysis, because RUPA §301(1) mirrors UPA §9(1) and RUPA §401(f) mirrors UPA §18(e). RUPA's indemnification provision does not refer to "reasonably," but agency law easily fills that gap.[24] In sum, absent a contrary agreement, a RUPA partner is authorized to make those commitments that are "incidental to, usually

---

22. Under both pre- and post-UPA case law, a partner's agent status is that of a general agent. Restatement §14A, comment *a*. See section 2.6.2 for a definition of a general agent.
23. Restatement §35. See section 2.2.3 (actual authority: express and implied).
24. RUPA §104(a) and Comment.

accompany . . . , or are reasonably necessary to accomplish"[25] all tasks within "the ordinary course of the business of the partnership."[26]

An implied but important limit.   A partner's actual authority to bind the partnership has an important limit. If a partner knows or has reason to know that another partner would object to a proposed commitment, the first partner has no actual authority to commit the partnership, unless the partnership agreement provides otherwise or the partners have already voted on the matter.

This limitation follows from UPA §18(h) and RUPA §401(j) and the law of agency. Under both UPA §18(h) and RUPA §401(j) disputes among partners are to be settled by a vote of the partners.[27] Under agency law, an agent's authority ceases when the agent no longer has reason to believe that the authority exists. Since partnership law mandates a vote on disputed matters, a partner's awareness of a disagreement means that the partner can no longer reasonably believe the authority exists.

> *Example:* Rachael, Sam, and Carolyn form a chicken farming partnership, but the partnership agreement does not specify who may commit the partnership to sell chickens. One day Carolyn overhears Sam discussing a sale of 500 chickens to an established customer. Before Sam can close the deal, Carolyn says, "I don't think we should sell to that customer. They're on the verge of bankruptcy." Sam has no authority to make the deal. He must refer the matter to a vote of the partners.

> *Example:* Sam does have the partners' vote, and he and Rachael vote in favor of continuing to sell to that customer on a "C.O.D." basis. Sam closes the deal with the customer. The next week Carolyn learns that Sam proposes to sell another 1,000 chickens to the customer. She again objects. Since a partner vote has already settled the matter, Sam's awareness of Carolyn's objection does not remove Sam's authority.[28]

§9.5   The Right to Participate in Decision Making and to Veto Some Decisions

§9.5.1   *The Basic Default Structure*

The basic approach.   When partners disagree, under the UPA's default rules:

- the partners resolve the disagreement by a vote,[29]

---

25. Restatement §35.
26. RUPA §401(c).
27. See section 9.5 for a detailed discussion of these provisions.
28. These Examples address Sam's *actual authority* to commit the partnership. For a discussion of a partner's *power* to bind the partnership, see Chapter Ten.
29. UPA §18(h); RUPA §401(j).

- each partner has one vote, regardless of how much each partner has contributed to the partnership and regardless of how much each partner works in the partnership's business,[30] and
- some disputes are resolved by majority vote, while other actions require unanimity.[31]

Determining what vote is required — UPA. Three UPA provisions comprise the default rules for determining the vote required for resolving disagreements among the partners. UPA §§9(3) and 18(g) list particular matters requiring unanimous consent. UPA §18(h) provides a general rule for disagreements not covered by UPA §§9(3) or 18(g).

Particular matters requiring unanimous approval. Under UPA §9(3), unless a partnership agreement provides otherwise, the following actions require unanimous approval:

- assigning the partnership's property in trust to creditors or in return for the assignee's promise to pay the partnership's debts;
- disposing of the good will of the business;
- doing any other act which would make it impossible to carry on the partnership's ordinary business;
- confessing a judgment against the partnership;
- submitting a claim by or against the partnership to arbitration.

UPA §18(g) adds another matter: "No person can become a member of a partnership without the consent of all the partners."

The general rule of UPA §18(h). For matters not covered by UPA §§9(3) or 18(g), the general rule of §18(h) appears simple enough:

> Any difference arising as to ordinary matters connected with the partnership business may be decided by a majority of the partners; but no act in contravention of any agreement between the partners may be done rightfully without the consent of all the partners.

Example: Rachael, Sam, and Carolyn form a partnership to raise chickens and eventually have a disagreement about where to buy their chicken feed. Rachael wants to buy from Eli's Feed and Stock. Both Sam and Carolyn prefer Rebecca's Ranching Necessities. On this ordinary matter, covered by neither UPA §9(3) nor §18(g), Sam and Carolyn will prevail. Each partner has one vote, UPA §18(e), and a majority vote controls, UPA §18(h).

---

30. UPA §18(e) and (h); RUPA §401(f) and (j).
31. UPA §§18(h) and 9(3); RUPA §401(j).

Figure 9-2. How the Set of "Extraordinary" Matters Overlaps Only Partially the Set of "Acts in Contravention"

extraordinary acts   acts in contravention

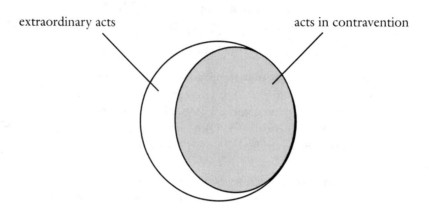

Example: The Rachael-Sam-Carolyn partnership buys chicken feed from Rebecca's Ranching Necessities. Later a dispute develops over the quality of the feed. Rebecca proposes submitting the dispute to binding arbitration. Sam and Carolyn think arbitration is a good idea, but Rachael objects. Rachael's objection means that none of the partners has the right to commit the partnership to the arbitration. Under UPA §9(3) unanimity is necessary.[32]

The problem of the omitted category.   The rule of UPA §18(h) is problematic, because its language omits a category of conduct: matters that are not "ordinary" (i.e., that are highly unusual or significant) but that do not involve "an act in contravention" of a partnership agreement. See Figure 9-2.

Example: For five years the Rachael-Sam-Carolyn partnership profitably raises and sells chickens. Then Rachael and Sam decide the partnership should "branch out" into raising cattle. Cattle raising involves significantly different equipment, feed, skills, and contacts than chicken farming and would require the partnership to invest a substantial amount of money in purchasing equipment and stock. Carolyn objects to the change, but nothing in the partnership agreement limits the scope of the partnership's business. The decision on expansion is not "ordinary," but neither would expansion contravene an express provision of the partners' agreement.

The case law has resolved this conundrum by generally holding that extraordinary changes require unanimous consent. Some cases hold that a deci-

---

32. As for the power to commit the partnership to binding arbitration, see section 10.2.6.

sion to depart substantially from past practices actually does contravene an agreement, because the past practices imply an agreement among the partners. Other cases pay less homage to the language of §18(h), recognize the omitted category, and establish a rule for it. Noting that a partnership is a *voluntary* association and that each partner is *personally* liable for debts arising from the partnership's operations, these cases hold as a matter of policy that each partner must consent to any fundamental change in a partnership or its operations.

Determining what vote is required — RUPA. RUPA's rule is simpler. The list of decisions categorically requiring unanimous consent has been winnowed down to one item: the admission of a partner.[33] The "omitted category" has been expressly included as requiring unanimous consent:

> A difference arising as to a matter in the ordinary course of business of a partnership may be decided by a majority of the partners. An act outside the ordinary course of business of a partnership and an amendment to the partnership agreement may be undertaken only with the consent of all of the partners.[34]

The boundary between "ordinary" and "extraordinary." The precise boundary between "ordinary" and "extraordinary" is easier to find in a diagram than in actual cases or other real-life situations. A few generalizations are possible, however, and they are equally applicable under the UPA and RUPA. Substantial changes to the nature of the partnership's business are likely to require unanimous consent. So too are decisions to increase substantially the size of the business, where that increase requires a significant increase in the liability exposure of each partner. Changes in the standards for admitting new partners or expelling old ones probably also require unanimity.[35]

> *Example:* Robert, Martin, and John have a partnership that invests in real estate. Each partner contributed $50,000 to get the business going, and for the five years of its existence the partnership has invested in properties averaging approximately $100,000 each in value. The partnership agreement does not mention any limit on the size of any single investment. Robert and Martin wish to have the partnership buy a large apartment building that has just come on the market. To buy the building, the partnership will have to assume a $1.2 million mortgage. Although the purchase would not contravene any express provision of the partnership agreement, it would fundamentally change the nature of the partnership business and significantly increase each partner's exposure

---

33. RUPA §401(i). RUPA §301, the analog to UPA §9, contains nothing of UPA §9(3).

34. RUPA §401(j).

35. For a discussion of partner expulsion, see sections 11.2.1, 11.7.2, and 11.9.2.

to personal liability. Most likely, Robert and Martin need John's consent to rightfully make this extraordinary decision.

§9.5.2 *The Special Problem of Defrocking a Partner*

As explained previously,[36] absent a contrary agreement each partner has some actual authority (i.e., some right vis-à-vis fellow partners) to commit the partnership to third parties. Suppose that the other partners wish to take away that right, that is, they wish to defrock the partner. As between the partners,[37] may they do so by majority vote? Or is unanimous consent necessary?

Defrocking most likely requires unanimous consent. Recall that, absent a contrary agreement, each partner has an equal right to "conduct" the partnership business. Conducting business typically involves making binding commitments to third parties. Therefore, taking away a partner's right to bind the partnership would seem to constitute an extraordinary act. Moreover, if the particular partner has for some time exercised the right to bind, that pattern of conduct may imply an authority-granting agreement. In that event, defrocking would constitute "an act in contravention." Under either view, unanimity is required.

The would-be defrockers are not totally without recourse. If a partner's irresponsible actions are getting the partnership in trouble, the fellow partners may bring the partnership to an end or, under RUPA, seek a court order expelling the partner.[38]

§9.5.3 *The Special Problem of Management Deadlock*

What happens when the partners are in disagreement, a majority vote is necessary to resolve the disagreement, and no majority is possible? This problem arises most often in two person partnerships.

> **Example:** Alice and Ariel have a partnership that operates a grocery store. They have for several years purchased bread from National Bakery. Alice decides that the bread is inferior and the price too high. She wants to find a new supplier. Ariel thinks that both the bread and the price are fine. This is certainly an "ordinary" matter, but neither partner can muster a majority vote.

The cases hold that the partner proposing the change loses. As one authority put it, "[I]f the partners are equally divided, those who forbid a

---

36. Section 9.4.

37. As to whether taking away the right will affect the defrocked partner's power to bind the partnership, see section 10.2.7.

38. See section 11.9.2. Under the UPA, expulsion is possible if provided for in the partnership agreement. UPA §31(1)(d).

change must have their way."[39] This rule is consistent with both the UPA and RUPA; each requires at least a majority to take action in the event of a dispute. How the rule works in practice, however, can depend on how the partners conceptualize the matter in dispute.

> *Example:* Alice and Ariel are meeting to discuss Alice's opposition to buying bread from National Bakery. Ariel says, "What's at issue is your idea that we discontinue using National. I vote no. There's no majority, so you lose." Alice says, "Oh no. You don't understand. What's at issue is where we buy bread this week. You're proposing National. I vote no. There's no majority, so you lose. And there will be no majority until you agree on another supplier."

If the deadlock concerns a substantial matter, the partners can resolve the problem by dissolving the partnership.[40]

§9.6   Agreements That Change Management Rights

§9.6.1   *Importance and Ubiquity*

The statutory management rules are not for everyone. One of the great advantages of the partnership form is its flexibility, and almost every partnership with a formal partnership agreement varies the management rules in some way. Moreover, the course of conduct among partners can imply agreements about management rights.

The following is a nonexclusive list of important areas in which partners often vary the default management rules provided by the UPA and RUPA:[41]

- delegating to one partner or a committee of partners some or all decisions on the conduct of the business
- changing the "one partner/one vote" rule (e.g., weighting each partner's vote proportionally to capital contributed to the partnership, or allocating more votes to partners who work full time in the business)
- changing the unanimous consent requirements (e.g., allowing the admission of new partners on a two-thirds vote of the current partners, or by approval of a management committee)
- requiring super-majority votes for important decisions (e.g., major financial commitments)
- creating a right to expel partners

---

39. Lindley, A Treatise on the Law of Partnership, ch. II, §24-8 at 403 (1924), quoted in Summers v. Dooley, 481 P.2d 318, 321 (Idaho 1971).

40. The mechanics depend on whether the partnership is "at will" and also on whether the UPA or RUPA applies. See Chapter Eleven.

41. Partners may also by agreement alter the other default rules, such as the rules on profit sharing, no remuneration for labor. See generally Chapter Eight.

- requiring partners to seek approval before making certain kinds of commitments on behalf of the partnership
- delegating to a management or executive committee the right to bind the partnership to any significant obligations

Example: The partnership agreement of Sachs & Harris, a 100-partner law firm, provides for the annual election of a five-partner "Management Committee" and includes the following two provisions:

Admission of New Partners: The Management Committee shall in its sole discretion determine whether to admit any new member to the partnership. A vote of four of the five members of that Committee is necessary to admit a new partner. . . .

Authority to Advance Costs: Whenever a partner begins representation on a new matter, that partner will report in writing to the Management Committee whether in that partner's judgment it will be necessary for the firm to advance costs in the matter.[42] If the partner wishes to have authority to advance costs, the report must identify the types of costs to be incurred and state an estimate of the total costs to be advanced prior to final disposition of the matter. The Management Committee will promptly set a maximum amount of costs which may be advanced on the matter and will inform the partner of that authority. No partner has authority to advance any costs except as authorized consistent with this procedure.

Agreements among partners can go very far to change the management structure of a partnership. Beyond even delegating management authority, *inter se* agreements can even delegate the right to amend the partnership agreement itself.

Example: The partnership agreement of Sachs & Harris contains the following provision:

Amendments: This Partnership Agreement may be amended only upon a majority vote of the members of the Management Committee followed by a 2/3 majority vote of all Partners.

§9.6.2 *Limits on Inter Se Agreements That Restructure Management*

Under the UPA.   Under the UPA, agreements that restructure management face three constraints. First, although agreements can waive certain fiduciary duties and define others, no agreement among partners can remove

---

42. Law firms often pay third parties for costs such as court filing fees and transcripts of depositions, and then re-bill the clients for those costs. This practice is known as *advancing costs.*

totally the fiduciary obligations that partners owe each other.[43] Second, the more fundamental the obligation involved, the more likely is judicial scrutiny. For example, a court will examine carefully any agreed-upon restrictions on a partner's right to information.[44] A restriction is most likely to be upheld if it (i) has some important justification, (ii) is not overbroad, and (iii) does not leave the partners who lack access vulnerable to oppression.

Third, dicta in at least one noted case suggests that partners may have the *nondelegable* right to consent to fundamental changes in the partnership agreement.[45] That is, if a proposed amendment will fundamentally alter either the nature of the partnership or the partner's stake in the venture, then:

- even though the partnership agreement purports to allow amendment with less than unanimous consent,
- nonetheless each partner may have to consent to the amendment.[46]

Example: The Sachs & Harris Partnership Agreement provides for amendment upon a majority vote of the Executive Committee, coupled with a 2/3 vote of all partners. The Agreement initially provided that any partner could be expelled without cause upon a 4/5 majority vote of the Executive Committee, confirmed by a 2/3 majority vote of all partners. The expelled partner had a right to be "cashed out" of the partnership within 30 days of the expulsion date. An amendment to the Partnership Agreement, adopted by a majority vote of the Executive Committee and a 2/3 vote of the partners, changed the expulsion provision in three important ways: (i) the votes required were reduced to a simple majority of the Executive Committee and the partners, (ii) the partnership was given the right to cash out the expelled partner through installment payments over a two-year period, and (iii) the cash out amount was reduced. If a partner who voted against the change challenged the amendment, a court might hold the amendment invalid. Because the amendment so significantly increased the risks of expulsion for individual partners, perhaps—despite the amendment procedure stated in the Partnership Agreement—each partner had a right to veto the change.

Under RUPA. The strictures under RUPA are similar to those under the UPA, but RUPA purports to collect in one place and state expressly all the limits on the power of the partnership agreement. RUPA §103(a) provides that: "Except as otherwise provided in subsection (b), relations among the partners

---

43. Section 9.8 discusses partners' fiduciary duty, and section 9.9 focuses on agreements which waive, limit, or define fiduciary duty.

44. See section 9.2 (partner's right of access to information) and section 9.8.5 (full disclosure).

45. McCallum v. Asbury, 393 P.2d 774 (Or. 1964).

46. Id. *McCallum* has been noted by commentators but not followed by courts. Indeed, a few cases flatly contradict it.

and between the partners and the partnership are governed by the partnership agreement." Subsection (b) contains ten restrictions. The one directly relevant here appears in subsection (b)(2). A partnership agreement may not "unreasonably restrict the right of access to books and records under Section 403(b)."[47]

Subsection (b) also limits the power of the partnership agreement to curtail fiduciary duties and the obligation of good faith and fair dealing.[48] Those duties and that obligation therefore overhang the contents and enforcement of each provision in every RUPA partnership agreement.

§9.6.3 *Effect of Inter Se Agreements on Third Parties*

In some circumstances partners' *inter se* management agreements can increase a third party's ability to hold the partnership liable. In other, more restricted circumstances, an *inter se* agreement can undercut a third-party claim.

Increasing the third party's ability to hold the partnership liable.   If a partnership agreement gives a partner the right to act for the partnership on particular matters, then within that specified scope the partner has actual authority. A partner who acts within actual authority binds the partnership as a matter of agency law. There is no need to rely on any of the special rules that partnership law contains for binding the partnership to third parties.[49]

Undercutting a third party's claim.   Just as a partnership agreement can convey actual authority, so too an agreement can negate that authority. If a partner who lacks actual authority purports to bind the partnership to a third party, and that third party knows of the lack of authority (or, under RUPA, knows or "has received a notification that the partner lacked authority"), then the partnership is not bound.[50]

§9.7   Management Duties

§9.7.1 *Duty to Furnish Services*

Does and should a duty exist?   As previously discussed,[51] absent a contrary agreement each partner has a right to participate in partnership affairs. Is

---

47. That right is discussed in section 9.2.2.

48. Fiduciary duty is discussed in section 9.8. RUPA's provision on the obligation of good faith and fair dealing is discussed in section 9.8.4. The relationship between these concepts and partnership agreement is discussed in section 9.9.

49. Chapter Ten discusses those rules. Of course, if actual authority is not conceded, the cautious lawyer (and law student) will also consider the partnership law rules.

50. UPA §9(4); RUPA §301(1). See sections 10.2 and 10.3. In this respect, RUPA §401(k) is inaccurate when it states: "This section does not affect the obligations of a partnership to other persons under Section 301."

51. See section 9.3.

there also a duty to participate? Is each partner obligated to furnish labor, services, or some other form of effort to the partnership business?

Some, mostly older cases suggest that such a duty exists. However, neither the UPA nor RUPA contains any support for the notion, and the case law authority may reflect an antiquated notion of the typical partnership. Perhaps at one time it made sense to imply a duty to provide services, because with only rare exceptions partnerships consisted exclusively of active partners. For a partner to decline to serve, therefore, defeated the reasonable expectations of the copartners.

Today, however, it makes far less sense to imply a duty to serve merely from partner status. While partnerships with exclusively active partners still predominate, passive partners are by no means rare. The advent of LLPs probably increases the likelihood of passive partners.

Of course, partners may by express agreement create a duty to be active, and their behavior in the formation or conduct of the partnership may imply a duty as well.[52] But no duty should be presumed on account of partnership status alone.

Remedies for breach of the duty. A partner who breaches a duty to provide services may be held liable for the cost of hiring someone else to perform the services or for the reasonable value of the services withheld. If the withheld services are crucial to the business, the copartners may obtain a court order bringing the partnership to an end.[53] In that case, the breaching partner would probably be liable for damages caused by the partnership's premature demise.

§9.7.2 Duty of Care

When a partner does act in the partnership business, does the partner have a duty to the partnership to act carefully? If a partner's mistake damages the partnership, is the partner liable to the partnership for the resulting harm?

Some commentators have argued that the answer to these questions should be "no." They assert that partners can adequately protect themselves by carefully choosing and then carefully monitoring their copartners. The law,

---

52. For example, it seems reasonable to expect services from a partner who has contributed neither money nor other property to the partnership.

53. UPA §32(1)(d) requires a court to dissolve a partnership if "[a] partner wilfully or persistently commits a breach of the partnership agreement, or otherwise so conducts himself in matters relating to the partnership business that it is not reasonably practicable to carry on the business in partnership with him." RUPA §801(5)(ii) has similar language: "A partnership is dissolved . . . on application by a partner, [upon the occurrence of] a judicial determination that . . . another partner has engaged in conduct relating to the partnership business which makes it not reasonably practicable to carry on the business in partnership with that partner." RUPA also provides for the expulsion of miscreant partners, see section 11.7.2, but expulsion will not remedy the lack of crucial services.

however, is to the contrary under both the UPA and RUPA. RUPA §404(c) provides:

> A partner's duty of care to the partnership and the other partners in the conduct and winding up of the partnership business is limited to refraining from engaging in grossly negligent or reckless conduct, intentional misconduct, or a knowing violation of law.

An official Comment explains that "[t]he standard of care imposed by RUPA is that of gross negligence, which is the standard generally recognized by the courts"[54] under the UPA. Partners have a duty to avoid gross negligence and wilful misconduct. They are not, however, liable for ordinary mistakes in judgment.

> *Example:* Alvin, a partner in a partnership of surgeons, makes a mistake during an operation and is later found to have committed malpractice (i.e., ordinary negligence). Under UPA §13 and RUPA §305(a) the partnership is liable to the patient,[55] and the plaintiff chooses to collect from the partnership rather than Alvin personally. The partnership cannot recover from Alvin. Alvin would be liable to the partnership only if the partnership could show that he had been grossly negligent or had engaged in wilful misconduct.

Under both the UPA and RUPA, a partner's duty of care is less than that of a paid agent.[56] The rationale may be that, unlike a principal, a partner in a general partnership is assumed to be actively involved in the business and assumed, therefore, to be better positioned than a principal to watch out, supervise and, when necessary, intervene. Or, the gross negligence standard may reflect the influence of corporate law's business judgment rule.

The partnership agreement may change the duty of care, but (at least under RUPA) may not "unreasonably reduce" it.[57]

§9.8   Partner's Fiduciary Duty of Loyalty

§9.8.1   *The Beauty, Ubiquity, Influence, and Vagueness of Cardozo's Language*

Partners owe each other a fiduciary duty of loyalty, and the touchstone of analysis in this area is a beautiful passage in Justice Cardozo's opinion in *Meinhard v. Salmon*:[58]

---

54. RUPA §404, Comment 3.
55. See section 10.4.
56. Paid agents have a duty to exercise ordinary care. See section 4.1.4.
57. RUPA §103(b)(4).
58. 164 N.E. 545 (N.Y. 1928).

Joint adventurers, like copartners, owe to one another, while the enterprise continues, the duty of the finest loyalty. Many forms of conduct permissible in a workaday world for those acting at arm's length, are forbidden to those bound by fiduciary ties. A trustee is held to something stricter than the morals of the market place. Not honesty alone, but the punctilio of an honor the most sensitive, is then the standard of behavior.

Although *Meinhard v. Salmon* involved a joint venture rather than a partnership, Cardozo's words are equally applicable to partnerships.[59] Indeed, those words are probably the most often quoted passage in all of partnership law. They instruct courts to approach partner selfishness with a critical eye.

Beyond that general instruction, however, Cardozo's words are quite vague. It is one thing to say in general, "be your brother's keeper," but how does the principle apply when, for instance, your brother wants to watch the opera, you want to watch the football game, and your house has only one TV and no VCR? What does "the punctilio of an honor the most sensitive" mean when the two partners in an at-will partnership are discussing a change in profit shares because one partner believes she is bringing in most of the business?[60]

The law of partner loyalty can be divided into two categories, and in one of those categories some pretty specific rules augment and define Cardozo's "punctilio." The first category consists of issues relating to the conduct or interests of the partnership's business. In that category partner selfishness is not allowed unless the other partners consent. The second category consists of issues relating to differences of interests between or among partners. In that category the rules are less stringent and less clear. Section 9.8.3 discusses "partner versus partnership" issues, and section 9.8.5 discusses "partner versus partner" issues. Section 9.9 examines the extent to which partner agreements can change, waive, or eliminate partner fiduciary duties. Section 9.8.2 provides on overview of the differences and similarities between the UPA and RUPA in this fundamentally important area of partnership law.

§9.8.2 *UPA, RUPA, and the Fiduciary Duty of Loyalty*

During the ten years NCCUSL spent drafting, debating, and adopting RUPA, no issue generated more controversy than the new Act's treatment of the fiduciary duty of loyalty. In form, RUPA differs from the UPA in at least seven ways:

- While under the UPA the duty of loyalty is mostly a matter of case law, RUPA codifies the subject.

---

59. As explained in section 7.2.6, in most jurisdictions the law of joint ventures is essentially identical to the law of partnerships.

60. Recall from section 7.2.6 that in an at-will partnership any partner has the right to call an end to the partnership at any time. That right will have an inevitable impact on negotiations between partners.

- While under the UPA the duty of loyalty is an open-ended legal category, RUPA's formulation purports to be exclusive and exhaustive.
- While UPA §21(1) expresses the scope of a partner's loyalty duty by referring generally to "any transaction connected with the formation, conduct, or liquidation of the partnership," RUPA:
  - expressly encompasses self-dealing[61] and competition;[62]
  - ends at dissolution the restriction on competition;[63] and
  - entirely excludes formation activities from the duty of loyalty;[64]
- While UPA cases generally consider a partner's duty of loyalty to include the duty to volunteer information, RUPA ousts disclosure duties from the realm of fiduciary duty.[65]
- While the UPA nowhere mentions any general duty of good faith,[66] RUPA §404(d) provides: "A partner shall discharge the duties to the partnership and the other partners under this [Act] or under the partnership agreement and exercise any rights consistently with the obligation of good faith and fair dealing."
- While RUPA is silent as to a partner's right to act in his, her, or its own self-interest, RUPA §404(e) states: "A partner does not violate a duty or obligation under this [Act] or under the partnership agreement merely because the partner's conduct furthers the partner's own interest."
- While the UPA is silent on the extent to which the partnership agreement can alter or eliminate fiduciary duties, RUPA §103(b) expressly prohibits elimination and provides standards for evaluating attempted alterations.

It remains to be seen whether these formal differences matter practically and substantively. Of all the differences, the most controversial is embodied in RUPA §404(a), which provides that "The only fiduciary duties a partner owes to the partnership and the other partners are the duty of loyalty and the duty of care set forth in subsections (b) and (c)," and in RUPA §404(b), which introduces three specific prongs of the duty of loyalty with the phrase "A partner's duty of loyalty to the partnership and the other partners is limited to the following . . ."

Fiduciary duty originated as an equitable concept, and courts have always taken a flexible, expansive approach to defining the obligations of a fiduciary. Critics of RUPA §§404(a) and (b) believe that the words "only" and "limited" will cripple, or at least hamstring, a court's ability to deal with ingenu-

---

61. RUPA §404(b)(2).

62. RUPA §404(b)(3).

63. RUPA §404(b)(3) (requiring a partner to "refrain from competing . . . before the dissolution of the partnership).

64. All three paragraphs of subsection (b) refer to the "conduct" or the "conduct and winding up" of the partnership business. In contrast with UPA §21, RUPA §404(b) never uses the word "formation."

65. See section 9.2.

66. UPA §3(1) uses the concept of "bad faith" to define "knowledge."

ously structured improprieties. Defenders of RUPA's approach respond that subsection (b) properly defines a partner's fiduciary duties and that the obligation of good faith and fair dealing exists to capture and control other improperly opportunistic behavior.

§9.8.3 *Partner versus Partnership Duty of Loyalty*

In matters relating to partnership affairs, the UPA and RUPA have very similar views of a partner's duty of loyalty: in general, a partner may not profit at the expense—either direct or indirect—of the partnership. In particular, without the consent of fellow partners,[67] a partner is prohibited from:

- competing with the partnership
- taking business opportunities from which the partnership might have benefitted or that the partnership might have needed
- using partnership property for personal gain
- engaging in conflict-of-interest transactions

Under the UPA, these restrictions begin with partnership formation and continue until the partnership terminates. Under RUPA, the restrictions apply to the conduct of the partnership business, and the non-competition restriction ends when the partnership dissolves. The other restrictions remain until the partnership terminates.[68]

Noncompetition. RUPA §404(b)(3) expressly requires each partner "to refrain from competing with the partnership in the conduct of the partnership business before the dissolution of the partnership." UPA §21(1) contains very broad language which includes a noncompete requirement:

> Every partner must account to the partnership for any benefit, and hold as trustee for it any profits derived by him without the consent of the other partners from any transaction connected with the formation, conduct, or liquidation of the partnership. . . .

To engage in a competing business is to engage in "transaction[s] connected with the . . . conduct . . . of the partnership."[69] The "account/trustee" language in §21 means that a partner who violates the noncompete rule must disgorge to the partnership any profits made through the violation.

> *Example:* Michael is a partner in a company that provides business consulting services throughout the United States. While on a skiing

---

67. See section 9.9.

68. Under both the UPA and RUPA, dissolution does not terminate a partnership. Instead, the partnership enters a period of "winding up" and terminates only when winding up is complete. See sections 11.2.1 and 11.9.1.

69. In some circumstances, the competition might relate to formation or liquidation of the partnership.

vacation in Colorado, Michael meets Dorothy, who seeks some business advice. Michael at first declines, explaining, "I'm on vacation." He suggests that Dorothy use the services of another partner and offers to call his office and arrange matters. Dorothy, however, insists on Michael's services and offers to pay double his usual charges. Michael finally agrees. He takes a day out of his vacation, provides Dorothy the advice she needs, and pockets a large fee. The fee belongs to the partnership, even though (i) Michael did the work "on his own time," (ii) Michael tried to steer Dorothy to another partner, and (iii) Dorothy insisted on Michael performing the services and rejected Michael's suggestion that she consult with another partner. None of those facts are relevant under UPA §21. The work Michael did was precisely the type of work the partnership does, and Michael's dealings with Dorothy therefore constituted a "transaction connected with the . . . conduct . . . of the partnership." UPA §21. For Michael to retain the fee would be to set himself as a competitor to the partnership.

The result is the same under the RUPA, although RUPA §404(b)(3) does not contain the "account/trustee" language. Under generally applicable principles of fiduciary duty, a constructive trust will arise if Michael seeks to retain the fee.[70]

Taking business opportunities.   A partner's duty of loyalty also prevents a partner from taking business opportunities from the partnership, unless the copartners consent. Protected opportunities include not only those from which the partnership might have profited but also those which the partnership might have needed. The business opportunity duty somewhat overlaps the noncompetition duty: to compete with the partnership is to seek and take opportunities (i.e., customers) from which the partnership might have benefitted. But the opportunity rule also has independent scope.

> *Example:* Alice, a partner in a biotechnology partnership, knows that the partnership is looking to rent new office and laboratory space. She happens to know of a building, in the ideal location, suitable to house the firm's special equipment. She learns that the owner is willing either to lease or to sell. Alice decides that the building would make a fine personal investment, so she buys it for herself. She leases the building to a company that does not compete with the partnership, and later she re-sells the building at a profit. She must account to the biotechnology partnership for whatever profit she made on the building. Although Alice did not engage in directly competitive activity, the building could

---

70. See section 4.1.7 (constructive trust and disgorgement as remedies for an agent's breach of the duty of loyalty). The "account/trustee" language does appear in RUPA §404(b)(1), but that section is narrower than UPA §21(1).

have been a fruitful opportunity for the partnership. Under UPA §21, Alice must therefore "hold as trustee . . . any profits derived . . . from [this] transaction connected with the . . . conduct . . . of the partnership." Under RUPA §404(b)(1), the result is the same and the language more direct: Alice must "account to the partnership and hold as trustee for it any property, profit, or benefit . . . derived from a use by the partner of partnership property, including the appropriation of a partnership opportunity."

Like other aspects of the duty of loyalty, the opportunity rule can be waived by copartners' informed consent. Unless the partnership agreement provides otherwise, such consent must be unanimous.[71] However, a partner may be able to avoid the unanimity requirement by presenting the opportunity to the partnership and having the partnership vote on taking the opportunity for itself. Arguably such a decision is an ordinary matter, and a majority vote will control.[72] If the majority rejects the opportunity and a partner then proceeds individually, the partnership will have a difficult time persuading a court to order disgorgement.

Using partnership property for personal gain. UPA §25(2)(a) and RUPA §401(g) each prohibit a partner from using partnership property for personal purposes without copartner consent. UPA §21(1) and RUPA §404(b)(1) each require a partner to disgorge any gain obtained, without the consent of the other partners, from any personal use of partnership property.

> *Example:* Alex is a partner in a landscaping company that works exclusively on commercial projects. On weekends, without the permission of his copartners, Alex uses company equipment to do landscaping at private homes. He must disgorge his profits to the partnership. They result from his use of partnership property.

This rule is subject to a *de minimis* requirement. For example, a partner in an accounting firm who occasionally uses the firm's telephones to talk with a stockbroker will not have to disgorge profits made from stock trading.

Conflict of interest. A partner has a conflict of interest when the partner causes or allows the partnership to do business with:

- the partner him-, her-, or itself,
- a closely-related member of the partner's family,
- an organization in which the partner has a material financial interest, or
- any other person whose interests are adverse to the partnership.

---

71. See section 9.9.
72. UPA §18(h); RUPA §401(j). See section 9.5.1.

Example: Alice is a partner in a biotechnology partnership that is look-ing to rent new laboratory space. Alice happens to own a building, in the ideal location, suitable to house the firm's special equipment. If Alice leases or sells the building to the partnership, she will be "on both sides of the deal." She has a conflict of interest.

Transactions like the one just described are often called *self-dealing.*

RUPA §404(b)(2) specifically prohibits conflicts of interest and self-dealing. Each partner must "refrain from dealing with the partnership in the conduct or winding up of the partnership business as or on behalf of a party having an interest adverse to the partnership." The broad "account/trustee" language of UPA §21(1) establishes the same prohibition under that statute.

Remedies.   A partner who breaches the fiduciary duty of loyalty must dis-gorge all profits gained through the disloyal act. It is not necessary for the partnership to prove damages in order to obtain disgorgement. However, if the partnership can prove damages, the partnership may also bring a damage action. In a self-dealing situation, the partnership may rescind any executory portion of a contract tainted with partner conflict-of-interest.[73]

§9.8.4 *Obligation of Good Faith and Fair Dealing*

Unlike the UPA, RUPA includes among the duties of partners the obligation of good faith and fair dealing: "A partner shall discharge the duties to the partnership and the other partners under this [Act] or under the partnership agreement and exercise any rights consistently with the obligation of good faith and fair deal-ing."[74] The obligation is *not* a fiduciary duty but warrants mention here because it may serve to capture improprieties which escape RUPA's list of loyalty duties.[75]

The official Comment to RUPA §404 characterizes the obligation as con-tract based ("a contract concept, imposed on the partners because of the consen-sual nature of a partnership"[76]) and as lacking any "separate [or] independent" content. "It is an ancillary obligation that applies whenever a partner discharges a duty or exercises a right under the partnership agreement or the Act."[77]

Noting that " '[g]ood faith' clearly suggests a subjective element, while 'fair dealing' implies an objective component,"[78] the Comment "acknowledges that "[t]he meaning of 'good faith and fair dealing' is not firmly fixed under present law."[79] The Comment then puts the best possible face on indefinite-

---

73. For the procedures to be followed in bringing both damage actions and claims for equitable relief, see section 9.10.
74. RUPA §404(d).
75. See section 9.8.2.
76. RUPA §404, Comment 4.
77. RUPA §404, Comment 4.
78. RUPA §404, Comment 4.
79. RUPA §404, Comment 4.

ness by explaining: "It was decided to leave the terms undefined in the Act and allow the courts to develop their meaning based on the experience of real cases."[80]

> *Example:* The partnership agreement of Thomas Company establishes Sharon as the managing partner and gives her "the right, in her sole discretion, to decide whether to admit any person as a partner." The partnership needs additional capital, and Harry offers to contribute it on very favorable terms if the partnership admits him as a partner. Sharon's discretion in the matter is subject not only to the duty of care[81] but also to the obligation of good faith and fair dealing.

§9.8.5 *Differences of Interest Between and Among Partners*

The *inter se* context. According to Cardozo, partners may not use tactics appropriate to "arm's length" transactions in their inter se dealings. But even if partners are never fully at arm's length, they are nonetheless occasionally on opposite sides of the negotiating table. In such circumstances, self-interest is inherent and inevitable. It therefore cannot be *per se* evil.[82]

UPA cases recognize this reality, and RUPA §404(e) makes the point explicitly: "A partner does not violate a duty or obligation under this [Act] or under the partnership agreement merely because the partner's conduct furthers the partner's own interest."

In the *inter se* context, only excessive self-interest is wrongful, and questions about excess fall generally into two main categories:

- partner-to-partner transactions (when partners engage each other in partnership-related financial transactions), including:
  - formation of the partnership (under the UPA but not RUPA)
  - renegotiation of profit shares, particularly in an at-will partnership
  - sale or purchase of a current partner's interest in the partnership
- partners' exercise of discretion vis-à-vis copartners, including:
  - exercise of a right created by the partnership agreement to expel a partner "without cause"[83]

---

80. RUPA §404, Comment 4.

81. See section 9.7.2. The phrase "sole discretion" probably does not suffice to limit the duty of care. Courts tend to construe narrowly any language asserted to restrict a fiduciary duty. In any event, RUPA §103(b)(4) prevents a partnership agreement from "unreasonably reduce[ing] the duty of care." See section 9.9.1.

82. See RUPA §404, Comment 1 ("Arguably, the term 'fiduciary' is inappropriate when used to describe the duties of a partner because a partner may legitimately pursue self-interest.").

83. Partnership agreements often authorize a specified majority of partners (or, in some agreements, a specified majority of a management committee) to expel a partner without having to state or possess "cause." Under such agreements, if the required majority decides that a partner should be out, the partner is out. There is no obligation to prove that the partner did anything wrong. See the more detailed discussion in this section and in section 11.7.2.

— rightfully calling an end to a partnership, when the end disadvantages one partner and advantages another[84]

On any such occasion, one partner's interests will inevitably be adverse to another's. For example, if several partners seek to buy out one of their copartners, that copartner will want as high a buy-out price as possible. The would-be buyers, naturally enough, will want a low price. Similarly, when one partner wishes a higher profit share, any gain must come at the expense of some other partner or partners.

The issues raised by no-cause expulsion and ending an at-will partnership are more complicated. In each situation, the acting partner or partners apparently have absolute discretion. The law appears to entitle them to act for any reason they choose—even if their actions benefit them to the prejudice of copartners.

How the UPA and RUPA approach the issue.   The UPA and RUPA differ in how they approach partner-to-partner duties. UPA §21 pertains only to a partner's duty to the partnership, so UPA rules in this area come exclusively from case law—including Cardozo's famous opinion in *Meinhard v. Salmon*.

Under RUPA the situation is more complex. Like UPA §21, RUPA's duty of loyalty provision, §404, pertains only to a partner's duty to the partnership:

- subsection (b)(1)—"to account to the partnership and hold as trustee for it . . ."
- subsection (b)(2)—"to refrain from dealing with the partnership . . . as or on behalf of a party having an interest adverse to the partnership"
- subsection (b)(3)—"to refrain from competing with the partnership . . ."

What complicates matters is that, unlike the UPA, RUPA insists that its statutory treatment of the duty of loyalty is exhaustive.[85] As a result, any partner-to-partner duties under RUPA must have some other, non-fiduciary source.

RUPA §403 is one such source, detailing each "partner's rights and duties with respect to information."[86] RUPA §404(d), the statutory obligation of good faith and fair dealing, must perforce be the other.

---

84. Under the UPA default rules, this situation exists only in an at-will partnership. See section 11.2.1. A comparable situation exists, however, when one partner wrongfully dissolves a term partnership. Under UPA §38(2)(b), the other partners then have the right to preserve the partnership assets and carry on the business until the end of the original term—but only if all the remaining partners agree. Section 11.4.2. Under RUPA, the situation exists always in an at-will partnership, RUPA §801(1), and often in a partnership for a definite term or particular undertaking. RUPA §801(2)(i). Section 11.9.3.

85. RUPA §404(b) begins with the phrase "A partner's duty of loyalty to the partnership and the other partners is *limited* to the following." (Emphasis added.)

86. See section 9.2.2.

What the UPA and RUPA require. Although RUPA case law in this area is still scant, neither the statutory text nor the Comments indicate any intention to depart from prior law. It is therefore likely that courts will use RUPA §§403 and 404(d) to produce substantive rules consistent with UPA case law.[87] Under both the UPA and RUPA, therefore, when partners' interests are potentially or actually adverse, a partner is obliged to: (i) provide full disclosure (which is a well-defined concept) and (ii) engage in "fair dealing" (which is not).

Full disclosure.
In partner-to-partner transactions. A partner selling a partnership interest to a fellow partner, or buying a partnership interest from a fellow partner, has an affirmative duty to disclose any material information that:

- relates to the value of the partnership interest or the partnership itself, and
- could not be learned by examining the partnership books.

The partner who possesses the information must volunteer it. "You didn't ask" is no excuse.[88]

> *Example:* Samantha and Todd are partners in a real estate investment partnership. The partnership has a term of ten years, but after five years Samantha wants to get her money out. Todd offers to buy her out and names what appears to be a reasonable price. Samantha does not know, however, that Todd has received a very good offer on one of the partnership's parcels. Todd does not volunteer the information, and Samantha accepts Todd's offer. Samantha has a claim against Todd. Under the UPA, he breached his fiduciary duty by failing to disclose information relating to the value of the partnership which could not be learned by reviewing the partnership's books.
>
> As to RUPA, the analysis must pick its way through the relevant statutory provisions, but the result is the same. The sale involves the transfer of Samantha's transferable interest and therefore involves Samantha's exercise of a right under RUPA §503(a)(1).[89] Todd has therefore violated RUPA §403(c)(1) by failing to furnish, without demand, "information concerning the partnership's business and affairs reasonably required for the proper exercise of [Samantha's] rights . . . under . . . this [Act]."

---

87. Remedies may be a different matter. See the discussion at the end of this section.

88. The partner's obligation differs substantially from the situation of a party to an arm's length transaction. In an arm's length transaction, a party may not misrepresent information, but—absent some special relationship—the party has no duty to volunteer. Partnership is a special (i.e., fiduciary) relationship.

89. See section 8.8.4.

When partners exercise discretion vis-à-vis copartners.   When a partner rightfully dissolves a partnership, the general disclosure requirements continue as the partnership winds up its business.[90] When partners expel a copartner, the expelled copartner's right to information may, in contrast, be quite restricted. The same provision of the partnership agreement that authorizes the expulsion may expressly or implicitly deny the expelled partner any right to an explanation for the expulsion.[91]

Fair dealing.   The vague concept of "fair dealing" has two aspects: process and substance. The process aspect concerns the manner in which partners deal with each other. The substance aspect concerns the fairness of the outcome of partner-to-partner dealings.

In partner-to-partner transactions.   As a matter of *process,* partners are obliged to deal with each other in a candid, noncoercive manner. They have, as just discussed, a duty of full disclosure. They must also avoid exacting agreements through threats or other forms of intimidation. Conduct which in an arm's-length relationship would *not* amount to actionable duress or procedural unconscionability may nonetheless suffice to invalidate a transaction between partners.

As a matter of *substance,* the cases speak of a partner's obligation to provide a "fair price" in partner-to-partner transactions. However, almost without exception "unfair price" cases are also "nondisclosure" cases. That is, the partner who agreed to the bad deal did so in the absence of material information that the other partner possessed and failed to disclose. It seems unlikely that a court would use "unfair price" to overturn a partner-to-partner deal if the partner who benefitted from the deal made full disclosure and avoided any abusive negotiating tactics.

In deference to freedom of contract, a partner who complies with the process aspect of "fair dealing" in a partner-to-partner transaction should not have to worry about the substantive aspect. Any *post hoc* attack on the fairness of the outcome should be rejected as "buyer's (or seller's) remorse" or "20/20 hindsight."

When partners exercise discretion vis-à-vis copartners.   The process aspect of "fair dealing" has little relevance to a partner's right to dissolve a partnership. To cause the end of the partnership, a partner must manifest *express will.*[92] This manifestation typically involves giving notice to fellow partners, but there is no fiduciary duty to consult with them before making the decision or to hear them out if they object to ending the partnership. Process-fair dealing likewise has little relevance when a partner is expelled under a partnership agreement.

---

90. Chapter Eleven discusses in detail the process by which a partnership comes to an end.

91. For a detailed discussion of expulsion, see section 11.7.2.

92. UPA §31(1)(b); RUPA §801(1) and (2)(i).

Those doing the expelling must comply with any process requirements stated in the agreement, but fiduciary duty does not impose additional requirements. Unless the partnership agreement so provides, fair dealing does not mean "due process," a warning, an opportunity to be heard, or even a statement of reasons. Substance-fair dealing has slightly greater impact in controlling partners' exercise of discretion. Partners may not end a partnership or effect an expulsion for the malicious purpose of depriving a fellow partner of benefits, if:

- the fellow partner had a right to expect the benefits,
- the benefits would have naturally accrued to the fellow partner absent the exercise of discretion, and
- the exercise of discretion transfers the benefits to the partner or partners exercising the discretion.

Succeeding with a claim based on this substantive aspect of fair dealing is not easy. The claimant partner must show conduct amounting to expropriation or unjust enrichment.[93]

Remedies.   Under the UPA, a court has available the full panoply of remedies for breach of the duty of loyalty: damages, disgorgement (constructive trust), recission. Under RUPA, in contrast, the analysis is more complex and perhaps somewhat limited. As explained earlier in this section, under RUPA partner-to-partner duties come not from the duty of loyalty but rather from RUPA §§403 and 404(d). Neither of these provisions expresses a fiduciary duty.

As a result, punitive damages will likely be unavailable, and courts will have to combine common law concepts such as fraudulent nondisclosure and fraud in the inducement in order to set aside tainted transactions. Concepts of unjust enrichment may empower a court to order disgorgement.

§9.9   The Impact of Agreements on Partner Fiduciary Duty

§9.9.1   *Limits on Agreements*

Like other facets of partners' inter se relationships, partner fiduciary duties are subject to contrary agreement. Unlike other inter se facets, however, these duties are not completely default rules. There is a limit to the changes agreements can make.

Unfortunately, under both the UPA and RUPA the extent of those limits is unclear. Some duties can be completely waived and therefore may also be

---

93. For further discussion of this vague and rarely-satisfied standard, see sections 11.7.1 and 11.7.2.

changed or limited. For example, the duties under UPA §21(1) all give way with "the consent of the other partners," and under UPA §18(h) the partnership agreement can provide that less-than-unanimous consent constitutes "the consent of the other partners."

Likewise, under RUPA §103(b)(3)(ii) "all of the partners or a number or percentage specified in the partnership agreement may authorize or ratify, after full disclosure of all material facts, a specific act or transaction that otherwise would violate the duty of loyalty." In addition, under RUPA §103(b)(3)(i) "the partnership agreement may identify specific types or categories of activities that do not violate the duty of loyalty, if not manifestly unreasonable." Under RUPA §103(b)(5) "the partnership agreement may prescribe the standards by which the performance of the obligation [of good faith and fair dealing] is to be measured, if the standards are not manifestly unreasonable." In no event, however, may a RUPA partnership agreement "eliminate" the duty of loyalty or the obligation of good faith and fair dealing.[94]

Under case law, a UPA partnership agreement is likewise powerless to eliminate the duty of loyalty, but under both the UPA and RUPA it is difficult to determine exactly when a substantial limitation amounts to an elimination. Note, for example, that RUPA §103(b)(3)(ii) does not require that the authorization or ratification be by disinterested partners. An interested partner that participates in the authorization or ratification process is subject to the obligation of good faith and fair dealing, but RUPA §404(e) provides that a "partner does not violate a duty or obligation under this [Act] . . . merely because the partner's conduct furthers the partner's own interest."

In this area of law, as in many others, "pigs get fat and hogs get slaughtered." Attempts to waive process fair dealing in partner-to-partner transactions will likely be ineffective, as will attempts to authorize the expropriating use of discretion. In contrast, agreements that authorize partners to compete with the partnership, or permit self-dealing by a managing partner, are commonplace and ordinarily enforceable.

§9.9.2 *Ambiguous, Oral, and Implied Agreements*

Under both the UPA and RUPA, agreements or conduct purporting to waive or alter partner fiduciary duties are carefully scrutinized and strictly construed. The duties are fundamental to the character of a partnership and protect important interests which are potentially vulnerable to abuse. Ambiguity is construed against the purported alteration or waiver, not only because the person asserting the alteration or waiver has often drafted language at issue[95] but also because the waiver must be established by clear and convincing evidence.

---

94. RUPA §103(b)(3) and (5).

95. The reason reflects the contract doctrine of *contra proferentem*. Black's Law Dictionary (7th ed. 1999) defines the term as naming "[t]he doctrine that, in interpreting documents, ambiguities are to be construed unfavorably to the drafter."

Under RUPA the same approach is likely to be applied to attempts to "prescribe the standards by which the performance of the obligation [of good faith and fair dealing] is to be measured."[96]

Neither the UPA nor RUPA requires agreements altering or waiving fiduciary duties to be in writing, but alleged oral agreements can produce wasteful and expensive "swearing contests." Courts can infer waivers from the conduct of the partners, but such inferences do not come easily. Insisting on clear and definitive evidence, courts are wary of making too much out of mere acquiescence to past conduct.

> *Example:* Alice, a partner in a biotechnology partnership, knows that the partnership is looking to rent new office and laboratory space. She happens to know of a building, in the ideal location, suitable to house the firm's special equipment. She learns that the owner is willing either to lease or to sell. Alice decides that the building would make a fine personal investment, so she buys it for herself. Her partners later discover the transaction but make no objection. Two years later, when the partnership is looking for additional laboratory space Alice again buys an opportune location for herself. This time her partners object, and under either UPA §21 or RUPA §404(b)(1) their objection is valid. Their acquiescence to the first transaction did not waive Alice's duties as to the second transaction.

§9.10   Enforcing Inter Se Obligations

Action for an accounting.   When one partner raises a breach of duty claim against another, the resulting dispute can be exceedingly complicated. Any situation nasty enough to produce litigation is likely to signal the end of the partnership. If so, it may be impossible (or at least extremely difficult) to determine the breach of duty of claim without also settling accounts generally among all the partners.[97]

To keep this complexity within bounds, partnership law provides an equitable action for an accounting. The accounting sorts out the partners' various claims and rights and avoids piecemeal adjudication.

According to much UPA case law, an accounting is generally a condition precedent to bringing a claim for damages arising out of the partnership's affairs or business.[98]

---

96. RUPA §103(b)(5).

97. Sections 11.5.3-11.5.5 discuss the rules that apply to settle partner accounts when the partnership comes to an end.

98. Some exceptions do exist to the UPA's condition precedent rule, including claims between the partners that do not relate to the partnership business and claims that are so simple that no accounting is necessary.

Example: The whoopee cushion partnership of Larry, Moe, and Curley has fallen on hard times. Larry accuses Moe of failing to use his best efforts, as promised in the partnership agreement, to secure new clients. Curley claims Larry has taken excessive draws against profits and owes money to the partnership. Moe believes that the partnership owes him $5,000 in reimbursement for customer entertainment expenses. None of the partners can pursue their claims unless their prayer for relief includes an accounting.

RUPA takes a different approach:

(b) A partner may maintain an action against the partnership or another partner for legal or equitable relief, *with or without an accounting* as to partnership business, to:

(1) enforce the partner's rights under the partnership agreement;

(2) enforce the partner's rights under this [Act] . . . ; or

(3) enforce the rights and otherwise protect the interests of the partner, including rights and interests arising independently of the partnership relationship.[99]

According to the official Comment, this change "reflects the increased willingness courts have shown to grant relief without the requirement of an accounting, in derogation of the so-called 'exclusivity rule.' "[100]

Partner standing to sue fellow partner for damage to the partnership. To the extent a partnership is considered an entity separate from its partners,[101] it might appear that only the partnership itself (or a partner asserting a derivative claim[102]) has standing to sue a partner whose misconduct has injured

---

99. RUPA §405(b) (emphasis added).

100. RUPA §405, Comment 2.

101. See section 7.2.7.

102. Derivative claims most commonly occur and are perhaps most easily understood in the corporate context:

[A] shareholder asserts a derivative claim to vindicate the rights of the corporation. A wrongful act has depleted or devalued corporate assets or has undercut the corporate business. The shareholder has suffered harm only indirectly, as a consequence of damage done to the corporation. The wrongful conduct relates to the shareholder only through the medium of the corporation, i.e., by reducing the value of the shareholder's stock. For example, when those in control of the corporation act negligently, or waste or misappropriate corporate assets, it is the corporation, not the shareholder, that first suffers the loss. Likewise, if a corporate director takes for him or herself a business opportunity that properly belongs to the corporation, it is the corporation, not the shareholder, that has lost the opportunity and any attendant profits.

In essence, a derivative plaintiff seeks to derive standing from the injury to the corporation and to represent the corporation's interests in the derivative lawsuit.

Daniel S. Kleinberger and Imanta Bergmanis, Direct vs. Derivative, or What's a Lawsuit Between Friends in an "Incorporated Partnership"? 22 William Mitchell L. Rev. 1203, 1214-1215 (1996). For further discussion, see section 13.5.6.

the partnership. Under the UPA, however, the aggregate concept prevails in this context, and such claims are typically sorted out through an accounting.

Although RUPA takes a pure entity approach, one of its official Comments flatly rejects derivative claims. "Since general partners are not passive investors like limited partners, RUPA does not authorize derivative actions, as does [the Revised Uniform Limited Partnership Act], Section 1001."[103] The same Comment asserts that under RUPA §405(b) "a partner may bring a direct suit against the partnership or another partner for almost any cause of action arising out of the conduct of the partnership business."[104]

PROBLEM 72

A 30-partner law firm has a partnership agreement that delegates most management decisions to a five-partner Executive Committee elected annually by all the partners. The partnership agreement states a formula for determining each partner's profit share and allocates to the Executive Committee the exclusive authority to apply the formula and determine the profit shares. The formula allows the Executive Committee some discretion but depends very heavily on objective factors such as billable hours, payments received from clients, and clients brought to the firm.

A partner is dissatisfied with the profit share he received this year and wishes to see the partnership records the Executive Committee used in determining shares for all the partners. The Committee claims that this information "relates to the individual performance of the several partners and is therefore confidential." The Committee offers to show the partner only the records directly relevant to him. The partner accurately points out that the formula requires the Committee to compare the performance of all the partners. He insists on seeing all the relevant records. Who is right under the UPA? Under RUPA?

EXPLANATION

Under the UPA the partner is right. UPA §20 provides that "[p]artners shall render on demand true and full information of all things affecting the partnership to any partner." The partner has made demand, and the records are connected to the fundamental partnership question of profit shares. Given that connection, they certainly contain "information of . . . things affecting the partnership."

The delegation of management authority to the Executive Committee makes no difference to this issue. A partner's right to information can be waived by agreement, but the agreement must be specific to be effective.[105]

---

103. RUPA §405, Comment 2.

104. RUPA §405, Comment 2.

105. There is a counterargument, based on the delegation of management authority to the Executive Committee. That delegation establishes a system of profit allocation that, arguably at least, requires confidentiality in order to work. When the partners agreed to the delegation of authority, they implicitly agreed to the necessary confidentiality.

The partner is also right under RUPA. RUPA §403(b) provides categorically that: "A partnership shall provide partners and their agents and attorneys access to its books and records. . . . The right of access provides the opportunity to inspect and copy books and records during ordinary business hours."[106]

PROBLEM 73

Bernard and Suzanne form a partnership to run a dance school for children ages 4 to 14. Their partnership agreement delegates all artistic control to Bernard, and states that "all business decisions shall be decided by Suzanne in her sole discretion." The school sells ballet and tap shoes to its students, at a very healthy mark-up. Bernard thinks the shoes should be sold at cost. "We make our money from our teaching," he says. "We are not shopkeepers." Under RUPA, does Suzanne have a right to continue to sell at a mark-up, despite Bernard's objections? Under the UPA?

EXPLANATION

Yes, under either statute. Although under RUPA §401(j) partners decide any "difference arising as to a matter in the ordinary course of business" by majority vote, that provision is a default rule. These partners have agreed to allocate all business decisions to Suzanne. Therefore, on matters such as the price of shoes Bernard no longer has "equal rights in the management and conduct of the partnership business."[107]

The result is identical under the UPA. UPA §§18(e) (equal management rights) and (h) (disagreements as to ordinary matters decided by majority vote) are both subject to the partnership agreement.

PROBLEM 74

Larry, Moe, and Curley form a partnership to operate a whoopee cushion factory. Larry invests $100,000, Moe, $80,000, Curley, $20,000. They agree that (i) each will work full time in the business, (ii) each will receive a salary of

---

106. If the partnership had not reduced the information to record form, the outcome might be different. The partnership could assert RUPA §403(c)(2), which provides that "Each partner and the partnership shall furnish to a partner . . . on demand, any other information concerning the partnership's business and affairs, *except to the extent the demand or the information demanded is unreasonable or otherwise improper under the circumstances.*" (Emphasis added.) The partner could counter, however, that the information was "reasonably required for the proper exercise of the partner's rights . . . under the partnership agreement" and therefore was categorically obtainable under RUPA §403(c)(1) (requiring the disclosure, without demand, of "any information concerning the partnership's business and affairs reasonably required for the proper exercise of the partner's rights and duties under the partnership agreement or this [Act])".

107. RUPA §401(f). Without the partnership agreement, the partners would be deadlocked. See section 9.5.3.

$20,000 (separate from whatever profits they may receive), and (iii) none will withdraw their capital for at least three years. They make no other specific agreements.

At the end of the first year of operation, the partnership has a profit (after salaries) of $100,000. Larry and Moe want to distribute profits in proportion to the partners' respective contributions—50 percent to Larry, 40 percent to Moe, and 10 percent to Curley. They assert that profits are an ordinary part of partnership business and that therefore a majority vote controls. Are they correct?

EXPLANATION

No. UPA §18(a) provides for partners to share profits equally, "subject to any agreement between them." To change the default rule requires unanimous consent, not a mere majority vote.

The result is identical under RUPA §§401(b) (default rule of profit shares) and 103(a) (subject to exceptions not relevant here, partnership agreement controls relations inter se the partners).

PROBLEM 75

This Problem is based on a children's poem by Eugene Field:

> Wynken, Blynken, and Nod one night
>   Sailed off in a wooden shoe—
> Sailed on a river of crystal light,
>   Into a sea of dew.
> "Where are you going, and what do you wish?"
>   The old moon asked the three.
> "We've come to fish for the herring fish
>   That live in this beautiful sea;
>   Nets of silver and gold have we!"
>   Said Wynken,
>   Blynken,
>   And Nod.

Assume that Wynken, Blynken, and Nod are partners in a RUPA partnership. Since the inception of the partnership, Wynken, Blynken, and Nod have always given the same answer to the old moon's question. If Wynken and Blynken want to have the partnership take up vegetable farming, and Nod opposes the idea, what result?

EXPLANATION

Absent a contrary agreement, RUPA §401(j) governs this type of situation. If the dispute over vegetable farming is a "difference arising as to a matter in the ordinary course of business," then the majority rules and Wynken and Blynken will prevail. If the dispute is "outside the ordinary course of business" or in contravention of the partnership agreement, taking up vegetable farming will require unanimous consent and Nod will prevail.

The facts suggest that Nod will prevail. The partners' repeated answers to the old moon would support a finding that the partnership's ordinary course of business is fishing. In addition, the same facts could evidence an implied-in-fact agreement among the partners that the partnership will confine itself to fishing. In either case, RUPA §401(j) would require unanimous agreement to take up vegetable farming.[108]

PROBLEM 76

Oscar is a partner in a UPA partnership formed, in the words of the partnership agreement, "for the purpose of investing in real estate." The agreement contains no other limitation on the scope of the partnership's business. In the five years since its formation, the partnership has invested exclusively in residential real estate located in either Minnesota or Iowa. While on vacation in Hawaii, Oscar comes across an attractive investment opportunity in an office building located there. Without informing his partners or obtaining their consent, Oscar uses his own money and buys the building. Two years later, while the partnership is still in existence, Oscar sells the building and makes a profit of $300,000. When the other partners learn of the transaction they insist that Oscar share the profits with the partnership. Must he?

EXPLANATION

Probably. The profits certainly come from "investing in real estate," and so appear "connected with the . . . conduct of the partnership." Oscar's partners will therefore prevail under UPA §21(1), unless Oscar can show that the partnership's practice of investing solely in residential real estate impliedly limited the scope of the partnership business.[109]

PROBLEM 77

Same facts as Problem 76, except that:

(1) Two weeks before his trip to Hawaii, Oscar attended a partnership meeting at which the partners reviewed the partnership's then-current finances.

(2) During that review, it was apparent that the partnership had on hand only sufficient funds to meet operating expenses and did not have any cash available to make any further investments.

(3) Before purchasing the Hawaii building, Oscar telephones you, his attorney, and asks "Am I going to be in trouble with that partnership if I buy this building?"

What advice should you give Oscar?

---

108. UPA §18(h) would involve the same analysis and produce the same result.
109. RUPA §404(b)(1) would involve the same analysis and produce the same result.

EXPLANATION

Despite the partnership's current "cash poor" situation, the Hawaii building may still be a partnership opportunity. If made aware of the opportunity, the partners may choose to raise the necessary cash by, for example, selling some of the partnership's current holdings or borrowing against those holdings. Oscar's safest course therefore is to disclose the situation to his copartners and either (i) obtain their unanimous consent for him to take the opportunity personally or (ii) obtain a vote of the partners rejecting the opportunity.

If Oscar can obtain unanimous consent, the first approach is better. It has the virtue of certainty. The second approach rests on the argument that (i) a decision to take or reject a business opportunity is an ordinary matter and is therefore subject to a majority vote under UPA §18(h), and (ii) the fact that a partner wishes to take the opportunity individually does not transform the decision into an extraordinary matter requiring unanimous consent.[110]

PROBLEM 78

Same facts as Problem 76, except that:

(1) At a partnership meeting that took place three weeks before the Hawaii trip, the partners rejected by a vote of 3-2 a proposal to invest in an office building in Minneapolis.

(2) One of the partners who voted against the proposal expressed the opinion that the partnership should "stick with residential real estate."

Will these new facts change the outcome of the partnership's disgorgement claim?

EXPLANATION

No. Neither the partnership's decision to reject an opportunity nor one partner's opinion on the subject generally will change the scope of matters "connected with the . . . conduct of the partnership."[111] If that scope does in fact include commercial real estate, then only an amendment to the partnership agreement can put such investments beyond the partnership's reach.[112]

PROBLEM 79

Same facts as Problem 76 except that:

(1) The office building is located in Minneapolis.

---

110. Again, the analysis under RUPA is parallel. See RUPA §§404(b)(1) and 401(j).

111. UPA §21(1).

112. The result would be the same under RUPA §404(b)(1). Although arguably Oscar's "profit . . . [was not] derived by the partner in the conduct . . . of the partnership business," given the scope of the partnership's business Oscar's purchase constituted "the appropriation of a partnership opportunity."

(2) Oscar first discovers the building while inspecting several apartment complexes owned by the partnership and while driving in a car owned by the partnership.
(3) The partnership agreement limits investments to residential real estate.

Will these new facts change the outcome of the partners' disgorgement claim?

EXPLANATION

Yes. Oscar will not have to disgorge, even though his investment is tangentially "connected with the . . . conduct . . . of the partnership [and ensues] from . . . use by [Oscar] of its property." UPA §21(1). Oscar discovered the opportunity while engaged in the partnership's business and while driving the partnership's car. However, a de minimis rule applies to UPA §21. Because the connection is so insubstantial, and because the opportunity is so clearly beyond the partnership's scope, the partnership has no claim.[113]

PROBLEM 80

Same facts as Problem 76, except that:

(1) Instead of making a profit of $300,000, Oscar loses $100,000.
(2) The partnership agreement provides that all investment decisions will be made by majority vote.
(3) The partnership agreement requires all partners to share partnership losses equally.

Can Oscar get any reimbursement from his copartners?

EXPLANATION

No. The reach of UPA §18(b), the UPA's indemnification provision, is different from the reach of UPA §21(1). UPA §18(b) obligates the partnership to "indemnify every partner in respect of payments made and personal liabilities reasonably incurred by him in the ordinary and proper conduct of its business, or for the preservation of its business or property." Oscar's investment satisfies neither condition. He acted outside the "ordinary and proper conduct" of the partnership business (i.e., without the authority of a partner vote) and did not act to preserve partnership "business or property." Oscar therefore must bear his losses alone, even though he might have been obliged to share his profits.[114]

---

113. RUPA §404(b)(1) would involve the same analysis and produce the same result.
114. The analysis and result would be the same under RUPA. Although the language of RUPA §401(c) differs somewhat from the language of UPA §18(b), the differences are immaterial here. See section 8.4.

PROBLEM 81

Sweeney & Todd, a large metropolitan law firm, has been growing steadily and now has 50 partners. Plans call for adding another 40 partners over the next five years. Under the current partnership agreement all partners have one vote on all matters, including the annual election of the firm's management committee. Some of the more senior partners wish to give greater control to partners who have been with the firm at least ten years. Is such an arrangement lawful under the UPA and RUPA? If so, how might it be accomplished?

EXPLANATION

Such an arrangement is certainly lawful. UPA §18 and RUPA §401 each state default rules, and each allows partners to shape their management structure virtually as they see fit. The partnership agreement could, for example, give extra votes to partners who have been with the firm at least ten years. Or, the agreement could create two separate classes of partnership interests, allocate the "senior" interests to partners who have been with the firm at least ten years, and reserve specified management matters to partners holding senior interests.

To establish either structure, the partners would have to amend the partnership agreement. Unless the agreement provides for amendment on a less-than-unanimous basis, all the current partners will have to agree to any change. See RUPA §401(j).

PROBLEM 82

In addition to its 50 partners, Sweeney & Todd has 50 associates and 125 other employees. The partnership agreement dates from when the firm had only ten partners and requires unanimous consent for any amendment.

The firm's elected Management Committee wishes to implement a sexual harassment policy for dealing with complaints from firm employees. Upon the advice of counsel experienced in employment law, the Committee wishes to implement a policy that provides for confidential investigations of employee complaints and allows the Committee to impose discipline, either confidential or public, on any employee found to have engaged in harassing conduct. (This particular policy will not apply to partners. The Committee hopes soon to propose a policy on that subject.)

The Committee is quite concerned about confidentiality. "Leaks" can discourage employees from making complaints, ruin ongoing investigations, and subject the firm to damages for defamation. The Committee wants to make sure that only partners on the Management Committee will have access to information relating to complaints made, determinations reached, and sanctions imposed under the policy.

Are there any partnership law "wrinkles" to the Committee's concern under the UPA and RUPA?

EXPLANATION

Yes. As to the UPA, §20 may give each partner a right to the information the Committee seeks to protect. Claims of sexual harassment are exceedingly serious, and their proper handling is essential to the welfare of the partnership. Obversely, poor handling of a complaint could imperil both the partnership and the partners.[115] The complaint information is therefore "information of . . . things affecting the partnership" and subject to disclosure to any partner on demand.

Since the partnership agreement can only be amended through unanimous consent, under the UPA the only solution to this problem is to have each partner waive his or her right to the problematic information.

A similar "wrinkle" exists under RUPA §403. If the information is retained in the partnership's books and records, absent a contrary agreement each partner has a categorical right of access. RUPA §403(b). If the partnership never memorializes the information—a dangerous option under employment law—each partner still has an unbridled right of access to the extent the information is "reasonably required for the proper exercise of the partner's rights and duties under the partnership agreement or [RUPA]." RUPA §403(c)(1).

The partnership agreement can place reasonable restrictions on access to partnership books and records and can completely eliminate the access rights granted by RUPA §403.[116] However, in the stated situation the partnership agreement can be amended only with unanimous consent. Under RUPA, therefore, the partnership's best hope is to argue that (i) information about these matters has not been memorialized into the partnership's books and records; (ii) because these matters are within the authority of the Management Committee and information concerning them is not "reasonably required for the proper exercise of the partner's rights and duties" and therefore not within RUPA §403(c)(1); and (iii) under RUPA §403(c)(2), the partner has no right of access because—due to the importance of confidentiality—"the demand or the information demanded is unreasonable or otherwise improper under the circumstances."

PROBLEM 83

Same facts as in Problem 82, except that the partnership agreement provides: "This Agreement may be amended at any time upon the vote of 3/5 of the members of the Management Committee and the vote or written consent of a majority of all partners." Can Sweeney & Todd protect the complaint information through a nonunanimous amendment of the partnership agreement?

---

115. Recall that, except in an LLP, partners are personally liable for the debts of the partnership. UPA §15. See section 7.3.

116. RUPA §103(b)(2) limits the partnership agreement's power to curtail access to books and records, but RUPA §103 contains no restrictions on curtailing access to the other information covered by RUPA §403.

EXPLANATION

Probably. The analysis is the same under both the UPA and RUPA. There is some UPA dicta to the effect that, despite agreements to the contrary, all partners must consent to changes that affect their fundamental rights. That dicta should not be problematic here. Although the duty to render information is a core fiduciary duty, the contemplated waiver is limited in scope, is well defined, and will clearly serve the partners' overall interests.

PROBLEM 84

Xena, Gabriel, and Ares, Inc. (a corporation in which Xena is the sole stockholder) and Gabriel are going to form a RUPA partnership, with Xena to act as the active, managing partner. Xena wishes the partnership agreement to provide that it is not a breach of the duty of loyalty for her to cause the partnership to retain Ares, Inc. to furnish services to the partnership regardless of the amount Xena causes the partnership to pay for those services. As Xena's lawyer, you have advised her that the desired provision might fail the "manifestly unreasonable" standard of RUPA §103(b)(3)(i). Paraphrasing J.P. Morgan, Xena exclaims, "I don't hire lawyers to tell me what I can't do. I hire them to tell me how to do what I want to do." She adds, "Find me another way." Do so.

EXPLANATION

RUPA §103(b)(3)(ii) may offer you that way. It states that "a number or percentage [of partners] specified in the partnership agreement may authorize or ratify, after full disclosure of all material facts, a specific act or transaction that otherwise would violate the duty of loyalty." If the partnership agreement provides for ratification of self-dealing transactions by a 2/3 majority of the partners, the votes of Xena and Ares, Inc. will suffice to ratify the partnership's contracts with Ares, Inc. RUPA §103(b)(3)(ii) does *not* require that the ratifying partners be disinterested and is not subject to the manifestly unreasonable standard applicable to RUPA §103(b)(3)(i). If Xena and Ares, Inc. ratify a grossly unfair fee, their votes could be attacked as a breach of the duty of care. However, RUPA's gross negligence standard is substantially more lenient than the duty of loyalty as applied to self-dealing transactions.

10

The Power to Bind the Partnership

§10.1 Overview

The UPA and RUPA use the same basic approach to determine when and how the conduct of a partner binds the partnership. RUPA does introduce one novel concept—publicly filed statements delineating the actual authority of particular partners—but otherwise the RUPA power-to-bind provisions mostly mirror their UPA analogs.[1] The table on the following page lists and compares those power-to-bind rules of the UPA and RUPA.

Of these various attribution rules, UPA §9 and RUPA §301 require the most attention. They provide rules for binding the partnership in contract and are therefore the key provisions for analyzing most business transactions. Moreover, they provide the conceptual basis for some of the other attribution rules. The reach of UPA §11, for instance, depends on how that provision interacts with §9.[2]

---

1. UPA §10 (Conveyance of Real Property of the Partnership) and RUPA §302 (Transfer of Partnership Property) contain special rules for transferring real property owned by a partnership. Those rules rest on the more general provisions of UPA §9 and RUPA §301 and relate mostly to the formalities of title transfer.

2. See section 10.7. See also UPA §10 (providing rules for the conveyance of a partnership's real property and repeatedly referring to "the provisions of paragraph (1) of section 9").

power to bind through a partner's . . .	UPA provision	RUPA provision
contractual undertakings and similar acts	§9	§301 (drawn closely from UPA §9)
wrongful act	§13	§305(a) (drawn closely from UPA §13)
breach of trust	§14	§305(b) (intended to encompass UPA §14 claims)
knowledge, notice	§3 (definition of knowledge) §12 (attribution rule)	§102 (modeled on UCC, Article 1 definitions)
admission	§11	omitted (concept not even mentioned in a Comment)
effect of publicly filed statements	n/a	comprehensive system providing constructive notice

§10.2   Binding the Partnership in Contract —UPA §9

§10.2.1 The Paragon of Complexity

UPA §9 is a complex and somewhat problematic provision, which, fortunately, has been simplified and improved in RUPA §301. For several reasons, it makes sense to begin by understanding UPA §9. First, that provision continues to be the law in almost 20 states. Second, RUPA §301 can be understood only in historical context. Its improvements make most sense when compared to UPA §9, and its remaining problems all derive from that section. Third, many limited liability company statutes incorporate UPA §9 language to provide power-to-bind rules for members and managers of LLCs. (These statutes were enacted before the widespread acceptance of RUPA).[3]

UPA §9 provides:

---

3. Chapter Thirteen discusses limited liability companies, and section 13.5.4 considers the power of LLC members to bind the LLC..

§9. *Partner Agent of Partnership as to Partnership Business*

(1) Every partner is an agent of the partnership for the purpose of its business, and the act of every partner, including the execution in the partnership name of any instrument, for apparently carrying on in the usual way the business of the partnership of which he is a member binds the partnership, unless the partner so acting has in fact no authority to act for the partnership in the particular matter, and the person with whom he is dealing has knowledge of the fact that he has no such authority.

(2) An act of a partner which is not apparently for the carrying on of the business of the partnership in the usual way does not bind the partnership unless authorized by the other partners.

(3) Unless authorized by the other partners or unless they have abandoned the business, one or more but less than all the partners have no authority to:

(a) assign the partnership property in trust for creditors or on the assignee's promise to pay the debts of the partnership,

(b) dispose of the good-will of the business,

(c) do any other act which would make it impossible to carry on the ordinary business of a partnership,

(d) confess a judgment,

(e) submit a partnership claim or liability to arbitration or reference.

(4) No act of any partner in contravention of a restriction on authority shall bind the partnership to persons having knowledge of the restriction.

The difficulty in mastering UPA §9 comes from three sources: (1) the section states a very intricate set of rules, (2) at key points the section uses language carelessly, and (3) much of the case law is superficial and unenlightening.

The intricacy exists because UPA §9 contains multiple rules that run in opposite directions. UPA §9's basic structure reflects a common but unfortunate tendency of lawyers to write rules in the mode of "two steps forward, but one step back."[4] UPA §9 follows this "cha-cha" approach by providing two rules that establish a partner's power to bind and three rules that confine that power:

- *the "agency law" empowering rule (§9(1), first clause)*, which invokes (albeit ambiguously) the law of agency
- *the "apparently/usual" empowering rule (§9(1), second clause)*, which is partnership law's analog to apparent authority

---

4. Asked to define a bagel, for example, a lawyer might say, "A bagel is a thick disc of baked dough with rounded edges, provided however that, notwithstanding the foregoing, the center of the disc does not contain dough." A less intricate definition might be "a ring of baked dough."

- *the "not apparently/usual" constraining rule (§9(2))*, which looks like the "flip side" of the "apparently/usual" empowering rule but which serves to substantially undercut the "agency law" empowering rule
- *the "no authority" constraining rule (§9(1), third and fourth clauses, §9(4))*, which is apparently so important that the UPA states it twice
- *the "unanimous consent" constraining rule (§9(3))*, which is the clearest of all the five rules

As for careless use of language, UPA §9 deals sometimes with the power to bind, sometimes with the right to bind, and sometimes with both at once. Worse, the section does not always make clear when it is doing which. For example, terms "authority" and "authorized" appear six times in the section, with no express indication whether they encompass apparent and inherent as well as actual authority.

As for unenlightening case law, many of the cases apply UPA §9 without much analysis, neglecting important nuances and focusing on individual parts of the rules out of context. It is impossible to construe UPA §9 in a way that reconciles all or even most of the cases.

Some of the case law confusion relates to the role of agency law under UPA §9. The provision's first clause seems to incorporate all of agency law's attribution rules,[5] and many courts invoke those rules uncritically. As a result, many cases fail to consider how, if at all, the rest of UPA §9 constrains the application of agency law rules.

To avoid the same failing, the following analysis begins with the components of UPA §9 that belong exclusively to partnership law.

§10.2.2 The "Apparently/Usual" Empowering Rule

The basic rule.   The second clause of §9(1) reads in pertinent part: "the act of every partner . . . for apparently carrying on in the usual way the business of the partnership of which he is a member binds the partnership. . . ." A third party claimant who seeks to use this language must that show that:

- at the time of the transaction
- it reasonably[6] appeared to the claimant that the partner's act was:
  —for carrying on the business of the partnership and
  —for doing so "in the usual way."

A partner's apparently/usual power is analogous to the agency law concept of apparent authority, with the partnership's admission of the partner

---

5. That clause reads: "Every partner is an agent of the partnership for the purpose of its business. . . ." See also UPA §4(3) ("The law of agency shall apply under this act.")

6. Although the statute does not mention reasonableness, the case law does.

constituting the principal's manifestation. Apparently/usual power is therefore analogous to "apparent authority by position."

Like apparent authority, apparently/usual power concerns itself with appearances, reasonably interpreted.[7] It is possible, therefore, for a partner to have apparently-usual power while lacking actual authority.

> *Example:* Ventura Company is a partnership that trades agricultural commodities, and for many years the Company has traded in tobacco. This year, on personal moral grounds, the partners unanimously decided to stop. Subsequently, however, one of the partners backslides and makes a contract for the partnership to buy 50,000 pounds of tobacco. The apparently/usual power of UPA §9(1) probably binds the partnership to the contract. Although a tobacco contract is no longer "the usual way" for Ventura to do business, the contract likely appeared "usual" to the third party. If so, the partnership is bound.[8]

The apparently/usual rule's focus on appearances gives rise to four questions: (1) Must the partner's act appear "usual" for that particular partnership, or merely for partnerships of the same type? (2) Does the rule apply when the partnership does not appear at all, that is, when the partnership's involvement is undisclosed? (3) Does the rule apply even though both the appearances and the acting partner are deceiving, that is, when the partner purports to act for the partnership but instead takes personally the benefits of the transaction? (4) Are some actions so extraordinary that they can never be apparently/usual?

Subissue #1: Whose usual way?   The phrase "the usual way" is ambiguous. Some cases hold that the third party must establish that the partner's act appeared usual *for the particular partnership.* Other cases hold that the third party must or may establish that the partner's act appeared usual *for similar partnerships.*

The following Example shows the tension between these two interpretations.

> *Example:* Al, a partner in the Ventura Company, purports to purchase on Ventura's behalf 50,000 bushels of sunflowers from Acme Agriculture. Ventura Company later repudiates the transaction, asserting that Al had no

---

7. Some cases treat the apparently/usual power as reflecting inherent agency power, but these cases have difficulty making sense of the word "apparently."

8. A company that "trades" commodities buys and sells the right to take delivery of the commodities. Occasionally the company may itself take delivery of an order, but usually the company tries to match each "take delivery" contract with a "make delivery" contract. If the company correctly predicts how prices will move, it matches well and profits. For example, on Monday the company buys from a farmer the right to receive 5,000 bushels of sunflower seeds for $5.79 per bushel. On Wednesday, after a big storm damages crops in sunflower country, the company is able to sell its right to receive those 5,000 bushels for $6.00 per bushel. The company has made a profit of $1,050 (less commissions charged for the buying and selling). If the company predicts poorly, it will lose money.

right to commit Ventura to such a large purchase. Acme invokes the apparently/usual power of §9(1) and offers to prove that: partners in commodities trading partnerships often make 50,000 bushel commitments, so therefore at the time of the transaction it appeared to Acme that Al was acting "in the usual way" for partnerships engaged in similar activities. In contrast, according to Ventura, Acme should instead prove that at the time of the transaction it appeared to Acme that Al was acting "in the usual way" *for the Ventura Company,* and, in proving that appearance Acme should not be able to rely solely on the custom of similar partnerships.

Subissue #2: The partnership must be apparent.   A partner may transact business on behalf of a partnership without disclosing the partnership's existence to the third party. In those circumstances, other attribution rules may bind the partnership to the third party,[9] but the "apparently/usual" power will not. Whatever "the usual way" means, the statute certainly requires that the partner's act *appear to be* "for . . . carrying on . . . the business of the partnership of which he is a member."

> *Example:* Al, a partner in the Ventura Company, buys a computer for the partnership to use in its offices. It is quite usual for Ventura partners to make such purchases, and indeed Ventura partners have previously made such purchases from this seller. However, the seller does not know that Al is a partner in Ventura, and Al does not mention the partnership. Instead, Al signs an installment contract in his own name. The apparently/usual power will not bind the partnership,[10] because the seller cannot satisfy the "appearance" element. The partnership was undisclosed, and the seller could not reasonably have believed that the purchase was connected in some way with the business of a partnership.

Subissue #3: The partnership need not benefit.[11]   Since appearance is what matters, the apparently/usual rule may apply even though the partner's act actually benefits the partner rather than the partnership.[12]

> *Example:* Al is a partner in the Ventura Company. Purporting to act for the Company, Al buys a computer on credit from a computer store. Ventura partners have made such purchases from the computer store in the past. This time, however, Al does not deliver the computer to the partnership. Instead, he resells the computer to a friend and pockets the

---

9. For example, a partner with actual authority may bind the partnership even though the partnership is undisclosed. See section 10.2.4.

10. Other doctrines probably will. See sections 10.2.4 and 10.2.8.

11. The cases and the commentators do not all agree on this point.

12. While the *first* clause of UPA §9(1) empowers a partner to act only "for the purpose of [the partnership's] business," the "apparently/usual" rule contains no such restriction. The first clause of §9(1) is discussed at section 10.2.4.

cash. The computer store may nonetheless collect from the Ventura Company. From the perspective of the computer store Al's act in buying the computer was "for apparently carrying on in the usual way the business of the partnership." The partnership is therefore bound.

This interpretation is not universally accepted, but it (i) seems compelled by the language of the statute, (ii) finds support in the case law, and (iii) comports with analogous tenets of apparent authority.[13] Moreover, the interpretation serves basic notions of efficiency and fairness. It is generally easier for members of a partnership to monitor each other than for third parties to inquire deeply into the bona fides of every partner who reasonably appears to be acting for the partnership. If a partner's dishonesty causes loss, that loss should fall on those better positioned to avoid it.

Subissue #4: Acts considered not "apparently/usual." Through the early twentieth century, partnership law used an overarching concept to address the apparently/usual issue—namely, the concept of a "trading" partnership. Trading partnerships were involved in trade; their businesses consisted of buying and selling goods. In contrast, nontrading partnerships sought profits through means then considered less mercantile, such as the provision of professional services. In the view of many courts, certain commercial acts, such as borrowing money, could be "apparently/usual" for a trading partnership but were quite out of character for a nontrading partnership.

Today, even partnerships of professionals are intensely commercial in their outlook, and the trading/nontrading distinction is obsolete. Lawyers do marketing studies, physicians face a "health care financing system," and architects think about the bottom line. Services providers of all types worry about "cash flow," and borrowing money under a line of credit is hardly extraordinary.[14]

The demise of the trading/nontrading distinction leaves the apparently/usual rule without any overarching tool of analysis. The case law does, however, suggest that the following categories of acts are not "apparently/usual" regardless of the type of partnership involved:

- having the partnership guarantee the debts of some other person or entity
- paying or assuming the debt of a partner
- giving away significant partnership property

This list is not exhaustive, nor is each category a per se rule. Ultimately, the apparently/usual issue is always a question of fact.

---

13. See section 2.3.

14. Under a line of credit, a borrower may borrow as it sees fit (typically from a bank) for the purposes specified in the line of credit agreement, so long as the amount borrowed does not exceed the credit limit stated in the agreement and the customer makes timely payments of the interest required by the agreement.

§10.2.3 The "Flip Side" Constraining Rule: Not "Apparently/Usual" and No Actual Authority

Under UPA §9(2) a partner lacks the power to bind the partnership if:

- the partner is not "authorized by the other partners" (i.e., if the partner lacks actual authority[15]), and
- the partner's act "is not apparently for the carrying on of the business of the partnership in the usual way."

Example: Sara is a partner in Ventura Company. Under the partnership agreement, Sara has no authority to commit Ventura to any trades. Sara makes a purchase of soybeans in her own name from a farmer who is unaware of the partnership's existence. Under UPA §9(2), Sara's act cannot bind Ventura, because (i) the act was not "apparently/usual" and (ii) Sara lacked actual authority.[16]

Although both the "apparently/usual" empowering rule of UPA §9(1) and the "not apparently/usual" constraining rule of UPA §9(2) have a common component, the constraining rule does not follow automatically from the empowering rule. The empowering rule states conditions under which a partner's act binds the partnership, but that rule does not itself foreclose other empowering conditions. UPA §9(2) performs that function. Taken together the two "apparently/usual" rules mean that:

- a partner who has actual authority binds the partnership within the scope of that authority, regardless of what appears to the third party, and
- a partner who lacks actual authority can bind the partnership *only* by satisfying the "apparently/usual" empowering rule.

§10.2.4 The Agency Law Empowering Rule

The first clause of UPA §9(1) states: "Every partner is an agent of the partnership for the purpose of its business. . . ." This clause invokes agency law principles as a separate basis for holding a partnership responsible for the acts of a partner. When a partner acts "for the purpose of [the partnership's] business," the partner as agent may bind the partnership.[17] Thus, even when the "appar-

---

15. In this context "authorized" must mean "actually authorized," otherwise the subsection would swallow its own tail.

16. If, however, the partnership later accepts the benefits of the deal, the partnership will be bound to some extent. Acceptance may indicate ratification, which would bind the partnership to the deal itself. Short of ratification, acceptance may oblige the partnership to respond in quantum meruit for the reasonable value of benefits accepted. See section 10.2.8.

17. The entity/aggregate debate, see section 7.2.7, sometimes surfaces in this context, with some authorities contending that each partner is an agent for all the other partners. UPA §9(1) expressly takes the entity approach, referring to the partner's act as binding "the partnership."

ently/usual" power does not work, a partnership may still be bound under agency rules unless a UPA §9 constraining rule provides to the contrary.

This section analyzes a partner's *agency* power to bind the partnership, considering in turn a partner's actual authority, apparent authority, and inherent power.

Actual authority.   Although often a partner who acts with actual authority also satisfies the "apparently/usual" rule, a partner who acts with actual authority[18] binds the partnership regardless of appearances.

> *Example:* Al is a partner in the Ventura Company and has the actual authority to make equipment purchases for the partnership. Without mentioning the Company, he buys a computer for the Company to use in its offices. He even signs an installment contract in his own name. The partnership is obligated on the contract, even though the "apparently/usual" power does not apply. Agency law attributes Al's act to the partnership, and Al's actual authority defeats the "not apparently/usual" constraining rule of UPA §9(2).

Apparent authority.   Apparent authority cannot extend the power to bind of a partner *qua* partner[19] beyond the scope of UPA §9(1)'s apparently/usual power. Any extension would contravene UPA §9(2).

However, apparent authority can apply if the circumstances would establish apparent authority for a non-partner.

> *Example:* Al, a partner in the Ventura Company, approaches Acme Agricultural and offers to buy 100,000 bushels of birdseed for the partnership. Acme's Vice President of sales knows from experience that Ventura deals only in commodities suitable for human consumption. The Vice President telephones Beatrice, Ventura's Managing Partner, who says, "It's okay. We've authorized Al to try a few experiments in birdseed. It's not our usual practice, but this trade is okay." Satisfied, the Vice President agrees to Al's offer. Ventura Company later repudiates the deal, and Acme learns that, contrary to Beatrice's assertion, Al had no actual authority. The partnership agreement expressly limits the partnership to trading commodities suitable for human consumption.
>
> Is Ventura Company bound? Al had no actual authority. The Ventura Partnership Agreement expressly limits the company's business to trading in human consumables and prohibits the Managing Partner from authorizing other kinds of trading. Acme cannot invoke Al's "apparently/usual" power, because it did *not* appear to the Vice President that Al's act was "for apparently carrying on in the usual way the business of the partnership."

---

18. Section 9.4 discusses the actual authority of a partner.

19. *Qua* means "as," signifies "in the capacity or role of," and indicates that the stated proposition is limited to the particular role being discussed.

However, a claim of apparent authority is more promising. By placing Beatrice in the position of Managing Partner, the partnership gave her the apparently/usual power[20] to describe to third parties the authority of her fellow partners, including Al.[21] Her statement to the Vice President concerning Al's authority was therefore a manifestation attributable to the partnership. From that manifestation Acme (through its agent, the Vice President) reasonably believed that Al was authorized to bind the partnership.

The same circumstances would have clothed a non-partner with apparent authority, so Al had apparent authority and Ventura is bound. Al's apparent authority was not *qua* partner but rather as a person whom the managing partner held out as having authority to bind the partnership.

Inherent agency power.[22]   One rule of inherent agency power might be useful with regard to partners—namely, the inherent power of a general agent who acts for an undisclosed principal. According to Restatement §194:

> A general agent[23] for an undisclosed principal authorized to conduct transactions subjects his principal to liability for acts done on his account, if usual or necessary in such transactions, although forbidden by the principal to do them.[24]

Suppose a partner acts for an undisclosed partnership. Actual authority might exist, but suppose the partner acts beyond or contrary to that authority? Apparently/usual power will not apply, because by hypothesis the partnership does not "appear." But Restatement §194 might work. Unless the partnership agreement provides to the contrary, each partner is a general agent of the partnership.[25]

However, the same impediment exists here as with apparent authority—i.e., UPA §9(2). When a partner's act is neither authorized nor apparently/

---

20. And perhaps also the inherent agency power. See below.

21. Beatrice certainly lacked actual authority to give the description she gave, since she could not reasonably have believed that the partnership wished her to incorrectly describe Al's authority.

22. As explained in section 2.6, the Restatement (Second) uses the term "inherent agency power" as a catch-all category for attribution rules that sometimes succeed when actual authority, apparent authority, and estoppel all fail.

23. "A general agent is an agent authorized to conduct a series of transactions involving a continuity of service." Restatement §3(1). "One who is an integral part of a business organization and does not require fresh authorization for each transaction is a general agent." Restatement §3, comment *a*.

24. Similar inherent power exists when the principal of the general agent is disclosed. Restatement §161. However, in the partnership context that power probably does not reach any situations other than those already covered by the apparently/usual power.

25. This conclusion follows both from the first clause of UPA §9(1) and from the scope of a partner's actual authority, as explained in section 9.4. See also Restatement §14A, comment *a*.

usual, the act "does not bind the partnership"—not even through inherent agency power. In sum, inherent agency power adds nothing to a partner's power to bind the partnership.

$10.2.5 The "No Authority" Constraining Rule

UPA §9(4) and the last lines of §9(1) state the same rule. Regardless of the "apparently/usual" empowering rule, the partnership is not bound if (i) the partner acts without actual authority, and (ii) at the time of the act the third party knows of the lack of authority.

> *Example:* To finance its commodities purchases the Ventura Company establishes a $4 million line of credit with the First National Bank. When Ventura applies for the line of credit the Bank asks for and receives a copy of the Partnership Agreement. The Agreement specifies that the signatures of two partners are necessary to commit the partnership to borrow money. Four months later, Al approaches the Bank to arrange a loan outside the line of credit to finance the partnership's purchase of a $10,000 server for the partnership's network. A loan officer approves the loan, and Al signs the loan agreement on behalf of the partnership. The partnership is not bound. Although Al's act may appear "apparently/usual," under the Partnership Agreement he lacks the actual authority to borrow the money. Having received a copy of the Agreement, the Bank knows of that lack.[26] According to both §§9(1) and 9(4), therefore, the partnership is not bound.[27]

$10.2.6 The "Unanimous Consent" Constraining Rule

Under UPA §9(3), unless the other partners have abandoned the business, a partner needs either *actual* authority or unanimous consent from copartners to:

(a) assign the partnership property in trust for creditors or on the assignee's promise to pay the debts of the partnership
(b) dispose of the good will of the business
(c) do any other act which would make it impossible to carry on the ordinary business of a partnership
(d) confess a judgment
(e) submit a partnership claim or liability to arbitration or reference

In these specified areas, a partner who lacks the authority to bind the partnership also lacks the power to bind.

If a partner lacks actual authority, the copartners' unanimous consent can remedy the situation. If the consent precedes the partner's act, the consent

---

26. As for how a bank could "know" something, see sections 2.4.4 and 2.4.8.
27. However, the partnership will be bound either through ratification or in quantum meruit if it accepts and retains the loan proceeds. See section 10.2.8.

creates actual authority. If the consent follows the act, the consent amounts to ratification. In either event, the partner's act becomes rightful and can therefore bind the partnership.

> **Example:** The Ventura Company, a commodities trading partnership, has a dispute with one of its customers. The customer suggests to Sara, one of Ventura's partners, that the parties settle the dispute through binding arbitration. The Ventura Partnership Agreement makes no mention of arbitration, and the other partners have not authorized Sara to agree to arbitration. Nonetheless, Sara agrees. At this point, regardless of what might appear apparently/usual to the customer, Ventura is not bound. UPA §9(3)(e).
>
> Sara later discusses the matter with her fellow partners and, at her insistence, they all agree to the arbitration. Now the Ventura Company is bound to arbitrate. The partners' unanimous consent ratified Sara's initially unauthorized act.

§10.2.7 The Problem of "Defrocking" a Partner

Suppose a partner begins to run amok, committing the partnership in inappropriate transactions. Can the partnership eliminate that partner's *power* to bind the partnership without expelling the partner or seeking judicial dissolution of the partnership?[28]

The only sure method is to trigger the no-authority constraining rule of UPA §§9(1) and 9(4). To securely "defrock" a partner, the partnership must (i) eliminate the partner's *actual authority* to bind the partnership, and (ii) make sure that potential third parties know of the lack of authority.

Eliminating a partner's actual authority to bind the partnership is certainly problematic and arguably impossible, unless the partnership agreement provides for such action.[29] Even if the partnership manages to end the actual authority, disseminating that information can be a daunting task. If the partnership has kept good records, it can notify current and past customers and vendors.[30] But what about the world at large? Unlike other provisions of the UPA, §9(4) does not provide for public notice as a substitute for knowledge.[31]

In sum, defrocking a fellow partner of authority is fully effective only against third parties who get the message. Actual authority claims will be cut off regardless, but the apparently/usual power will be unimpaired wherever

---

28. For a discussion of these avenues of recourse, see sections 11.7.2 and 11.8.

29. See section 9.5.2.

30. Under UPA §3 notice is not equivalent to knowledge, but a properly sent communication should raise a strong inference that the recipient has actual knowledge.

31. See, e.g., UPA §35(1)(b)(II) providing for advertising the fact of dissolution "in a newspaper of general circulation."

the message fails to reach. In an extreme situation, under the UPA the only practical recourse may be to bring the partnership to an end.[32]

§10.2.8 The Import of the Partnership's Receipt of Benefits

Under ordinary contract and agency law principles, a partnership's acceptance of benefits from a transaction can bind the partnership to that transaction under theories of ratification,[33] quantum meruit, or unjust enrichment.

§10.3 Binding the Partnership in Contract — RUPA §301

§10.3.1 RUPA and UPA Compared

RUPA "retains the basic principles reflected in UPA Section 9(1)"[34] and also maintains that section's basic structure. However, RUPA §301 is considerably shorter than UPA §9:

> SECTION 301. PARTNER AGENT OF PARTNERSHIP. Subject to the effect of a statement of partnership authority under Section 303:
>
> (1) Each partner is an agent of the partnership for the purpose of its business. An act of a partner, including the execution of an instrument in the partnership name, for apparently carrying on in the ordinary course the partnership business or business of the kind carried on by the partnership binds the partnership, unless the partner had no authority to act for the partnership in the particular matter and the person with whom the partner was dealing knew or had received a notification that the partner lacked authority.
>
> (2) An act of a partner which is not apparently for carrying on in the ordinary course the partnership business or business of the kind carried on by the partnership binds the partnership only if the act was authorized by the other partners.

Length is not the only difference between the two provisions. RUPA §301 differs from UPA §9 in six noteworthy ways. RUPA §301:

1. replaces the UPA's "apparently/usual" formulation with the phrase "for apparently carrying on in the ordinary course" — a change in wording that does not affect meaning;[35]

---

32. See section 9.5.2.

33. See section 2.7.

34. RUPA §301, Comment 2.

35. According to RUPA §301, Comment 2, "No substantive change is intended. . . . The UPA and the case law use both terms without apparent distinction."

2. delineates a partner's "apparently/ordinary" power by referring both to "the ordinary course [of] the partnership business" and to "business of the kind carried on by the partnership";
3. eliminates as inflexible the "unanimous consent" constraining rule of UPA §9(3);
4. eliminates as redundant UPA §9(4)—a change that has no effect on meaning;[36]
5. modifies the "no authority" constraining rule, so that it applies not only if the third party knew that the partner lacked actual authority but also if the third party "had received a notification that the partner lacked authority;"
6. establishes a system of recorded statements of authority, and limitations of authority, which can significantly affect both the apparently/ordinary empowering rule and the "no authority" constraining rule.

The following sections discuss each of the substantive changes in detail.

§10.3.2 Changing the Referent for Delineating a Partner's "Apparently/Ordinary" Power

RUPA §301(1) delineates a partner's apparently/ordinary power by referring both to "the ordinary course of the partnership business" and to "business of the kind carried on by the partnership." This change resolves the question of "whose usual way" which exists under UPA §9. According to a RUPA Comment, "The UPA is ambiguous on this point, but there is some authority for an expanded construction in accordance with the so-called English rule."[37]

§10.3.3 Eliminating the "Unanimous Consent" Constraining Rule

UPA §9(3) lists five extraordinary acts for which no partner can have apparently/usual power. RUPA §301 eliminates that list in the interests of "afford[ing] more flexibility."[38]

The change will have its greatest effect on matters covered by UPA §9(3)(e)—i.e., submitting partnership claims to arbitration. When the UPA was promulgated in 1914, arbitration was disfavored. Today, arbitration is a commonplace species of "alternative dispute resolution," and it therefore

---

36. The "unless" clause of "Section 301(1) fully reflects the principle embodied in UPA Section 9(4) that the partnership is not bound by an act of a partner in contravention of a restriction on his authority known to the other party." RUPA §301, Comment 5.
37. RUPA §301, Comment 2.
38. RUPA §301, Comment 4.

"seems archaic that the submission of a partnership claim to arbitration always requires unanimous consent."[39]

In general, eliminating UPA §9(3) "leaves it to the courts to decide the outer limits" of a partner's apparently/ordinary power.[40] However, this change is not expected to alter outcomes very much. "Most of the acts listed in UPA Section 9(3) probably remain outside the apparent authority of a partner under RUPA, such as disposing of the goodwill of the business. . . ."[41]

§10.3.4 Modifying the "No Authority" Constraining Rule

RUPA §301(1) modifies the "no authority" constraining rule, so that it applies not only if the third party knew that the partner lacked actual authority but also if the third party "had received a notification that the partner lacked authority." Under RUPA §102(d), "A person receives a notification when the notification: (1) comes to the person's attention; or (2) is duly delivered at the person's place of business or at any other place held out by the person as a place for receiving communications."[42]

As between a partnership and third party, this change shifts somewhat the risk arising from a partner's unauthorized act.[43]

Example: In the Rachael-Sam-Carolyn chicken-breeding partnership, each partner has the authority to purchase chickens for the partnership. During a cash flow crunch, however, the partners by a 2-1 vote decide not to buy any chickens during the next 30 days. The partnership sends a letter to each of its regular suppliers, stating, "For your convenience in scheduling, we are informing you that we will not be making any purchases during the next 30 days. We look forward to making further orders after this brief hiatus."

One week later, however, Carolyn finds what she considers a "golden opportunity" to purchase 500 chicks, cheap, from Gili's Golden Hens, one of the partnership's regular suppliers. Carolyn places an order on behalf of the partnership, and Gili accepts the order. The partnership's "hiatus" letter is sitting unopened on Gili's desk.

---

39. RUPA §301, Comment 4.

40. RUPA §301, Comment 4.

41. RUPA §301, Comment 4.

42. This definition closely resembles the definition in UPA §3(2) for giving notice. See section 10.6. The difference is in the operative provision—i.e., RUPA §301(1)'s "no authority constraining rule" refers to knowledge or receipt of notification, while UPA §9's "no authority constraining rule" refers only to knowledge.

43. Of course, a partner who acts without actual authority will be liable to the partnership for any resulting damages, see section 4.1.2, and, if the partnership is not bound, will be liable to the third party for breach of the warranty of authority. See section 4.2.2.

Under the UPA, the partnership is probably bound. Carolyn lacked actual authority, but she had apparently/usual power. At the relevant moment Gili had no "knowledge of the fact that [Carolyn had] no such authority." UPA §9(1). Under UPA §3, a person has knowledge of a fact not only through "actual knowledge thereof but also when he [or she] has knowledge of such other facts as in the circumstances shows bad faith." However, Gili's failure to promptly open her mail does not amount to "bad faith."

Under RUPA §§301(1) and 102(d), in contrast, the partnership is probably *not* bound. The partnership's "hiatus" letter is a "notification" which has been "duly delivered at the [Gili's] place of business."

§10.3.5 *Establishing a System of Recorded Statements that Can Significantly Affect the Operation of RUPA §301*

In general.   One of RUPA's major innovations is to establish a system of publicly filed statements to provide what is often termed "constructive notice." RUPA §303, which provides for statements of partnership authority, is a central part of RUPA's new system, and RUPA §301(1) is expressly subject to RUPA §303. Statements filed under RUPA §303 can significantly affect both the apparently/ordinary empowering rule and the "no authority" constraining rule.

Under RUPA §303, a statement of partnership authority "must be executed by at least two partners,"[44] must contain certain basic information about the partnership[45] and "may state the authority, or limitations on the authority, of some or all of the partners to enter into other transactions on behalf of the partnership and any other matter."[46] As to the effects of such statements, RUPA §303's approach is intricate, almost byzantine. Understanding the section's origins helps in deciphering its meaning.

Transfers of real property.   "The most important goal of the statement of authority is to facilitate the transfer of real property held in the name of the partnership."[47] For decades (perhaps centuries) prior to RUPA, real property

---

44. RUPA §105(c).
45. According to RUPA §303(a)(1):

    a statement of partnership authority . . . must include:
       (i)   the name of the partnership;
       (ii) the street address of its chief executive office and of one office in this State, if there is one;
       (iii) the names and mailing addresses of all of the partners or of an agent appointed and maintained by the partnership for the purpose of ["maintain[ing] a list of the names and mailing addresses of all of the partners and mak[ing] it available to any person on request for good cause shown"]; and
       (iv) the names of the partners authorized to execute an instrument transferring real property held in the name of the partnership . . .

46. RUPA §301(2).
47. RUPA §303, Comment 2.

lawyers had lamented the difficulty of opining on a chain of title when a partnership was part of the chain. A lawyer giving a title opinion prefers to have his or her opinion rest on the public record as much as possible. Before RUPA, there was no way for the public record to indicate the authority of a partner to transfer title to real estate owned in the name of a general partnership. When NCCUSL began working on RUPA, real property lawyers urged NCCUSL to fix the problem.

RUPA §303 reflects that urging. Statements pertaining to authority to transfer real property held in the name of the partnership are the core of the section:

- Any statement of partnership authority *must* contain "the names of the partners authorized to execute an instrument transferring real property held in the name of the partnership,"[48] even if the purpose of the statement is to provide information on some other subject.
- A properly filed "grant of authority to transfer real property held in the name of the partnership . . . is conclusive in favor of a person who gives value without knowledge to the contrary, so long as and to the extent that [there is no properly filed] statement containing a limitation on that authority."[49]
- If a statement limiting "the authority of a partner to transfer real property held in the name of the partnership" is properly filed, a "person not a partner is deemed to know of [the] limitation."[50]

Example: The Rachael-Sam-Carolyn chicken-breeding partnership owns in its own name a parcel of land in Dakota County, where the partnership conducts most of its operations. Rachael and Carolyn have executed a statement of partnership authority stating that Sam has the authority to make contracts pertaining to all assets of the partnership, including all land owned in the partnership name. The statement has been filed with the Secretary of State and a certified copy has been recorded with the Dakota County Registrar of Deeds. The partnership agreement (which is not on file) prohibits Sam from taking any action "which would make it impossible to carry on the ordinary business of the partnership."[51]

On behalf of the partnership, Sam enters into an agreement with Lotem-Maor, Inc. to sell the Dakota County land for $1.5 million. The partnership is bound. Although Sam lacked both actual authority and apparently/ordinary power, a properly filed statement grants him the authority and "is conclusive in favor of a person who gives value without

48. RUPA §303(a)(1)(iv).

49. RUPA §303(d)(2).

50. RUPA §303(e).

51. The observant reader may be thinking, "I've seen that language somewhere." It is taken, essentially verbatim, from UPA §9(3)(c).

knowledge to the contrary."[52] The corporation's promise to pay $1.5 million is "value," and there are no facts to indicate that the corporation knew anything about the restriction contained in the partnership agreement.

Example: The Ofek-Noam Company ("the Company") is a RUPA general partnership that purchases land and subdivides it for sale to home builders. The partnership owns a large parcel of land in Dakota County. Suzanne and Gili are the Company's managing partners. Eli is a partner whose participation in management, according to the partnership agreement, is limited to voting on matters of major policy. Suzanne and Gili have executed a statement of partnership authority stating that Eli has no authority to act on behalf of the Company in any matter, including the transfer of real property held in the name of the partnership." The statement has been filed with the Secretary of State and a certified copy has been recorded with the Dakota County Registrar of Deeds.

Despite the partnership agreement, Eli purports to enter into a contract to sell some of the Dakota land to a home building firm. The Company is not bound, even if the firm could establish that Eli had apparently/ordinary power. Under the partnership agreement, Eli lacked the actual authority to enter into the transaction. Due to the statement of partnership authority, the home building firm "is deemed to know of a limitation on the authority of [Eli] to transfer real property held in the name of the partnership."[53] Thus the "no authority" constraining rule of RUPA §301(1) applies: "the partner had no authority to act for the partnership in the particular matter and the person with whom the partner was dealing knew [under RUPA §303(e)] . . . that the partner lacked authority."

When real property is involved, proper filing means:

- filing the statement "in the office of [the Secretary of State],"[54]

  plus

- having "a certified copy of a filed statement of partnership authority recorded in the office for recording transfers of that real property."[55]

Other transactions and other matters. A statement of partnership authority may also "state the authority, or limitations on the authority, of some

---

52. RUPA §301(d)(2).

53. RUPA §303(e). Eli will be liable to the home building firm for breach of the warranty of authority. See section 4.2.2 (agency law warranty of law) and RUPA §104(a) (supplemental principles of law and equity).

54. RUPA §105(a).

55. RUPA §303(d)(2).

or all of the partners to enter into other transactions on behalf of the partnership and any other matter."[56] In this context, proper filing involves only filing "in the office of [the Secretary of State]."[57]

The effect of an "other matter" filing is more limited than in the real property context and, moreover, the limitation tilts *against* the partnership:

- "a grant of authority contained in a filed statement of partnership authority is *conclusive in favor of a person who gives value* without knowledge to the contrary, so long as and to the extent that a limitation on that authority is not then contained in another filed statement"[58] but has no effect in favor of the partnership; and
- "a person not a partner is not deemed to know of a limitation on the authority of a partner merely because the limitation is contained in a filed statement."[59]

Example: Recall the Ofek-Noam Company partnership, whose partnership agreement excludes Eli from the management of the business and whose managing partners have filed a statement of partnership authority stating that Eli has no authority to act on behalf of the Company in any matter. Eli nonetheless enters into a contract on the partnership's behalf with 3ality, Inc., to provide 3D imaging of the topography of land subdivided by the partnership. If Eli's act comes within his apparently/ordinary power, the partnership is bound. The filed statement that Eli has no authority has no effect. 3ality, Inc. "is not deemed to know of a limitation on the authority of a partner merely because the limitation is contained in a filed statement."[60]

Changing and cancelling statements of authority.   A statement granting authority can be cancelled by filing a statement of cancellation[61] and can be nullified by filing a statement containing a statement of limitation which contradicts the grant.[62] "Unless earlier canceled, a filed statement of partnership authority is canceled by operation of law five years after the date on which the statement, or the most recent amendment, was filed with the [Secretary of State]."[63]

---

56. RUPA §303(a)(2).

57. RUPA §105(a).

58. RUPA §303(d)(1) (emphasis added).

59. RUPA §303(f).

60. RUPA §303(f).

61. RUPA §303 does not directly authorize statements of cancellation, but RUPA §§303(d)(1), (d)(2), and (g) assume that such statements exist.

62. RUPA §303(d)(1) and (2).

63. RUPA §303(g).

§10.4 Binding the Partnership Through a Partner's Wrongful Acts (UPA §13; RUPA §305(a))

§10.4.1 *The Attribution Rule*

UPA §13 and RUPA §305(a) each provide a rule for attributing certain "wrongful" acts or omissions of a partner to the partnership. "Section 305(a) . . . is derived from UPA Section 13,"[64] and the provisions state very similar rules.

If UPA §13 attributes a partner's act to the partnership, "the partnership is liable therefor to the same extent as the partner so acting or omitting to act." RUPA §305(a) provides, more directly, that the "partnership is liable for loss or injury caused." Under both provisions, the partnership's liability includes any penalty incurred. Under UPA §13, the attribution rule applies both to torts of negligence and intentional torts but does not apply to wrongs by one partner to another. The RUPA rule is broader, applying not only to "a wrongful act or omission" but also to "other actionable conduct" (i.e., no-fault torts) and encompassing injuries suffered by fellow partners as well as by third parties. In tabular form:

provision	nature of partner's conduct	connection of partner's conduct to the partnership
UPA §13	"any wrongful act or omission"	"in the ordinary course of the business of the partnership or with the [actual] authority of his copartners"
RUPA §305(a)	"a wrongful act or omission, or other actionable conduct"	"in the ordinary course of business of the partnership or with [the actual] authority of the partnership"[65]

Wrongful but ordinary?   How can an act or omission be wrongful and still be "in the ordinary course" or actually authorized? Whenever a claimant invokes UPA §13 or RUPA §305(a), won't the partnership argue that, while the "rightful" version of the partner's conduct may be "ordinary course" or authorized, the wrongful conduct is not? Won't the partnership say, for example, "Yes, it's normal and proper for our partners to describe our products, but it is both extraordinary and unauthorized for them to make misrepresentations when doing so"?

---

64. RUPA §305, Comment 1.

65. Although the phrase " 'with the authority of the partnership' . . . is intended to include a partner's apparent, as well as actual, authority," RUPA §305, Comment, the apparent authority is not relevant to the comparison with UPA §13. Including apparent authority serves to "bring[] within Section 305(a) the situation covered in UPA Section 14(a)." Id. See section 10.5.

Although superficially attractive, such arguments should fail. The proper question under both UPA §13 and RUPA §305(a) is not whether the specific *wrongful* act *is* "ordinary course" or authorized, but rather whether that *type* of act, *if done rightfully, would be.* For example, the question is not whether attending a Chamber of Commerce luncheon and then driving negligently back to the office meets the scope requirement, but rather whether attendance and nonnegligent driving would do so. Similarly, the question is not whether a partner's inaccurate disparagement of a competitor's product meets the scope requirement, but rather whether an accurate criticism of the product would be "ordinary course" or authorized.[66]

> *Example:* Al, a partner in the Ventura Company, believes that the partnership should branch out and begin importing *paté de fois gras.* The other Ventura partners are not so sure, but they do agree that Al should journey to Paris to investigate possible vendors. While driving to the airport, Al negligently hits another car, causing $10,000 in damages. The partnership is liable under UPA §13 or RUPA §305(a), whichever applies. Although Al's trip was not "in the ordinary course of the business," he had actual authority to make the trip.

> *Example:* In the course of discussing a soybean trade with a customer, Al offers to sell (for the partnership) 20,000 bushels "99% free of vermin infestation." Al knows that the soybeans in question actually have a troublesome eight-percent infestation rate. The partnership is legally responsible for Al's misstatement. Since Al's intentional misrepresentation (a wrongful act) occurred in the ordinary course of the business of the partnership, UPA §13 or RUPA §305(a) (whichever applies) will attribute the misrepresentation and any resulting liability to the Ventura Company partnership.[67]

§10.4.2 UPA §13 and RUPA §305(a) Compared to Respondeat Superior

UPA §13 and RUPA §305(a) state a rule of vicarious liability, and in that general respect they resemble the agency doctrine of respondeat superior:[68] A first legal person (the partnership or the master, as the case may be) becomes liable

---

66. This distinction parallels rules of agency law. See section 2.6.3 (agent has inherent power to bind principal with inaccurate statement if agent has actual authority to make accurate statement on the same subject).

67. In this context the misrepresentation is viewed as tortious, and UPA §13 and RUPA §305(a) attribute to the partnership the liability resulting from Al's tort. There may be contract consequences as well. If Al's misstatement came within his apparently/usual (UPA §9(1)) or apparently/ordinary power (RUPA §301(1)), the customer may succeed with a claim either for recission or breach of warranty.

68. For a discussion of respondeat superior, see section 3.2.

on account of the tortious conduct of a second person[69] (the partner or the servant agent), without the claimant needing to establish that the first person is at fault or directly responsible for the claimed harm. All that a claimant need show is:

- that the second person (the partner or the servant agent) incurred tort liability, and
- that the first and second person stand in a specified relationship to each other (partner/partnership or servant/master).

There is one major difference, however. Under respondeat superior the claimant must show that the master had the right to control the means by which the tortfeasor performed his, her, or its functions. This showing is crucial to establishing servant status.[70] The partnership rules have no parallel requirement. UPA §13 and RUPA §305(a) apply regardless of whether the tortfeasor is the most subservient junior partner or the most dictatorial managing partner.

§10.5   Binding the Partnership Through a Partner's Breach of Trust (UPA §14; RUPA §§305(a) and (b))

§10.5.1 *The Attribution Rule*

The UPA version.   If a partner misapplies (e.g., steals, converts, loses) a third party's money or other property, UPA §14 attributes the loss to the partnership if either:

- the *partner* received the money or other property while "acting within the scope of his apparent authority," §14(a), or
- the *partnership* received the money or other property "in the course of its business" and the partner misapplies the property "while it is in the custody of the partnership," §14(b).

The second prong of UPA §14's either/or criterion applies to situations in which the partnership and its business are truly connected to the third party's property. The first prong applies to situations in which the partnership and its business merely appear to be involved.

> *Example:* Chris, an attorney in a law partnership, represents a hospital in a malpractice case. Chris arranges a settlement, and the hospital sends a check, made out to the partnership, to cover the settlement amount and Chris's fees. Chris takes the entire amount for himself.

---

69. UPA §13 does not encompass no-fault torts. See section 10.4.1.
70. For a discussion of the criteria for establishing servant status, see section 3.2.2.

The law partnership is liable to the hospital. The position of partner in a law firm probably creates by itself the apparent authority to receive settlement checks. If so, UPA §14(a) applies. In any event, UPA §14(b) applies because (i) receiving settlement checks is undoubtedly within "the course of [a law partnership's] business," (ii) Chris probably had actual authority and undoubtedly had "apparently/usual" power to receive the check for the partnership, so under UPA §9(1) the partnership received and had custody of the check, and (iii) Chris misapplied the check while it was "in the custody of the partnership."

RUPA version. RUPA replicates both prongs of UPA §14. UPA §14(a) is replicated in RUPA §305(a), where the phrase "with authority of the partnership" encompasses "a partner's apparent, as well as actual, authority, thereby bringing within Section 305(a) the situation covered in UPA Section 14(a)."[71]

UPA §14(b) is replicated in RUPA §305(b), which "is drawn from UPA Section 14(b), but has been edited to improve clarity."[72] Arguably at least, RUPA §305(b) also expands the rule's reach. For UPA §14(b) to apply, the *partnership* must have received the money or property and the partner must have misapplied the money or property while the money or property was in the partnership's "custody." RUPA §305(b) applies when "a partner receives or causes the partnership to receive money or property" and makes no mention of the misapplication having to occur while the partnership has custody.

§10.5.2 A Core Concern of UPA §14—Defalcations by Professionals

Many of the most interesting cases under UPA §14 have involved defalcations by partners in professional partnerships, and the same is likely to be true under RUPA. For example, a partner in a law firm induces a grieving widow to entrust him with the investment of her late husband's estate and then steals the funds. A partner in an accounting firm supervises a client's accounts receivable and then embezzles funds collected from the client's customers. In each case the partnership, while perhaps sympathizing with the victim, asserts that such fund handling involved is foreign to the normal business of the partnership.

The older leading cases deny recovery against the partnership. Rationales include:

- The mere fact of partner status does not constitute a "holding out" that a partner is authorized to handle the funds on behalf of the partnership. Therefore, without some other manifestation of authority attributable to the partnership, no apparent authority exists. Therefore no UPA §14(a) liability. (Nor would there have been any liability under the "apparent authority" aspect of RUPA §305(a).)

---

71. RUPA §305, Comment.
72. RUPA §305, Comment.

- The fund handling is not within "the course of [the partnership's] business." Therefore no UPA §14(b) liability. (Nor would there have been any liability under RUPA §305(b), because the partner was acting neither "in the course of the partnership's business [n]or . . . with authority of the partnership.")
- The fund handling is not "within the ordinary course of the business of the partnership" and is not "authorized by [the] copartners." Therefore no UPA §13 liability. (Nor any liability under the ordinary course and "actual authority" aspects of RUPA §305(a).)

Some of the newer cases allow recovery, or at least reverse a summary judgment in favor of the defendant partnership. Rationales include:

- Apparent authority should be determined from the perspective of the client, not the profession. It may, for instance, be unreasonable for a fellow lawyer to believe that a partner in a law firm has authority to act as an investment advisor. But the proper question is whether a *client* might reasonably have that belief.
- In modern professional practices, handling funds may indeed occur in the course of the partnership's business, especially when the client entrusts the funds to a partner in connection with advice or services that themselves clearly constitute traditional "course of business" matters.
- When professionals are involved, the need to protect the public and to hold professionals to high standards of responsibility argue for an expansive interpretation of vicarious liability provisions.

Example: Brad is a partner in a law firm partnership governed by RUPA. Shirley retains Brad to help her business "work out" from some serious financial difficulties. She entrusts Brad with $100,000, to be used for legal fees and for paying Shirley's creditors. Brad suggests to Shirley that, rather than letting the money "sit around," she should allow him to invest it for her. "We do it all the time," he says, "especially when a client has a lot of money just waiting." Shirley agrees. Brad then uses the money for his own purposes. After Shirley discovers the loss, she learns that the firm never invests funds for clients and that Brad had no authority from the firm to accept the money for investment purposes.

The partnership may be liable to Shirley. From her perspective, Brad may have had apparent authority to receive the funds on the partnership's behalf. If so, RUPA §305(a) applies (wrongful act of partner acting with the apparent authority of the partnership) and the partnership is liable. RUPA §305(b) might apply as well. Shirley proffered the money in connection with traditional legal work to be done by Brad, so arguably at least the partnership received the money "in the course of the partnership's business." The analysis would be similar under the UPA. If Brad had apparent authority to receive the funds, UPA §14(a) would apply. As for UPA §14(b), the course of business element is the same as under RUPA §305(b). However, under UPA §14(b) Shirley must also show that Brad misapplied the property "while it [was] in the custody of the partnership." Here appearances matter. If Brad's acceptance of the money was "apparently for carrying on the business of the partnership . . . in the usual way," UPA §9(1), his possession of the money gave the partnership "custody." If so, under UPA §14(b) "[t]he partnership [would be] bound to make good the loss."

§10.6 Binding the Partnership Through Information Known or Received by a Partner (UPA §12; RUPA §102(f))

§10.6.1 *The Attribution Rules*

UPA §12 attributes to the partnership "notice" made to a partner and "knowledge" possessed by a partner. RUPA §102(f) attributes to a partnership a "partner's knowledge, notice, or receipt of a notification of a fact relating to the partnership." Comparing the two provisions is somewhat tricky, because what UPA §12 means by "notice" is not what RUPA means by notice and because RUPA §102(f) relies on three defined terms while UPA §12 relies on only two. The following chart provides the necessary comparison.

type/source of information	UPA	RUPA
knowledge	"A person has 'knowledge' of a fact . . . not only when he has actual knowledge thereof, but also when he has knowledge of such other facts as in the circumstances shows bad faith." UPA §3(1)[73]	"A person knows a fact if the person has actual knowledge of it." RUPA §102(a)
receipt of information	"A person has 'notice' of a fact . . . when the person who claims the benefit of the notice: (a) States the fact to such person, or (b) Delivers through the mail, or by other means of communication, a written statement of the fact to such person or to a proper person at his [i.e., such person's] place of business or residence." UPA §3(2)	"A person receives a notification when the notification: (1) comes to the person's attention; or (2) is duly delivered at the person's place of business or at any other place held out by the person as a place for receiving communications." RUPA §102(d)

---

73. The phrase "shows bad faith" probably means "shows intentional, bad faith ignorance of the fact."

type/source of information	UPA	RUPA
reason to know	no defined term	"A person has notice of a fact if the person: (1) knows of it; (2) has received a notification of it; or (3) has reason to know it exists from all of the facts known to the person at the time in question." RUPA §102(b)

The relevant substantive law determines the significance of any attributed information.

> *Example:* Dorothy buys 500 chickens from the Rachael-Sam-Carolyn chicken-breeding partnership. She later claims damages, asserting that she had a particular purpose in mind, that the partnership knew of that purpose, and that the chickens were not suitable to that purpose. Carolyn did, in fact, know of that purpose. Depending on whether the UPA or RUPA governs the partnership, either UPA §12 or RUPA §102(f) will determine whether Carolyn's knowledge binds the partnership. The law of sales will determine what significance, if any, that attributed knowledge has for Dorothy's claim.

Rule for attributing knowledge. The attribution analysis for partner knowledge is more complicated than for notice. According to UPA §12, the attribution rule varies depending on whether the partner with knowledge is "acting in the particular matter":

> . . . the knowledge of the partner acting in the particular matter, acquired while a partner or then present to his mind, and the knowledge of any other partner who reasonably could and should have communicated it to the acting partner, operate as . . . knowledge of the partnership, except in the case of a fraud on the partnership committed by or with the consent of that partner.

If a UPA partner *is* acting in the matter, subject to an exception for fraud,[74] the partner's knowledge inescapably binds the partnership. UPA §12 attributes both (i) knowledge "acquired while a partner" and (ii) knowledge acquired earlier if at the time of the action the acting partner still retains the knowledge.[75]

---

74. Discussed in section 10.6.2.

75. Id. The precise language is: "acquired while a partner or then present to his mind."

The knowledge of a UPA partner *not* acting in a particular matter binds the partnership only if the partner "reasonably could and should have communicated it to the acting partner." The Official Comment to §12 explains the rationale:

> It seems clear that . . . the partnership should be charged [with the nonacting partner's knowledge] only when the partner having "knowledge" had reason to believe that the fact related to a matter which had some possibility of being the subject of partnership business and then only if he was so situated that he could communicate it to the partner acting in the particular matter before such partner give[s] binding effect to his act.[76]

Example: At a trade show Rebecca happens to meet Sam of the Rachael-Sam-Carolyn chicken-breeding partnership and mentions to him that she "buys supplies for a new regional restaurant chain, Fast Food, Inc." Rebecca is only one of dozens of people Sam meets at the trade show. Moreover, Fast Food's restaurants are far away from the partnership's breeding farm. Sam therefore does not mention Rebecca to his fellow partners.

A month later Rebecca contacts Rachael and commits to buy 5,000 chickens. Although Rebecca is in fact acting as agent for Fast Food, Inc., she does not disclose that fact to Rachael. When Rachael commits the partnership to sell the chickens, Rachael believes that the contract is with Rebecca.

Fast Food later repudiates the contract, and Rebecca so informs Rachael. Acting for the partnership, Rachael insists that Rebecca personally honor the contract. (Rachael correctly asserts that an agent who executes a contract on behalf of an undisclosed principal is personally liable on the contract.[77]) Rebecca responds that the principal was not undisclosed, that Sam knew of her relationship with Fast Food, and that Sam's knowledge binds the partnership.

Rebecca's argument will most likely fail. Sam was not "acting in the particular matter" of the contract, UPA §12, and at the time of contract formation Sam did not have "reason to believe that the fact [of Rebecca's agent status] related to a matter which had some possibility of being the subject of partnership business." UPA §12, Official Comment. Sam's knowledge, therefore, is not attributable to the partnership.

---

76. The rationale here parallels the rationale for attributing to a principal an agent's knowledge concerning a matter within the agent's actual authority while not attributing an apparent agent's knowledge concerning a matter within the apparent agent's apparent authority. In the former situation, the agent has a duty to communicate the information to the principal. In the latter, the apparent agent has no such duty. See sections 2.4 (attribution rules for information) and 4.1.5 (duty of agent to provide information to principal).

77. See section 4.2.1 (liability of agent who enters into a contract on behalf of an undisclosed principal).

RUPA's rule on attribution of partner knowledge makes no distinction between a partner who acts in the matter and one who does not. Subject to the same fraud exception as exists under the UPA, a RUPA "partner's knowledge . . . of a fact relating to the partnership is effective immediately as knowledge by . . . the partnership."[78]

> *Example:* In the trade show Example just given, under RUPA Sam's knowledge of Rebecca's status will bind the chicken-breeding partnership *assuming that at the relevant moment Sam still knows that fact.* "Knowledge is cognitive awareness,"[79] so if Sam has forgotten the partnership no longer knows.

Under both the UPA and RUPA, attribution of a partner's knowledge occurs regardless of whether the partner shares the knowledge with fellow partners.

Rule for attributing information received or delivered.   The UPA and RUPA rules on this point are quite similar, although, as shown above, the two statutes use different defined terms. Subject to the exception for fraud,[80] UPA §12 attributes to a UPA partnership "[n]otice to any partner of any matter relating to partnership affairs." Subject to the same exception, RUPA §102(f) attributes to a RUPA partnership a "partner's . . . receipt of a notification of a fact relating to the partnership." The UPA concept of "notice" and the RUPA concept of "receipt of a notification" are for the most part functionally identical, although the congruence is not complete.

> *Example:* Vladi is the managing partner of the Waterville Ski Company, a general partnership which owns and operates several ski slopes. The Company has an important contract with Michael, its principal ski instructor, which requires Michael to give four weeks notice to terminate the contract. Michael attempts to give notice by sending a letter to Vladi's home address, although Vladi does not normally do business from that address. If the letter is delivered to Vladi's home, the notice is effective under the UPA. Under UPA §3(2)(b), Vladi, as partner, "has 'notice' of [the contents of the letter] . . . when the person who claims the benefit of the notice [i.e., Michael] . . . [d]elivers through the mail . . . a written statement of the fact to [Vladi] at his . . . residence." Under UPA §12, notice to Vladi is notice to the partnership.
>
> The result is different under RUPA §102(f). There the concept is "receipt of notification," and, under RUPA §102(d), delivery through the mails must occur "at the person's place of business or at any other place held out by the person as a place for receiving communications."

---

78. RUPA §102(f).
79. RUPA §102, Comment.
80. See section 10.6.2.

For RUPA purposes, therefore, Vladi has not received a notification, and there is nothing for RUPA §102(f) to attribute to the partnership.

Under both the UPA and RUPA, the attribution occurs regardless of whether the partner to whom information is delivered is aware of the delivery, and regardless of whether the partner who has notice (UPA) or receives a notification (RUPA) communicates the information to fellow partners.

Example: The First Regional Bank has extended a line of credit to the Ventura Company but now wishes to deny the Company any additional borrowing against the credit. The line of credit agreement requires the Bank to give the Company 48 hours advance notice. When Al, a Ventura partner, comes to the Bank to make a deposit, the Bank manager hands him a letter about "no further borrowing." Al neglects both to read the letter and to inform his fellow partners. Nonetheless, the Bank has complied with the agreement. Under UPA §3(2), the Bank gave notice to Al by delivering the letter to him. Under RUPA §102(d)(1), Al has received a notification. Regardless of whether Al actually passes the information on:

- under UPA §12, notice to Al is notice to the partnership;
- under RUPA §102(f), a notification received by Al is a notification received by the partnership and, under RUPA §102(b)(2), a "person [including a partnership] has notice of a fact if the person . . . has received a notification of it."

Rule for attributing information a partner has reason to know. RUPA handles this category of information by using the defined term "notice," defining the term to include information that a partner "has reason to know . . . it exists from all of the facts known to the [partner] at the time in question,"[81] and providing that a "partner's . . . notice . . . of a fact relating to the partnership is effective immediately as . . . notice to . . . the partnership."[82] The UPA has no comparable provisions. The closest the UPA comes is to attribute a partner's knowledge to the partnership and to define knowledge to include situations in which a person "has knowledge of such other facts as in the circumstances shows [the person's ignorance to be in] bad faith."[83]

---

81. RUPA §102(b). The definition of notice also includes known information and information contained in a notification that has been received. In this context, however, those aspects of the definition are redundant, because RUPA §102(f) separately addresses those two categories of information.

82. RUPA §102(f).

83. UPA §3(1).

§10.6.2 The "Partner Fraud on the Partnership" Exception

The attribution rules of UPA §12 and RUPA §102(f) do not apply "in the case of a fraud on the partnership committed by or with the consent of [the] partner" whose knowledge or receipt of notice is to be attributed. In this context the concept of "fraud" probably includes a breach of the partner's duty of loyalty (sometimes called "equitable fraud"). Fraud blocks the attribution even if the third party was ignorant of the fraud and has no reason to know of it.

> *Example:* Seeking to preclude the Ventura Company from additional borrowing against its line of credit, the First Regional Bank delivers a written "no more borrowing" notice to Al, a partner. For some time Al has been borrowing from the line of credit in the partnership's name but for his own personal benefit. Neither the Bank nor the partnership are aware of Al's misconduct. Because Al is committing "a fraud on the partnership," notice to him is not notice to the partnership.

§10.7 Binding the Partnership Through Partner Admissions (UPA §11)

§10.7.1 The Rule

The UPA contains one information attribution rule for which RUPA provides no parallel: UPA §11, concerning admissions of a partner.

An admission is (i) a statement by a party to a lawsuit or a person who becomes a party to a lawsuit, (ii) made outside of court (and typically before the trial), (iii) which is subsequently recounted in court (by someone who heard the statement),[84] (iv) to be used as evidence against the person who originally made the statement. UPA §11 attributes to the partnership any "admission or representation made by any partner concerning partnership affairs within the scope of his authority as conferred by this act" and makes the attributed information admissible in court as "evidence against the partnership."[85]

§10.7.2 The Reach of the Rule

The reach of UPA §11 depends on two questions of interpretation, both related to the phrase "within the scope of his authority as conferred by this act." The first question concerns the meaning of the word *authority*. In some other UPA contexts, *authority* signifies *actual authority*. Here, the cases and commentaries make clear, the word means *power*, particularly a partner's power to bind the partnership as reflected in UPA §9.[86]

---

84. Or, in the case of a written admission, by someone who has read the admission.

85. This rule is significant, because it allows litigants to enter out-of-court statements into evidence without having to satisfy the exceedingly complex rule on "hearsay."

86. A partner's *power* to bind the partnership includes both the partner's actual authority, section 10.2.4, and the partner's "apparently/usual" power, section 10.2.2.

The second question is more difficult and concerns the referent for the problematic phrase as a whole. Does the phrase "within his authority as conferred by this act" refer to "an admission or representation" or to "partnership affairs"?

If the former, then UPA §11 is to be interpreted as if it began: "An admission or representation *made* by a partner within the scope of his authority as conferred by this act. . . ." If the latter, UPA §11 is to be interpreted as if it began: "An admission or representation made by a partner concerning partnership affairs *which are* within the scope of his authority as conferred by this act. . . ."

The former, narrower interpretation would make UPA §11 totally redundant of UPA §9(1). Not surprisingly, therefore, both the Comment to UPA §11 and the cases favor the latter, broader interpretation.[87] As a result, comments made by a partner incidental to any "empowered" transaction bind the partnership. So do comments made after a transaction by a partner with the power to engage in that type of transaction.

> *Example:* The Rachael-Sam-Carolyn chicken-breeding partnership is disputing with Eli's Feed and Stock the amount still outstanding on a chickenfeed bill. Each partner has the power to enter into such transactions, although Carolyn actually placed the order in question. In a discussion with the partnership's bookkeeper, Sam says, "And, oh yes, we still owe $500 to Eli's." UPA §11 applies to Sam's statement, regardless of whether Sam has any authority to speak on behalf of the partnership.

§10.7.3 Two Places Where UPA §11 Will Not Reach

Admissions that a partnership exists.   An alleged partner's admission that a partnership exists is not admissible against the other alleged partners to prove that the partnership does in fact exist. This rule follows from the language of UPA §11, which refers to statements "made by any partner." To successfully invoke UPA §11, therefore, the third party must first show—at least prima facie[88] and through independent evidence—that a partnership did exist and that the maker of the admission was in fact a partner in that partnership.

Admissions that conduct is ordinary partnership business.   As discussed above,[89] determining whether a partner's tortious act was "in the ordinary course of business" can be crucial to determining whether the partnership is vicariously liable for the partner's tort. According to the case law under UPA

---

87. The Comment states: "Admissions . . . concerning a particular matter should bind the partnership only where the partner has authority to act in the particular matter."

88. For an explanation of prima facie, see section 7.4.2, n.55.

89. See section 10.4.1.

§11, a third party cannot use a partner's admission to establish "ordinary course."

PROBLEM 85

In the aftermath of a bitter divorce, Ronald goes into partnership with Robert in a donut shop. Ronald wishes to hide his income from his ex-wife, so he and Robert agree that Ronald will be a very "silent" partner. Ronald will provide 60 percent of the capital and will share in all major decisions. Robert will handle all transactions with third parties. He will appear to third parties as the sole owner of the business. Accordingly, after consultation with Ronald, Robert signs a long-term lease for a building in which the donut shop will operate.

The business eventually fails, and only afterwards does the lessor discover the relationship between Robert and Ronald. If RUPA applies, can the lessor hold the partnership liable on the lease? Under the UPA?

EXPLANATION

Yes, under either statute. The arrangement between the partners gave Robert actual authority to sign the lease on behalf of the partnership. The fact that the partnership was undisclosed is therefore immaterial.

PROBLEM 86

The Ventura Company partnership agreement gives wide-ranging authority to Beatrice, the partnership's managing partner. However, all decisions to initiate or settle litigation must be approved by a majority vote of the partners. On two occasions during the past five years, Beatrice has recommended to the partners that the partnership arbitrate a dispute, and on each occasion the partners approved.

Ventura has a dispute with Central California Soybean ("CCS") concerning a particular trade. No suit has been filed, but litigation seems inevitable. Aware that Ventura has arbitrated disputes in the past, CCS proposes arbitration. Beatrice agrees, this time without consulting the other partners. In determining whether Ventura is bound to arbitrate the dispute, does it matter which general partnership statute applies?

EXPLANATION

Yes. Under the UPA, Ventura is not bound. Under RUPA, the partnership might well be.

Under UPA §9(3)(e), part of the UPA's "unanimous consent" constraining rule, no partner has the power to "[s]ubmit a partnership claim or liability to arbitration" unless either all the partners consent or the partner agreeing to arbitration has actual authority to do so. In this instance, the other partners have not consented, and under the partnership agreement Beatrice lacks actual authority to agree to arbitration on her own. The partnership's past practices conform with and confirm this interpretation of the partnership agreement. To obtain actual authority, Beatrice needs the consent of a majority of her partners.[90]

RUPA, in contrast, has no "unanimous consent" constraining rule, and RUPA §301, Comment 4 states that "it seems archaic that the submission of a partnership claim to arbitration always requires unanimous consent." Because CCS is "[a]ware that Ventura has arbitrated disputes in the past," Beatrice's act is probably within her "apparently/ordinary" power. If so, the partnership is bound to arbitrate.

PROBLEM 87

Two brothers, Caleb and Adam, operate a farm as an ordinary general partnership, known as AdCal Farming Company. The two brothers are well respected. Their partnership is well known in the community, as is the fact that each partner regularly makes equipment purchases for the partnership business.

One day, Caleb goes to the local Ford dealer and buys a $25,000 Ford pick-up truck on credit, signing the purchase agreement "AdCal Farming Company, by Caleb, general partner." In fact, the truck has nothing to do with the partnership business. Caleb has decided to give up farming and go "on the road." The truck is for his personal use. Under RUPA, may the Ford dealer hold *Adam* liable on the purchase agreement?

EXPLANATION

Yes. Adam is liable under RUPA §306(a) because the partnership is liable under RUPA §301(1). Caleb's truck purchase was "for *apparently* carrying on in the ordinary course of the partnership business."[91] The dealer knew Caleb to be a partner and saw nothing unusual in an individual AdCal partner committing the partnership to an equipment purchase. To the contrary, the partnership had a reputation for doing business this way. Moreover, Caleb asserted that he was acting for the partnership, and nothing in Caleb's reputation gave the dealer any reason to doubt that assertion.

PROBLEM 88

Hiview Company is a UPA partnership that operates a drive-in movie theater. Rachael, its managing partner, purports to sell the land where the theater is located to a development company. The partnership agreement authorizes the managing partner to "make all management decisions in the ordinary course

---

90. CCS may well have believed that Beatrice's agreement to arbitrate was apparently/usual. However, since UPA §9(3) applies, the apparently/usual question is immaterial.

91. Emphasis added.

of the business." Has Rachael's action bound the partnership? Would the analysis change under RUPA?

EXPLANATION

For three reasons, under the UPA Rachael has not bound the partnership. Her "ordinary course" actual authority does not extend to the extraordinary decision to sell the crucial assets of the business. Her doing so could not have appeared "apparently/usual" to the buyer. Her doing so runs afoul of UPA §9(3)(c) (partner lacks power to do "any . . . act which would make it impossible to carry on the ordinary business of a partnership," unless partner has actual authority or all partners agree).

The analysis is the same under RUPA, except that RUPA contains no analog to UPA §9(3)(c).

PROBLEM 89

Illegitimus, Non, and Carborundum have formed a RUPA partnership as a "hand-shake deal" and gave explicit thought to only two issues. First, they agreed that the sole purpose of the partnership would be to function as a locator of "spot" grapes for the makers of wine. Second, they agreed that they would share equally all profits from the partnership.

Locators of spot grapes play an important part in the production of non-vintage wines.[92] From time to time vineyards producing nonvintage wine find themselves short of a particular type of grape that they want to add to a mixture of other grapes. Locators of spot grapes are in the business of knowing which vineyards have a need for which types of grapes and which vineyards have a surplus of that type of grape. Based on this knowledge they act to get surplus grapes to the vineyards that need them.

The overwhelming majority of locators act only as agents, never taking a position in grapes. This means that when they have a customer who needs a particular type of grape, they locate a supply of those grapes in another vineyard. Then, acting merely as the agent of the customer who needs the grapes, they arrange for the sale of grapes from the vineyard with the surplus to the vineyard with the need. In this conventional approach, the locator never takes title to the grapes and never commits itself to pay for the grapes.

The partnership carries on its business at variance with this typical pattern. On occasion, it will buy and take title to surplus grapes held by a vineyard, speculating that it (i.e., the partnership) can find another vineyard to which it can resell the grapes. Although with this approach the partnership faces greater risk than it would if it followed the conventional pattern, the potential rewards are greater. Where it takes a position and then resells the

---

92. The practices described in this Problem do not necessarily correspond to actual commercial practices.

grapes, the partnership charges a mark-up that exceeds the amount of commission the partnership would have received for simply acting as a locator agent.

When Illegitimus, Non, and Carborundum began the partnership they needed start-up capital. Illegitimus contributed $30,000. Non and Carborundum each contributed $10,000. Each year the partners have fully drawn out all profits. They have never withdrawn any capital.

Last spring Non and Carborundum became concerned about some of the deals that Illegitimus had made. At a regularly scheduled partnership meeting, they voted to prohibit Illegitimus from making any further purchases of grapes on behalf of the partnership. They expressly allowed him to continue arranging deals of the more conventional sort, that is, where the partnership would act only as an agent. Illegitimus objected to and voted against the limitation.

Soon after the meeting, Illegitimus took a buying tour out into the countryside and visited Schekainery Vineyard. The owner of the vineyard, Sally Schekainery, knew generally of the partnership and of Illegitimus's status as a partner. She had no particular knowledge about the partnership or about its business practices, and had never done business with the partnership before. During the visit Illegitimus learned that the Schekainery Vineyard had several tons of surplus of a particular variety of red grape. Illegitimus believed, and reasonably so at the time, that several regular clients of the partnership would soon need this grape. Over dinner he began to negotiate with Sally for a price, and eventually Illegitimus and Sally agreed to a price of $5,000 per ton for 8 tons, to be delivered within the next 30 days. The next morning Sally wrote a memorandum expressing the deal, and Illegitimus signed on behalf of the partnership.

As it turned out, several of the clients whom Illegitimus had in mind did not need that particular variety of grape. Moreover, throughout the entire valley, vineyards that needed to purchase the grapes were able to purchase easily at a price significantly below the price Illegitimus had committed to pay. When Non and Carborundum learned what Illegitimus had done, they wrote to Sally (1) explaining that Illegitimus had no authority to act for the partnership in this matter, and (2) stating that the partnership had no interest in purchasing the grapes. As evidence of Illegitimus's lack of authority, they enclosed a certified copy of the minutes of the meeting at which Non and Carborundum voted to "defrock" Illegitimus of his authority to enter into this particular type of transaction.

Sally consulted an attorney, who advised her to warn the partnership that (1) she intended to hold them to the contract, and (2) if they did not take delivery as agreed, she would mitigate her damages by selling the grapes elsewhere and would then file suit against the partnership for any difference between the mitigation price and the contract price. Hearing no response from the partnership, she proceeded as she had indicated. The difference amounted to $20,000. Sally sued the partnership. What result?

EXPLANATION

The partnership will be liable if either (i) Illegitimus's act was "apparently/ordinary," or (ii) Illegitimus had actual authority to make the deal.

Sally's apparently/ordinary claim will fail. She cannot show that Illegitimus's act appeared for "carrying on in the ordinary course the partnership business or business of the kind carried on by the partnership." RUPA §301(1). As to businesses "of the kind carried on by the partnership," industry practices suggest that Illegitimus's act should have appeared quite unusual. As to reasonable appearances and the ordinary course of *this* partnership's business, Sally has no evidence to offer. She knew nothing in particular about this partnership. She could only suppose that its commercial practices resembled those of similar partnerships.

Sally will probably fare better with her actual authority claim. Illegitimus certainly had authority to make comparable deals when the partnership began, and it is unlikely that a mere majority vote of the partners could have ended that authority. Defrocking a partner seems an extraordinary act, requiring unanimous consent. The partners' 2-1 vote did not suffice.[93]

The partnership could, however, advance a less aggressive interpretation of the 2-1 vote that, ironically, could give Sally difficulty. The partnership could argue that (i) the vote and the discussion that preceded it informed Illegitimus that his partners would differ with him anytime he contemplated making a purchase of spot grapes; (ii) Illegitimus therefore knew that any grape purchase he might contemplate would involve a "difference arising as to a matter in the ordinary course of business of [the] partnership," to be decided in each particular instance by majority vote, RUPA §401(j); and (iii) as with any such difference, knowledge of the difference eliminated the acting partner's authority pending resolution "by a majority of the partners." Id.

If this latter interpretation prevails, the partnership will not be liable.

PROBLEM 90

Suppose that immediately after the 2-1 vote, Non and Carborundum executed and properly filed a statement of partnership authority indicating that Illegitimus lacked the authority to purchase any grapes on behalf of the partnership. Would this fact change the result?

EXPLANATION

No. The statement does not concern "authority to transfer real property held in the name of the partnership," RUPA §§303(d)(1) and (e), and therefore "a person not a partner is not deemed to know of a limitation on the authority of

---

93. The facts about capital contributions are red herrings. In the default mode, capital contributions have no impact on partner voting power. Absent a contrary agreement, each partner has a single vote. RUPA §401(f). See section 9.5.1.

a partner merely because the limitation is contained in a filed statement."
RUPA §303(f).

PROBLEM 91

Since graduating from law school five years ago, Able, Baker, and Charlene
have practiced law in a partnership that is not an LLP. The partners "cover" for
each other during vacations, and the partnership has in place a system for
avoiding conflicts of interests. Otherwise, however, each partner is responsible for his or her own files. Three years ago, Attorney Able filed a consumer
fraud lawsuit in state district court against Defendant, Inc. Consumer fraud
was one of Able's principal areas of practice, but in this instance the claims
were frivolous. Able had signed the complaint without having made any investigation into the facts.

Neither Baker nor Charlene had any involvement in the case. Indeed,
Baker was not even aware that the case had been filed. The court eventually
dismissed the lawsuit and, citing Rule 11 of the state Rules of Civil Procedure,
ordered Able to pay Defendant, Inc. the $7,000 in attorney's fees which De-
fendant, Inc. had incurred in defending the lawsuit. The court specifically
found that Able had violated Rule 11 by "failing to make a 'reasonable inquiry' into the facts before filing a complaint that was neither 'well grounded
in fact' nor 'warranted by existing law or a good faith argument for the extension, modification, or reversal of existing law.' " The court of appeals affirmed
the award against Able. Under the UPA, can Defendant, Inc. hold Baker and
Charlene personally liable for the Rule 11 award? Under RUPA?

EXPLANATION

Baker and Charlene are liable jointly and severally under UPA §15(a), because
the partnership is liable for the award under UPA §13.[94]

To establish the partnership's liability under UPA §13, Defendant, Inc.
must show that (i) it suffered harm from a partner's wrongful act or omission,
and (ii) the conduct occurred either (a) in the ordinary course of the partnership's business or (b) with the authority of the other partners. Able was a
partner, and filing a frivolous lawsuit is clearly a wrongful act. Defendant will
therefore have no trouble on the first element of UPA §13. As to the second
element, Defendant can actually meet both requirements of the either/or test.
The business of the partnership ordinarily included the filing of lawsuits.
Therefore, when Able filed the frivolous claim, he was "acting in the ordinary
course of business of the partnership." Able was also acting with actual authority. UPA §18(e) gives all partners "equal rights in the . . . conduct of the
partnership business." The partners augmented this statutory authority by

---

94. This liability may be subject to an exhaustion requirement. See section 7.3.1
(some jurisdictions require third parties to exhaust partnership assets before asserting
UPA §15 claims against individual partners).

granting each partner autonomous authority over his or her own files. It is not clear from the facts whether the partners agreed to this grant expressly, but the way they conducted their business certainly implied an agreement.

The fact that Baker and Charlene had no part in this misconduct is irrelevant to Defendant, Inc.'s claim. UPA §13 states a rule of vicarious liability, and UPA §15 states a rule of liability by status.

The analysis and results are the same under RUPA. Only the citations differ: UPA §15(a) → RUPA §306(a); UPA §13 → RUPA §305(a); UPA §18(e) → RUPA §401(f).

PROBLEM 92

Mrs. Rouse recently lost her husband. He left a small estate, mostly in cash. The widow is an elderly lady who throughout her life left business affairs to her husband. She confides to her lawyer, Mr. Pollard, that she does not know how best to invest the funds.

Mr. Pollard has been a lawyer for 20 years, and for the past 15 years has served as the Rouse family lawyer. For the past 16 years he has been a partner in the law firm of What, Me and Worry. The firm is organized as a general partnership. Mr. Pollard tells Mrs. Rouse, "My dear lady, I would be delighted to handle your investment decisions for you. Place yourself in my hands. Entrust your funds to our firm. We have quite a bit of experience in such matters."

Mrs. Rouse agrees to "put the money with the firm." She writes a check for almost the entirety of her assets. At Mr. Pollard's direction, she makes the check payable to him.

Unfortunately, Mr. Pollard is a crook. The law firm of What, Me and Worry does not handle investments for clients. Indeed, law firms in general do not ordinarily serve as investment advisors. Mr. Pollard deposits Mrs. Rouse's check in his personal checking account and appropriates her money to his own use. For a few months he sends her checks drawn on his personal account purporting to represent a return on her investments. Then his financial house of cards topples, and his fraud is exposed.

Mr. Pollard goes into bankruptcy and thence into jail. Mrs. Rouse sues the law firm partnership for return of the money she entrusted to Mr. Pollard. What result under the UPA and under RUPA?

EXPLANATION

Whether Mrs. Rouse will prevail depends on how liberal a view the court takes of UPA §14(b) and RUPA §305(b).

Neither UPA §13 nor the "actual authority" aspect of RUPA §305(a) can help Mrs. Rouse. To successfully invoke either of those provisions she must show either that Mr. Pollard handled her funds in the ordinary course of the business of the partnership, or that he did so with actual authority. Mrs. Rouse can make neither showing. The law firm never acted as an investment advisor and never authorized Mr. Pollard to do so.

For similar reasons Mrs. Rouse will be unsuccessful invoking UPA §14(b). For that provision to apply, the partnership must have received the money "in the course of its business." Arguably at least, the *partnership* never received the money at all. Moreover, "the course of its business" did not include investing clients' funds.

Mrs. Rouse may fare better under UPA §14(a) and RUPA §305(b). She can certainly show that Mr. Pollard, a partner, misapplied her money. It is only doubtful whether she can show that Mr. Pollard received the money within the scope of his apparent authority.

Under the older case law, Mrs. Rouse would likely lose on this point. The older cases suggest, almost as a matter of law, that no reasonable client can believe that a lawyer has the authority to handle client funds for investment purposes. More modern cases, however, treat the question as one of fact. They do not simply assume that every reasonably prudent client understands the limitations on a law firm's business.

Mrs. Rouse may therefore be able to prevail by proving that (i) Mr. Pollard had apparent authority by position, and (ii) despite Mr. Pollard's direction that the check be made out to him personally, Mrs. Rouse was reasonable in believing that Mr. Pollard's authority extended to handling client funds for investment. Mr. Pollard's assertions about the firm's business and his own authority would not suffice as manifestations of the firm, but they could help show the reasonableness of Mrs. Rouse's belief. The long relationship of trust and confidence between Mr. Pollard, as a partner of the firm, and the Rouse family would also support Mrs. Rouse's reasonableness argument.

If Mrs. Rouse prevails on the apparent authority issue, under either UPA §14(a) or RUPA §305(b), the partnership will be liable.

PROBLEM 93

For the past 15 years Lucille, Phyllis, and William have operated a fishing guide business from a piece of lakefront property near the Canadian border. They operate the business as a general partnership, share in all the work, make business decisions by consensus, and share profits equally.

The partnership rents rather than owns its lakefront location. The lease has a two-year term and renews automatically unless either party gives written notice of nonrenewal "at least 90 days but no more than 120 days in advance of the renewal date."

The lease was up for renewal last January 1. On the preceding September 15th the lessor handed a written notice of nonrenewal to William. The notice was in an envelope and the lessor did not say specifically what the envelope contained. The lessor did say, "William, this is important. Don't put it aside."

Unfortunately, William did just that. Unbeknownst to the lessor or William's partners, William was suffering a relapse into alcoholism. He lost the envelope, forgot its existence, and never mentioned it to Lucille or Phyllis. The first they learned of the lessor's intention was on November 15th, when the lessor telephoned to discuss "transition issues." The November 15 conversation occurred too late to constitute valid notice of nonrenewal. Under the UPA, did the lost letter constitute valid notice to the partnership? Under RUPA?

EXPLANATION

Yes, under either statute. Under UPA §3(2)(b), the lessor gave notice to William by "deliver[ing] a written statement" to William. It is irrelevant that William never read the statement. Under UPA §12, "[n]otice to any partner of any matter relating to partnership affairs . . . operate[s] as notice to . . . the partnership." It is also irrelevant that the partner never mentioned the notice to any other partner. UPA §12 contains an exception applicable "in the case of a fraud on the partnership committed by or with the consent of [the] partner" receiving notice. However, William's dereliction of duty does not constitute fraud.

The analysis is similar and the results are the same under RUPA. Under RUPA §102(d)(1), William has received a notification. Regardless of whether William actually passes the information on, under RUPA §102(f) a notification received by William is a notification received by the partnership. Under RUPA §102(b)(2), a "person [including a partnership] has notice of a fact if the person . . . has received a notification of it."

PROBLEM 94

Their dispute over the nonrenewal notice convinces Lucille, Phyllis, and William to buy a piece of lakefront property. After William regains sobriety, the three partners locate an apparently suitable parcel on another lake. They negotiate with the parcel's owner ("the seller") and eventually sign a contract on behalf of the partnership. During the negotiations, the seller assures all three partners that "this lake is real quiet. There's no rule against motorboats, but almost no one ever uses them here." That representation is central to the partners' decision to have the partnership buy the land.

After the contract is signed, Phyllis learns that motorboats are quite common on the lake and that during the summer months waterskiing is the dominant lake activity. The partnership seeks to rescind the contract, asserting fraud in the inducement.

In the relevant jurisdiction, a party asserting fraud in the inducement must show not only a material misstatement and reliance, but also that the reliance was reasonable. The seller contends that the partnership could not have reasonably relied on his assertions because "Two years ago William was over here all the time, and he saw all the motorboats and the water skiing all over the lake."

His memory prompted by the seller's contention, William acknowledges it as true. Just as truthfully he states that (i) he visited the lake on vacation and not on partnership business, and (ii) his recent bout with alcohol had suppressed all memory of that vacation.

Assuming that the UPA applies and the seller's representations about the quiet and the lack of significant motorboat activity were false and material, what result on partnership's fraud in the inducement theory? Any difference under RUPA?

EXPLANATION

If the UPA applies, the partnership will lose.

The outcome turns on UPA §12 and its rule for attributing a partner's knowledge to the partnership. William was "acting in the particular matter," so the rule will attribute to the partnership any "knowledge acquired while a partner or then present to his mind." UPA §12. Although at the time of the negotiations and contract formation, William's knowledge about the motor boats was not "present to his mind," that phrase is in the disjunctive with the phrase "acquired while a partner." That is, any knowledge the acting partner acquires while a partner is attributed to the partnership, regardless of whether the acting partner happens to remember the information at the critical moment. The phrase "then present to his mind" serves only to limit attribution of information acquired before the partner became a partner. Therefore, William's dormant knowledge of the motor boat traffic is attributed to the partnership and defeats the partnership's claim of reasonable reliance.

Under RUPA, in contrast, the partnership might prevail. RUPA §102(f) will attribute William's knowledge, if any, to the partnership, but it is arguable that at the relevant moment William had no relevant knowledge. Under RUPA §102(a), "knowledge" is confined to actual knowledge, and "[k]nowledge is cognitive awareness." RUPA §102, Comment. Temporary memory loss due to alcohol abuse might well negate "cognitive awareness."

PROBLEM 95

The Ventura Company ("Ventura") is a general partnership that manufacturers widgets. Although Ventura has five partners, the partnership agreement provides that one of the partners, Maurice, is the managing partner and has sole authority to manage all partnership business. Ventura has a long-term contract with Rolande, Inc. ("Rolande"), under which Rolande supplies framjets to Ventura. (Ventura incorporates one framjet into each widget Ventura makes.) The Ventura-Rolande contract requires that Ventura "inform Rolande of any defect in any framjet supplied under this contract, within 30 days after Ventura knows of the defect, or be barred from any remedy for such defect."

One day, Alan, one of the other four partners in Ventura, happens to be walking through Ventura's factory and happens to notice that an entire pallet of Rolande framjets are defective. Alan assumes, however, that Maurice has procedures in place to check incoming products and therefore does not mention the defects to anyone.

Unfortunately, neither Maurice nor anyone else connected with Ventura notices the defect until 35 days later. In the ensuing legal struggle between Ventura and Rolande, is Ventura better off under the UPA or under RUPA?

EXPLANATION

Ventura is far better off under the UPA. Under RUPA §102(f), Alan's knowledge of the defect is immediately attributable to the partnership, regardless of the fact that Alan is not involved in partnership operations. In contrast, that fact matters under UPA §12. Because Alan is not "the partner acting in the particular matter [of checking for and informing Rolande of defects]," his knowledge of the defects is attributed to the partnership only if he "reasonably could and should have communicated it to the acting partner." Obviously, Alan could have communicated his knowledge to Maurice, but it is at least arguable that Alan acted reasonably in assuming that Maurice had established appropriate inspection procedures. If Alan's assumption was reasonable, Rolande cannot satisfy the "should have communicated" requirement and Alan's knowledge of the defects did not start the clock on the 30-day notice period.

PROBLEM 96

For many years Harry has owned and operated a delivery service. When Harry's son, Joe, turns 21, Harry takes him into the business as a partner in a partnership governed by the UPA. Father and son agree to split profits 70/30. They have a clear understanding that, for at least the next five years, Harry is in charge of all dealings with customers, and that Joe's role is to make deliveries and pick-ups and to maintain the partnership's books.

One day Joe delivers a truckload of sensitive environmental testing equipment to an environmental clean-up company. The next day the company's manager calls Joe to complain that the equipment is damaged, apparently from having been bounced around in transit. Joe says, "Ah . . . that must have happened when I hit that giant pothole on Route 66." If the clean-up company sues the partnership for damage to the equipment, will Joe's statement be admissible as a partnership admission?

EXPLANATION

Yes. Joe had authority to make deliveries, so his statement was "[a]n admission made by [a] partner concerning partnership affairs within the scope of his authority as conferred by this act." UPA §11. His admission is therefore "evidence against the partnership." Id.

The partnership might argue that (i) the phrase "within the scope of his authority as conferred by this act" refers not to the subject matter of the partner's comment but rather to comment-making itself; (ii) the agreement between Joe and Harry deprived Joe of actual authority to comment to customers, and therefore (iii) if the clean-up company wants to use Joe's comment against the partnership, the clean-up company has to show that Joe had other "authority as conferred by this act," that is, "apparently/usual" power to make comments.

That argument should fail. It rests on an interpretation of UPA §11 that ignores the provision's Official Comment and, moreover, would make the provision redundant of UPA §9(1).

11

Partner Dissociation and Partnership Dissolution

§11.1 The UPA and RUPA

In both the UPA and RUPA, the most elaborate provisions concern:

- partner dissociation—the separation of a partner from the partnership, and
- partnership dissolution—the point at which a partnership stops functioning as a forward looking enterprise and begins to wind up its business.

Elaborate provisions are necessary because those two topics implicate numerous interrelated issues, including:

1. the management rights of a partner who has dissociated;
2. the management rights of the other partners after a partner has dissociated;
3. the power to bind of a partner who has dissociated;
4. the power to bind of the other partners after a partner has dissociated;
5. in an ordinary general partnership, the liability of a partner who has dissociated for the debts of the partnership incurred:
   a. before the dissociation
   b. after the dissociation;
6. the relationship between partner dissociation and partnership dissolution;

7. the question of whether dissolution (and eventual termination) of the partnership as a legal organization (whether entity or aggregate) will result in the liquidation or the continuation of the business;

8. the manner of winding up a dissolved partnership, including how to settle accounts with third parties and among the partners.

The concepts of dissociation and dissolution also comprise the area of greatest difference between the UPA and RUPA.[1] Although the *structure* of the UPA's approach can be discerned in RUPA's approach, RUPA has departed radically from the UPA's basic *premise*. Under the UPA, the dissociation of any partner necessarily causes the dissolution of the partnership. Under RUPA, that is not true. Consequently, while the RUPA provisions in this area have a somewhat similar architecture to the UPA provisions, RUPA rules produce consequences markedly at odds with the consequences produced by the rules of the UPA.

It is therefore necessary to study each set of rules separately, so that each is understood as a system. The first part of this chapter deals in detail with the UPA rules, the second with RUPA's, and the third provides a comparison.[2]

§11.2   UPA—Foundational Notions

§11.2.1   *Four Fundamental Concepts*

Partnership dissolution under the UPA raises complex and interrelated issues. To keep those issues straight, you must keep in mind four fundamental concepts: (i) the dissociation of any partner causes dissolution of a UPA partnership; (ii) dissolution does not end the partnership but instead puts the partnership into a period of winding up; (iii) the eventual end of a partnership is not necessarily the end of the partnership's business; (iv) under the UPA, a partner always has the power (but not necessarily the right) to dissolve the partnership.

Dissociation causes dissolution.   The UPA has a long list of "Causes of Dissolution,"[3] but the core concept is that the dissociation of any partner from

---

1. The UPA does not use the term "dissociation," but the word is useful shorthand for the UPA concept of "any partner ceasing to be associated in the carrying on . . . of the business." UPA §29. RUPA uses the word repeatedly without specifically defining it. See, e.g., RUPA §601 (listing causes of dissociation) and Comment 1.

2. Readers who are only concerned with RUPA may be tempted to skip the UPA materials. Certainly the RUPA materials can stand alone, but RUPA—like any other statute—is best understood in light of the circumstances that gave rise to its promulgation. The RUPA provisions discussed in this chapter are therefore best understood by those who also understand the UPA provisions which preceded them.

3. UPA §31, titled "Causes of Dissolution," lists in its six paragraphs nine different events or actions that cause dissolution. The list is actually longer, however, because

the partnership triggers dissolution. Dissolution "is the change in the relation of the partners caused by any partner ceasing to be associated in the carrying on . . . of the business."[4]

Although you should familiarize yourself with all the listed causes of dissolution, you may want to note particularly the following situations:

- *Express Will Dissolution of an At-Will Partnership*—If the partners have not agreed to continue the partnership until the end of some particular term or undertaking, then each partner has the power and the right to cause dissolution at any time simply by withdrawing, resigning, retiring, or otherwise making known his, her, or its *express will*.[5]
- *Express Will Dissolution of a Partnership for a Term or Undertaking*—Even if the partners have agreed to a partnership for a "definite term or particular undertaking,"[6] each partner retains the *power* to cause dissolution merely by making known his, her, or its express will.[7] The resulting dissolution will be premature and wrongful, that is, "in contravention of the agreement between the partners,"[8] but it will occur nonetheless.[9]
- *Dissolution by Expelling a Partner*—An expelled partner has been dissociated, so expulsion causes dissolution. A partnership agreement can authorize expulsion, but it cannot prevent expulsion from causing dissolution.[10]
- *Dissolution by the Death or Bankruptcy of a Partner*—Death obviously changes the deceased's relationship to fellow partners. The changes caused by bankruptcy are less permanent but often just as fundamental. Either event causes dissolution. In neither event is the dissolution wrongful.[11]

UPA §31(6) incorporates another list of causes from UPA §32. The eight different causes listed in UPA §§31(1)-31(5) are all automatic and "self-actuating." If a listed event or action occurs, the partnership is dissolved. In contrast, UPA §32 lists grounds upon which "the court shall decree dissolution." A claim of dissolution under UPA §31 can nonetheless result in judicial intervention. Partners sometimes litigate over whether a dissolving event did in fact occur. See sections 11.4.2, 11.5.4, and 11.5.5 (significance of the distinction between wrongful and rightful dissolution). They also litigate in an effort to sort out the consequences of dissolution. See section 9.10 (action for accounting).

4. UPA §29.

5. UPA §31(1)(b).

6. UPA §31(1)(a).

7. UPA §31(2).

8. Id.

9. For the distinction between wrongful and rightful dissolution see infra this section. For the consequences of the distinction, see sections 11.4.2, 11.5.4, and 11.5.5.

10. UPA §31(1)(d) (dissolution is caused "[b]y the expulsion of any partner from the business bona fide in accordance with such a power conferred by the agreement between the partners"). For a discussion of UPA expulsion issues, see section 11.7.2.

11. UPA §§31(4) (death) and 31(5) (bankruptcy).

- *Expiration of a Term or Undertaking*—If the partnership agreement includes a specific term or a particular undertaking, the expiration of the term or the accomplishment of the undertaking automatically causes dissolution.[12]

Dissolution does not end the partnership.   Dissolution is not itself the end of the partnership; it is merely the beginning of the end. Dissolution means that the partnership as a legal construct has no future, other than to finish in one way or another the work it has already begun and to settle accounts among the partners.

The finishing of business and the settling of accounts is called "the *winding up* of partnership affairs,"[13] and dissolution automatically puts the partnership into the winding up phase. To wind up its business with outside *obligees,* the partnership must perform or otherwise satisfy the obligations. If, for example, dissolution occurs with a project underway for a customer, during winding up the partnership will complete the project, arrange to have someone else (including one of the partners, a successor partnership, or some other successor business) complete the project, or obtain the customer's permission to abandon the project.

For outside *obligors,* during winding up the partnership will receive performance, assign the right to receive performance, or release performance of the obligation. For example, during winding up a partnership will try to collect all of its accounts receivable (i.e., money which customers owe the partnership for products sold or services rendered). For amounts owed but not yet due, the partnership may try to collect early, offering to accept a reduced amount in return for early payment. Or, the partnership may sell to someone else (including one of the partners, a successor partnership, or some other successor business) the right to collect the debt when it comes due.

Winding up also involves settling accounts among the partners. If the partners have an agreement on the subject, that agreement will govern. Otherwise, UPA default rules will control this final reckoning.

When winding up has finished, the partnership is actually and legally at an end. There are no papers to be filed or magic words to be said.[14] The end of function marks the end of existence.

The end of the partnership is not necessarily the end of the partnership business.   There is a difference between the legal construct the law calls a

---

12. UPA §31(1)(a).

13. UPA §30.

14. In this respect the death of a partnership resembles its creation. See section 7.2 (no special formalities needed to create a partnership). There may, however, be some paperwork following dissolution. To protect themselves against future liabilities, partners of a dissolved UPA partnership may wish to give notice of the dissolution to third parties who have done business with the partnership and to the public generally. See section 11.3.3.

partnership and the business that can be carried on under the partnership form. As both a theoretical and practical matter, the "partnership business" is distinct from the legal form. It is therefore possible for a particular partnership to dissolve, wind up, and terminate while the partnership business continues.

Whether the business continues depends on whether the partners have so agreed. In the default mode, the UPA gives every partner the right to require liquidation,[15] but partners often relinquish this right by agreement. Such agreements can be made either before or after the dissolution. Often the same agreement that forms the partnership also dictates what will happen after dissolution.

Whenever made, business continuation agreements typically provide for a successor partnership to take over from the dissolved partnership. The successor partnership may consist of some or all of the members remaining from the dissolved partnership and may also include some "new blood."

A partner always has the power (but not necessarily the right) to dissolve a partnership. Among the inevitable causes of dissolution is the "express will" of a partner. Under UPA §§ 31(1)(b) and 31(2), any partner can dissolve the partnership at any time simply by manifesting a desire to do so. For centuries the law has characterized partnership as a voluntary arrangement, and a partner's power to dissolve reflects and preserves that character.

The power cannot be eliminated by agreement. Indeed, the power exists even when its exercise will breach an agreement. "[T]he express will of any partner at any time" dissolves a partnership, even though the dissolving partner is acting "in contravention of the agreement between the partners."[16]

Having the power to dissolve is not, however, the same as having the right to dissolve. Dissolutions that contravene a partnership agreement are "wrongful" rather than "rightful."[17] Moreover, in some jurisdictions an opportunistic dissolution can be wrongful even though the dissolving partner has not breached any specific provision of the partnership agreement. As will be discussed in detail below,[18] the wrongful/rightful distinction can significantly influence the nature of the winding up process.

§11.2.2 Following the UPA Three-Ring Circus: Three Pathways of Postdissolution Concerns

Understanding what happens when a UPA partnership dissolves is a lot like watching a three-ring circus. Three different things are happening at once, and it

---

15. In liquidation, the partnership sells off all its assets (e.g., its buildings, equipment, accounts receivable, good will) either as a whole or piecemeal. See section 11.4.1. If a partner *wrongfully* dissolves the partnership, that partner may lose the right to compel liquidation. See section 11.4.2.

16. UPA §31(2).

17. A comparable distinction exists between wrongful and rightful terminations of agency relationships. See section 5.2.

18. See sections 11.4.2, 11.5.4, and 11.5.5.

is almost impossible to have them all in view simultaneously. It is nonetheless useful to understand that they are all occurring. Under the UPA, the three post-dissolution rings (or pathways) concern: (i) how the partnership is managed during winding up, (ii) what happens to the partnership business, and (iii) what happens to the partners. The following sections deal with each pathway in turn.

§11.3   Management Issues During Winding Up

When a partnership dissolves, it does not immediately disappear. It lingers to wind up its affairs. Winding up can occur quickly, as when a successor partnership takes over, or may be quite lengthy, as when an extensive and complicated business is sold off in pieces. In any event, the same two basic categories of management issues exist both during winding up and before dissolution: (i) inter se the partners, who has the right to manage the business and make commitments on its behalf; (ii) as between the partnership and third parties, what acts of individual partners suffice to bind the partnership.

§11.3.1 Inter Se Issues

Actual authority to manage the partnership during winding up.   UPA §37 states the default rule: "the partners who have not wrongfully dissolved the partnership [have] the right to wind up the partnership affairs."[19] UPA §37 does not say what happens if those partners disagree, but presumably UPA §18(h) applies. Under UPA §18(h) differences over "ordinary matters" are settled by majority vote, while acts "in-contravention of any agreement between the partners" require unanimous consent.[20]

As explained previously,[21] UPA §18(h) fails to expressly provide a rule for matters not "in contravention" but nonetheless extraordinary. During winding up, this omitted category may cause serious problems. Some winding up matters will be clearly ordinary—for example, deciding where to buy supplies. Others, such as deciding whether to compromise a claim or sell an important partnership asset, may be unprecedented.

Some courts have solved the problem by holding that extraordinary matters can become ordinary during the winding up process.

Example: Larry, Moe, and Curley have an at-will partnership that owns and races a single racehorse. Fed up with Moe's abuse, Curley quits. The

---

19. When no partners survive into the winding up period, "the legal representative of the last surviving partner, not bankrupt" may wind up. UPA §37.
20. See section 9.5.1.
21. See section 9.5.1.

partnership accordingly dissolves, and Moe insists on liquidation. A third party offers $100,000 for the race horse. Larry and Curley vote yes. Moe votes no. Predissolution, selling the partnership's key asset would have required unanimity. But in winding up, selling off assets is probably "an ordinary matter." If so, Larry and Curley's majority vote prevails.

Example: The Larry-Moe-Curley racehorse partnership has a partnership agreement that states in part: "During winding up, Moe will have the sole authority to dispose of partnership assets." Under the agreement, when dissolution occurs, Moe's actual authority expands while the actual authority of Larry and Curley constricts.

UPA §37 also provides that "any partner, his legal representative or his assignee, upon cause shown, may obtain winding up by the court." The provision does not specify what constitutes cause, but courts have held that waste, fraud, and gross mismanagement justify the appointment of a receiver to wind up the partnership. Whether mere dissension among the partners justifies appointing a receiver is an open question. Even a partner who wrongfully dissolved the partnership can seek court intervention under UPA §37.

Except for the provision on "winding up by the court," the rules of UPA §37 can be altered or displaced by an agreement of the partners.

Authority to commit the partnership to new business. Dissolution deprives all partners of actual authority to transact new business. "Except so far as may be necessary to wind up partnership affairs to complete transactions begun but not then finished, dissolution terminates all [actual] authority of any partner to act for the partnership."[22]

The precise timing of the deprivation depends on the cause of dissolution. If the act of some partner is responsible, then each partner's "new business" authority terminates upon knowledge of the dissolution.[23] When a partner's death or bankruptcy causes dissolution, each partner's "new business" authority ends upon knowledge or notice of the death or bankruptcy.[24] With all other causes, "new business" authority ends at the moment of dissolution.[25] The end of "new business" actual authority does not necessarily end the partners' power to bind the partnership as to new business.[26]

---

22. UPA §33.
23. UPA §§33(1)(b) and 34(a).
24. UPA §§33(1)(a) and 34(b).
25. UPA §33(1)(a).
26. UPA §§33(2) and 35(1)(b). See section 11.3.2.

§11.3.2 *The Power to Bind the Partnership After Dissolution*

UPA §35 describes the postdissolution power of a partner to bind the partnership. UPA §35(1) states empowering rules, and UPA §35(3) states constraining rules.[27] For a partner's postdissolution act to bind the dissolved partnership, the act must (i) qualify under one of the rules of UPA §35(1) and (ii) not be disqualified under any of the rules of UPA §35(3).

The empowering rules of UPA §35(1).   The empowering rules of UPA §35(1) establish two categories of postdissolution partner acts: (i) acts "appropriate for winding up partnership affairs or completing transactions unfinished at dissolution,"[28] and (ii) acts that would bind the partnership if dissolution had not occurred.[29]

Under UPA §35(1) (a), acts in the former category bind the partnership, subject to the constraining rules of UPA §35(3).

> *Example:* A partner in a dissolved autobody partnership orders paint so the partnership can finish work on cars already in the shop. This is an "act appropriate for . . . completing transactions unfinished at dissolution," and UPA §35(1)(a) applies.

> *Example:* The same partner, with a view toward settling the partners' accounts with each other, hires an accountant to put a value on partnership assets. This is an "act appropriate for winding up partnership affairs," and UPA §35(1)(a) applies.

> *Example:* The same partner accepts a new "rush" order on a '67 Corvette and hires a "detailing" expert to do the fancy paintwork. Neither the rush order nor the new hire qualifies under UPA §35(1)(a).

The rule for the second category—"transactions which would bind the partnership if dissolution had not taken place"—is considerably more complicated. The rule has two branches, depending on whether the third party extended credit to the partnership before dissolution. If so, under UPA §35(1)(b)(I), the third party must show that (i) absent dissolution the partner's act would have bound the partnership, and (ii) at the time of the partner's act the third party had "no knowledge or notice of the dissolution."[30]

> *Example:* A partner in a dissolved bodyshop partnership accepts a new, "rush" order on a '67 Corvette and hires a detailing expert to do the

---

27. UPA §35(2) limits the personal liability of individual partners for certain postdissolution obligations of the partnership, and UPA §35(4) makes clear that UPA §35 does not affect liability created under UPA §16 (partnership by estoppel). For an explanation of partnership by estoppel, see section 7.5.

28. UPA §35(1)(a).

29. UPA §35(1)(b).

30. UPA §35(1)(b)(I).

fancy paintwork. The expert has worked for the partnership before, always billing the partnership after completing the work. No one has notified the expert that the partnership is dissolved, and she is unaware of that fact. Assuming that the partner's act of hiring the expert would have bound the partnership before dissolution, UPA §35(1)(b)(I) applies.

If the third party did not extend credit to the partnership before dissolution, under UPA §35(1)(b)(II) the third party must show that (i) it knew of the partnership prior to dissolution, (ii) at the time of the partner's act it had no knowledge or notice of the dissolution, (iii) at the time of the partner's act there had been no public notice of the dissolution (through advertisement in a newspaper of general circulation in the partnership's place(s) of business), and (iv) absent dissolution the partner's act would have bound the partnership.[31]

> *Example:* A partner in a dissolved bodyshop partnership accepts a new, "rush" order on a '67 Corvette, and the owner of the Corvette seeks to hold the partnership to the deal. Another partner has sent letters announcing the partnership's dissolution to all the bodyshop's suppliers and customers and has published the announcement in the city's main newspaper. The Corvette's owner has never been a customer before, never received a copy of the letter, never read the newspaper announcement, and was unaware of the dissolution when the first partner accepted the rush order. Even assuming the first partner's act of accepting the order would have bound the partnership before dissolution, accepting the order does not qualify under UPA §35(1)(b)(II). The owner had not extended credit to the partnership before dissolution, and "the fact of dissolution had . . . been advertised in a newspaper of general circulation in the place . . . at which the partnership business was regularly carried on."[32]

Under both branches of UPA §35(1)(b), the third party must show that the partner's act would have bound the partnership absent dissolution. To make that showing, the third party invokes the same rules that apply predissolution—namely, UPA §9.

The constraining rules of UPA §35(3). UPA §35(3) contains three constraining rules. The first two are straightforward. A partner's postdissolution act cannot bind the partnership if (i) dissolution occurred because it was unlawful to carry on the partnership business and the partner's act is not appropriate for winding up (UPA §35(3)(a)), or (ii) the partner doing the act is bankrupt (UPA §35(3)(b)).

> *Example:* A partner in an autobody partnership files for personal bankruptcy, causing the partnership to dissolve. The same partner then or-

---

31. UPA §35(1)(b)(II).
32. UPA §35(1)(b)(II).

ders paint so the partnership can finish work on cars already in the shop. Although this is an "act appropriate for . . . completing transactions unfinished at dissolution," UPA §35(1)(a) does not bind the partnership. Because the acting partner is bankrupt, the partnership can invoke UPA §35(3)(b) to override UPA §35(1)(a).

The third constraining rule is more important as a practical matter and decidedly more complex. The third rule determines whether a partner's *unauthorized* postdissolution act binds the partnership.[33]

Like the empowering rule of UPA §35(1)(b), this constraining rule of UPA §35(3)(c) has two branches, depending on whether the third party extended credit to the partnership before dissolution. If so, UPA §35(3)(c)(I) bars a third party from recovering only if the third party had "knowledge or notice of [the partner's] want of authority." If the third party had not extended credit to the partnership before dissolution, UPA §35(3)(c)(II) bars a third party from recovering if either the third party had "knowledge or notice of [the partner's] want of authority" or there has been public notice of the partner's lack of authority (through advertisement in a newspaper of general circulation in the partnership's place(s) of business).

> *Example:* Larry, Moe, and Curley have a partnership that owns and races a single racehorse. The partnership agreement provides that (i) the partnership has a term of five years, (ii) after dissolution Moe will handle all discussions with third parties interested in buying the horse, and (iii) any decision to sell the horse following dissolution will be made by a majority vote of the partners. When the partnership dissolves, it places an announcement in all the major racing publications. The announcement states in part: "We are dissolving our partnership and looking for buyers for our horse. All interested parties should contact Moe."
>
> Despite the partnership agreement, Curley starts looking for potential buyers on his own. He finds a hot prospect who has never previously done business with the partnership, has not seen the announcement in the trade papers, and is unaware that Curley is acting for a dissolved partnership. After a half-hour of hard bargaining, Curley and the prospect agree that the prospect will buy the horse for $75,000.
>
> Despite the partnership agreement and the public announcement, the partnership is bound. Curley's act is "appropriate for winding up partnership affairs,"[34] and so qualifies under the empowering rule of UPA §35(1)(a). Curley's lack of authority does not negate this power, because under UPA §35(3)(c)(II) the prospect had "no knowledge or

---

33. The power to bind is not the same as the actual authority to act. For a discussion of the latter, see section 11.3.1. Lack of authority also figures in a pre-dissolution UPA constraining rule. See section 10.2.5 (discussing the "no authority" constraining rule under UPA §9).

34. UPA §35(1)(a).

notice of [Curley's] want of authority" and the public notice about Moe was not in a newspaper of general circulation. (Since the third party had not extended credit to the partnership before dissolution, UPA §35(3)(c)(II) is the relevant constraining rule.)

§11.3.3 Partner Self-Protection: The Importance of Notice

Whether a partner's postdissolution act binds the partnership to a third party often depends on what the third party knows or has notice of. Therefore, following dissolution a partnership can limit its liability for unauthorized acts by promptly "spreading the word" both about the dissolution and about any limitations on the winding up authority of particular partners.[35]

To spread the word effectively, the partnership should (i) run an advertisement in "a newspaper of general circulation" published in the partnership's regular place(s) of business, stating the fact of dissolution and detailing any limitations of partner authority, and (ii) send a letter, containing the same information as the advertisement, to all third parties that have provided goods or services to the partnership. The advertisement will limit claims by those who have not previously extended credit to the partnership.[36] Technically, the letter need only go to those who have previously "extended credit to the partnership,"[37] but it may be difficult to determine from the partnership records which businesses have extended credit and which have acted solely on a cash basis. It is better to be overinclusive and safe than underinclusive and sorry.

§11.4 The Fate of the Partnership Business

§11.4.1 The Fundamental Decision: Whether to Liquidate

The most fundamental decision after any UPA dissolution is whether the partnership business will be liquidated or continued.[38] From a business standpoint, liquidation usually produces inferior results. Unless a buyer can be found for the business as a whole, the partnership will have to sell off its assets piecemeal. Usually, a business is much more valuable as a going concern, so a piecemeal sale will produce an inferior payout. Moreover, liquidation sales are often in the nature of fire sales—everything must go within a relatively short

---

35. A partner can also spread the word and would be well advised to do so if the partnership fails to act promptly.

36. UPA §§35(1)(b)(II) and 35(3)(c)(II).

37. UPA §§35(1)(b)(I) and 35(3)(c)(I).

38. A decision to continue the business does not relieve the dissolved partnership of its obligations to its creditors or release the partners of the dissolved partnership from their personal liability on those obligations. See section 11.5.2. The decision does, however, affect the way in which the partners settle accounts with the outside world and with each other. See sections 11.5.3-11.5.5.

period of time, and potential buyers know it. As a result, the seller rarely gets top dollar.

Despite the practical problems with liquidation, the UPA default rules conduce toward that result. Following a rightful dissolution, absent a contrary agreement UPA §38(1) gives every partner the right to have the assets of the partnership liquidated and the partners paid in cash.[39] In the default mode, the right to compel liquidation also exists following a wrongful dissolution unless all the partners who did not wrongfully dissolve agree to carry on the business of the partnership and meet certain other statutory requirements.[40]

§11.4.2 Who Decides

Although the decision whether to liquidate or continue affects third parties, the decision itself is an inter se matter. Like all inter se matters, it is subject to the agreement of the partners. Agreement may precede or follow the dissolution.

> *Example:* Rachael, Sam, and Carolyn have a partnership that operates a chicken-breeding farm. There is no written partnership agreement and no commitment to continue the partnership for any particular time or undertaking. One day Carolyn decides that she is getting out of chicken farming and going to attend art school. Carolyn's friend, Suzanne, expresses an interest in joining the business. After discussing the matter, Rachael, Sam, Carolyn, and Suzanne agree that Suzanne will buy "Carolyn's share." Suzanne joins the business, Carolyn leaves for art school, and chicken breeding continues through the successor partnership of Rachael, Sam, and Suzanne. Carolyn's withdrawal has dissolved the old partnership, but Rachael, Sam, and Carolyn have each agreed not to compel liquidation.

Where the partners have not agreed, the UPA default rules govern. Which particular rule applies depends on whether the dissolution was rightful or wrongful.

Following a *rightful* dissolution, liquidation is the typical default result. Under UPA §38(1), "each partner . . . , unless otherwise agreed, may have the partnership property applied to discharge its liabilities, and the surplus applied to pay *in cash* the amount owing to the respective partners."[41] An exception exists when "dissolution is caused by expulsion of a partner, bona fide under the partnership agreement." In that event, the expelled partner has no right to force liquidation if the continuing partners (i) "cash out" the expelled

---

39. In extraordinary circumstances, courts may divide the partnership's assets in kind. In general, however, valuation problems cause the law to disfavor in-kind division of assets. See section 11.5.3.

40. UPA §§38(2)(b), 38(2)(c)(II). A wrongful dissolution occurs when a partner dissolves in violation of the partnership agreement. See section 11.2.1. In some jurisdictions a breach of fiduciary duty can also cause a wrongful dissolution. See section 11.7.

41. Emphasis added.

partner without liquidating the business,[42] and (ii) cause the expelled partner to be released from (not merely indemnified for) personal liability for the debts of the dissolved partnership.[43] Authority is divided as to whether the estate of a deceased partner can force liquidation. The language of UPA §38(1) implies that the estate has no such right, but language in UPA §41(3) points the other way.[44] The cases are also divided.

Following a *wrongful* dissolution, the analysis is a bit more complicated. Under UPA §38(2), the first choice belongs to the partners who did not wrongfully dissolve:

> The partners who have not caused the dissolution wrongfully, if they all desire to continue the business in the same name, either by themselves or jointly with others, may do so, during the agreed term for the partnership. . . .[45]

The remaining partners must agree unanimously and in addition must "indemnify [the wrongful dissolver] against all present or future partnership liabilities" (with the indemnity backed by a bond approved by a court) *and either* cash out the wrongful dissolver immediately[46] *or* promise to pay the cash-out amount at some later date and obtain a court-approved bond to secure the payment. If these criteria are met, the continuing partners "may possess the partnership property" and use it for the rest of the dissolved partnership's original term.[47]

If these conditions are not met, each partner—including the wrongful dissolver—has the right to demand liquidation just as if the dissolution had been rightful.[48]

---

42. For how the cash-out amount is calculated, see section 11.5.4.

43. For the difficulties involved in obtaining a release, see section 11.5.2 (effect of dissolution on the liabilities of partners). Absent a contrary agreement, each of the nonexpelled partners retains the right to compel liquidation. Ordinarily, however, the same agreement that provides for expulsion overrides UPA §38(1) generally. As a result, the nonexpelled partners lose their right to compel liquidation, and the expelled partner may lose the right to be released from partnership liabilities.

44. UPA §38(1) states only that "each *partner*" has a right to compel liquidation. The right does not extend to "persons claiming through [partners] in respect of their interests in the partnership." That latter category (persons claiming through partners) includes the estate of a deceased partner. In contrast, UPA §41(3) refers to "the business of the dissolved partnership [being] continued . . . *with the consent of* the retired partners or *the representative of the deceased partner.*" (Emphasis added.)

45. UPA §38(2)(b).

46. For how the cash-out amount is calculated, see section 11.5.5 (settling accounts among partners following wrongful dissolution).

47. UPA §38(2)(b).

48. UPA §§38(2)(a)(I) (following wrongful dissolution, "Each partner who has not caused dissolution wrongfully shall have (I) All the rights specified in paragraph (1) of this section . . .") and 38(2)(c)(I) (following wrongful dissolution, if the partnership business is not continued under §38(2)(b), wrongful dissolver has "all the rights of a partner under paragraph (1)," subject to any claims for damage on account of wrongful dissolution).

§11.4.3 *Continuing the Business Through a Successor Partnership (An Example)*

The following Example may help you follow the various issues inherent in a decision to continue the business of a dissolved partnership through a successor partnership.

> *Example:* Three law students, Charlotte, Paul, and Sophie, form a UPA partnership to sell used law textbooks. They place no term on the partnership, agreeing instead to continue "just as long as we all want to." The three partners rent a room in their law school, take books from fellow students on consignment, open a partnership checking account, and do a profitable business. After a year, Sophie is nearing graduation and wants to "get her money out." She dissolves the partnership.
>
> Charlotte and Paul want to continue the bookstore business and decide to bring in Jacob to take Sophie's place. To carry on the bookstore business, Charlotte, Paul, and Jacob form a successor partnership. Although Sophie has the legal right to force liquidation of the dissolved partnership's business, Charlotte and Paul convince her to take a cash settlement instead. As part of the winding up process of the dissolved partnership:
>
> 1) the dissolved partnership settles Sophie's accounts by cashing her out (that is, by paying her the settlement amount);
> 2) Charlotte and Paul take rights in the successor partnership as settlement of their respective accounts in the dissolved partnership;[49]
> 3) the dissolved partnership arranges to transfer its rights and obligations (including, e.g., its lease with the law school) to the successor partnership; and
> 4) the successor partnership agrees to hold Sophie harmless from any liabilities arising from either the dissolved or successor partnership.[50]

When winding up ends, the Charlotte-Paul-Sophie partnership terminates; it no longer exists. Its business, however, continues on. With the same suppliers, the same customers and two of the same partners, Charlotte, Paul, and Jacob operate that business "at the same old stand."

The following terms will be useful in keeping straight the legal issues raised when the business of a UPA partnership continues despite dissolution:

---

49. For a detailed discussion of settling accounts among partners, see section 11.5.3-11.5.5.

50. This undertaking is part of the settling of accounts among the partners. See section 11.5.4.

- *Dissociated Partners*—Partners of the dissolved partnership, who are not continuing in the business as members of the successor partnership. In the Example above, Sophie is a dissociated partner. (The UPA calls such withdrawal "retirement," a term which is confusing because of its lay association with senior citizen status and warm climates.)
- *Continuing Partners*—Partners of the dissolved partnership, who are continuing in the business as members of the successor partnership. In the Example above, Charlotte and Paul are continuing partners.
- *New Partners*—Partners of the successor partnership, who were not members of the dissolved partnership. In the Example above, Jacob is a new partner.

§11.4.4 Settling Accounts with Third Parties

The dissolution of a partnership does not abrogate obligations between the dissolved partnership and third parties. Indeed, half of the winding up process consists of resolving those obligations.[51]

When the partnership business is being liquidated. If the partnership business is being liquidated, resolving relations with third parties is theoretically quite simple. Winding up continues until the partnership has completed all performance as an obligor and received all performance as an obligee.

As a practical matter, however, such completion may be difficult and time consuming. For example, not all amounts owed the partnership can be collected immediately. Some obligations may not be due yet, and some obligors may be "slow pays." To the extent prompt collection is impractical, the partnership may either sell the right to collect to a third party, assign the collection right to one of the partners,[52] or simply abandon the obligation.

For obligations the dissolved partnership owes to third parties, two pathways exist. The partnership can either pay off or otherwise perform its obligations, or it can delegate the responsibility to someone else. Delegation may be especially attractive for long-term obligations, such as constructing a building. For a dissolved partnership that has long-term obligations, delegation is the only alternative to a very extended period of winding up.[53]

When the partnership business is being continued. When the partnership business is being continued by a successor partnership, the theoretical

---

51. The other half consists of settling accounts among the partners. See sections 11.5.2-11.5.5.

52. Typically as part of an agreed-upon settling of accounts among the partners.

53. Delegating an obligation does not by itself release the dissolved partnership or its partners. If the delegatee fails to perform, the obligor may proceed against those partners—even if the dissolved partnership has long since ceased to exist. Moreover, if the obligation arises from a contract, the contract may purport to prohibit or restrict delegation. See section 4.4.3 for a discussion of these issues in the agency context.

structure is far more complex, although from a practical perspective the transition from the dissolved partnership to the successor partnership can be seamless.

Resolving obligations owed to the dissolved partnership is usually simple enough. The dissolved partnership assigns its rights to the successor partnership.[54] Resolving obligations owed to third parties is more complicated. The dissolved partnership could in theory perform all these obligations. However, if the obligations are large relative to the assets of the business, that approach would require at least partial liquidation, which in turn would cripple the successor partnership's ability to function. Moreover, as discussed above, some obligations require drawn out performance. Typically, therefore, the dissolved partnership resolves its obligations to third parties by delegating them to the successor partnership.

Contract law applies to these delegations. In some instances the transfer of responsibility may require the obligee's consent.[55] In all instances, the mere transfer of responsibility does not discharge the dissolved partnership from its obligations. As a matter of contract law, discharge occurs only if the obligee consents to a novation with the successor partnership.[56] An economically rational obligee will not agree to a novation without receiving something in return.

> **Example:** Alex, Bernice, Carl, and Donald form a partnership to do carpentry work. To equip themselves they borrow $10,000 from First State Bank at the then current rate of 6 percent. Two years later Alex dissolves the partnership. He is willing to let the others continue the business, so long as he is released from any personal liability to the bank. Over the past two years interest rates have risen, so the going rate is now 9 percent. If Bernice, Carl, and Donald are creditworthy without Alex, then the bank may well release Alex, provided the interest rate on the loan is reset nearer to or at 9 percent.

---

54. Complexity develops if the dissolved partnership's rights are not assignable. Certain rights to receive payments are assignable despite anything to the contrary in the contract giving rise to the rights. See UCC §§2-210 and 9-406(d) and (f). Most experienced partnership practitioners are aware, however, of Fairway Development Co. v. Title Ins. Co. of Minnesota, 621 F. Supp. 120 (Ohio 1985), in which a federal district court held that a successor partnership could not benefit from a title insurance policy issued to the predecessor partnership.

55. Some contracts expressly prohibit delegation without the obligee's consent, and contract law sometimes validates such provisions. See section 4.4.3 (delegation of performance to an agent).

56. See section 2.7.5. As a matter of partnership law, delegation to the successor partnership may lead to release of dissociated partners, i.e. those partners of the dissolved partnership who are not members of the successor partnership. See section 11.5.2.

§11.4.5 Successor Liability When a Successor Partnership Continues the Business of a Dissolved Partnership

If a successor partnership continues the business of a dissolved partnership, then both contract law and partnership law make the successor partnership liable for the obligations of the dissolved partnership. The agreement transferring the business typically calls for the successor partnership to assume the obligations of the dissolved partnership, and, as a matter of contract law, creditors of the dissolved partnership can enforce the assumption agreement as third party beneficiaries. Even without an assumption agreement, if the successor partnership includes any continuing partners (i.e., any members from the dissolved partnership), UPA §41 makes the successor partnership liable for the debts of the dissolved partnership as a matter of partnership law.[57]

This successor liability extends to all the partners in the successor partnership,[58] with one exception. The liability created by *partnership law* for *new partners* is limited. Under UPA §41(7), "The liability of a third person becoming a partner in the partnership continuing the business, under this section, to the creditors of the dissolved partnership shall be satisfied out of partnership property only." Although the language of the statute is confusing, the phrase "a third person" refers to persons who are members of the successor partnership but were not members of the dissolved partnership. In other words, newcomers have no *personal* liability for the debts of the dissolved partnership. The entire value of their interest in the successor partnership may be consumed in paying those old debts, but those debts do not put a newcomer's personal assets at risk.[59]

UPA §41(7) expressly limits its reach to "liability . . . under this section," so a newcomer's protection relates only to liability arising from UPA §41. Since successor partnerships typically agree to assume the obligations of the dissolved partnership, liability typically arises not only from UPA §41 but also from contract law. The protections of UPA §41(7) do not extend to liability arising from contract law.

> *Example:* Charlotte, Paul, and Sophie form a partnership to operate a used bookstore in the law school. When Sophie nears graduation, she dissolves the partnership. Jacob joins Charlotte and Paul, and they form a successor partnership to carry on the business of the dissolved partnership. En masse the professors assign new editions, the market for used

---

57. UPA §§41(1), (2), (3), (5), and (6). If the entity continuing the business includes no continuing partners, then the successor entity is liable for the debts of the dissolved partnership only if it has promised to assume those debts. UPA §41(4).

58. This personal liability follows from UPA §15. In some UPA states, the UPA has been amended to provide for LLPs. If the successor partnership is an LLP, its partners are not personally liable for its debts. See section 14.1.1.

59. Those assets are at risk, of course, for all other debts of the successor partnership. UPA §15.

books plummets, and the bookstore goes under. The business can no longer make its lease payments to the law school.

Under UPA §41(1), "the creditors of the . . . dissolved partnership are also creditors of the partnership . . . continuing the business." Therefore, the law school can pursue the successor partnership for the lease payments. Under UPA §15, the law school can also pursue the successor partnership's partners.[60] If the law school bases its claims solely on UPA §41, the personal assets of Jacob (the newcomer) are not at risk, due to UPA §41(7). Jacob's protection under UPA §41(7) will be of no use, however, if the successor partnership contractually assumed the lease obligation of the dissolved partnership. (In any event, Charlotte, Paul, and Sophie are liable as partners of the dissolved partnership.)[61]

§11.5   The Impact of Dissolution on the Partners

§11.5.1   *Impact on Partners' Fiduciary Duties*

Since dissolution does not end the partnership, dissolution does not end the partners' reciprocal fiduciary duties.[62] Indeed, these duties can take on a special importance if the partners seek to negotiate an agreement to continue the business or to buy each other out.[63]

§11.5.2   *Impact on Partners' Personal Liability*

Dissolution by itself does nothing to change the partners' personal liability for the debts of the dissolved partnership. In the words of UPA §36(1), "The dissolution of the partnership does not of itself discharge the existing liability of any partner." Discharge *will* occur, however, under two circumstances that may follow from dissolution.

Postdissolution discharge by agreement with the creditor.   UPA §36(2) states "A partner is discharged from any existing liability upon dissolution of the partnership by an agreement to that effect between himself, the partnership creditor, and the person or partnership continuing the business. . . ." Presumably under such an agreement "the person or partnership continuing the business" will assume responsibility for the discharged partner's obligations.

---

60. In some jurisdictions, the law school will first have to exhaust partnership assets. See section 7.3.1. If the successor partnership is an LLP, the law school will have no claim against the partners. See section 14.2.2.

61. See section 11.5.2.

62. For a discussion of these duties, see section 9.8.

63. For a more detailed discussion of this point, see section 9.8.5.

UPA §36(2) also states that an agreement to discharge a member of the dissolved partnership "may be inferred from the course of dealing between the creditor having knowledge of the dissolution and the person or partnership continuing the business." The statute provides no guidance on what factors support an implied agreement. At least one case suggests, however, that a creditor risks implied discharge by acting as if the dissociated partner is no longer liable.

Example: A farmer borrowed money from a finance company and secured the debt by giving the finance company a mortgage on some farmland and a security interest in some farm equipment. The farmer subsequently sold the land and equipment (subject to the financing company's interests) to a partnership on credit. One of the partners then withdrew from the partnership, and the other continued the business. The dissociated partner assigned all his interests in the partnership to the continuing partner. From these facts the court implied an agreement by the continuing partner to assume the obligations of the dissociated partner. The court found an implied agreement by the farmer to release the dissociated partner based on the following facts: (i) the farmer learned that the dissociated partner had withdrawn from the partnership business; (ii) the continuing partner signed an agreement to assume the farmer's obligations to the finance company, but the dissociated partner did not and apparently the farmer did not insist on the dissociated partner's signature; (iii) when the continuing partner was unable to make a payment on the debt to the finance company, the continuing partner and the farmer agreed to sell off some farm equipment to reduce that debt. The dissociated partner was not consulted.[64]

Discharge by material alteration in the obligation. Under UPA §36(3) a creditor may inadvertently discharge partners from their predissolution liabilities. Discharge occurs if (i) someone has agreed to assume the obligations of the dissolved partnership, (ii) the creditor knows of the agreement, and (iii) the creditor consents to a material change in the obligation.

Most of the cases under UPA §36(3) concern the meaning of "material alteration." Many of those cases use analogies from surety law.[65] Changes found to be material under UPA §36(3) include: extension of time to pay a debt; renewal of a promissory note, agreement to surrender leased premises in advance of the surrender date stated in the original lease. Changes found not to be material include: assignment to the creditor of accounts receivable as additional security for the debt (no change in the nature of the obligation, no possible prejudice to dissociated partner); failure of creditor to immediately sue business to collect on overdue account (no consented-to change in the obligation).

---

64. Gjovik v. Strope, 401 N.W.2d 664 (Minn. 1987).

65. Absent a contrary agreement, a creditor releases a surety if the creditor and principal agree to a material change in the underlying obligation.

§11.5.3   Settling Accounts Among Partners When the Business Is Liquidated

When the business is being liquidated, settling accounts among the partners is a crucial part of winding up. An agreement among the partners can govern this inter se matter.

> *Example:* Burt and Dorothy form a partnership to raise and race thoroughbred horses. The partnership has a term of five years. Burt provides all the money to buy the horses, and Dorothy contributes her considerable expertise as a trainer. Profits are split 60 percent to Dorothy, 40 percent to Burt. The partnership agreement states in part:

> > *Distribution of assets following dissolution:* Upon dissolution the partnership shall pay or secure the discharge of all liabilities which it owes. Any remaining partnership property—other than horses—shall be sold and the net proceeds divided according to the partners' respective profit shares. All horses shall become the property of Burt.

In the absence of an agreement, UPA §§38, 40, and 42 supply the default rules. Which particular rules apply depends on whether the business is being continued or liquidated and on whether the dissolution was wrongful or rightful.

When the partnership business is to be liquidated following a rightful dissolution, UPA default rules provide a theoretically simple approach for distributing the assets of the partnership and settling accounts among the partners. Property that a partner has merely loaned or rented to the partnership returns to the partner as the partnership business comes to an end.[66] The assets that belong to the partnership are marshalled and liquidated.[67] From those assets:

- outside creditors are paid off;
- inside creditors (i.e., partners who have made loans or leased property) are paid off;
- partners are repaid their invested capital (i.e., the value of any property they have contributed to the partnership, plus any profits previously allocated to the partners and left in the business, less any returns of capital previously made); and
- any remaining funds are divided, as profit, according to each partner's ordinary profit percentages.[68]

---

66. See sections 8.6.2-8.6.3 (distinguishing property contributed to the partnership from property merely loaned, leased, or furnished).

67. UPA §38(1).

68. UPA §40(b). The UPA rule that sets priorities among creditors has little practical significance. For the UPA rule to be significant, the partnership must lack sufficient

If the partnership has insufficient funds to pay its creditors and repay capital contributions, then the partners must pay into the partnership according to their respective obligations to share losses.[69]

The UPA expressly provides for the settling of accounts among partners in cash.[70] Division of assets in kind raises significant problems of valuation and so is disfavored. Partners may of course agree to settle accounts with each other through an in-kind asset distribution, but absent such an agreement in-kind distribution is permissible only to avoid great unfairness or extraordinary waste.

> *Example:* A partnership grew Christmas trees on land rented from one of the partners. When the partnership dissolved, growing trees, not ready for harvest, were a substantial partnership asset. Liquidation was impractical; to order the trees harvested and sold would have wasted the asset. Instead the court divided the growing trees between the partners.

The function of partners' capital accounts in dissolution.   As part of the settling up process, partners are paid the amounts owed "in respect of capital."[71] The bookkeeping devices which track the amount the partnership owes each partner "in respect of capital . . ." are called "capital accounts." Property contributed to the partnership increases the contributing partner's capital account by an amount equal to the fair market value of the asset as of the time of contribution. Payments made to partners as return of capital decrease their respective capital accounts. Postcontribution depreciation or appreciation of a contributed asset does not affect the contributing partner's capital account. The contribution severs the contributor's direct connection to the asset; subsequent vicissitudes in the asset's value are for the partnership's account.[72]

When the partnership dissolves and the partners settle accounts, each partner receives as a return of capital the amount in his, her, or its capital account. If the partnership has neither made nor lost money, has experienced neither depreciation nor appreciation in its assets, and has generated no saleable good will, then the sum of the capital accounts at dissolution will equal the net worth of the firm.

Such equality is by no means the norm, however. If, for example, the firm's assets have appreciated in value, then the net worth of the firm will exceed the sum of the partners' capital accounts. Any surplus remaining after paying creditors and discharging the capital accounts is profit—to be distributed according to the partners' respective profit shares.

---

funds to pay all its creditors. In that event, however, the partnership would be bankrupt and federal bankruptcy law would preempt the UPA's rule on creditor priority.

69. UPA §§40(a)(II) and 40(d).

70. UPA §38(1).

71. UPA §40(b)(III).

72. See section 8.6.3.

In contrast, if the firm has lost money or its assets have depreciated, then at dissolution the sum of the capital accounts will exceed the firm's net worth. The loss or depreciation will have affected the firm's assets, but not the separate claims of the partners to be repaid the value of their respective contributions. The partners will have to contribute additional funds to the partnership, either to permit a full return of capital or at least to adjust the capital accounts so that losses are shared appropriately.[73]

The following Example, modeled in simplified form on *Langness v. "O" Street Carpet Shop, Inc.*,[74] illustrates how capital accounts and UPA §§38(1) and 40 determine each partner's return when the partnership business is liquidated following rightful dissolution.

> *Example:* Three individuals, *A, B,* and *C,* form a partnership. They agree to share profits equally. *A* contributes $14,000. *B* contributes the vendee's interest in a real estate purchase agreement. At the time, the fair market value of the real estate is $65,000. The purchase agreement sets a price of $56,000, so the value of the contribution is $9,000. *C* makes no capital contribution, providing instead legal services in the drafting of the partnership agreement. At that point the capital accounts would stand as follows:
>
> | | |
> |---|---|
> | *A* | $14,000 |
> | *B* | 9,000 |
> | *C* | 0 |
>
> (*C*'s providing of legal services qualifies *C* for a share of the profits, but not for any credit in *C*'s capital account.)[75]
>
> *An Interim Return of Capital:* Soon after, by agreement, *B* receives $8,000 as a return of capital. The capital accounts would then stand at:
>
> | | |
> |---|---|
> | *A* | $14,000 |
> | *B* | 1,000 |
> | *C* | 0 |
>
> *Interim Capital Contributions:* The partnership later purchases the property subject to the purchase agreement, and *B* and *C* each contribute $2,000 in cash to be used toward the down payment. The capital accounts would then stand at:
>
> | | |
> |---|---|
> | *A* | $14,000 |
> | *B* | 3,000 |
> | *C* | 2,000 |

---

73. UPA §40(d). Absent a contrary agreement, partners share losses equally. UPA §18(a). See section 8.3.1.

74. 353 N.W.2d 709 (Neb. 1984).

75. UPA §18(f). See section 8.5.

Interim Losses: The next year the partnership suffers a $6,000 operating loss. The partners have no explicit agreement on loss sharing, so under UPA §18(a) they share losses "according to [their respective] share in the profits." The capital accounts would then stand at:

A	$12,000
B	1,000
C	0

Dissolution and Settling up Among the Partners: Later the partnership sells the real estate, making a profit of $46,000 on the sale. The partnership then dissolves, owing $3,000 to outside creditors. The sale profits are the partnership's only asset. Under UPA §40(b)(I), the "first" $3,000 of the $46,000 goes to pay the creditors. Then, under UPA §40(b)(III), A and B receive the value of their respective capital accounts. The three partners then divide the remaining $30,000 equally, according to their original agreement on sharing profits.

Assets of the partnership	$46,000
Less payment to creditors; per §40(b)(I)	(3,000)
Available prior to return of capital	43,000
Less discharge of A's capital account; per §40(b)(III)	(12,000)
Less discharge of B's capital account; per §40(b)(III)[76]	(1,000)
Remaining for distribution as profits; per §40(b)(IV)	30,000

Per agreement, each partner receives one third ($10,000) of the profits. Total payout per partner:

A	$22,000	(capital account of $12,000, plus profits of $10,000)
B	11,000	(capital account of $1,000, plus profits of $10,000)
C	10,000	(no capital to return; profits of $10,000)

Settling accounts following wrongful dissolution. If the business is being liquidated following a wrongful dissolution, the settling of accounts among the partners is the same as if the dissolution were rightful—except that the wrongfully dissolving partner's share may be decreased by the amount of damages due the other partners "for breach of the [partnership] agreement."[77]

---

76. The capital claims of A and B have equal priority.

77. UPA §§38(2)(c)(I) and (2)(a)(II). In addition, the wrongful dissolver has no right to wind up the partnership. UPA §37. See section 11.3.1.

§11.5.4 *Settling Accounts Among Partners When the Business Is Continued: Rightful Dissolution*

Settling accounts by express agreement.   For the partnership business to continue after dissolution, there must be some agreement among the partners. The agreement can be made before or after dissolution, and, if the dissolution is wrongful, need not include the wrongful dissolver. But some agreement there must be; the default mode is liquidation.[78]

The agreement that provides for the continuation of the business will normally govern how the partners will settle their accounts. Indeed, any business continuation agreement should at minimum address the following five topics:

i. the transfer of the rights and obligations of the dissolved partnership to the successor partnership;

ii. the conversion of the continuing partners' rights in the dissolved partnership to rights in the successor partnership;

iii. the compensation of the dissociated partner for that partner's rights in the dissolved partnership;

iv. the indemnification or (if possible) the release of the dissociated partner for debts of the dissolved partnership; and

v. the indemnification of the dissociated partner for debts of the successor partnership.

The possibility of a tacit agreement to continue the business.   If a partner rightfully dissociates from a partnership and fails to seek liquidation of the partnership business, a court may decide that the partner tacitly consented to a continuation of the business. One case found implied consent even though, throughout the period of supposed acquiescence, the dissociated partner sought to have the continuing partners buy out his interest. Such a result is not preordained, however. For example, in another case another court rejected the tacit consent argument even though liquidation was delayed for years following dissolution. During the delay a lawsuit was pending, challenging the partnership's ownership of important assets. The court treated the delay as a long, drawn-out wind up.

Compensating the dissociated partner.   A finding of tacit agreement does stave off liquidation but leaves open, among other issues, the question of how to compensate the dissociated partner.[79] The same issue exists when all the

---

78. See section 11.4.2 (partners' rights to compel liquidation).

79. In theory, a finding of tacit agreement also leaves open the question of what interests the continuing partners will have in the successor partnership. In practice, however, the conduct of the continuing partners often reflects an understanding on that point. If not, it seems reasonable to assume that the continuing partners intend their respective interests to be the same in the successor partnership as they were in the old.

partners expressly agree to continue the business but neglect the compensation issue.[80]

For these situations, UPA §42 provides a default rule, essentially treating the value of the dissociated partner's interest in the dissolved partnership as a loan to the successor partnership. Under UPA §42:

a. the value of the dissociated partner's interest in the dissolved partnership is calculated as of the date of dissolution;

b. as compensation for the business's use of that value from the date of dissolution to the date the successor partnership cashes out the dissociated partner, the dissociated partner receives (at the dissociated partner's election) either:

    i. interest on that value, or

    ii. a share of the profits attributable to the successor partnership's "use of [the dissociated partner's] right in the property of the dissolved partnership."

The language of UPA §42 leaves open at least seven important questions. The relevant case law is scarce, and much of the reasoning is muddy. Following are the seven troubling questions and the author's view of the answers.

1. How long may the successor partnership wait to cash out the dissociated partner? In some circumstances, the dissociated and continuing partners may expressly or impliedly agree on a pay-out deadline. If not, the law must give the successor partnership some breathing room. An obligation to immediately cash out the dissociated partner could force the continuing partners to liquidate the business in order to come up with the necessary cash.[81]

2. Must the successor partnership make interim payments to the dissociated partner pending the cash out? The cases do not contemplate interim payments, because they all involve actions for an accounting.[82] In each of these actions, the continuing partners had disputed the cash out amount and had made no interim payments. Nothing in the cases penalizes the continuing partners for failing to make interim payments. Nor does anything in the law prevent the partners from agreeing on interim payments.

3. When does the dissociated partner elect between the interest option and the profit sharing option? The dissociated partner may wait until an accounting reveals both the value of the partnership at dissolution and the value of the disso-

---

80. The same issue also exists when the business of a wrongfully dissolved partnership is continued without the agreement of the wrongful dissolver. See section 11.5.5.

81. The cases do not directly address this question, because they do not concern disputes about the timing of the cash out. Instead, they involve disputes relating to the amount of the payment due or whether any payment was due at all.

82. For an explanation of the action for an accounting, see section 9.10.

ciated partner's interest. If the dissociated partner has to bring an accounting action to obtain the cash out, then the dissociated partner can delay the election until the partner can determine which option will be the more lucrative. The dissociated partner's right to delay election creates an incentive for the continuing partners to cash out the dissociated partner as soon as possible.

4. May the dissociated partner change the election?   A representative of a deceased partner's estate may lack the authority to make a binding election before an accounting has revealed the value of the partnership and the value of the deceased partner's interest. Otherwise, it appears that a dissociated partner is stuck with the election once made. It does not make sense for a dissociated partner to make an election prior to cash out unless the continuing business is making interim payments.

5. How is the interest rate determined?   There is very little authority on this point. Among the arguable positions: the legal rate for interest on judgments, the legal rate for prejudgment interest, and the amount the successor partnership would have to pay to borrow funds in an arm's length transaction.

6. How is the profit share calculated?   The case law and commentaries indicate that the profit share equals the ratio of the value of the dissociated partner's interest in the partnership at dissolution to the value of the entire partnership at dissolution, regardless of the profit share enjoyed by the dissociated partner prior to dissolution.

> **Example:** When Sophie dissolves her used bookstore partnership with Charlotte and Paul, the partnership's net worth is $10,000 and Sophie's capital account is at $5,000. Sophie agrees that the business will be continued without liquidation but no agreement is made on compensating Sophie for her interest. If Sophie chooses the profit sharing option, her share of the successor partnership's profits will be 50 percent ($5000/$10,000), even though in the dissolved partnership the partners shared profits equally.

7. How long may the business continue before fully cashing out the dissociated partner?   Under the aegis of UPA §42 the successor partnership may continue the business indefinitely, subject of course to the power of the members of the successor partnership to dissolve that partnership. If the continuing partners do not pay the dissociated partner the cash out amount (plus interest or profit), then the dissociated partner can sue to collect the amount due. The dissociated partner can proceed against both the partners of the dissolved partnership and against the successor partnership and its members.[83] But the

---

83. See section 11.4.5.

dissociated partner will proceed "as an ordinary creditor"[84] and will therefore have no special rights to compel liquidation of the business of the successor partnership.

§11.5.5 Settling Accounts Among Partners When the Business Is Continued: Wrongful Dissolution

The default "package" for the wrongful dissolver. Following a wrongful dissolution, the partnership business may be continued either (i) by agreement of all of the partners or (ii) under UPA §38(2)(b), by the unanimous consent of the partners who did not wrongfully dissolve. In the former instance, the partners' agreement will likely set the pay-out rights of the wrongful dissolver. In the latter instance, UPA §38(2) provides the wrongful dissolver a compensation package consisting of three elements:

- the right (at the option of the continuing partners) either to be cashed out immediately or to be cashed out later (with the delayed payment guaranteed),
- the right to be protected against personal liability for partnership debts, and
- if the cash-out payment is not immediate, the right to compensation on account of the delay.

Calculating the cash-out amount. When the default package applies, UPA §38(2)(c)(II) requires that "the value of [the wrongful dissolver's] interest in the partnership" be ascertained. The calculation proceeds as if the dissolution were rightful,[85] with two important exceptions:

- "in ascertaining the value of the [wrongfully dissolving] partner's interest the value of the good-will of the business shall not be considered,"[86] and
- the value of the wrongful dissolver's interest is to be decreased by "any damages caused to his co-partners by the [wrongful] dissolution."[87]

Timing and securing the payment. If the wrongful dissolver has a large stake in the partnership, requiring immediate payment of the cash-out amount might interfere with or even preclude the continuation of the business. The UPA therefore allows the continuing partners an option. They can either pay the wrongful dissolver immediately, or they can delay payment until the end of the original term of the dissolved partnership.

---

84. UPA §42.
85. See section 11.5.4.
86. UPA §38(2)(c)(II).
87. Id.

If the continuing partners delay payment, they must "secure the payment by bond approved by the court."[88] That is, they must obtain a guarantee from a bonding company stating that, if the successor partnership fails to pay the cash out amount when due, the bonding company will make payment to the wrongful dissolver. The statute does not specify whether the bond must be for the full amount of the obligation and does not indicate whether the bond can require the wrongful dissolver to first try to collect from the members of the successor partnership. Presumably the court granting approval to a proposed bond would consider these matters.

Except for the bond, a wrongful dissolver awaiting payment has the status of "an ordinary creditor."[89] UPA §42 applies, and the wrongful dissolver appears to have no greater rights to interim payments than does any rightfully dissociated partner who becomes subject to that provision.[90]

Protecting the wrongful dissolver from partnership debts.   UPA §38(2)(b) plainly requires that the continuing partners "indemnify [the wrongful dissolver] against all . . . future partnership liabilities." The statute's approach to current liabilities is less clear. UPA §38(2)(b) requires indemnification "against all present . . . partnership liabilities," but UPA §38(2)(c) entitles the wrongful dissolver "to be released from all existing liabilities of the partnership." Neither the statute nor its official comments explain the inconsistent language. The major commentators note but do not resolve the problem.

From the perspective of the wrongful dissolver, the release approach is certainly superior. The indemnity does nothing to the underlying obligation; the obligee is still entitled to pursue the wrongful dissolver. The indemnity is therefore only as good as the solvency of the indemnitor.

From the perspective of the continuing partners, the release approach may be impractical. Generally, obligees are unwilling to release partners without receiving full payment or perhaps an increase in interest rates. After all, why should the obligee give up something—the right to pursue the wrongful dissolver—without getting something in return?

Rationale for protecting the wrongful dissolver from liability.   It makes sense for the continuing partners to protect the wrongful dissolver against future partnership liabilities, because the wrongful dissolver will have no part in the creation of those liabilities. At most, if the cash-out payment is delayed, the wrongful dissolver will relate to the continuing business as an ordinary creditor.

The rationale for protecting the wrongful dissolver against existing liabilities is more complex and is best explained with an Example.

---

88.   UPA §38(2)(b).

89.   UPA §42.

90.   See section 11.5.4 (UPA §42 governs when rightfully dissociated partner agrees to have the partnership business continue without liquidation but overlooks the compensation issue).

Example: George, Bernard, and Shaw form a partnership with a term of five years to sell widgets. They agree to share profits equally. After three years George wrongfully dissolves the partnership. Bernard and Shaw decide to continue the business under UPA §38(2).

The value of George's interest (the cash-out amount) must therefore be ascertained. The partnership's assets, other than good will,[91] are as follows:

Assets	
Cash	$50,000
Accounts Receivable	35,000
Orders in, but not yet billed	5,000
TOTAL	$90,000

Liabilities	
Loan due to the bank	$25,000
Accounts payable	5,000
TOTAL	$30,000

VALUE OF PARTNERSHIP: $90,000 − $30,000 =	$60,000

To keep the analysis as simple as possible, assume that none of the partners has anything in his capital account.[92] The $60,000 value is therefore all surplus (i.e., as yet undistributed profit) to be divided equally per the original partnership agreement. George's share is $20,000. This figure is reached by *subtracting liabilities from assets* and then dividing by 3. In effect, the $20,000 figure assumes that the partnership will pay its $30,000 in liabilities, and George's cash-out amount has been decreased by his share of those liabilities. In essence, therefore, George has already "paid" his share. He should be protected against having to pay again.

§11.6 Avoiding UPA Dissolution by Agreement (A Specious Idea)

According to the language of the UPA, certain events automatically and inevitably cause dissolution. Under UPA §31(4), for example, "Dissolution is caused . . . by the death of any partner." Under UPA §31(1)(d) the expulsion of a partner under a power conferred by the partnership agreement likewise causes dissolution. Unlike many other provisions of the UPA, these provisions are not by their terms subject to contrary agreement by the partners.

---

91. Good will is excluded from the calculation. UPA §38(2)(c)(II). See above in this section.

92. For an explanation of capital accounts, see section 11.5.3.

Despite any partnership agreement to the contrary, the occurrence of the specified event triggers dissolution.

Nonetheless, some partnership agreements seek to avoid disruption to the partnership business by ignoring the statutory language. These agreements provide that the dissociation of a partner does not cause dissolution.

> *Example:* The law firm of Tinkers, Evers, and Chance has a partnership agreement which provides, in part:
>
> > Neither the death, retirement, resignation, or withdrawal of any partner shall dissolve this partnership but the partnership will buy out the dissociated partner's interest in the partnership as provided in paragraph Z of this agreement.

Although there are cases upholding these agreements in disputes among the partners, such agreements are dangerous. The conflict between the language of the agreement and the language of the statute invites litigation.

Moreover, ignoring the UPA's approach to dissolution subjects the dissociated partner to an added risk of personal liability if the partnership business continues. The UPA provides a panoply of protections for the dissociated partner, but all those protections revolve around the concept of dissolution:

   i. UPA §§33 and 34 end the actual authority (though not the power) of the continuing partners to bind the dissolved partnership (and thereby the dissociated partner) on obligations related to new business.[93]
   ii. UPA §35 limits the power of the continuing partners to bind the dissolved partnership (and thereby the dissociated partner).[94]
   iii. UPA §36 provides, under certain circumstances, for the dissociated partner to be discharged from personal liability for debts of the dissolved partnership.[95]
   iv. UPA §15 imposes personal liability on the dissociated partner only for the debts of the dissolved partnership and not for the debts of any successor partnership.[96]

If dissolution does not occur, these protections do not arise.

The answer for partners trying to avoid business disruption is to provide for rather than preclude dissolution. A well-drafted partnership agreement ensures continuity by providing for the partnership business to be continued even as the partnership itself is wound up and terminated.[97]

---

93. See section 11.3.1.

94. See section 11.3.2.

95. See section 11.5.2.

96. See section 7.3 (partner's personal liability results from status as a partner in the partnership).

97. See section 11.4.3.

§11.7 Wrongful Dissolution Without Breach of Agreement

§11.7.1 Wrongful Dissolution of a Partnership at Will

As indicated so far throughout this chapter, under the UPA the distinction between rightful and wrongful dissolution has great significance. The simplest and clearest example of a wrongful dissolution is dissolution "[i]n contravention of the agreement between the partners . . . by the express will of any partner."[98] For instance, a partner who purposely withdraws from a term partnership before the end of the term is a wrongful dissolver.[99]

It might seem impossible to have a wrongful dissolution of a partnership at will. After all, the essence of an at-will partnership is that every partner has the right as well as the power to dissolve the partnership at any time. Yet a few cases have held to the contrary. These cases all involved egregious situations, in which the dissolution either made possible a substantial and unfair economic advantage for the dissolving partner or threatened significant and unfair economic disadvantage to the other partners.

The cases that have granted relief have dealt with the at-will issue in one of two ways: (i) by finding an implied agreement for a particular term or undertaking, or (ii) by holding that partners have an implied agreement not to injure each other through breach of fiduciary duty. *Vangel v. Vangel*,[100] for example, considered a partnership formed by three brothers to purchase and operate a citrus ranch. One brother was unable to furnish his share of the down payment for the ranch, so the other two brothers advanced his share. The borrower was to repay his brothers "only out of funds accumulated from the operation of the ranch or realized from its sale."[101] The court acknowledged that the partnership agreement "does not mention the term of the partnership."[102] It held, however, that the borrowing arrangement "seems to negate any idea of a partnership at will for it cannot be assumed that it was the intention of the parties that the borrower was at liberty to walk out of the partnership until the loan had been repaid from either the operation or the sale of the ranch."[103] This holding meant that the partnership was for a particular undertaking[104] and made the dissolution premature and wrongful.

---

98. UPA §31(2).

99. The dissolution is not wrongful, however, if the partner dissociates through death or bankruptcy. UPA §§31(4) and 31(5).

100. 254 P.2d 919, 925 (Cal. App. 1953), *appeal (on other grounds) after remand*, 282 P.2d 907 (Cal. App.), *rev'd in part and aff'd in part*, 291 P.2d 25 (Cal. App. 1955).

101. 254 P.2d at 921.

102. Id. at 925.

103. Id.

104. UPA §31(1)(a). The undertaking was the paying off of the loan.

Other decisions have gone further, implying a fiduciary duty limit on dissolution even in partnerships that are genuinely at will. *Page v. Page*[105] is perhaps the leading case. It involved a linen supply partnership, which after eight unprofitable years seemed about to turn the corner; the air force had established a base in the vicinity. Just then, one of the partners dissolved the partnership. The other partner feared that his own weak financial position and lack of management experience in the business would enable the dissolving partner to pick up the business of the dissolved partnership without providing fair compensation.

The California Supreme Court rejected the claim that the partnership had an implied term to continue until the losses of previous years had been recouped. It held instead that:

> If . . . it is proved that [the dissolving partner] acted in bad faith and violated his fiduciary duties by attempting to appropriate to his own use the new prosperity of the partnership without adequate compensation to his co-partner, the dissolution would be wrongful and the [dissolving partner] would be liable under [the California equivalent of UPA §38(2)(a)] (rights of partners upon wrongful dissolution) for violation of the implied agreement not to exclude defendant wrongfully from the partnership business opportunity.[106]

§11.7.2 *Wrongful versus Rightful Dissolution in the Context of Expulsion*

Under UPA §31(1)(d), "the expulsion of any partner from the business bona fide in accordance with such a power conferred by the agreement between the partners" automatically dissolves the partnership. Such dissolution is ordinarily rightful, even if the agreement allows "no cause" expulsion.[107]

Example: The partnership agreement among nine physicians who practice medicine together states in part:

> *Expulsion:* A partner will be expelled from the partnership if six of the partners vote to expel that partner. There is no requirement that the partners voting for expulsion state a reason or give the expelled partner an opportunity to be heard. The expulsion will take effect when notice of the vote is given the expelled partner. As full compensation for his or her interest in the partnership, the expelled partner will receive an amount determined under Paragraph X of this Agreement.

---

105. 359 P.2d 41 (Ca. 1961) (en banc).

106. Id. at 45.

107. Under most no-cause provisions, the expelling partners need not even state a reason, or give the expelled partner an opportunity to be heard. They just have to prove that the agreed upon number of partners voted for expulsion.

Although such "guillotine" provisions may at first glance seem harsh, they rest on a solid rationale. The success of a partnership often depends on the ability of the partners to work together. If, as sometimes happens, one of the partners becomes troublesome or is otherwise undermining the business, an expulsion provision allows the partnership to save the business without destroying it.[108]

The "no cause" aspect of an expulsion provision can be very important, because otherwise the partnership may have to go through the time-consuming, costly, and bitter process of proving partner misconduct. No-cause provisions help avoid litigation (what is there to litigate about?) and allow for the immediate, surgical removal of a problem partner. No-cause provisions also reflect the idea that if—for whatever reason—most of the partners decide they no longer want to work with one of their colleagues, then that decision by itself is adequate reason to separate the unwanted partner from the business.

The notion of wrongful "no-cause" expulsion. In a few reported cases, expelled partners have challenged their expulsion as wrongful, asserting that the expelling partners have breached fiduciary duty by acting either in bad faith or without "due process." These challenges have generally failed, with the courts holding either that the plain language of the partnership agreement allows no-cause expulsion or that the expelled partner has failed to prove bad faith.

A claim for wrongful dissolution might exist if an expelled partner could prove the type of expropriating bad faith contemplated in *Page,* supra. *Page* involved dissolution of an at-will partnership rather than no-cause expulsion, but the situations seem analogous. The rationale that led the *Page* court to constrain a partner's seemingly absolute discretion to dissolve an at-will partnership might apply to constrain partners' seemingly absolute discretion to vote expulsion.

For very large partnerships and those with very "junior" (i.e., powerless) partners, there may be another constraint as well. If the expelled partner is a member of a protected class, he or she may be able to contest the expulsion under federal and state anti-discrimination laws. These statutes generally protect "employees," and, formally at least, partners are not employees. However, the larger the partnership and the more junior the partner, the more the situation resembles employment. Most of the cases raising this issue have involved large law and accounting firms and large brokerage houses, and the courts have focussed primarily on the amount of management authority and responsibility enjoyed by the partner claiming employee status. So far most decisions have gone against the plaintiff, but the courts' analysis has left the door open.[109]

---

108. To be useful, the provision must be accompanied by an agreement allowing the remaining partners to continue the business of the old partnership. Otherwise, unless the continuing partners can get the expelled partner released from personal liability on the debts of the dissolved partnership, the expelled partner will have the right to force liquidation of the business. UPA §38(1). See section 11.4.2, n.43. Getting the expelled partner released from liability may be very difficult. See section 11.5.2.

109. See Daniel S. Kleinberger, Magnificent Circularity and the Churkendoose: LLC Members and Federal Employment Law, 22 Okla. City U.L. Rev. 477 (1997), reprinted at 40 Corporate Practice Commentator 379 (1998).

§11.8   Judicial Dissolution

UPA §32 provides several bases for a court to "decree a dissolution." The most interesting are UPA §§31(1)(d) and (e) and UPA §31(2). UPA §32(1)(d) makes dissolution by decree of court available on "application by or for a partner" when another "partner willfully or persistently commits a breach of the partnership agreement, or otherwise so conducts himself in matters relating to the partnership business that it is not reasonably practicable to carry on the business in partnership with him." UPA §32(1)(e) permits a partner to apply for judicial dissolution when "[t]he business of the partnership can only be carried on at a loss."

UPA §31(2) permits "a purchaser of a partner's interest" (i.e., an assignee or a person who has purchased through a foreclosure of a charging order) to petition for dissolution "(a) [a]fter the termination of the specified term or particular undertaking, [and] (b) [a]t any time if the partnership was a partnership at will when the interest was assigned or when the charging order was issued." The rationale seems to be that a third party's right to a liquidating distribution "vests" when the third party acquires the interest (or, in the case of a charging order, acquires the equivalent of a lien on the interest).[110]

§11.9   RUPA—Foundational Notions

§11.9.1 Four Foundational Concepts

Although RUPA's provisions on partner dissociation and partnership dissolution are as elaborate as the UPA's, RUPA's approach is simpler to follow because it tilts *toward* continuity and away from dissolution. RUPA's approach rests on four major concepts:

- The dissociation of a RUPA partner does *not* necessarily cause the dissolution of a RUPA partnership.
- RUPA contains a "switching provision"[111]—if a partner's dissociation results in dissolution, the "switch" activates Article 8 (dissolution and winding up); if not, the "switch" activates Article 7 (buy out of dissociated partner and continuation of the partnership).
- RUPA provides for statements of dissociation and dissolution, the public filing of which significantly affects power-to-bind and personal liability issues.

---

110. This rationale corresponds to contract law principles pertaining to assignment. See, e.g., Restatement (Second) of Contracts §338(1) ("Discharge of an Obligor After Assignment . . . [N]otwithstanding an assignment, the assignor retains his power to discharge or modify the duty of the obligor to the extent that the obligor performs or otherwise gives value until but not after the obligor receives notification that the right has been assigned and that performance is to be rendered to the assignee").

111. RUPA §603, Comment 1 (describing RUPA §603(a)).

- Almost all of RUPA's provisions on dissociation and dissolution are subject to change by the partnership agreement, making it possible for a RUPA partnership to be almost as indissoluble as a corporation.

§11.9.2 Dissociation Described

Events causing dissociation. Under RUPA, partner dissociation is a pivotal term and carries forward a UPA concept—namely, that "any partner ceasing to be associated in the carrying on as distinguished from the winding up of the [partnership's] business" is an event significant both to the partner and the partnership.[112] RUPA does not directly define "dissociation," but RUPA §603 lists ten events "upon the occurrence" of which a "partner is dissociated from a partnership." The ten events divide roughly into four categories:[113]

1. "the partnership's having notice of the partner's express will to withdraw as a partner or on a later date specified by the partner";[114]
2. an event specified in the partnership agreement as causing dissociation;[115]
3. expulsion
   a. as provided in the partnership agreement;[116]
   b. by unanimous vote of the other partners; if
      i. it is unlawful to carry on the business with the to-be-expelled partner,[117]
      ii. the partner being expelled no longer has any economic stake in the business, because "there has been a transfer of all or substantially all of that partner's transferable interest in the partnership,"[118] or
      iii. the partner being expelled is a corporation or partnership which has lost its right to take on new business;[119]

---

112. UPA §29. The significance to the partnership is that dissociation can result in dissolution. See section 11.9.3. The connection between dissociation and dissolution reflects the aggregate view of partnership. See sections 7.2.7 and 13.3 (discussing the "continuity of life" factor under the now-defunct Kintner Regulations on tax classification).

113. If subcategories are counted separately, there are 20 separate circumstances.

114. RUPA §601(1). "Notice" is a defined term. See RUPA §102(b), discussed in section 10.6.1.

115. RUPA §601(2).

116. RUPA §601(3). "The expulsion can be with or without cause. As under existing law [i.e., the UPA], the obligation of good faith under Section 404(d) does not require prior notice, specification of cause, or an opportunity to be heard." RUPA §601, Comment 4.

117. RUPA §601(4)(i).

118. RUPA §601(4)(ii). RUPA §503(a)(2) is not to the contrary. It provides that the transfer of a partner's transferable interest "does not *by itself* cause the partner's dissociation." (Emphasis added.)

119. RUPA §601(4)(iii).

  c. by court order, if the partner being expelled has engaged in seriously wrongful conduct;[120]

 4. the partner's ability to participate in the partnership affairs comes to an end, or the partner's economic stake in the partnership comes to an end,[121] including

  a. the partner becoming a debtor in bankruptcy or taking other, non-bankruptcy actions which indicate insolvency;[122]

  b. if the partner is an individual, the individual's ability to participate in partnership affairs coming to an end, either by:

   i. death, or

   ii. mental incompetency, as indicated either by:

    (1) "the appointment of a guardian or general conservator," or

    (2) "a judicial determination that the partner has otherwise become incapable of performing the partner's duties under the partnership agreement";[123]

  c. if the partner is a trust or estate, its economic stake in the partnership coming to an end by the distribution (typically to the beneficiaries) of the partner's "entire transferable interest in the partnership";[124]

  d. "termination of a partner who is not an individual, partnership, corporation, trust, or estate."[125]

Example: Dardale Company is a RUPA general partnership, with three partners: Amos, Eli and Alan. The partnership is at-will, and the partnership agreement does not alter RUPA's provisions on dissociation. Following an intense meeting of the partners, Amos is walking home with Eli and says, "I'm tired of all this nonsense. I'm done. I quit." At that moment, Amos is dissociated. Eli has notice of Amos's "express will," RUPA §102(b)(1) (defining "notice" to include knowledge), and notice to a partner is notice to the partnership. RUPA §102(f).[126] Therefore, "the partnership [has] notice of [Amos's] express will to withdraw as a partner."

Example: Same situation, except that Dardale Company is a partnership formed for a particular term or undertaking. Amos is dissociated, although the dissociation may be wrongful (as explained below).

---

120. RUPA §601(5).

121. RUPA §§601(6)-(10). RUPA uses this category in its definition of wrongful dissociation, RUPA §602(b)(2)(i) (discussed below), and in its provision on partnership dissolution, RUPA §801(2)(i), discussed in section 11.11.

122. RUPA §601(6).

123. RUPA §601(7).

124. RUPA §§601(8) and (9).

125. RUPA §601(10). Note that RUPA treats partnerships and corporations differently than estates, trusts, and other non-individual legal persons.

126. See section 10.6.1.

Example: Same situation, except that instead of quitting, Amos sells his entire transferable interest to Paul. Amos is not dissociated. However, if Alan and Eli vote to expel Amos, he will be expelled and thereby dissociated. RUPA §601(4)(ii). Paul does not have a vote, because he is not a partner. RUPA §§401(i) (person becomes a partner only with the consent of all the partners)[127] and 503(a)(3) (transferee has no rights in management).[128]

Consequences of dissociation, whether wrongful or rightful, whether or not dissolution results. Many of the consequences of partner dissociation depend on whether the dissociation is wrongful or rightful and on whether dissolution results from the dissociation. One consequence applies regardless—"the partner's duty of loyalty [not to compete with the partnership before dissolution] terminates."[129]

Rightful versus wrongful dissociation. RUPA §602(b) expressly defines and carefully delimits "wrongful" dissociation:

(b) A partner's dissociation is wrongful only if:

(1) it is in breach of an express provision of the partnership agreement; or

(2) in the case of a partnership for a definite term or particular undertaking, before the expiration of the term or the completion of the undertaking:

(i) the partner withdraws by express will, unless the withdrawal follows within 90 days after another partner's dissociation by death or otherwise under Section 601(6) through (10) [dissociation because either the partner's ability to participate in the partnership affairs has come to an end, or the partner's economic stake in the partnership has come to an end] or wrongful dissociation under this subsection;

(ii) the partner is expelled by judicial determination under Section 601(5);

(iii) the partner is dissociated by becoming a debtor in bankruptcy; or

(iv) in the case of a partner who is not an individual, trust other than a business trust, or estate, the partner is expelled or otherwise dissociated because it willfully dissolved or terminated.

Example: Dardale Company is a RUPA general partnership, with four partners: Amos, Eli, Alan, and Paul. The partnership is for a term of ten

---

127. See section 9.5.
128. See section 8.8.4.
129. RUPA §603(b)(2).

years, and the partnership agreement does not alter RUPA's provisions on dissociation. Following an intense meeting of the partners, Amos is walking home with Eli and says, "I'm tired of all this nonsense. I'm done. I quit." Amos's dissociation is wrongful, because it occurs "by express will" of a partner "before the expiration of the term" of the partnership. RUPA §602(2)(b)(i).

Example: As soon as Alan learns that Amos has quit, Alan announces that he is also quitting. Like Amos's dissociation, Alan's dissociation comes before the expiration of the partnership's term. However, Alan's dissociation is not wrongful, because it comes "within 90 days after another partner's . . . wrongful dissociation." RUPA §602(2)(b)(i).

RUPA §602(b) effectively rejects cases like *Page* and *Vangel*.[130] Under RUPA, a dissociation is not wrongful merely because it constitutes a breach of fiduciary duty or the obligation of good faith and fair dealing. Such a breach may be separately actionable, but the consequences that attach to "wrongful dissociation" do not apply.

Consequences of wrongful dissociation.   There are several consequences when a partner wrongfully dissociates:

- the wrongfully dissociated partner "is liable to the partnership and to the other partners for damages caused by the dissociation";[131]
- in a partnership for a term or undertaking, the dissociation creates the possibility of partnership dissolution, which occurs if "within 90 days after a partner's . . . wrongful dissociation . . . the express will of at least half of the remaining partners [is] to wind up the partnership business";[132]
- if the partnership continues (i.e., does not dissolve), the wrongfully dissociated partner is not entitled to any payout until the end of the original term "unless the partner establishes to the satisfaction of the court that earlier payment will not cause undue hardship to the business of the partnership"; and[133]
- if the dissociation results in dissolution of the partnership, the wrongfully dissociated has no right to participate in winding up.[134]

Example: Amos's premature and wrongful departure from the Dardale Company causes the partnership to have to hire an employee to provide the technical expertise that Amos had been providing. Dardale's cost for this employee exceeds what Amos was receiving as a partner. The extra

---

130. See section 11.7.1.
131. RUPA §602(c).
132. RUPA §801(2)(i).
133. RUPA §701(h), discussed in section 11.10.5.
134. RUPA §803(a), discussed in section 11.11.

expense puts the partnership into a "cash poor" situation. Amos is liable in damages to the partnership to the extent of the extra expense.[135] Moreover, Amos is not entitled to any payout until the end of the original term.[136]

Power of partnership agreement over dissociation. With only two exceptions, RUPA §601 is a default rule. The partnership agreement can change or omit each of the listed causes of dissociation, except that the partnership may not eliminate a partner's power to dissociate[137] nor vary the right of a court to expel a partner.[138] As a result, the partnership agreement can dramatically restrict the circumstances under which a partner may exit a RUPA partnership.

In addition, as explained in Comment 2 to RUPA §602, because RUPA §602(b) is also "merely a default rule, the partnership agreement may eliminate or expand the dissociations that are wrongful or modify the effects of wrongful dissociation."

§11.9.3 The Nexus Between Partner Dissociation and Partnership Dissolution

Under the UPA, the dissociation of any partner inevitably causes dissolution.[139] The situation under RUPA is dramatically different. First, the statutory provisions that connect partner dissociation and partnership dissolution are merely default rules. The partnership agreement can sever the nexus completely, or to any lesser extent the partners desire. Second, even with the default rules in place, not every dissociation causes dissolution. Dissolution follows dissociation only in two circumstances:

- in an at-will partnership, the "express will" dissociation of a partner who has not been previously dissociated through some other cause[140]
- in a partnership for a term or undertaking

---

135. RUPA §602, Comment 3: "The partnership might also incur substantial expenses resulting from a partner's premature withdrawal from a term partnership, such as replacing the partner's expertise or obtaining new financing."

136. RUPA §701(h). If Amos has not previously paid the partnership for the damage caused by his wrongful association, the damage amount will be offset against his payout. RUPA §701(c).

137. RUPA §103(b)(6).

138. RUPA §103(b)(7). Despite this restriction, under federal law, a partnership agreement can probably subject expulsion matters to arbitration. "Any other interpretation would put this Act at odds with federal law. See Southland Corp. v. Keating, 465 U.S. 1 (1984) (holding that the Federal Arbitration Act preempts state statutes that seek to invalidate agreements to arbitrate) and Allied-Bruce Terminix Cos., Inc. v. Dobson, 513 U.S. 265 (1995) (same)." Uniform Limited Partnership Act (2001), §110, Comment to Subsection (b)(9) (discussing a comparable provision).

139. See section 11.2.1.

140. RUPA §801(1).

—"the express will of at least half of the remaining partners to wind up the partnership business"

—manifested "within 90 days after a[nother] partner's dissociation by death or otherwise under Section 601(6) through (10)[141] or wrongful dissociation under Section 602(b)"[142]

Example: The Sachs Company is a RUPA at-will partnership, whose partners are Todd, Teri, Mikki, and Samantha. After Todd transfers his entire transferable interest to Jeff, the remaining partners vote unanimously to expel Todd. Todd has no right to cause dissolution of The Sachs Company.

Example: The Sachs Company is a RUPA partnership, with a term of ten years. Its partners are Todd, Teri, Mikki, and Samantha. Todd quits the partnership, and two weeks later Teri, Mikki, and Samantha meet to decide what to do with the partnership. Mikki and Samantha vote to dissolve, and Teri votes to continue. The partnership is dissolved.

§11.9.4 The "Switching Provision"—RUPA §603(a)

Different consequences follow from a partner's dissociation, depending on whether the dissociation results in dissolution of the partnership. RUPA §603(a) segregates those consequences from each other by functioning as a switching provision: "If a partner's dissociation results in a dissolution and winding up of the partnership business, [Article] 8 applies; otherwise, [Article] 7 applies."

Example: The Sachs Company is a RUPA partnership, with a term of ten years. Its partners are Todd, Jeff, Teri, Mikki, and Samantha. Todd quits the partnership, but during the next 90 days the remaining partners do not vote to dissolve the partnership. A few months later, as permitted by RUPA §801(2)(ii),[143] all the remaining partners unanimously vote to dissolve the partnership. Todd wishes to be involved in winding up the partnership, but he has no right to be. Even assuming Todd's dissociation was not wrongful, RUPA §803(a) is the only provision permitting a dissociated partner to participate in winding up. That provision is not available to Todd, because it is part of RUPA's [Article] 8. That Article applies to Todd only if *his* "dissociation results in a dissolution and winding up of the partnership business."

---

141. These provisions refer to dissociation which occurs either because the partner's ability to participate in partnership affairs has come to an end, or the partner's economic stake in the partnership has come to an end.

142. RUPA §801(2)(i).

143. This provision is discussed in section 11.11.

§11.10 Dissociation That Does Not Cause Dissolution

§11.10.1 Overview

When a partner's dissociation does not result in partnership dissolution, the partnership business continues without interruption and the partnership itself continues as the same entity that existed before the dissociation. The dissociated partner has no further role in management[144] and no further fiduciary duties.[145] A dissociated partner does, however, have a lingering power to bind the partnership and, unless the partnership is an LLP, a lingering exposure to personal liability for future partnership obligations. Unless the partnership agreement provides otherwise, the partnership must cause the dissociated partner's interest to be bought out at a price determined under a statutory formula and must indemnify the dissociated partner against all partnership liabilities. Subject to an exception derived from the UPA, the dissociation does not discharge the dissociated partner from liability for partnership obligations.

§11.10.2 Statement of Dissociation

As part of its system of public filings,[146] RUPA provides for the filing of a statement of dissociation, "stating the name of the partnership and that the partner is dissociated from the partnership."[147] Either the dissociated partner or the partnership may file the statement.[148] If filed by the partner, the statement must be executed by that partner.[149] If filed by the partnership, the statement "must be executed by at least two partners."[150]

If properly filed, a statement of dissociation functions as a statement limiting the authority of the dissociated partner[151] and, in addition, gives constructive notice of the partner's dissociation.[152] As with statements of authority under RUPA §303, statements of dissociation are to be filed "in the office of [the Secretary of State]."[153] For a statement of dissociation to have its full effect with regard to real property owned in the name of the partnership,

---

144. RUPA §603(b)(1).

145. RUPA §§603(b)(2) and (3).

146. See section 10.3.5.

147. RUPA §704(a).

148. Id.

149. RUPA §105(c).

150. Id.

151. See sections 10.3.5 and 11.10.3.

152. See sections 11.10.3 and 11.10.4 for the operative significance of this constructive notice.

153. RUPA §105(a). The brackets indicate NCCUSL's recognition that in some states the central filing office is not the Secretary of State.

"a certified copy of a filed statement . . . [must be] of record in the office for recording transfers of that real property."[154]

As soon as that recording is done, the dissociated partner loses all power to transfer real property owned in the name of the partnership.[155] With regard to any other lingering power of the dissociated partner to bind the partnership and any lingering exposure the dissociated partner may have to personal liability for future partnership obligations, "a person not a partner is deemed to have notice of the dissociation 90 days after the statement of dissociation is filed" with the Secretary of State.[156]

§11.10.3 Dissociated Partner's Lingering Power to Bind

When a partner dissociates and the partnership does not dissolve, the dissociated partner loses any "right to participate in the management and conduct of the partnership business."[157] However, consistent with notions of apparent authority, a dissociated partner's "apparently/ordinary" power to bind the partnership lingers after the dissociation and can continue for up to two years. Under RUPA §702(a), a dissociated partner's act binds the partnership if:

- before the dissociation the act would have bound the partnership under RUPA §301; and
- at the time the other party enters into the transaction:
  —less than two years has passed since the dissociation;
  —the other party does not have notice of the dissociation and reasonably believes that the dissociated partner is still a partner;
  —fewer than 90 days have passed since the filing of a statement of dissociation;[158] and
  —if the transaction involves the transfer of real property owned in the name of the partnership, "a certified copy of [a] filed statement . . . [of dissociation is not] of record in the office for recording transfers of that real property."[159]

Example: The Ofek-Noam Company ("the Company") is a RUPA general partnership that purchases land and subdivides it for sale to home builders. The Company has three partners—Suzanne, Eli, and Gili— and for years all three have acted for the partnership in selling land to

---

154. RUPA §303(e).

155. RUPA §704(b).

156. RUPA §704(c). For a detailed explanation of how this notice curtails the power to bind and personal liability, see sections 11.10.3 and 11.10.4, respectively.

157. RUPA §603(b)(1).

158. "For the purposes of [terminating a dissociated partner's lingering power to bind the partnership], a person not a partner is deemed to have notice of the dissociation 90 days after the statement of dissociation is filed." RUPA §704(c).

159. RUPA §303(e), referred to by RUPA §702(a)(3).

home builders. The partnership has filed a statement of authority with the Secretary of State, indicating that each partner has the authority to transfer land owned in the name of the partnership. The partnership owns a large parcel of land in Dakota County, and a certified copy of the statement of authority has been recorded with the Dakota County Registrar of Deeds.

Acting pursuant to the partnership agreement, Gili and Suzanne expel Eli from the partnership. They then execute and file a statement of dissociation with the Secretary of State and record a certified copy of the statement with the Dakota County Registrar of Deeds. Two days later, Eli purports to enter into a contract to sell some of the Dakota land to a home building firm. The Company is not bound, even if the firm could establish that Eli's act "would have bound the partnership under Section 301 before [the] dissociation" of Eli.[160] "A statement of dissociation is a limitation on the authority of a dissociated partner for the purposes of Section 303 . . . (e.)" Therefore, RUPA §702(a)(3) bars the firm's claim because the firm "is deemed to have knowledge [of the limitation of Eli's authority] under Section 303(e)."

Example: A month after his expulsion, Eli purports to buy a new car for the Ofek-Noam Company. The Company has regularly purchased company cars from this particular dealer, and often Eli has acted for the Company. The dealer has no idea that Eli has been expelled from the partnership. Eli purchases the car on credit, takes a $1500 "manufacturer's incentive" in cash, and takes delivery of the car. The Company is bound. Before the dissociation Eli's act would have bound the Company under RUPA §301, the dealer had neither knowledge nor notice of Eli's dissociation, the transaction does not involve real property owned in the name of the Company, and fewer than 90 days have passed since the partnership filed the statement of dissociation.

Example: Same facts as the immediately prior Example, except that the transaction occurs 91 days after the filing of the statement of dissociation. The partnership is not bound.

A partner's lingering power to bind has nothing to do with actual authority. If the act of a dissociated partner binds the partnership, the "dissociated partner is liable to the partnership for any damage caused to the partnership arising from [the] obligation."[161] Like the lingering power itself, this liability is consistent with agency law principles.[162]

---

160. RUPA §702(a).
161. RUPA §702(b).
162. See section 4.1.2 (agent liable to principal for acting without authority).

§11.10.4 *Dissociated Partner's Liability for Partnership Obligations*

Partnership obligations incurred before dissociation.   In this context, RUPA continues much of the UPA approach:

> A partner's dissociation does not of itself discharge the partner's liability for a partnership obligation incurred before dissociation. . . . A dissociated partner is released from liability for a partnership obligation if a partnership creditor, with notice of the partner's dissociation but without the partner's consent, agrees to a material alteration in the nature or time of payment of a partnership obligation.[163]

Partnership obligations incurred after dissociation—lingering liability. Because third parties may deal with a partnership believing that a dissociated partner is still a partner, RUPA §703(b) creates a "lingering liability" rule whose structure mirrors the structure of the rule creating a lingering power to bind. Under RUPA §703(b), a "partner who dissociates without resulting in a dissolution and winding up of the partnership business is liable as a partner to the other party in a [post-dissociation] transaction" if at the time the other party enters into the transaction:

- the partnership is not an LLP,
- less than two years has passed since the dissociation,
- the other party does not have notice of the dissociation and reasonably believes that the dissociated partner is a still a partner,
- fewer than 90 days have passed since the filing of a statement of dissociation, and
- if the transaction involves the transfer of real property owned in the name of the partnership, "a certified copy of the filed statement . . . [is not] of record in the office for recording transfers of that real property"[164]

Example: Four months after expelling Eli from the Ofek-Noam Company, the Company sells to a home builder a lot from the Company's Dakota County parcel, giving a warranty deed. The builder has previously dealt with the Company and believes Eli to be one of the partners. Eli is liable for the partnership obligations created by the warranty deed.

Example: Same situation, except that a week after being expelled Eli executes and files with the Secretary of State a statement of dissociation. He is not liable for the partnership obligations created by the warranty deed. A "person not a partner is deemed to have notice of the dissociation 90 days after the statement of dissociation is filed." RUPA §704(c).

---

163. RUPA §703(a) and (d). For the UPA approach, see section 11.5.2.
164. RUPA §303(e), referred to by RUPA §703(b)(3).

As result, Eli is protected under RUPA §703(b)(3); the home builder "is . . . deemed to have had notice under Section 704(c)."

As part of the mandatory buyout discussed below, a dissociated partner is entitled to be indemnified "against all partnership liabilities, whether incurred before or after the dissociation," except for partnership liabilities that result from the dissociated partner's lingering power to bind.[165]

§11.10.5 *Buyout of the Dissociated Partner*

Dissociated partner's entitlement. If a partner's dissociation does not result in dissolution, RUPA §701 provides as a default rule that the dissociated partner is entitled to be bought out: "the partnership shall cause the dissociated partner's interest in the partnership to be purchased." Unless otherwise provided in the partnership agreement, "[t]he buyout is mandatory. The 'cause to be purchased' language is intended to accommodate a purchase by the partnership, one or more of the remaining partners, or a third party."[166]

Determining the buyout price. RUPA §701(b) and (c) provide the default rule for determining the buyout price:

- assume the partnership was terminated on the date of dissociation[167]
- calculate the amount the partnership would have received for its assets on that date, both through liquidating those assets piecemeal and through a "sale of the entire business as a going concern"[168]
- using the higher of those two values, calculate the amount that would have been due the dissociated partner (taking into account all liabilities of the partnership)[169]
- subtract from that amount any "[d]amages for wrongful dissociation . . . and all other amounts owing, whether or not presently due, from the dissociated partner to the partnership"[170]

---

165. The indemnification obligation makes sense because (i) the buy out price presupposes the payment of all existing liabilities, and (ii) the dissociated partner should be not accountable for liabilities incurred after he, she or it ceases to be a partner. For more discussion of the first rationale, see section 11.5.5 (discussing the point in the context of UPA §38(2)).

166. RUPA §701, Comment 2.

167. RUPA §701(b).

168. RUPA §701(b). "Liquidation value is not intended to mean distress sale value. Under general principles of valuation, the hypothetical selling price in either case should be the price that a willing and informed buyer would pay a willing and informed seller, with neither being under any compulsion to deal. . . . UPA Section 38(2)(c)(II) provides that the good will of the business not be considered in valuing a wrongfully dissociating partner's interest. The forfeiture of good will rule is implicitly rejected by RUPA." RUPA §701, Comment 3.

169. RUPA §702(b).

170. RUPA §701(c).

- add to that amount interest "from the date of dissociation to the date of payment"[171]

Timing of and tendering the payment.   If the partnership is for a term or undertaking and the dissociation was premature and wrongful, the partnership is presumptively entitled to defer payment:

> A partner who wrongfully dissociates before the expiration of a definite term or the completion of a particular undertaking is not entitled to payment of any portion of the buyout price until the expiration of the term or completion of the undertaking, unless the partner establishes to the satisfaction of the court that earlier payment will not cause undue hardship to the business of the partnership. A deferred payment must be adequately secured and bear interest.[172]

In all other situations, unless otherwise agreed, the partnership "shall pay, or caused to be paid, in cash" its estimate of the buy out price "120 days after a written demand for payment."[173]

The payment must be accompanied by specified financial information, "an explanation of how the estimated amount . . . was calculated" and a written notice warning that the estimate becomes final unless "within 120 days . . . the dissociated partner commences an action to determine the buyout price."[174] If the partnership is exercising its right to defer payment, it must provide the same information (including the warning) together with "a written offer to pay the amount it estimates to be the buyout price . . . stating the time of payment, the amount and type of security for payment, and the other terms and conditions of the obligation."[175]

Power of the partnership agreement.   Section 701 is entirely subject to the partnership agreement:

> The Section 701 rules are merely default rules. The partners may, in the partnership agreement, fix the method or formula for determining the buyout price and all of the other terms and conditions of the buyout right. Indeed, the very right to a buyout itself may be modified, although a provision providing for a complete forfeiture would probably not be enforceable.[176]

---

171. RUPA §701(b).

172. RUPA §701(h). This right to "lock in" the financial interest of a partner who wrongfully dissociates parallels the right provided by UPA §38(2) with regard to a wrongful dissolver. See section 11.5.5.

173. RUPA §701(e).

174. RUPA §702(g).

175. RUPA §701(f). For the mechanics of an action by a dissociated partner to determine the buy out price or contest deferral, see RUPA §701(i).

176. RUPA §701, Comment 3.

§11.11 Dissociation That Causes Dissolution

§11.11.1 Overview

If a partner's dissociation results in dissolution, RUPA's approach is quite similar to the UPA's.[177] Dissolution does not end the partnership but instead commences a period of winding up.[178] "The partnership is terminated when the winding up of its business is completed."[179] Unless the partnership agreement provides otherwise, any "partner who has not wrongfully dissociated may participate in the winding up of the partnership's business." Each partner's duty "to refrain from competing with the partnership" ends at dissolution,[180] but the other fiduciary duties and the obligation of good faith and fair dealing remain in effect.

In winding up its business the partnership:

- may preserve the partnership business or property as a going concern for a reasonable time, prosecute and defend actions and proceedings, whether civil, criminal, or administrative, transfer the partnership's property, settle disputes by mediation or arbitration, and perform other necessary acts; and
- must discharge the partnership's liabilities, settle and close the partnership's business, and marshall the assets of the partnership and distribute the net proceeds to the partners "in cash."[181]

The settling of accounts among partners is essentially the same as under the UPA, except that (i) under RUPA debts owed by the partnership to partners are treated the same as debts owed to third parties,[182] and (ii) RUPA expressly refers to each partner having an account reflecting the partner's contributions, share of partnership profits, distributions and share of losses,[183] and then uses that concept to describe the "Settlement of Accounts and Contributions Among Partners."[184]

In one substantive departure from the UPA, RUPA §802(b) permits a partnership to "undo" its dissolution "[a]t any time . . . before the winding up of its business is completed." This "180" requires the waiver by "all of the partners, including any dissociating partner other than a wrongfully dissociat-

---

177. See sections 11.2–11.5.

178. RUPA §802(a).

179. RUPA §802(a).

180. RUPA §404(b)(3).

181. RUPA §§803(c), 807(a).

182. RUPA §807(a). The UPA gives higher priority to obligations owed to third parties. See section 11.4.4.

183. RUPA §401(a).

184. RUPA §807. The extended Example provided in section 11.5.3 is thus equally useful for understanding settling accounts under RUPA. (That Example does not include any debts owed to partners.)

ing partner" of "the right to have the partnership's business wound up and the partnership terminated."[185] In that event "the partnership resumes carrying on its business as if dissolution had never occurred,"[186] except that "the rights of a third party . . . may not be adversely affected."[187]

§11.11.2 *Partner's Power to Bind During Winding Up*

Like the UPA, RUPA specifically deals with the power of partners to bind the partnership during winding up. RUPA's approach is, however, far simpler and allows for the public filing of a statement of dissolution. RUPA §804 provides that, subject to the effect of a statement of dissolution:

> a partnership is bound by a partner's act after dissolution that:
>
> (1)   is appropriate for winding up the partnership business; or
>
> (2)   would have bound the partnership under Section 301 before dissolution, if the other party to the transaction did not have notice of the dissolution.

In this context, the phrase "a partner's act" includes an act by the partner whose dissociation resulted in the dissolution.[188]

The filing and function of a statement of dissolution under Article 8 is roughly analogous to the filing and function of a statement of dissociation under Article 7. "After dissolution, a partner who has not wrongfully dissociated may file a statement of dissolution stating the name of the partnership and that the partnership has dissolved and is winding up its business."[189]

The effect of the filed statement varies depending on whether the transaction at issue involves the transfer of real property owned in the name of the partnership. If so, as soon as "a certified copy of the filed statement . . . is of record in the office for recording transfers of that real property,"[190] the statement has the immediate effect of "restrict[ing] the authority of all partners to real property transfers that are appropriate for winding up the business."[191]

---

185. RUPA §802(b).

186. RUPA §802(b)(1).

187. RUPA §802(b)(2).

188. This conclusion follows from the fact that many such partners will have the right to participate in winding up, RUPA §803(a) ("a partner who has not wrongfully dissolved may participate") and from the fact that no statement of dissociation may be filed when Article 8 applies. RUPA §§603(b) (switching provision) and 704 (providing for statement of dissociation).

189. RUPA §805(a). The statement is not filed by the partnership and therefore does not require the signatures of two partners. RUPA §105(c). In some circumstances, it would be impossible to obtain the signature of two partners who had not wrongfully dissociated—i.e., a two-person partnership for a term, where one partner wrongfully dissociates before the end of the term.

190. RUPA §303(e), referred to by RUPA §806(b).

191. RUPA §805, Comment 2. The statement has this effect because it "is a limitation on authority for the purposes of Section 303(e)." RUPA §805(b).

A filed statement of dissolution also has the immediate effect of canceling all previously filed statements of partnership authority granting authority.[192] In addition, ninety days after filing, a statement of dissolution "operates as constructive notice conclusively limiting the apparent authority of partners to transactions that are appropriate for winding up the business."[193]

> *Example:* The Ofek-Noam Company ("the Company") is a RUPA general partnership that purchases land and subdivides it for sale to home builders. The Company has three partners—Suzanne, Eli, and Gili—and for years all three have acted for the partnership in selling land to home builders. The partnership has filed a statement of authority with the Secretary of State, indicating that each partner has the authority to transfer land owned in the name of the partnership. The partnership owns a large parcel of land in Dakota County, and a certified copy of the statement of authority has been recorded with the Dakota County Registrar of Deeds.
>
> The partnership dissolves, and Gili files a statement of dissolution with the Secretary of State and records a certified copy with the Dakota County Registrar of Deeds. Two days later, Eli purports to enter into a contract to grant another developer a five-year option on the Dakota County parcel. The Company is not bound:
>
> - Granting a five-year option is hardly "appropriate for winding up the partnership business," so the partnership is not bound under RUPA §804(1).
> - Even if the developer could establish that Eli's act "would have bound the partnership under Section 301 before dissolution," the partnership is not bound under RUPA §804(2).[194] "A state-

---

192. RUPA §805(b). It is unclear whether this cancellation affects statements of authority granting a partner authority to transfer real property owned in the partnership name, if no certified copy of the statement of dissolution is filed in the office for recording transfers of that real property. Arguably, the certified copy on record in that office must lose its efficacy when the underlying filing (i.e., the filing of which it is a copy) is cancelled. However, RUPA §303(d)(2) provides:

> A grant of authority to transfer real property held in the name of the partnership contained in a certified copy of a filed statement of partnership authority recorded in the office for recording transfers of that real property is conclusive in favor of a person who gives value without knowledge to the contrary, *so long as and to the extent that a certified copy of a filed statement containing a limitation on that authority is not then of record in the office for recording transfers of that real property.*

(Emphasis added.)

193. RUPA §805, Comment 3. The statement has this effect because "[f]or the purposes of Sections 301 and 804, a person not a partner is deemed to have notice of the dissolution and the limitation on the partners' authority as a result of the statement of dissolution 90 days after it is filed." RUPA §805(c).

194. RUPA §804(2). The Dakota County parcel is a major operating asset of the partnership. It is at best arguable whether a five-year option on such an asset comes within a partner's apparently/ordinary power. See section 10.3.

ment of dissolution cancels a filed statement of partnership authority for the purposes of Section 303(d) and is a limitation on authority for the purposes of Section 303(e)." Therefore, the developer cannot invoke the previously filed and recorded statement of authority and "is deemed to have knowledge" that each partner's authority to transfer real property is limited to transactions appropriate for winding up the partnership business.[195]

Example: Same facts as in the previous example, plus (i) winding up The Ofek-Noam Company is a lengthy process, and (ii) six months into that process, Gili orders on behalf of the Company $5000 worth of gifts explaining to the vendor, "These are to promote our relationship with our long time customers." The Company is not bound. The gifts are clearly not "appropriate for winding up the partnership business,"[196] and RUPA §804(2) does not help the would-be seller because the would-be seller had "notice of the dissolution." Under RUPA §805(c), "a person not a partner is deemed to have notice of the dissolution . . . 90 days after [a statement of dissolution] is filed."

§11.12   Other Causes of Dissolution

Like the UPA, RUPA provides a number of events of dissolution that are not connected to the dissociation of a partner. These events include:

- in a partnership for a term or undertaking
  —"the expiration of the term or the completion of the undertaking"[197]
  —"the express will of all the partners to wind up the business" before the expiration or completion[198]
- an event that the partnership agreement establishes as causing dissolution[199]
- "on application by a partner, a judicial determination that: (i) the economic purpose of the partnership is likely to be unreasonably frustrated; (ii) another partner has engaged in conduct relating to the partnership business which makes it not reasonably practicable to carry on the business in partnership with that partner; or (iii) it is not otherwise reasonably practicable to carry on the partnership business in conformity with the partnership agreement"[200]

---

195. The phrase "deemed to have knowledge" comes from RUPA §303(e), which applies to this situation under RUPA §805(b).
196. RUPA §805(1).
197. RUPA §801(2)(iii).
198. RUPA §801(2)(ii).
199. RUPA §801(3).
200. RUPA §801(5).

- "on application by a transferee of a partner's transferable interest, a judicial determination that it is equitable to wind up the partnership business: (i) after the expiration of the term or completion of the undertaking, if the partnership was for a definite term or particular undertaking at the time of the transfer or entry of the charging order that gave rise to the transfer; or (ii) at any time, if the partnership was a partnership at will at the time of the transfer or entry of the charging order that gave rise to the transfer"[201]

The grounds for judicial dissolution on application by a partner mirror the grounds for judicial expulsion under RUPA §601(5) and are derived in part from the UPA and in part from the Revised Uniform Limited Partnership Act. The grounds for judicial dissolution on application by a transferee come from UPA §32(2), but "[t]he requirement that the court determine that it is equitable to wind up the business is new."[202] Allowing a transferee to seek dissolution is a major exception to the general rule that transferees have no right to meddle in the management of the partnership.

> *Example:* Larry, Moe, and Curley agree to form a partnership with a term of five years. Two years later, Moe's transferable interest becomes subject to a charging order and is eventually transferred to Shemp, a non-partner, in a foreclosure sale.[203] Moe dissociates from the partnership, but neither Larry and Curley wants to dissolve the partnership before the expiration of its original term.[204] They continue with their original business plan, under which they each take small salaries for the work they do, while "plowing back" all profits into the business. When the end of the five-year term approaches, Larry and Curley decide that the business is "on the cusp of a great opportunity." They believe that "with a little staying power, a little delayed gratification, we might make it big, big, big." They agree therefore to extend the partnership's term for another three years. As soon as the original five-year term expires, Shemp may go to court seeking an order dissolving the partnership despite Larry's and Curley's agreement to the contrary. Shemp's chances are greatest if Larry's and Curley's plans to "make it big, big, big" are very risky or if the court considers the extension of the partnership term a bad faith effort to deprive Shemp of the value of his transferable interest.

---

201. RUPA §801(6).

202. RUPA §801, Comment 9. In this respect, RUPA §801(6) seems to correspond with Restatement (Second) of Contracts §338(2) ("DISCHARGE OF AN OBLIGOR AFTER ASSIGNMENT. . . . So far as an assigned right is conditional on the performance of a return promise, and notwithstanding notification of the assignment, any modification of or substitution for the contract made by the assignor and obligor in good faith and in accordance with reasonable commercial standards is effective against the assignee. The assignee acquires corresponding rights under the modified or substituted contract.").

203. For a discussion of charging orders, see section 8.8.4.

204. See section 11.9.3.

The partnership agreement may not vary the power of a court to order dissolution on application by either a partner or transferee.[205]

§11.13   Dissociation and Dissolution—UPA and RUPA Compared

The following chart shows how the UPA and RUPA approach the key issues of partner dissociation and partnership dissolution. Unless marked by an asterisk (*) each provision is a default rule, subject to change by the partnership agreement.

Issue	UPA	RUPA
"dissociation" used as a statutory term of art	no	yes*
events of dissociation	labeled "Causes of Dissolution" and listed in §31*	labeled "Events Causing Partner's Dissociation" and listed in §601
rightful and wrongful dissociation distinguished	yes, characterized as causing "wrongful dissolution"; e.g., §§37, 38(2)	yes, "wrongful dissociation" defined in §602(b)
partner has power to dissociate even when wrongful	yes, §31(2)*	yes, §602(a)*
effect of partner dissociation on partnership entity/aggregate	partnership inevitably dissolves, §29*	dissolution not inevitable, §603(a); if no dissolution, post-dissociation partnership is the same entity which existed before dissolution*
other causes of partnership dissolution	yes, primarily: termination of term or undertaking, §31(1)(a), unanimous consent of partners, §31(1)(c), judicial intervention (including on behalf of assignees), §32*	essentially the same: termination of term or undertaking, §801(2)(iii), unanimous consent of partners, §801(2)(ii), judicial intervention (including on behalf of transferees, although, RUPA, unlike the UPA, requires transferees to show that "it is equitable to wind up the partnership business"), §§801(5) and (6)*

---

205. RUPA §103(b)(8).

Issue	UPA	RUPA
effect of partner dissociation on partnership business	must be wound up, unless: (i) in rightful dissolution all partners agree to continue the business in a successor organization, §38(1); (ii) in wrongful dissolution, all partners except the wrongful dissolver agree to continue the business in a successor partnership, §38(2)(b)	none, if partnership not dissolved; must be wound up if partnership dissolved, unless by agreement some partners continue the business in a successor entity
effect of partner dissociation on partner fiduciary duties	duties continue through winding up	if dissociation does *not* => dissolution, fiduciary duties of dissociated partner end, §603(b)(2) and (3);
		whenever dissolution occurs, noncompete duties of all partners end, §404(b)(3)
dissociated partner's role in management	may participate in winding up, unless dissociation caused wrongful dissolution, §37	if dissociation does *not* => dissolution, dissociated partner has no further participation in partnership affairs, §603(b)(1)
		if dissociation => dissolution, dissociated partner may participate in winding up, unless dissociation was wrongful, §803(a)
post-dissociation power to bind of dissociated partner	lingering power to bind, subject to the complex rules of §35, and especially §35(3)(c)*	if dissociation does *not* => dissolution, lingering power to bind is subject to the somewhat less complex rules of §702 and the effect of a filed statement of dissociation, §704*; if dissolution occurs later from some other cause, a filed statement of dissolution will also affect lingering power to bind, §804*
		if dissociation => dissolution, lingering power to bind is subject to the somewhat less complex rules of §804 and the effect of a filed statement of dissolution, §805*

table continues

Issue	UPA	RUPA
effect of partner dissociation of dissociated partner's personal liability for pre-dissociation obligations of the partnership	dissolution does not discharge the liability, but discharge is possible by agreement under §36(2) or, under §36(3), if the creditor agrees to a material change in the obligation*	dissociation does not discharge the liability, but discharge is possible under the material change rule, §703(d)*
dissociated partner's liability for post-dissociation obligations of the partnership or the partnership business	liable, just like other partners, for partnership obligations incurred during winding up; not liable for partnership obligations incurred by successor organization that continues the partnership business unless partnership by estoppel applies, §§16 and 35(4)*	if dissociation does *not* => dissolution, lingering liability under §703; filing of a statement of dissociation, §704 can significantly curtail the exposure*
ability to "lock in" the interest of a partner who has prematurely and wrongfully dissociated from a partnership for a term or undertaking	requires unanimous consent of the remaining partners to continue the business, §38(2)(b)	yes, unless within 90 days after the wrongful dissociation a majority of the remaining partners decide to dissolve the partnership, §801(2)(i), or, if the partnership continues, the wrongfully dissociated partner can prove that prompt pay out "will not cause undue hardship to the partnership," §701(h)
impact of wrongful dissociation on valuation of dissociated partner's interest	partnership valued excluding good will, §38(2)(c)(II); dissociated partner's share decreased by damages caused by wrongful dissolution, §38(2)(a)(II)	partnership valuation includes good will, §701(b); dissociated partner's share decreased by damages caused by wrongful dissolution, §701(c)
settling of accounts after dissolution	according to the Rules for Distribution, §40	essentially the same as per UPA, according to Settlement of Accounts and Contributions Among Partners, §807
presence of a "switching provision" among the rules governing dissociation and dissolution	no, because dissociation inevitably causes dissolution	yes, under §603(a): [Article 7] governs if dissociation does *not* => dissolution; [Article] 8 governs if dissociation => dissolution*

Issue	UPA	RUPA
role of publicly filed statements	none	if dissociation does *not* => dissolution, statement of dissociation curtails dissociated partner's lingering power to bind and lingering liability, §§702-704*
		if dissociation => dissolution, statement of dissolution curtails power to bind of all partners, §§804, 805*

§11.14 Merger and Conversion

§11.14.1 Merger

"Merger" was originally a corporate concept, and for many decades corporate statutes have provided a mechanism under which one or more corporations can be subsumed (and therefore disappear) into another corporation. The very concept is foreign to the "aggregate" notion of general partnerships,[206] and the UPA contains no merger provisions. RUPA, in contrast, provides that a RUPA general partnership "may be merged into one or more [general] partnerships or limited partnerships."[207] Some RUPA states have amended their laws to allow partnerships to merge not only with other partnerships but also with corporations and limited liability companies (so-called "cross entity mergers").[208] Some UPA states have amended their laws to allow general partnerships to participate in mergers.

The basic structure of a merger is the same regardless of the entities or statutes involved:

- the owners of each participating entity (often called a "constituent" entity) must approve the proposed "plan of merger" according to approval mechanisms specified in the entity's governing statute;[209]
- effectuating the merger involves the filing of specified documents with specified public officials;

---

206. See section 7.2.7.

207. RUPA §905(a).

208. The merger of an entity taxed as a partnership into a corporation has very significant tax consequences, as does the merger of an entity taxed as a corporation into an entity taxed as a partnership. For a detailed discussion, see Carter G. Bishop & Daniel S. Kleinberger, Limited Liability Companies: Tax and Business Law (Warren, Gorham & Lamont, Supp. 2002-1), chapter 12.

209. For a constituent corporation, board of director approval is also required.

- when the merger takes effect, each entity being merged into the "surviving" entity ceases to exist by operation of law; and
- all the assets and obligations of each disappearing entity vest by operation of law in the surviving entity.

RUPA follows this basic blueprint, providing in section 905 for the "Merger of Partnerships" and detailing in section 906 the "Effect of Merger."

RUPA and most other partnership merger provisions differ from the corporate blueprint in one very important respect. Corporate law long ago discarded the notion that mergers should require the unanimous consent of all owners (i.e., shareholders). In place of each shareholder's veto rights, modern corporate statutes provide generally for merger by the consent of the majority of shareholder voting power, subject to each shareholder's right to:

- dissent—i.e., formally vote against a proposed merger, and
- seek appraisal—i.e., have his, her, or its stock interest purchased by the surviving entity at fair value, as defined by statute, if the merger succeeds.

In contrast, RUPA and most other partnership merger provisions omit any dissent and appraisal provisions and instead provide—as a default rule—that all partners must consent to any merger involving the partnership.[210]

When the default rule remains in place, this approach gives each partner a veto right over any merger. On the other hand, displacing the default rule can involve substantial traps for the unwary.

> *Example:* Hook Company ("Hook") is a RUPA general partnership with 15 partners. Hook owns and operates several suburban shopping malls and has an excellent opportunity to expand its business by merging with another RUPA partnership, T-Belle Company ("T-Belle"), which has 10 partners. Under the proposed merger, (i) T-Belle would merge into Hook (and therefore disappear), (ii) all of T-Belle's assets and liabilities would transfer by operation of law to Hook, and (iii) T-Belle's partners would become partners in Hook. The merger cannot take place unless *every single member of both partnerships agrees.*

> *Example:* Smee Company ("Smee") is a RUPA partnership whose partnership agreement (i) provides that the partnership has a term of 30 years and (ii) permits Smee to participate in a merger "upon the approval of partners owning 60 percent of the interests in profits." The required approval is obtained for a merger in which Smee is the surviving entity. In the view of Mr. Pan, one of Smee's partners, the merger is a bad idea because the merger significantly increases Smee's risk of failure and therefore each partner's exposure to personal liability in the event

---

210. RUPA §905(c)(1).

Smee becomes insolvent. No matter how reasonable Mr. Pan's view, he has no palatable options.[211]

Two other partnership-specific aspects of merger also warrant mention. One relates to the lingering personal liability of a partner following a merger. The other relates to the lingering power to bind of a partner following a merger. These two very complicated issues have no analog under corporate law, because a corporate shareholder *qua* shareholder has neither personal liability for the corporation's obligations nor any apparent authority by position to bind the corporation. RUPA addresses these two issues in several subsections of Section 906 fairly described as recondite.[212]

§11.14.2 Conversions

Conversions are a relatively recent development in the law of business organizations. "In a statutory conversion an existing entity changes its form, the jurisdiction of its governing statute or both. . . . In contrast to a merger, which involves at least two entities, a conversion involves only one. The converting and converted organization are the same entity."[213]

The UPA has no conversion provisions. RUPA provides both for the conversion of a general partnership to a limited partnership[214] and for the conversion of a limited partnership to a general partnership.[215] Some RUPA states have amended their laws to allow partnership-related conversions also to involve corporations and limited liability companies. Some UPA states have similarly amended their laws.[216] In effect and purpose, a conversion is identical to a merger in which an existing entity arranges for the creation of a new, shell entity (of a different type, or governed by the law of a different state) and then merges into that new entity. As a result, the issues raised by conversions are parallel to those raised by mergers.

---

211. Dissociation would be wrongful, see section 11.9.2, would have no effect on Mr. Pan's exposure for partnership liabilities incurred before dissociation, and only limited effect on his exposure for partnership liabilities incurred after dissociation. See section 11.10.4.

212. RUPA §906(c), (d), and (e). The new uniform limited partnership act takes a somewhat more direct but still complicated approach to these issues. See ULPA (2001), §§1111 (Liability of General Partner after Conversion or Merger) and 1112 (Power of General Partners and Persons Dissociated as General Partners to Bind Organization after Conversion or Merger).

213. ULPA (2001), §1102, Comment.

214. RUPA §902.

215. RUPA §903.

216. The conversion of an entity taxed as a partnership into a corporation has very significant tax consequences, as does the conversion of an entity taxed as a corporation into an entity taxed as a partnership. For a detailed discussion, see Carter G. Bishop & Daniel S. Kleinberger, Limited Liability Companies: Tax and Business Law (Warren, Gorham & Lamont/RIA 1994–2002), chapter 12.

PROBLEM 97

John, Jacob, and Susan form an investment partnership with a term of five years. For the first two years everything goes fine. Then Jacob says to his partners, "I want out. I want my money out—now." Is Jacob's departure wrongful? Is the partnership dissolved?

EXPLANATION — UPA

Even though the partners (Jacob included) promised each other to maintain the partnership for five years, Jacob's "express will" causes a dissolution. Because that dissolution breaches Jacob's promise—that is, because the dissolution is in contravention of the partnership agreement—the dissolution is wrongful. UPA §31(2).

EXPLANATION — RUPA

Jacob's departure is a wrongful dissociation. "A partner's dissociation is wrongful . . . if . . . in the case of a partnership for a definite term or particular undertaking, before the expiration of the term or the completion of the undertaking . . . the partner withdraws by express will." RUPA §602(b)(2)(i). The partnership is not dissolved, unless within 90 days of Jacob's dissociation either John or Susan manifests the "express will" to dissolve. RUPA §801(2)(i) (wrongful dissociation does not result in premature dissolution of a term partnership absent "the express will [manifested within 90 days of the dissociation] of at least half of the remaining partners to wind up the partnership business").

PROBLEM 98

John, Jacob, and Susan form a five-year investment partnership. Two years later John dies. Is the partnership dissolved? If so, was the dissolution wrongful or rightful?

EXPLANATION — UPA

The death of a partner automatically dissolves the partnership. UPA §31(4). John's death and the resulting dissolution disappoints the expectations of Jacob and Susan but does not breach the partnership agreement or violate some other legally enforceable duty owed by John to his partners. Therefore, the dissolution is rightful.

EXPLANATION — RUPA

John's death is a dissociation, RUPA §601(7)(i), but it is not wrongful. RUPA §602(b). The partnership is not dissolved, unless within 90 days of Jacob's dissociation either John or Susan manifests the "express will" to dissolve. RUPA §801(2)(i).

PROBLEM 99

John, Jacob, and Susan form an investment partnership with a five-year term. One of the partnership's assets is a classic car, which is in basically good shape but will require considerable mechanical work if it is to be profitably sold. Two years into the partnership John quits the partnership. He then hires a mechanic to prepare the classic car for sale. The mechanic is unaware of the partnership and is likewise unaware that John has quit the partnership. Is the partnership bound by John's act?

EXPLANATION — UPA

Most likely yes. When John quit the partnership, the partnership dissolved. UPA §31(2). If the partnership is to be wound up through liquidation, John's act is probably "an act appropriate for winding up partnership affairs." Under UPA §35(1)(a) such acts bind the dissolved partnership. Because the mechanic is unaware of the dissolution, the constraining rules of UPA §35(3)(c) cannot apply.

The answer under UPA §35(1)(a) might be different if Jacob and Susan plan to continue the partnership business under UPA §38(2)(b) and intend to wind up the affairs of the dissolved partnership by transferring them (and the dissolved partnership's assets) to a successor partnership. In that case, John's act would not be appropriate for winding up purposes.

EXPLANATION — RUPA

The partnership is not bound if the partnership is not dissolved. John's dissociation is wrongful, RUPA §602(b)(2)(i), but the partnership is not dissolved absent "the express will [manifested within 90 days of the dissociation] of at least half of the remaining partners to wind up the partnership business." RUPA §801(2)(i). If the partnership does not dissolve, RUPA §702 will determine John's power to bind the partnership. RUPA §702(1) negates any such power, because "at the time of entering into the transaction the other party"—i.e., the mechanic—did not "reasonably believe[] that the dissociated partner was then a partner."

If John's dissociation does result in dissolution, RUPA §804 will determine his power to bind the dissolved partnership. In that event, the partnership might be bound, because preparing the car for sale might well be "appropriate for winding up the partnership business." RUPA §804(1).[217]

PROBLEM 100

Able and Baker have a partnership at will which buys finished cloth from mills and resells it to garment manufacturers. For the past two years the partnership

---

217. RUPA §804(2) would not apply, because John was not authorized to act for the partnership, RUPA §803(a) and the partnership was undisclosed. Therefore, John's act "would [not] have bound the partnership under Section 301 before dissolution." See section 10.3 (explaining that RUPA §301 binds a partnership through a partner's actual authority and through apparently/ordinary power).

has regularly bought cloth from Inventive Design Outlet, Inc. ("IDO"), using purchase orders signed by either partner. The terms of the sale have been "net 30 date of shipment," that is, payment is due 30 days after the goods are shipped.

On January 15, Baker says to Able, "This partnership is over." On that day the partnership has a few outstanding obligations to provide cloth to various manufacturers, and the partnership has sufficient cloth in stock to cover those obligations.

On January 17 Able signs and sends a purchase order to IDO for $50,000 worth of wool cloth. IDO promptly wires back its acceptance. Two days later the president of IDO telephones the partnership's offices to express appreciation for the order. Able is not in, so the president speaks to Baker. Upon hearing of the order Baker exclaims, "That order is no good. Able had no right to issue it. We dissolved this partnership two days before." The president of IDO quite accurately explains that IDO "knew nothing of any dissolution" and asserts, "That order is good. You're stuck with it."

Did Able's purchase order bind the partnership?

EXPLANATION — UPA

The partnership is bound. While under UPA §33 Able lacked authority to bind the partnership in matters of new business, under UPA §35(1)(b) she had the power to do so. Her actions in sending the purchase order bound the partnership under UPA §35(1)(b)(I).

Since the partnership was at will, Baker's January 15 statement caused a dissolution. Dissolution being caused by an act of the partner, Able lost her authority to bind the partnership for new business as soon as she knew of the dissolution — i.e., immediately. UPA §§33(1)(b) and 34(a). The facts indicate that Able's order represented new business; at the time of the order the partnership had already covered its outstanding obligations to customers. Therefore, Able was acting without authority.

Under UPA §35, however, a partner can have the power to bind a dissolved partnership even if he or she lacks the authority to do so. Since Able's order constituted new business, UPA §35(1)(b) applies. (UPA §35(1)(a) is inapposite, because Able's order was not an "act appropriate for winding up partnership affairs or completing transactions unfinished at dissolution." The partnership had on hand ample cloth to finish all predissolution orders.)

Under UPA §35(1)(b)(I) a partner's postdissolution commitment binds the partnership if: (i) the commitment would have bound the partnership prior to dissolution, (ii) the third party had previously extended credit to the partnership, and (iii) the third party had no knowledge of the dissolution.

The given facts meet all three criteria. Able's issuing of the order was an act "for apparently carrying on in the usual way the business of the partnership," UPA §9(1), so the transaction would indeed have bound the partnership prior to dissolution.[218] IDO had previously extended credit to the

---

218. See section 10.2.

partnership (the "net 30" term), and, as IDO's president indicated, IDO received and accepted the order unaware of the dissolution.

None of the "de-powering" exceptions of UPA §35(3) apply. The only exception remotely connected to the facts is found in UPA §35(3)(c) (partner lacks authority and creditor had notice or knowledge of the lack of authority). Able did lack authority, but IDO was totally unaware of that fact. Able's lack of authority stemmed from the dissolution, and when IDO accepted the order it had neither knowledge nor notice of the dissolution.

EXPLANATION — RUPA

The partnership is bound. The January 15 statement dissolved the partnership, RUPA §801(1), and therefore RUPA §804 controls each partner's power to bind during winding up. Although the January 17 order was not "appropriate for winding up the partnership business," RUPA §804(1), before the dissolution the order would have been within Baker's apparently/ordinary power. IDO "did not have notice of the dissolution," so the partnership is bound under RUPA §804(2).

PROBLEM 101

John, Jacob, Sara, and Susan form an investment partnership with a term of five years. John prematurely and wrongfully quits the partnership, and Susan does not want to continue the business without John's participation. Jacob and Sara do want to continue, and Susan is willing to wait for her money (assuming Jacob and Sara guarantee it and she is compensated for her wait). However, John demands liquidation. The partnership agreement does not address the situation. Can John compel liquidation?

EXPLANATION — UPA

Yes. John's departure caused a wrongful dissolution, UPA §31(2), but Susan's desire not to participate in a successor venture costs Jacob and Sara their right to continue the partnership business under UPA §38(2)(b). That provision allows business continuation only if all the remaining partners agree. Since UPA §38(2)(b) does not apply, under UPA §§38(2)(c)(I) and 38(1) each of the partners (including John) has the right to insist on liquidation.

EXPLANATION — RUPA

No. John's departure is a wrongful dissociation, RUPA §602(b)(2)(i), but the partnership is not dissolved. RUPA §801(2)(i) (requiring the "express will of at least half of the remaining partners"). Suzanne has the right to dissociate herself, RUPA §602(b)(2)(i) (wrongful dissociation of one partner in a term partnership gives other partners the right to withdraw within 90 days), but even that withdrawal will not cause dissolution.

John does have a buy out right under RUPA §701. However, under RUPA §701(h) payment is not due "until the expiration of the term . . . , unless the partner establishes to the satisfaction of the court that earlier payment will not cause undue hardship to the business of the partnership."

In contrast, if Susan dissociates, her dissociation is not wrongful, and she is entitled to be paid "within 120 days of a written demand for payment." RUPA §701(e).

PROBLEM 102 (UPA ONLY)

Three law students, Charlotte, Paul, and Sophie, form a partnership to operate a used bookstore at their law school. Nearing graduation, Sophie dissolves the at-will partnership. Charlotte and Paul decide, with Sophie's consent, to continue the business. They bring Jacob into the business and with him form a successor partnership. The dissolved partnership assigns its lease with the law school to the successor partnership. The law school consents to the assignment but does not agree to release the dissolved partnership.

Always attentive to legal niceties, Charlotte decides that the students who consigned their used books to the old partnership should be informed that the successor partnership is taking over. On credit, she buys a $40 ad in the law school newspaper. The ad proclaims "A Changing of the Guard" and explains the change.

Charlotte, Paul, and Jacob decide that the bookstore should expand its "product line." They write to a supplier of the dissolved partnership, inform that supplier of their new arrangement, and buy on credit $500 worth of study aids for resale to the students.

(1)   The bookstore falls on hard times and fails to pay its rent to the law school. Whom can the law school hold liable?

(2)   No one pays for the study aids. Whom can the vendor hold liable?

(3)   No one pays for the ad in the law school paper either. Whom can the paper hold liable?

EXPLANATION

These facially simple questions have some rather complicated answers. To keep the answers coherent, it is helpful to separate the obligors into the three groups described in section 11.4.3:

- *The Dissociated Partner*—A partner of the dissolved partnership, who is not continuing in the business as a member of the successor partnership. Sophie is a dissociated partner.
- *The Continuing Partners*—Partners of the dissolved partnership, who are continuing in the business as members of the successor partnership. Charlotte and Paul are continuing partners.
- *The New Partner*—A member of the successor partnership, who was not a member of the dissolved partnership. Jacob is a new partner.

(1) The lease. All four individuals are liable.

Liability of Sophie (Withdrawing Partner)—The lease obligation is clearly a debt of the dissolved partnership. Absent a novation, even a withdrawing partner like Sophie remains liable for such debts. UPA §36(1) and §36(2). (There has been no material alteration in the obligation, so UPA §36(3) does not apply even if the creditor was aware that the successor partnership had assumed the responsibilities of the dissolved partnership.) If the school actually pursues Sophie on this debt, then she will probably have an action against the successor partnership and its partners. Typically, the same agreement by which the old partners provide for the continuation of the business also obliges the successor partnership to hold harmless the withdrawing partner from any further liabilities related to the dissolved partnership.

Liability of Charlotte and Paul (Continuing Partners)—On three different grounds, Charlotte and Paul are liable on this debt. First, like Sophie, they are liable as members of the dissolved partnership. Second, under UPA §41(1), the debts of the dissolved partnership are also the debts of the successor partnership, and, per UPA §15, Charlotte and Paul are liable as members of the successor partnership. (UPA §41 does not limit their UPA §41 liability, because they are not new to the business.) Third, the successor partnership's assumption by contract of the dissolved partnership's obligations makes Charlotte and Paul, as members of the successor partnership, liable for this debt.

Liability of Jacob (New Partner)—Jacob is also liable on the lease to the school, but only on two grounds, not three. Unlike Charlotte and Paul, Jacob is not liable as a member of the dissolved partnership, but he *is* liable due to the operation of UPA §§41(1) and 15. However, unlike Charlotte and Paul, Jacob benefits from UPA §41(7)'s limitation on liability. Jacob is a partner new to the business. Finally, like Charlotte and Paul, Jacob is liable under contract law theory.

(2) The study aids.

Liability of Sophie (Withdrawing Partner)—This debt is exclusively a debt of the successor partnership, so Sophie, who is not a member of that partnership, is not liable. UPA §35(1)(a) does not bind the dissolved partnership, because the new purchase is not "appropriate for winding up." UPA §35(1)(b) cannot bind the dissolved partnership, because the supplier had notice of the dissolution. The only other possible theory of liability is UPA §16, but nothing in the facts supports the notion of partnership by estoppel.

Liability of Charlotte and Paul (Continuing Partners)—All three partners of the successor partnership agreed to expand the product line, so the study aids purchase binds the partnership. Under UPA §15 Charlotte and Paul are liable for the resulting debt as members of the successor partnership.

Liability of Jacob (New Partner)—Jacob is personally liable for this debt as a member of the successor partnership.

(3) The newspaper ad.

Liability of Sophie (Withdrawing Partner) — The question of Sophie's liability turns on whether this debt is part of the winding up of the dissolved partnership, or part of the business of the successor partnership. If the former, Sophie is liable. If the latter, she is not. (UPA §35(1)(b) will not apply because the ad itself provided the vendor notice of the dissolution.)

With the facts stated, it is impossible to characterize the debt. The person who placed the ad had authority to act for and power to bind both the dissolved partnership, UPA §§37 and 35(1)(a), and the successor partnership, UPA §§18(e) and 9(1). The ad's purpose was ambiguous. Was it intended to announce the demise of the dissolved partnership (hence, winding up) or to advertise the advent of the new one (hence, an act of the successor partnership)? Or both?

Liability of Charlotte and Paul (Continuing Partners) — Charlotte and Paul are liable no matter how this debt is characterized. If it is a winding up debt of the dissolved partnership, then the analysis is the same as for the lease. If instead the debt is directly a debt of the successor partnership, then Charlotte and Paul are liable because they are members of that successor partnership.

Liability of Jacob (New Partner) — Jacob is liable no matter how this debt is characterized. If it is a winding up debt of the dissolved partnership, then the analysis is the same as for the lease. If instead the debt is directly a debt of the successor partnership, then Jacob is liable because he is a member of that successor partnership.

PROBLEM 103

Jacob, Paul, and Leah form a partnership at will. They do not discuss how the business will be handled after dissolution. Later, Leah dissolves the partnership. She demands that the assets be liquidated so that she can have her share. Jacob and Paul object that liquidating the assets will cause everybody to lose value. Can Leah successfully insist on a liquidation? What argument can Jacob and Paul make against liquidation? What additional facts could strengthen Jacob and Paul's position?

EXPLANATION — UPA

Leah can most likely compel liquidation. Since the partnership was at will, under UPA §31(1)(b) Leah's express will caused a rightful dissolution. Under UPA §38(1), absent an agreement to the contrary, following a rightful dissolution each partner has the right to compel liquidation.

Jacob and Paul might argue for an in-kind division of assets, but to succeed they will have to show something beyond the general proposition that liquidations usually do not bring best value.

With some additional facts Jacob and Paul might also argue that the partnership had an implied term (not yet expired) or that Leah's dissolution somehow breached her duty of loyalty (e.g., by allowing her to appropriate an opportunity that otherwise the partnership would have enjoyed). Either showing would saddle Leah with the status of "wrongful dissolver." In that case, under UPA §38(2) Jacob and Paul could avoid liquidation by opting to continue the business.

EXPLANATION — RUPA

Leah may successfully insist on liquidation. Under RUPA §807(a), the net proceeds of winding up are to be paid to the partners "in cash."

Jacob and Paul might be able to delay the inevitable by arguing for a slow winding up in order to maximize the net proceeds. They will not, however, succeed with any claim of breach of the duty of loyalty. There is no indication that Leah is acting for any reason other than her own legitimate self interest. According to RUPA §404(e): "A partner does not violate a duty or obligation under this [Act] or under the partnership agreement merely because the partner's conduct furthers the partner's own interest."

PROBLEM 104

Last year Theodora became a partner in the law firm of Grand, Summit and St. Clair. The firm has 150 attorneys, including 85 partners. When Theodora became a partner, she signed the partnership agreement. That agreement states in part:

> Any member may be expelled from the firm by a two-thirds majority vote of the executive committee, and the committee need not have, state, or demonstrate good cause, nor need the committee afford the member being expelled any opportunity to be heard.

On May 1 of this year Theodora gave a speech, widely reported in the local media, on the abortion issue. The next day the president of one of the law firm's most important clients called the firm and complained vociferously to a senior partner about Theodora's speech. The president said, "Where did you guys get that crazy lady? We're not going to be able to entrust our business to a firm that gets publicly branded on this issue and can't keep its people in the office doing what they're supposed to be doing."

Although Theodora is an excellent lawyer, this is not the first complaint the firm has received about her outspoken public remarks. On May 3 the firm's nine-member executive committee meets and votes 7-2 to expel Theodora. Can Theodora establish that the expulsion was wrongful? Is the partnership dissolved?

EXPLANATION — UPA

The expulsion dissolves the partnership. Theodora is certainly "ceasing to be associated [with the other partners] in the carrying on . . . of the business." UPA §29.

The expulsion is probably not wrongful. The partnership's executive committee acted under the authority of the partnership agreement. This seems to be an expulsion "bona fide in accordance with such a power conferred by the agreement between the partners." UPA §31(1)(d).

The firm's failure to state its reasons for expulsion or to accord Theodora a hearing are not likely to change the result. By signing the partnership agreement, Theodora (like the rest of the partners) agreed to accept no-cause, "no process" expulsion.

Nor will Theodora succeed if she claims that the expulsion is wrongful because it violated the constitutional guarantee of due process. The firm is a private organization, and unlike the government, has no constitutional obligation to accord due process. For the same reason, it is likely irrelevant that the expulsion has penalized Theodora for speaking out. The First Amendment does not apply to private organizations. It is therefore not wrongful to expel a partner on account of the notoriety or even the content of his or her speech.

All is not necessarily lost for Theodora, however. Perhaps the expulsion was wrongful because it was unlawful. Was the executive committee motivated in part by the characterization of Theodora as a "crazy lady"? Would the firm have been so quick to expel a male partner? If Theodora can show that the expulsion reflected sex discrimination and that, despite her formal status as a partner, her real role was that of an employee, then she will have demonstrated not only sex discrimination but also wrongful dissolution.

EXPLANATION — RUPA

The expulsion does not dissolve the partnership, even if the partnership is an at-will partnership. The expulsion itself does not cause dissolution, RUPA §801, and an expelled partner cannot dissolve an at-will partnership. RUPA §801(1) (in "a partnership at will, [dissolution is caused by] the partnership's having notice from a partner, *other than a partner who is dissociated under Section 601(2) through (10),* of that partner's express will to withdraw as a partner" (emphasis added); "expulsion pursuant to the partnership agreement" is listed in §601(3)).

As to wrongful expulsion, the analysis is the same as under the UPA, buttressed by RUPA §404(e) ("A partner does not violate a duty or obligation under this [Act] or under the partnership agreement merely because the partner's conduct furthers the partner's own interest.")

PROBLEM 105

In 1995 four friends, Albert, Bernice, Carl, and Donald, form a partnership to do carpentry work in single-family residential construction. They make no written agreement, but after an evening-long discussion Bernice finally says, "So that's what we're going to do. Let's do carpentry work on houses; we'll all be in it together. Share and share alike." The other three agree, and they all shake hands on the deal.

For the five years following that agreement, their partnership operates very successfully. The partners make good livings and also put a substantial amount of the partnership's revenues toward purchasing two company trucks and state of the art carpentry equipment. The partnership's success impresses local banks, and the partnership obtains a line of credit with two of them. Each line of credit allows the partnership to borrow as it wishes up to a pre-determined limit.

For its first five years the partnership decides by consensus which projects to bid on. In 2002 the partners have for the first time a serious disagreement about whether to bid on a particular project. The disagreement concerns a residential development called "The Eagan project." Albert objects to bidding on the Eagan project because he believes that both the profit margins and the developer's quality standards are too low. The other three partners disagree, perhaps in large part because recently the partnership has had difficulty finding work. The partners vote 3-1 to bid on the project, and the bid is successful. Albert grumbles, "I don't like this. This is not the way we've always made our decisions, and this project is not our kind of business." However, he does show up at the worksite, and for three weeks he works side by side with Bernice, Carl, and Donald.

Then, three weeks into what the partners expect to be a three-month project, Albert announces, "I've had it. I don't like this work; never did. I'm outta here. I'm going to Alaska. I've got a chance to get in on the ground floor of a new fishing business."

That evening Albert, Bernice, Carl, and Donald meet, and Bernice, Carl, and Donald declare that they intend to finish the Eagan project and "maybe keep going after that." Albert reiterates that he is leaving the project and the partnership. He adds that he wants the partnership to turn over his share of the money tied up in the partnership trucks and other equipment.

What is the status of the partnership?

EXPLANATION — UPA

It is dissolved. Albert's "express will" is clearly to dissociate himself from carrying on the partnership business. Under either UPA §31(1)(b) (rightful dissolution of an at-will partnership) or UPA §31(2) (wrongful dissolution), that express will causes dissolution.

EXPLANATION — RUPA

The partnership is likely dissolved. Albert's "express will" has dissociated him as a partner, RUPA §601(1), the partnership is probably a partnership at-will,[219] and, as such, is dissolved by "having notice from a partner . . . of that partner's express will to withdraw as a partner." RUPA §801(1).

---

219. It is possible to argue that the partnership becomes a partnership for a particular undertaking each time the partnership agrees to take on a new project. See the Explanations to the next Problem.

PROBLEM 106

Is Albert's decision to dissociate wrongful?

EXPLANATION — UPA

Most likely not. The original, oral partnership agreement specified "no definite term or particular undertaking." Therefore, under UPA §31(1)(b) Albert's express will caused a rightful dissolution.

The fact that Albert may be leaving for greener pastures does not make the dissolution wrongful. According to some cases, a partner's duty of loyalty may constrain the right to dissolve at will. But these cases all involve the dissolving partner's exploitation of assets or opportunities that belong to or are closely associated with the partnership. Those cases would not apply here. There is no apparent connection between the partnership's carpentry business and Albert's fishing prospects.

It is possible to argue, however, that Albert dissolved wrongfully because he contravened an implied agreement not to dissolve with a partnership project underway. Under this analysis, each decision by the partners to undertake a project would transform their partnership at-will into a partnership for that "particular undertaking." Albert's dissolution would therefore be premature and wrongful. UPA §31(2).

If so, Albert would lose the right to wind up the partnership, UPA §37. Beyond that, however, nothing would change. Dissolution does not end even an at-will partnership; the partnership continues until it has wound up its affairs, including ongoing projects.

EXPLANATION — RUPA

The analysis here mirrors the UPA analysis. If the partnership was at will, Albert's dissociation was not wrongful. RUPA §602(b).

As to the argument that the partnership became a partnership for a particular undertaking each time the partnership agreed to take on a new project, that argument would render Albert's dissociation wrongful, RUPA §602(b)(2)(i), and would deprive him of the right to participate in winding up. RUPA §803(a).

PROBLEM 107

Assume that the partners had originally agreed to a partnership term of seven years. Given this change in facts, is there any way for Albert to avoid the label of "wrongful dissolver" or "wrongfully dissociated partner" (RUPA)?

EXPLANATION — UPA

Probably not. Albert might be able to claim that the decision to bid on the Eagan project violated implied agreements (created through the partners' course of dealing with each other) on the type of work to be done by the partners (e.g., no low budget, low quality jobs) and on the decision-making process to be used by the partners (e.g., projects selected by consensus only). That argument would allow Albert to claim that the decision to bid on the Eagan project constituted a wrongful dissolution.

That argument would probably fail, however, because Albert eventually consented to the Eagan project. By showing up to work on the project, Albert at least acquiesced in the decision. That acquiescence probably satisfies the requirement of UPA §18(h) that an "act in contravention of any agreement between the partners may be done rightfully [with] the consent of all the partners." Moreover, the mere violation of the partnership agreement does not dissolve the partnership. Albert's partners did not exclude him from the partnership business; he excluded himself.[220]

EXPLANATION — RUPA

The analysis here is similar to the analysis under the UPA. Under RUPA §401(j), Albert can argue not only that the Eagan project violated an implied agreement but also that the project was "outside the ordinary course of business of [the] partnership."[221]

PROBLEM 108

Assuming that the partnership had no specific term, can Albert force the partnership to immediately give him his share of the money tied up in the trucks and equipment?

EXPLANATION — UPA AND RUPA

Not at least until the Eagan project is finished. Under either statute, Albert's strongest position is to claim that the partnership is dissolved. Even assuming dissolution, the trucks and equipment are partnership property. Regardless of whether the dissolution is rightful, Albert cannot compel liquidation until, as part of winding up, the partnership has performed or otherwise discharged its obligations on the Eagan project.

PROBLEM 109

Two days after his announcement, Albert leaves for Alaska. Before leaving he writes to all the companies that had previously sold materials to the partnership. In his letters he states, "The original partnership is dissolved. I am no

---

220. Albert might have sought judicial dissolution under UPA §32(1)(d) (dissolution by decree of court available when a "partner willfully or persistently commits a breach of the partnership agreement, or otherwise so conducts himself in matters relating to the partnership business that it is not reasonably practicable to carry on the business in partnership with him").

221. As for judicial dissolution, RUPA §801(5)(ii) and (iii) are the analogs to UPA §32(1)(d).

longer associated with the business. I am not responsible for any of its debts." Bernice, Carl, and Donald continue to work on the Eagan project. As they continue the work, they make purchases necessary to finish the project. For example, they buy wood costing $10,000 from the Wabasco Wood Company, which happens to be a new supplier. Assuming that the partnership is not an LLP, is Albert personally liable for this debt?

EXPLANATION — UPA

Yes. This purchase is clearly an "act appropriate for . . . completing transactions unfinished at dissolution." As such, the purchase binds the dissolved partnership under UPA §35(1)(a). UPA §15 makes Albert personally liable for the partnership debt.

EXPLANATION — RUPA

Yes. The purchase "is appropriate for winding up the partnership business." RUPA §804(1). Albert is personally liable under RUPA §306(a), although his liability is subject to the exhaustion rule of RUPA §307(d).

PROBLEM 110

Bernice, Carl, and Donald also buy nails after Albert's departure. They buy from Nantucket Nail Emporium, which previously sold the partnership nails on a "net 30 date of shipment" basis (i.e., payment due within thirty days of shipment). Bernice, Carl, and Donald order and receive nails costing $600 before the Emporium receives Albert's letter, and they order and receive nails costing $1,100 after the letter arrives. Is Albert personally liable for these amounts?

EXPLANATION — UPA

Yes—under UPA §35(1)(a). The analysis is the same as for Problem 109. Albert's letter is irrelevant to the analysis under UPA §35(1)(a). Nothing in that provision concerns the third party's knowledge of the dissolution.

Albert's letter would have made a difference if the $1,100 worth of nails ordered after the letter arrived were used for new business. In that case, under UPA §35(1)(b)(I) the nail order would not have bound the dissolved partnership.

EXPLANATION — RUPA

The analysis here is the same as under the UPA. Under RUPA §804(1), notice of dissolution is irrelevant to the power of a partner to bind a dissolved partnership through "an act . . . appropriate for winding up the partnership business."

PROBLEM 111

Bernice, Carl, and Donald fare poorly on the Eagan project. Within a month after Albert leaves, the business falls behind in its payments to both banks. One bank, the First Bank, promptly sends written notice to the partnership, complaining about the delay in payments. Prior to Albert's departure, the partnership had borrowed the full $50,000 available under the First Bank line of credit. After receiving the notice, Bernice, Carl, and Donald meet with an officer of the First Bank to explain what has been happening. To help the continuing partners "get back on their feet," the bank agrees to a four-month moratorium on payments on the loan. Is Albert personally liable on the debt to the First Bank?

EXPLANATION — UPA

Possibly not. Under UPA §36(1), the dissolution by itself does not discharge him, but UPA §36(3) may. Under that latter provision, a discharge occurs if the continuing partners agree to assume the dissociated partner's liability, the creditor knows of that agreement, and the creditor agrees to a material alteration in the "nature or time of payment" of the obligation. If the continuing partners agreed to assume Albert's responsibility, and if the explanation and discussion with the Bank officer caused the Bank to know of the assumption agreement, then UPA §36(3) is probably satisfied. A four-month moratorium is probably a material change in the "time of payment."

EXPLANATION — RUPA

Yes. Although RUPA contains a provision analogous to UPA §36(1), that provision appears in [Article] 7 and applies only when a partner's dissociation does not result in dissolution. RUPA §603(a). Under RUPA §802(a), "a partnership continues after dissolution" and, accordingly, the partnership's obligations continue as well. The only question is whether the revised obligation is an obligation of the dissolved partnership—i.e., whether the act of Bernice, Carl, and Donald bound the partnership. The answer is yes. Since all of the funds were borrowed before Albert's departure, obtaining the moratorium was "appropriate for winding up the partnership business." RUPA §804(1). Albert is personally liable under RUPA §306(a), although his liability is subject to the exhaustion rule of RUPA §307(d).

PROBLEM 112

The other bank, the Second Bank, does not initially object to or even take note of the late payments. Bernice, Carl, and Donald decide to "let sleeping dogs lie." Indeed, they decide to undertake new projects and to fund them they actually borrow additional money under the line of credit. Before Albert's departure, the partnership had borrowed $40,000. To fund the new projects, Bernice, Carl, and Donald draw down the final $30,000 available under the original line of credit agreement. Is Albert personally liable for any of the $70,000?

EXPLANATION — UPA

Yes—for all of it. As to the first $40,000, Albert is liable under UPA §15, and UPA §36(3) will not save him. Even if the continuing partners agreed to assume Albert's liability and the $30,000 draw down constituted a material change in the nature of the obligation, there is no basis for finding that the Second Bank knew of the assumption agreement. Indeed, the Second Bank was not even aware of the dissolution; Albert notified only "companies which had previously sold materials to the partnership."

Albert is also liable as to the $30,000 draw-down, per UPA §35(1)(b)(I). The draw-down would have bound the partnership prior to dissolution; the Second Bank had previously extended credit to the partnership; and the Second Bank had no notice or knowledge of the dissolution.

EXPLANATION — RUPA

For the reasons stated in the RUPA Explanation to Problem 111, Albert is liable on the initial $40,000. Albert is probably also liable on the final $30,000.

As to the $30,000, the Second Bank will likely argue that: (i) when the money was borrowed, the original partnership was still winding up; (ii) the Bank had no notice of the dissolution; (iii) borrowing the money would have bound the partnership under RUPA §301 before the dissolution, and therefore (iv) under RUPA §804(2) the partnership is bound even though the money was used for new projects. If the partnership is bound, under RUPA §306(a) Albert is liable.

Even if Bernice, Carl, and Donald were acting as members of a new partnership when they borrowed the $30,000, Albert may still be liable. By leaving in place the line of credit and not informing the Second Bank that he had quit the partnership, Albert "purports to be a partner, or consents to being represented by another as a partner, in a partnership" now actually consisting of Bernice, Carl, and Donald. RUPA §308 (Liability of Purported Partner). Albert, as "the purported partner[,] is liable to a person to whom the representation is made [i.e., the Second Bank], if that person, relying on the representation, enters into a transaction with the actual . . . partnership." Id. The pivotal question is whether the Second Bank allowed the $30,000 to be borrowed "relying on the representation"—i.e., whether the Bank would have closed or somehow modified the line of credit if it had known of Albert's departure.

PROBLEM 113

Concerned that Bernice, Carl, and Donald will continue to undertake new projects for which he may be responsible, Albert seeks your advice on preventative measures. Advise him.

EXPLANATION — UPA

Albert must bring the fact of his departure to the knowledge of each third party that "extended credit to the partnership" prior to Albert's departure. UPA §35(1)(b)(I). For all other third parties, it will suffice to advertise "the fact of dissolution . . . in a newspaper of general circulation in the place (or in each place if more than one) at which the partnership business was regularly carried on." UPA §35(1)(b)(II).

EXPLANATION — RUPA

Albert should immediately file a statement of dissolution, as provided in RUPA §805. The statement's protective effect will begin 90 days after filing. RUPA §805(c). There is no need to record a certified copy of the statement, because the partnership does not own any real property.

To protect himself during the 90 days following the filing, Albert should send a notification announcing the dissolution to as many potential customers, vendors, and other third parties as he can identify. Doing so will allow him to invoke RUPA §804(2), which provides that, postdissolution, no partner has the power to bind the partnership through acts not appropriate for winding up "if the other party to the transaction [has] notice of the dissolution."

Advertising the dissolution will trigger the protections of RUPA §804(2) only to the extent that the advertisement comes to the attention of a third party or creates a situation in which a third party "has reason to know" that dissolution has occurred. RUPA §102(b) (defining "notice of a fact").

12

Limited Partnerships

§12.1   Overview

A limited partnership is an entity, organized under the auspices of a state statute and structured by that statute to allow one or more managing owners (general partners) to run an enterprise built on money and other property contributed by those owners and one or more passive owners (limited partners).

§12.1.1 *Limited Partnerships Distinguished from General Partnerships*

Ordinary limited partnerships differ from ordinary general partnerships[1] in six fundamental ways:

1. *Creation*—Creating a limited partnership involves special formalities: namely, the filing of a "certificate of limited partnership" with the public official or office specified in the state limited partnership act.
2. *Types of Partners*—A limited partnership has two types of partners: general partners and limited partners. A limited partnership must have at least one general partner and one limited partner.
3. *Personal Liability*—Like the partners of an ordinary general partnership, the general partners of an ordinary limited partnership are personally liable for the partnership's debts. Limited partners are not personally liable except in extraordinary circumstances.

---

1. The terms "ordinary limited partnerships" and "ordinary general partnerships" are used to distinguish these more traditional forms of organization from the shielded entities known respectively as "limited liability limited partnerships" (LLLPs) and "limited liability partnerships" (LLPs). LLLPs and LLPs are discussed in Chapter Fourteen.

4. *Management*—Except as otherwise provided in the partnership agreement, both the right to manage and the power to bind a limited partnership are reserved to the general partners. Limited partners are essentially passive investors.

5. *Profit and Loss Sharing*—Except as otherwise provided in the partnership agreement, partners in a limited partnership share profits and losses essentially in proportion to their respective capital contributions.

6. *Dissolution*—Except as otherwise provided in the partnership agreement, the dissociation of a limited partner does not dissolve the partnership, and the dissociation of a general partner merely threatens the partnership with dissolution.

§12.1.2 *Limited Partnership Statutes*

Every limited partnership is formed under and governed by some state limited partnership statute. The National Conference of Commissioners of Uniform State Laws[2] has promulgated four versions of the Uniform *Limited* Partnership Act: the original Act in 1916 ("ULPA"), the Revised Uniform Partnership Act in 1976 ("RULPA—1976"), the 1985 amendments to RULPA ("RULPA"), and an entirely new Uniform Limited Partnership Act in 2001 ("ULPA (2001)"). Most states now have in effect some version of RULPA—1976 or RULPA. Section 12.2 will focus on RULPA (i.e., the 1985 version), and Section 12.3 will discuss ULPA (2001).

§12.2   RULPA

§12.2.1 *Not a "Stand Alone" Statute*

Although RULPA covers numerous issues peculiar to limited partnerships, the statute does not purport to be exhaustive. It does not "stand alone"; instead it is "linked" to the UPA: "In any case not provided for in this [Act] the provisions of the Uniform Partnership Act govern."[3]

> *Example:* Rachael, Sam, and Carolyn are the general partners in a limited partnership that owns several apartment buildings. For some time the partnership has used Joe's Maintenance for routine maintenance work. Rachael and Carolyn wish to replace Joe's with RMV Dorothy &

---

2. This is the same organization that promulgated the Uniform Partnership Act and the Revised Uniform Partnership Act. See section 7.1.2.

3. RULPA §1105. RULPA also expresses this dependence on UPA more particularly. For example, RULPA §403 provides that a general partner in a limited partnership has the same rights, power, and liabilities as a partner in a general partnership. For its part, the UPA, §6(2), provides that "this act shall apply to limited partnerships except in so far as the statutes relating to such partnerships are inconsistent herewith." In states which have adopted RUPA and repealed the UPA, this link is problematic. See section 12.3.1.

Co., but Sam disagrees. RULPA provides no rules for this type of management disagreement, so the UPA governs. In particular, UPA §18(h) applies to this "ordinary matter."[4]

§12.2.2 Formalities of Creating a RULPA Limited Partnership

In order to form a RULPA limited partnership the would-be general partner[5] must first select a state of organization—that is, a state under whose limited partnership statute the limited partnership will be established and governed. Most limited partnerships are organized under the law of the state in which the partnership does all or most of its business, but it is not legally necessary to do so. Indeed, if a limited partnership does business in more than one state, the partnership will necessarily do business outside its state of organization.[6]

After choosing a state of organization, the general partner must invoke that state's limited partnership statute by filling a "certificate of limited partnership" with that state's secretary of state.[7] Each general partner must sign the certificate,[8] which must contain: (1) the limited partnership's name, (2) the name and business address of each general partner, (3) the latest date on which the limited partnership will dissolve,[9] and (4) the address of the office and the name and address of an agent designated to receive service of process on behalf of the limited partnership.[10]

The certificate may include other information, but most certificates contain only the bare minimum required by statute.[11] The certificate is a public

---

4. Under UPA §18(h), differences as to ordinary matters are decided by majority vote, with each partner having one vote. See section 9.5. The rule is a default rule. See section 7.1.4.

5. For the sake of convenience, this section refers to a sole general partner, although many limited partnerships have more than one general partner.

6. A limited partnership that does business in states other than its state of organization must register in each of those other states as a "foreign limited partnership." RULPA §§101(4) (defining the term) and 902 (requiring registration of foreign limited partnerships). With respect to its state of organization, a limited partnership is considered a "domestic" limited partnership. RULPA §101(7). Both the nomenclature and the registration requirement parallel those applicable to corporations. See, e.g., Revised Model Business Corporation Act §§1.40(4) (defining domestic corporation), 1.40(10) (defining foreign corporation), and 15.01 (requiring foreign corporations to obtain a certificate of authority before transacting business).

7. RULPA §201(a).

8. RULPA §204(a)(1).

9. This date effectively sets the term of the partnership. Other events may dissolve the partnership before this date. See section 12.2.7. Some RULPA states have deleted this requirement, in order to facilitate the formation of so-called "family limited partnerships." See section 12.4.

10. RULPA §201(a).

11. Both ULPA and the 1976 version of RULPA required greater disclosure in the certificate. See, e.g., ULPA §§2(1)(a)(vi) (requiring disclosure of each limited partner's capital contribution) and 2(1)(a)(ix) (requiring disclosure of each limited

document, and business people usually prefer to keep their business arrangements as confidential as possible. The key document for a limited partnership is therefore the partnership agreement. Although RULPA does not expressly require a partnership agreement, almost all limited partnerships have one. It is the partnership agreement, not the certificate of limited partnership, that details the rights, responsibilities, and relationships of the partners.

If the certificate of limited partnership substantially complies with the limited partnership statute, filing the certificate brings the partnership into existence either immediately or at a later date specified in the certificate.[12] Once formed, a limited partnership is a legal entity, distinct from its co-owners. It is not an aggregate of its partners.[13]

§12.2.3 *Personal Liability of RULPA Partners*

Each general partner in an ordinary limited partnership is personally liable for the partnership's debts, just as if the partnership were an ordinary general partnership.[14] Limited partners face no such automatic liability. They can, however, be liable in the following special circumstances:

1. *Wrongful personal conduct*—If a limited partner engages in wrongful conduct on behalf of the limited partnership and that conduct causes actionable injury, the limited partner is liable to the person injured.[15]
2. *Unfulfilled promise to contribute*—If a limited partner makes an enforceable promise to contribute to the limited partnership, the limited partner is liable to the partnership on that promise.[16]
3. *Wrongfully returned contributions*—If the limited partnership has returned all or part of a limited partner's contribution and the return violated the partnership agreement or left the partnership insolvent, then for six years afterwards the limited partner is liable to the partnership for the amount of the wrongful return.[17]
4. *Properly returned contributions*—If (a) the limited partnership has returned all or part of a limited partner's contribution without violating the partnership agreement and without leaving the partnership insolvent, and (b) the limited partnership cannot pay creditors "who ex-

---

partner's profit share), and RULPA (1976) §§201(a)(5) (requiring disclosure of each partner's capital contribution) and 201(a)(9) (requiring disclosure of each partner's right to receive distributions).

12. RULPA §201(b).

13. Compare the mixed entity/aggregate nature of a UPA general partnership, discussed in section 7.2.7.

14. RULPA §403(b).

15. Compare section 4.2.3 (agent liable for tortious conduct).

16. RULPA §502(b). For an explanation of partner contributions, see section 8.6.

17. RULPA §§608(b) (stating the general rule) and 607 (prohibiting distributions that leave the limited partnership effectively insolvent).

tended credit to the limited partnership during the period the contribution was held by the partnership," then for one year after the return the limited partner is liable to the partnership for whatever amount of the returned contribution is necessary to pay those creditors.[18]

5. *Use of limited partner's name*—If a limited partner allows its name to be used in the name of the limited partnership and a third party extends credit to the partnership without knowing that the limited partner is not a general partner, then the limited partner is liable to that third party on the transaction as if the limited partner were a general partner.[19]

6. *Mistaken belief in limited partner status*—If (a) a person makes a contribution to an enterprise, believing in good faith that the contribution is made as a limited partner, but (b) either no limited partnership exists or the certificate of limited partnership erroneously identifies the person as a general partner, and (c) when the person learns of the problem, the person either formally withdraws from the enterprise or has the certificate corrected, then the person is not categorically liable as a general partner in the enterprise. However, if before the person takes corrective action a third party transacts business with the enterprise, believing in good faith that the person is a general partner, then the person is liable on that transaction as if a general partner.[20]

7. *Participation in control*—If (a) a limited partner "participates in the control of the business" of the limited partnership, (b) that conduct causes a third party to reasonably believe that the limited partner is a general partner, and (c) with that belief the third party transacts business with the limited partnership, then the limited partner is liable to the third party as if a general partner.[21]

The last-mentioned rule—known as the "control rule"—has been the most litigated. Under both ULPA and the 1976 version of RULPA, it was impossible to draw any bright line or find any safe harbors for limited partner conduct. The current version of RULPA contains a lengthy list of activities that do not constitute participating in control. The list includes not only specific items (e.g., being an agent or employee of the partnership,[22] acting as a

---

18. RULPA §§608(a) (stating the general rule) and 607 (prohibiting distributions that leave the limited partnership effectively insolvent).

19. RULPA §303(d). This rule does not apply if the limited partner's name is the same as a general partner's or if the limited partnership had used the name before the limited partner became a limited partner.

20. RULPA §304(b).

21. RULPA §303(a) ("if [a] limited partner participates in the control of the business, he [or she] is liable only to persons who transact business with the limited partnership reasonably believing, based upon the limited partner's conduct, that the limited partner is a general partner").

22. RULPA §303(b)(1).

consultant to the general partner[23]) but also a very general provision that protects any right of control granted to the limited partners by the partnership agreement.[24]

> *Example:* Rebecca persuades Vladi to invest $10,000 in a business. The business is supposedly a limited partnership, with Rebecca as the general partner and Vladi as the limited partner. Vladi makes the investment, but Rebecca does not file any certificate of limited partnership. Subsequently, Michael sells 5,000 widgets to the business, having been assured by Rebecca that "the company is good for it and besides both Vladi and I are on the hook as general partners." When Vladi later learns of Rebecca's misstatement, he immediately confronts her and causes her to file a proper certificate of limited partnership. Vladi is nonetheless liable to Michael as a general partner. (Circumstance #6 on page 405)

> *Example:* Suzanne is the sole general partner of a limited partnership, but she relies heavily on the services of Paul, who is both a limited partner and the partnership's purchasing manager. In his capacity as purchasing manager Paul causes the partnership to buy 500,000 widgets from Rolande. The contract price is large, and it seems to Rolande that Paul has complete discretion in the matter. Rolande accordingly assumes that Paul is a general partner. The limited partnership has filed a certificate of limited partnership, and Paul is not listed as a general partner. No matter how reasonable Rolande's assumption, Paul is not personally liable on the widget transaction. He was acting as an employee of the partnership and is therefore within one of the safe harbors provided by RULPA. (Circumstance #7 on page 405)

§12.2.4 Management

The default management structure of a limited partnership is easily described. The general partners manage the business, and only the general partners have the power *qua* partners to bind the partnership.[25] Because of their management role, general partners owe fiduciary duties of loyalty and care to the partnership.

Limited partners are essentially passive. They do have the right to information about the partnership business,[26] may have the opportunity to consent to avoid or cause dissolution,[27] and in extraordinary circumstances can

---

23. RULPA §303(b)(2).
24. RULPA §303(b)(6)(ix).
25. Limited partners may have the power to bind the partnership as a matter of agency law. See Chapters Two and Three.
26. RULPA §305.
27. See section 12.2.7.

bring derivative suits to assert partnership claims against the general partners.[28] They do not, however, have any say in the ordinary operations of the
partnership.

> *Example:* Ventura, LP, is a RULPA limited partnership. Sarah is its sole
> general partner, and Alan is one of its limited partners. Purporting to act
> on behalf of Ventura, Alan signs a contract "Ventura, LP, by Alan, one of
> its partners." Even if the contract is well within the ordinary scope of
> Ventura's business, Ventura is not bound. Alan is merely a limited part-
> ner and, as such, lacks the power to bind the limited partnership.

> *Example:* Same facts, except that the other party to the contract reason-
> ably believes that Alan is a *general* partner and that belief is based on
> some manifestation legally attributable to Ventura. Under principles of
> agency law, Alan has the apparent authority to bind the limited partner-
> ship.[29]

The partnership agreement can enlarge the management role of the limited partners and can also shape the management prerogatives and responsibilities of the general partners. For example, some limited partnership
agreements give the limited partners the right to remove the general partners.

§12.2.5 Profit and Loss Sharing

RULPA's default rules on profit and loss sharing differ both structurally and
substantively from the UPA and RUPA rule. Both the UPA and RUPA provide simply that the partners share profits per capita (i.e., equally) and losses
according to profit share.[30] RULPA addresses the *allocation* of profits and
losses (which is important for bookkeeping and tax purposes) separately from
the sharing of actual *distributions*. However, the default rule is the same under
both rubrics. Subject to the partnership agreement, profits and losses are allocated and distributions are shared in proportion to "the value . . . of contributions made by each partner to the extent they have been received by the
partnership and have not been returned."[31]

---

28. RULPA §§1001-1004. In a derivative suit, a limited partner asserts standing to
enforce the partnership's rights. Protecting the partnership's rights—whether by litigation or otherwise—is a management matter and therefore ordinarily the province of
the general partners. Derivative plaintiffs typically assert, however, that the general
partners cannot be trusted to protect the partnership's interests because the general
partners are or will be defendants. For a more detailed discussion of derivative claims,
see section 13.5.6.

29. See sections 2.3 (apparent authority) and 10.2.4 (apparent authority of the
power-to-bind of general partners).

30. UPA §18(a); RUPA §401(b). See section 8.3.1.

31. The same language appears in RULPA §§503 (sharing of profits and losses) and
504 (sharing of distributions).

Example: Ofek, Lotem, Maor, and Noam are partners in a limited partnership. Ofek and Lotem are the general partners, each having contributed $10,000. Maor and Noam, the limited partners, contributed $50,000 and $40,000, respectively. Noam subsequently received $10,000 as a partial return of her contribution. The partnership agreement provides that Ofek and Lotem will each receive $50,000 per year as a management fee but says nothing about profits, losses, and distributions. The partnership will therefore allocate profits and losses and make distributions according to the following percentages:

Ofek	10%
Lotem	10%
Maor	50%
Noam	30%

§12.2.6 Transfer of Partnership Interests

Like ULPA (1916), RULPA—1976, the UPA, and RUPA, RULPA follows the "pick your partner" rule. Unless the partnership agreement provides otherwise, no partner, whether general or limited, may transfer its management authority to another person or substitute another person for itself as a partner without the consent of all the other partners.[32] Absent a contrary agreement, a partner may freely transfer its financial rights.[33]

§12.2.7 Partner Dissociation and Partnership Dissolution

In a general partnership, each partner has the power to dissociate at any time. Under the UPA, any dissociation inevitably causes dissolution and immediately puts the partnership into winding up.[34] As part of winding up, absent a contrary agreement each partner has the right to be paid the value of its interest in the partnership.[35]

A general partner in a limited partnership also has the power to "withdraw" at any time,[36] but that withdrawal does not necessarily cause dissolution. The limited partnership can avoid dissolution if either (1) the partnership has at least one remaining general partner, the partnership agreement allows the remaining general partners to continue the partnership, and the remaining general partners do so, or (2) within 90 days after the withdrawal, *all* the remaining partners (limited as well as general) agree in writing to continue the partnership.[37]

---

32. RULPA §702.

33. RULPA §702.

34. See section 11.2.1. The situation is different under RUPA. See section 11.9.3.

35. For a detailed discussion of partner dissociation and partnership dissolution in a general partnership, see Chapter Eleven.

36. RULPA §602. RULPA uses the term "withdrawal" to refer to partner dissociation. RULPA §402.

37. RULPA §801(4). If there is no remaining general partner, then the limited partners must also consent to appoint at least one new general partner. Id. Influenced by

If a general partner's withdrawal does result in dissolution, the consequences are comparable to the dissolution of a general partnership. If the partnership avoids dissolution, the dissociated general partner has a right, subject to the partnership agreement, to be paid "within a reasonable time after withdrawal, the fair value of his [or her] interest in the limited partnership."[38] A limited partnership agreement could conceivably freeze in the interest of a general partner who withdraws in breach of the partnership agreement.[39] In any event, if the withdrawal breached the partnership agreement, the payout amount is subject to any damages caused by the breach.[40]

In contrast to general partners, limited partners have no omnipresent power to dissociate. Whether they ever have that power depends on whether the partnership agreement states in writing a particular term for the partnership and whether the agreement provides in writing for limited partner withdrawal. If the partnership agreement does neither, then a limited partner can withdraw by giving at least six months written notice to each general partner.[41] If the partnership agreement states a particular term, then a limited partner can withdraw only if allowed by the agreement. If the partnership agreement provides for limited partner withdrawal, then—regardless of whether the agreement states a particular term—a limited partner can withdraw only as provided in the agreement. In tabular form:

	Limited Partnership Agreement Provides for Limited Partner Withdrawal	*Limited Partnership Agreement Does Not Provide for Limited Partner Withdrawal*
Limited Partnership Agreement Provides for Particular Term for Partnership	limited partner can withdraw only as provided in partnership agreement	limited partner cannot withdraw
Limited Partnership Agreement Does Not Provide for Particular Term for Partnership	limited partner can withdraw only as provided in partnership agreement	limited partner can withdraw on six months' written notice.

tax classification developments related to limited liability companies, see section 13.3, some RULPA states have amended their RULPA dissolution provisions to lower the quantum of consent needed to avoid dissolution following the withdrawal of a general partner.

38. RULPA §604 (brackets in the original).

39. Compare UPA §38(2) (if a partner wrongfully dissolves a general partnership, the remaining partners may delay that partner's payout and use the resources in a successor partnership). For a discussion of UPA §38(2), see section 11.5.5.

40. RULPA §602.

41. RULPA §603. This situation seems unlikely to occur, since RULPA §201(a)(4) requires the certificate of limited partnership to state a definite term. In light of RULPA §603, the term will be repeated in most limited partnership agreements.

The withdrawal of a limited partner does not cause or even threaten dissolution.[42] A limited partner who withdraws does have the right to be paid out within a reasonable time, unless the partnership agreement provides otherwise.[43]

For reasons related to so-called "family limited partnerships," some RULPA states have amended their version of RULPA to eliminate a limited partner's power to withdraw or to freeze in a limited partner's financial interest even after withdrawal.[44]

§12.3   ULPA (2001)[45]

§12.3.1 The Development of ULPA (2001)

Because RULPA is linked to the UPA, NCCUSL's promulgation of RUPA raised questions about RULPA. "RUPA differs substantially from the UPA, and the drafters of RUPA expressly declined to decide whether RUPA provides a suitable base and link for the limited partnership statute."[46]

In 1997 an NCCUSL drafting committee began considering what modifications to make to RULPA. The drafting committee quickly decided to develop a new, stand alone statute to replace RULPA. The committee determined that linkage "has not been completely satisfactory, because the consequences of linkage are not always clear" and because "in some instances the 'not inconsistent' rules of the UPA can be inappropriate for the fundamentally different relations involved in a limited partnership."[47] The committee also decided that a stand alone act would "promote clarity and coherence in the law of limited partnerships" by recognizing that "the modern limited partnership involves fundamentally different relations than those involved in 'the small, often informal, partnership' that is '[t]he primary focus of RUPA.' "[48] In particular, a stand alone act would "rationalize future case law, by ending the automatic link between the cases concerning partners in a general partnership and issues pertaining to general partners in a limited partnership."[49]

---

42. RULPA §801 (stating causes of dissolution and not mentioning the withdrawal of a limited partner). The partnership agreement could make a limited partner's withdrawal a cause of dissolution. See RULPA §801(2) (allowing the partnership agreement to specify additional events that cause dissolution).

43. RULPA §604.

44. Section 12.4 discusses family limited partnerships.

45. This section is derived from the Prefatory Notes and official Comments to ULPA (2001), which were drafted by the author in his capacity as Reporter to the NCCUSL Drafting Committee for ULPA (2001).

46. ULPA (2001), Prefatory Note, The Decision to "De-Link" and Create a Stand Alone Act.

47. Id.

48. Id., quoting RUPA, Prefatory Note.

49. ULPA (2001), Prefatory Note, The Decision to "De-Link" and Create a Stand Alone Act.

The drafting process took four years (during which the new Act was colloquially and temporarily referred to as "Re-RULPA"). In August 2001, NCCUSL gave final approval to ULPA (2001).

§12.3.2 Basic Purpose, Assumptions, and Approach

The basic purpose, assumptions and approach of ULPA (2001) are best summarized in the first section of the Act's Prefatory Note:

> The new Act has been drafted for a world in which limited liability partnerships and limited liability companies can meet many of the needs formerly met by limited partnerships. This Act therefore targets two types of enterprises that seem largely beyond the scope of LLPs and LLCs: (i) sophisticated, manager-entrenched commercial deals whose participants commit for the long term, and (ii) estate planning arrangements (family limited partnerships). This Act accordingly assumes that, more often than not, people utilizing it will want:
>
> - strong centralized management, strongly entrenched, and
> - passive investors with little control over or right to exit the entity
>
> The Act's rules, and particularly its default rules, have been designed to reflect these assumptions.[50]

§12.3.3 Overview of Major Differences Between RULPA and ULPA (2001)

There are 12 major differences between RULPA and ULPA (2001). In contrast to RULPA, ULPA (2001):

1. is a stand alone act, as previously explained, incorporating essentially verbatim many important provisions from RUPA;[51]
2. provides constructive notice, 90 days after appropriate filing, of general partner dissociation and of limited partnership dissolution, termination, merger, and conversion;[52]
3. has a perpetual duration, subject to change by the partnership agreement (and to earlier dissolution following the dissociation of a general partner and otherwise by partner consent);[53]

---

50. ULPA (2001), Prefatory Note, The Act's Overall Approach. Chapter Thirteen discusses limited liability companies. Section 14.2 discusses limited liability partnerships.

51. For example, ULPA (2001) incorporates RUPA's provisions on the power of a general partner to bind the partnership. ULPA (2001), §§402 (general partner agent of limited partnership) and 403 (limited partnership liable for general partner's actionable conduct), incorporating respectively RUPA §§301 and 305.

52. In this respect, ULPA (2001) follows the example of RUPA. See sections 10.3.5 (RUPA statements of authority), 11.10.2 (RUPA statements of dissociation) and, 11.11.2 (RUPA statements of dissolution).

53. ULPA (2001), §§104(c) and 802(2) and (3).

4. expressly delineates the permissible scope and effect of the partnership agreement;[54]

5. provides a complete, corporate-like liability shield for limited partners "even if the limited partner participates in the management and control of the limited partnership";[55]

6. permits a limited partnership to be a limited liability limited partnership (LLLP), and thereby makes a complete, corporate-like liability shield available to general partners;[56]

7. gives limited partners the power but not the right to dissociate before the limited partnership's termination and allows the partnership agreement to eliminate even the power;[57]

8. eliminates any pre-termination pay out to dissociated partners, unless the partnership agreement provides otherwise;[58]

9. eschews the UPA's open-ended approach to general partner fiduciary duties and incorporates essentially verbatim RUPA's provision on fiduciary duty and the obligation of good faith and fair dealing;[59]

10. provides for judicial expulsion of a general partner, although the partnership agreement can negate this provision;[60]

11. makes dissolution following a general partner's dissociation less likely, by replacing RULPA's unanimous consent rule with a two-pronged approach:

    a. if at least one general partner remains, no dissolution unless "within 90 days after the dissociation . . . partners owning a majority of the rights to receive distributions as partners" consent to dissolve the limited partnership;[61]

    b. if no general partner remains, dissolution occurs upon the passage of 90 days after the dissociation, unless before that deadline limited partners owning a majority of the rights to receive distributions owned by limited partners consent to continue the business and admit at least one new general partner and a new general partner is admitted;[62] and

12. authorizes a limited partnership to participate in mergers and conversions.[63]

---

54. ULPA (2001), §110.

55. ULPA (2001), §303. See section 12.3.4.

56. ULPA (2001), §§102(9), 201(a)(4), and 404(c). Section 14.3 discusses limited liability limited partnerships.

57. ULPA (2001), §§601(a) and 601(b)(1).

58. ULPA (2001), §§602(3) (limited partners) and 605(5) (general partner).

59. ULPA (2001), §408. In contrast with RUPA, ULPA (2001), §408(b)(3) provides that a general partner's non-compete duties continue during winding up.

60. ULPA (2001), §603(5).

61. ULPA (2001), §801(3)(A).

62. ULPA (2001), §801(3)(B).

63. ULPA (2001), Article 11. Section 11.14 explains mergers and conversions involving partnerships.

§12.3.4 Complete Shield for Limited Partners

ULPA (2001), §303 rejects the "control rule" of limited partner liability[64] and states:

> An obligation of a limited partnership, whether arising in contract, tort, or otherwise, is not the obligation of a limited partner. A limited partner is not personally liable, directly or indirectly, by way of contribution or otherwise, for an obligation of the limited partnership solely by reason of being a limited partner, even if the limited partner participates in the management and control of the limited partnership.

The official Comment explains: "In a world with LLPs, LLCs and, most importantly, LLLPs, the control rule has become an anachronism."

> *Example:* Ventura, LP is an ULPA (2001) limited partnership which initially has two general partners, Maurice and Rolande. Although Maurice dissociates, the limited partnership does not dissolve. To assist Rolande on an interim basis, two limited partners, Suzanne and Alan, become deeply involved in the management of the limited partnership. Even if a third party extends credit to the limited partnership believing Alan and Suzanne to be general partners, they are not liable for Ventura's obligations.[65]

As is the case with any liability shield, the limited partner's shield protects only against liability asserted "solely by reason of being" an owner of an entity.[66] As a result, the shield is irrelevant to (and therefore does not protect against) a limited partner's liability arising from (i) wrongful personal conduct; (ii) unfilled promises to contribute; (iii) improperly received distributions; and (iv) a mistaken belief that one is, in fact, a limited partner.[67]

§12.3.5 Freezing in the Transferable Interests of Dissociated Partners

Like RUPA, ULPA (2001) refers to the financial rights of partners as their "transferable interest." Under ULPA (2001), unless the partnership agreement provides otherwise, a partner who dissociates before the termination of a limited partnership becomes merely the transferee of his, her, or its own transferable interest.

---

64. See section 12.2.3.

65. If someone has misrepresented Alan's and Suzanne's status to the third party, the third party may have a claim for misrepresentation.

66. See section 14.2.3 (discussing this point in detail in the context of limited liability partnerships).

67. Compare section 12.2.3 (personal liability of RULPA limited partners). Under ULPA (2001), use of a limited partner's name in the name of the limited partnership does *not* put the limited partner at risk of personal liability. ULPA (2001), §108(a).

Example: Oscar is a limited partner in a ULPA (2001) limited partnership. When Oscar dies, his transferable interest will be distributed to his heirs according to estate law. There will be no payout to his heirs; they will acquire only whatever rights Oscar had to receive distributions.

Example: Cornflakes, LP is an ULPA (2001) limited partnership which initially has two general partners, Oscar and Felix. Oscar also owns a limited partner interest. Oscar's transferable interest as a general partner allocates to him the right to 1 percent of all distributions. His transferable interest as a limited partner allocates to him the right to 5 percent of all distributions.

Pursuant to the limited partnership agreement, Oscar is expelled as a general partner (but not as a limited partner). The limited partnership does not dissolve. Oscar continues to own the 5 percent as a limited partner (with whatever management rights may accompany that interest). He holds his 1 percent profits interest, however, as a mere transferee.

§12.3.6 *The Nexus Between General Partner Dissociation and Limited Partnership Dissolution*

Taking advantage of the tax classification flexibility created by the Internal Revenue Service in 1997,[68] ULPA (2001) significantly attenuated the nexus between general partner dissociation and limited partnership dissolution. ULPA (2001), §801(3) provides:

a limited partnership is dissolved, and its activities must be wound up, . . .

(3) after the dissociation of a person as a general partner:

(A) if the limited partnership has at least one remaining general partner, the consent to dissolve the limited partnership given within 90 days after the dissociation by partners owning a majority of the rights to receive distributions as partners at the time the consent is to be effective; or

(B) if the limited partnership does not have a remaining general partner, the passage of 90 days after the dissociation, unless before the end of the period:

(i) consent to continue the activities of the limited partnership and admit at least one general partner is given by limited partners owning a majority of the rights to receive distributions as limited partners at the time the consent is to be effective; and

ii) at least one person is admitted as a general partner in accordance with the consent; . . .

---

68. For a detailed discussion of the IRS's revolutionary "check the box" regulations, see section 13.3.

Example: Cornflakes, LP is an ULPA (2001) limited partnership which initially has two general partners, Oscar and Felix. Felix's transferable interest as a general partner allocates to him 2 percent of all distributions. Oscar's transferable interest as a general partner allocates to him the right to 1 percent of all distributions. Oscar also owns a limited partner interest, which allocates to him the right to 5 percent of all distributions. Other limited partners in the aggregate own the right to receive 82 percent of all distributions. Non-partner transferees in the aggregate own the right to receive 10 percent of all distributions.

Oscar dissociates from the limited partnership and hopes for dissolution. Oscar consents to dissolve the limited partnership as do other limited partners owning in the aggregate 39 percent of the rights to receive distributions. The limited partnership is not dissolved. ULPA (2001), §801(3)(A)(i) requires consent "by partners owning a majority of the rights to receive distributions as partners" (emphasis added). The calculation is as follows:

Felix as general partner	2%
Oscar as limited partner	5%[69]
Other limited partners	82%
Total relevant percent	89%
Majority needed to dissolve	>44.5%
Percent consenting to dissolution	44%
Oscar as limited partner (5%) + other limited partners (39%)	

§12.3.7 *Dissolution by Consent of the Partners*

Perhaps paradoxically, it is easier under ULPA (2001) than under RULPA to dissolve a limited partnership by consent of the partners. RULPA §801(3) requires "the written consent of all partners." In contrast, ULPA (2001), §801(2) states that the limited partnership is dissolved upon "the consent of all general partners and of limited partners owning a majority of the rights to receive distributions as limited partners at the time the consent is to be effective."

Example: XYZ is a limited partnership with three general partners, each of whom is also a limited partner, and five other limited partners. Rights to receive distributions are allocated as follows:

Partner #1 as general partner	3%
Partner #2 as general partner	2%
Partner #3 as general partner	1%
Partner #1 as limited partner	7%
Partner #2 as limited partner	3%
Partner #3 as limited partner	4%

---

69. After Oscar's dissociation, he owns as a mere transferee the transferable interest (1 percent) he formerly owned as a general partner. ULPA (2001), §605(a)(5).

> Partner #4 as limited partner   5%
> Partner #5 as limited partner   5%
> Partner #6 as limited partner   5%
> Partner #7 as limited partner   5%
> Partner #8 as limited partner   5%
> Several non-partner transferees, in the aggregate 55%

Distribution rights owned by persons as limited partners amount to 39 percent of total distribution rights. A majority is therefore anything greater than 19.5 percent. If only partners 1, 2, 3, and 4 consent to dissolve, the limited partnership is not dissolved. Together these partners own as limited partners 19 percent of the distribution rights owned by persons as limited partners—just short of the necessary majority. For purposes of this calculation, distribution rights owned by non-partner transferees are irrelevant. So, too, are distribution rights owned by persons as general partners. (However, dissolution under this provision requires "the consent of all general partners.")[70]

§12.3.8 Detailed Comparison of RULPA and ULPA (2001)

The following table[71] compares some of the major characteristics of RULPA and ULPA (2001). In most instances, the rules involved are "default" rules—i.e., subject to change by the partnership agreement.

Characteristic	RULPA	ULPA (2001)
relationship to general partnership act	linked, §§1105, 403; UPA §6(2)	de-linked (but many RUPA provisions incorporated)
permitted purposes	subject to any specified exceptions, "any business that a partnership without limited partners may carry on," §106	any lawful purpose, §104(b)
constructive notice via publicly filed documents	only that limited partnership exists and that designated general partners are general partners, §208	RULPA constructive notice provisions carried forward, §103(c), plus constructive notice, 90 days after appropriate filing, of: general partner dissociation and of limited partnership dissolution, termination, merger and conversion, §103(d)
duration	specified in certificate of limited partnership, §201(a)(4)	perpetual, §104(c); subject to change in partnership agreement

---

70. This Example is taken verbatim from the Comment to ULPA (2001), §801, Paragraph (2).

71. This table appears at the end of the Prefatory Note to ULPA (2001) and is used by permission of the Reporter.

Characteristic	RULPA	ULPA (2001)
use of limited partner name in entity name	prohibited, except in unusual circumstances, §102(2)	permitted, §108(a)
annual report	none	required, §210
limited partner liability for entity debts	none unless limited partner "participates in the control of the business" and person "transact[s] business with the limited partnership reasonably believing . . . that the limited partner is a general partner," §303(a); safe harbor lists many activities that do not constitute participating in the control of the business, §303(b)	none, regardless of whether the limited partnership is an LLLP, "even if the limited partner participates in the management and control of the limited partnership," §303
limited partner duties	none specified	no fiduciary duties "solely by reason of being a limited partner," §305(a); each limited partner is obliged to "discharge duties . . . and exercise rights consistently with the obligation of good faith and fair dealing," §305(b)
partner access to information— required records/ information	all partners have right of access; no requirement of good cause; Act does not state whether partnership agreement may limit access; §§105(b) and 305(1)	list of required information expanded slightly; Act expressly states that partner does not have to show good cause; §§304(a), 407(a); however, the partnership agreement may set reasonable restrictions on access to and use of required information, §110(b)(4), and limited partnership may impose reasonable restrictions on the use of information, §§304(g) and 407(f)
partner access to information— other information	limited partners have the right to obtain other relevant information "upon reasonable demand," §305(2); general partner rights linked to general partnership act, §403	for limited partners, RULPA approach essentially carried forward, with procedures and standards for making a reasonable demand stated in greater detail, plus requirement that limited partnership supply known material information when limited partner consent sought, §304; general partner access rights made explicit, following ULLCA and RUPA, including obligation of limited partnership and general partners to volunteer certain information, §407; access rights provided for former partners, §§304 and 407

table continues

Characteristic	RULPA	ULPA (2001)
general partner liability for entity debts	complete, automatic and formally inescapable, §403(b) (n.b.—in practice, most modern limited partnerships have used a general partner that has its own liability shield; e.g., a corporation or limited liability company)	LLLP status available via a simple statement in the certificate of limited partnership, §§102(9), 201(a)(4); LLLP status provides a full liability shield to all general partners, §404(c); if the limited partnership is not an LLLP, general partners are liable just as under RULPA, §404(a)
general partner duties	linked to duties of partners in a general partnership, §403	RUPA general partner duties imported, §408; general partner's non-compete duty continues during winding up, §408(b)(3)
allocation of profits, losses and distributions	provides separately for sharing of profits and losses, §503, and for sharing of distributions, §504; allocates each according to contributions made and not returned	eliminates as unnecessary the allocation rule for profits and losses; allocates distributions according to contributions made, §503 (n.b.—in the default mode, the Act's formulation produces the same result as RULPA formulation)
partner liability for distributions	recapture liability if distribution involved "the return of . . . contribution"; one year recapture liability if distribution rightful, §608(a); six-year recapture liability if wrongful, §608(b)	following ULLCA §§406 and 407, the Act adopts the RMBCA approach to improper distributions, §§508 and 509
limited partner voluntary dissociation	theoretically, limited partner may withdraw on six months' notice unless partnership agreement specifies a term for the limited partnership or withdrawal events for limited partner, §603; practically, virtually every partnership agreement specifies a term, thereby eliminating the right to withdraw (n.b.—due to estate planning concerns, several States have amended RULPA to prohibit limited partner withdrawal unless otherwise provided in the partnership agreement)	no "right to dissociate as a limited partner before the termination of the limited partnership," §601(a); power to dissociate expressly recognized, §601(b)(1), but can be eliminated by the partnership agreement
limited partner involuntary dissociation	not addressed	lengthy list of causes, §601(b), taken with some modification from RUPA

Characteristic	RULPA	ULPA (2001)
limited partner dissociation—payout	"fair value . . . based upon [the partner's] right to share in distributions," §604	no payout; person becomes transferee of its own transferable interest, §602(3)
general partner voluntary dissociation	right exists unless otherwise provided in partnership agreement, §602; power exists regardless of partnership agreement, §602	RULPA rule carried forward, although phrased differently, §604(a); dissociation before termination of the limited partnership is defined as wrongful, §604(b)(2)
general partner involuntary dissociation	§402 lists causes	following RUPA, §603 expands the list of causes, including expulsion by court order, §603(5)
general partner dissociation—payout	"fair value . . . based upon [the partner's] right to share in distributions," §604, subject to offset for damages caused by wrongful withdrawal, §602	no payout; person becomes transferee of its own transferable interest, §605(5)
transfer of partner interest—nomenclature	"Assignment of Partnership Interest," §702	"Transfer of Partner's Transferable Interest," §702
transfer of partner interest—substance	economic rights fully transferable, but management rights and partner status are not transferable, §702	same rule as RULPA, but §§701 and 702 follow RUPA's more detailed and less oblique formulation
rights of creditor of partner	limited to charging order, §703	essentially the same rule as RULPA, but, following RUPA and ULLCA, the Act has a more elaborate provision that expressly extends to creditors of transferees, §703
dissolution by partner consent	requires unanimous written consent, §801(3)	requires consent of "all general partners and of limited partners owning a majority of the rights to receive distributions as limited partners at the time the consent is to be effective," §801(2)
dissolution following dissociation of a general partner	occurs automatically unless all partners agree to continue the business and, if there is no remaining general partner, to appoint a replacement general partner, §801(4)	if at least one general partner remains, no dissolution unless "within 90 days after the dissociation . . . partners owning a majority of the rights to receive distributions as partners" consent to dissolve the limited partnership, §801(3)(A); if no general partner remains, dissolution occurs upon the passage of 90 days after

table continues

Characteristic	RULPA	ULPA (2001)
		the dissociation, unless before that deadline limited partners owning a majority of the rights to receive distributions owned by limited partners consent to continue the business and admit at least one new general partner and a new general partner is admitted, §801(3)(B)
filings related to entity termination	certificate of limited partnership to be cancelled when limited partnership dissolves and begins winding up, §203	limited partnership may amend certificate to indicate dissolution, §803(b)(1), and may file statement of termination indicating that winding up has been completed and the limited partnership is terminated, §203
procedures for barring claims against dissolved limited partnership	none	following ULLCA §§807 and 808, the Act adopts the RMBCA approach providing for giving notice and barring claims, §§806 and 807
conversions and mergers	no provision	Article 11 permits conversions to and from and mergers with any "organization," defined as "a general partnership, including a limited liability partnership; limited partnership, including a limited liability limited partnership; limited liability company; business trust; corporation; or any other entity having a governing statute . . . [including] domestic and foreign entities regardless of whether organized for profit." §1101(8)
writing requirements	some provisions pertain only to written understandings; see, e.g., §§401 (partnership agreement may "provide in writing for the admission of additional general partners"; such admission also permitted "with the written consent of all partners"), 502(a) (limited partner's promise to contribute "is not enforceable unless set out in a writing signed by the limited partner"), 801(2) and (3) (dissolution occurs "upon the	removes virtually all writing requirements; but does require that certain information be maintained in record form, §111

Characteristic	RULPA	ULPA (2001)
	happening of events specified in writing in the partnership agreement" and upon "written consent of all partners"), 801(4) (dissolution avoided following withdrawal of a general partner if "all partners agree in writing")	

§12.4 Family Limited Partnerships

One of the major uses of limited partnerships is the so-called "family limited partnership." A family limited partnership is an estate planning vehicle whose use requires very sophisticated planning under some very abstruse IRS regulations concerning estate and gift tax. The details of that planning and those regulations are far beyond the scope of this chapter, but it is worthwhile to note several points that have influenced the developments in limited partnership statutes:

1. When a person makes a noncharitable gift of major value, the gift is subject to a gift tax, with the amount of tax based on the fair market value of the gift. To determine fair market value, the law tries to determine the price a hypothetical willing buyer and willing seller would agree on, with neither facing any compulsion to make a deal.

2. A major purpose of a family limited partnership is to allow wealthy members of one generation to gift property to a younger generation in a way that enables the donor to claim substantial discounts in the fair market value of the gift.

3. If a family limited partnership owns substantial assets, the would-be donors can

    a. serve as general partners of the limited partnership, thereby keeping control of the assets during their lifetime, while

    b. gifting limited partner interests to members of younger generations, and

    c. claiming large discounts on the fair market value of the gifts because

        i. a limited partner has no right to force distributions or dissolution (which would produce a payout via winding up and liquidation),

        ii. the general partner is not subject to removal and completely controls operations, and therefore

        iii. the hypothetical willing buyer would not pay a large amount for the limited partner interest.

From the perspective of valuation discounts, the more locked in (i.e., illiquid) a limited partner interest is, the better. And, because the IRS regulations will disregard any restrictions on liquidity created by agreement,[72] the illiquidity must be built into the default rules of the limited partnership statute.

To accommodate this perspective, a number of RULPA states have amended their version of RULPA to protect limited partnerships from dissolution, prevent limited partners from withdrawing, and lock in a limited partner's transferable interest even if the limited partner does withdraw. ULPA (2001) has incorporated all those approaches, giving each limited partnership a perpetual term,[73] attenuating the nexus between general partner dissociation and limited partnership dissolution,[74] depriving limited partners of the right to dissociate,[75] permitting the partnership agreement to eliminate a limited partner's power to dissociate[76] and providing that a partner who dissociates is not entitled to any payout on account of having dissociated.[77]

PROBLEM 114

Rosebud, LP is a limited partnership with a term of 30 years. Ten years into the term, an opportunity arises to sell all the partnership's assets and make a substantial profit. All the limited partners wish to take advantage of this opportunity, but the sole general partner believes that greater returns will be available if the limited partnership continues in existence until the end of its 30-year term. Under RULPA, can the limited partners bring about the sale of the partnership's assets? Under ULPA (2001)?

Explanation

No, under either statute. With exceptions not relevant here, both statutes vest all management authority in the general partner. Moreover, neither statute permits the limited partners to cause the premature dissolution of the limited partnership and thereby force the general partner to sell the assets as part of winding up. Under RULPA §801(3), dissolution by partner consent requires "the written consent of all partners." ULPA (2001), §801(2) requires "the consent of all general partners and of limited partners owning a majority of the rights to receive distributions as limited partners."

---

72. The rationale for disregarding what are called "applicable restrictions" is that in a family limited partnership the family will agree to disregard the restrictions when it suits the family's purposes.

73. ULPA (2001), §104(c).

74. ULPA (2001), §801(3).

75. ULPA (2001), §§601(a) and 601(b)(1).

76. ULPA (2001), §110(b).

77. ULPA (2001), §§602(3) (limited partner) and 605(5) (general partner).

PROBLEM 115

Wife is the sole general partner of a limited partnership. Husband, who is retired, assists Wife in running the business by working as the unofficial office manager of the limited partnership's principal place of business. Husband's efforts are voluntary and are not compensated. Husband owns a limited partner's interest in the partnership, which is reflected in the partnership agreement. The partnership agreement does not indicate that Husband has any role in managing the limited partnership.

A trade creditor of the limited partnership, knowing that Wife is a general partner and seeing that Husband performs key administrative functions, believes that Husband is also a general partner. The trade creditor maintains an "open account" with the limited partnership—i.e., delivering products and invoicing the limited partnership for payment after delivery.

The limited partnership becomes insolvent, still owing the trade creditor substantial amounts. If the limited partnership is organized under RULPA, does the trade creditor have a valid claim against Husband? What if the limited partnership is organized under ULPA (2001)?

EXPLANATION

The trade creditor may have a valid claim under RULPA, §303(a). Husband is a limited partner who, arguably at least, has "participate[d] in the control of the business." The trade creditor has "transacted business with the limited partnership reasonably believing, based upon the limited partner's conduct, that the limited partner [was] a general partner."

However, Husband may qualify for one of the safe harbors of RULPA §303(b). Husband's best chance is to assert RULPA §303(b)(1) and claim that he was merely "being . . . an agent . . . of the limited partnership."[78]

The result is clearer under ULPA (2001) §303: "A limited partner is not personally liable, directly or indirectly, by way of contribution or otherwise, for an obligation of the limited partnership solely by reason of being a limited partner, even if the limited partner participates in the management and control of the limited partnership."

PROBLEM 116

XYZ Limited Partnership ("XYZ") is managed by a sole general partner, ABC, Inc. ("ABC"), which is itself a corporation. ABC is the general partner of several different limited partnerships and, by a resolution of its board of directors, has authorized Shapiro, its Executive Vice President, to act for ABC in all matters within the ordinary course of ABC's responsibilities as the general partner of XYZ. Shapiro is also a limited partner in XYZ.

---

78. It should not matter that Husband worked without pay. A gratuitous agent is just as much an agent as a paid agent. See section 1.2.5.

Purporting to act on behalf of XYZ, Shapiro signs a contract for 18 months of janitorial services at the building where XYZ maintains its headquarters. Is XYZ bound by Shapiro's act?

EXPLANATION

Yes. Although under both RULPA and ULPA (2001) Shapiro *qua* limited partner lacks the power to bind XYZ, Shapiro is also the authorized agent of the XYZ's general partner. In that capacity, Shapiro has the power to bind XYZ.

Because Shapiro was acting within the actual authority conferred on him by the resolution of ABC's board of directors, Shapiro's act is deemed an act of ABC. As the sole general partner of XYZ, ABC probably has the actual authority and certainly has the apparently/usual or apparently/ordinary power to bind XYZ to a janitorial contract.[79]

PROBLEM 117

Same facts as Problem 116. Does Shapiro's substantial involvement in the management of XYZ expose him to liability for XYZ's obligations?

EXPLANATION

The answer is the same under both RULPA and ULPA (2001)—no. Under ULPA (2001), a limited partner does not risk personal liability simply by participating in control of the business. ULPA (2001), §303. As for RULPA, Shapiro's activities come within the safe harbor protection of §303(b) ("being an officer . . . of a general partner that is a corporation").

---

79. If the limited partnership is governed by RULPA, per RULPA §403(a) "a general partner of a limited partnership has the rights and powers . . . of a partner in a partnership without limited partners"—i.e., UPA §9(1) applies and with it the concept of apparently/usual power. See section 10.2. If the limited partnership is governed by ULPA (2001), per ULPA (2001) §402(a) a general partner has apparently/ordinary power to bind the partnership. See section 10.3 (discussing this power in the context of RUPA §301).

13

Limited Liability Companies and the Revolution in Unincorporated Business Organizations[1]

§13.1 The Modern World of Unincorporated Business Organizations

§13.1.1 Entity Proliferation

Before 1988, the U.S. world of unincorporated business organizations had two main players: ordinary general partnerships (discussed in Chapters Seven to Eleven) and ordinary limited partnerships (discussed in Chapter Twelve). Today, limited liability companies ("LLCs") are increasingly prominent, most general partnerships should be limited liability partnerships ("LLPs"), and the new Uniform Limited Partnership Act (2001) provides for limited liability limited partnerships ("LLLPs"). To make sense of this "alphabet soup" requires understanding what caused the world of unincorporated business organizations to change so dramatically.

---

1. Some of this chapter is based on materials in Carter G. Bishop & Daniel S. Kleinberger, Limited Liability Companies: Tax and Business Law, (Warren, Gorham & Lamont/RIA 1994-2002) ("Bishop & Kleinberger"), Chapter 1. Materials used with permission of the authors.

The driving force was the desire to solve the "the tax-shield conundrum"—i.e., to create an entity which

- as a matter of tax law would be classified as a partnership with each owner treated as a partner, while
- as a matter of non-tax law would shield each of the owners from the automatic personal liability of a general partner.

The change began with the invention of limited liability companies.

§13.1.2 Essence of the Limited Liability Company

The limited liability company (LLC) is a relatively new, hybrid form of business entity that combines the liability shield of a corporation with the federal tax classification of a partnership. A creature of state law, each LLC is organized under an LLC statute that creates the company, gives it a legal existence separate from its owner or owners (called "members"), shields those members from partner-like vicarious liability, governs the company's operations, and controls how and when the company comes to an end. The essence of an LLC is the coexistence of partnership tax status with corporate-like limited liability.

LLCs were revolutionary when they first appeared, and it was a new interpretation of federal tax law that made the revolution possible. In 1988, the Internal Revenue Service issued Revenue Ruling 88-76, declaring that a Wyoming LLC would be taxed as a partnership—despite the company's corporate-like liability shield.

Revenue Ruling 88-76 applied the four-factor test of the now-defunct "Kintner" tax classification regulations,[2] and those regulations constrained both the structure of LLCs and the growth of the LLC phenomenon. Over the next nine years, the Service gradually relaxed many of the constraints and, effective January 1, 1997, threw them out almost entirely. The "check-the-box" regulations jettisoned Kintner's four factors, providing federal partnership tax status for virtually any multi-owner business entity formed under a state statute unless that statute refers to the entity as a corporation.[3] The regulations also dealt with single member LLCs ("SMLLC"), deeming them "disregarded entities" for federal income tax purposes and providing that the economic activities of an SMLLC are treated as if directly undertaken by the SMLLC's sole member.[4]

---

2. The Kintner regulations are summarized in section 13.3.1.

3. See Classification of Certain Business Entities, 61 Fed. Reg. 66,584, 66,590 (1996), codified at 26 CFR §301.7701-3.

4. The IRS would not accord partnership tax status to single owner entities, reasoning that a partnership must have two or more owners. *Corporate* tax status is available to any LLC which prefers it. The regulations have the colloquial name "check the box" for a very simple reason: "Under 'check-the-box,' each domestic entity—other than one organized pursuant to a corporate or joint stock statute—determines its own tax status simply by checking or not checking a box [on an IRS form]. Indeed, unless an unincorporated organization elects otherwise, it will be taxed as a partnership" unless it has but one owner,

The LLC thus eliminated the tax-shield conundrum—i.e., the trade-off between liability protection and tax status that had bedeviled practitioners and entrepreneurs for decades. Today, all 50 states and the District of Columbia have LLC statutes, and, as of 1995, more than 210,000 LLCs have been formed.

§13.2 The Need for Limited Liability Companies: The Tax-Shield Conundrum

§13.2.1 *The Conundrum Explained*

To understand the tax-shield conundrum requires understanding the characteristics of the corporate liability shield and the advantages of partnership tax classification.

Corporate liability shield. In a corporation, the owners (called "shareholders" or "stockholders") are not, merely on account of ownership status, liable for the obligations of the corporation. They are thus "shielded" from the automatic liability by status which comes with being a partner in an ordinary general partnership[5] or a general partner in an ordinary limited partnership.[6]

Example: Athos, Porthos, and Aramis form a corporation ("Fencing, Inc.") to teach fencing. They are its shareholders, and, as shareholders, they elect themselves to the corporation's board of directors.[7] The board elects Athos as chief executive officer, Porthos as Executive Vice President, and Aramis as chief financial officer. Acting through one of its duly authorized officers, the corporation then rents a building to serve as its headquarters and teaching center. Under agency law principles, the corporation is bound to the lease.[8] Athos, Porthos, and Aramis, in contrast, are not. Shareholders *qua* shareholders are not personally liable for corporate obligations.

Example: Same facts, except Athos, Porthos, and Aramis form an ordinary general partnership. They are each personally liable on the lease.

Example: Same facts, except Athos, Porthos, and Aramis form an ordinary limited partnership, with Aramis as the sole general partner. Athos

---

in which case the organization is simply disregarded for federal income tax purposes. Bishop & Kleinberger, §1.01[3][e] at 1-15.

5. See section 7.3.
6. See section 12.2.3.
7. The board of directors is the top decision-making component of a corporation.
8. See section 2.2.4 (agent acting for disclosed principal).

and Porthos do not involve themselves in managing the business, although they are employed as fencing instructors.[9] Aramis is personally liable on the lease; Athos and Porthos are not.

The shield does not protect a shareholder from liability resulting from the shareholder's own conduct. Moreover, the "shield" protects the shareholders, not the corporation. Indeed, the entire point of the shield is to prevent the corporation's obligations from being automatically imputed to the shareholders. Nonetheless, common usage refers to "the corporate shield" or "the corporation's shield" or "the corporate liability shield."

> *Example:* Acting as an employee of Fencing, Inc., Porthos gives fencing lessons to individual students. Distracted by personal concerns, he negligently inflicts a leg wound. The corporate shield is irrelevant to the student's tort claim against Porthos. That claim has nothing to do with Porthos's status as a shareholder but rather arises from his own misconduct. Likewise, the shield is irrelevant to the student's respondeat superior[10] and direct liability claims against the corporation.[11]

The corporate shield is not completely impermeable. When a dominant shareholder has abused the corporate form, in the interests of justice courts will "pierce the veil" protecting the shareholder and impose personal liability for the corporation's debts. Piercing claims are rarely successful, however, and the corporate shield is an extremely important advantage of the corporate form of business organization.[12]

Partnership tax classification.   All business organizations are subject to the provisions of the Internal Revenue Code concerning income tax.[13] For any organization with two or more owners, the threshold question under those provisions is whether the organization will be classified (and therefore taxed) as a partnership or a corporation.

In most situations partnership tax status is preferable, because corporate shareholders face "double taxation" on any dividends they receive. An ordinary "C corporation"[14] is a taxable entity; it pays dividends out of its after-tax "earnings and profits." Those dividends are taxed when received by

---

9. See section 12.2.3 (explaining how, under RULPA, a limited partner risks personal liability from being overly involved in the business and describing a list of safe harbors).

10. See section 3.2 (discussing respondeat superior). The conduct of a person *qua* shareholder is not attributable to the corporation, but the conduct of a servant (who happens to be a shareholder) may be.

11. See section 4.4.1.

12. See section 13.5.7 for further discussion of piercing.

13. Business organizations are also subject to state tax codes, and in most matters pertaining to this chapter most state income tax regimes follow the federal approach.

14. So-called because it is taxed under Subchapter C of the Internal Revenue Code.

the shareholders. In essence, the profits comprising those dividends are taxed twice.

Partners avoid this double taxation, because, unlike a corporation, a partnership is not a taxable entity. For income tax purposes, partnerships are "pass through" entities. Partnership profits (whether distributed or not) are deemed to pass through to the partners, who pay tax on them. Partnership losses also pass through and can serve as deductions on each partner's own tax return. In contrast, the losses of an ordinary corporation stay with the entity, and are useful only if the entity later enjoys a profit.

Example: In its most recent taxable year, Fencing, Inc. made a profit of $100,000 and would like to distribute all its profits to its shareholders. Assuming a corporate tax rate of 25 percent, an individual tax rate of 20 percent, and that Athos, Porthos, and Aramis own the same number of shares of stock (and therefore share dividends equally), the calculations and results are:

Taxable Corporate Profit	100,000
Less Corporate Income Tax	(25,000)
Available for Distribution	75,000
Dividend to Each Shareholder	25,000
Less Individual Income Tax	(5,000)
Net to Each Shareholder	20,000
Allocation of Profits	
to Federal Government	**40,000**
(corp. 25,000; ind. 3 × 5,000)	
to shareholders	**60,000**

Example: Same facts, except that Athos, Porthos, and Aramis have formed a partnership.[15] The calculations and results are:

Profit	100,000
No Partnership Income Tax	(0)
Available for Distribution	100,000
Distribution to Each Partner	33,333[16]
Less Individual Income Tax	(6,667)[17]
Net to Each Partner	26,666
Allocation of Profits	
to Federal Government	**20,001**
(ind. 3 × 6,667)	
to partners	**79,998[18]**

---

15. For present purposes, it does not matter whether the partnership is a general partnership or a limited partnership.

16. Rounded, for simplicity's sake.

17. Rounded.

18. One dollar is unaccounted for, due to rounding.

Comparison of Examples

	Corporation	Partnership
Federal government's "share"	40,000	20,001
Owners' share (aggregate)	60,000	79,998

A partnership's "pass through" character brings other advantages as well; the disadvantage has always been on the non-tax side—i.e., personal liability. Prior to the advent of limited liability companies, limited liability partnerships, and limited liability limited partnerships, an organization could obtain partnership tax classification only if at least one partner was liable for the business's debts. Put another way, entrepreneurs who wanted the complete, corporate shield had to pay some form of tax cost for the protection. In its simplest manifestation, that cost consisted of double taxation of a business's profits. Thus: the tax-shield conundrum.

§13.2.2 Dealing with the Conundrum—Pre-LLC

For many years there have been several widely used vehicles for mitigating the effects of the tax-shield conundrum. To retain partnership tax status while minimizing liability risk, entrepreneurs could resort to an ordinary limited partnership with a corporate general partner.[19] To maintain a full corporate shield while obtaining some of the advantages of partnership tax status, entrepreneurs could use an S corporation[20] or try to "zero out" the profits of a C corporation. None of these approaches was fully satisfactory.

Ordinary limited partnerships.   An ordinary limited partnership's liability shield can approach the corporate version, but only at the cost of (i) tying up capital, and (ii) at least before ULPA (2001), depriving most of the partners of any significant role in management. Under federal tax regulations in effect before January 1, 1997,[21] and most state limited partnership acts before ULPA (2001), each limited partnership had to have at least one general partner and that general partner had to be personally liable for the limited partnership's debts. As a matter of state law, that general partner could be a corporation, but before January 1, 1997, that approach raised tax classification issues. For a limited partnership with a corporate general partner to be sure of being taxed as a

---

19.   I.e., having the general partner be a corporation.

20.   So-called because its owners have elected to have the corporation taxed under Subchapter S of the Internal Revenue Code.

21.   For an explanation of the dramatic change made effective January 1, 1997, by the "check the box" regulations, see section 13.3.

partnership, the net worth of the corporate general partner (exclusive of the general partner's interest in the limited partnership) had to equal 10 percent of the total contributions of all limited partners. Complying with this requirement diverted capital that could otherwise be engaged in the business. Even after January 1, 1997, using a thinly capitalized corporate general partner raises the possibility of liability through piercing the veil of the corporate general partner.

As for the limited partners, except under ULPA (2001) their shield is safe only if they stay out of management. Limited partners risk personal liability if they are too involved in the business. At the same time, however, limited partners can lose some of the tax benefits of partnership losses if they do not materially participate in the business.

S corporations. An S corporation provides a full corporate liability shield with some of the benefits of pass-through tax status. Like a partnership, an S corporation generally pays no tax on its earnings, and its profits and losses are passed through and taxed directly to its shareholders. However, there the similarity to partnerships ends. S corporations face significant constraints that do not apply to partnerships. Subchapter S significantly limits who can own interests in the enterprise, what kind of business the enterprise may conduct, and how the enterprise may structure its finances. Moreover, decisions which make sense for an S corporation's business may have untoward tax consequences for the corporation's shareholders.

Restrictions on owners. For most practical purposes, all shareholders in an S corporation must be either U.S. citizens or resident aliens. Subchapter S therefore rules out a long list of potential owners and investors, including all corporations, investment banks, venture capital firms, and most foreign nationals. Moreover, an S corporation may not have more than 75 shareholders.

Restrictions on businesses. Subchapter S also rules out a long list of business types and structures. For example, a corporation may not obtain or retain S status if it is a foreign corporation, a bank or savings and loan association, or an insurance company.[22]

Restrictions on financial structure. An S corporation may have only one class of stock. This requirement precludes flexible allocations of profits, restricts the type of debt the corporation may issue, hampers efforts to gradually shift control of family-owned businesses, and, in general, makes passive investment very difficult to structure.[23]

---

22. Also prohibited: a possessions corporation, a domestic international sales corporation (DISC) or former DISC, or a regulated investment company (RIC), real estate investment trust (REIT), or real estate mortgage investment conduit (REMIC).

23. The "one class of stock" restriction pertains to economic rights but not to governance rights.

Untoward consequences for owners.   Unlike a partnership, an S corporation is not a complete pass-through entity. As a result, S corporations contain a number of traps for the unwary. For example, distributions to shareholders of appreciated property trigger a gain to the corporation and hence to the shareholders.[24]

C corporations and "zeroing out."   A corporation that cannot, or chooses not to, elect S status can try to avoid double taxation by "zeroing out." To "zero out," the C corporation makes ostensibly deductible payments to shareholder-employees, thereby reducing or eliminating corporate profits. These payments can be made in a number of ways; the simplest are salaries and bonuses.

This approach is not risk-free, however. The Internal Revenue Service may view the payments as disguised dividends, especially where (1) the payments are excessive compared with the value of the services rendered to the corporation,[25] (2) the payments are proportional to the shareholders equity interests,[26] or (3) capital is a material income-producing factor for the business and the corporation is not paying reasonable dividends.[27] Even when successful, zeroing out techniques provide none of the other advantages of pass-through tax status.

---

24. Appreciated property is property whose fair market value (FMV) exceeds the corporation's tax "basis" in the property. This situation can occur because the value of the property has increased since the time the corporation acquired it, or because the value of the property has decreased by an amount less than the amount of tax deductions taken by the corporation on account of the property. Suppose, for example, that Fencing, Inc. owns three antique epées, each purchased by the corporation several years ago for $1,000 (giving the corporation a tax basis of $1,000 in each epée), and each epée is now worth $2,000. If the corporation decides to distribute one epée to each of its shareholders as a dividend "in kind," and assuming (for the sake of simplicity) that the corporation has taken no deductions on account of the epées, each of the shareholders will incur $1,000 of taxable gain ($2,000 FMV minus $1,000 basis). Other "traps" include: (i) the basis of a shareholder's stock is not increased to take into account any corporate debt, thereby limiting the shareholders' ability to take advantage of passed-through losses; (ii) when a shareholder dies, the basis of the assets of the corporation is not adjusted to reflect the estate's stepped-up basis, thereby putting the estate at risk of realizing unexpected and (in an economic sense) phantom gains.

25. This factor suggests that part of the payments are not genuinely salary for the EMPLOYEE/shareholder but rather a disguised return on the ownership interest of the SHAREHOLDER/employee.

26. Unless the shareholder employees are all doing work whose fair market value just happens to be in proportion to the shareholders' stock holdings, this factor suggests that the payments are "in respect of" the ownership interests (i.e., distributions, and taxable as such) rather than in compensation for services.

27. If capital—i.e., assets owned by the corporation—plays an important role in producing revenue, dividends should provide the owners of the corporation a return on (i.e., compensation for) the investment reflected in those assets. If the corporation is not paying appropriate dividends, it may be disguising as salary payments that which should properly be considered a return on investment—i.e., dividends.

§13.3 Invention and Development of the LLC

§13.3.1 Wyoming Starts a Revolution

Wyoming began the LLC revolution by taking seriously the Internal Revenue Service's "Kintner" Regulations on tax classification. Before January 1, 1997, those regulations determined how to classify unincorporated business organizations and were biased toward finding partnership status. The regulations identified four key corporate characteristics (limited liability, continuity of life, free transferability of ownership interests, centralized management), and classified an unincorporated organization as a corporation only if the organization had three or more of the corporate characteristics. Although limited liability may seem to be the hallmark corporate characteristic, the Kintner Regulations contained no "super" factor. Each characteristic was as significant as another.

The Wyoming legislature sought to resolve the "tax-shield conundrum" by exploiting that aspect of the Kintner Regulations. Enacted in 1977, the Wyoming LLC Act gave every Wyoming LLC a full, corporate-like liability shield and partnership-like characteristics as to entity management, continuity of life, and transferability of ownership interests. Like a general partnership, a Wyoming LLC was managed by its owners. Like a limited partnership, a Wyoming LLC risked dissolution if one of its owners ceased to be an owner. As in both a general and a limited partnership, an ownership interest in a Wyoming LLC was not freely transferable; an LLC member had the right to transfer only the economic aspect of the ownership interest. If the Kintner Regulations meant what they said, then a Wyoming LLC would be accorded partnership tax status.

§13.3.2 IRS Response to Wyoming; Common Characteristics of Early LLCs

The IRS took over ten years to acknowledge the consequences of its own tax classification regulations. Revenue Procedure 88-76 classified a Wyoming LLC as a partnership, and caused legislatures around the country to consider seriously the LLC phenomenon. For the most part, Wyoming's early emulators were faithful copiers, imposing through their LLC statutes the same basic structure as ordained in the Wyoming statute.

This fidelity gave the earliest LLCs some common characteristics—at least to the extent they followed the default blueprint of their respective LLC statutes. In the default mode, an LLC:

- was managed by its members in their capacity as members;
- was threatened with dissolution each time a member dissociated; and
- allowed its members to freely transfer the economic rights associated with membership, but prohibited them from transferring their membership interest in toto (or any management rights associated with membership) without the consent of all the other members.

In the first respect, LLCs resembled general partnerships.[28] In the second respect, LLCs resembled a limited partnership that had lost a general partner.[29] In the third respect, LLCs resembled both general and limited partnerships.[30]

§13.3.3 Increasing Flexibility of Form; IRS Bias Toward Manager-Managed LLCs

This characteristic picture began to lose focus in 1989 as the IRS began to loosen its approach to tax classification. In a series of public and private rulings, the IRS allowed for increasing flexibility of form, especially as to the continuity of life characteristic. This characteristic had done much to keep a "family resemblance" among LLCs because, until 1989, every LLC "blessed" by the IRS had lacked that characteristic. Then, the IRS began to accept both (1) a shrinking of the categories of member dissociation that threatened dissolution and (2) a decrease in the quantum of member consent necessary to avoid dissolution following member dissociation. As a result, LLC organizers had a greater variety of structures from which to choose.

At the same time, however, the IRS's pronouncements on continuity of life and free transferability of interests were conducing towards a new characteristic LLC structure. Beginning with Private Letter Ruling 9210019, the IRS revealed a bias toward manager-managed LLCs.[31] In contrast to a member-managed LLC, a manager-managed LLC could achieve partnership tax status while enjoying significant protection from business disruption and significant control over member exit rights. In both official and unofficial ways, the IRS suggested that, for purposes of tax classification, LLCs were properly analogized to limited partnerships rather than to general partnerships.

§13.3.4 Revenue Procedure 95-10

In 1994, the IRS issued Revenue Procedure 95-10 and made its earlier suggestion a matter of policy. Revenue Procedure 95-10 purported to provide guidelines for LLCs seeking advance assurance of partnership tax status under the Kintner Regulations, but in essence merely provided a series of safe harbors. Those safe harbors rested heavily on the limited partnership analogy. For example, under Revenue Procedure 95-10, a manager-managed LLC whose manager was also a member could avoid the corporate characteristic of continuity of life even if only that manager's dissociation as a member threatened dissolution of the LLC. That dissociation/dissolution nexus paralleled the approach of RULPA, under which (in the default mode) the dissociation of a

---

28. See section 9.1.

29. See section 12.2.7.

30. See sections 8.8.4 and 12.2.6.

31. Although state LLC statutes permitted manager-managed LLCs to have non-member managers, the IRS pronouncements concerned manager-managed LLCs whose manager or managers were also members.

limited partner has no effect on the partnership's existence, but the dissociation of a general partner threatens the partnership with dissolution.

Similarly, under Revenue Procedure 95-10, a manager-managed LLC whose manager was also a member could avoid the corporate characteristic of free transferability even though only the manager possessed the authority to approve the transfer of a member's complete membership interest. This structure went beyond the default rules of RULPA (which require the consent of all the remaining partners), but it paralleled the IRS's longstanding approach to transferability of interests in limited partnerships.

Although Revenue Procedure 95-10 also offered some safe harbors for member-managed LLCs, those harbors carried greater non-tax risks, especially as to business continuity. For instance, for a member-managed LLC to be assured of an advance ruling that it lacked continuity of life, it was necessary for the dissociation of any member to threaten dissolution. Revenue Procedure 95-10 did not require unanimous consent to avoid dissolution; a mere majority in interest sufficed. However, for these purposes, majority in interest meant a majority of both the capital and profit interests. As a result, a member-managed LLC that sought to avoid continuity of life under Revenue Procedure 95-10 could face various governance anomalies, including (1) effective veto power resting with holders of large capital accounts and (2) incongruity between member voting power generally and member voting power on the crucial issue of dissolution avoidance.

§13.3.5 LLC Characteristics After "Check-the-Box"

Revenue Procedure 95-10 might well have pushed LLCs into the limited partnership mold if the IRS had not subsequently decided to do away with the Kintner Regulations. Effective January 1, 1997, the Treasury Department adopted a "check-the-box" tax classification regime. Under "check-the-box," each domestic entity—other than one organized pursuant to a corporate or joint stock statute—determines its own tax status simply by checking or not checking a box. Indeed, unless a multi-member, unincorporated business organization elects otherwise, it will be taxed as a partnership.

Thus, under "check-the-box," the tax status of an unincorporated organization no longer depends on any of the Kintner factors or any other attribute of the organization's structure.[32] Accordingly, except for a special rule for publicly traded partnerships,[33] tax classification no longer dictates organiza-

---

32. Although the "check-the-box" regulations were undoubtably a response to LLCs, they apply equally to other unincorporated business organizations. As a result, they have led to changes in the law of limited partnerships, see section 12.3, and to the growth of limited liability partnerships and limited liability limited partnerships. See Chapter Fourteen.

33. Under this rule, which has very few exceptions, if an organization has numerous owners and the ownership interests are publicly traded, the organization is taxed as a corporation. The "check-the-box" regulations have no effect on this rule.

tional structure. The IRS even countenances one-member LLCs, whose tax status was previously doubtful given the IRS view that a "partnership" necessarily has at least two "partners." Under "check-the-box," a single member LLC is simply disregarded for income tax purposes, and all of the entity's income tax affairs are treated as pertaining to the LLC's sole member.

With tax classification constraints removed, LLC varieties will proliferate, and any "family resemblance" among LLCs will attenuate. Indeed, "check-the-box" caused many states to amend their respective LLC statutes to take advantage of the newly permitted flexibility. These amendments have included:

- eliminating the requirement that an LLC have at least two members and authorizing one-member LLCs;
- authorizing operating agreements in one-member LLCs;[34]
- allowing LLCs to have perpetual existence;
- making member dissociation more difficult, either by (1) depriving members of the power to dissociate or (2) subjecting members who withdraw prematurely to damage claims;
- changing the relationship between member dissociation and entity dissolution, either by (1) providing that, in the default mode, member dissociation does not even threaten dissolution or (2) changing the quantum of consent necessary to avoid dissolution following a member's dissociation.

§13.4   Common Elements of Contemporary LLCs

Despite the great flexibility brought on by the "check-the-box" regulations, it is possible to identify some essential LLC characteristics and to describe a range of possibilities for other important attributes. Even after "check-the-box," every LLC:

- is organized under a state statute other than a corporation statute, which allows the LLC to exist as a legal person and provides rules (many of them "default" rules) for structuring, governing, and operating the entity;[35]
- comes into existence through the filing of a specified public document (typically called "articles of organization") with a specified state agency;

---

34. As explained in section 13.4, an LLC operating agreement functions like the partnership agreement in a limited partnership.

35. According to a "choice of law" rule called the "internal affairs doctrine," the internal affairs of an entity should be governed by the law of the state under whose statute the entity is created. So, for example, a dispute among members of a limited liability company formed under the Delaware LLC statute would be governed by that statute—regardless of where the LLC does business and regardless of where the members reside.

- exists as a legal entity, separate from its owners;
- has a full, corporate-like liability shield to protect its owners against automatic, vicarious liability for the debts of the enterprise.

Example: Three individuals, Voltaire, Rousseau, and Marat, go into business with the expressed intention of forming a limited liability company. They draft and sign articles of organization, and Marat is given the task of actually filing the document. Unfortunately, Marat drops the document in his bath, is too embarrassed to tell Voltaire or Rousseau, and never files the document. The business is conducted as if the papers had been filed. In all its dealings with third parties, the business styles itself VRM, LLC. The business is not an LLC. To create an LLC requires the filing of articles.[36]

Example: Jeff creates an LLC, becomes its sole member and contributes to the LLC a parcel of real estate. On behalf of the LLC Jeff then applies for a zoning variance. When the zoning authority denies the application, Jeff files a formal appeal *in his own name.* The appeal is properly rejected, because Jeff is not the owner of the land. The LLC is.[37]

Example: A contractor sued a subcontractor for damages, including emotional distress. The court rejected the emotional distress claim outright, stating: "[The contractor] is a limited liability company. As such, its owners are entitled to certain legal rights and protections. It is a fictional "person" for legal purposes. [The contractor] has cited no authority which would allow it to be treated as a natural person that would be capable of experiencing emotions such as mental stress and anguish. The damages, if any, due to [the contractor] from [the subcontractor], are due to it as a fictional person, and may not be recovered by its owners. . . ."[38]

In almost every LLC, an agreement among the members determines the LLC's governance structure and provides its key operating rules. This agreement is analogous to a partnership agreement and most LLC statutes call it the "operating agreement."[39] An operating agreement can encompass any and all of the following topics:

---

36. If creditors of the business seek to hold the owners personally liable for the business's debts, the owners *may* be able to analogize from corporate law and claim entity status de facto or by estoppel. See Bishop & Kleinberger, §6.02[2][d].

37. This Example is based on Reid v. Town of Hebron, 1996 WL 634254, at *3 (Conn. Super. Ct. 1996), discussed in Bishop & Kleinberger, §5.05[1][e].

38. This Example and the quoted language are from All Comp Constr. Co., LLC v. Ford, 999 P.2d 1122, 1123 (Okla. Ct. App. 2000), discussed in Bishop & Kleinberger, §5.05[1][e].

39. Some LLC statutes label this agreement the "limited liability company agreement." At least one statute uses the term "member control agreement."

- *membership*—requirements and rights for admitting a new member, both as to memberships obtained directly from the limited liability company and as to memberships obtained as a transferee from a current member; transferability of membership interests; conditions and consequences of member dissociation
- *governance*—management structure (i.e., shifting the default structure from member-managed to manager-managed, or vice versa); classes of membership interests; voting rights of members; number of managers; qualifications, selection procedures, and duties for managers; matters reserved for member decision
- *finance*—amount and status of member contributions; consequences for nonperformance of a contribution promise, including the power of the limited liability company to compromise its claims; amount and timing of interim distributions; priorities in liquidating distributions; distributions in kind
- *dissolution*—events which trigger dissolution; ability of the limited liability company to avoid dissolution following member dissociation; authority to manage winding up; preferences in liquidating distributions[40]

Most LLC statutes permit an LLC to merge with other business entities and many now permit an LLC to convert into another form of entity. Many LLC statutes no longer require an LLC to have a specified "term" or duration, and many of these statutes expressly state that an LLC may have "perpetual" duration or existence.

LLC governance structure runs the gamut from a New England town-meeting style (with decisions made through discussion and consensus among all members) to an enterprise dominated autocratically by a single managing member. Some LLCs use corporate-style governance, and two state LLC statutes provide that arrangement as the default structure. Most LLC statutes dichotomize governance between "member-managed" LLCs and "manager-managed" LLCs. Governance in a member-managed LLC resembles governance in a general partnership. Governance in a manager-managed LLC resembles governance in a limited partnership.[41]

Great flexibility exists as to the rights and roles of LLC members in the LLC. To comply with IRS tax accounting requirements for partnerships, members' interests must continue to reflect a capital account and a profit percentage. In other respects, however, there will be no such paradigmatic construct. In some LLCs, members are unremittingly passive—their governance

---

40. This list is from Bishop & Kleinberger, §5.06[2][a][ii].

41. The resemblance is not complete. For example, managers in a manager-managed LLC are not required by statute to be members, although they usually are. In contrast, the managers of a limited partnership—i.e., the general partners—are necessarily partners.

rights scant and their financial rights preferred.[42] Other members have a "hands on" role in their LLC. Depending on the operating agreement, that role ranges from intermittent to constant; responsibilities range from the most senior, supervisory of management duties to the most prosaic of day-to-day work.

> *Example:* Hobbes, LLC is a manager-managed LLC with five members and a single manager. According to the LLC's articles of organization and operating agreement, the manager, who is also a member, has "full and complete authority to make all decisions concerning the operations and business of the LLC, except (i) requiring members to make additional contributions; (ii) selling all or substantially all of the company's assets or taking or failing to take any other action that makes it impossible to carry on the company's business, and (iii) dissolving the Company."

> *Example:* Jefferson, LLC is a member-managed LLC with five members. According to the LLC's articles of organization and operating agreement, "the Company will be managed exactly as if the Company was a general partnership organized under the Revised Uniform Partnership Act, and each member will have the same rights to manage and participate in the business as if she, he, or it were a partner in a general partnership organized under the Revised Uniform Partnership Act."

§13.5 Salient Issues for LLCs

§13.5.1 How Much Information Must Be Disclosed in the Articles of Organization

Early LLC statutes required significant disclosure via the filed articles of organization, including, e.g., the value of contributions made or promised by each member and name and address of each member of a member-managed LLC. This amount of disclosure was far greater than is required to form a corporation under the laws of most states, and today most LLC statutes require far less information.

§13.5.2 Resolving Conflicts Between an LLC's Articles of Organization and Operating Agreement

All LLC statutes empower the articles of organization *and* the operating agreement to structure an LLC and, in particular, determine the relationship

---

42. Such members have rights that, in substance, resemble those of preferred shareholders. Preferred stock typically has some sort of preference or priority with regard to distribution rights but often lacks any voting power.

inter se the members. An LLC's articles of organization and its operating agreement should of course be compatible, harmonized, and synchronized. However, human beings being imperfect, it is inevitable that conflicts will sometimes exist.

Some LLC statutes address this problem expressly. For example, the Uniform Limited Liability Company Act ("ULLCA") §203(c) states:

> if any provision of an operating agreement is inconsistent with the articles of organization: (1) the operating agreement controls as to managers, members, and members' transferees; and (2) the articles of organization control as to persons, other than managers, members and their transferees, who reasonably rely on the articles to their detriment.

Some LLC statutes lack any general provision on the subject but do reserve specified matters to the articles of organization. A conflict pertaining to one of those matters is easily resolved, because the operating agreement provision is of no effect.

Example: Merrimac, LLC is organized under an LLC statute which states that a limited liability company is managed by its members unless the articles of organization provide for management by one or more managers. Merrimac's articles are silent on this subject, but its operating agreement states "Until removal by a vote of 3/5 of the members or her resignation, Grant Monitor shall be the sole manager of this Company." Merrimac is not a manager-managed LLC.[43]

Where the LLC statute provides no guidance at all, the ULLCA approach (quoted above) makes the most policy sense. "Absent statutory commands to the contrary, the articles of organization are mere outward-looking formalities, while the operating agreement is the members' fundamental document."[44] Therefore:

- the articles of organization should control in favor of any third party who has reasonably relied on the articles
  - because people should be able to rely on information an entity inserts into "the public record"
- the operating agreement should control among members and transferees
  - because members have assented to the operating agreement and should know better than to rely on a publicly filed document that conflicts with their private agreement, and
  - because transferee rights are completely derivative of member rights

---

43. Members favoring the manager structure could argue that the operating agreement implies an obligation for each member to do whatever may be necessary to amend the articles.

44. Bishop & Kleinberger, §5.06[2][c].

§13.5.3 Written versus Oral Operating Agreements[45]

Some LLC statutes require an LLC's entire operating agreement to be in writing; some state the requirement directly, while others define "operating agreement" to be a written agreement. Some LLC statutes contain no overall writing requirement but do require particular aspects of the agreement to be written.

> *Example:* The Oklahoma LLC statute defines operating agreement as "*any* agreement of the members as to the affairs of a limited liability company and the conduct of its business," Okla. Stat. Ann. tit. 18, §2001(16) (emphasis added). However, the statute's provision on distribution of assets during winding up states that: "Except as provided *in writing* in the articles of organization or operating agreement, [payout] to members and former members [is allocated] first for the return of their contributions and second respecting their membership interests, in proportions in which the members share in distributions." Okla. Stat. Ann. tit. 18, §§2040(2) and (3) (emphasis added).

Even if the relevant LLC statute permits oral operating agreements, it is usually foolhardy to indulge in such informality. Memories are subjective and frail enough when no money is at stake. If members dispute the contents of an oral operating agreement, the informality will serve mainly to enrich the litigating attorneys.

§13.5.4 Power of Members qua Members to Bind the LLC

Like any other legal "person," an LLC can be bound through the acts of its agents. However, a member of an LLC is not necessarily an agent of the LLC. Whether the act of a member *qua* member can bind an LLC depends first on the LLC statute under which the LLC is organized and then, to the extent the statute fails to answer the question, on the application by analogy of principles of agency and partnership law.

Basic statutory approach.   Most LLC statutes state a member's power to bind the LLC to contracts and in similar transactions by replicating UPA §§9(1) and (4).[46] If the LLC is managed by its members, the power-to-bind attaches to the members as members. If the LLC is managed by managers, the power-to-bind attaches to managers (and not to the members *qua* members). Typically, the articles of organization provide the switching mechanism, because the articles determine whether an LLC is member-managed or manager-managed.

---

45. This section is based on Bishop & Kleinberger, §5.06[3][c].

46. For an in-depth discussion of UPA §9(1) and (4), see section 10.2. LLC statutes generally do not pick up the refinements of RUPA §301, see section 10.3, because most were adopted before RUPA's approach had become well established.

Example: The Arizona LLC statute, A.R.S. §29-654 (member or manager as agent), provides:

A. Unless the articles of organization of a limited liability company provide that management is vested in one or more managers:

1. Each member is an agent of the limited liability company for the purpose of carrying on its business in the usual way.

2. The act of each member, including the execution in the name of the limited liability company of any instrument, for apparently carrying on in the usual way the business of the limited liability company of which he is a member binds the limited liability company unless the acting member has in fact no authority to act for the limited liability company in the particular matter and the person with whom he is dealing has knowledge of the fact that the member has no such authority.

B. If the articles of organization of a limited liability company provide that management is vested in one or more managers:

1. A member is not an agent of the limited liability company for the purpose of its business solely by reason of being a member except to the extent that authority has been delegated to the member by the sole manager or managers or by the provisions of an operating agreement.

2. Each manager is an agent of the limited liability company for the purpose of carrying on its business in the usual way.

3. The act of each manager, including the execution in the name of the limited liability company of any instrument, for apparently carrying on in the usual way the business of the limited liability company of which he is a manager binds the limited liability company unless the acting manager has in fact no authority to act for the limited liability company in the particular matter and the person with whom he is dealing has knowledge of the fact that the manager has no such authority.

C. An act of a member or manager that is not apparently for carrying on the business of the limited liability company in the usual way does not bind the limited liability company unless authorized in fact by the limited liability company in the particular matter.

D. An act of any member, manager, employee, officer or other agent of a limited liability company in violation of a restriction on authority does not bind the limited liability company to persons with knowledge of the restriction.

Such statutes have the quietly revolutionary effect of imposing on third parties the burden of checking the public record.

Example: Purporting to act on behalf of Revolution, LLC, an Arizona limited liability company, Robespierre signs an agreement to purchase equipment from Guillotine, Inc. Robespierre signs the agreement: "Robespierre, member of Revolution, LLC, on behalf of Revolution, LLC." Guillotine has had past dealings with the LLC, which has been member-managed. However, Revolution recently amended its articles of organization to become a manager-managed LLC and Robespierre is not a manager. Guillotine has not checked the public record and believes that Revolution is still member managed. Under A.R.S. §29-654(B)(1), Revolution, LLC is not bound to the agreement.[47]

Burdening third parties in this way is fundamental under Article 9 of the UCC[48] and in the realm of real property transactions, but until recently had no role in resolving power-to-bind questions. RUPA statements of dissolution and dissociation now create a "check the public record" burden for third parties dealing with RUPA partnerships, but those statements at least have a delayed impact.[49] RUPA statements of authority provide constructive notice only with regard to real property transactions.[50]

Attribution of members torts.   UPA §9 is only part of the UPA's attribution rules for partners, but no LLC statute contains any provision analogous to UPA §§13 and 14.[51] Indeed, no LLC statute contains any provision expressly addressing the nexus between a tort of a member or manager and the liability of the LLC.

It is no solution to apply LLC versions of UPA §9 to such torts. That approach would wrench the provisions out of their historical context and ignore the core statutory language:

> The core rule of UPA §9 is the "apparently/usual" power, that is, the power of a person to bind the limited liability company through an act apparently for carrying on the business of the limited liability company in the usual way. This core formulation makes great sense when considering a contractual undertaking, but makes virtually no sense when considering torts. Appearances are often key to inducing a third party to enter into a contract, but they are rarely relevant to a third party subjecting itself to a tort.[52]

The proper solution is to apply principles of agency law, in particular the notion of enterprise liability:

> It is inevitable that in doing their work, either through negligence or excess of zeal, agents will harm third persons or will deal with them in unauthorized ways. It would be unfair for an enterprise to have the benefit of the work of its agents without making it responsible to some extent for their excesses and failures to act carefully. The answer of the common law has been the creation of special agency powers or, to phrase it other-

---

47. It might be possible to argue that, as a matter of agency law, Robespierre had lingering apparent authority to bind. See sections 2.3 and 5.3.1. If the LLC is not bound, Robespierre will be liable for breach of the warranty of authority. See section 4.2.2.

48. Article 9 governs "security interests."

49. See sections 11.10.2 and 11.11.2.

50. See section 10.3.5.

51. These latter sections attribute to a general partnership the torts of a partner. See sections 10.4 and 10.5.

52. Bishop & Kleinberger §7.07[1].

wise, the imposition of liability upon the principal because of the unauthorized or negligent acts of its servants and other agents.[53]

This rationale supports the doctrine of respondeat superior[54] and is also reflected in UPA §§13 and 14 and RUPA §305. Although the wording differs from context to context, the basic concept is essentially the same:

- *When*
  - — a tort is committed by a person
  - — who acts on a regular basis on behalf of an entity
  - — as an integral part of that entity, whether as a servant agent or as an owner furnishing services, and
  - — the tort occurs within the ordinary course of the entity's business or within the scope of the person's authorized responsibilities
- *then* the enterprise—i.e., the entity—is liable for the tort.

The same rationale supports applying the same concept to hold a member-managed limited liability company liable for torts committed by its members and to hold a manager-managed limited liability company liable for the torts committed by its managers. (In a manager-managed LLC, the torts of a non-managing member should be attributed to the LLC only if some rule of agency law so provides.)

> *Example:* Revolution, LLC is a member-managed LLC that operates a bar. Robespierre, one of its members, is tending bar one night and is overzealous in trying to control an unruly patron. If Robespierre is liable to the patron for the tort of battery, the LLC is liable as well. Robespierre—a member in a member-managed LLC—was bartending on behalf of the LLC, and dealing with unruly patrons is part of *both* the ordinary course of a bar's business and the authorized responsibilities of a bartender.[55]

> *Example:* Revolution, LLC is a *manager*-managed LLC that operates a bar. Robespierre, one of its non-manager members, stops by the bar one night, officiously confronts an unruly patron, and commits a battery. The LLC is *not* liable for Robespierre's tort.[56]

> *Example:* Revolution, LLC is a manager-managed LLC that operates a bar. Robespierre, one of its non-manager members, is employed by Revolution, LLC as a parttime bartender. While tending bar one night,

---

53. Restatement (Second) of Agency §8A, comment *a* (1958).

54. See section 3.2.4.

55. Under the rule stated above, either one of these connections would suffice. For an explanation of how intentional torts can come within "scope of employment," see section 3.2.6. For an explanation of how a wrongful act can be within the "ordinary course" of a business, see section 10.4.1.

56. The LLC might be liable for failing to protect a business invitee, but that liability would be a matter of general tort law and have nothing to do with Revolution's status as a limited liability company or Robespierre's status as a member.

Robespierre is overzealous in trying to control an unruly patron. If Robespierre has committed the tort of battery, the LLC is liable to the patron under the doctrine of respondeat superior.

§13.5.5 *Fiduciary Duties Within LLCs*

Although LLC statutes differ substantially in how they address fiduciary duties, a few generalizations are possible. As is the case with those who manage a limited partnership or a corporation, those who manage a limited liability company owe *to the entity* the fiduciary duties of loyalty and care. Whether the members of an LLC owe each other duties of loyalty or fair dealing depends both on the state of organization and the operating agreement.

> *Example:* Mille Lacs, LLC is organized under the Minnesota Limited Liability Company Act, which provides (as a default rule) that each LLC is to be managed by a board of governors and recognizes "the duty that all members in a closely held limited liability company owe one another to act in an honest, fair, and reasonable manner in the operation of the limited liability company."[57] That duty applies to all members, regardless of whether they are elected to the board of governors.

> *Example:* Falcon, LLC is manager-managed limited liability company organized under the Georgia LLC statute. That statute provides that: "Except as otherwise provided in the articles of organization or a written operating agreement, a person who is a member of a limited liability company in which management is vested in one or more managers, and who is not a manager, shall have no duties to the limited liability company or to the other members solely by reason of acting in his or her capacity as a member."[58] It appears that non-managing members owe no fiduciary duties to fellow members, or the LLC.

That appearance may be misleading, however, at least in some circumstances.

> *Example:* Falcon, LLC is managed by three non-member managers, each elected by the members by majority vote and subject to removal also by majority vote. Two members, Turner and Fonda, have in the aggregate 60 percent of the votes, and they always act in concert. As a result they elect the managers and effectively control them. Under principles of agency law, Turner and Fonda may owe manager-type duties to the LLC.[59]

---

57. Minn. Stat. §322B.833, subd. 4.

58. Ga. Stat. 14-11-305(1).

59. This Example is based on the analysis presented in Bishop & Kleinberger, §10.09[2][b][i], which in turn relies on a corporate case, Sinclair Oil Corp. v. Levien, 280 A.2d 717 (Del. 1971).

Power of the operating agreement to reshape or eliminate fiduciary duties.   Many LLC statutes authorize the articles of organization or operating agreement to eliminate liability for damages for breach of duty, but this exculpatory power is essentially limited to breach of the duty of care. The statutes typically prohibit exculpation for (i) breach of the duty of loyalty, (ii) acts or omissions not in good faith or which involve intentional misconduct or a knowing violation of law, and (iii) any transaction from which the breaching party derives an improper personal benefit.

Some LLC statutes take a different approach, expressly exalting members' freedom of contract and exculpating those who rely in good faith on an agreement among the members. For example, Delaware's LLC statute provides:

> To the extent that, at law or in equity, a member or manager or other person has duties (including fiduciary duties) and liabilities relating thereto to a limited liability company or to another member or manager or to another person that is a party to or is otherwise bound by a limited liability company agreement:
>
> (1) Any such member or manager or other person acting under the limited liability company agreement shall not be liable to the limited liability company or to any such other member or manager or to any such other person for the member's or manager's or other person's good faith reliance on the provisions of the limited liability company agreement; and
>
> (2) The member's or manager's or other person's duties and liabilities may be expanded or restricted by provisions in the limited liability company agreement.[60]

Delaware has been the national leader in exalting freedom of contract as to fiduciary duties, although to date no case has been decided under the LLC Act provision just quoted. That provision derives, however, from a provision in Delaware's limited partnership statute, and that provision has been applied by Delaware courts. Although respectful of the statutory mandate, those courts have made clear that the "good faith reliance" provision is not a safe harbor for oppressive conduct.

> *Example:* A law firm is organized as a limited liability company under an LLC statute that exalts freedom of contract and contains a "reliance" provision just like Delaware's. The LLC has ten members. Its operating agreement provides that profits will be allocated only when realized, specifies that any member may be expelled at any time without cause by a two-thirds vote of the other members, states that such expulsion is "in the sole discretion of members constituting two-thirds of the members,"

---

60. Del. Code Ann., tit. 6 §18-1101(c).

and sets a formula for paying out an expelled member. Just as the firm is about to realize a very large contingency, seven of the members "gang up" on the other three and purport to expel them. The sole motivation is to grab a larger share of the contingency. Despite statutory provisions that authorize limitations on liability, vouchsafe reliance on the operating agreement, and exalt freedom of contract, and despite the express language of the operating agreement—no court would countenance such expropriating conduct.[61]

§13.5.6 Breach of Fiduciary Duty and the Distinction Between Direct and Derivative Claims in an LLC

Nature and origin of derivative claims.   Because an LLC is an entity distinct from its members, most breaches of fiduciary duty will directly injure the LLC rather than its members.

> *Example:* Robespierre is the managing member of Revolution, LLC, a manager-managed LLC with five members, each of whom has an equal share in the company's profits and has made an equal contribution to the company's capital. As a result of Robespierre's grossly negligent management, the LLC suffers a million dollar loss. Although the value of each member's interest has diminished by approximately $200,000, none of the members have been *directly* injured. Instead, they have each suffered a loss *because* the LLC has suffered a loss.

Under U.S. law, "standing" to sue for an injury generally belongs to the person who has been directly injured. In the law of corporations and limited partnerships, this general proposition means that claims for injury to the entity belong to the entity and, normally, must be brought by the entity in its own name. The same is true for limited liability companies.

But what is to be done when the person who has allegedly injured the entity is the same person who normally manages the entity?

> *Example:* The other members of Revolution, LLC learn of Robespierre's incompetence and the resulting (direct) damage to the LLC and (indirect) damage to the value of their respective membership interests. They first demand that Robespierre "make good the loss" to the LLC, and, when he refuses, they demand that he cause the LLC to sue him for the damages. Raising his eyebrows, Robespierre responds, "I am the manager, and in my judgment such a suit is not in the best interests of the company."

To resolve such situations, courts long ago exercised their equitable powers and recognized "derivative" claims—i.e., claims brought by the owners of

---

61. This Example is taken from Bishop & Kleinberger, §10.09[4][b][v].

the entity, on behalf of the entity, over the objections of those who normally manage the entity. The standards for bringing derivative claims are now codified, both in statutes and in rules of civil procedure. Those standards, which apply to LLCs, include the "contemporaneous ownership" requirement and the "demand" requirement. To satisfy the "contemporaneous ownership" requirement, the person bringing a derivative suit must be an owner of the entity (e.g., a corporate shareholder, a partner in a limited partnership, a member of an LLC) when the suit begins and must have been an owner when the conduct giving rise to the action occurred (or must have obtained ownership status after that time by operation of law). To satisfy the demand requirement, the person bringing a derivative suit must either:

- first make a demand on those managing the entity (requesting that they cause the entity to bring the desired suit) and allow those managers a reasonable time to investigate, decide, and respond, or
- plead and eventually establish that the managers were so tainted with conflict of interest as to make demand "futile."

Except in unusual circumstances, all proceeds from a derivative suit belong to the entity, not the owner or owners who brought the suit. However, if a derivative action is successful in whole or in part, the court may award the plaintiff reasonable expenses, including reasonable attorney's fees, from the proceeds of the suit.

Distinguishing between direct and derivative claims in an LLC.   The rule for distinguishing between direct and derivative claims in an LLC is the same as with any other entity: the claim belongs to the person first injured.

Example: In the case of Robespierre's gross negligence, the damage first affects the LLC and, accordingly, the claim belongs to the LLC. If the other members wish to sue Robespierre, they must bring a derivative claim.

Example: The operating agreement of Revolution, LLC provides that each year the manager shall distribute to each member at least enough funds to cover the member's tax liability arising from the member's share of LLC profits.[62] As managing member, Robespierre fails to make the required distribution. Each member has a direct claim against Robespierre. His failure does no harm to the LLC but does directly injure each member.

Breach of operating agreement does not necessarily create a direct claim.   "In ordinary contractual situations it is axiomatic that each party to a contract has standing to sue for breach of that contract."[63] However, an LLC

---

62. In an LLC taxed as a partnership, each member is taxed on his, her, or its share of profits regardless of whether the profits are actually distributed. See section 13.2.1.

63. ULPA (2001), §1001, Comment to subsection (b).

operating agreement is not an ordinary contractual situation, because an operating agreement is both a contract among the members and the basic "charter" of the entity. Often, therefore, an operating agreement will state the duties of those who manage the LLC. Breach of those duties will directly harm the LLC and not the individual members. In those situations, members will have to bring a derivative claim to enforce the operating agreement.

§13.5.7 The LLC Liability Shield and "Piercing the Veil"

The LLC's liability shield is derived from corporate law, and the corporate concept of "piercing the veil" is already well established in the realm of LLCs. The piercing doctrine recognizes that

> while limited liability generally benefits society, entrepreneurs sometimes use the shield abusively. When abuse occurs, courts will not allow the miscreants to find shelter behind the shield. In the words of Justice Cardozo, to avoid "a fraud upon the law. . . . unity is ascribed to parts which, at least for many purposes, retain an independent life, for the reason that only thus can we overcome a perversion of the privilege to do business in a corporate form."[64]

Recognizing instances of "perversion" is a fact-intensive task. In the corporate realm, courts have focused on a number of factors, including whether

- the entity was the alter ego or "mere instrumentality" of a dominant owner
- the dominant owner used the entity shield not merely for the legitimate purpose of limiting personal liability but somehow to promote a fraud or injustice
- the entity was undercapitalized, i.e., lacked enough assets to meet the obligations normally to be expected to arise from the entity's operations
- the dominant owner
  - disregarded the entity's economic separateness (e.g., by commingling entity and personal funds, commingling entity and personal business records, or using the entity's credit to obtain personal loans)
  - siphoned funds from the entity (e.g., through inappropriately timed or sized distributions of profits, or by unsecured loans to the owner)
  - disregarded the entity's governance "formalities" (e.g., by ignoring requirements for meetings, or allowing owners to usurp the functions formally allocated to managers)

---

64. Bishop & Kleinberger, §6.03[1], quoting Berkey v. Third Ave. Ry., 155 N.E 58, 61 (N.Y. 1926).

Some LLC statutes expressly recognize the piercing doctrine, and case law suggests that courts will apply the doctrine as a matter of equity even without statutory authority.[65] All the corporate piercing factors will be relevant in LLC piercing cases, except perhaps "disregard of governance formalities." Most LLCs lack the elaborate management structure of a corporation, so disregard of organizational formalities is less likely to occur. However, to the extent an LLC operating agreement establishes formal decision making structures and a controlling member disregards them, "disregard of governance formalities" could be a significant factor in an LLC piercing case.

PROBLEM 118

Under local law "a person may represent him or herself in court, but no person who is not an attorney licensed to practice in this state may represent another person." Todd Morgan has formed Todd, LLC, of which he is the sole member. Todd, LLC is the lessee on a lease with SamMik, Inc., and SamMik has sued Todd, LLC in small claims court for nonpayment of rent. May Todd Morgan, who is not an attorney, represent Todd, LLC in small claims court?

EXPLANATION

No. An LLC and its members are separate persons. If Todd Morgan were to represent Todd, LLC, the representation would involve a "person who is not an attorney licensed to practice in this state . . . representing another person."

PROBLEM 119

If Todd, LLC defaults on its lease payments, may SamMik sue Todd Morgan for the amount due?

EXPLANATION

Not unless Todd Morgan has guaranteed the LLC's payment or SamMik can establish grounds to "pierce the veil." An LLC member is not liable for the LLC's debts merely on account of being a member.

PROBLEM 120

Three individuals, Voltaire, Rousseau, and Marat, go into business with the expressed intention of forming a limited liability company. They draft and sign articles of organization, and Marat is given the task of actually filing the document. Unfortunately, Marat drops the document in his bath, is too embarrassed to tell Voltaire or Rousseau, and never files the document. The business is conducted as if the papers had been filed. In all its dealings with third parties, the business styles itself VRM, LLC.

---

65. This result makes sense, because "piercing" originated as an equitable doctrine, without any statutory authority.

After about a year, Marat and Voltaire discover that Rousseau has diverted almost all of the company's assets into a separate company that he owns by himself. Rousseau defends by inter alia asserting that (i) the company should be treated as a limited liability company de facto, and (ii) the resulting shield should protect him from personal liability on Marat's and Voltaire's claims. Is Rousseau correct?

EXPLANATION

No. Even if the relevant jurisdiction accepts the notion of LLC de facto, the LLC shield protects members from automatic liability for the LLC's obligations and has nothing to do with liability of a member for his own misconduct.

PROBLEM 121

Roundhead, LLC is manager-managed limited liability company organized under an LLC statute that negates any power-to-bind of a non-managing member of a manager-managed LLC. Cromwell is the LLC's sole manager. Cromwell wants the LLC to rent a luxury box at the arena that houses the local professional basketball team. Busy with other matters, Cromwell asks Charles, a non-managing member, to reserve the box. Charles does so in his own name. Is Roundhead, LLC bound?

EXPLANATION

Yes, although Charles had no power to bind Roundhead, LLC in his capacity as a member, he was acting as the agent for an undisclosed principal.[66] (As sole manager of the LLC, Cromwell certainly had the authority to establish an agency relationship between Roundhead and Charles.)

PROBLEM 122

Same facts, as in Problem 121, plus the LLC statute provides that "a person who is a member of a limited liability company in which management is vested in one or more managers, and who is not a manager, shall have no duties to the limited liability company or to the other members solely by reason of acting in his or her capacity as a member." After reserving the luxury box, Charles declines to sign it over to Roundhead. Does the quoted statutory language protect Charles from a claim by Roundhead?

EXPLANATION

No. Roundhead's claim is for Charles's breach of his duties as an agent[67] and not "solely by reason of acting in his or her capacity as a member."

---

66. See section 2.2.4.
67. See sections 4.1.1 (duty of loyalty) and 4.1.3 (duty to obey instructions).

PROBLEM 123

Marat, Rousseau, and Voltaire form MRV, LLC, a manager-managed LLC, and, with the consent of all members, the LLC retains a corporation owned by Marat to serve as the non-member manager. The agreement between the LLC and the corporation permits the LLC to terminate the management contract on 30 days' notice without cause, while the LLC's operating agreement states that for the first two years of the LLC's operation, the LLC will terminate the management contract only if (i) all three members agree, or (ii) "good cause" exists and two members agree. After only six months, Rousseau and Voltaire vote to cause the LLC to terminate the management contract. Marat promptly files suit against Rousseau and Voltaire, alleging that "good cause" did not exist, the termination therefore breached the operating agreement, and "the termination of the management contract will significantly prejudice MRV, LLC by depriving it of experienced and effective management." Is Marat's claim direct or derivative?

EXPLANATION

Derivative, because the harm alleged is to the LLC, not to Marat directly. (The result might be different if Marat were to claim that the termination prejudiced him directly by depriving him of the revenue that would have come to him through payments to his corporation.[68])

---

68. This Problem is based on Carson v. Lynch Multimedia Corp., 123 F. Supp. 2d 1254, 1259-1260 (D. Kan. 2000).

14

Limited Liability Partnerships and Limited Liability Limited Partnerships

§14.1 Overview: Terminology and Origins

§14.1.1 *Terminology*

Limited Liability Partnership (LLP). A *limited liability partnership:*

- is a *general* partnership that has invoked the limited liability partnership provisions of its governing general partnership statute
- by filing with a specified public official a specified document (typically called "a statement of qualification" or a "registration")
- thereby becoming a limited liability [general] partnership and eliminating partially or completely the automatic personal liability of each partner for each partnership obligation.

Under some state statutes, a limited liability partnership is called a registered limited liability partnership. The term "limited liability partnership" is abbreviated *LLP* and, except in statutory provisions, the abbreviation is used far more often than the term itself.

The term "liability shield" is typically used to refer to the liability protection provided the partners of an LLP. As discussed in more detail below,[1] a plurality of LLP statutes provides a "full shield" for the partners—completely eliminating a partner's liability *qua* partner for the partnership's obligations. The other LLP statutes provide only a "partial shield"—leaving in place some of a partner's automatic liability for partnership obligations.

Limited Liability Limited Partnership (LLLP).   A *limited liability limited partnership:*

- is a *limited* partnership that has invoked the limited liability limited partnership provisions of its state partnership law
- by filing with a specified public official a specified document
- thereby becoming a limited liability limited partnership and eliminating completely the automatic personal liability of each general partner for each partnership obligation and, under most statutes, also eliminating the "control rule" liability exposure for all limited partners.[2] The term "limited liability limited partnership" is abbreviated *LLLP* and, except in statutory provisions, the abbreviation is used far more often than the term itself. The abbreviation is usually pronounced "triple–L–P."

The term "liability shield" is used in this context too. With regard to *general* partner liability, all LLLP provisions are full shield provisions.

§14.1.2   *Origins of LLPs and LLLPs*

The advent of limited liability companies had a ripple effect on the law of general and limited partnerships. Put most simply: if a limited liability company could shield *its* owners from automatic, vicarious liability for the enterprise's debts and still be taxed as a partnership, why not provide a comparable liability shield for general partners? Once the IRS acknowledged that its Kintner Regulations meant what they said, there was nothing in tax law to deter state legislatures from providing for both limited liability [general] partnerships—LLPs—and limited liability limited partnerships—LLLPs.[3]

There remained non-tax forces of inertia, however. Most importantly, from a non-tax and historical perspective a general partner's liability seemed inherently and inescapably the hallmark of partnership law. It took five years after the IRS's seminal ruling on LLCs for any state legislature to authorize limited liability partnerships. Moreover, the first LLP shield was decidedly inferior to an LLC or corporate shield.

Today, in contrast, the limited liability partnership is firmly established and widespread, and the limited liability limited partnership is only a few

---

1. See section 14.2.2.

2. See sections 12.2.3 and 12.3.4.

3. For a discussion of the Kintner tax classification regulations, see section 13.3.1. The "check the box" regulations, discussed in section 13.3.5, removed any shadow of tax classification doubt, even for the most conservative of tax practitioners.

steps behind. All states authorize LLPs, and a plurality of LLP statutes now provide a shield that is essentially indistinguishable from an LLC or corporate shield. More than 15 states provide for LLLPs, and under the new Uniform Limited Partnership Act (2001), a limited partnership can originate as or become an LLLP simply by including a one-line statement in the certificate of limited partnership.[4]

§14.2   Limited Liability Partnerships (LLPs)

§14.2.1 *Origin and Development*

In 1991, Texas enacted the first LLP legislation, which was targeted to help professional firms (especially firms of accountants and lawyers) and which provided a liability shield that makes sense only in that context.[5] The shield was available only to general partnerships and protected only against a partner's vicarious liability[6] for

> debts and obligations of the partnership arising from errors, omissions, negligence, incompetence, or malfeasance committed in the course of the partnership business by another partner or a representative of the partnership not working under the supervision or direction of the first partner at the time the errors, omissions, negligence, incompetence, or malfeasance occurred.[7]

The shield thus gave partners no protection whatsoever against contract-based partnership obligations. Even as to tort-based partnership obligations, the shield was ineffective if the partner invoking the shield:

> (a) was directly involved in the specific activity in which the errors, omissions, negligence, incompetence, or malfeasance were committed by the other partner or representative; or
>
> (b) had notice or knowledge of the errors, omissions, negligence, incompetence, or malfeasance by the other partner or representative at the time of occurrence.[8]

---

4. ULPA (2001), §201(a)(4).

5. See Carter G. Bishop & Daniel S. Kleinberger, Limited Liability Companies: Tax and Business Law (Warren, Gorham & Lamont/RIA 1994-2002) ("Bishop & Kleinberger"), §15.01[3][a] at 15-6 to 15-9.

6. Like all shields, this LLP shield offered no protection against (and, indeed, was irrelevant to) claims arising from a partner's own conduct. See section 14.2.3.

7. Tex. Rev. Civ. Stat. Ann. art. 6132b, §15(2), quoted in Bishop & Kleinberger, §15.01[3][a] at 15-7.

8. Tex. Rev. Civ. Stat. Ann. art. 6132b, §15(2), quoted in Bishop & Kleinberger, §15.01[3][a] at 15-7. Note that these exceptions can but do not necessarily involve any directly culpable conduct by the partner. It is possible, for example, for an individual to be "directly involved in the specific activity in which . . . negligence" occurs without the individual being negligent. Likewise, an individual can have "knowledge or notice" of a co-worker's negligence without the individual being negligent.

In addition, the efficacy of the shield was conditioned *inter alia* on the partnership carrying specified amounts of malpractice insurance.

In 1992 and 1993, a few states followed Texas's example, and in 1993 Texas clarified and refined its statute. The next major development occurred elsewhere, however.

In 1994, first Minnesota, then New York enacted "full shield" LLP provisions—enabling partners in a general partnership to have the same liability protection available to LLC members and corporate shareholders.[9]

Prior to 1996, LLP provisions were all UPA-based. RUPA was just beginning to gain acceptance, and, moreover, as originally promulgated RUPA had no LLP provisions. In 1996, NCCUSL amended RUPA to provide for "full shield" LLPs,[10] and since that time many states have taken the "full shield" approach. Today, all states provide for LLPs; more than 20 provide for a full shield.

§14.2.2 *Essential Characteristics*

Most LLP statutes now reflect RUPA, so most LLP statutes have nearly identical provisions. Under RUPA:

i.   An ordinary general partnership becomes an LLP by first obtaining the requisite quantum of consent from its partners and then filing a "statement of qualification" with a specified public official.[11]

ii. Unless the partnership agreement provides otherwise, the quantum of partner consent necessary to approve becoming an LLP is the same quantum of consent as is necessary to approve an amendment to the partnership agreement "except, in the case of a partnership agreement that expressly considers obligations to contribute to the partnership, [the LLP approval quantum is] the vote necessary to amend those provisions."[12]

iii. The statement of qualification "must be executed by at least two partners,"[13] must be accompanied by whatever filing fee is required by statute,[14] and must contain: "(1) the name of the partnership; (2) the

---

9. 1994 Minn. Sess. Law Serv. ch. 539, §12, amending Minn. Stat. Ann. §323.14(2); 1994 NY Laws ch. 576, §8, amending N.Y. Partnership Law §26.

10. RUPA, Uniform Partnership Act—Quick Chronology.

11. RUPA §§1001(b) and (c).

12. RUPA §1001(b). As to why this provision makes special reference to contribution obligations, see section 14.2.6.

13. RUPA §105(c).

14. Most LLP statutes require a small filing fee—typically less than $200—which must be paid when the general partnership first becomes an LLP and each time the LLP files an annual report or (under non-RUPA statutes) renews its registration. A few states, however, impose significantly higher filing fees. Delaware, for example, imposes a fee of $100 per partner, subject to an annual limit of $120,000, for both the initial statement of qualification and each subsequent annual report. Del. Code Ann. tit. 6, §15-1207(a)(3). This fee will be a substantial expense for any LLP with numerous partners, such as a large accounting firm.

street address of the partnership's chief executive office and, if different, the street address of an office in this State [i.e., the State under whose law the general partnership is becoming an LLP], if any; (3) if the partnership does not have an office in this State, the name and street address of the partnership's agent for service of process; (4) a statement that the partnership elects to be a limited liability partnership; and (5) a deferred effective date, if any."[15]

    iv. An LLP's name must include specified designators—i.e., phrases or abbreviations that reflect the partnership's status as a limited liability partnership. "The name of a limited liability partnership must end with "Registered Limited Liability Partnership", "Limited Liability Partnership", "R.L.L.P.", "L.L.P.", "RLLP," or "LLP"."[16]

    v. An LLP must file an annual report with the same public official that receives the statement of qualification. The annual report contains minimal information; its function is merely to keep current the public record.[17]

    vi. When a statement of qualification takes effect, a full liability shield arises. "An obligation of a partnership incurred while the partnership is a limited liability partnership, whether arising in contract, tort, or otherwise, is solely the obligation of the partnership. A partner is not personally liable, directly or indirectly, by way of contribution or otherwise, for such an obligation solely by reason of being or so acting as a partner."[18]

Example: For several years Locke, Hobbes, and Calvin have been operating a business as an ordinary general partnership governed by RUPA.

---

15. RUPA §§1001(c)(1)-(5).

16. RUPA §1002. This provision does not directly require that an LLP use its special designator when transacting business. Failure to do so, however, may result in personal liability for the person acting on behalf of the LLP on the agency law theory that the person is not acting for a fully (or correctly) disclosed principal. See Bishop & Kleinberger, §6.04[5] at S6-34 (discussing the issue in the context of limited liability companies).

17. RUPA §1003(a) requires the annual report to state the LLP's name; the street address of the LLP's chief executive office and, if different, the street address of an in-state office, if any; and, if the LLP does not have an in-state office, the name and street address of the LLP's agent for service of process. Failure to file the annual report can result in revocation of an LLP's statement of qualification, which in turn ends the partnership's status as an LLP and removes the liability shield. RUPA §§1003(c) and (d). However, revocation does not occur automatically. A specified public official must take action—giving the LLP "at least 60 days' written notice of intent to revoke the statement [of qualification]." RUPA §1003(c). Even after revocation, a general partnership can retroactively regain its LLP status (and retroactively re-establish the LLP shield) by properly applying for "reinstatement" of the revoked statement of qualification. RUPA §§1003(e) and (f). Reinstatement nullifies the effect of revocation *ab initio* ("as if the revocation had never occurred"). RUPA §1003(f). Subsection (f) does not expressly preserve the rights of third parties who may have relied on the revocation, but principles of estoppel will likely provide that protection.

18. RUPA §306(c). As to why this provision makes special reference to contribution obligations, see section 14.2.6.

They have no formal partnership agreement and have not previously agreed how to go about changing their inter se relationship. On March 1 of this year, Hobbes suggests that the partnership become an LLP. Calvin agrees, but Locke wants to "think it over for a few days." At that point the partnership cannot become an LLP. Under RUPA §1001(a), the decision to become an LLP requires the same consent as is required for amending the partnership agreement. This partnership has no agreement as to amending the partnership agreement, so RUPA §401(j) applies and requires unanimous consent.

Some RUPA states have nonuniform provisions explicitly stating that the liability shield does not protect a partner from liability for the partner's own misconduct or from liability for the misconduct of a person directly supervised by the partner. The former exception is unnecessary because an LLP shield by its terms addresses only a partner's liability *qua* partner for obligations *of the partnership*. The latter exception is significant, however, because it goes beyond holding a partner liable for the partner's own misconduct. The "supervisee" exception appears not only to preserve a partner's liability *qua* partner for a partnership obligation resulting from a supervisee's misconduct but to do so without even requiring the claimant to prove that the partner's supervision was negligent or otherwise deficient.

As to LLP provisions not based on RUPA, the principal variations are that:

- under approximately 15 LLP statutes, the shield protects a partner only as to partnership obligations resulting from the malpractice or similar tort committed by a person other than the partner (leaving the partner liable *qua* partner for partnership obligations arising in any other way, including through contract);[19]
- many statutes expressly provide that the shield does not protect a partner from liability for the partner's own misconduct or from liability for the misconduct of a person directly supervised by the partner;
- some statutes require each LLP to maintain specified levels of liability insurance;
- a few states require an LLP to renew its registration annually.

All these provisions are foot prints from the early days of LLPs.[20]

---

19. Some of these statutes limit the shield protection to partnership obligations resulting from malpractice and other torts. Others provide protection against partnership obligations arising from all malpractice claims, regardless of whether the claim sounds in tort or contract.

20. See section 14.2.1.

§14.2.3   No Protection for the Partnership and No Effect on Partner's Own Misconduct

What is true for the LLC and corporate shields is equally true for the LLP shield. The LLP shield protects the partners, not the partnership; indeed, the entire point of the shield is to prevent the partnership's obligations from being automatically imputed to the partners. Also, the LLP shield does not protect against liability resulting from a partner's own conduct.

> **Example:** Fencing, LLP is a RUPA limited liability partnership, and Porthos is one of its partners. One day, while conducting the partnership's ordinary business and giving a fencing lesson to an individual student, Porthos becomes distracted by personal concerns. As a result, he negligently inflicts a leg wound on the student. The LLP shield is irrelevant to the student's tort claim against Porthos. The claim arises from Porthos's own misconduct and does not seek to impose on Porthos a partner's liability for an obligation of the partnership. Likewise, the shield is irrelevant to the student's RUPA §305(a) claim against the partnership.[21]

§14.2.4   Effects of LLP Status on the Partnership and of Dissolution on LLP Status

Becoming or ceasing to be an LLP.   A limited liability partnership is a general partnership with an LLP shield. Donning or doffing the shield has considerable importance for the general partnership's partners but does not remake the underlying business organization. Whether that underlying organization is viewed as an aggregate or an entity:[22]

- the organization's becoming an LLP does not create a new partnership, and
- the organization's ceasing to be an LLP does not dissolve or terminate the existing partnership.[23]

Partnership dissolution.   Partnership dissolution has no effect on the partnership's LLP status. RUPA makes this point explicitly,[24] but the same rule ap-

---

21. See section 10.4.1.

22. On the entity/aggregate distinction, see section 7.2.7.

23. As to a RUPA LLP, see RUPA §§201(b) and 1003(d) and Comment to RUPA §201.

24. RUPA §1001(e). The Comment expands on the point: "[L]imited liability partnership status remains even though a partnership may be dissolved, wound up, and terminated. Even after the termination of the partnership, the former partners of a terminated partnership would not be personally liable for partnership obligations incurred while the partnership was a limited liability partnership."

plies even under LLP provisions that lack comparable language. By definition, dissolution does not end a partnership,[25] and the UPA dissolution provisions nowhere refer to terminating LLP status.

The situation is different, however, when a dissolved LLP winds up its business by transferring its assets, obligations, and operations to a successor general partnership. As explained in Chapter Eleven, for most purposes the transition can be and often is seamless.[26] However, the successor partnership is not the same organization as the dissolved partnership, which means that the successor partnership is *not* an LLP unless either (i) the successor partnership itself files to become an LLP, or (ii) the LLP statute automatically transfers the dissolved partnership's LLP status to the successor partnership. Few LLP statutes provide for automatic transfer, and the transition to a successor partnership often occurs without the partners paying much attention or even recognizing that a transition is occurring. As a result, especially in UPA states, gaps in the shield seem likely.

> **Example:** Jay, Alfred, and Proofrock are partners in a general partnership governed by the law of a state that has grafted LLP provisions to the UPA. The partnership has filed the necessary document to be an LLP. On April 1, Jay decides to leave the partnership, and Alfred, Proofrock, and he informally agree that (1) the business will continue without interruption, and (2) Jay will be bought out at a specified price, payable in specified installments. No one thinks to do any paperwork other than a simple letter memorializing the buy-out arrangement. On May 5, a customer slips and falls while on the business's premises. On May 15, Alfred and Proofrock file the necessary document for their partnership to be an LLP. On May 20, a second customer slips and falls while on the business's premises. As to the tort claim of the first fallen customer, the partnership is not an LLP unless the LLP statute automatically transfers the LLP status of a dissolved partnership to a successor partnership. As to the second fallen customer, the partnership is an LLP in any event.

§14.2.5   *When Partnership Obligations Are Incurred*

RUPA §306(c) applies an LLP's liability shield to partnership obligations "incurred while the partnership is a limited liability partnership" and non-RUPA LLP statutes have similar language. If a general partnership is an LLP throughout its existence, the question of when a partnership is "incurred" never arises. If the question does arise, the answer can be quite complex.

---

25. See sections 11.2.1.
26. See section 11.4.4.

The text of RUPA provides no clue, but the notion of a partnership obligation being "incurred" derives ultimately from UPA §17, which states the liability of a "person admitted as a partner into an existing partnership" for partnership obligations "incurred" before the partner's admission.[27] Cases under UPA §17 are not numerous, but they suggest that a partnership's obligations in contract are incurred when the contract is first made.

The official Comment to RUPA §306 offers the following approach:

- partnership obligations arising in contract are "incurred" when the contract is made[28]
- unless the parties otherwise agree, modifications to a contract do not "re-set" the "incurred date" even as to the subject matter of the modification[29]
- partnership obligations arising in tort are "incurred" when the tortious conduct occurs and not when the tort victim suffers injury; "[t]his interpretation prevents a culpable partnership from engaging in wrongful conduct and then filing a statement of qualification to sever the vicarious responsibility of its partners for future injury or harm caused by conduct that occurred prior to the filing."[30]

§14.2.6 The Contribution Conundrum

In an ordinary general partnership, partners share losses inter se, and both the UPA and RUPA require partners to contribute to the partnership so as to effectuate that loss sharing.[31] Many partnership agreements also establish contribution obligations among the partners, sometimes merely replicating and sometimes varying the statutory default rules.

In the context of an LLP, however, contribution is problematic. The problem is best explained by example.

---

27. RUPA §306(b) continues the UPA rule: "A person admitted as a partner into an existing partnership is not personally liable for any partnership obligation incurred before the person's admission as a partner."

28. This aspect of the suggested approach is consistent with the case law under UPA §17.

29. This aspect of the suggested approach appears to come from Minn. Stat. §323.14, subd. 6 (repealed), part of Minnesota's pre-RUPA provisions on LLPs.

30. RUPA §306, Comment 3.

31. UPA §18 states: "Each partner . . . must contribute toward the losses . . . sustained by the partnership according to his share in the profits." See also UPA §40(a)(II) (a dissolved partnership's assets include the partners' respective contribution obligations). RUPA §807(b) provides that, following a partnership's dissolution: "A partner shall contribute to the partnership an amount equal to any excess of the charges over the credits in the partner's account. . . ."

Example: Fencing, LLP is a RUPA limited liability partnership, and
Porthos is one of its partners. He and his co-partners, Aramis and
Athos, share profits and losses equally. One day, while conducting the
partnership's ordinary business and giving a fencing lesson to an individual student, Porthos becomes distracted by personal concerns. As a
result, he negligently inflicts a serious leg wound on the student. The
student successfully sues both Porthos and the partnership for
$90,000. The partnership has no funds to pay the judgment, and—be-
cause the partnership is an LLP—the partners are not, merely on account of partner status, responsible for the partnership's obligation to
the student. Porthos, however, is directly liable for his own negligence.
Porthos also has a claim against the partnership for $90,000 in indem-
nification.[32] If the partnership cannot meet that indemnification obligation, Porthos has suffered a loss in the conduct of the partnership
business. If Aramis and Athos are obliged to contribute to the partnership so as to equalize the loss among the three partners, that obligation
effectively defeats the purpose of the LLP liability shield. Assuming for
the sake of simplicity that there are no other losses to be shared among
the partners, Aramis and Athos will each have to contribute $30,000
to the partnership, the resulting $60,000 will be in theory available to
Porthos but in practice will be garnered by the student as a judgment
creditor of Porthos, the partnership, or both.[33]

RUPA pays considerable attention to this issue, and RUPA §§306(c),
807(b), 807(c), and 1001(b) each specifically refer to a partner's contribution
obligations. Section 1001(b) links the consent necessary to become an LLP to
the consent necessary to amend any partnership agreement provisions pertaining to contribution.[34] RUPA §§807(b) and (c) each make a partner's contribution obligations subject to RUPA §306(c). RUPA §306(c) shields an
LLP's partner from liability *qua* partner for a partnership obligation, whether
a claim is asserted "directly or indirectly, by way of contribution or otherwise."
Section 306(c) even overrides contribution obligations that the partners

32. "In cases of partner misconduct, Section 401(c) sets forth a partnership's obligation to indemnify the culpable partner where the partner's liability was incurred in the
ordinary course of the partnership's business." RUPA §306, Comment 3. See section
8.4.

33. RUPA §807(f) provides: "An assignee for the benefit of creditors of a partnership
or a partner, or a person appointed by a court to represent creditors of a partnership or
a partner, may enforce a partner's obligation to contribute to the partnership."

34. The link is a default rule. If the partnership agreement contains no provision pertaining to contribution, or if the partnership agreement does not provide an amendment mechanism specific to the agreement's provisions on contribution, §1001(b)
links to the consent mechanism generally applicable for amending the partnership
agreement.

may have chosen to state in their partnership agreement before the partnership became an LLP.

As a result of these provisions

- RUPA's loss sharing provisions remain intact *as to capital losses suffered by the partners;*
- RUPA's contribution provisions will never create a hole in the LLP shield; and
- a partnership agreement's provisions on contribution will jeopardize the shield only if adopted or reaffirmed after the general partnership becomes an LLP.

Example: Holmes and Watson are partners in a general partnership that has been an LLP throughout its existence. When the partnership begins, Holmes contributes $30,000 and Watson contributes $10,000. The partners agree to share profits equally. The partnership muddles along and eventually dissolves, never having made any profit and never having distributed any money or other property to either partner. After marshaling its assets, the dissolved partnership owes creditors $100,000 and has only $70,000 to pay them. *A fortiori* there is no money to distribute to the partners as a return of their respective contributions. In order for each partner to have an equal loss (i.e., $20,000), Watson must contribute an additional $10,000 to the partnership, which will then distribute the money to Holmes. Holmes will then have suffered a $20,000 loss: $30,000 contribution (loss), less $10,000 distributed. Watson will also have suffered a $20,000 loss: an initial contribution of $10,000 (loss), and a winding up contribution of $10,000 (also a loss). Watson's contribution is *not* available to the partnership's unsatisfied creditors.

In somewhat simplified form, the accounting works as follows. By hypothesis, over the course of its existence the partnership suffered a loss of $70,000. (The partnership began with $40,000 of contributed capital, which is all gone, and has unsatisfied liabilities of $30,000.) Each partner's share of the losses is charged against the partner's capital account,[35] but in determining a partner's obligation to contribute there is "exclud[ed] from the calculation charges attributable to an obligation for which the partner is not personally liable under Section 306."[36] In effect, therefore:

---

35. RUPA §401(a)(2).
36. RUPA §807(b).

Holmes	capital contribution	30,000	
	share of losses protected by §306(c)	(15,000)	(disregarded for purposes of contribution among partners)
	capital account before settling accounts among partners — excluding losses protected by §306(c)	30,000	(since the partnership has no funds to return partner contributions, this positive number reflects a loss that Holmes will suffer)
	action needed to equalize losses among partners	10,000	distribution from partnership
Watson	capital contribution	10,000	
	share of losses protected by §306(c)	(15,000)	(disregarded for purposes of contribution among partners)
	capital account before settling accounts among partners — excluding losses protected by §306(c)	10,000	(since the partnership has no funds to return partner contributions, this positive number reflects a loss that Watson will suffer, but n.b. the loss is 20,000 less than Holmes's)
	action needed to equalize losses among partners	10,000	contribution to the partnership

§14.2.7   Piercing the Veil

Although only a few LLP statutes specifically contemplate the doctrine of "piercing the veil," piercing will nonetheless be part of the law applicable to LLPs. Piercing is, after all, an equitable doctrine which originated and exists in the corporate realm as "exclusively a case law phenomenon."[37] That case law has already helped establish the piercing doctrine as part of the law of limited liability companies,[38] and there is every reason to expect the same phenomenon with LLPs.[39]

---

37. Bishop & Kleinberger, §6.03[3] at 6-29 (discussing piercing and LLCs).

38. See section 13.5.7.

39. Bishop & Kleinberger, §6.03[3] at 6-29. The case for piercing is, if anything, stronger for LLPs than for corporations and limited liability companies, because LLP

§14.3 Limited Liability Limited Partnerships

§14.3.1 Origins and Current Availability

Like LLPs, LLLPs began in Texas. In 1993, Texas amended its general and limited partnership statutes to permit a limited partnership to invoke the LLP provisions of the general partnership statute and thereby become a registered limited liability limited partnership.[40] Several other states promptly followed suit, and over the next decade the following pattern developed:

1. Several states expressly permitted a limited partnership to invoke the LLP provisions of the state's general partnership statute.[41]
2. A few states provided for LLLPs directly, solely through language in the limited partnership statute.
3. A few states expressly precluded a limited partnership from being an LLLP.
4. Most state partnership statutes did not expressly address the issue.

As to the first and second categories, by 2002 more than 15 states had authorized the existence of limited liability limited partnerships, although at least initially in a few of these states the LLLP shield protected only general and not limited partners.[42]

As to the fourth category, despite the statutory silence it is possible to argue "based on the language of the UPA, RUPA, and RULPA" that a limited partnership may invoke the LLP provisions of its state's general partnership act, at least to provide a liability shield for the limited partnership's general partners.[43]

---

statutes uniformly lack any provisions imposing liability either on owners or managers for distributions which left the entity insolvent or which were otherwise improper. *Compare, e.g.,* Rev. Mod. Bus. Corp. Act §8.33 (directors' liability for unlawful distributions) and ULLCA §407 (liability for unlawful distributions both for those who assent and those who knowingly receive).

40. Bishop & Kleinberger, §15.01[4] at 15-18.

41. Most such statutes refer to "limited liability limited partnerships" but a few lump both general and limited partnership under the term "limited liability partnership." See, e.g., Ariz. Rev. Stat. §29-308(C), Ga. Code §14-8-2(6.1), and Tex. Civ. Stat. Art. 6132a-1, §2.14. For simplicity's sake, this book uses the term "limited liability limited partnership" and the abbreviation "LLLP."

42. See Bishop & Kleinberger, §15.03[3][b] at 15-73 to 15-74. As explained in section 12.2.3, in an ordinary limited partnership a limited partner's regular liability shield is subject to the "control rule," which in some circumstances exposes a limited partner to personal liability for a limited partnership obligation. If an LLLP shield applies to a limited partner, the shield overrides and renders moot the control rule.

43. See Bishop & Kleinberger, §15.03[2] at 15-70 for a detailed explanation.

In 2001, NCCUSL promulgated its new Uniform Limited Partnership Act and sought to bring clarity, simplicity, and uniformity to this issue. ULPA (2001)

- defines a limited liability limited partnership simply as "a limited partnership whose certificate of limited partnership states that the limited partnership is a limited liability limited partnership";[44]
- requires the certificate of limited partnership of each limited partnership to state "whether the limited partnership is a limited liability limited partnership";[45]
- uses essentially verbatim the language of RUPA's *LLP* shield to establish a full corporate and LLC-like *LLLP* shield;[46]
- eliminates the "control rule" and provides a full corporate and LLC-like liability shield for all limited partners regardless of whether the limited partnership is an LLLP.[47]

§14.3.2   Name Requirements

Like the name of an LLP, the name of an LLLP must include specified phrases or abbreviation so as to designate the limited partnership's special status. The designator requirements vary depending on whether the relevant statute refers to limited liability limited partnerships or, instead, treats an LLLP as merely a subset of LLPs. The Iowa statute exemplifies the former approach and the Texas statute the latter:

> [Iowa] The name of a limited liability limited partnership must end with "Registered Limited Liability Limited Partnership", "Limited Liability Limited Partnership", "R.L.L.L.P.", "L.L.L.P.", "RLLLP", or "LLLP".[48]

> [Texas] [The name of a limited partnership that has filed as an LLP under the general partnership act's LLP provision must have] as the last words or letters of its name the words "Limited Partnership" or the abbreviation "Ltd." followed by the words "registered limited liability partnership" or the abbreviation "L.L.P."[49]

ULPA (2001) provides:

> The name of a limited partnership that is not a limited liability limited partnership must contain the phrase "limited partnership" or the abbreviation "L.P." or "LP" and may not contain the phrase "limited liability

---

44. ULPA (2001) §102(9).
45. ULPA (2001) §201(a)(4).
46. ULPA (2001) §404(c).
47. ULPA (2001) §303.
48. Iowa Code Ann. §487.1302.
49. Tex. Civ. Stat. Art. 6132a-1, §2.14(3).

limited partnership" or the abbreviation "LLLP" or "L.L.L.P." The name of a limited liability limited partnership must contain the phrase "limited liability limited partnership" or the abbreviation "LLLP" or "L.L.L.P." and must not contain the abbreviation "L.P." or "LP."[50]

§14.3.3 *Piercing and Dividend Recapture*

An LLLP provides a full, corporate and LLC-like liability shield. There is no reason why this shield should be immune from the equitable doctrine of piercing the veil.[51]

As to distribution recapture, most current LLLP provisions rest on some version of RULPA, which provides for recapture of both rightfully and wrongfully made distributions.[52] The shield is inapposite to a partner's recapture liability, because the liability is not asserted "solely" on account of partner status. In this respect, LLLPs are less protective than LLPs, which typically do not provide for distribution recapture.[53]

PROBLEM 124

Fezzik, Vincini, and Buttercup are partners in an ordinary general partnership governed by RUPA. Fezzik is a very wealthy individual, while Buttercup has only modest means and Vincini is nearly judgment proof. The partnership agreement (i) names Fezzik as "managing partner"; (ii) authorizes him to make all decisions on behalf of the partnership that pertain to "ordinary operations and activities"; (iii) allocates profits 65 percent to Fezzik, 20 percent to Buttercup, and 15 percent to Vincini; (iv) requires unanimous consent of the partners to amend the partnership agreement; and (v) does not mention the idea of a limited liability partnership. Does Fezzik have the authority, either as managing partner under the partnership agreement or as the owner of a majority of the profits interest, to cause the partnership to become an LLP?

EXPLANATION

No. Under RUPA §1001(b), unless the partnership agreement provides otherwise, the decision to file a statement of qualification requires the same quantum of consent as an amendment to the partnership agreement. This partnership agreement does not address becoming an LLP but does require unanimous consent for an amendment. Fezzik's role as managing partner and his ownership of 65 percent of the profits interests are both irrelevant.

---

50. ULPA (2001) §108(b) and (c).

51. For an explanation of this point in the context of LLPs, see section 14.2.7. For a discussion of the factors courts use in determining piercing claims, see section 13.5.7.

52. See section 12.2.3. ULPA (2001) §§508 and 509 take a more corporate-like approach but nonetheless retain some recapture exposure.

53. See section 14.2.7, n.39.

PROBLEM 125

Same facts as Problem 124, plus the following. Fezzik suggests to Buttercup and Vincini that the partnership become an LLP. Buttercup readily agrees, but Vincini refuses. Vincini says to Fezzik, "You're going to have to make it worth my while to get my agreement. The shield doesn't much matter to me. They can't get blood from a stone. But you, Mr. Moneybags, you've got a lot to lose. If you want my agreement, you'll have to transfer me 5 percent of the profits." Does Fezzik have any claim against Vincini?

EXPLANATION

Possibly. Fezzik might succeed with a claim that Vincini has breached the obligation of good faith and fair dealing stated in RUPA §404(d). Fezzik would characterize Vincini as withholding consent solely for the purpose of extorting a transfer from Fezzik. Vincini would invoke RUPA §404(e) and argue that he is *entitled* to engage in "conduct [which] furthers [his] own interests." Fezzik would respond that:

 i. RUPA §404(e) in its entirety provides that "A partner does not violate a duty or obligation under this [Act] or the partnership agreement *merely* because the partner's conduct furthers the partner's own interest" (emphasis added);
 ii. more is involved here than mere self-interest;
 iii. LLP status could in no way prejudice Vincini, and Vincini was not protecting any legitimate self-interest by refusing his consent; and
 iv. Vincini was, in fact, using his veto power and Fezzik's concern about personal liability to coerce Fezzik.

PROBLEM 126

Same facts as Problem 124, except that Vincini states only the following reason for refusing to consent. "You're the managing partner and the success of this business depends fundamentally on you. I like the idea of you having to worry about personal liability if things go badly wrong. I think it keeps you on your toes, and it's part of the deal we made going in." Assuming that Vincini is being honest in his explanation, does Fezzik have any claim against Vincini?

EXPLANATION

No. Vincini's conduct and explanation meet both the subjective and objective standards of good faith and fair dealing.[54] Vincini's motivation is honest and reasonable. He is not seeking to coerce Fezzik into changing their agreement. To the contrary, he is merely protecting what he honestly and reasonably sees as part of the agreement.

---

54. See section 9.8.4.

Table of Statutes

Uniform Limited Partnership Act (ULPA 1916)

Revised Uniform Limited Partnership Act (RULPA)

Table of Restatements

Index

Index